MANAGING INDIVIDUAL AND GROUP BEHAVIOR IN ORGANIZATIONS

McGraw-Hill Series in Management

Keith Davis and Fred Luthans, *Consulting Editors*

MANAGING INDIVIDUAL AND GROUP BEHAVIOR IN ORGANIZATIONS

Daniel C. Feldman
University of Florida

Hugh J. Arnold
University of Toronto

McGraw-Hill Book Company

*New York   St. Louis   San Francisco   Auckland   Bogotá   Hamburg
London   Madrid   Mexico   Montreal   New Delhi
Panama   Paris   São Paulo   Singapore   Sydney   Tokyo   Toronto*

This book was set in Aster by Black Dot, Inc. (ECU).
The editors were Kathi A. Benson and Peggy Rehberger;
the designer was Joan E. O'Connor;
the production supervisor was Phil Galea.
The drawings were done by ECL Art Associates, Inc.
R. R. Donnelley & Sons Company was printer and binder.

MANAGING INDIVIDUAL AND GROUP BEHAVIOR IN ORGANIZATIONS

890DOCDOC89

ISBN 0-07-020386-5

Library of Congress Cataloging in Publication Data
Feldman, Daniel C.

   Managing individual and group behavior in organizations.

   (McGraw-Hill series in management)
   Includes bibliographies and indexes.
   1. Organizational behavior.   2. Management.
I. Arnold, Hugh J.   II. Title.   III. Series.
HD58.7.F44   1983   658.3   82-17245
ISBN 0-07-020386-5

DEDICATED TO OUR PARENTS

CONTENTS

PREFACE

This book is about managing individual and group behavior in organizations. Effective handling of employees has always been an important part of management. Today declining productivity, increased competition from abroad, and rising expectations of employees entering the work force have made effective management of individual and group behavior even more critical. In this book we will be describing the day-to-day problems managers face at work, presenting theories and research on why individuals and groups in organizations behave the way they do, and suggesting some guidelines on how to manage individual and group behavior in organizations more effectively.

ORGANIZATION

The text consists of twenty chapters, divided into eight sections: *Introduction; Integrating the Individual and the Organization; Motivation, Satisfaction, and Performance; The Design of Work; Leadership in Organizations; Managerial Processes; Groups in Organizations;* and *Conclusions.*

In general, we have tried to cover primarily "individual" topics, such as job satisfaction, before primarily "group" topics, such as group dynamics. Also, we have tried to follow, where possible, the "life cycle" of employees' careers. Thus, the first topic we cover is selecting employees; next we examine motivating effective performance; and then later, we examine performance appraisal.

BOOK CONTENT

We have covered in the text the major topics in the areas of individual and group behavior in organizations. In so doing we have tried to integrate the perspectives and findings of a wide range of social science disciplines. Professors and students in a variety of courses—organizational behavior, personnel, human resource management, and managing groups in organizations—will find the book appropriate for their purposes.

We also believe readers of the book will be able to study topics in individual and group behavior in more depth than generally available in management text books. In the sections on individual behavior, for instance, there are two chapters each on selection, motivation, leadership, and job design. We also devote whole chapters to topics often omitted entirely from organizational behavior books, or treated only briefly: socialization and careers; designing reward systems; job satisfaction; quality of working life; communication; managerial decision making; and performance appraisal.

Another important feature of the book's content is its extensive coverage of groups. Rather than having a couple of cursory overview chapters on groups, the book has a whole section focusing on groups and group behavior in organizations. Frequently ignored topics such as norms, conformity, deviance, cohesiveness, group performance, group decision-making, and autonomous work groups are all covered here, and in substantial detail. We also try to point out how groups influence what is traditionally thought of as "individual behavior in organizations." For example, we discuss attribution processes in both the selection and performance appraisal chapters, social comparison processes in the motivation and job satisfaction chapters, and dissonance-reduction processes in the decision-making and communication chapters.

PEDAGOGY

There are several features of the book designed to facilitate student learning. For instance, each chapter concludes with both a summary that outlines the key points of the chapter and a series of review questions about the major topics covered. These summaries and review questions should clarify and help students remember the important issues.

In addition, we have included in each chapter a section titled *Managerial Implications*. Each of these sections is intended to help students make the connection between theory and application. Throughout the book we have tried to deal with relatively sophisticated concepts in an understandable and accessible writing style, buttressed by plenty of examples. Moreover, we have tried to present a coherent point of view about what we know about individual and group behavior in organizations, rather than letting students flounder in a catalogue of briefly described theories. Finally, while we have avoided a cookbook approach to management we have tried to give the reader some well-reasoned guidelines on how to manage individual and group behavior in organizations more effectively. The "Managerial Implications" sections address the oft-heard complaint that social science research has too much approach and not enough arrival.

Eleven cases are included at the end of the text. These cases have been carefully chosen to help students relate the textbook material to real situations in real organizations. Each case illustrates several different topics, and points out the relationships among important management issues.

There is also an accompanying instructor's manual, which provides exam questions for each chapter, answers to the discussion questions, and transparency masters, as well as detailed information about how to use each case to teach a variety of topics.

ACKNOWLEDGMENTS

We were fortunate to have had such excellent assistance from our editors, our colleagues, and our secretaries. Kathi Benson and Peggy Rehberger, our editors at McGraw-Hill, were supportive at every stage in the project, from initial conception to the final production. Fred Luthans, our consulting editor, provided consistently constructive suggestions for improving the manuscript. We also received many useful comments from outside reviewers: John Wanous, Michigan State University; Roy Lewicki, Duke University; Ricky Griffin, Texas A&M University; Wayne Cascio, University of Colorado-Denver; James McElroy, Iowa State University; Ed Nevis, Massachusetts Institute of Technology; Peter Dubno, New York University; Robert Paul, Kansas State University; and Frederick Greene, Manhattan College.

Our colleagues at the University of Florida, University of Toronto, and Northwestern University have given us helpful feedback on various portions of the book. Bob House and Martin Evans, in particular, commented in detail on several chapters in the text, and we benefitted substantially from their efforts. Richard Hackman, Doris St. Clair, and Robert Warren gave us valuable advice at the outset of the project that helped us get off to a good start.

Our secretaries have typed the manuscript with care and attention. We appreciate their efforts all the more, knowing how illegible our handwriting can be and how many deadlines they had to meet. We especially want to thank Barbara Washington, Lisa Herrman, Connie Carrol, Hilda Lopez-Urgell, and Barbara Long at the University of Florida; Edith Kosow and Rexie Florov at the University of Toronto; and Thelma Soderling, Martha Fenton, and Vonnie Lorber at Northwestern University.

Finally, we are especially grateful to Clara Arnold, whose friendship and love have been a constant source of encouragement.

Daniel C. Feldman
Hugh J. Arnold

PART ONE

INTRODUCTION

CHAPTER 1

INTRODUCTION TO MANAGING INDIVIDUAL AND GROUP BEHAVIOR IN ORGANIZATIONS

Managing individual and group behavior in organizations is a difficult and complex task.

In large part, this is because of the many different roles managers have to play.[1] First of all, managers are responsible for coordinating the activities of a wide range of people: subordinates, clients, business associates, and suppliers. Second, managers are responsible for processing much of the information relevant to the activities of their work units: gathering information, evaluating its usefulness, and disseminating it through the appropriate channels. Third, managers have a lot of responsibility for decision making: initiating new products, resolving conflicts, allocating resources, and hiring and firing personnel. In short, managers have to accomplish many tasks but have only limited time in which to do them.

Another reason managing individual and group behavior in organizations is a difficult and complicated job is the widespread folklore about the

[1]Henry Mintzberg, "The Manager's Job: Folklore and Fact," *Harvard Business Review,* July-August 1975, pp. 55–61.

nature of managerial work.[2] While folklore has it that managers spend a lot of time doing systematic planning, study after study has shown the opposite to be true. Managers seem to jump from issue to issue and from person to person, continually responding to the needs of the moment rather than reflecting on the future. While folklore has it that managers have no regular duties to perform, the research suggests that managers do spend a lot of time doing low-level activities, often because they are so short-staffed. Managers are overburdened with obligations, but cannot easily delegate even routine tasks. While folklore has it that managers value and prefer sophisticated management information systems, most managers strongly favor the verbal media—namely, telephone calls and meetings. Managers rely heavily on this "soft" information, as well as on hearsay and speculation. Thus, the manager's day is marked by a series of brief, face-to-face encounters on a variety of organizational issues demanding immediate attention—and not by long periods of reflective planning on key strategic issues using sophisticated data.

Third, managing individual and group behavior in organizations is a lot more difficult than many students may expect because universities do not adequately prepare future managers for the world they will enter. New managers' expectations often exceed reality, eliciting feelings of frustration, anxiety, underutilization, and disappointment. In school, all too often theory becomes separated from practice; students are prepared for the world as it should be rather than the way it actually is.

GOALS OF THE BOOK

Our objectives in the book are threefold. First, we hope to describe the day-to-day problems managers face as they try to influence individuals and groups in organizations. Second, we hope to help the reader understand more fully why individuals and groups in organizations behave the way they do. Third, we hope to give students some guidelines on how to manage individual and group behavior in organizations more effectively.

Throughout the book we have drawn on insights from the field of *organizational behavior*. Organizational behavior is the study of human behavior, attitudes, and performance within organizational settings. It is an interdisciplinary field: it draws on concepts from a variety of behavioral sciences, such as social and clinical psychology, the sociology of organizations, labor relations, cultural anthropology, industrial engineering, and industrial psychology.

The field of organizational behavior has two distinct orientations in its approach to the study of organizations, and both are represented in this

[2]Ibid., pp. 49–54.

book. One orientation seeks out ways to improve and encourage effective performance; the other seeks out ways to make work environments more humane and satisfying. We have tried in each chapter to bring both orientations to bear on the issue at hand. Organizational behavior as a field has also valued the use of scientific method and evidence over supposition and intuition. That perspective is present here as well. We have seen too many managers burned too many times by what William McGuire at Yale calls *bubba psychology*—what everybody's bubba (grandmother) knows to be true, but isn't.

CONTENT

We have also tried to choose topics that are both theoretically interesting and practically important. Besides this introductory section, the book has seven sections, composed of nineteen chapters. The earlier chapters cover issues of individual behavior in organizations; the later chapters cover issues of group behavior. We'd like to briefly introduce here the topics and issues we'll be considering in more detail in later chapters.

Part II: Integrating the Individual and the Organization

In this section of the book we will explore how individuals initially link up with organizations and subsequently sustain those links through a series of job changes.

In Chapters 2 and 3, our focus is on how organizations recruit and select new employees. In "Assessing Jobs and Job Applicants," we'll be examining a variety of methods for assessing the strengths of applicants, such as selection interviews, personality tests, biographical information blanks, and assessment centers. For instance, do selection interviews really predict performance? Can executive recruiters really "psych out" job candidates? What other selection devices might be more reliable? In "Making Selection Decisions," we'll discuss how EEOC and Affirmative Action plans have influenced how selection decisions are made in organizations today. We'll also look at some predictive models organizations can use to increase their chances of hiring job applicants who will prove successful on the job.

In Chapter 4, "Socialization and Careers," we will first examine selection from the point of view of the individual. How do people choose careers? What determines which job an individual will accept? Then we'll explore organizational socialization—the types of training and orientation that new recruits undergo that facilitate their adjustment to the organization. Why do some new recruits "fit in", while other, equally competent recruits fall by the wayside? Finally, we'll discuss the middle and later stages of employees' careers. Is a "mid-life" crisis inevitable? What can individuals and organizations do to prevent plateaued or obsolescent performance?

Part III: Motivation, Satisfaction, and Performance

In this section of the book, we will explore what motivates employees to perform well and what makes them satisfied with their jobs. We will also look at the consequences of high employee motivation and satisfaction for organizations.

In Chapters 5, 6, and 7 we will focus on motivation. In "Motivation: Employee Needs, Perceptions, and Expectations," we will discuss three factors that largely determine whether people feel motivated: Do employees feel they have sufficient skills and can exert enough effort to perform effectively? Do employees value the rewards they can obtain for performing effectively? Do employees feel they are being rewarded fairly relative to coworkers? In "Motivating Individual Performance", we will look at three strategies managers can use to increase employee motivation: setting goals, reinforcing behaviors that are desired by the organization, and providing positive role models for subordinates. In "Designing Reward Systems," we'll explore how organizations can implement reward systems to obtain the maximum possible benefits for themselves and for their members. We will give particular attention to pay as a motivator and will discuss in some detail recent innovations in designing compensation plans. For instance, what happens to satisfaction with pay when there is no secrecy about pay rates? Why do employees undervalue fringe benefits and what can organizations do about it?

In Chapter 8 we will explore job satisfaction—both its causes and its consequences. For instance, we'll look at why pay is such an important source of job satisfaction but working conditions are not. We'll examine, too, why the happy worker is not necessarily the more productive worker but why job satisfaction is related to turnover and absenteeism. We'll also explore here the relationship between job satisfaction and unions: Why do people join unions and file grievances if unionized? In addition, the chapter considers the recent decline in national job satisfaction and what it reflects about changes in the work force and workplace. Finally, we'll explore how job satisfaction surveys can be used more effectively and for a wider range of purposes than has traditionally been the case.

Part IV: The Design of Work

In this section we will examine the impact that the design of work has on the motivation, satisfaction, and performance of organization members.

In Chapter 9, "Job Design," we will focus on the design of work for individuals. First, we'll review several of the more well-known approaches to the design of work, particularly scientific management, job rotation, and job enlargement. Then we'll turn to some more recent developments in job design, including a model that draws attention to the five "core" job characteristics that particularly motivate individuals to perform well. Union problems at the Lordstown plant have brought job design to the national attention, but the research has been equivocal about its success. We'll thus discuss when job design will influence employee motivation and satisfaction most strongly. Finally, we'll examine how to diagnose job design problems more readily, and what steps to take to insure successful implementation of job design projects.

In Chapter 10, "Quality of Work Life: The Design of Work Groups," we come at the problem of job design from a slightly different perspective. Rather than focusing upon individual organization members and the design of jobs for individuals, we'll be examining the issue of work design for groups. We'll pay particular attention to such factors as the group's technology, the membership of the group, and group norms about performance. Two of the most significant and innovative group job design efforts, the Topeka plant of General Foods and Volvo's Kalmar plant, are analyzed in some detail.

Part V: Leadership in Organizations

In Chapters 11 and 12 we will examine the nature of leadership in organizations. In "Leadership: Personality and Behavior" we will examine what personality characteristics predict leadership and what behaviors of leaders contribute to leadership effectiveness. Are leaders more aggressive? self-confident? intelligent? extraverted? Do successful leaders behave more autocratically or democratically? We'll discover that while no single trait or set of traits will consistently predict who will become leaders, traits like initiative, self-confidence, and persistence are more common in successful leaders. As for effective leadership behaviors, we'll examine why employee-oriented leadership generally leads to increased subordinate satisfaction and why production-oriented leadership generally leads to increased productivity.

In "Contingency Models of Leadership," we'll examine how different situations in organizations demand different types of leadership. For instance, if subordinates are working on highly ambiguous jobs with few policies and procedures, directive leadership will increase motivation and performance. Directive leadership here will help subordinates understand what they need to do in order to perform effectively. The same directive leadership with subordinates working on highly routine jobs, on the other hand, will simply create frustration and resentment. We'll pay particular attention here to the uses, misuses, and abuses of participation.

Part VI: Managerial Processes

In this section we will examine the functions traditionally seen as the most critical parts of management jobs: decision making, communication, and performance appraisal.

In Chapter 13, "Managerial Decision Making," we will look at how managers make decisions in real organizational situations. "Rational" decision making rarely works because there are too many goals to maximize, too many alternative courses of action to consider, and too much data to synthesize. Instead, decision makers have only "bounded rationality," which limits their capacity to generate and analyze alternatives. Most managers don't look for the best alternative but for an alternative that is "good enough." We'll pay particular attention to decision making procedures that facilitate the development and evaluation of realistic alternative courses of action.

In Chapter 14, "Communication," we will examine how managers give information to subordinates and persuade them to modify their behavior. We look at these questions: How can managers make sure people pay attention to their communication? How do jargon and nonverbal cues distort the exchange of information? What factors determine whether the information managers give subordinates is seen as true? What types of communication styles are most effective?

In Chapter 15, "Performance Appraisal," we will look at how managers evaluate employee performance. We will be interested here in both performance appraisal instruments and performance appraisal interviews. For instance, we'll look at a wide variety of evaluation forms traditionally used in organizations to appraise employees (e.g., graphic rating scales, single global evaluations, and ranking methods) and some difficulties inherent in these traditional methods. Then we'll examine some new techniques that are more effective, such as MBO and Behaviorally Anchored Rating Scales (BARS). We'll also explore more productive ways of giving subordinates feedback so that they will be less defensive and more willing to change their behavior.

Part VII: Groups in Organizations

In this section, we will examine the ways in which groups influence the thoughts, feelings, and behaviors of their members.

In Chapter 16, "Introduction to Group Dynamics," we will describe the different types of groups people belong to in organizations, and what makes some groups more cohesive than others. We'll also explore here the nature of group norms—the informal rules and regulations created and enforced by group members. We'll look at how norms like goldbricking and quota restriction develop and what they tell managers about underlying group dynamics.

In Chapter 17, "Conformity and Deviance," we will look at the circumstances under which individuals are most likely to conform to group norms. When will people give in to group pressure, and when will they resist? We'll also explore deviance: Who gets scapegoated in groups? Why are groups hesitant to reject group deviants? Using some examples from foreign policy decision-making fiascos, we'll discover why groups need to tolerate more deviance without dismissing the offenders out of hand.

Chapter 18 focuses on group performance and group decision making. Groups can potentially enhance the productivity of members in a variety of ways—by increasing their job-relevant knowledge and skills, by increasing the intensity with which they work, and by increasing the level of their job satisfaction. However, groups can also cause problems of decreased motivation and coordination. We will pay particular attention to identifying those situations where groups will create synergy, i.e., situations where there will be some "value added" by bringing together individuals to work on a common task. We will also look at the impact groups have on the accuracy, creativity, and riskiness of decisions. For instance, we'll discuss why brainstorming groups generally prove unsuccessful in organizations, and why Nominal and Delphi groups show greater promise.

Chapter 19, "Intergroup Behavior and Managing Conflict," examines a different aspect of group behavior. Here the focus is on the relationships *between* groups in organizations and what causes hostilities to arise in the relationships between them. We'll discuss both what causes intergroup conflict and the dynamics that occur between groups that are experiencing such conflict. Much of this chapter is devoted to conflict-resolution strategies such as smoothing, forcing a solution, appealing to superordinate goals, bargaining, using representatives, and confrontation. These strategies vary greatly in terms of how openly they address the conflict, and we provide some guidelines for when each type of resolution strategy is most appropriate.

Part VIII: Conclusion

In our concluding chapter, "Future Prospects in Organizational Behavior," we will summarize the key points of the book, speculate on future developments in the field of organizational behavior, and highlight the consistent themes that run throughout the book.

A FINAL NOTE

Textbook authors are often influenced by what they liked (and disliked) about the textbooks they used as students themselves. We have been no exception. We remember all too vividly reading books overloaded with jargon, mind-numbing descriptions of research methodology, and uninterpretable results. Books we read sometimes seemed to be getting around to saying something which they never actually came out with.

Consequently, we have tried throughout this book to deal with relatively sophisticated concepts in an understandable and accessible writing style, rather than simplifying ideas to trivialities and dressing them up with jargon. We have also tried to integrate the material as much as possible, so that readers will not feel they are doing a semester-long Rubik's cube, trying to figure out how to get all the different theories lined up appropriately. We have devoted as much effort to describing organizations as they are as we have to describing how we would like them to be. Finally, we have tried to make clear and explicit the implications of organizational behavior theory for the practice of management. In short, we have tried to write a book that reflects both our enthusiasm about the field of organizational behavior and the excitement of actually managing individual and group behavior in organizations.

PART TWO

INTEGRATING THE INDIVIDUAL AND THE ORGANIZATION

CHAPTER 2

ASSESSING JOBS AND

JOB APPLICANTS

The effectiveness of any organization is critically influenced by the quality of its members. As a result, the methods an organization employs for determining the kinds of people it needs, for assessing people who apply for jobs, and finally for making selection decisions regarding whom to hire and whom to reject are extremely important.

The process of selecting new organization members can be thought of as a matching process with two simultaneous goals. First, the organization seeks to match as closely as possible its own needs with the capabilities of the prospective member. There must be a good fit between what the organization needs done and what the individual is capable of doing. Obtaining a good match on this level requires the organization to analyze carefully what its requirements are and then to screen applicants in such a way that there is maximum likelihood that the applicant has the skill, ability, training, and experience necessary to meet the organization's needs and demands. In addition, the selection process must also attempt to match what the organization has to offer the prospective employee with the legitimate needs and demands of the applicant. The individual-organization relationship is not a one-way process. Individuals have expectations about what organizations can provide them with regarding things such as security, pay, prestige, challenge, opportunities for learning and development, opportunities to make friends, and so on. An effective selection system must seek to match these expectations of the individual with the capabilities of the organization to meet them.

This chapter and the next focus on the techniques available to organizations for identifying and selecting competent new members who are well suited to the demands and opportunities which exist in the organization. In this chapter we look at how organizations go about assessing jobs and job applicants. Obviously, obtaining a good match or fit between the person and the job requires that the organization analyze carefully what it needs in a new employee, as well as whether any given job applicant appears likely to meet those needs or not.

JOB ANALYSIS

Before the process of choosing new organization members can get off the ground, the organization must address the question "What are we looking for?" No set of complex assessment techniques, sensitive interviewing skills, or sophisticated decision-making procedures will help an organization make sound staffing decisions if the entire process has not begun with a careful and detailed analysis of exactly what it is that the organization needs in a prospective employee. Selection is a matching process, and making good matches requires careful attention to both sides of this process. In this case, it means careful attention to the nature of the position to be filled, as well as to the nature of the prospective employee. Thus, the starting point of the selection process, and the starting point of our discussion of it, must be the development of techniques that the organization can employ for answering the question "What are we looking for?" We'll begin our discussion by defining some of the terms that frequently arise in this area. After getting the terminology straight we then present the various methods which can be employed in analyzing jobs and discuss a couple of specific examples of job analysis systems.

Job Analysis Defined

In looking at how terms have come to be defined in this area, it is important to keep in mind that the primary goal of the selection process from the organization's point of view is finding an individual who is capable of competently carrying out the tasks and activities associated with the position being filled. This primary goal has resulted in an emphasis upon the *behavior* of current or potential incumbents of a position in the definitions of terms. If we want to be able to find someone who is capable of *doing* the job well, we must first have a very clear and specific description of what it is that needs to be *done*. As a result, definitions of what constitutes a *job* and what constitutes *job analysis* are *behavior-centered*, i.e., they focus upon the observable actions and behaviors of members of the organization.

In line with this emphasis upon what people actually do in organizations, we can usefully adopt the following definition of a job: "A *job* is a relatively homogeneous cluster of work tasks carried out to achieve some essential and enduring purpose in an organization. A job is a grouping of tasks that appear to 'go together' in some meaningful sense—tasks similar in kind or content, tasks posing common requirements, or tasks for which the only common ground is that employees who perform one task X are likely also to perform another task Y" (Dunnette, 1966, p. 69). This definition of a job has the advantage of being specific and concrete and helps us to focus upon what *behaviors* are required for effective performance of the job.

With a definition in hand of what constitutes a job, we can move on to define job analysis. "*Job analysis* consists of defining the job and discovering what the job calls for in employee behaviors" (Dunnette, 1966, p. 69). A slightly more detailed definition that is consistent with this has been provided by the U.S. Department of Labor (1944, p. 1). "Job analysis is defined as the process of determining, by observation and study, and reporting pertinent information relating to the nature of a specific job. It is the determination of the tasks that comprise the job and of the skills, knowledges, abilities, and responsibilities required of the worker for successful performance and which differentiate the job from all others."

From these definitions we can see that there are really two aspects to the process of job analysis. The first aspect consists of a careful and systematic delineation of the tasks and activities to be performed by the job incumbent. This aspect of job analysis is sometimes referred to as the development of a *job description*. The second aspect of job analysis involves discovering what employee behaviors are necessary to carry out these tasks, and what employee characteristics are likely to be associated with the capability of successfully performing these behaviors. This latter

FIGURE 2-1
The dual matching process of organizational selection.

facet of job analysis is sometimes referred to as the development of a *job specification.*

Schneider (1976) has also recently drawn attention to an important distinction between two different basic approaches to the job analysis process. His distinction is consistent with the overall approach to selection depicted in Figure 2-1, which we described at the beginning of the chapter as seeking simultaneously to match: (1) the demands of the organization for competent performance with the skills and abilities that the individual has to offer; and (2) the needs of the individual for meaningful social, personal, and material rewards with the capability of the organization to meet these legitimate needs.

Achieving the first match between organizational needs and individual abilities implies the need for the *job requirements* approach to job analysis. The vast majority of the literature on job analysis implicitly assumes this approach. Our discussion of job analysis up to this point and our definitions of the term exemplify the job requirements approach.

The second type of job analysis technique, called the *worker rewards* approach, focuses upon our second matching process, i.e., the need for a match between the individual's needs and desires and the capability of the organization to fulfill them. The worker rewards approach implies a need for the organization to analyze carefully not only what it requires of a job incumbent, but also what the job and the organization have to offer the potential incumbent in terms of social satisfaction, opportunities for challenge, growth and development, and concrete rewards such as pay and promotion opportunities.

This distinction is an important one. An optimal selection system must seek a match between individual and organization on both levels. In the remainder of this chapter, we will continue our focus on the job requirements approach to selection. We will return to the worker rewards approach in subsequent chapters on reward systems and job design. In these chapters we will dwell at length upon how the organization's methods of rewarding employees and the nature of the jobs which employees perform have a critical impact upon the fit between individual and organization, and ultimately upon the effectiveness of the organization as a whole.

Methods of Job Analysis

A variety of methods are available for conducting job analyses. Each method has certain strengths and weaknesses associated with it (Prien & Ronan, 1971). The method most appropriate for any given situation will depend upon a number of factors, such as the nature of the job being analyzed, the resources available for conducting the job analysis, and the size of the organization. We will present several of the most commonly used methods and briefly comment on their strengths and weaknesses. In reviewing the methods, it is important to keep in mind that the goal of job analysis is the development of as clear and accurate a statement as possible of the nature of the job, the behaviors required of the incumbent in the performance of the job, and the personal characteristics necessary for effective job performance.

Observation

Perhaps the most obvious and straightforward method of job analysis is observation of people performing the job. It should be possible to learn a great deal regarding what the job requires of an incumbent by carefully observing individuals carrying out the tasks involved in their jobs. Observation is indeed a useful technique for job analysis and forms an integral part of many job analysis programs. However, it is not without its shortcomings. Some of the shortcomings can be overcome by careful design and implementation; others are inherent to the method and hence unavoidable.

There are two factors in the category of avoidable problems. The first is the need for some systematic and standardized method of recording the job analyst's observations. Without this, job analysis by observation becomes highly idiosyncratic and it becomes extremely difficult to develop job analyses which are comparable from job to job and from analyst to analyst. The second factor is the need to observe systematically the performance of a number of different job incumbents. The goal of job analysis is to analyze the requirements of the job; it is not to appraise the performance of a given incumbent. The more latitude the job permits the incumbent in how job requirements are fulfilled, the more important it is to observe a variety of incumbents.

While these problems can be overcome by careful planning and implementation, there are several problems with observational methods which are inherent to the method and hence unavoidable. First, the mere presence of an observer may alter the behavior of the job incumbent. The result may be an analysis of the job "as performed in the presence of a job analyst," rather than an analysis of the job as it is actually performed on a day-in, day-out basis. It is impossible to predict precisely how and in what direction the presence of an observer may influence the behavior of a job incumbent. A second problem with observation as a method for job analysis lies in the fact that it is not feasible or practical for all types of jobs. The value of observation tends to be highest for jobs whose components are primarily physical rather than mental and whose job cycle time is relatively short. If the requirements of a job are primarily mental (e.g., engineers, writers, designers) there is little overt behavior for a job analyst to observe and record. Further, if the cycle time of a job is long, even if the work is primarily physical, it might require months or years of observation to obtain a composite picture of all of the requirements of a job (e.g., metal workers building turbines for power generation may work for months or even years on a single unit). In such circumstances, observation is clearly inefficient and not to be recommended.

Interviews

A great deal of information can be obtained by interviewing job incumbents, either individually or in small groups, regarding the behavioral requirements of their position and the personal characteristics necessary for effective performance. Interviews have the advantage of being much more economical of the analyst's time than observation, particularly in the case of jobs with a long cycle time. Interviews are also much more appropriate and useful in the analysis of jobs having a significant mental component. Just as with observation, the utility and validity of interviews is dependent upon: (1) the use of a systematic method of eliciting and recording information about the job from interviewees; and (2) insuring that an adequate sample of incumbents has been interviewed to provide a relatively complete and objective picture of the job requirements.

Interviews also have weaknesses. Just as job incumbents may change or distort their job behavior in the presence of an observer, incumbents may distort what they say to an interviewer about the requirements of a job. The interviewee may be trying to second-guess the purpose of the interview and provide information that places the incumbent in the best possible light. The validity of the information obtained in interviews will depend in part upon the ability of the interviewer to establish rapport with the person being interviewed. Finally, interviews lack some of the richness of observation. A verbal description of a job and the requirements it places upon an incumbent can never completely capture all of the nuances and complexities of the workplace. For this reason, interviews are frequently used in combination with observation of actual job behavior.

Questionnaires and Checklists

A variety of questionnaires and checklists to be completed by job incumbents has been designed and employed for job analysis. Such questionnaires and checklists have two unique advantages that are their primary strengths. First, they provide standardized information in response to a fixed set of items or questions about the job. This standardization facilitates tremendously the ability of the job analyst to: (1) pool the responses of a large number of job incumbents; and (2) compare different jobs with one another on a standard set of common characteristics or dimensions. The second strong advantage of questionnaires and checklists is their relative economy of the analyst's time. It is feasible for a job analyst to have 100 job incumbents simultaneously complete a questionnaire in less than the amount of time required to observe one job or interview a single job incumbent.

At the same time, of course, questionnaires and checklists are not without their shortcomings. In particular, they lack the flexibility of interviews to probe unique aspects of a job, and they lack the richness of description available only from first-hand observation of job performance. As with the previously discussed techniques, they are also subject to distortion by the individuals completing the questionnaires and checklists.

Other Techniques

Observation, interviews, and questionnaires do not exhaust the list of methods available for job analysis, although they are the most commonly employed and generally applicable techniques. There are a number of additional alternatives worthy of brief mention.

A conference of experts can be employed to develop a job analysis. The "experts" involved in such a conference are usually a combination of experienced job analysts and line managers directly familiar with the job being analyzed. This method has the advantage of being relatively economical and also avoids potential bias in information provided by current job incumbents. Its primary weakness lies in the fact that job incumbents inevitably know more than anyone else about the requirements of their jobs. Failure to seek and incorporate their inputs generally results in an imperfect or incomplete analysis.

A job analysis can also be developed by referring to previous analyses of the same or similar jobs in the organization, as well as by reference to additional sources of job descriptions such as the *Dictionary of Occupational Titles*, published by the U.S. Department of Labor, which contains brief descriptions of over 30,000 jobs. Such a technique, though frequently helpful, will almost always yield incomplete and inaccurate job analyses, since very few jobs are identical to one another in all respects and the requirements of jobs tend to change with time.

A final and somewhat extreme technique of job analysis requires that the job analyst do the job being analyzed. While such a technique undoubtedly provides the analyst with the most intimate and complete familiarity with the job that is possible, it is likely to be infeasible in most situations due to the time required and the skill demands of all but the lowest-level positions.

Examples of Job Analysis Systems

Most large organizations have developed their own composite system for carrying out job analyses. In order to provide some feeling for what a job analysis looks like in practice, we will briefly describe two carefully developed and widely used job analysis systems.

U.S. Department of Labor Approach

The *Handbook for Analyzing Jobs* published by the U.S. Department of Labor (1972) outlines a detailed and comprehensive method for analyzing jobs. The approach involves a combination of observation of job behavior, interviews with job incumbents, and expert judgments on the part of the job analyst. The procedure results in a job being classified on four major dimensions.

The first dimension is called *worker functions*. Here the job is classified on the basis of the specific functions performed by the incumbent with regard to data, people, and things. The twenty-four particular functions included in this dimension are summarized under these three headings in Table 2-1. Second, the job is assigned to one of a hundred possible *work fields*, e.g., cooking, building, recording. Third, the major outcomes or results produced by the job are identified and the job is assigned to one of fifty-five categories of *materials, products, subject matter,* or *services*, e.g., business service. Fourth, the *worker traits* which are appropriate for performing the job are estimated by the analyst. Ratings are provided on a total of six traits: training time, aptitudes, temperaments, interests, physical demands, and environmental conditions. This classification is supplemented by additional information regarding things such as the education, training, and experience necessary for the job, as well as a fairly detailed narrative description of the actual tasks performed on the job.

The Department of Labor system has the advantage of providing a relatively comprehensive standardized package which can be employed for job analysis. It has the disadvantages of being rather cumbersome, requiring considerable initial training of analysts, and being fairly dependent for its completeness on the qualitative data contained in the narrative descriptions of the tasks performed on the job.

TABLE 2-1
Worker functions employed in the U.S. Department of Labor job analysis system

Data	People	Things
0 Synthesizing	0 Monitoring	0 Setting up
1 Coordinating	1 Negotiating	1 Precision working
2 Analyzing	2 Instructing	2 Operating-controlling
3 Compiling	3 Supervising	3 Driving-operating
4 Computing	4 Diverting	4 Manipulating
5 Copying	5 Persuading	5 Tending
6 Comparing	6 Speaking-signaling	6 Feeding-offbearing
	7 Serving	7 Handling
	8 Taking instructions-helping	

SOURCE: U.S. Department of Labor, Manpower Administration, *Handbook for Analyzing Jobs,* Washington, D.C.: U.S. Government Printing Office, 1972, p. 73. Used by permission.

Position Analysis Questionnaire (PAQ)

The PAQ developed by McCormick and his colleagues (McCormick, Mecham, & Jeanneret, 1972) is a questionnaire that permits the job analyst to carry out a purely quantitative analysis of a job. No narrative descriptions or qualitative judgments are included in the analysis. The questionnaire itself consists of a total of 194 items. Each item describes a single "element" of work and asks the respondent to indicate the degree to which that element is present in the job being analyzed. The questionnaire can be filled out either by the job incumbents themselves, or by job analysts based upon their observations of the job and interviews with incumbents. The 194 elements are designed to assess six broad categories of work activity: (1) information input, e.g., use of written materials; (2) mental processes, e.g., coding/decoding; (3) work output, e.g., use of keyboard devices; (4) relationships with other persons, e.g., interviewing; (5) job context, e.g., working in high temperatures; and (6) other job characteristics, e.g., working irregular hours.

The PAQ has been used with a wide variety of jobs. The results of analyses of over 500 different jobs with the PAQ indicate that jobs tend to have five basic dimensions along which they differ.

1. Having decision-making/social responsibilities.
2. Performing skilled activities.
3. Being physically active/related environmental conditions.
4. Operating vehicles/equipment.
5. Processing information. (McCormick & Tiffin, 1974, pp. 54–55)

The PAQ's reliance upon quantitative responses to standardized items has a number of advantages. First, it reduces the extent to which job analysis is dependent upon the qualitative personal judgments of the analyst. Second, it permits jobs to be compared with one another quantitatively rather than purely qualitatively. Finally, it provides organizations with the scope to group jobs together systematically on the basis of a common set of underlying dimensions.

Future Developments in Job Analysis

Equal employment opportunity legislation guidelines, and judicial decisions regarding discrimination in the selection process (discussed in detail in Chapter 3) have resulted in a greatly increased emphasis upon the need for organizations to maintain objective job analyses. Under certain conditions organizations can be required to produce evidence of valid job analyses in order to justify their selection systems. An outcome of this important role for job analysis has been increased attention to new and improved approaches to conducting job analyses (e.g., Cornelius & Lyness, 1980; Lopez, Kesselman, & Lopez, 1981). This heightened interest in job analysis will no doubt continue as organizations become increasingly sensitive to the validity of their selection procedures.

ASSESSING APPLICANTS

A systematic job analysis puts the organization in the position of having a clear, well-defined picture of what it is looking for in a prospective employee. The job analysis outlines exactly what a person occupying the job must do and also indicates the types of personal characteristics and traits that a person should have in order to be capable of doing the things that the job requires. However, a systematic job analysis, while an obvious necessity, is clearly not sufficient to insure that the organization makes sound selection decisions. In order to assure a good match between its requirements and the capabilities of its members, the organization requires methods of assessing the skills, abilities, characteristics, and traits of applicants. In other words, even when an organization has answered the question "What is it we are looking for?", it must then address the question "How can we tell when we have found it?" The answer to this question lies in the design and implementation of appropriate and informative methods of assessing the characteristics and capabilities of prospective members of the organization. In what follows we will present a number of the most common of these assessment techniques and discuss the strengths and weaknesses of each. Prior to undertaking this discussion, however, we must first briefly review several important qualities that measures of applicant characteristics must possess if they are to be helpful in making sound personnel selection decisions.

Reliability and Validity of Measurement

The process of assessing job applicants can be thought of as a measurement process. When faced with a person who has applied for a job, the organization wishes to "measure" the extent to which that person possesses the personal traits, characteristics, or qualities necessary for successful job performance. An inherent problem involved in this process lies in the fact that it is extremely difficult to develop accurate and precise methods of measuring the extent to which individuals possess traits and characteristics such as intelligence, sociability, decision-making capacity, and so on. Thus, organizations must be extremely conscious of the quality of the measurement techniques which they are employing in order to insure that they are obtaining reasonably accurate measures of the personal characteristics which they are interested in. In addition, they must also insure that the personal characteristics they are measuring are in fact related to successful performance of the job. The assessment of the extent to which measures of applicants' personal characteristics fulfill these requirements involves an examination of the *reliability* and *validity* of the measures employed.

Reliability

The term *reliability* refers to the extent to which a method of measuring the personal characteristics of an applicant yields stable and consistent results. Stability and consistency of results are desirable, since this indicates that the measurement technique is in fact yielding true measures of some underlying characteristic of the applicant. If a measurement technique were found to yield highly variable and inconsistent results, this would lead us to suspect that the technique is not really measuring any true underlying characteristic of the applicant, but instead is generating only random, uninterpretable, and uninformative data.

The reliability of a measurement technique can be assessed in either of two ways. First, the *stability* of the measurements over time can be determined. This approach, often referred to as *test-retest reliability*, involves obtaining measures of individuals at two times and assessing the extent of agreement between the two sets of measures. The degree of agreement between the two sets of measures provides an index of the reliability of the measurement technique, since if it is yielding true measures of applicant characteristics, the measures should not change from one time to another. This method of determining measurement reliability is obviously applicable only to those measures of personal characteristics of applicants that would not be expected to change over time.

The second method of determining a measure's reliability involves the assessment of the internal *consistency* of the measure itself. Most measures of personal characteristics consist of a number of different questions or items. If the different items are all generating true measures of the same underlying personal characteristic of the applicant, then all of the items should yield consistent results that are in agreement with each other. The internal consistency test of reliability can be applied even to measures of characteristics expected to change over time.

Validity

The term *validity*, when applied to measures of personal characteristics of job applicants, generally has to do with the extent to which measures really are measuring what we think they're measuring. There exists a multitude of different types of validity. We'll discuss the three types of validity most relevant to our discussion of the personnel selection process.

1. Content Validity. *Content validity* refers to the extent to which a group of experts agrees that the questions or items included in a measurement device are truly representative of the entire universe of content which the device is attempting to measure. In the case of a paper-and-pencil measure

of a personality trait, the assessment of content validity requires a judgment of the degree of representativeness of the items included in the test. In the case of a job ability test, content validity would be determined by the extent to which the content of the ability test was adequately representative of the overall content of the job. While the assessment of content validity is only judgmental, content validity is an important and desirable characteristic of a measurement device. The judgments involved in assessing content validity are those of experts in the field, and these judgments are made against a specified criterion (the representativeness of the items or questions employed).

2. Construct Validity. *Construct validity* refers to the extent to which a measurement technique is truly measuring the underlying characteristic it is intended to measure. The determination of the construct validity of a measure is important since without it we have no assurance that our measurement devices are in fact measuring the personal characteristics of job applicants that we wish to measure. Quantitative statistical techniques have been developed for the determination of the construct validity of measures (Campbell & Fiske, 1959).

3. Criterion-Related Validity. *Criterion-related validity* refers to the extent to which measures of applicants' personal characteristics are in fact related to performance on the job for which the applicant is being considered. The term *criterion-related validity* is employed since this aspect of validity has to do with the relationship between measures of an applicant's personal characteristics and measures of some *criterion* of job performance. The extent to which a measure possesses criterion-related validity can be determined quantitatively by examining the degree of correlation between the measure and the subsequent criterion of job performance. Clearly, a high degree of criterion-related validity is a desirable characteristic of any method of assessing an applicant's personal charateristics for purposes of making personnel selection decisions.

The Selection Interview

We begin our discussion of methods of assessing job applicants with the selection interview, since it is probably the most widely used assessment technique and is the one with which almost everyone has some first-hand personal experience.

The selection interview has been the object of a good deal of study and much controversy. Its popularity as an assessment device with managers and practitioners is almost equaled by its lack of popularity, indeed its downright bad reputation, among scholars and researchers. The following statement by two eminent researchers is representative of the esteem in which the interview is held by this group:

> The personnel interview continues to be the most widely used method for selecting employees, despite the fact that it is a costly, inefficient, and usually invalid procedure. . . . It is almost always treated as the final hurdle in the selection process. (Dunnette and Bass, 1963)

Our goal in discussing the selection interview will be to provide a reasonably balanced picture of the interview as a method of assessing job applicants. First we'll explore the negative side of the controversy to show why the interview has come into such disrepute among systematic researchers. Next, we'll present some of the positive attributes of the interview, factors which have led to its pervasiveness and popularity among practitioners. We'll conclude our discussion with some suggestions for improving the validity and utility of the interview as an assessment device.

The Negative Side

The typical unstructured selection interview tends to be quite unreliable. When several people are each asked to interview the same applicant, there tends to be very little agreement among the interviewers in their assessments of the applicant. This disagreement applies to the interviewers' assessments of what attributes or characteristics the applicant possesses, as well as the interviewers' judgments of whether the applicant would be successful or not if hired (Valenzi & Andrews, 1973). This seems to imply that the assessments generated from unstructured interviews depend as much or more upon the attitudes and opinions of the interviewer as they do on the characteristics of the interviewee. This is not a desirable situation.

Common sense dictates that if the unstructured interview is unreliable it must also be invalid. If several interviewers disagree on the characteristics and potential of an interviewee (which means the interview is unreliable), it is impossible that all of their assessments are correct and accurate (which means that the interview as an assessment device must be invalid). Systematic empirical research confirms what common sense dictates. The judgments of interviewers arising from unstructured selection interviews tend to be very poor in terms of both: (1) their accuracy of assessing whether the applicant does or does not possess particular personal characteristics; and (2) the accuracy of their estimates of the future success or failure of the applicant if hired (Wright, 1964).

Why is it that unstructured selection interviews tend to fare so badly when the accuracy and consistency of the assessments they generate are closely examined? Two large-scale research programs have attempted to come up with some answers to this question. Their results throw a great deal of light on problems with the selection interview and help guide us to some suggestions for its improvement.

The first research project was carried out at McGill University and involved an extensive study of interviewing recruits to the Canadian Armed Forces (Webster, 1964). The second large-scale project studied applicants for positions in the life insurance industry and was conducted for the Life Insurance Marketing and Research Association (LIMRA) by Carlson and his colleagues (Carlson, Thayer, Mayfield, and Peterson, 1971).

The results of these research projects, along with a description of their implications, are summarized in Table 2-2. These systematic studies lead to the following rather unflattering picture of the "typical" selection interview.

1. Interviewers have their own personal stereotypes of what constitutes a "good" employee or how a potential "good" employee should appear in an interview situation. These stereotypes generally differ from interviewer to interviewer and bear no necessary relationship to a true or valid profile of a good potential employee.
2. Interviewers tend to make an accept-or-reject decision very early in the interview (often in the first 5 to 10 minutes) and then spend the remainder of the interview seeking out information which confirms this initial impression. The notion of the interviewer as a detached and objective analyst of the interviewee's strengths and weaknesses appears to be more myth than reality.
3. Negative information supplied by an applicant tends to have a much greater impact upon an interviewer's judgments than does positive information. Negative and positive aspects are not equally weighted and traded off against one another. The negative is given much more weight.
4. An interviewer's judgments regarding an applicant are not determined solely by the applicant's characteristics but are also influenced by: (a) the relative strength or weakness of immediately preceding interviewees; and (b) the presence or absence of quotas or numbers of applicants who *must* be hired. When an average applicant is interviewed immediately following one or more below-average applicants, the average applicant tends to be rated well above average. The same process works in reverse if an average applicant has the misfortune to follow immediately after an outstanding applicant. Similarly, when interviewers have been given quotas of minimum numbers of people who must be hired, applicants with only average potential tend to be rated well above average in order to permit the interviewers to meet their quotas.
5. Experience as an interviewer does *not* result in interviewers' judgments becoming more accurate and valid, unless the interviewers are supplied with systematic feedback regarding the strengths, weaknesses, successes, and failures of those people whom they have interviewed. When such feedback is not provided, interviewers do not improve their accuracy and validity, although they do become much more confident that their inaccurate and invalid judgments are accurate and valid.

TABLE 2-2
Results of two major research projects on the selection interview with their implications for the use of interviews

Webster (1964)	Carlson et al. (1971)	Implications
1. Interviewers seem to develop stereotypes about a good applicant and seek to match interviewees with their stereotype.	1. Interviewers agree on which facts they *say* they consider in making decisions, and can agree on the goodness or badness of an interviewee's record, but they do not agree on whether they should *hire* the person. Interviewers thus seem to have different stereotypes of the good employee; only some stereotypes are shared by interviewers.	1. Provide interviewers an accurate picture of the "good" employee so that all interviewers can work with the same stereotype. Put the stereotype in behavioral terms and require the interviewer to make a prediction about job behavior.
2. Unfavorable information about an interviewee is more influential on the interviewer's decision than favorable information.	2. The impact of the favorability of information is a function of the characteristics of the people *already* interviewed and/or the others with whom the interviewee is presented; an average applicant after or among poor applicants is rated above average. Further, when "bodies" are needed (when the interviewer has a quota to fill) an average applicant receives a higher rating. Interviewers agree more on unfavorable applicants.	2. Require interviewers to consider all *relevant* information in making decisions.
3. Interviewer decisions are affected by whether the information is provided a little piece at a time or all at once.		3. Do not give interviewers quotas for bodies.
4. Biases for or against an interviewee are established early in the interview.	3. The impact of factual information on the interviewer's judgment is a function of (1) whether the interviewer follows a structured interview schedule and (2) whether the interviewer takes notes. Those who do neither seem to make decisions based on a global impression ("halo"). Interviewers differ in their ability to "spread out" interviewees on the basis of the information they receive.	4. Require interviewers to use a standardized, highly structured interview schedule and to take extensive notes to be used *later* in making their decisions. The guidelines should concentrate on assessment of factual material, not on evaluations.
4 Experienced interviewers can agree on the rankings (from best to worst) to be given a group of interviewees.	4. Only highly structured interviews generate information that enables interviewers to agree with each other; experience is not the important element *unless interviewers receive feedback on their interviews*. Then more experienced interviewers are more reliable. Experience also makes the interviewer less susceptible to external pressure such as quotas (see number 2 above). Those interviewers who can "spread out" applicants based on the information they receive also tend to agree more with each other on the rankings of applicants; factual information helps the process.	5. Make sure the information to be sought *in the interview and* the interviewer have been validated. Provide feedback to interviewers on their performance so they can engage in self-correction behavior. Some people seem to be better users of information than others.

SOURCE: *Staffing Organizations* by Benjamin Schneider. Copyright © 1976 Scott, Foresman and Company. Reprinted by permission.

There are obviously many serious problems with the selection interview. However, the picture is not totally bleak. Selection interviews also have a number of strengths and positive characteristics. We'll look at some of these strengths and then discuss how the strengths of the interview can be accentuated and the weaknesses minimized.

The Positive Side

The popularity of the interview has not occurred by accident. Organizations are well aware that interviews have a variety of positive characteristics which they would be very reluctant to give up (Miner & Miner, 1977).

1. The interview gives the organization an opportunity to provide information to the applicant regarding the specific position in particular and the organization in general. This mutual information-sharing aspect of the interview is essential if a good "fit" is to be obtained. Sometimes this aspect of the interview may consist largely of discussing specific terms of employment, while in other cases (e.g., an outstanding applicant or a very tight labor market) the organization may be seeking to "sell" itself to the applicant.
2. The interview may be used as a public relations device by the organization to help project a positive image to all applicants. This public relations function may be particularly important in the case of applicants who are eventually refused employment, to attempt to insure that they are not left with a totally negative impression of the organization.
3. One of the interview's greatest assets is its flexibility. It provides the organization with an opportunity to fill in the gaps of missing or incomplete information which may be required for a decision. This flexibility also permits the applicant to draw attention to any relevant strengths which other assessment devices may have failed to bring to light.
4. The interview does permit interviewers to make assessments of their ability to get along with the applicant. This may be valuable if an interviewer will be an interviewee's immediate superior if the person is hired. Interviewers must take care, however, not to overgeneralize from the relatively short and circumscribed interview situation to an ongoing, long-term work relationship. Interviewers must also exercise caution in assessing an interviewee's overall ability to "get along with other people" from their impression of how the interviewee "got along" with the interviewer.
5. Finally, the interview may in certain cases be the only appropriate or acceptable form of assessment available. In most professions, and for very senior positions in organizations, the most desirable potential candidates for a position may be unwilling to subject themselves to any other form of assessment (such as application blanks or employment tests). In such cases the interview, for all its weaknesses, may be all that is available.

With these positive characteristics of interviews in mind we now turn to a discussion of how an organization might best design its interviewing procedures to accentuate the potential strengths and minimize the potential weaknesses.

Suggestions for Improving the Interview

Improving the value of the interview as a method of assessing applicants requires attending carefully to the negative aspects of the interview and taking all possible steps to minimize each potential negative factor. The *implications* column of Table 2-2 outlines what some of these steps might look like. We'll expand a bit more fully upon each of these suggestions.

1. **Use Trained Interviewers.** Effective interviewing requires specific skills in asking questions, probing, listening, recording unbiased information, and so on. Most people don't have such skills unless they have been provided with training and direction. Competent interviewing is not something that "anybody" can do effectively.

2. **Provide a Complete Job Analysis.** A major problem with the interview is that each interviewer has a different stereotype of the ideal candidate. This problem is overcome if all interviewers are provided with a clear description of what the job requires of a person and what personal characteristics are likely to be indicative of success (Osburn, Timmreck, & Digby, 1981).

3. **Use a Structured Interview Format.** The long list of woes of the interview applies to *unstructured* interviews. It is in unstructured interviews that interviewers tend to make snap decisions and put too much emphasis on negative information. The interview can be made much more systematic and objective if a specific structure for the interview is laid out and adhered to by all interviewers. Such a structure may take the form of a list of topics to be covered and the order in which they should be covered. In other cases the structure may specify the actual questions to be asked. Evidence from the life insurance industry indicates that structured interviews can contribute valuable information and increase the validity of selection decisions (Mayfield, Brown, & Hamstra, 1980).

4. **Keep a Structured Written Record of Each Interview.** Human memory is very limited and very fallible. Keeping a written record of every interview in a structured format insures that the information generated by the interview will be accurately maintained in a fashion which facilitates the systematic comparison of everyone interviewed.

5. **Use Multiple Interviewers.** We all tend to see the world somewhat differently; some of us pick up on some factors while others focus on quite different characteristics of whatever we're presented with. The same

applies to interviewers and their perceptions of job applicants. The use of multiple interviewers permits the organization to have greater confidence in areas on which there is consensus and to explore areas of disagreement among interviewers to arrive at the most accurate possible picture of the applicant (Grove, 1981; Rothstein & Jackson, 1980). Naturally, the drawback of using multiple interviewers is the greater cost and consumption of time involved.

6. Avoid Quotas. The evidence is clear that when interviewers are told they "must" find a certain number of suitable candidates, they do. However, they do this by lowering their standards of what they consider to be suitable and end up recommending candidates of lower quality and potential. The solution is straightforward. Don't set quotas. Let the quality of the applicants, not some artificial quota, determine who is recommended and who is not.

7. Use the Interview as One Aspect of an Overall Selection System. When the foregoing recommendations are implemented, the interview can become a valuable source of information to be taken into account in making selection decisions. This is the appropriate role for the interview in the selection process. The interview must not be used as the sole basis for assessing applicants, nor should the interviewer be the sole decision maker regarding who is hired and who is not.

Recent research on the employment interview indicates that approaches incorporating the above suggestions can result in the interview becoming a useful and valid source of information for making selection decisions. One approach, labeled the *situational interview*, has been shown to have high reliability and substantial validity for predicting subsequent job performance (Latham, Saari, Pursell & Campion, 1980).

Tests

It is terribly seductive to imagine that an organization could give a job applicant a short, objectively scored test of some kind and on the basis of the results accurately predict whether, and to what extent, the applicant would perform effectively if hired. Tests have the advantages of being quick, inexpensive, and objective. These advantages, combined with the appeal of the assumption that it "should" be possible to design tests which predict job performance accurately, have resulted in the development of a tremendous number of tests for use in personnel selection.

Tests have also come in for their fair share of criticism, particularly from people who are skeptical of the ability of tests to assess what someone is "really like." This criticism frequently takes the form of people poking fun at psychological tests. For example, William Whyte's book *The Organization Man* contains an appendix on "How to Cheat on Personality

Tests," and Fran Lebowitz in *Metropolitan Life* has written her own version of psychological tests to assess people for the jobs of Pope, Heiress, Political Dictator, Social Climber, and Empress. The Social Climber test is included in Figure 2-2 so you can assess how well suited you might be for this occupation.

The types of tests used for selection in organizations can be broadly classified into two categories. The classification is based upon the view that a person's performance in an organization is determined jointly by a combination of the person's motivation and ability. In ordinary everyday

FIGURE 2-2
A humorous example of a selection test for the job of "Social Climber." (SOURCE: Fran Lebowitz, *Metropolitan Life*. New York: Elsevier-Dutton, 1974. Used by permission.)

1. When alone I most often. . .
   a. Read.
   b. Watch television.
   c. Write sonnets.
   d. Build model planes.
   e. Call the Beverly Hills Hotel and have myself paged.

2. Were a female friend to say something particulary amusing I would most likely. . .
   a. Say, "Hey, that was really funny."
   b. Laugh delightedly.
   c. Giggle uncontrollably.
   d. Say, "You're so like Dottie."

3. When the phone rings I am most likely to answer by saying. . .
   a. "Hello, how are you?"
   b. "Oh, hello."
   c. "Hi."
   d. "Oh, hi, I was just listening to one of Wolfgang's little symphonies."

4. If my house or apartment was on fire the first thing I would save would be. . .
   a. My son.
   b. My cat.
   c. My boyfriend.
   d. My mention in *Women's Wear Daily*.

5. I consider dining out to be. . .
   a. A pleasure.
   b. A nice change.
   c. An opportunity to see friends.
   d. A romantic interlude.
   e. A career.

6. My idea of a good party is. . .
   a. A big, noisy bash, with lots of liquor and lots of action.
   b. Good talk, good food, good wine.
   c. A few close friends for dinner and bridge.
   d. One to which I cannot get invited.

7. If I were stranded alone on a desert island and could have only one book I would want. . .
   a. The Bible.
   b. The Complete Works of William Shakespeare.
   c. *The Wind in the Willows*.
   d. Truman Capote's address book.

8. Some of my best friends are. . .
   a. Jewish.
   b. Negro.
   c. Puerto Rican.
   d. Unaware of my existence.

9. As far as I am concerned, a rose by any other name is. . .
   a. Still the same.
   b. A flower.
   c. A color.
   d. A scent.
   e. A Kennedy

terms, a person must be both "willing" (have the motivation), and "able" (have the ability), if he or she is to be an effective performer in an organization. In line with this view, the tests which have been developed to assess job applicants are usually classified into: (1) tests of motivation; and (2) tests of ability.

There is both good news and bad news regarding the capability of tests to predict job performance. Most of the good news has to do with the tests of ability, and it is to these which we turn first.

Ability Testing

The notion of testing and measuring differences among people in their ability has a long history, dating back to the initial ideas of Sir Francis Galton who wrote a book entitled *Hereditary Genius* in 1869. The approach really gathered steam with the work of Binet in the late 19th and early 20th centuries. Binet developed the first carefully constructed and empirically validated test of intelligence, a test which served as the forerunner of most modern approaches to the measurement of intellectual ability.

In the years since these pioneering efforts a vast number of tests have been developed to measure a staggering variety of different types of job-related abilities. A systematic review of all of these different approaches is available in a variety of sources (Dunnette, 1966; Ghiselli, 1966, 1973; Guion, 1965; Schneider, 1976). For our purposes, it will suffice to summarize briefly the different types of ability tests under the following general headings.

1. *Intellectual ability,* often simply referred to as *intelligence.* A wide variety of tests exist, each of which contains a number of specific subcomponents of intellectual ability, e.g., verbal reasoning, numerical ability, memory, abstract reasoning.
2. *Spatial and mechanical ability.* The ability to perceive and cope with physical and mechanical tasks.
3. *Clerical ability.* The ability to perform systematic clerical operations.
4. *Motor ability.* The ability to perform tasks requiring physical activity, precision, and coordination.
5. *Interpersonal ability.* The ability to get along with others and manage relationships with others constructively.
6. *Personal decision-making ability.* The ability to cope effectively with organizational decision-making responsibilities.

Much research has been conducted on the capacity of ability tests to predict subsequent job behavior. In general, the results indicate that ability tests can be helpful in predicting who will subsequently be successful on the job. Up until very recently it was also felt that a test which was a good predictor of success for one job would not necessarily be a useful predictor for another job (Ghiselli, 1973). However, recent research indicates that the validities of aptitude and ability tests are in fact highly general from job to job (Schmidt, Hunter & Caplan, 1981; Schmidt, Hunter & Pearlman, 1981; Schmidt, Gast-Rosenberg & Hunter, 1980; Callender & Osburn, 1980; Pearlman, Schmidt & Hunter, 1980). These findings will very likely have the impact of increasing the use of aptitude and ability tests for selection purposes in the future (Schmidt & Hunter, 1980).

Motivation Testing

It would be extremely handy for an organization to have a short test which would sort out the ambitious, highly motivated "go-getters" from the lazy, lackadaisical "drones." Unfortunately, such a test does not exist. However, a considerable amount of effort has been put into attempts to develop tests which could predict the level of motivation of prospective employees. Although the results of such efforts have generally been less successful than comparable attempts at measuring abilities, some promising results have been obtained.

Tests designed to assess levels of motivation fall into two general categories: (1) tests which measure a person's pattern of *interests*; and (2) tests which measure various aspects of a person's *personality*.

There are two carefully developed and widely distributed interest tests, the Strong-Campbell Interest Inventory [or SCII, an updated version of the Strong Vocational Interest Blank (SVIB)], and the Kuder Preference Records: Occupational and Vocational (Kuder O and Kuder V). The SCII yields a profile of a person's interests in a wide variety of different occupations. A person's responses can be compared to the average responses of actual members of each occupation to assess the degree of similarity between the person's interests and those of occupation members. While the SCII has been shown to be quite useful in predicting which occupation a person will enter, it has not been shown to predict a person's level of motivation or performance on any given job. A similar pattern of results has emerged regarding the Kuder Preference Records as well (Dunnette and Aylward, 1956). Some interesting recent research has however succeeded in uncovering relationships between patterns of vocational interests and effective police performance (Johnson & Hogan, 1981). These recent findings may stimulate further research into the relationship of vocational interests to job performance.

On the personality side of the motivation-testing approach, results are a bit more promising for certain occupations. A wide variety of paper-and-pencil tests of personality have been developed. Among the most widely used tests in selection situations are the California Psychological Inventory (CPI), the Edwards Personal Preference Schedule (EPPS), and the Self-Description Inventory (SDI). These tests generally yield a series of scores for the applicant on a number of different personality dimensions, such as dominance, extraversion, self-assurance, and decisiveness. The results of a review of the average validities for different occupations of various personality tests indicate that measures of personality characteristics can be useful predictors of job performance in certain occupations, but have a more limited role in predicting success in other occupations (Ghiselli, 1973). For example, personality measures tend to have good validities in predicting success in sales occupations. Additional recent research also indicates the viability of predicting success of police officers on the basis of scores on the CPI (Mills & Bohannon, 1980).

Biographical Information Blanks (BIBs)

Almost every organization uses some type of application form for assessing applicants for most jobs below senior management levels. However, organizations differ widely in the kinds of information that they obtain on application blanks and in the extent to which they systematically utilize this information in making selection decisions.

The basic rationale behind the use of biographical information in choosing among job applicants is summarized in the maxim that "The best predictor of future behavior is past behavior." In fact, the argument for the validity of biographical information as a predictor of job success can be made in a somewhat more sophisticated manner. Biographical and personal history information can provide extremely reliable data regarding the ability of an applicant to engage in the types of behavior necessary for successful performance of the job. Thus, biographical data items should serve as valid predictors of job success to the extent that they provide an assessment of: (1) whether an applicant has previously occupied positions similar to the current opening; and (2) the adequacy of the applicant's performance in such similar situations in the past.

BIBs obtain basic demographic information regarding an applicant (name, address, date of birth, marital status, etc.), plus information regarding factors such as educational history (schools attended, with dates, degrees, or certificates obtained), job-related training experiences, and work history (including items such as job titles, duties, level in the organization, tenure, supervisory responsibilities, salary, and reason for leaving). Some forms ask for additional information, usually in multiple-choice format, regarding factors such as individual achievements, hobbies, health, family experiences, and social relationships. Three factors must be kept in mind in designing a BIB.

1. Items should only be included which have the potential of providing information regarding the applicant's past behavior in situations which bear some similarity or generalizability to the types of situations to be encountered on the job.
2. Items should only be included which will actually be used in the selection process. BIBs have a tendency to grow with the passage of time. While it is always feasible (and perhaps desirable) to add new

items to an existing BIB, it is also feasible (and equally desirable) to delete unnecessary or unused items.

3. Items should only be included which do not violate fair employment practices legislation and which do not constitute an unwarranted invasion of the privacy of the applicant (further discussion of these issues is contained in Chapter 3).

In order for the BIB to contribute maximally to improving the accuracy and validity of selection decisions, systematic empirical research must be done into the relationship between responses to items on the BIB and subsequent success on the job. A separate analysis must be carried out for *each job* for which the BIB is to be used. This systematic research involves studying the degree of relationship (if any) between responses to the items contained in the BIB and subsequent job success, ignoring or eliminating those responses which are not related to success and developing a weighting scheme for those items which are related to successful performance. Items with the strongest relationship to subsequent success are given the greatest weight in influencing the selection decision, those with a weaker relationship are given lower weights, and so on. Once these weights have been determined from a careful analysis of one group of applicants, they must be double checked on another group of applicants before they are actually used for making selection decisions (this double-checking procedure is known as *cross-validation*). It is essential that: (1) all of the above steps be carried out; (2) the procedure be conducted separately for each distinct job or family of jobs for which the weighted BIB is to be used; and (3) the procedure be repeated every few years (or more frequently if the requirements of the job change) to insure the weighting procedure continues to be valid.

When these steps are adhered to and carefully implemented, BIBs can be impressive predictors of success on the job. In fact they consistently outperform *all* of the other standard methods of assessing applicants, and they generally do so at lower cost as well. Table 2-3 summarizes results from a comparison of BIBs with intelligence and personality tests in terms

TABLE 2-3
Percentages of validities of biographical information blanks, intelligence tests, and personality tests exceeding certain values

Validities	BIB	Intelligence	Personality
Above 0.50	55	28	12
Above 0.40	74	51	22
Above 0.30	97	60	42

SOURCE: Adapted from James J. Asher, "The biographical item: Can it be improved?" *Personnel Psychology*, 1972, *25*, 255, 256. Used by permission.

of their capacity to predict subsequent job performance (Asher, 1972). The term *validities* in the table refers to the correlation coefficients observed between the predictor of job performance and a subsequent criterion measure of job performance. Validity coefficients greater than 0.50 are considered to be very high, those over 0.40 are high, and those exceeding 0.30 are still valuable and useful. The superiority of BIBs is clear. BIBs have been employed successfully in the selection of clerical personnel, industrial research scientists, managers, food sales managers, life insurance salesmen, and unskilled employees.

Assessment Centers

Assessment centers are a relatively recent development on the selection scene. Up to now they have tended to be used most widely for the purpose of assessing current members of the organization in order to identify managerial potential and promotability. However, they are clearly feasible as an assessment technique for use in selecting among applicants for managerial positions, and some organizations do in fact use assessment centers for this purpose.

An assessment center is a method of assessing managerial potential; the term does not refer to any particular physical location. An assessment center can be conducted on the premises of the organization doing the assessing or at some offsite location such as a hotel or a special training and assessment facility maintained by the organization.

An assessment center is usually from 1½ to 3½ days in duration. During this period a group of candidates (usually from ten to fifteen in number), referred to as assessees, engage in a wide variety of structured activities under the observation of a group of trained assessors. The group of assessors is generally composed of a combination of senior managers from the organization who have been given special training in assessment techniques, and several professional psychologists who are experts in assessment center methodology.

The assessments of candidates that are generated by an assessment center are based upon some combination of the following methods.

1. Personal history forms filled out by assessees, i.e., some form of biographical information blank which records work experience, educational history, special accomplishments, and so on.
2. In-depth structured interviews of each candidate conducted by two or more assessors.
3. Systematic written records based on observations of the candidate's performance in a variety of structured experiences and exercises.
4. Analysis by professional psychologists of results of a variety of psychological tests.
5. Peer evaluation of each assessee by the other candidates in the assessment center.

6. Composite judgments by assessors based upon their overall impression of each candidate derived from extensive observation and interaction.

During an assessment center, candidates spend the majority of their time engaged in various structured experiences and exercises. The design of the exercises is based upon the nature of the managerial position or positions for which the candidates are being assessed. The goal is to create situations in the assessment center whose demands most closely simulate the demands of the actual managerial job. By placing candidates in such simulated situations and systematically observing their reactions, it is possible to assess as objectively as possible the candidate's current ability to engage in the behaviors required for successful performance of the position.

The exercises and simulations employed in any given assessment center can take a wide variety of forms. Among the most frequently used techniques are the following.

1. ***In-Basket Exercise.*** Candidates play the role of managers who have just moved into new positions in a hypothetical organization. The candidates are given large quantities of material that simulates the contents of their in-baskets on the first morning in their new positions. The in-baskets contain memos, reports, telephone messages, urgent requests for meetings, complaints, and so on. The candidates are then given a very limited amount of time to work through the contents of the in-basket, making decisions, responding to requests, setting priorities, etc. Each candidate's responses are subsequently evaluated by assessors on a set of criteria and given a numerical score.

2. ***Leaderless Group Discussions.*** Candidates work together as a group on some simulated managerial problem that requires a group meeting. Within the group no individual has been clearly assigned a leadership role. A typical simulation requires each participant to play the role of a manager of a different geographical region of a company. The managers are meeting to discuss who is the best candidate for a promotion to the managerial ranks. Each participant has one subordinate whom he or she feels is the best candidate and whom they would like to see receive the promotion. The discussion is observed by the assessors, who maintain a written record of the participants' behavior on a variety of dimensions such as willingness to listen to others, openness to alternatives, ability to communicate effectively, and tendency to adopt a leadership role.

3. ***Interpersonal Role-Play Exercises.*** Candidates work in pairs on simulated role-play situations designed to assess candidates' abilities to listen, to communicate effectively, to handle disagreement and conflict constructively, to handle problem employees, etc. An example is a simulated appraisal interview in which the boss has been provided with incomplete information about his or her subordinate's perform-

ance. The exercise permits an assessment of the boss's ability to draw out information from the subordinate, to listen effectively, to overcome barriers to communication set up by differences in rank, and to use the appraisal interview as an opportunity for constructive coaching and development.

4. *Case Analyses.* Candidates are provided with a written case study of an organization and are asked either to write an analysis of the case or to prepare themselves for a group discussion of the case. In the former situation the written analyses are scored, while in the latter observers make a record of the quality of the candidate's participation in the disucssion.

5. *Oral Presentation.* Candidates are required to make a speech on some topic. The presentation may be either immediately observed and evaluated by assessors, or it may be videotaped for subsequent careful evaluation.

Throughout the assessment center, assessors are required to maintain copious notes on their observations and to write up their impressions and evaluations systematically. After the conclusion of assessment center activities for those being assessed, the assessors remain together as a group for an additional several days. During this time the assessors share their evaluations of each candidate, pooling them with the other sources of data which have been employed. There are two outcomes of this procedure. The first is a detailed report on the candidate for use by the organization in making its selection or promotion decisions. The second is a summary of findings and results which is fed back directly to the candidate personally by at least one of the assessors.

Overall, assessment centers have an impressive record of validity in predicting subsequent successful managerial performance. Byham (1970), in a review of twenty-three studies, reports validity coefficients for assessment centers ranging from 0.27 to 0.64. Further, in the studies reviewed, the assessment centers outperformed other assessment techniques in twenty-two of the twenty-three studies. In the twenty-third study it performed as well as the alternative techniques. Other, more recent, analyses of the validity of assessment centers have also tended to yield generally supportive results (Huck, 1973; Howard, 1974; Klimoski & Strickland, 1977). There is also evidence that the utilization of assessment centers is increasing rapidly (Kraut, 1973).

The impressive performance of assessment centers in predicting managerial effectiveness should not be surprising. They can be seen to incorporate a number of desirable characteristics.

1. They permit an assessment to be based upon observation of a relatively large sample of the applicant's *actual behavior.*

2. Applicants' behavior is observed in *situations* which are designed to mirror as closely as possible the requirements and demands of the actual job situation.
3. Assessments are based upon the composite judgments of several assessors. Pooling the judgments of a number of raters helps avoid personal biases, mistaken impressions, and unfounded inferences.

A primary impediment to the use of assessment centers is their cost. They are expensive because of: (1) extensive design and development costs; (2) rental or ownership costs of appropriate assessment facilities; (3) lost work time for assessors (usually relatively senior managers); and (4) lost work time for assessees. This latter issue of time required of assessees also presents problems in using assessment centers for selecting new applicants, since applicants must be willing to take several days away from their current employers in order to attend the assessment center. Although there can be no doubt about the high cost of conducting assessment centers, some researchers have begun to argue that the payoffs to organizations resulting from improved selection decisions may more than repay the seemingly high initial costs of conducting assessment centers (Cascio & Silbey, 1979). Organizations need to analyze carefully how well their current selection systems are working and how critical to the organization's success are the jobs for which individuals are being selected.

Organizations may be able to deal with the cost issue to a certain extent by employing assessment center results for a variety of purposes. In addition to their use for personnel selection, the results of assessment centers can also be extremely useful for placement, training, development, and career planning activities. However, the evidence to date does not yet indicate that organizations are utilizing assessment center results to the fullest possible extent for these multiple purposes (Alexander, 1979).

MANAGERIAL IMPLICATIONS

Our discussion of the issues involved in the analysis of jobs and the assessment of job applicants leads to a variety of managerial implications for the effective handling of the employee selection process. In this section we outline these implications for the handling of job analysis and applicant assessment in turn.

Job Analysis

With job analysis, as with most other aspects of our study of organizations, it is not possible to prescribe the one "right" way of doing things (Prien, 1977;

Levine, Bennet, & Ash, 1979). What is "best" or most appropriate for one organization may not be appropriate for another (Levine, Ash, & Bennet, 1980). It is possible, however, to describe some generally desirable characteristics of any job analysis system, and also to draw attention to some of the factors which must be taken into account in choosing the most appropriate method for a given organization.

1. ***Managers need to insure that job analyses are behavior centered.*** From the outset of our discussion of job analysis we stressed the importance of job analysis focusing upon actual behaviors necessary for effective job performance. We must have a clear idea of what an individual must actually be capable of doing in order to perform effectively before we can meaningfully begin the selection process.

2. ***The organization's job analysis system must be reliable.*** Job analysis procedures must be reliable to be useful. If a system is reliable, two different analysts analyzing the same job will arrive at the same conclusions regarding the requirements of the job. Similarly, a reliable system will yield the same results if the same job is analyzed at two different times. Focusing upon specific well-defined job behaviors permits higher degrees of reliability to be attained. Careful training of job analysts to insure uniformity also improves reliability.

3. ***Managers should implement job analysis procedures which are repeatable at reasonable cost.*** Jobs, and the requirements that jobs place upon their incumbents, are not static but tend to change over time. In order to be useful for selecting new employees, a job analysis must be up-to-date and reflect the demands of the position as it exists right now. This implies a need to repeat job analyses as changes occur in the organization in order to insure that the analyses are current. This in turn implies that in choosing a job analysis technique, an organization should choose a method that it can afford to use as frequently as is necessary. The frequency of conducting job analyses, and hence the salience of the cost criterion, will depend upon the degree to which the organization is dynamic and changing.

4. ***Managers should focus their job analysis procedures upon areas of greatest need and potential payoff.*** Although it might feel reassuring to know that an up-to-date job analysis is available (and will continue to be available) for every job in the organization, this is not always feasible. When it is not, resources should be focused upon those jobs for which a good job analysis will have greatest payoffs for the organization's selection system. Generally, this will imply the desirability of focusing upon those jobs for which there are the largest number of incumbents and for which there is the highest degree of turnover. A job analysis system should be chosen with these high payoff areas in mind.

5. ***Organizations should take into account alternative uses of job analysis.*** Our focus in this chapter has been the selection of new members of the

organization, and our discussion of job analysis was undertaken to indicate how the organization must go about analyzing what it needs from a new employee before it begins screening applicants and making selection decisions. At the same time, it is important to be aware of the fact that job analyses can have many uses in organizations in addition to their important role in the selection process. Job analyses can serve as the basis for setting wage and salary scales, designing training programs, appraising job performance, and analyzing the effectiveness of selection systems. Thus, job analyses play an integral role in a wide variety of personnel management programs, and this range of uses and programs must be taken into account when designing or choosing a job analysis system.

Assessing Applicants

Our discussion of alternative techniques for the assessment of job applicants analyzed the nature of each technique, its strengths and weaknesses, and the evidence regarding its validity as a selection device. Following is a brief summary of the primary implications of this discussion which managers should keep in mind in deciding whether and how to employ each of the techniques.

1. ***Managers should make use of the selection interview carefully and judiciously.*** Interviews are clearly here to stay. Their positive features, combined with their absolute entrenchment in the hiring processes of most organizations, make it foolhardy to suggest that their use be discontinued. However, the interview as a selection device is fraught with problems and pitfalls, many of which can be minimized or overcome by training interviewers, standardizing the structure of the interview, keeping systematic written records, and using multiple interviewers whenever possible.
2. ***Tests, when carefully constructed and validated, can aid in the assessment process.*** Carefully designed ability tests can frequently improve the quality of selection decisions. Motivation tests, while helpful for some types of jobs, are less generally valid. The capacity of any test to predict subsequent performance must be systematically evaluated by the organization. In addition, organizations must determine whether a test adds anything to their ability to predict success over and above that provided by alternative selection devices (such as a biographical information blank).
3. ***Managers should consider biographical information blanks (BIBs) as a potentially effective and efficient assessment tool.*** BIBs, when carefully developed, properly weighted, and systematically validated, demonstrate an impressive ability to predict job success. Their validity is particularly impressive in light of their low cost and relative ease of construction and validation.
4. ***Assessment centers are a valid but expensive technique for identifying managerial talent.*** Assessment centers have demonstrated a consistent ability

to identify potential for success in managerial jobs. Their primary drawbacks are their high cost and their awkwardness for assessing job applicants who are not currently members of the organization. Whether the costs involved are justified will depend upon the amount of improvement the assessment center offers over currently used selection techniques as well as the importance to the organization of the jobs for which applicants are being selected.

SUMMARY

From the organization's standpoint, the goal of the process of selecting new members is to optimize the fit between what the organization requires as effective job behavior and what skill, ability, and motivation the individual is capable of providing. This implies two primary prerequisites to an effective selection system. The first prerequisite is the development of techniques which permit the systematic analysis of exactly what it is that the organization needs, i.e., job analysis. The second component is the design of methods of assessing job applicants to determine what their skills, abilities, and motives are.

The process of systematically determining what is required of a job incumbent is known as job analysis. A job analysis provides a summary of exactly what activities and behaviors the person occupying the job must be capable of performing and also indicates the types of personal characteristics felt to be desirable in a person performing the job. A variety of methods exist for conducting job analyses. In practice, job analyses are frequently based upon some combination of observations of the work as it is being performed, as well as descriptions of the work collected from incumbents via interviews and questionnaires. Systematic, up-to-date, and reliable job analyses are an essential prerequisite to the design of an effective personnel selection system.

Once a job analysis is available to describe clearly what type of person the organization requires, the next step is the development of methods of assessing job applicants to find out whether or not they fit the picture of what is required. The most commonly used methods of assessing job applicants are interviews, tests, and biographical information blanks (BIBs). Interviews, though used almost universally, suffer from a variety of biases and shortcomings which tend to make them poor predictors of job success. However, techniques are available for making interviews more systematic and more useful as an assessment technique. Tests of ability tend to be systematically, though not always strongly, related to job performance. Personality tests, on the other hand, are much less frequently predictive of subsequent success on the job. BIBs, when carefully developed and systematically employed, serve as very good predictors of job performance and are extremely cost effective. A fourth, less frequently used method of assessing applicants is the assessment center. Assessment centers appear extremely promising, though their primary drawback is their high cost.

REVIEW QUESTIONS

1. Describe the dual matching process of organizational selection.
2. What is the organization's primary goal in the design of its selection system?
3. What is a job analysis?
4. Briefly describe three alternative techniques for conducting a job analysis.
5. What factors should an organization take into account in choosing a method of carrying out job analyses?
6. Compare and contrast two widely used methods of collecting information on job applicants. What are the strengths and weaknesses of each?
7. Discuss why the selection interview is such a poor predictor of job success. How can the selection interview be improved to increase its ability to predict success on the job?
8. Would you recommend the use of interviews if you were in charge of designing an organization's selection procedures? If so, why? If not, why not?
9. Discuss several different types of ability tests and indicate the extent to which each type is a good predictor of job success.
10. Why are personality tests generally poor predictors of job performance?
11. Why should a biographical information blank be a good predictor of job performance?
12. What is an assessment center? What are the primary strengths and weaknesses of assessment centers for personnel selection?
13. Do you feel that it is inherently unwise or unfair for an organization to make selection decisions without seeing the applicant in person in an interview? Discuss and defend your position.
14. What types of organizations in what types of circumstances do you feel should be particularly concerned about the quality and accuracy of their personnel selection procedures? Justify your position.

REFERENCES

Alexander, L. D. An exploratory study of the utilization of assessment center results. *Academy of Management Journal*, 1979, *22*, 152–157.

Asher, J. J. The biographical item: Can it be improved? *Personnel Psychology*, 1972, *25*, 251–269.

Byham, W. C. Assessment centers for spotting future managers. *Harvard Business Review*, 1970, *48*, 150–167.

Callender, J. C., & Osburn, H. G. Development and test of a new model for validity generalization. *Journal of Applied Psychology*, 1980, *65*, 543–558.

Campbell, D. T., & Fiske, D. W. Convergent and discriminant validation by the multitrait-multimethod matrix. *Psychological Bulletin*, 1959, *56*, 81–105.

Carlson, R. C., Thayer, P. W., Mayfield, E. C., & Peterson, D. A. Improvements in the selection interview. *Personnel Journal,* 1971, *50,* 268–274.

Cascio, W. F., & Silbey, V. Utility of the assessment center as a selection device. *Journal of Applied Psychology,* 1979, *64,* 107–118.

Cornelius, E. T., III, & Lyness, K. S. A comparison of wholistic and decomposed judgment strategies in job analyses by job incumbents. *Journal of Applied Psychology,* 1980, *65,* 155–163.

Dictionary of occupational titles, (3d ed.). Washington, D.C.: U.S. Government Printing Office, 1965.

Dunnette, M. D., *Personnel selection and placement,* Belmont, Calif.: Wadsworth, 1966.

Dunnette, M. D., & Aylward, M. S. Validity information exchange, No. 9–21. *Personnel Psychology,* 1956, *9,* 245–247.

Dunnette, M. D., & Bass, B. M. Behavioral scientists and personnel management. *Industrial Relations,* 1963, *2,* 115–130.

Ghiselli, E. E. *The validity of occupational aptitude tests.* New York: Wiley, 1966.

Ghiselli, E. E. The validity of aptitude tests in personnel selection. *Personnel Psychology,* 1973, *26,* 461–478.

Grove, D. A. A behavioral consistency approach to decision making in employment selection. *Personnel Psychology,* 1981, *34,* 55–64.

Guion, R. M. *Personnel Testing.* New York: McGraw-Hill, 1965.

Howard, A. An assessment of assessment centers. *Academy of Management Journal,* 1974, *17,* 115–134.

Huck, J. R. Assessment centers: A review of the external and internal validation. *Personnel Psychology,* 1973, *26,* 191–212.

Johnson, J. A., & Hogan, R. Vocational interests, personality, and effective police performance. *Personnel Psychology,* 1981, *34,* 49–54.

Klimoski, R. J., & Strickland, W. J. Assessment centers—Valid or merely prescient? *Personnel Psychology,* 1977, *30,* 353–360.

Kraut, A. J. Management assessment in international organizations. *Industrial Relations,* 1973, *12,* 172–182.

Latham, G. P., Saari, L. M., Pursell, E. D., & Campion, M. A. The situational interview. *Journal of Applied Psychology,* 1980, *65,* 422–427.

Lebowitz, Fran. *Metropolitan life.* New York: Elsevier-Dutton, 1974.

Levine, E. L., Ash, R. A., & Bennett, N. Exploratory comparative analysis of four job analysis methods. *Journal of Applied Psychology,* 1980, *65,* 524–535.

Levine, E. L., Bennett, N., & Ash, R. A. Evaluation and use of four job analysis methods for personnel selection. *Public Personnel Management,* 1979, *8,* 146–151.

Lopez, F. M., Kesselman, G. A., & Lopez, F. E. An empirical test of a trait-oriented job analysis technique. *Personnel Psychology,* 1981, *34,* 479–502.

Mayfield, E. C., Brown, S. H., & Hamstra, B. W. Selection interviewing in the life insurance industry: An update of research and practice. *Personnel Psychology,* 1980, *33,* 725–740.

McCormick, E. J., Mecham, R. C., & Jeanneret, P. R. *Technical Manual for the Position Analysis Questionnaire (PAQ).* West Lafayette, Ind.: PAQ Services, 1972.

McCormick, E. J., & Tiffin, J. *Industrial Psychology,* (6th ed.). Englewood Cliffs, N.J.: Prentice-Hall, 1974.

Mills, C. J., & Bohannon, W. E. Personality characteristics of effective police officers. *Journal of Applied Psychology*, 1980, *65*, 680–684.

Miner, J. B., and Miner, M. G. *Personnel and industrial relations: A managerial approach*, (rev. ed.). New York: Macmillan, 1977.

Osburn, H. G., Timmreck, C., & Digby, D. Effect of dimensional relevance on accuracy of simulated hiring decisions by employment interviewers. *Journal of Applied Psychology*, 1981, *66*, 159–165.

Pearlman, K., Schmidt, F. L., & Hunter, J. E. Validity generalization results for tests used to predict job proficiency and training success in clerical occupations. *Journal of Applied Psychology*, 1980, *65*, 373–406.

Prien, E. P. The function of job analysis in content validation. *Personnel Psychology*, 1977, *30*, 167–174.

Prien, E. P., & Ronan, W. W. Job analysis: A review of research and findings. *Personnel Psychology*, 1971, *24*, 371–396.

Rothstein, M., & Jackson, D. N. Decision making in the employment interview: An experimental approach. *Journal of Applied Psychology*, 1980, *65*, 271–283.

Schmidt, F. L., Gast-Rosenberg, I., & Hunter, J. E. Validity generalization results for computer programmers. *Journal of Applied Psychology*. 1980, *65*, 643–661.

Schmidt, F. L., & Hunter, J. E. The future of criterion related validity. *Personnel Psychology*, 1980, *33*, 41–60.

Schmidt, F. L., Hunter, J. E., & Caplan, J. R. Validity generalization results for two jobs groups in the petroleum industry. *Journal of Applied Psychology*, 1981, *66*, 261–273.

Schmidt, F. L., Hunter, J. E., & Pearlman, K. Task differences as moderators of aptitude test validity in selection: A red herring. *Journal of Applied Psychology*, 1981, *66*, 166–185.

Schneider, B. *Staffing organizations*. Pacific Palisades, Calif.: Goodyear, 1976.

U.S. Department of Labor, Manpower Administration, *Handbook for analyzing jobs*. Washington, D.C.: U.S. Government Printing Office, 1972.

U.S. Department of Labor, U.S. Employment Service. Occupational Analysis and Industrial Services Division. *Training and reference manual for job analysis*. June, 1944.

Valenzi, E. R., & Andrews, I. R. Individual differences in the decision process of employment interviewers. *Journal of Applied Psychology*, 1973, *58*, 49–53.

Webster, E. C. *Decision making in the employment interview*. Montreal: Industrial Relations Center, McGill University, 1964.

Whyte, W. H., Jr. *The organization man*. New York: Simon & Schuster, 1956.

Wright, O. R., Jr. Summary of research on the selection interview since 1964. *Personnel Psychology*, 1969, *22*, 391–413.

CHAPTER 3
MAKING SELECTION DECISIONS

In the previous chapter we looked at methods which organizations can use for analyzing jobs on the one hand and for assessing the characteristics of applicants for those jobs on the other. The point of the whole procedure is to try to assure as close a match as possible between what the organization needs done and what the individual is capable of doing. However, analyzing jobs and assessing applicants are really only the preliminary steps in the selection process. The most critical phase in the process occurs when the organization must determine how to make use of all of the information which has been generated in order to arrive at a *decision* regarding whether or not to offer employment to a particular applicant. From the organization's standpoint the entire procedure eventually boils down to having to choose between one of two options: the applicant either is or is not offered a position in the organization. The organization thus must develop some mechanism for translating the myriad bits of information about each applicant into a decision either to hire or not to hire.

In this chapter we deal with three major issues regarding the personnel decision-making process. We first examine the legal environment of selection decisions and constraints which the legal framework places upon the organization's hiring process. Next, we examine the two major approaches which organizations can employ for synthesizing information on job applicants in order to arrive at a decision to hire or reject an applicant. Finally, we analyze a variety of selection system design issues and explore their implications for the effectiveness and efficiency of the organization's system of selecting new members.

THE LEGAL ENVIRONMENT OF SELECTION DECISIONS

In recent years in the United States a wide variety of federal legislation, executive orders, guidelines, and court decisions have had a tremendous impact upon how organizations can and do make their hiring decisions. An understanding and awareness of what these factors are and how they influence the selection process is essential to the effective management of the process.

Relevant Legislation

The key piece of legislation relevant to the selection process is Title VII of the Civil Rights Act of 1964 (as amended in 1972). Title VII prohibits discrimination on the basis of race, sex, religion, and national origin in personnel decisions. In addition, the act created the Equal Employment Opportunity Commission (EEOC) as a federal agency for the purpose of administering and enforcing Title VII. Under the terms of the original act, the EEOC was responsible for investigating charges of discrimination and attempting to arrive at voluntary resolutions via negotiation, persuasion, and conciliation. The EEOC was not given the power, however, to take cases to court. This changed when the act was amended in 1972. The power of the EEOC was greatly enhanced under this amendment, which now permits the commission to take alleged violators to court if a complaint cannot be resolved voluntarily.

Federal Guidelines

In 1978 the federal *Uniform Guidelines on Employee Selection Procedures* were issued jointly by the Equal Employment Opportunity Commission, the Department of Labor, the Department of Justice, and the Civil Service Commission. This single set of uniform guidelines replaced the previous EEOC guidelines of 1970, as well as the Federal Executive Agency Guidelines of 1976.

The guidelines are specifically written to apply to almost any selection procedure which an organization might employ. According to the guidelines, a selection procedure is "Any measure, combination of measures or procedure used as a basis for any employment decision." The guidelines go on to point out that the definition of a selection procedure can range "from traditional paper and pencil tests, performance tests, training programs, or probationary periods and physical education and work experience requirements through informal or casual interviews and unscored application forms." In other words, almost any applicant assessment technique which an organization might choose to employ is covered by the guidelines.

The guidelines do not require employers to carry out validation studies of the relationship between scores on a selection device and subsequent measures of job performance for every selection system they employ. Rather, validation studies must be conducted only when there is evidence of the *adverse impact* of a selection procedure upon one of the classes protected under Title VII. Adverse impact upon a group is defined as existing when the selection rate of applicants from that group for a given job is less than 80 percent of the selection rate of the group having the highest selection rate. Thus, adverse impact would exist if it were the case that, on average, 20 percent of the males who applied for a given job were hired, while only 10 percent of females applying for the same job were hired. In such a situation, the guidelines would require that the selection rate for females be at least 16 percent (80 percent of the 20 percent selection rate for males) in order to indicate that no adverse impact was occurring.

There are two difficulties associated with this *80 percent* definition of adverse impact. First, it can have the effect of encouraging a quota system of hiring, since it tells employers that they need not go to the trouble and expense of validating their selection procedures as long as they hire an adequate proportion of individuals from the classes protected by Title VII. Second, the guidelines themselves equivocate on whether or not the 80 percent guideline is or is not *the* standard for determining adverse impact. While in one section the guidelines state that the 80 percent rule constitutes "a practical means of determining adverse impact in enforcement proceedings," a later section states that "smaller differences in selection rates may nevertheless constitute adverse impact where they are significant in both statistical and practical terms." Thus employers are left in the position of not knowing clearly when and under what circumstances validation studies may be required.

When a selection procedure has been shown to have an adverse impact, the guidelines provide the employer with the option of either discontinuing its use or providing validation evidence that the procedure is in fact job-related. Employers have the option of presenting evidence of criterion-related validity, content validity, or construct validity. Evidence of criterion-related validity is most desirable. Employers choosing to provide evidence of content validity must be in possession of detailed and systematic job analyses in order to demonstrate the relevance of the content of the selection procedure to the job for which it is being used. Finally, although the guidelines technically indicate that evidence of construct validity is permissible, they also specify that in addition to producing evidence of construct validity, an employer must also present evidence that the measures of the construct are in fact related to job performance. In other words, an employer choosing to demonstrate construct validity must *also* demonstrate criterion-related validity. Thus, although the guidelines technically permit criterion-related validity, content validity, and construct validity, in practice the details of the procedures specified in the guidelines operationally require evidence of either criterion-related validity or content validity.

Landmark Cases and Their Implications

Griggs v. Duke Power Co.

Probably the single most important and most well known case relevant to the employee selection process is *Griggs v. Duke Power Co.*, which came before the U.S. Supreme Court in 1971. The employer (Duke Power Co.) required individuals applying for jobs above the rank of common laborer to have a high school education. The company also employed an intelligence test and a mechanical aptitude test in selecting employees. The company had never conducted validation studies of any type to determine whether any of these selection devices were valid or not. Two key pieces of information were before the Court in this case. First, the selection requirements were shown to screen out proportionately more black employees than white employees. Second, there was no evidence that the company had adopted these selection requirements with any *intent* to discriminate against black employees. Thus, the key issue which the Court had to decide was whether an employment practice had to be *intended* to discriminate in order to be prohibited under the law, or whether only the adverse outcome of discrimination, regardless of intent, constituted a violation of the law. The Court clearly and unanimously found that a lack of intent to discriminate does *not* constitute a defense of an employment practice which in effect is discriminatory. In the words of the Chief Justice, "Good intent or absence of discriminatory intent does not redeem employment procedures or testing mechanisms that operate as built-in headwinds for minority groups and are unrelated to measuring job capability." Thus, the *Griggs* case established the fundamental proposition that once it has been shown that an organization's employment practice has an adverse effect on individuals of a particular race, sex, religion, or national origin, then what is legally termed a *prima facie* case has been made out against the employer. In other words, once adverse effect on a protected class has been demonstrated, the burden of proof falls on the organization to present evidence that the employment practice is job-related. If the organization cannot produce such evidence, then it is guilty of an unfair employment practice and is subject to a variety of penalties, including provision of back pay to members of the adversely affected group.

However, since in the *Griggs* case the employer had presented no evidence whatsoever of the job-relatedness of its employment practices, this case did not help clarify what types of evidence an organization must be able to produce to demonstrate that an employment practice is in fact job-related.

Albemarle Paper Co. v. Moody

The case of *Albemarle Paper Co. v. Moody*, decided by the Supreme Court in 1975, dealt specifically with the issue of the kind of evidence that an organization must produce to show the job-relatedness of its employment practices. In this case, the organization had been utilizing several standard selection tests with cutoff scores derived from published national norms for the tests. In addition, following the *Griggs* decision the organization had conducted a "quick and dirty" validation study which produced some positive correlations between the tests and job performance, but which obviously contained a variety of flaws and shortcomings from a rigorous scientific viewpoint.

In this case the Court held that merely *some* evidence of job-relatedness was inadequate and that in fact the organization must show that selection devices are job-related by a preponderance of the evidence. In addition, and of considerable significance, the Court appeared to indicate that the only way for an organization to provide such evidence was by proving compliance with the 1970 EEOC *Guidelines on Testing and Selection*. These guidelines required that all types of selection devices be subjected to criterion-related validation, and ruled that evidence of construct or content validity would be acceptable only in exceptional circumstances.

Washington v. Davis

Some further clarification of the types of validation evidence an organization must produce was provided by the Supreme Court's decision in *Washington v. Davis* in 1976. This decision indicated some retreat from an apparent requirement of the *Albemarle* decision of strict adherence to the 1970 EEOC guidelines.

The case involved a charge that an aptitude test used by the District of Columbia in the selection of policemen screened out blacks disproportionately and hence was discriminatory unless it could be shown to be job-related under the *Griggs* principle. The key portion of the decision has to do with how an organization may demonstrate that its selection devices are job-related. While noting that it is not sufficient for an employer merely to demonstrate that a challenged selection practice has *some* rational basis, the Court held that "it is necessary that the challenged practice be 'validated' in terms of job performance *in any one of several ways*" [emphasis added]. In addition, the Court observed that "it appears beyond doubt by now that there is *no single method* for appropriately

validating employment tests for their relationship to job performance"
[emphasis added]. Thus the *Washington* decision indicated a retreat from
the strong endorsement of the 1970 EEOC guidelines contained in the
Albemarle decision. The decision appears to open up the possibility that
evidence of construct or content validity may be an acceptable indicator of
job-relatedness. The 1978 *Uniform Guidelines* are consistent with this
position, since they indicate that employers may produce evidence of
criterion-related validity, content validity, or construct validity.

Sex Discrimination

Under Title VII it is illegal to discriminate in the hiring process on the
basis of an applicant's sex. However, exceptions are permitted to this
general rule when an employer can demonstrate that sex is a "bona fide
occupational qualification reasonably necessary to the normal operation
of that particular business or enterprise" (this exception, known as the
b.f.o.q. exception, is in fact applicable to any of the prohibited grounds of
discrimination in addition to sex).

Immediately after the passage of Title VII, many employers attempted
to defend discriminatory hiring practices on the basis of the b.f.o.q.
exception. However, the EEOC and the courts have tended to adopt a very
narrow interpretation of the b.f.o.q. exception. In the case of sex discrimination, the b.f.o.q. exception has tended to be permitted in only two types
of situations. First, sex can be employed as a basis for employee selection
when sex is an essential determinant of authenticity or genuineness in
carrying out the job, as in the case of actors or actresses. Second, sex of
applicants can be taken into account in order to maintain community
standards of propriety and morality, as in the case of washroom attend-
ants for example. More important perhaps, the EEOC has indicated that
application of the b.f.o.q. exception is *not* warranted for: (1) refusing to
hire a woman because of her sex due to assumptions regarding the
comparative employment characteristics of women in general; (2) refusing to hire a person based on stereotyped characterization of the sexes; or
(3) refusing to hire a person because of the preferences of coworkers, the
employer, clients, or customers.

Age Discrimination

The Age Discrimination in Employment Act (ADEA) of 1976 (as amended
in 1978) was designed to promote employment opportunities for individuals in the 40 to 70 age range (this is the only group to whom the act
applies). Among other things, the act makes it illegal to fail or refuse to
hire an individual between the ages of 40 and 70 on the basis of his or her
age. Thus, if an organization has applicants for a position who fall into this
age range, their age cannot be taken into account in making selection

decisions. Age could be taken into account if all applicants were under 40 or over 70 (although an organization is not permitted to achieve this type of situation by discouraging applicants from the 40 to 70 age range).

The Act does permit exceptions if age can be shown to be a "bona fide occupational qualification" (b.f.o.q.) or if discrimination is based on "reasonable factors other than age" (e.g., physical fitness). For example, a refusal by bus lines to hire drivers over age 40 was found to be justified when the companies were able to demonstrate that driving skills tend to deteriorate beyond this age and that there is no reliable method of assessing such skill deterioration other than on the basis of age. As in the case of Title VII, the burden of proof is on the employer to demonstrate that discrimination on the basis of age is justified. The demands for proof, however, appear to be somewhat less stringent for jobs involving public safety such as bus drivers, airline pilots, fire fighters, and police officers.

Affirmative Action

The process of selecting organization members can also be influenced by the existence of an affirmative action program in the organization. Under Executive Orders 11246 and 11375, organizations having contracts or subcontracts with the U.S. federal government are required to develop and implement affirmative action programs.

The orders require affected employers to conduct a *utilization analysis* on a job-by-job basis. A utilization analysis involves determining the number and percentage of women and minorities in each job and then comparing their representation or utilization in the organization to their availability in the labor market. If a group is found to be underutilized, the organization must establish goals and timetables for the selection, promotion, and training of members of the underutilized groups. Further, the employer must be able to demonstrate that a *good-faith effort* is made to achieve the goals laid out in the affirmative action progam (what constitutes a good-faith effort has recently begun to be investigated, cf. Marino, 1980). The existence of an affirmative action program in an organization can thus have a significant impact upon the organization's selection decisions.

ALTERNATIVE APPROACHES TO SELECTION DECISIONS

In order to arrive at actual selection decisions on job applicants, organizations require some method or technique for combining and synthesizing all of the information available on job requirements on the one hand and job applicants on the other. In this section we explore the two basic alternative approaches which organizations can adopt to the selection decision-making process.

Intuitive Judgment versus Systematic Combination

There are two basic options available to an organization for combining information about applicants in order to arrive at selection decisions (Meehl, 1954). One option, which we are labeling *intuitive judgment* (and frequently referred to as the *clinical* approach to decision making), requires someone in the organization to review all of the information on an applicant and then to make a hiring decision based upon his or her best judgment derived from an overall impression of the applicant. The second option, labeled *systematic combination* (and often known as the *statistical* approach), requires all of the information on an applicant to be expressed in numerical terms. This information is then simply added up, with the more important pieces of information (i.e., the best predictors of success) being given greater weight than less important pieces of information. The hiring decision is then based purely upon the final score assigned to the applicant resulting from this systematic combination of numerical scores.

The vast majority of selection decisions in organizations are made by intuitive judgment. This is the case for a number of reasons. First, many organizations are unaware that there is any alternative to using their best judgment to arrive at a final selection decision. Second, while some may be aware of the existence of systematic data combination techniques, they may lack the knowledge or resources to implement the systematic combination technique. Third, some people are of the opinion that it is dehumanizing to reduce a job applicant to a series of numbers and then to make an important decision based solely on those numbers. Finally, some personnel decision makers hold strong beliefs that their intuitive judgment is excellent and could never be excelled by a system lacking their personal brand of sensitivity and insight into the nature of people.

While the pervasiveness of intuitive judgment as a method of making personnel decisions is quite understandable, it is also extremely unfortunate. The evidence is now overwhelming that systematic combination is vastly superior to intuitive judgment as a method of making valid personnel selection decisions. We'll look briefly at two sources of this evidence.

Meehl (1965) reviewed a total of fifty-one different studies which permitted a comparison of intuitive judgment versus systematic combination as methods of making decisions. These studies were not all restricted to personnel selection decisions in organizations, but also included studies of predictions of things such as academic success, success in military training, psychiatric diagnosis, and medical diagnosis. The results are stunning. In thirty-three of the fifty-one studies (i.e., about 65 percent) systematic combination of numerical data yielded better predictions than did intuitive judgment. *All* of the remaining eighteen studies were judged to be a tie. There was not a single example of intuitive judgment outperforming systematic combination (Goldberg, 1968; Lindzey, 1965).

Further evidence of the superiority of systematic combination is contained in Sawyer's (1966) review of forty-five studies comparing intuitive judgment and systematic combination. Sawyer's method of classifying the studies is very helpful since it draws attention to an important distinction. That distinction is between the method of *combining* information which is employed (intuitive judgment versus systematic combination), and the method of *collecting* information which is employed (which could be subjective or objective or both). Subjective methods of collecting information are those which require some interpretation on the part of the person who is collecting the information. Examples of subjective methods are selection interviews and observations of behavior in assessment centers. Objective methods require no interpretation on the part of the person collecting the information; for example, biographical information blanks and ability tests.

Our discussion in this section has to do with comparing different approaches to *combining* information. However, Sawyer's distinction is helpful for two reasons. First, it helps us keep the distinction between method of collecting information and method of combining information clearly in mind. Second, it permits us to compare the accuracy of predictions both for different methods of combining information (our primary concern here) and for different methods of collecting information (an additional issue of interest).

Sawyer classified each of the forty-five studies he reviewed on the basis of both its method of combining information and its method of collecting information. We'll look in detail at the six major classifications summarized in Table 3-1.

When information collected subjectively is combined intuitively the overall method employed is referred to as *pure judgment*, e.g., a hiring

TABLE 3-1
Six alternative approaches to making personnel selection decisions*

Method of collecting information	Method of combining information	
	Intuitive judgment	Systematic combination
Subjective	Pure judgment 20%	Combined ratings 43%
Objective	Judgmental interpretation 38%	Pure systematic 63%
Both	Judgmental composite 26%	Systematic composite 75%

*Percentages indicate the frequency with which each approach was as good as or better than any of the alternative approaches.

SOURCE: Adapted from Jack Sawyer, "Measurement *and* prediction, clinical *and* statistical," *Psychological Bulletin*, 1966, *66*, 192. Copyright by the American Psychological Association. Adapted by permission of the author.

decision made judgmentally by a personnel officer based solely upon an interview. When subjectively collected information is combined systematically (e.g., when interviewers must supply numerical ratings of applicants which are then combined according to some systematic validated procedure), the situation is labeled *combined ratings*. *Judgmental interpretation* occurs when an "expert" studies objective sources of information (such as a biographical information blank and the results of ability tests) and makes a selection decision based upon his or her best judgment. When such objective information is combined systematically, a *pure systematic* system is being employed. Finally, we have situations in which both subjective and objective sources of information are employed, such as when an applicant has filled out a biographical information blank, taken ability tests, and been interviewed. When the person who has done the interviewing (or who has otherwise been involved in the interpretation of subjective information) makes decisions based on his or her judgment, the method is labeled *judgmental composite*. When all of the sources of information are used as input to a systematic combination technique, we say that a *systematic composite* technique is being employed.

Sawyer compared the different techniques with one another to determine the degree to which each method was as good or better than each of the other techniques and expressed this comparison as a percentage. The higher the percentage, the better the technique. The results of these comparisons are summarized in Table 3-1. The findings are clear and unequivocal. Regardless of the method by which information was collected, systematic combination of the data *always* outperforms intuitive judgment. This superiority varies from a minimum difference of 25 percent (when all the information is objective) to a maximum of 49 percent (when both subjective and objective information are employed). It is also interesting to note that when systematic combination is employed, pure objective information results in better predictions than pure subjective information, but a combination of both subjective and objective information results in the best possible predictions. A similar pattern is not evident when intuitive judgment is employed. Intuitive judgment based purely on objective information is superior to intuitive judgment based solely on subjective information. However, when the intuitive judge is provided with both subjective and objective information, the performance of the judge is worse than when only objective information is supplied.

Why Systematic Combination Is Superior

The evidence is unambiguous that better, more accurate decisions are made when information is combined systematically than when decision makers rely solely on their intuitive judgment. Why is this the case and what does it imply for the design of an organization's selection systems?

There is nothing magical about systematically combining numerical information which causes it to outperform intuitive judgment. Rather it appears that systematic combination works so well because it is, as its name implies, systematic, reliable, and not prone to some of the distortions and biases of human judgment (Dawes, 1979; Dawes & Corrigan, 1974). A great deal of research on human judgment indicates that people, regardless of their training or their good intentions, have some severe limitations.

1. People have limited memory capacity and a limited ability to take information into account simultaneously when making decisions.
2. People engage in selective attention and retention of information. We are not capable of attending to all of the information which comes in to us, nor are we capable of remembering all of the information with which we are presented. When selection decisions are made by intuitive judgment, the decisions are thus based upon the particular pieces of information about the applicant which the decision maker attended to and can still remember.
3. People unconsciously distort information to make their impressions consistent with one another. Thus, if an applicant has created an overall positive impression, the intuitive judge will tend to distort negative information about the applicant in a positive direction (or vice versa if an overall negative impression was created).
4. People make mistakes. Even if an intuitive judge is consciously attempting to take all of the information systematically into account, errors are frequently made. Too much emphasis may be placed on a minor point, or too little on a major one. Information may be inadvertently overlooked.

These are some of the reasons why systematic combination of numerical information always performs at least as well as, and usually outperforms, intuitive judgment. A systematic combination method can take into account as many pieces of information as have been shown to be related to job success, it will weight each piece of information appropriately and identically for each applicant, and it will not distort, change, or omit any of the pieces of information which are put into it.

SELECTION SYSTEM DESIGN

Up to this point we have reviewed the basic elements and issues involved in the process of selecting new organization members. In this final section we will briefly address the implications of our discussion and recommendations for the overall design of personnel selection systems in organizations.

Perhaps the most simplistic conclusion to be drawn from our discussion would be to urge every organization to do all of the things which we have recommended: to conduct systematic job analyses frequently and carefully; to develop and validate a whole battery of predictors for each job in the orgnization; and to design, test, and update methods for systematically combining information about applicants to arrive at selection decisions.

Such an interpretation has a distinctly "ivory tower" ring to it. While it may be true that in an ideal world an organization should attempt to do all of these things, in the real world organizations must also attend to the costs associated with improving their selection systems, and the benefits which they may anticipate as a result of any improvements. In what follows we will provide a framework within which an organization can systematically evaluate the costs and benefits associated with various techniques in designing a selection system.

The Different Outcomes of Personnel Decisions

From the organization's standpoint, the entire selection process eventually comes down to a single yes or no decision regarding each applicant. The organization decides either to hire the applicant or to reject the applicant.

Job applicants, on the other hand, can be thought of as falling into two groups: those who are capable of achieving an adequate level of competence in job performance and those who are not. The goal of the organization's selection system is to distinguish these two groups from one another. The better the selection system is at distinguishing the two groups, the better the organization's selection decisions will be.

If we put together the fact that applicants are either competent or incompetent to perform the job with the fact that the organization can either hire or reject each applicant, we can see that there are a total of four possible outcomes associated with the selection decision an organization makes regarding each job applicant (Wiggins, 1973). These four outcomes are diagrammed in Figure 3-1.

When the organization decides to hire an applicant who turns out to

FIGURE 3-1
The four outcomes of an organization's personnel selection decisions.

Type of Applicant		reject	hire
	competent	Successful competitor	Successful employee
	incompetent	Correct rejection	Problem employee

Organization's Decision

be competent, the outcome for the organization is the addition of a new successful employee. A second positive outcome occurs when the organization rejects an applicant who does not have the ability to perform the job effectively. However, just as there are two types of correct decisions which the organization can make, there are also two types of errors which can be made. The first and most obvious error occurs when the organization mistakenly decides to hire an applicant who does not have the necessary competence and who turns out to be a problem employee. The second, less obvious, error occurs when the organization rejects a person with the necessary competence who subsequently becomes a successful employee with a competing organization.

Breaking down the outcomes of an organization's personnel decisions into these four categories has two major advantages. First, it provides a basis upon which an organization can classify and examine its personnel decisions in order to analyze what proportions are correct and incorrect from the organization's standpoint. Second, each of the four categories of outcomes has a different cost or benefit associated with it for the organization. By clearly identifying these categories the organization puts itself in a position to: (1) think carefully and specifically about what these costs and benefits are; and (2) make informed decisions about the extent to which it can foresee increased benefits or reduced costs associated with improvements in its ability to make correct decisions.

Assessing How Good a Selection System Is

There are two approaches to assessing how good a selection system is. The first approach considers all four possible outcomes of selection decisions as outlined in Figure 3-1. The second approach concerns itself only with those persons actually hired by the organization.

The first approach involves the assessment of the total proportion of correct decisions arrived at using a selection system. Correct decisions are those in which a competent person is hired or an incompetent person is rejected (the top right and bottom left entries in Figure 3-1). Incorrect decisions arise when a competent person is rejected or an incompetent person is hired (top left and bottom right of Figure 3-1). Assessing how good a selection system is by this method requires identifying how many people fall into each of the four categories, adding together the numbers falling into the two "correct" categories, and dividing this number of correct decisions by the total number of applicants (i.e., the total number of decisions made). The larger the proportion of correct decisions, the better the selection system. The advantage of this approach is that it is comprehensive, taking into account all of the potential outcomes of a selection decision. The problem with the approach lies in the difficulty of determining who among those rejected by the organization were in fact "correct rejections," and who in fact did have the potential to perform competently and are now performing successfully with another organization. Thus, this approach is comprehensive and complete but often difficult to implement in practice.

The second approach ignores those who were rejected by the organization and focuses solely upon those persons hired. The goodness of a selection system is assessed by determining the proportion of applicants hired who are subsequently judged to be successful employees. The higher the proportion of successful employees hired using a particular selection system, the better the system. No attention is paid to the potential cost to the organization of failing to hire applicants who had the competence to perform effectively but were rejected. While the approach ignores this potential cost, it has the advantage of requiring only information which is generally readily available, i.e., a classification of employees hired using a particular selection system into successful employees and problem employees.

Which approach an organization adopts in assessing how good its selection system is depends upon several factors. The first approach has the advantage of being more complete and taking into account all of the various costs and benefits of selection decisions. Its major shortcoming lies in the need to classify rejected applicants into those who were correct rejections and those who would have been competent if hired and hence were incorrectly rejected. The choice of method of assessment hinges upon the difficulty of making this classification of rejected applicants and the importance of this classification to the organization.

In many situations it may be all but impossible to do anything other than guess at the proportions of rejected applicants who have subsequently been successful. This is particularly true for lower-level jobs in the organization. However, there will be some situations (e.g., professional sports teams) where it will be clearly (and sometimes painfully) obvious when someone who was rejected was in fact a potentially competent or even outstanding performer. In general, the rule of thumb must be that if an organization can only guess at the proportion of rejects subsequently successful or unsuccessful, it should probably ignore this group and employ the second approach to assessing its selection systems.

However, there is another factor which must also be taken into account. That factor is the cost to the organization of failing to hire a potentially competent employee. Again, for many organizations, particularly at lower levels, this cost may be minimal. However, the cost may be extremely high in situations in which either: (1) individuals with the skills to be successful are extremely rare and hard to find; or (2) an individual with the skills to be successful may be capable of doing serious harm to the organization if hired by a competing organization. When either of these situations obtains, it is essential that the organization take into account the costs associated with rejecting a potentially competent person. In these cases, the organization must also adopt the first approach to assessing its selection systems, an approach which addresses all four possible outcomes of personnel decisions.

Factors Influencing the Proportion of Correct Decisions Made

There are a number of factors which influence the proportion of correct decisions made with any personnel selection system. Some are straightforward, while others are a bit less obvious. All must be taken into account in determining whether the investment of resources in selection systems by the organization can be expected to pay dividends.

Validity of Selection Methods

This is the most obvious factor which influences the proportion of correct decisions made using any personnel selection system. Validity in this context refers to the strength of the relationship between an applicant's scores on the assessment techniques employed in the selection system and the applicant's subsequent performance on the job. The stronger the relationship, the more valid the selection system is said to be. It follows necessarily, then, that the more valid the selection system, the higher the proportion of correct hiring decisions made with that system.

Does this imply that all organizations should be investing resources in improving the validity of their selection systems for all jobs? Not necessarily. While high levels of validity are always desirable, the validity of selection techniques is not the only factor influencing the proportion of correct decisions made with that system. Before determining whether investment aimed at increasing validities is justified, the organization must take into account two additional factors which influence the proportion of correct decisions made.

Number of Applicants per Opening

If an organization were to advertise a position paying a six-figure salary for someone to travel the world sampling the quality of service at the world's best hotels and restaurants, the organization would quite likely be inundated with enthusiastic applicants. On the other hand, the flow of applicants would probably be rather sparse if the position advertised were for someone to staff a radar listening post in the high Arctic at a minimal salary. Although these examples are rather extreme, they are meant to draw attention to the fact that the number of applicants for a position will vary with the nature of the job, its location, the salary offered, and so on.

The average number of applicants per opening (often referred to as the *selection ratio*) is extremely important to take into account in determining whether any payoffs can be expected from improvements in the organization's selection systems. A selection system is only of value to an organization if there exists a reasonable number of applicants to choose from. If very few people tend to apply when a job becomes vacant, the organization finds itself in the position of having to hire almost anyone willing to accept the position. In this type of situation investment in the design of valid selection devices would be wasteful since the devices could not be used or would have to be ignored. In general, the overall value to an organization of a valid personnel selection system increases with the number of applicants which can be expected per opening.

Likelihood that Anyone Could Perform Adequately

It is probably a safe bet that almost any normal, healthy adult possesses the skills necessary to perform adequately the job of dishwasher in a restaurant. On the other hand it is probably extremely unlikely that just anyone off the street would be capable of performing adequately as an astronaut on a mission to the moon. In the case of the dishwasher, a series of highly valid selection instruments will be of no value whatsoever, since they will not be telling us anything that we don't already know, i.e., that the applicant is capable of washing dishes. In the case of the astronaut, carefully validated selection devices will be essential in helping us identify that small number of individuals possessing the skills and abilities necessary for successful performance.

Although our examples present extreme cases, they are indicative of a general fact regarding the potential payoffs to the organization from improved selection systems. As the likelihood goes up that almost anyone applying for a job will be capable of performing it adequately, the payoffs to the organization from valid selection techniques go down. If almost all applicants can be expected to have the skills required for a position, then a selection system has to be very good and very sensitive to pick out that small group of people who lack the necessary skills. In such cases, it is extremely rare that the investment required in a valid selection system will result in any noticeable improvement in the proportion of successful applicants hired. On the other hand, when a position requires a highly unique and specialized set of skills, even selection devices of relatively low validity will be extremely helpful to the organization in screening out unacceptable applicants.

Overall Considerations in Selection System Design

It is probably fair to say that there is room for improvement in the selection systems employed for the vast majority of jobs in almost every organization. Does this then imply that all organizations should be putting more money into improving their personnel selection systems? Again, the answer is not necessarily. A decision to invest resources in improved personnel selection systems should be treated no differently than any other organizational investment decision. The appropriate question thus is not "Can we improve our selection systems if we invest additional resources in them?" The answer to that question is almost always yes. However, the appropriate question is *"How much* improvement in our selection systems can we anticipate *at what costs?"* An answer to this question depends directly upon the issues raised in our preceding discussion. We will highlight these essential issues by reviewing a series of central questions which must be taken into account in designing an organization's selection systems and determining the optimal degree of organizational investment in personnel selection. These questions must be reviewed for each job or family of jobs in the organization.

1. ***How well is the current system working?*** An answer to this question requires a systematic assessment of the proportion of correct decisions being made with the current selection system. It's essential that the assessment be careful and systematic. People's guesses, impressions, and intuitions are frequently quite inaccurate. A system which is currently yielding a high proportion of correct decisions is not a likely candidate for investment in improvements.

2. ***What are the payoffs associated with correct decisions and the costs associated with errors?*** For certain jobs, making a correct decision to hire a subsequently successful person may have very high positive payoffs for the organization. Conversely, making the mistake of either hiring someone who is inappropriate or failing to hire a top-notch person may be extremely costly. In such situations, even small increments in the validity of a selection system may be worth the investment to the organization. This is frequently the case with very senior positions in the organization.

3. ***Is there a sufficient flow of applicants for openings to justify a comprehensive selection system?*** If the organization must virtually accept everyone who applies, there is little payoff associated with having a selection system. The higher the proportion of applicants to openings, the greater the potential benefit of a selection system.

4. ***Are the skills required sufficiently rare to justify a comprehensive selection system?*** If almost everyone possesses the necessary skills, there is little to be gained from a selection system. As the skills become rarer the payoffs associated with a comprehensive selection system increase.

5. ***How much better is the selection system than the least-cost alternative?*** Determining how "good" a return on investment of organizational resources a selection system gives requires some baseline for comparison. An appropriate method is to compare the proportion of correct decisions made with a given selection system to the proportion of correct decisions which would be made if applicants were hired

randomly (e.g., by flipping a coin) or on a first-come, first-served basis. Such a comparison can also provide a basis for determining how high the validities of selection devices must be if they are to result in a higher proportion of correct decisions.

MANAGERIAL IMPLICATIONS

Our discussion of the issues involved in the process of making personnel selection decisions has a variety of implications for management practice.

1. **Managers must be aware of the relevant legal constraints on personnel selection decisions.** The number and complexity of laws, guidelines, and judicial decisions which influence what an organization can and cannot do in the selection process have been increasing at an enormous rate. In order to insure that hiring practices are in compliance with legal requirements, managers in general and personnel managers in particular must work hard at staying up to date and well informed on legal developments. Failure to do so can have such serious consequences for the organization as expensive and time consuming law suits, negative publicity, and potentially extremely costly back-pay settlements for all members of an adversely affected class. Some excellent suggestions regarding how organizations can go about designing effective equal employment opportunity programs are provided by Lockwood (1974).
2. **Managers should seriously consider adopting the systematic combination approach to making selection decisions.** The evidence is clear-cut and unequivocal that the systematic combination approach to decision making is superior to intuitive judgment. Managers need to recognize this fact and begin using systematic combination techniques in making personnel decisions.
3. **Personnel managers should be focusing their attention on designing decision-making systems, rather than on making the decisions themselves.** The clear superiority of systematic combination over intuitive judgment implies that the appropriate role of the personnel manager is *not* to be making selection decisions but to be focusing on the design, implementation, and validation of systematic methods for collecting and combining information about job applicants. The particular pieces of information to be combined, and the amount of weight given to each, must be carefully determined for different jobs, and the degree of success of the systematic techniques must be continuously evaluated and updated.
4. **The quality of current selection techniques needs to be systematically analyzed and areas of potential improvement identified.** While it is true that there will always be room for improvement in *any* selection system,

managers must analyze problems and opportunities in a realistic fashion. The validities of selection systems must be compared not to "perfect" systems but to realistic alternatives. In addition, applicant flows and skill requirements need to be taken into account in order to insure that organizational investments in improved selection systems pay off in a higher proportion of correct hiring decisions.

SUMMARY

A tremendous variety of laws, guidelines, and judicial decisions must be taken into account by organizations in the design of their personnel decision-making procedures. Title VII of the Civil Rights Act of 1964 (as amended in 1972) prohibits discrimination in hiring on the basis of race, sex, religion, or national origin. The U.S. *Uniform Guidelines on Employee Selection Procedures* lays out the conditions under which organizations must be prepared to demonstrate the validity of their selection procedures and indicates the types of evidence of validity which are acceptable. In addition, a variety of Supreme Court decisions have influenced the selection process. Perhaps of greatest importance is the principle that lack of intent to discriminate does not constitute a defense of a selection procedure that has the effect of discriminating unfairly against a particular group.

The process of putting together all of the available information about job applicants in order to arrive at a final selection decision has usually been done in the mind of the person making the hiring decision. This method is known as *intuitive judgment.* An alternative method known as *systematic combination* requires the organization to express all of the information about each applicant in numerical form and to develop a method of systematically combining this information to yield a final "score" for each applicant. Hiring decisions are then based upon who obtains the best score. The research evidence clearly indicates the superiority of the systematic combination technique. In studies which have compared the two methods intuitive judgment has *never* been shown to perform better than systematic combination and usually performs considerably worse.

Finally, the organization needs to adopt a systematic approach to designing its selection systems. Such a systematic approach has a number of components. First, the proportions of correct and incorrect decisions resulting from an existing selection system must be determined. Second, the organization must attend to both the costs associated with making incorrect selection decisions and the benefits which accrue from making correct decisions. Third, an analysis must be undertaken to determine the level of the flow of applicants for vacant positions and the skill level of these applicants relative to the demands of the positions. All of this information must be simultaneously taken into account in order to determine whether or not an investment of resources by the organization in improving its selection techniques would pay concrete dividends to the organization as a whole.

REVIEW QUESTIONS

1. Describe briefly the key pieces of federal legislation which have an impact upon the employee selection process in the United States.
2. What types of selection procedures are covered by the *Uniform Guidelines on Employee Selection Procedures*?
3. Under what circumstances must an organization be prepared to produce evidence of the validity of its selection procedures? What types of evidence of validity are acceptable?
4. Is a selection procedure acceptable as long as the organization did not intend to use the procedure to discriminate unfairly? Discuss.
5. What is a "bona fide occupational qualification" (b.f.o.q.)? What types of factors are and are not considered to be a sound basis for b.f.o.q. exceptions to the requirement that organizations not discriminate on the basis of an applicant's sex?
6. What do you feel is the appropriate role for the government in the regulation of the selection process?
7. Compare and contrast intuitive judgment and systematic combination as techniques for making selection decisions.
8. Discuss some of the reasons why systematic combination always performs as well as, or better than, intuitive judgment as a method of making decisions.
9. Why do you think that managers might be resistant to the implementation of systematic combination techniques for personnel selection? Are such sources of resistance justified? How might they be overcome?
10. What are the four different outcomes that can follow an organization's decision to select or reject an applicant?
11. What are two different approaches to assessing the proportion of correct decisions arising from a personnel selection system?
12. How does the number of applicants per opening influence the design of an organization's selection system?
13. How does the likelihood that anyone could adequately perform a job influence selection system design?
14. Is it always desirable for an organization to invest its resources in improving the validity of its selection systems? Why, or why not?

REFERENCES

Albemarle Paper Co. v. Moody, 422 U.S. 405 (1975).

Dawes, R. M. The robust beauty of improper linear models in decision making. *American Psychologist*, 1979, *34*, 571–582.

Dawes, R. M., & Corrigan, B. Linear models in decision making. *Psychological Bulletin*, 1974, *81*, 95–106.

Goldberg, L. R. Seer over sign: The first "good" example? *Journal of Experimental Research in Personality*, 1968, *3*, 168–171.

Griggs v. Duke Power Co., 401 U.S. 424 (1971).

Holt, T. Personnel selection and the Supreme Court. In W. C. Hamner & F. L. Schmidt, *Contemporary problems in personnel* (Rev. ed.). Chicago: St. Clair Press, 1977.

Lindzey, G. Seer versus sign. *Journal of Experimental Research in Personality*, 1965, *1*, 17–26.

Lockwood, H. C. Equal employment opportunities. In D. Yoder & H. G. Heneman, Jr., (Eds.), *ASPA handbook of personnel and industrial relations*, (Vol. I) *Staffing policies and strategies*. Washington, D.C.: The Bureau of National Affairs, Inc., 1974.

Marino, K. E. A preliminary investigation into the behavioral dimensions of affirmative action compliance. *Journal of Applied Psychology*, 1980, *65*, 346–350.

Meehl, P. E. *Clinical versus statistical prediction: A theoretical analysis and a review of the evidence*. Minneapolis: University of Minnesota Press, 1954.

Meehl, P. E. Seer over sign: The first good example. *Journal of Experimental Research in Personality*, 1965, *1*, 27–32.

Sawyer, J. Measurement *and* prediction, clinical *and* statistical. *Psychological Bulletin*, 1966, *66*, 178–200.

Uniform guidelines on employee selection procedures. *Federal Register*, 1978, *43*(166).

Washington v. Davis, 426 U.S. (1976).

Wiggins, J. S. *Personality and prediction: Principles of personality assessment*. Reading, Mass.: Addison-Wesley, 1973.

CHAPTER 4
SOCIALIZATION AND CAREERS

This chapter addresses the major issues in career development. We are interested here not only in the jobs and job changes organizations plan for employees, but also in employees' "subjective careers"—the aspirations, satisfactions, and self-conceptions employees themselves have about the jobs they hold (Hall, 1976). Integration of individuals and organizations does not occur once and for all at the time of selection; it needs to be continuously reachieved as individuals move up and through a series of jobs in organizations.

In this chapter we look first at some of the important changes that have occurred recently in how we think about our careers. Second, we explain the "joining-up" process: how individuals and organizations seek each other out and decide whether there is a good fit between individual skills and needs and organizational demands and opportunities. Third, we examine organizational socialization and early career issues. Here we look at how organizations train, orient, and seek to influence the values and attitudes of new recruits. We examine here, too, the special needs of individuals early in their careers and the special demands put on them by organizations. In the fourth and final section, we consider middle- and later-career issues: the impact of transfers and promotions, middle-life transitions, plateaued and obsolescent performance, and other problems and challenges unique to older, more experienced workers.

CAREERS IN ORGANIZATIONS

In *The Organization Man*, the classic critique of corporate life in America, William H. Whyte attacked the lack of control executives and managers were exerting over their own careers. In the organizations Whyte described in 1957, career success was largely determined by willingness to conform to organizational values and expectations, both at work and at home. Corporations valued individuals who were willing to get along by going along.

Twenty-five years later, we find a very different situation. Consider these remarks from respondents to a recent survey on what Americans "really want from their jobs" (Renwick et al., 1978):

> "In my case (36-year career with the same organization) I deliberately chose, at my 27th service year, to 'shoot my way' into organizational-development consultation. This required considerable personal risk, abandoning my former technological field (engineering administration). . . . While I enjoy my work and am involved in a client-centered way, I try—and usually succeed—in keeping my ego involvement low."

> "My present husband and myself left Baltimore, Maryland, two and a half years ago to live in Olds, Alberta, Canada, because he wanted a better life. He left a lucrative dental practice, a wife, and two children; he was in *Who's Who in the East*. I left a husband and a child because of the pressures you talk about in your article. It is a *very* difficult decision to leave, but we have never regretted it. We have two stores and a dental practice . . . but we go camping practically every weekend. We really enjoy life and each other. . . ." (p. 65):[1]

These comments reflect some of the important changes over the last 25 years in how we think about careers.

1. No longer does the term career pertain only to individuals in high-status or rapid-advancement occupations. The term career has in a sense been "democratized"—*careers* now refers to the sequence of jobs people hold during their work histories, regardless of occupation or organizational level (Hall, 1976). Executives have careers, but so do executive secretaries.
2. No longer does the term career refer only to job changes of vertical mobility, moving up in an organization. While a large majority of

[1]From *Psychology Today Magazine.* Copyright 1978 by Ziff-Davis Publishing Company. Reprinted by permission.

workers are still striving for advancement, there are increasing numbers of people who are turning down more responsible jobs to remain in positions they currently hold and enjoy. There are now more frequent career moves of horizontal, and sometimes downward, mobility.

3. No longer is the term career synonymous with employment in one occupation or in one organization. Today there is evidence that more and more individuals are experiencing what Hall (1976) calls "multi-careers," career paths that include two or three different fields and two or three different organizations.

4. No longer is it assumed that the organization has unilateral control over the individual's career. Colleges, graduate schools, the government, and the media have all made individual employees more sensitive to the benefits which can be reaped from being active in planning and managing their own careers. To maintain valued employees, organizations, too, have become more responsive to individuals' demands and employees' needs. There is more emphasis on planning and less emphasis on "seeing how things turn out" on the part of both the individual and the organization.

In recent years there has also been increased interest in what has been called the "psychological contract." As defined by Kotter (1973), this psychological contract is an implicit contract between an individual and an organization that specifies what each expects to give and receive from the other in their relationship. The individual brings to the employer a set of career goals and a set of expectations about the job and the organization (e.g., challenging work, salary, chances for advancement), as well as a set of skills to utilize at work. The organization offers a job that demands certain employee abilities, but it also has other expectations of new recruits as well—such as time, energy, commitment, and loyalty to the organization (Lewicki, 1981). The research has consistently shown that where good matches are achieved, employees are less likely to leave their jobs voluntarily and are more likely to experience higher job satisfaction and exhibit greater productivity. Let's look more closely now at how individual career goals and expectations are formed initially and how individuals seek out and join new organizations.

THE JOINING-UP PROCESS

Individuals will be motivated to accept a particular job to the extent that they: (1) can visualize themselves in the job; (2) value the rewards that the job offers; and (3) expect they can get the job and perform it successfully. The more positive each of these factors, the more likely the individual will be attracted to and accept a job offer.

Developing a Career Identity

Before the individual starts considering specific jobs, he or she goes through a period where career or occupational choice occurs. At the very minimum, career choice involves "day-dreaming, forecasting future situations . . . seeing [oneself] in many different situations and predicting [one's] actions in them" (Clausen, 1968, p. 9).

Social Background

The first major factor that influences career identity is a person's social background. Research suggests there is a high correlation between the occupational level of fathers and the aspired occupational level of children. For example, people with parents with little formal education and doing unskilled work are most likely to wind up in occupations at or just above that level. Children of managerial and professional parents are much more likely to end up in managerial or professional positions.

Personality Development

The second major factor that influences career identity is personality development, the needs that people acquire as children. For instance, Anne Roe's research (1957) suggests that the desire for social contact developed during childhood strongly influences career choice. Individuals are more likely to be "people-oriented" in their vocational preferences if their parents were very attentive to them during their childhood; persons with neglecting or rejecting parents tended to be less people-oriented in their career choices. Her research suggests that jobs involving social science knowledge and business contact, for instance, tend to attract more people-oriented individuals than do physical science or technical jobs.

Perhaps John Holland's research (1973) on the link between personality orientation and career selection is the most well known in this area. Holland suggests that people gravitate toward work environments that are consistent with their personal orientations. He has identified six personality types and has shown which occupations each personality type will be most attracted to (see Table 4-1). Further empirical research on Holland's model has confirmed not only that personality orientation is a good predictor of career choice but also that when there is a match between personality type and occupation, individuals are less likely to change careers. For example, *enterprising* personality types are both more likely to go into management jobs and to remain in those jobs over time.

As the individual gets older, the search for a career or a job becomes more structured and involves conscious consideration of *specific* occupations and organizations (Ginzberg et al., 1951). The individual weighs the factors and alternatives involved in choosing occupations and organizations, testing self-perceptions against the realities of work environments.

TABLE 4-1
Holland's hexagonal model of the relationships among the occupational personality types

Personal orientation	Occupational environment
1. **Realistic:** Involves aggressive behavior, physical activities requiring skill, strength, coordination	⟶ Forestry, farming, architecture
2. **Investigative:** Involves cognitive processes (thinking, organizing, understanding) rather than affective activities (feeling, acting, emotional)	⟶ Biology, mathematics, ocean-ography
3. **Social:** Involves interpersonal rather than intellectual or physical activities	⟶ Clinical psychology, foreign service, social work
4. **Conventional:** Involves structural, rule-regulated activities and subordination of personal needs to an organization or person of power and status	⟶ Accounting, finance
5. **Enterprising:** Involves verbal activities to influence others, to attain power and status	⟶ Management, law, publications
6. **Artistic:** Involves self-expression, artistic creation, expression of emotions, and individual activities	⟶ Art, music education

SOURCE: Reprinted with permission from John L. Holland's *Making Vocational Choices: A Theory of Careers.* Englewood Cliffs, N.J.: Prentice Hall, 1973, p. 23.

Super (1957) describes how individuals look at what they have done well in at school, in part-time jobs, and in hobbies, and then seek out jobs that satisfy their self-concepts of what they are competent in.

Developing Personal Values

As people are developing some ideas about what careers and jobs they would like to have, they are simultaneously developing some values about the different opportunities careers and jobs offer.

The Influence of Parents and Teachers

The first major source of influence on how these values develop is parents and teachers. Blau and his associates (1956) found that parents and teachers influence personal values in two ways: (1) they control how much information children get about various occupations (e.g., requirements for entry, rewards offered, and opportunities for advancement); and (2) they affect how children evaluate the different kinds of rewards offered by different types of occupations. Parents send subtle cues to their children not only about the worth of different occupations ("big business is the backbone of the country" or "big business is out to get the little guy") but also about whether the rewards from jobs are worth the effort to get them ("if you're a doctor, you've got it made for life" or "no job is worth staying in school 10 years for").

Societal Influences

As people mature, they become much more sensitive to the broader societal prescriptions about what it means to work in a particular career or organization (e.g., "advertising is creative" or "IBM means 'I've been moved' "). Hall (1976) points out the important impact of both the labor economy and the political environment during this stage. For instance, during the Sputnik era and the "missile gap" scare of the early 1960s, the demand for scientists escalated and more and more people chose to go into engineering and physical sciences. During the anti-Vietnam War era of the late 1960s, burgeoning antibusiness fervor turned more people away from management schools and into the law, which was seen as a more noble way of influencing society (see Charles Reich's *The Greening of America*).

A short note about which factors are most important in job choice decisions: A survey by Renwick and Lawler in 1978 revealed that characteristics of intrinsically motivating jobs (such as opportunities to learn and chances to develop skills) were listed as most important, while factors such as pay and chances for promotion were rated much lower (see Table 4-2).

How can we reconcile these findings with the common observation that people gravitate toward high-paying jobs? A study by Arnold and Feldman (1981) suggests that social desirability plays a big role in determining what people say they value in jobs. Social desirability is the tendency to make statements about oneself that are socially acceptable. The data suggest that people who are very high on social desirability tend to overreport to others the importance of having interesting and challenging work and tend to underreport to others the importance of pay and fringe benefits. They find it more awkward to say they work mainly for money than to say they work because they like a job. Thus, when M.B.A.s were asked to rank what was important to them in jobs, job characteristics like "using skills and abilities" came out on the top of the list, with pay in the middle. However, when the results were controlled for a social desirability response bias, pay came out number one.

Renwick and Lawler's study also suggests that people develop an internal standard of what they consider to be adequate compensation. If pay falls below that level, then money becomes more important than interesting work; if wages or salary are above this level, then having a challenging job becomes much more important.

TABLE 4-2
What you really want from your job

"How satisfied are you with each of the following aspects of your job? And how important to you is each of them?"

Respondents were asked to choose among different degrees of importance and satisfaction for each job feature. Based on averages of their responses, the numbers below rank each from 1 (most important to the group or most often satisfying) to 18 (least important or least often satisfying).

	Importance	Satisfaction
Chances to do something that makes you feel good about yourself	1	8
Chances to accomplish something worthwhile	2	6
Chances to learn new things	3	10
Opportunity to develop your skills and abilities	4	12
The amount of freedom you have on your job	5	2
Chances you have to do things you do best	6	11
The resources you have to do your job	7	9
The respect you receive from people you work with	8	3
Amount of information you get about your job performance	9	17
Your chances for taking part in making decisions	10	14
The amount of job security you have	11	5
Amount of pay you get	12	16
The way you are treated by the people you work with	13	4
The friendliness of people you work with	14	1
Amount of praise you get for job well done	15	15
The amount of fringe benefits you get	16	7
Chances for getting a promotion	17	18
Physical surroundings of your job	18	13

SOURCE: "What You Really Want From Your Job" by P. A. Renwick, E. E. Lawler, & the *Psychology Today* staff. *Psychology Today*, 1978, *11* (12), 56. Copyright 1978 by the Ziff-Davis Publishing Company. Reprinted by permission.

Developing Expectations

Another factor can influence why people don't all gravitate toward the highest-paying job. As Porter, Lawler, and Hackman (1975) suggest, there is a "reality" principle operating: if people don't expect they could get the job or if they couldn't perform it well if they got it, they will not be motivated to seek out the job. People will try to join organizations to which they have the highest expectations of gaining entry (Glueck, 1969; Feldman & Arnold, 1978).

Probably the most informative and illuminating study done on individual expectations about jobs and organizations was done at Carnegie-Mellon University during the 1960s (Vroom, 1966; Vroom & Deci, 1971). M.B.A. students were asked to rate the jobs they were considering according to their perceived instrumentality for the attainment of fifteen goals, ranked in order of their importance. They were also asked to state their probability estimates of how likely they were to obtain each of these fifteen outcomes or goals. When it came time to choose a particular job offer, 76 percent of the M.B.A. students picked the organization which had been most instrumental in meeting the most job goals. Research since this study has been clear and consistent that job-choice decisions are based both on a person's values and goals and on individual expectations about what the organization will be like. From among the offers of employment extended to an individual, he or she is most likely to select the offer that is expected to provide the greatest rewards (Pieters, Hundert, & Beer, 1969).

We know much less about *how* individuals gather information about jobs and organizations. As is discussed in Chapter 13, the decision-making process is much more one of "satisficing" rather than "optimizing" (Simon, 1964). Individuals do not seek out all the information which is available about each job and do not consider all the alternatives and consequences of their choices, if for no other reasons than information overload and incapacity to process so much information. Sorenson, Rhode, and Lawler (1975) suggest that information from teachers and from present and past employees generally carries the most weight (particularly if they are personal friends of the applicant), while advertisements and campus recruiters seem to be more biased and less influential. We also know that individuals have more unrealistic expectations about the intrinsic aspects of their jobs, such as opportunities to grow and develop on jobs (Dunnette, Campbell, & Hakel, 1967; Wanous, 1977). These are the characteristics which are both the hardest to describe and the most abstract.

Why the Joining-Up Process Can Fail

Despite the importance of obtaining a good initial fit between an individual and an organization, frequently the fit is not achieved for a variety of reasons.

Differences in Expectations
Organizations and recent college graduates often have systematic differences in expectations. Graduating college seniors and M.B.A. students have higher expectations of advancement opportunities and increased responsibility than organizations are prepared to give to them. Also, these new entrants into the work force have very different ideas from their

employers on how to sell ideas and get things done and about how important and practical "theoretical" knowledge is (Kotter, 1973). One management student remarked about his graduate education: "I feel like one of those confused baby squirrels running around outside College Hall—I'm scurrying about collecting acorns for winter, but I have no idea yet of what winter will be like" (Feldman, 1980). Such differences in expectations lead to day-to-day frustrations on the part of both organizations and employees.

Individual Perceptions

The act of choosing a job seems to distort individual perceptions. When people are trying to gain entry into an organization, they may either unconsciously distort their own self-perceptions or consciously create false impressions to gain the approval of the recruiter (Feldman, 1980). This, too, increases the chance of a poor fit.

The Vroom and Deci job-choice study done at Carnegie-Mellon revealed further distortions of perception. The authors also found that immediately after deciding which organizations to enter, most people tended to perceive their chosen organization as even *more* attractive than they did before the choice. They also tended to perceive the rejected alternatives as even *less* attractive. These people were engaged in what is called *postdecision dissonance reduction*—justifying their choices by both *increasing* how positively they perceive their chosen organization and by *decreasing* how positively they evaluate the alternatives not chosen (Lawler et al., 1975; Soelberg, 1967). Consequently, it was difficult for people to backtrack to see how good or bad a job-choice decision they made was, and why.

In a very important study by Janis and Mann (1977), the authors point out that these distortions become even greater under conditions of high stress and high conflict. The decision maker bolsters his or her chosen course of action by: (1) exaggerating the favorable consequences of some favored alternatives; (2) minimizing unfavorable consequences of favored alternatives; (3) denying negative feelings about the risks the choice involves; and (4) exaggerating the time between the job choice and actually taking the job, thereby making less salient the long-range consequences of the decision (see Chapter 13).

Job Information

Organizations frequently do not give new recruits realistic information about the jobs being offered. As Wanous (1981) suggests, this is largely a result of the quality of information outsiders have when making choices and the impact of recruitment programs on expectations. For instance, Ward and Athos's 1972 study of recruiting at Harvard Business School revealed that many recruiters gave "glowing" rather than "balanced" descriptions, while a study of the automotive industry found that most people's expectations were not met in their actual job (Dunnette et al., 1973).

The negative consequences of unrealistic expectations are numerous. First of all, there is consistent evidence that unrealistic expectations lead to higher turnover (Weitz, 1956). Second, unrealistic job previews also affect performance. Gomersall and Myers (1966) found that anxiety about the unpredictability of new jobs debilitated performance in the first few months of employment. Finally, Feldman's study of hospital employees (1977) shows that having unrealistic expectations can decrease internal work motivation by decreasing chances that new recruits will obtain jobs they find intrinsically interesting and goals they find challenging.

Sex-Role Conflicts

There may be large differences between men and women in how they go about choosing jobs. In some surprising research, Matina Horner found evidence that some women have a "motivation to avoid success," a disposition to become anxious about achieving success because they expect negative consequences (such as social rejection and feelings of being unfeminine) as a result of succeeding (Horner, 1969). Women who are faced with a conflict between their internalized sex-role stereotype and their need for achievement often attempt to avoid situations where they are likely to succeed at work but experience "traditional" male resentment. This motive to avoid success is most salient among women in traditionally male-dominated fields (Tresmer, 1974).

Selection System Inadequacies

Organizational selection systems may fail to identify applicants with high potential for success. Sometimes this occurs because the organization has not done a systematic job analysis, so that recruiters are even unsure which talents are central to effective performance. At other times, functional managers and personnel recruiters do not clearly communicate with each other about the types of applicants that should be recruited, so that the most appropriate employees are not identified at a sufficiently high "hit rate." At still other times, management may have very poor measures of successful performance and poor predictors of good performance, and so organizations hire too many people who ultimately do not succeed because of inappropriate skills. Particularly with job applicants with no prior work experience, it is difficult to identify patterns of successful performance.

Managing the Joining-Up Process

Having described what happens during the job-choice process and why good matches often don't get made, let's look at how individuals and organizations can better plan for and manage this phase of career development.

Selection Programs

Organizations can improve selection programs to identify better job candidates. As we discussed in Chapters 2 and 3, the efficiency of the selection system in choosing recruits with appropriate skills can largely determine how well organization members will ultimately perform. Talking about the need to begin a "benign circle of development," Smith (1968) writes: "Launched on the right trajectory, people are likely to accumulate successes that strengthen the effectiveness of their orientation toward the world while at the same time they acquire the knowledge and skills that make their further success more probable. . . . Off to a bad start, on the other hand, they soon encounter failures that make them hesitant to try. . . . And they fall increasingly behind their fellows in acquiring the knowledge and skills that are needed for success on those occasions when they do try" (p. 277).

During selection, organizations primarily need to identify what skills are necessary for successful performance and then to develop good predictors of that performance. Despite the favorable evidence on more recent selection devices such as assessment centers, too many organizations are still relying on poor predictors like the interview to select new recruits. The AT&T Management Progress Study (Bray, Campbell, & Grant, 1974) is a prime example of a selection program that is sensitive to career development issues. In addition to providing reliable and valid selection data, AT&T's assessment centers provide data for career development programs as well.

Job Previews

Organizations can provide recruits with more realistic job previews. Although the benefits of realistic job previews have been clearly identified by several researchers, many organizations are still hesitant to give recruits undistorted information—mainly because they fear placing themselves at a competitive disadvantage with organizations that do not give realistic job previews (Wanous, 1981; Louis, 1981). However, there is substantial evidence that realistic job previews do not impair an organization's ability to recruit. Furthermore, the gains from lower turnover are substantial. Life and Casualty Insurance Company of Tennessee, Prudential Insurance, Southern New England Telephone, and West Point Military Academy are just a few of the organizations that have used realistic job previews successfully (Weitz, 1956; Youngerberg, 1963; Wanous, 1973; Macedonia, 1969). The "survival" rate of new recruits receiving realistic job previews is often 10 percent higher than that of other employees.

Giving realistic job previews does not mean that employers need to instigate feelings of discontent by relaying to new recruits every negative aspect of every personality or every work group. What giving realistic job previews implies, however, is giving a balanced description of the jobs. Potential employees should know the types of work they will most frequently be doing, have a reasonable idea of the types of advancement opportunities available and the timetable for when promotions are likely to occur, be familiar with what the general climate of the work group is like, and be aware of the demands the job will make on an employee's outside life.

Of course, many recruits give organizations misleading information about themselves; they, too, fear being at a competitive disadvantage, especially against candidates using a different game plan. Even so, honest disclosure on the part of both applicant and employer is essential to getting the socialization process off on the right foot (Ilgen & Seeley, 1974).

University-Employer Links

Organizations and universities can develop better links with each other. Increased collaboration between universities and employers could be mutually beneficial. Employers can provide career counselors with more accurate information about what the job markets in various occupations and geographical areas are like. Employing organizations can also provide feedback to universities on the skills and attributes that they are looking for in new recruits, and they can give career counselors better information about job and organizational demands to pass on to students. Employing organizations can also provide students access to practitioners through campus visits, class projects, internships, and guest speakers who can directly facilitate students' information searches about what skills they should be trying to acquire to obtain the types of jobs they want (Hall, 1976, p. 152).

Employers, too, stand to gain from university-organization links. Universities can provide employers with information on changing characteristics of graduates, as well as information on the changing labor market and salary demands of their students. Moreover, the campus personnel function can provide organizations with some feedback, especially on their recruitment policies and their "reputations" among students. In addition, companies can get a preview of some of the talent they might want to recruit heavily for later. Such mutual exchanges can lead to both more efficient job search on the part of students and more effective selection on the part of companies.

Job Information

Job applicants need to seek out more and better job-related information and process that information more effectively. There is currently available a variety of career self-assessment materials so that people making decisions about choosing jobs and careers can obtain a better handle on their own career goals, on perceived obstacles to those goals and how they could be overcome, and on what resources or personal contacts would be needed in attaining those goals. An excellent example of this type of career self-assessment material is Bolles's *What Color Is Your Parachute?*, a manual for career planning.

While certainly self-assessment is a good place to start in career development, exclusive reliance on self-insight and introspection can lead to some hazardous risks and bad decision making. As we suggested earlier, people tend to distort information about themselves and about potential employers when they make career and job choices, particularly under conditions of high stress and when several attractive alternatives are available.

Janis and Mann (1977) suggest several ways that job seekers can improve the quality of the data they receive. First, they can seek out information from a greater number of diverse sources and rely less exclusively on one or two informants. Second, they can seek out information on a wider range of alternatives, searching as carefully for negative data as for positive data. Third, job seekers can often benefit from the help of a respected individual—be it a career counselor, a friend, or a mentor—who will *confront* rather than allay the job seeker's anxieties during decision making. Such a person could raise questions about the significance of negative feedback the applicant might have received, encourage the applicant to seek different or better information, help the applicant assess how constrained the decision-making environment really is (e.g., is it really unnegotiable that a decision has to be made in two weeks?), and help the applicant project what the real consequences of the alternatives are. From the individual's perspective, then, making better job decisions is dependent not only on obtaining better information but also on developing better procedures for evaluating information.

ORGANIZATIONAL SOCIALIZATION AND EARLY CAREER ISSUES

Once organizations have selected new employees, there still remains the job of transforming new recruits from total outsiders of companies to participating and effective members of them. This transformation process is called organizational socialization.

Characteristics of Organizational Socialization

There is widespread agreement on the five most salient characteristics of socialization:

1. Change of attitudes, values, and behaviors
2. Continuity of socialization over time

3. Adjustment to new jobs, work groups, and organizational practices
4. Mutual influence between new recruits and their managers
5. Criticality of early socialization period

Change of Attitudes, Values, and Behaviors

Organizational socialization involves change. This change can include the relinquishing of certain attitudes, values, and behaviors or the acquisition of new self-images, new involvements, and new accomplishments. It almost always involves learning—learning the basic goals of the organization, the preferred means by which those goals should be attained, the basic responsibilities of the job, the required behavior patterns for effective performance, and organizational norms and values (Schein, 1968; Van Maanen, 1976).

Continuity of Socialization Over Time

The process of organizational socialization is generally seen as continuous; socialization does not occur at one point, but is achieved more slowly and over time (Erikson, 1950; Brim, 1966). Two corollary points are made about the continuity of the organizational socialization process. First, the process of socialization usually starts *before* a person actually enters an organization, with such activities as occupational choice, attraction to organizations, and selection. Second, a distinction is generally made between the "encounter" phase of socialization, where new hires see what the organization is really like and attempt to become participating members of it, and the "metamorphosis" stage, where the recruits actually settle down and make substantive adjustments (Van Maanen, 1976). In the encounter stage, employees get over their anxieties about being fired or feeling isolated from coworkers; in the metamorphosis stage, employees master their work and become really comfortable with coworkers.

Adjustment to New Jobs, Work Groups, and Organizational Practices

Organizational socialization involves not only adjusting to new jobs but also to new work groups and new organizational practices. Feldman (1981) refers to this as the *multiple socialization* of new organization members. Organizational socialization encompasses several distinct processes which occur simultaneously when new recruits enter organizations:

1. The development of work skills and abilities
2. The acquisition of appropriate role behaviors
3. The adjustment to the work group and its norms
4. The learning of organizational values

The different phases of socialization and the activities engaged in by individuals and organizations at each stage are outlined in Table 4-3.

TABLE 4-3
Organizational socialization

Anticipatory socialization	Encounter	Metamorphosis
	Individual	
Forming expectations; transmitting, receiving, and evaluating information Making decisions about employment	Learning new tasks Clarifying role set Evaluating one's progress in the organization Establishing new interpersonal relationships Learning organizational values	Mastery of job and role requirements Establishing comfortable, trusting work relationships Resolving conflicts between work life and home life Resolving conflicts between demands of work group and demands of other groups in the organization
	Organization	
Forming expectations; transmitting, receiving, and evaluating information Making decisions about employment	Training new employees Redefining jobs Evaluating employees' progress Orienting employees Influencing employees' values	Providing counseling Making career plans for new hires

SOURCE: Adapted from Daniel C. Feldman, "A contingency theory of socialization," *Administrative Science Quarterly*, 1976, *21*, 433–452.

Mutual Influence Between New Recruits and Their Managers

Organizational socialization is a two-way, mutual influence process between individuals and organizations. Some negotiation and modification of job expectations takes place, no matter how institutionalized the new recruit's role might be (Weiss, 1977; Toffler, 1981). Individuals do not completely change to meet the demands of the organization; the organization, too, changes its expectations and behaviors toward employees. Organizations reassess their pictures of newcomers: they redefine jobs to take advantage of particular strengths and minimize particular weaknesses; they plan for different types of training and orientation; they reconsider longer-term career plans for new recruits.

This mutual influence may be not only inevitable but also desirable. One of the most frequently cited indicators of an ineffective socialization is the lack of individual influence. Schein (1968) distinguishes between three basic responses to socialization: rebellion (the rejection of all behaviors, values, and norms), conformity (the acceptance of all behaviors, values, and norms), and creative individualism (the acceptance of only pivotal behaviors, values, and norms and the rejection of others). Schein convincingly argues that creative individualism is healthier both for new recruits and for their employers. Overconformity too often leads to sterile, bureaucratic behavior (Whyte, 1957).

Criticality of Early Socialization Period

The early organizational learning period is particularly critical to the entire process of career development (Van Maanen, 1976; Berlew & Hall, 1966). Ross Webber (1976) points out the early years of one's first permanent job can be marked by frustration and dissatisfaction from several sources. Many young managers detest being treated as "average," not unique, not special. Much of the planning and strategic work they have spent most of their graduate education doing is irrelevant in their first assignments, which are more routine and technical. Theoretical knowledge is often undervalued and political expediency overvalued, and many young managers become resentful of corporate politics.

In addition, sometimes new hires are frustrated by what they perceive to be incompetent first supervisors or supervisors who block their visibility and exposure. Young managers are disappointed that organizations do not respond as quickly to the market and the environment as they would like. The criteria for performance appraisal are less structured and more ambiguous than expected, and the performance evaluations they receive from supervisors are less frequent and less positive than hoped for. Promotions and challenging job assignments, too, come slower than expected.

The overall result of such problems is that new recruits become less committed to their work, and less optimistic about whether they are going to succeed within the organization (Hall, 1976; Bray et al., 1974). These problems are serious because the evidence is strong that there is a *career-success cycle* in which early career success paves the way for later accomplishments. Early success opens up further opportunities for achievement, but early failure results in debilitating anxiety and the loss of more interesting work assignments. For these reasons, we turn next to examining what organizations can do to design better organizational socialization programs and what strategies new recruits can use to ease their own adjustment into organizations.

Managing Organizational Socialization: The Organizational Perspective

Organizations can take more initiative in creating conditions for successful organizational socialization. There are several strategies organizations can use to design more effective organizational socialization programs.

Provide a Challenging First Job

Earlier we discussed the *career-success cycle,* where early task success paves the way for later task achievements (Berlew & Hall, 1966). There is also a *task-liking spiral:* task success leads to task liking and task liking leads to further task success (Korman, 1968; Locke, 1968). To obtain commitment over and above role requirements, organizations need to provide recruits with intrinsically motivating jobs.

Schein (1964) has found that one of the most important causes of a new member's disillusionment with the organization—and one of the most important reasons for quick turnover among the newly employed—is a work assignment that is either too easy or too difficult. The two job characteristics which are most important in new assignments are autonomy and responsibility (Van Maanen, 1976). Recruits need a sense of control over their work and a sense of satisfaction from executing projects or seeing them through to completion.

Provide Relevant Training

So often, training programs are geared to such general matters that they provide little of the specific information new recruits want and need. What many organizations need is not necessarily more training, but more focused training. Organizations need to put more thought into identifying job-relevant skills and providing training that will develop these skills. Packaged, or canned, training programs often aim at such a low common denominator that they fulfill no one's needs.

The need for training, of course, doesn't stop at entry-level jobs. As recruits take on additional responsibilities or new jobs, additional training will very likely be needed. This is particularly true because organizations tend to promote employees on their technical competence, even though the skills important in the current job may have no relationship to the demands of the next. Contrary to the Peter principle, perhaps people are not promoted to their level of incompetence; perhaps, instead, they are promoted to the level of their organization's incompetence in selection and training (Feldman, 1976).

Provide Timely and Consistent Feedback

Most managers recognize the importance of feedback in motivating employee behavior. Fewer recognize the relationship between giving feedback and the development of skills and abilities during socialization. Two attributes of the performance evaluation system have the greatest effect on socialization.

Timing. The probationary review not only provides feedback on work to date, but also signals the employee with the organization's initial "letting-in" response to their "breaking-in" efforts. When a full year goes by before the first feedback is given, high performers are kept needlessly waiting for affirmation. As a nurse in a study of the socialization of hospital employees remarked: "Even a well-trained pigeon should be positively reinforced more than once every 365 days" (Feldman, 1977). Good performers also frequently interpret no feedback as disinterest or disappointment.

As the socialization process progresses, however, new recruits do come to realize that a lot of the responsibility for getting feedback is theirs, and not the sole responsibility of others. A good example of this increase in perceived personal control is seen in Feldman's (1980) study of management students. Upon first entering management school, students saw themselves simply as passive receivers of feedback and thought that they had to sit patiently (or impatiently) for exam grades or comments on papers. However, as they progressed in the system, students discovered other ways of receiving feedback—by observing faculty reactions to them in class, by observing student reactions to their comments, by observing whether they were sought out by others to work on group projects. By the end of the first year, grades had become much less important to the students, and they were very much more active about seeking out feedback when needed. Students also began to take more personal responsibility for obtaining feedback.

Consistency and Equity. We know that when employees consider their performance ratings inequitable, they may begin to exert less effort because they don't see the link between working hard and getting the rewards they want (see Chapter 7).

One reason that ratings may be seen as inequitable is that performance standards are often quite subjective and open to supervisory interpretation. In the hospital socialization study mentioned above, for instance, the staff complained about being rated on dimensions like cooperation and initiative. With no behavioral anchors in rating employees, supervisors can really bias evaluations (and, indeed, ratings on these two dimensions were correlated over 0.90 with the overall supervisory rating). Without tangible criteria and objective performance measures, the organization leaves itself open to attack on charges of favoritism or bias. Without standardized evaluations across supervisors, organizations subtly encourage employees to request transfers to units supervised by "easier" evaluators. More important, however, an organization without good performance evaluation systems allows recruits to reject feedback—thus failing to learn from their experience—and to make short-run job changes that can adversely affect both their personal careers and the organization's work force (Feldman, 1977).

Select a Good First Supervisor to Be in Charge of Socialization

There is virtually no aspect of the socialization process that the supervisor cannot sabotage or smooth, depending on inclination and talent. There is even general evidence that a "Pygmalion effect" operates: a supervisor who has positive expectations about how a subordinate can perform and communicates that to the subordinate may actually facilitate the subordinate's performance. Yet, because new recruits generally enter organizations only sporadically, and often under conditions of low manpower, supervisors are sometimes unaware of the difficult problems the recruits face, and they themselves receive no guidance in how to deal with those problems.

In particular, immediate supervisors can help new recruits in the following ways: (1) directly training new recruits in job specifics—or at least doing a competent needs analysis so that training can be done elsewhere; (2) giving new recruits challenging first assignments to motivate them to grow and stay with the organization; and (3) using the opportunity of new recruits' entry to reallocate tasks and redesign work to create both more efficient and more satisfying work systems within the group. Supervisors also play a critical part in buffering newcomers from conflict, and providing coaching in how to deal with conflict. The organization's role here is to train supervisors to be more effective in "people processing" during socialization (Van Maanen, 1978; Feldman, 1980).

Design a Relaxed Orientation Program

Formal orientation programs are too often geared toward "selling the company" or creating organizational loyalty rather than toward dealing with the anxiety new recruits bring with them. Some of these formal programs provide a slick, packaged indoctrination to a company. Frequently considered "overkill," they are neither credible to, nor internalized by, newcomers. Such presentations more often overwhelm than relieve recruits who hesitate even more to ask questions. "Debasing" orientations similarly create additional anxiety.

On the other hand, a more relaxed orientation that deals with the immediate feelings of new organization members can be successful. One such easy-going orientation program (Gomersall & Myers, 1966) stressed making four points clear to the recruits:

  a. "Your opportunity to succeed is very good."
  b. "Disregard 'hall talk,' 'hazing,' and rumors."
  c. "Take the initiative in communication."
  d. "Get to know your supervisor."

The resulting communication was two-way, rather than one-way from management. The employees involved reached preestablished levels of competence a month earlier than expected, and their anxiety was reduced more quickly.

Place New Recruits in Work Groups with High Morale

Since the internalization of values and beliefs depends so heavily on the selective filtering of information in the work group, it makes sense to structure the socialization so that incumbents with the most constructive approach get first crack at new recruits (Van Maanen, 1978). If the organization climate is positive, for instance, having new recruits socialized by former occupants of similar roles is logical: a sense of continuity and stability can be maintained, and job incumbents can help new members understand their new situation. On the other hand, of course, if the image that will be presented to new recruits is unpleasant, this "serial" socialization can exacerbate an already negative situation by reinforcing negative feelings.

When there is interpersonal and intergroup conflict in a work area, new employees are confused and hold back from making friends or being trusting until they can better understand the tension they sense. Moreover, where there is a low level of trust and friendship in a group, older recruits may withhold information about supervisory personalities and preferences that is essential for new recruits to know in order to do their job well. For instance, nurses in the hospital study felt that some of the most important things to learn about their jobs were the moods and personalities of the doctors they worked with and the doctors' particular preferences about how medical and administrative procedures should be performed. On medical floors where there was a good deal of interpersonal conflict, new nurses had more difficulty both adjusting to the group and performing their jobs as the physicians wished (Feldman, 1977).

Socializing new organization members in groups can also increase morale. When a recruit is the only new person to join a work group, there may be a longer delay in breaking in and feeling accepted by others. One problem is that the recruit lacks recourse to others with whom to check out initial perceptions and reactions. As one hospital billing clerk remarked, "Every time I look up from my desk I feel like they're all staring at me, and I wonder who's holding the black ball." An apprentice or mentor relationship with an incumbent group member can help mitigate such feelings.

A group that is socialized together quite often develops a collective consciousness and a group pride. In the study on M.B.A. student socialization, students who were all assigned to the same classes were able to share problems and attempted solutions with each other. Moreover, such a group was more able to resist attempts by older members of the organization to influence them. In subtle ways, a group of recruits can actually socialize the "socializers," especially when they outnumber them (Feldman, 1980).

Managing Organizational Socialization: The Individual Perspective

While organizations certainly can and do exert a lot of influence over new recruits' careers, much of the responsibility for managing early careers still rests with the recruits themselves. Webber (1976) and Hall (1976) catalog some of the more important suggestions new recruits can follow in managing their own early careers.

1. ***Obtain a challenging job.*** Challenge and potential for career growth should weigh more heavily than shorter-term considerations such as marginal pay differences in making job choices. The growth and stretching which occurs in that first job can lead to even wider choices of better jobs later.

2. ***Be an outstanding performer.*** The evidence is strong and consistent that more rewarding opportunities open up' to the more outstanding performers. Learning the job as quickly as possible and training a replacement makes it easier to move on to more broadening assignments.

3. ***Actively manage your own career.*** It is important that new recruits be active in influencing decisions being made about their careers higher up the hierarchy. New recruits should be prepared to practice self-nomination, to make it known to superiors that they want a particular job and are prepared to work to qualify for it.

4. ***Seek out a sponsor in the organization.*** Ineffective, immobile bosses can really dead-end a subordinate's career. Recruits should try to develop relations with a mobile senior executive who can be a sponsor, and avoid becoming a crucial subordinate to an immobile supervisor. Of course, once again, being an outstanding performer greatly increases the chances of attracting the attention of the people who matter most in the organization.

5. ***Seek to broaden the scope of the job.*** Particularly in quickly growing organizations, responsibility will always somewhat exceed authority. Newcomers should avoid being trapped by formal, narrow job descriptions and should instead seek out additional responsibilities of interest and jobs with higher visibility.

6. ***Leave an organization at your own convenience.*** If problems develop, employees should leave before the situation deteriorates so badly that they get asked to leave. It is best to try to leave the first employer on good terms.

MIDDLE- AND LATER-CAREER ISSUES

The problems of plateaued performance, obsolescence, and ultimate withdrawal from the work force seem very distant and vague to eager, talented newcomers to organizations. These problems are very immediate and real to the people senior to them, however.

Consider the following monologue by Bob Slocum, the middle-aged, middle-manager protagonist of Joseph Heller's *Something Happened* (1974).

On days when I'm especially melancholy, I begin constructing tables of organization from standpoints of plain malevolence, dividing, subdividing, and classifying people in the company on the basis of envy, hope, fear, ambition, frustration, rivalry, hatred, or disappointment. I call these charts my Happiness Charts. These exercises in malice never fail to boost my spirits—but only for a while. I rank pretty high when the company is analyzed in this way, because I'm not envious or disappointed, and I have no expectations. At the very top, of course, are those people, mostly young and without dependents, to whom the company is not yet an institution of any sacred merit (or even an institution especially worth preserving) but still only a place to work, and who regard their present association with it as something temporary. . . .

Near the very bottom of my Happiness Charts I put those people who are striving so hard to get to the top. I am better off (or think I am) than they because, first, I have no enemies nor rivals (that I know of) and am almost convinced I can hold my job here for as long as I want to, and second, because there is no other job in the company I want that I can realistically hope to get. I wouldn't want Green's job; I couldn't handle it if I had it and would be afraid to take it if it were offered. There is too much to do. I'm glad it won't be me (I'm sure it won't be).

I am one of those people, therefore, most of whom are much older than I, who are without ambition already and have no hope, although I do want to continue receiving my raise in salary each year, and a good cash bonus at Christmastime. . . . (pp. 34–35)[2]

Consider, too, the reminiscences of Gaylord Freeman, recently retired chairman of the board of the First National Bank of Chicago (Terkel, 1980):

This January, I sat down in the afternoon and read a novel. That's the first one I read since I got out of school in 1934. I never felt I could waste a minute. It was cheating. I felt I had a terrible duty to the bank and a duty to society. It took a hell of a lot of my time. People are silly. I'm not as good as I was. I'm not as physically strong. I'm not as mentally sharp. I have a hell of a time with names. So I don't feel the same duty I had when I was a more efficient machine.

It's worse if you have been top dog. It's harder to retire than if you never were the boss. Business is so goddman competitive! The head of a business is really competing with everybody all the time, not only with his competitors. You're competing with your friends in other businesses, your dearest friends. It influences your life tremendously. And not necessarily in a good way. It tends to make business friendships not quite friendships.

The guy who's been intensely competitive all his life and then—click!— he's retired, it's hard for him to joyously admire the success of his associates,

---

[2]From Joseph Heller's *Something Happened.* Copyright 1974 by Alfred A. Knopf, Inc. Reprinted by permission.

his friends. He can't help feeling it's a little at his expense. Of course, it isn't. He's not in that league any more. This is a hard thing for many men to take. (pp. 20–21)[3]

Mid-Career Issues

The sorts of issues and concerns that older, more experienced employees have about their careers—and that organizations have about those employees—are very different from the issues and concerns of the early-career stage. This is true due to a variety of differences in the work and home environments of older employees.

Slower Transfers and Promotions

First of all, the speed at which employees get transferred and promoted slows down after the first few job changes. In large organizations that are "tall" (many levels of management relative to the total number of employees) employees will probably be able to pass fairly easily from one echelon to the next early in their careers. However, the number of echelons may be so great that individuals may increasingly feel they are a long way from the top as they reach middle age. Moreover, at each level, employees realize how much they overestimated the power and authority of that position: the difference between the amount of responsibility they have and the amount they want or need is a constant.

New Criteria for Transfers and Promotions

Second, employees realize that the criteria for which they were selected to enter the organization are not the same criteria on which they are being moved through the organization (Feldman & Brett, 1982). While entry decisions may be based on specific competences, job change decisions may be based on entirely different factors, such as being politically savvy, being personally compatible with the new boss, or just being in the right place at the right time when an unexpected opening appears.

Organizations also differ in how difficult it is to cross functional boundaries (Rosenbaum, 1979; Schein, 1971). Because most movement in organizations is vertical within departments, it is generally quite difficult to find openings at the same or a higher level in a different functional area. Moreover, it is tough to compete for those cross-functional jobs with people with years of experience in the same area. Thus, as employees find themselves on "the thin edge of the wedge" moving up in the organization, they can also find it equally difficult to get out of their own area and into others.

---

[3]From Studs Terkel's *American Dreams: Lost and Found.* Copyright 1980 by Pantheon Books. Reprinted by permission.

Different Work Activities and Demands

Third, for those employees who don't have the skills or the temperament for enlarged job responsibilities, the middle and waning years of their careers can seem bleak indeed. Dalton and his colleagues (1977) have developed a four-stage model of professional careers, illustrated in Table 4-4, that illuminates the different activities and job demands which organization members face at different career stages.

After the initial socialization period (stage I), professionals and managers enter stage II, where their central activity becomes being an independent contributor and serving as a colleague. In a still later stage, stage III, the person's main activities become influencing, guiding, directing, and developing other people. Persons in this stage play the critical role in helping others move through stage I. In the final stage, stage IV, the key identifiable characteristic activity is defining the direction of the organization or some major segment of it.

As the Dalton model suggests, each of the transitions from stage to stage involves some major psychological issues. Where in stage I dependence is an acceptable posture, independence is valued in stage II, and assuming responsibilities for others and exercising power are expected in the more mature career stages. People in all four stages make an important contribution to the organization, and some people in each stage are necessary for organizational effectiveness. However, Dalton's research also indicates that as people grow older they are less likely to be highly valued if they don't move beyond the early stages.

Threatening Work Environment

Fourth, the work environments for middle- and later-career-stage employees can seem very threatening. While the work environments which new

TABLE 4-4
Four career stages

	I	II	III	IV
Central activity:	Helping Learning Following directions	Independent contributor	Training Interfacing	Shaping the direction of the organization
Primary relationship:	Apprentice	Colleague	Mentor	Sponsor
Major psychological issues:	Dependence	Independence	Assuming responsibility for others	Exercising power

SOURCE: "The Four Stages of Professional Careers—A New Look at Performance by Professionals" by Gene W. Dalton, Paul H. Thompson, & Raymond L. Price. *Organizational Dynamics*, Summer 1977, p. 23. © 1977 by AMACOM, a division of American Management Associations. All rights reserved.

employees face are uncertain, most recruits are optimistic about the chances for success. For middle- and later-career-stage employees, there are several reasons for pessimism (Levinson, 1969; Hall, 1976).

These employees feel a growing sense of obsolescence. Young subordinates have more recent technical knowledge and need to be turned to increasingly for technical advice. Older employees are more worried about crises emerging beyond their control.

Moreover, there is increasing contraction of the hard-work period. The average age at which people become company presidents is decreasing. Therefore, people have less time to "make it." Older employees are caught between brighter, younger subordinates who are competing with them for promotions, and a tighter external job market for managers who don't make it in their own organizations.

Stress and Frustration

Finally, there are systematic personal problems for middle- and later-career employees that produce stress and frustration. People at different stages in their lives have different needs and goals, and feel vulnerable in different ways. With new, young employees there is a great need to test themselves, to demonstrate their competence, to establish their independence. As we discussed above, the establishment of oneself in early career years is far from painless. However, the mid-career years present a particularly stressful set of circumstances for workers (Levinson, 1969; Hall, 1976).

For people in intensely competitive careers, each year is a milepost. If they do not move on schedule, they lose out on experience, position, and the reputation for being a star. This means there is continuous anxiety and fear of defeat. Moreover, there is a shift in what society views now as the prime of life. Because society now values youth more than in the past, the attainment of success is partially offset by the loss of youth. Since only rarely can one have youth and achievement at the same time, there is something anticlimactic about middle-age success.

There is also significant anger at younger employees, who are receiving greater opportunities and more money than mid-career people received at the same stage in life. There is anger, too, that younger employees have more flexibility in their lives and do not operate under the accumulated constraints of more job and home responsibilities. Energy is drained as this anger is repressed and denied. Most significantly, there is increased awareness of physical aging and awareness of death. Many people over 40 report the feeling that "life is half over," that they now have as much or more time behind them as ahead of them. All of these sources of threat and anxiety, when they overlap acutely, can result in what has been called a *mid-life crisis*.

The transition from older employee to retirement can be equally frightening. Because work is such an important part of one's identity, especially for highly involved people, loss of one's work role can be devastating to self-concept. Loss of work can mean, too, loss of a structure to one's day, loss of chances for social interaction, and loss of something to keep one's mind off feelings of loneliness and thoughts of death (Sofer, 1970).

Managing Later Career Development

Many of the strategies individuals use to manage their early-career years continue to be appropriate throughout their work lives. Assessing and reassessing career goals, career planning, seeking out different and challenging work assignments, continuing training and educational activities, being proactive in creating new work opportunities—all of these can help employees avoid becoming obsolescent or "burned out."

The actions which organizations can take to facilitate later-career development fall into three categories: making job assignments, manpower planning, and personnel policies (Hall, 1976). Let's examine each of these in turn.

Job Assignments

Several times earlier we have discussed how important challenging first jobs are to new recruits. Unfortunately, in too many organizations employees are moved around too frequently in the early years of their careers and too seldom during later years (Feldman & Brett, 1982). Periodically rotating employees through different departments or functions later in their careers can facilitate employees learning new skills and new material and give them a new perspective and a fresh outlook on their jobs.

Dalton and his colleagues (1977) also suggest that organizations can employ *dual-ladder* career development. In dual-ladder organizations, professionals can progress along either a technical or a managerial hierarchy, receiving the types of training and job assignments most relevant to their career goals. This is becoming increasingly frequent in engineering and R&D firms.

Human Resource Planning

Organizations can also use human resource planning to facilitate career development. The most obvious way is at initial selection—estimating short- and long-run labor needs. Organizations want to avoid "understocking" the employee pool with promotable talent while avoiding being oversupplied with "fast-track" M.B.A.s frustrated at slow promotion opportunities.

Morgan, et al., (1979) also recommend the use of management development committees, composed of department heads, upper management, and personnel officials. Such committees annually review the strengths and weaknesses of each manager and develop with each employee a 5-year career plan. From the organization's point of view, such committees can generate information for the selection of new replacements. From the individual's point of view, such committees can help achieve a fit between individual and organizational goals. Moreover, the feedback contains ideas about interim job assignments and formalized training so the individual has definite steps to follow in an effort to reach career goals.

Wellbank and his associates (1978) discuss the importance of having carefully sequenced job assignments. Companies like AT&T and Sears have identified career paths to key target jobs (like store manager or product manager). Once employees have gone through some type of skills assessment and career goals have been discussed with higher management, rational job progressions and training needs can be outlined and planned.

Personnel Policies

Corporate policies on career counseling, continuing education, geographical relocation, and handling of obsolescent or plateaued employees all affect the quality of career development in organizations (Miller, 1978).

In "The Shape of Things to Come: A New Look at Organizational Careers," Van Maanen, Schein, and Bailyn (1977) write that career counseling is likely to be expanded in organizations. Assessment centers will be used not only to serve the needs of the organization, but also to serve the needs of individuals through counseling. Assessment centers permit employees to get more accurate data on their career chances; moreover, assessment center data can be used to plan training programs (see Chapter 2). Another form counseling can take is that of workshop programs to help people learn how to identify career goals and how to develop specific action steps toward implementing career plans.

Van Maanen and his colleagues (1977) also foresee increasing use of sabbaticals and flexible working hours for off-work activities, particularly continuing education. Law firms are already finding they must promise time for public service work (*pro bono publico*) in order to attract top law students. Many professional groups have pressed for legislation requiring continuing education as the price for continuing professional practice (Dalton et al., 1977). Other organizations provide time off and tuition to attend university-based educational programs. Such educational activities can move plateaued employees off dead center and prevent them from becoming obsolescent.

As the frequency of households where both marriage partners work increases, organizations have to come to terms with the constraints faced by employees offered geographical transfers and promotions. Hall and Hall (1978, 1979) find that rigid corporate relocation policies are giving way to case-by-case exceptions. Among the types of assistance organizations can provide such two-career couples are shorter work weeks or staggered schedules to allow couples to commute more easily, more training moves within the same geographical area, and increased efforts to find the spouse a job.

With employees who have plateaued and become obsolescent, the organization might consider giving these individuals "retraining" money when they leave, in an amount based on length of service. Proposed by Connor and Fielden (1973), this policy encourages "shelf-sitters" to update themselves or switch fields later in their careers. Early retirement plans, retirement planning, and flextime scheduling can also ease the transition of older employees out of the work force.

CAREER-DEVELOPMENT PROGRAMS

The types of suggestions which we have made about career development here are not just academic constructs, but are based on programs currently being implemented by some forward-looking organizations. Some of the most innovative programs are briefly described below.

Some Current Programs

3M
Minnesota Mining and Manufacturing currently has a 2-day management assessment program that helps employees identify career goals, developmental needs, and placement opportunities. Each program consists of about fifteen participants, chosen from young, nonmanagement employees who have volunteered or been nominated by management.

AT&T
Three career-development programs are in use in the telephone system. The first program is a 1-day assessment program for noncollege, nonmanagement people. This *early identification program* consists of a 1-day assessment program, followed by extensive feedback and career counseling by a trained professional. The second program, for high-potential female college graduates, combines assessment with career planning. Career plans, including target jobs, training needs, and interim assignments, are reviewed every 6 months. The third program focuses on training the supervisor in job restructuring, joint target setting, and appraisal skills.

Travelers Insurance
Travelers uses career-planning conferences for high-potential employees between their 3d and 7th years of employment. These conferences, usually a week long and conducted offsite, deal with career planning and re-

evaluation of personal and work lives of managers at the first plateau of their careers (Hall, 1976).

Lawrence Livermore Laboratory

A regular series of workshops involves the assessment of abilities, career-interest testing, and access to a career-information center. An interesting feature of the laboratory's program is the utilization of technical and scientific professionals, who also hold graduate degrees in counseling psychology, as career counselors (Miller, 1978).

MANAGERIAL IMPLICATIONS

As the programs at 3M, AT&T, Travelers Insurance, and Lawrence Livermore Laboratory suggest, it is possible for organizations to better manage the careers of individuals in organizations. What are the keys to these successful career development programs?

1. *First, organizations need to assess employees periodically throughout their careers to discover individual strengths that can be used in other jobs in the organization, and to remedy individual weaknesses which are preventing career movement.* Achieving a fit between individual skills and organization demands is not achieved at one time, but has to be achieved continuously. Without periodic assessment employees are more likely to become plateaued or obsolete, and organizations are more likely to find themselves with a lack of promotable talent.

2. *Second, organizations need to give employees more realistic information not only when they are making hiring decisions but also when they are making promotion decisions.* One of the key elements of successful career-development programs is giving participants realistic information about both the assessment program and the assessment results. Employees in these programs understand that participation does not mean automatic advancement. Moreover, these employees receive more accurate data on their chances for promotion.

    Some organizations play games with employees. They don't tell employees when they're on the fast track so the employees won't get cocky, and they don't tell employees when they're doing poorly so they won't quit before they can be replaced. However, frequent renegotiation of expectations renews the psychological contract so important to both parties.

3. *Third, career-planning activities are most successful when they are coordinated with other activities in human resource management—selection, training, human resource planning, and performance appraisal.* Career development succeeds best where it is not relegated to the periphery, but becomes integrated with other key personnel functions. For instance, initial

selection data can be used to develop socialization programs. Performance appraisal programs can provide useful data for the design of training programs. Both performance appraisal and training data can be utilized in making recommendations for job moves, and for estimating future labor needs.

4. *Finally, career development is most likely to succeed when immediate line supervisors are actively involved.* While personnel departments may structure the process of career-development programs, their actual content should be largely the responsibility of line management (Hall, 1976). The line supervisors are frequently in the best position to assess employee competence, provide relevant training, and engage in career counseling. Equal access to the assessment part of career-development programs can cut down on complaints about favoritism. While companies may focus extra attention later on high-potential employees, in the successful programs we discussed earlier each employee has the opportunity to volunteer to be assessed (and, frequently, to be reassessed).

SUMMARY

The chapter focuses on careers in organizations, the sequences of jobs people hold during their work histories. How we think about careers has changed substantially in the last 25 years: individuals are exerting more control over their own job assignments, and frequently plan career paths which include two or three different fields and two or three different organizations.

The joining-up process, and the setting up of the "psychological contract," are the first steps in career development. The person's social background and early personality development, labor market factors, and the political environment all influence a person's preferences for jobs. Improved selection programs, realistic job previews, better university-business links, and more sophisticated decision-making procedures can increase the likelihood of matching individual needs to organizational demands.

The second phase in career development is organizational socialization, where new recruits are transformed from total outsiders of companies to participating and effective members of them. Organizational socialization involves not only the development of work skills and abilities but also the acquisition of appropriate role behaviors, adjustment to the work group and its norms, and the learning of organizational values. Key elements of a good socialization program include: challenging job assignments; relevant training; timely, consistent feedback; well-trained, receptive first supervisors; relaxed, informal orientation programs; and placement of new recruits into work groups of high morale.

The middle and later years of a person's career present a different set of problems and challenges. It is more difficult to move up in the organization or to change functions than it is to gain entry into the organization. Later job assignments often require skills and interpersonal relationships which employees don't possess.

Mid-career people are conscious that they are no longer up-and-coming stars, that they are frequently competitive with their subordinates yet dependent on them for technical expertise, that their job mobility has decreased, and that their best years may lay behind, not ahead, of them. Rotating job assignments, more and better manpower planning, and innovative personnel policies can all address the issues of plateaued and obsolescent performance.

REVIEW QUESTIONS

1. What do we mean by the term *career*? How have the ways we think about careers changed in the last 25 years?
2. What is a *psychological contract*? Why is it important to match individual needs and organizational demands?
3. What factors determine whether an individual will be motivated to accept a particular job?
4. What role do expectations about future performance play in job choice?
5. Why does the joining-up process fail?
6. How can the selection and recruitment programs be better designed to facilitate good matches?
7. Why are realistic job previews so important?
8. What are the most important features of organization socialization? What do we mean by the phrase *multiple socialization of new organization members*?
9. Why do many recruits experience frustration and dissatisfaction in their initial employment period? Why are the early career years so important in overall career success?
10. What can organizations do to better design the socialization experience?
11. What can new recruits do to manage their own early careers better?
12. What factors make the mid-career years an especially frustrating period? What can organizations do to help employees avoid becoming obsolescent or "burned out"?
13. What are some examples of innovative career-development programs? What are the keys to designing successful career-development programs?
14. What are the greatest career obstacles you expect to face? Why? What can you do to overcome some of those obstacles?

REFERENCES

Arnold, Hugh J., & Feldman, Daniel C. Social desirability response bias in self-report choice situations. *Academy of Management Journal*, 1981, *24*, 377–385.

Berlew, David E., & Hall, Douglas T. The socialization of managers: Effects of expectations on performance. *Administrative Science Quarterly*, 1966, *11*, 207–223.

Blau, Peter M., Gustad, John W., Jesson, Richard, Parnes, Herbert S., & Wilcox, Richard C. Occupational choices: A conceptual framework. *Industrial and Labor Relations Review*, 1956, *9*, 531–543.

Bolles, Richard N. *What color is your parachute? A practical manual for job-hunters and career changers* (rev. ed.). Berkeley, Calif.: Ten Speed Press, 1981.

Bray, D. W., Campbell, R. J., & Grant, D. L. *Formative years in business*. New York: Wiley, 1974.

Brim, O. G., Socialization through the life cycle. In O. G. Brim & S. Wheeler (Eds.), *Socialization after childhood*. New York: Wiley, 1966.

Clausen, John A. (Ed.). *Socialization and society*. Boston: Little, Brown, 1968.

Connor, Samuel, & Fielden, John S. Rx for managerial fence-sitters. *Harvard Business Review*, 1973, *51*, 113–120.

Dalton, Gene W., Thompson, Paul H., & Price, Raymond L. The four stages of professional careers—A new look at performance by professionals. *Organizational Dynamics*, 1977, *6*, 19–42.

Dunnette, Marvin D., Campbell, John P., & Hakel, Milt D. Factors contributing to job satisfaction and job dissatisfaction in six occupational groups. *Organizational Behavior and Human Performance*, 1967, *2*, 143–174.

Dunnette, Marvin D., Arvey, Richard D., & Banas, Paul A. Why do they leave? *Personnel*, 1973, *3*, 25–39.

Erikson, E. H. *Childhood and society*. New York: Norton, 1950.

Feldman, Daniel C. A contingency theory of socialization. *Administrative Science Quarterly*, 1976a, *21*, 433–452.

Feldman, Daniel C. A practical program for employee socialization. *Organizational Dynamics*, 1976b, *5*, 64–80.

Feldman, Daniel C. Organizational socialization of hospital employees: A comparative view of occupational groups. *Medical Care*, 1977a, *5*, 799–813.

Feldman, Daniel C. The role of initiation activities in socialization. *Human Relations*, 1977b, *30*, 977–990.

Feldman, Daniel C. A socialization process that helps new recruits succeed. *Personnel*, 1980, *57*, 11–23.

Feldman, Daniel C. The multiple socialization of organization members. *Academy of Management Review*, 1981, *6*, 309–318.

Feldman, Daniel C., & Arnold, Hugh J. Position choice: Comparing the importance of job and organizational factors. *Journal of Applied Psychology*, 1978, *63*, 706–710.

Feldman, Daniel C., & Brett, Jeanne M. Coping with new jobs: A comparative study of new hires and job changers. *Proceedings of the National Academy of Management Meetings*, 1982.

Ginzberg, E., Ginzberg, S. W., Axelrod, W., & Herna, J. L. *Occupational choice: An approach to a general theory*. New York: Columbia University Press, 1951.

Glueck, William F. Decision-making: Organizational choice. *Personnel Psychology*, 1969, *22*, 171–183.

Gomersall, E. R., & Myers, M. S. Breakthrough in on-the-job training. *Harvard Business Review*, 1966, *44*, 62–72.

Hall, Douglas T. *Careers in organizations*. Pacific Palisades, Calif.: Goodyear Publishing, 1976.

Hall, Francine S., & Hall, Douglas T. Dual careers—How do couples and companies cope with the problems? *Organizational Dynamics*, 1978, *6*, 57–77.

Hall, Francine S., & Hall, Douglas T. *The two career couple*. Reading, Mass.: Addison-Wesley, 1979.

Heller, Joseph. *Something happened*. New York: Knopf, 1974.

Holland, John L. *Making vocational choices: A theory of careers*. Englewood Cliffs, N.J.: Prentice-Hall, 1973.

Horner, Matina. Fail: Bright women. *Psychology Today*, 1969, *3*, 36–41.

Ilgen, E. W., & Seely, W. Realistic expectations as an aid in reducing voluntary resignations. *Journal of Applied Psychology*, 1974, *59*, 452–455.

Janis, Irving L., & Mann, Leon. *Decision making*. New York: Free Press, 1977.

Korman, Abraham. Task success, task popularity, and self-esteem as influences on task liking. *Journal of Applied Psychology*, 1968, *52*, 484–490.

Kotter, John P. The psychological contract: Managing the joining-up process. *California Management Review*, 1973, *15*, 91–99.

Lawler, E. E., Kuleck, W. J., Rhode, J. G., & Sorenson, J. E. Job choice and post-decision dissonance. *Organizational Behavior and Human Performance*, 1975, *13*, 133–145.

Levinson, Harry. On being a middle-aged manager. *Harvard Business Review*, 1969, *47*, 51–60.

Lewicki, Roy F. Organizational seduction: Building commitment to organizations. *Organizational Dynamics*, 1981, *10*, 5–22.

Locke, Edwin A. Toward a theory of task motivation and incentives. *Organizational Behavior and Human Performance*, 1968, *3*, 157–189.

Louis, M. R. Surprise and sense making: What newcomers experience in entering unfamiliar organizational settings. *Administrative Science Quarterly*, 1980, *25*, 226–251.

Macedonia, R. M. Expectations—Press and survival. Unpublished doctoral dissertation, New York University Graduate School of Public Administration, 1969.

Miller, Donald B. Career planning and management in organizations. In Mariann Jellinek (Ed.), *Career management for the individual and the organization*. Chicago: St. Clair Press, 1978, 353–360.

Morgan, Marilyn A., Hall, Douglas T., & Martier, Alison. Career development strategies in industry. *Personnel*, 1979, *66*.

Pieters, G. R., Hundert, A. T., & Beer, M. T. Predicting organizational choice: A post hoc analysis. *Proceedings of the 76th Annual Convention of the American Psychological Association*, 1969, 573–574.

Porter, Lyman W., Lawler, Edward E., & Hackman, J. Richard. *Behavior in organizations*. New York: McGraw-Hill, 1975.

Reich, Charles. *The Greening of America*. New York: Random House, 1970.

Renwick, Patricia A., Lawler, Edward E., & the *Psychology Today* staff. What you really want from your job. *Psychology Today*, 1978, *11*, 53–65, 118.

Roe, Anne. Early determinants of vocational choice. *Journal of Counseling Psychology*, 1957, *4*, 212–217.

Rosenbaum, J. E. Tournament mobility: Career patterns in a corporation. *Administrative Science Quarterly*, 1979, *24*, 220–241.

Schein, Edgar H. How to break in the college graduate. *Harvard Business Review,* 1964, *42,* 68–76.

Schein, Edgar H. Organizational socialization and the profession of management. *Industrial Management Review,* 1968, *9,* 1–16.

Schein, Edgar H. The individual, the organization, and the career: A conceptual scheme. *Journal of Applied Behavioral Science,* 1971, *7,* 401–426.

Simon, Herbert A. On the concept of organizational goal. *Administrative Science Quarterly,* 1964, *9,* 1–22.

Smith, M. Brewster. Competence and socialization. In John A. Clausen (Ed.), *Socialization and society.* Boston: Little, Brown, 1968.

Soelberg, P. Unprogrammed decision making. *Industrial Management Review,* 1967, *8,* 19–29.

Sofer, Cyril. *Men in mid-career.* London: Cambridge University Press, 1970.

Sorenson, J. E., Rhode, J. G., & Lawler, E. E. The generation gap in public accounting. *The Accounting Review,* 1967, *42,* 553–565.

Super, Donald. *The psychology of careers.* New York: Harper, 1957.

Terkel, Studs. *American dreams: Lost and found.* New York: Pantheon, 1980.

Toffler, Barbara L. Occupational role development: The changing determinants of outcomes for the individual. *Administrative Science Quarterly,* 1981, *26,* 396–418.

Tresmer, David. Fear of success: Popular but unproven. *Psychology Today,* 1974, *7,* 82–85.

Van Maanen, John. Breaking in: Socialization to work. In Robert Dubin (Ed.), *Handbook of work, organization, and society.* Chicago: Rand McNally, 1976.

Van Maanen, John. People processing: Strategies of organizational socialization. *Organizational Dynamics,* 1978, *7,* 18–36.

Van Maanen, John, Schein, Edgar H., & Bailyn, Lotte. The shape of things to come: A new look at organizational careers. In Hackman, J. R., Lawler, E. E., & Porter, L. W. (Eds.), *Perspectives on behavior in organizations.* New York: McGraw-Hill, 1977.

Vroom, Victor H. Occupational choice: A study of pre- and post-decision processes. *Organizational Behavior and Human Performance,* 1966, *1,* 212–225.

Vroom, Victor H., & Deci, Edward L. The stability of post decisional dissonance: A follow-up study of the job attitudes of business school graduates. *Organizational Behavior and Human Performance,* 1971, *6,* 36–49.

Wanous, John P. Effects of a realistic job preview on job acceptance, job attitudes, and job survival. *Journal of Applied Psychology,* 1973, *58,* 327–332.

Wanous, John P. Organizational entry: The individual's viewpoint. In Hackman, J. R., Lawler, E. E., & Porter, L. W. (Eds.), *Perspectives on behavior in organizations.* New York: McGraw-Hill, 1977.

Wanous, John P. *Organizational entry.* Reading, Mass.: Addison-Wesley, 1981.

Ward, L. B., & Athos, A. G. *Student expectations of corporate life.* Boston: Division of Research, Graduate School of Business Administration, Harvard University, 1972.

Webber, Ross A. Career problems of young managers. *California Management Review,* 1976, *18,* 11–33.

Weiss, Howard M. Subordinate imitation of supervisor behavior: The role of modelling in organizational socialization. *Organizational Behavior and Human Performance,* 1977, *19,* 89–105.

Weitz, J. Job expectancy and survival. *Journal of Applied Psychology,* 1956, *40,* 245–247.

Wellbank, Harry L., Hall, Douglas T., Morgan, Marilyn A., & Hamner, W. Clay. Planning job progression for effective career development and human resources management. *Personnel,* 1978, *65.*

Whyte, William H., Jr. *The organization man.* Garden City, New York: Anchor, 1957.

Youngerberg, C. F. An experimental study of job satisfaction and turnover in relation to job expectations and self expectations. Unpublished doctoral dissertation, New York University Graduate School of Arts and Sciences, 1963.

PART THREE

MOTIVATION,

SATISFACTION,

AND PERFORMANCE

CHAPTER 5

MOTIVATION: NEEDS, PERCEPTIONS, AND EXPECTATIONS

If an organization is to be successful, its members must be both willing and able to perform their jobs competently. This piece of commonsense wisdom has been stated in somewhat more precise and systematic terms in the literature of organizational behavior. In this context it is stated that the performance of organization members is jointly determined by the members' *motivation* (the extent to which they are willing to perform well), and by their ability (the extent to which they possess the skills and abilities necessary to perform well). The idea that performance is *jointly* determined by both motivation and ability is important since it implies that, beyond a certain level, lack of ability cannot be compensated for by high motivation and, conversely, lack of motivation cannot be compensated for by high levels of ability. *Both* motivation and ability are necessary components of effective performance in organizations.

In this chapter and the next we focus on the motivation side of this issue. In so doing we will be seeking to develop ways of understanding why it is that some members of organizations are more willing than others to put forth high levels of effort in order to perform their jobs effectively. What is it that causes some people to be highly motivated achievers, while others lack drive and commitment? Why are some members of an organization always attempting to do their best, while others are trying to do as little as possible in order to get by?

A great deal of research has been aimed at trying to develop answers to motivational questions like these. In this chapter we begin our discussion of motivation in organizations with a brief review of the various meanings and definitions which have been attached to the term *motivation*. We then turn to a discussion of *need* theories of motivation—theories which attempt to explain motivation in terms of the needs experienced by organization members. From need theories, we go on to present equity theory and expectancy theory, both of which are known as *cognitive* theories of motivation. They get this label in light of the fact that they attempt to explain motivation in terms of people's thoughts, feelings, and perceptions regarding their jobs and the organization. Psychologists use the term *cognitions* to refer to people's thoughts, feelings, and perceptions; hence equity theory and expectancy theory are referred to as cognitive theories of motivation.

DEFINITIONS OF MOTIVATION

It's not at all uncommon to hear managers refer to problems in their organizations as "motivation problems." Managers frequently describe their problem employees as "lacking motivation," and may ask themselves how they can "get their people motivated" to perform more effectively. Researchers studying behavior in organizations also recognize the importance of motivation as a determinant of effective performance and have invested a great deal of effort in trying to understand and explain the causes and consequences of motivation.

Although there is a wide consensus among managers and researchers alike that motivation is a critical determinant of behavior in organizations, there is not nearly so much agreement regarding just exactly what the term motivation means or how it should be defined. Many attempts have been made to come up with a clear, concise, and relatively straightforward definition of motivation which would satisfy most people. Unfortunately, the attempts have not been particularly successful. However, even though there is no single widely accepted definition of the concept, there are a number of common themes which run through most attempts to clarify what it is we mean when we use the term motivation.

In general, the topic of motivation has to do with three broad questions regarding people's behavior:

1. What is it that gets behavior *started*?
2. What is it that determines the *magnitude* or *intensity* of behavior?
3. What is it that causes behavior to *stop*?

The first question has to do with the *choices* and *decisions* which people make regarding what they are going to do. What causes a person *to choose to do one thing rather than another*? In the context of understanding motivation in work organizations, this aspect of motivation addresses questions such as the following: What causes a person to report regularly for work each day rather than frequently calling in sick? What causes one person to attack difficult problems head-on, while someone else avoids and procrastinates for long periods? What causes some people to choose to engage in the activities encouraged by the organization, while others seem bent on doing just those things which have been discouraged or prohibited? In order to address motivational questions such as these, we need theories which help us understand how people go about making decisions and what factors influence the choices which they make regarding what they are going to do and not do.

Our second question addresses the issue of the *magnitude* or *intensity* of behavior. This aspect of motivation is probably the one most familiar from our commonsense understanding of the term. We're concerned here with understanding what factors cause some people to invest high levels of *effort* in the activities they undertake, while others appear much more lackadaisical or even lazy. Theories of motivation must concern themselves with explaining what factors underlie the various levels of effort invested in activities by different people. From an applied standpoint, managers are generally very interested in understanding and influencing the levels of effort of their employees.

Finally, the topic of motivation also has to do with the issue of what factors cause people at work to *stop doing one thing and start doing another*. Why is it that one person will absolutely refuse to stop working on a project until it is totally completed, while someone else will drop everything on the dot of quitting time and not be the least bit concerned that the work remains incomplete? Why will one person give up on a job at the first setback, while another person views each setback as a challenge and refuses to be deterred? A complete understanding of the nature of motivation in organizations demands that we be able to answer questions such as these.

NEED THEORIES

Need theories hypothesize that people have a variety of different needs and that those needs which are most important and salient to a person at any given time have a critical impact upon the person's motivation and behavior. Obviously, in order to provide us with any degree of concrete guidance and insight, such theories must be capable of specifying: (1) exactly what needs people have; (2) exactly which needs will be salient at any given time for any given person; and (3) exactly what types of behaviors an individual will engage in to fulfill or satisfy those needs which are salient. A theory outlining all of these factors would permit us to understand how and why a person's needs influence his or her motivation and performance in the organization. A review of three of the most important need theories can provide some useful insights into these issues.

Maslow's Need Hierarchy Theory

One of the most well known theories among practicing managers is the need hierarchy theory developed by Abraham Maslow (1954). This theory hypothesizes that there are five basic categories of needs and that a person is motivated to engage in behavior that will lead to the fulfillment of the need or needs which are most salient at a particular time. The needs are arranged in a hierarchy, from lower-level *deficiency* needs to higher-level *growth* needs. The five general classes of needs from the most basic to the highest are as follows:

1. ***Physiological needs.*** These refer to our most basic survival needs for food, water, and adequate shelter from the environment to permit our continued existence.
2. ***Safety needs.*** The second set of needs has to do with needs for physical and psychological safety from external threats to our well-being. These needs become salient when the basic physiological needs have been met.
3. ***Belongingness/social needs.*** The third level of needs refers to our needs for the company and companionship of other people and our need for a sense of personal belongingness. These needs for contact and interaction with other people are triggered once physiological and safety needs have been met.
4. ***Esteem needs.*** The fourth level of needs (the first of the so-called "growth" needs) has to do with our need for a sense of self-esteem and a feeling of personal self-worth. Such needs for personal recognition become salient only when all of the lower-order deficiency needs have been satisfied.
5. ***Self-actualization needs.*** The final and highest level in the hierarchy refers to needs for personal growth, the development of one's full potential, and the fulfillment associated with the accomplishment of all that of which one is capable. Self-actualization needs are unique in that once activated, they can never be fully satisfied or fulfilled. The more self-actualization needs are fulfilled, the stronger they become, according to the theory.

According to need hierarchy theory people move up the hierarchy of needs from lowest (physiological) to highest (self-actualization). The theory hypothesizes that the lowest level of needs which is deprived will be the dominant set of needs until they are fulfilled. Once the dominant needs are fulfilled the theory suggests that the next highest level of needs is activated and is predominant until it is fulfilled. This progression up the hierarchy proceeds all the way to self-actualization, the highest set of needs in the hierarchy. Self-actualization needs are insatiable according to the theory; the more a person satisfies his or her need for self-actualization, the stronger the need becomes for more self-actualization.

The need hierarchy theory implies that an individual will be motivated to engage in behavior which will lead to the fulfillment or satisfaction of the needs which are currently salient to that person. For example, if a person's physiological and safety needs are fulfilled but belongingness/ social needs are not, then an individual will be motivated to seek out opportunities for friendship and social interaction. Such opportunities will be highly rewarding and satisfying to that person. At the same time, the theory implies that a person in such a situation would *not* be motivated by things such as opportunities for self-development or self-fulfillment, since, according to the theory, needs for self-esteem and self-actualization are not activated until all three lower-order needs (including the belongingness/social needs) have been satisfied. Thus the general implication of the theory for managers in organizations is to determine what needs are unfulfilled and therefore salient for members of the organization, and then to provide organization members with opportunities to satisfy those needs contingent upon their effective performance.

As mentioned at the outset, the need hierarchy theory has enjoyed wide currency and popularity among practitioners over the past 20 years. Unfortunately, in spite of its considerable popular appeal, the theory has not stood up particularly well to systematic scientific scrutiny. A considerable amount of research has been conducted on the need hierarchy theory. This research has focused both on the issue of whether or not there are in fact five distinct categories of needs arranged in a hierarchy and on the issue of how people move from one level of needs to the next. A review of the research by Wahba and Bridwell (1976) draws fairly pessimistic conclusions with regard to both issues. As to whether there are in fact five distinct needs arranged in a hierarchy, the authors report that the results of the research taken together (Wahba & Bridwell, 1976):

> . . . provide no consistent support for Maslow's need classification as a whole. There is no clear evidence that human needs are classified in five distinct categories, or that these categories are structured in a specific hierarchy. There is some evidence for the existence of possibly two types of needs, deficiency and growth needs, although this categorization is not always operative. (p. 224)

Regarding the second issue of how people move from one level of needs to the next, these same authors report at best mixed support for the notions that the lowest level of unfulfilled needs is predominant and that the fulfillment of needs at one level leads to activation of needs at the next higher level. Overall there is no sound basis of empirical support for the existence of a five-level hierarchy of human needs through which a person systematically progresses from lowest to highest. Thus, although the Maslow need hierarchy has considerable intuitive appeal and has become quite well known, it does not provide a sound basis for understanding or predicting the motivation of individuals in organizations.

ERG Theory

The E, R, and G of ERG theory stand for existence, relatedness, and growth—the three sets of needs which are the focus of this alternative theory of human needs in organizations. ERG theory, developed by Alderfer (1972), argues along with Maslow that people do have needs, that these needs are arranged in a hierarchy, and that human needs are important determinants of what people are motivated to do in organizations. However, ERG theory differs from the Maslow need hierarchy theory in two important respects. First, and most obvious, is the fact that instead of a hierarchy of five needs, ERG theory hypothesizes only three. The correspondence between the needs hypothesized by the two theories is outlined in Table 5-1. Existence needs are roughly comparable to the physiological and safety needs of the Maslow theory and refer to people's needs for sustenance, shelter, and physical and psychological safety from threats to their well-being. Relatedness needs correspond approximately to the belongingness/social needs hypothesized by the need hierarchy theory and have to do with needs for personal relationships and interaction with other people. Growth needs are the ERG-theory counterpart to esteem needs and self-actualization needs contained in the Maslow theory. Growth needs refer to human needs to grow, develop, and fulfill one's potential by seeking new opportunities and overcoming new challenges.

TABLE 5-1
A comparison of need hierarchy theory and ERG theory

Need hierarchy theory	ERG theory
Physiological needs Safety needs	Existence needs
Belongingness/social needs	Relatedness needs
Esteem needs Self-actualization needs	Growth needs

The second way in which ERG theory differs from the need hierarchy theory lies in how ERG theory hypothesizes that people move through the different sets of needs. Need hierarchy theory hypothesizes a strict lock-step hierarchy with the lowest level of unfulfilled needs predominating, and the next level in the hierarchy being activated only when the current set of needs is satisfied. ERG theory is a good deal more flexible in that it permits the possibility that more than one set of needs may be activated at the same time. Further, ERG theory suggests that people may move down, as well as up, the three-step hierarchy of the theory. Thus, while satisfaction of needs at one level leads to progression to the next higher level of needs, the theory also suggests that as people become frustrated in their attempts to fulfill needs at one level, this frustration can lead to regression to the next lower level of needs. These relationships are diagrammed in Figure 5-1.

Although the greater flexibility of ERG theory is probably an accurate reflection of the complexity of human needs, this flexibility also means that the implications of ERG theory for management practice are less clear-cut than those of need hierarchy theory. ERG theory implies that individuals will be motivated to engage in behavior which will satisfy one of the three sets of needs hypothesized by the theory. In order to predict what behavior any given person will be motivated to engage in would require an assessment of that person to determine which of the three needs were most salient and most important to that person. The individual would then be predicted to engage in behavior which would lead to the attainment of outcomes with the capacity of fulfilling these salient needs.

ERG theory is newer than need hierarchy theory and has not yet attained such wide currency, nor such a high degree of research interest as has need hierarchy theory. Thus the empirical status of ERG theory must be said to be somewhat uncertain at the moment. Alderfer's research has

FIGURE 5-1
ERG Theory relationships among frustration, importance, and satisfaction of needs.
(SOURCE: Adapted from F. J. Landy and D. A. Trumbo, *Psychology of Work Behavior*, rev. ed., Homewood, Ill.: Dorsey, 1980. Used by permission.)

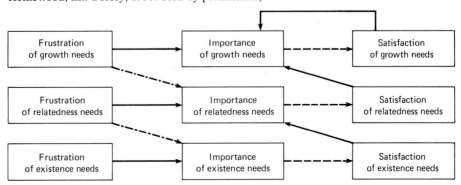

indicated some degree of support for the theory, but in general it is simply too early to pass judgment on the overall validity of the theory.

Other Need Theories

Although Maslow's need hierarchy theory is the most well known and widely applied need theory, it is certainly not the only theory of human needs, nor was it even the first. As early as 1938 Murray had developed what he termed a *manifest needs theory* which hypothesized some two dozen different needs, each of which, when activated, could have an impact upon a person's behavior. Murray's theorizing about needs has been subsequently extended and refined by the work of McClelland and Atkinson (Atkinson, 1964; McClelland, 1961; McClelland et al., 1953).

Some of the needs hypothesized by Murray are summarized in Table 5-2. As can be seen, the theory suggests that people possess an extremely wide variety of quite divergent types of needs. Unlike Maslow's theory, there is no suggestion that the needs are arranged into any sort of hierarchy, nor that certain needs must be fulfilled before others may be activated. Rather, it is argued that needs are primarily learned rather than inherited, that they tend to be activated by events or cues in the external environment, and that any combination of needs may be active or salient within a person at any particular time.

The inherent complexity of a theory containing such a large number of needs has both advantages and disadvantages. The primary advantage lies in the fact that a large set of needs provides a great deal of flexibility and specificity in explaining precisely what factors may be causing a person to engage in certain kinds of activities rather than others, to be attracted to certain types of situations and not others, and so on. At the same time, this complexity creates certain disadvantages from a practical standpoint, since if we wish to use the theory to explain and predict what a person will be motivated to do, we are faced with the herculean task of measuring simultaneously the strength of over twenty different needs. In light of the considerable difficulties inherent in such a task, there has been a tendency on the part of researchers to focus upon only one or some small number of the hypothesized needs. Those which have been the object of greatest attention are the *need for achievement*, the *need for affiliation*, and the *need for power*.

People with a strong need for achievement tend to set moderately difficult goals for themselves, engage in activities in which there is a moderate degree of risk that they may not succeed, seek out feedback on the quality and quantity of their performance, wish to be personally responsible for their actions, and generally are preoccupied with accomplishment and achievement. Such individuals will tend to find any of the preceding types of experiences to be motivating. Jobs which are highly challenging frequently provide opportunities for these kinds of experienc-

TABLE 5-2
Some of the Needs Hypothesized by Murray

Need	Characteristics
Achievement	Aspires to accomplish difficult tasks; maintains high standards and is willing to work toward distant goals; responds positively to competition; willing to put forth effort to attain excellence.
Affiliation	Enjoys being with friends and people in general; accepts people readily; makes efforts to win friendships and maintain associations with people.
Aggression	Enjoys combat and argument; easily annoyed; sometimes willing to hurt people to get his or her way; may seek to "get even" with people perceived as having harmed him or her.
Autonomy	Tries to break away from restraints, confinement, or restrictions of any kind; enjoys being unattached, free, not tied to people, places, or obligations; may be rebellious when faced with restraints.
Endurance	Willing to work long hours; doesn't give up quickly on a problem; persevering, even in the face of great difficulty; patient and unrelenting in work habits.
Exhibition	Wants to be the center of attention; enjoys having an audience; engages in behavior which wins the notice of others; may enjoy being dramatic or witty.
Harmavoidance	Does not enjoy exciting activities, especially if danger is involved; avoids risk of bodily harm; seeks to maximize personal safety.
Impulsivity	Tends to act on the "spur of the moment" and without deliberation; gives vent readily to feelings and wishes; speaks freely; may be volatile in emotional expression.
Nurturance	Gives sympathy and comfort; assists others whenever possible, interested in caring for children, the disabled, or the infirm; offers a "helping hand" to those in need; readily performs favors for others.
Order	Concerned with keeping personal effects and surroundings neat and organized; dislikes clutter, confusion, lack of organization; interested in developing methods for keeping materials methodically organized.
Power	Attempts to control the environment and to influence or direct other people; expresses opinions forcefully; enjoys the role of leader and may assume it spontaneously.
Succorance	Frequently seeks the sympathy, protection, love, advice, and reassurance of other people; may feel insecure or helpless without such support; confides difficulties readily to a receptive person.
Understanding	Wants to understand many areas of knowledge; values synthesis of ideas, verifiable generalization, logical thought, particularly when directed at satisfying intellectual curiosity.

Source: Adapted from the *Personality Research Form Manual*, published by Research Psychologists Press, Inc., P.O. Box 984, Port Huron, MI 48060. Copyright © 1967, 1974 by Douglas N. Jackson. Used by permission.

es and hence may be highly motivating to individuals who have a strong need for achievement.

Individuals with a high need for affiliation, on the other hand, tend to place greatest value upon human companionship and opportunities for obtaining personal reassurance from others. People with a high need for affiliation thus tend to be motivated to seek out personal approval, to conform to the wishes and expectations of those they admire, and to indicate a strong and sincere interest in the feelings of others. Such individuals will thus find opportunities for meaningful social interaction to be highly motivating.

Finally, the need for power refers to a desire to influence others and to exert a high degree of control over one's physical and social environment. People who are high in the need for power tend to try to influence other people directly via personal appeals or arguments and also frequently seek out positions of leadership in groups to which they belong. Such people find it motivating to be in situations which permit them to exert influence and control over others.

A great deal of research has been carried out on the need for achievement (Atkinson & Raynor, 1974), and a considerable number of studies have also examined the need for affiliation and the need for power (Birch & Veroff, 1966; Litwin & Stringer, 1968; Steers & Braunstein, 1976). Overall, this research indicates that these need concepts can be helpful in identifying individuals who will find different types of situations differentially motivating. In addition, some recent research has led to the development of new techniques for measuring the strength of these needs (Harrel & Stahl, 1981). The primary managerial implication of these need concepts is that people differ in the extent to which they experience needs for achievement, for affiliation, and for power. Hence it may be important for managers to assess the strength of these needs in their employees and to design motivational strategies in such a way that they permit employees to satisfy those needs which are strongest for each individual.

EQUITY THEORY

According to equity theory, the motivation of individuals in organizations is influenced by the extent to which they feel that they are being treated in a fair and equitable manner. When people feel that they are being treated in an inequitable, unfair fashion, the theory argues that they will be motivated to engage in activities aimed at restoring feelings of equitable treatment (Adams, 1965). There are two major components to the theory. First, the theory specifies the factors which influence the extent to which people feel that they are being equitably treated. Second, the theory outlines the kinds of activities which individuals might be motivated to engage in to restore feelings of equity when they are feeling inequitably or unfairly treated.

Determinants of Perceived Equity

According to equity theory, people are constantly engaged in making two types of comparisons. First, people compare the *inputs* that they make to their job to the *outcomes* that they receive from the job and from the organization. The term *inputs* refers to all of the things that an individual contributes to performing his or her job and includes a person's education, training, experience, time, effort, and so on. The term *outcomes* is equally general and is meant to cover all of the things the individual receives or obtains as a result of performing the job such as pay, promotions, praise, recognition, friendship, feelings of personal accomplishment, and so on.

The second comparison process that contributes to a person's feelings of equitable or inequitable treatment involves the comparison by the person of his or her own ratio of outcomes to inputs to the comparable ratio of outcomes to inputs of another person known as a *comparison other*. When a person perceives that his or her own ratio of outcomes to inputs is approximately equal to the corresponding ratio of the comparison other, a state of equity is said to exist. In such a situation the person will feel satisfied with the rewards that he or she is receiving, will feel that he or she is being fairly treated, and would be predicted to be motivated to continue doing the kinds of things he or she had been doing at work up to that point. A condition of perceived equity can be stated symbolically as follows, where p refers to the focal person and o refers to the comparison other.

$$\frac{\text{Outcomes}_p}{\text{Inputs}_p} = \frac{\text{Outcomes}_o}{\text{Inputs}_o}$$

Equity theory does not clearly specify who the comparison other will be or how an individual goes about choosing a comparison other. In fact, according to the theory, the comparison other need not actually be another person whom the individual knows personally. The comparison other could be another person, or even a group, with whom the person interacts directly, or it could be someone who interacts with some common third party, someone from a previous work situation, or even someone in a hypothetical work situation.

It is important to emphasize that equity theory hypothesizes the existence of *two* underlying comparison processes. According to equity theory, people do *not* merely compare their own outcomes to inputs and feel satisfied when these are perceived to be in balance with one another. Rather, they compare their own outcomes to inputs and then *compare this ratio* to the corresponding ratio of the comparison other. It is this second comparison process which determines whether or not people feel that they are being equitably treated. The basic idea of the theory is that people's feelings of fair and equitable treatment by the organization depend upon their feeling that what they are receiving from the organization in terms of valued outcomes is balanced fairly against the inputs they make to the organization. People determine whether the balance between inputs and outcomes is fair by comparing themselves to others and assessing what those others appear to be receiving in outcomes from the organization in return for the inputs being provided to the organization.

The theory argues that people will feel inequitably treated, and hence motivated to engage in activities aimed at restoring perceived equity, *both*: (1) when they feel their ratio of outcomes to inputs is *less* than that of the comparison other; and (2) when they feel their ratio of outcomes to inputs is *greater* than that of the comparison other.

The first situation, in which the person's perceived ratio of outcomes to inputs is *less* than that of the comparison other, can be diagrammed as follows:

$$\frac{\text{Outcomes}_p}{\text{Inputs}_p} < \frac{\text{Outcomes}_o}{\text{Inputs}_o}$$

This is a fairly straightforward prediction that people will feel unfairly or inequitably treated when they perceive that what they are receiving in outcomes from the organization in return for the inputs provided is less than what they perceive comparison others receiving in return for their inputs. Such a situation could arise, for example, if a person felt that the inputs to the organization provided by him or herself and the comparison other were identical, but the person perceived the comparison other receiving a higher level of outcomes from the organization for the same level of inputs. Equity theory predicts that the feelings of inequity generated by such situations will motivate people to engage in activities designed to restore feelings of equity.

The second type of inequity hypothesized by the theory occurs when people perceive their ratio of outcomes to inputs to be *greater* than the comparable ratio for comparison others. In diagrammatic form, the theory is saying that inequity occurs when:

$$\frac{\text{Outcomes}_p}{\text{Inputs}_p} > \frac{\text{Outcomes}_o}{\text{Inputs}_o}$$

This prediction is less straightforward and involves a hypothesis that individuals will feel uncomfortable or guilty if they perceive that their ratio of outcomes received in return for inputs provided is greater than the comparable level of outcomes obtained in return for inputs by comparison others. The theory argues that individuals in such situations will be motivated to engage in activities which will lead to a reestablishment of perceived equity.

Research on the theory's predictions regarding what causes people to feel inequitably treated has been generally supportive (Goodman & Friedman, 1971; Adams & Freedman, 1976). However, some questions have been raised about the validity of the theory's prediction of inequity occurring when people perceive their ratio of outcomes to inputs to be greater than that of the comparison other (Locke, 1976; Campbell & Pritchard, 1976). Recent research suggests that the prediction of perceived inequity under conditions of overpayment may only occur for individuals who are highly altruistic or who are high in what is termed "moral maturity" (Vecchio, 1981).

Methods of Restoring Equity

Equity theory outlines six alternative ways in which an individual may seek to restore feelings of equity. The six methods for resolving inequity are as follows.

1. *Altering inputs*, eg., people may choose to put more or less effort into the job.
2. *Altering outcomes*, eg., people paid on a piece-rate basis might increase their pay (an outcome) by producing a higher quantity of units of lower quality.
3. *Cognitively distorting inputs or outcomes.* Rather than actually changing inputs or outcomes, people might change their perceptions of what they are putting into or getting out of the organization. An example of cognitive distortion of inputs might be a person saying, "I used to think I only worked at an average pace, but now I realize I really work a lot harder than almost anyone else."
4. *Leaving the field.* This is equity-theory jargon for getting out of the situation creating the feelings of inequity by asking for a transfer or quitting the organization altogether.
5. *Taking actions designed to change the inputs or outcomes (either actual or perceived) of the comparison other.* Actions designed to change the actual inputs or outcomes of the comparison other could take the form of social pressure, for example saying to a coworker, "You shouldn't work so hard, it's not worth it." Changing the perceived inputs or outcomes of the comparison other is perhaps the easiest method of restoring equity, for example people might say to themselves, "I used to think that Joe was a lot smarter and more hardworking than I am, but now I realize that he's not."
6. *Changing the comparison other.* If comparing one's ratio of outcomes to inputs to that of a particular person creates uncomfortable feelings of

inequity, one may be able to restore equity by shifting the comparison to someone else.

Equity theory argues that perceived inequity creates feelings of discomfort and tension in a person and hence that a person experiencing such inequity will be motivated to restore equity via one of the preceding methods. Adams (1965) presents some general guidelines on how the characteristics of the inequitable situation will influence which method of equity restoration a person will be motivated to pursue. However, the theory has been criticized as not being sufficiently precise regarding which specific methods of restoring equity will be chosen in different circumstances (Mowday, 1979; Wicklund & Brehm, 1976). Such specificity will have to be developed in order to increase the applicability of equity theory by managers to the diagnosis and resolution of motivation problems in organizations. Current research on equity theory is attempting to deal with this issue by exploring the implications of perceived inequity for the performance of organization members (Lord & Hohenfeld, 1979; Duchon & Jago, 1981).

EXPECTANCY THEORY

Expectancy theory (sometimes referred to as expectancy-valence theory, instrumentality theory, or valence-instrumentality-expectancy (VIE) theory) hypothesizes that motivation is determined by: (1) a person's perceptions or beliefs regarding the relationship between his or her behavior and the outcomes or results of that behavior; and (2) the personal satisfaction or dissatisfaction which the person expects to experience as a result of obtaining those outcomes (Vroom, 1964; Lawler, 1973). The former set of perceptions or beliefs are referred to as *expectancies*, while the latter set of anticipated satisfactions are referred to as *valences*. Hence the terms *expectancy theory* and *expectancy-valence theory*.

The nature of the theory is summarized in Figure 5-2. As the figure indicates, the major components of the theory are two types of expectancies plus the valences of outcomes. We'll discuss each of these components of the theory in turn.

Effort → Performance Expectancy (E → P Expectancy)

The effort → performance, or E → P, expectancy refers to people's beliefs that their effort on a job will result in achieving a certain level of job performance. Expectancies are directly analogous to subjective probabilities and are expressed within the theory in probabilistic terms. Subjective probabilities can vary from 0.0 to 1.0. A subjective probability of 0.0 indicates that people believe that even if they exert a high level of effort, there is no chance whatsoever that they will attain a particular standard of performance. The opposite extreme is represented by a subjective probability or expectancy of 1.0 which indicates that people believe that it is absolutely certain that if they put forth the effort they will be able to perform effectively. Intermediate values of expectancy between the extremes of 0.0 and 1.0 indicate the strength of the belief that effort leads to performance. The larger the E → P expectancy (i.e., the closer it is to 1.0), the stronger is the belief that if one puts forth effort, one will perform effectively. Since the E → P expectancy is one component of the overall expectancy model of motivation, it also follows that the larger the E → P expectancy, the stronger is the person's motivation to perform.

Performance → Outcome Expectancy (P → O Expectancy)

The performance → outcome, or P → O, expectancy refers to a person's beliefs regarding the relationship between successfully achieving a given level of performance and the attainment of other types of outcomes. Since this component of the theory is also an expectancy, it too is conceived of as

FIGURE 5-2
Summary of the major components in expectancy theory.   (SOURCE: Adapted from D.A. Nadler and E. E. Lawler, III, "Motivation: A Diagnostic Approach," in J. R. Hackman, E. E. Lawler, III, and L. W. Porter, *Perspectives on Behavior in Organizations*, New York: McGraw-Hill, 1977. Used by permission.)

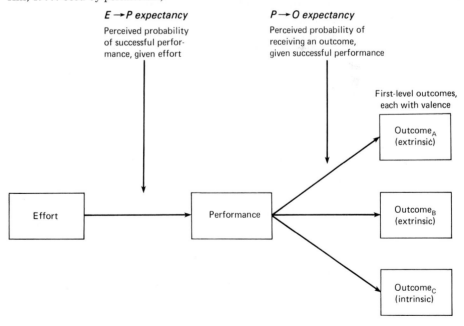

Motivation is expressed as follows: $M = [E \rightarrow P] \times \Sigma [(P \rightarrow O) (V)]$

a subjective probability. Just as in the case of the $E \rightarrow P$ expectancy, $P \rightarrow O$ expectancies can take on values from 0.0 to 1.0. The larger the value (the closer to 1.0), the stronger the person's belief that achieving the performance level will result in attaining the outcome.

Expectancy theory does not specify how many outcomes will have $P \rightarrow O$ expectancies associated with them in a person's mind, nor does the theory specify exactly which outcomes will be relevant in any given situation or for any given job. However, the theory does draw a distinction between two broad classes of outcomes associated with job performance. *Intrinsic* outcomes are outcomes attained or experienced by a person simply as a result of performing the job effectively. Intrinsic outcomes can be thought of as self-administered in that the job incumbent is not dependent upon the organization or upon any other person for the administration of these outcomes. Examples of intrinsic outcomes are feelings of competence, feelings of personal accomplishment, feelings of personal satisfaction, and so on.

The second class of outcomes is referred to as *extrinsic* outcomes. Extrinsic outcomes are outcomes that originate outside, or external to, the person and which are administered to the person by the organization or some member of the organization. Examples of extrinsic outcomes are things such as pay, promotions, verbal praise, and so on.

According to expectancy theory all of the outcomes, both intrinsic and extrinsic, which are salient to a person in the performance of his or her job have an influence upon the person's motivation. The extent to which each outcome influences motivation depends upon the strength of the $P \rightarrow O$ expectancy associated with that outcome. The stronger the $P \rightarrow O$ expectancy associated with a given outcome in the mind of the job incumbent, the greater the influence of that outcome on motivation.

Valence (V) of Outcomes

The final major component of the expectancy model is the *valence of outcomes*. The term *valence* is defined as the anticipated satisfaction or dissatisfaction that a person associates with attaining an outcome. Valence thus refers to the degree of satisfaction (positive valence) or dissatisfaction (negative valence) that a person anticipates will be experienced when an outcome is attained. Valence is defined in terms of anticipated satisfaction for two reasons. First, the actual satisfaction or dissatisfaction that a person experiences when an outcome is actually attained may or may not be equal to what was anticipated. Second, it is the anticipated satisfaction or dissatisfaction that will determine a person's motivation to put forth effort in order to attain the outcome. Hence the emphasis upon anticipated satisfaction and dissatisfaction in expectancy theory.

Since outcomes can be either satisfying or dissatisfying to a person, valences can take on both positive and negative values. The more a person anticipates a positive feeling of satisfaction from the attainment of an outcome (eg., obtaining a significant salary increase), the more positive the valence of that outcome would be for that person. Just the opposite holds for negatively valent outcomes. The more the person anticipates feeling dissatisfied or unhappy if an outcome is attained (eg., getting fired), the more negative the valence of that outcome would be for the person. Outcomes with valences near zero are outcomes about which a person does not have strong feelings one way or the other and which thus exert relatively little impact upon that person's motivation.

Combining the Factors

According to expectancy theory the three components of the model (the $E \rightarrow P$ expectancy, the $P \rightarrow O$ expectancies, and the valences of outcomes) all combine multiplicatively to determine a person's overall level of motivation. This multiplicative relationship is captured by the equation at the bottom of Fig. 5-2 which summarizes the expectancy model in algebraic form. The equation indicates that motivation is determined by the $E \rightarrow P$ expectancy (the expectancy that effort leads to performance) multiplied by the sum (the Greek letter Σ contained in the equation is the algebraic summation sign which symbolizes that the factors following it in parentheses are to be added together) of the products of the $P \rightarrow O$ expectancies (the expectancies that achieving the performance level will be followed by the attainment of valued outcomes) and the valences of the outcomes. The algebraic products of $P \rightarrow O$ expectancies and valences are computed for all of the valued outcomes which a person perceives to be contingent upon achieving the performance level.

The reason for hypothesizing that the components of the expectancy model combine multiplicatively is the belief that all three components of the model *must* be present if motivation is to be high. In the case of multiplying $P \rightarrow O$ expectancies and valences, the argument is that no matter how much someone values an outcome (no matter how high the valence), if the person perceives that there is no likelihood of attaining the outcome (a $P \rightarrow O$ expectancy of zero), then the outcome will have no impact on motivation. Conversely, no matter how strong the $P \rightarrow O$ expectancy that an outcome will be attained as a result of performance, if that outcome is not valued by the person (has zero valence), then there will be no impact on motivation. The theory also indicates that motivation is determined by the product of the $E \rightarrow P$ expectancy and the sum of the products of $P \rightarrow O$ expectancies and valences. This prediction is consistent with the view that no matter how many highly valued outcomes people perceive to be attainable if they perform at a certain level, if they perceive that they have no chance of performing at that level, regardless of their effort (i.e., $E \rightarrow P$ expectancy of zero), then they will not be motivated. Conversely, it doesn't matter if they are absolutely certain that they can achieve some level of performance (i.e., an E → P expectancy of 1.0), if they perceive no positively valent outcomes to follow from achieving the performance level, then there will be no motivation to put in the effort required to perform.

Consider a simple example to illustrate the multiplicative formulation of expectancy theory. Imagine a manager who has been given responsibility for a major project in the organization. Suppose the manager believes that there is a strong likelihood that if she works very hard, she will complete the project successfully and on time (i.e., she has a strong E → P expectancy, say, 0.8). Suppose further that she knows for certain that she will receive a significant salary bonus if the project is done on time (i.e., a P → O expectancy of 1.0 for a positively valent outcome whose valence might be +5). Finally, suppose that she also believes that she will have a fairly good chance of receiving a promotion if the project is completed successfully, a promotion that she values very highly (i.e., a moderately high P → O expectancy of 0.7 for a very positively valent outcome of valence +10). According to expectancy theory, her motivation to work hard to complete the project under these circumstances can be computed from the following formula: M = [E → P] × Σ [(P → O) (V)]. In this case then her motivation is: M = [0.8] × [(1.0) × (+5) + (0.7) × (+10)], or M = [0.8] × [5 + 7] = 9.6. Conversely, notice that because of the multiplicative formulation of the theory, if she believes that even by working hard she still had only about a 20 percent chance of completing the project successfully (i.e., an E → P expectancy of 0.2), her motivation to work hard on the project would be much lower: M = [0.2] × [5 + 7] = 2.4. Thus, the multiplicative formulation of expectancy theory captures the fact that *all* of the components of motivation must be present, and relatively strong, for motivation to be high. If any of the components is significantly reduced, so also is the person's overall level of motivation.

Expectancy Theory Research

A tremendous amount of research has been carried out to investigate the accuracy and validity of expectancy theory. Comprehensive reviews of this research have been conducted by Mitchell (1974) and by Campbell and Pritchard (1976). Research on the detailed components of the theory has been difficult due to the complexity of the theory itself and to the problems associated with adequately measuring all of its components (Lawler & Suttle, 1973; Schmidt, 1973). However, solutions to some of these methodological problems appear to be on the horizon (Arnold, 1981; Arnold & Evans, 1979; Ilgen, Nebeker, & Pritchard, 1981), and current research is helping clarify many of the areas of uncertainty (eg., León, 1981; Matsui, Okada, & Mizuguchi, 1981; Pecotich & Churchill, 1981; Schmitt & Son, 1981; Stahl & Harrell, 1981). Generally, the research indicates that all three components of the expectancy model (E → P expectancy, P → O expectancies, and valences) are positively and signficantly related to motivation and performance. Expectancy theory has been shown to have general validity as a model of motivation, and holds considerable promise for improving our ability to understand motivation in organizations.

MANAGERIAL IMPLICATIONS

The motivation of organization members to perform effectively is obviously a critical issue for every manager. The motivation theories discussed in this chapter have a variety of important implications for managers in their attempts to influence the motivation of those they manage.

1. ***Managers must be sensitive to the differences in needs and desires which exist among subordinates.*** Every member of an organization is an individual with a unique pattern of needs, values, and aspirations. As a result, what is motivating to one person may not be to another. Organizations and managers must recognize the uniqueness and individuality of organization members and take it into account in designing and implementing policies aimed at influencing the motivation and performance of organization members.

2. ***Managers must attempt to insure that employees are treated in a fair and equitable manner, and that employees feel they are being treated fairly and equitably.*** Equity theory helps draw attention to the fact that individuals in organizations compare themselves to one another and that the basis of such comparisons is the ratio of the outcomes they receive from the organization to the inputs they provide to it. Perceived inequity can be dysfunctional and demotivating to organization members. There are two clear implications for managers. First, managers must attempt to assure, as far as is possible, that individuals are fairly rewarded and compensated for their work and contributions to the organization. Reward and compensation practices must be fairly applied to *all* organization members. Second, managers must insure that the organization's system of rewarding employees for their work is *perceived* to be fair by employees. Even if an organization is in fact treating employees fairly and equitably, if the individuals affected do not *perceive* it to be so, they will *feel* inequitably treated and the manager will be faced with the dysfunctional consequences of such feelings.

3. ***Managers must clarify and increase individuals' perceptions that effort will lead to effective performance (the E→ P expectancy).*** If people are to be highly motivated, it is essential that they believe that exerting a high degree of effort will lead to a high level of performance. It is further essential that this belief be an accurate reflection of reality. An individual's $E \rightarrow P$ expectancy may be low for a variety of reasons, each of which has different implications for managerial action.
    a. The $E \rightarrow P$ expectancy may simply be inaccurate. As a result of lack of experience or lack of self-confidence people may not realize that if they

increase their effort they will indeed be able to perform more effectively. Such a situation requires the manager to clarify for the individual the fact that increased effort will in fact result in improved performance.

b.   The E → P expectancy may be low because it is unclear exactly where one should be putting one's efforts. As jobs become more complex and their demands more ambiguous, it becomes increasingly difficult for people to know which aspects of their jobs are of most importance and have the greatest payoffs. Such a situation requires the manager to clarify for the subordinate what is expected and to indicate clearly those aspects of the job for which increased effort will in fact lead to improved performance.

c.   The E → P expectancy may be low, not because the person lacks self-confidence, nor because it is unclear exactly which aspects of the job should be focused upon. A person's E → P expectancy may be low and at the same time quite accurate if that person lacks the skills and abilities necessary for effective performance. In this instance the manager must either move the person to a position for which he or she is competent or provide training to bring the person's ability up to the necessary level.

4.   ***Managers must clarify and increase individuals' perceptions that performance will lead to desirable outcomes (P→ O expectancies).*** According to expectancy theory, a high level of motivation to perform effectively depends in part upon the expectancies people hold regarding the consequences of effective performance. For the manager this has two important implications. First, it is necessary to insure that positively valent outcomes are in fact available to members of the organization contingent upon their achieving high levels of performance. This factor underlines the importance of carefully designed reward systems that make the receipt of valued outcomes conditional upon effective performance. The issues involved in reward system design are discussed in Chapter 7. Second, the manager must insure that organization members clearly understand and perceive these relationships between performing effectively and receiving valued outcomes. This implies the necessity of keeping employees informed and up-to-date regarding organizational reward systems, as well as the importance of insuring that rewards are in fact provided consistently and equitably in line with the expectations which have been created.

5.   ***Organizations need to employ outcomes which are highly positively valent to their members.*** The previously discussed steps aimed at clarifying and enhancing expectancies will have no impact upon motivation whatsoever if the organization does not or cannot provide the individual member with outcomes which that particular person values highly. The managerial implications of this fact are twofold. First, managers must take the time to determine what outcomes are in fact highly positively valued by their subordinates. The second implication is that once the highly positively valent outcomes have been identified, the manager must: (*a*) insure that the attainment of these outcomes is in fact contingent upon subordinates'

effective performance; and (*b*) make subordinates aware of the existence of these relationships.

SUMMARY

The issue of motivation in organizations has to do with understanding why people *choose* to do certain things rather than others at work and with what factors cause people to put variable amounts of *effort* or *intensity* into their work activities. A variety of theories have been developed to shed light on these issues.

Need theories attempt to explain motivation in terms of the needs experienced by individual organization members. Need theories argue that individuals are motivated to engage in activities which will result in the satisfaction of the needs which are strongest and most salient to the person at any given time. Maslow's need hierarchy theory argues that there are five categories of needs organized from the most basic physiological needs to the highest-order self-actualization needs. Alderfer's ERG theory suggests that individuals have needs for existence, relatedness, and growth. Many other needs and need theories have been developed, with special attention having been directed toward the need for achievement, the need for affiliation, and the need for power.

Equity theory is based on the premise that individuals compare themselves to one another on the basis of the ratio of outcomes they receive from the organization to the inputs they provide to the organization. Inequity exists when people perceive that their ratio of outcomes received in return for inputs provided is not in balance with the ratio of a *comparison other.* When people feel inequitably treated, they will be motivated to engage in any of a vareity of activities in order to restore a feeling of equity.

Expectancy theory argues that motivation is jointly determined by three factors: (1) a person's perception that putting in effort on a job will in fact result in successful performance of the job (the $E \rightarrow P$ expectancy); (2) a person's perception that successful performance on the job will in fact result in the attainment of valued outcomes (the $P \rightarrow O$ expectancies); and (3) the extent to which the person anticipates that he or she will find the attainment of the outcomes to be personally satisfying (the valence of outcomes). According to expectancy theory, a person's overall level of motivation is determined by the multiplicative combination of these three factors. The multiplicative formulation implies that *all* three components of motivation must be present and must be strong if a person is to be highly motivated to perform effectively.

REVIEW QUESTIONS

1. Why is motivation a critical issue of interest to managers in organizations?

2. What are the major components of most definitions of the term *motivation*?
3. Briefly describe Maslow's need hierarchy theory. What are the theory's strengths and weaknesses?
4. Describe the similarities and differences between Maslow's theory and ERG theory.
5. What differences would you predict in the work behavior of a person high on the need for achievement compared to another person high on the need for affiliation?
6. What do you think are the advantages and disadvantages in general terms of theories which attempt to explain motivation in organizations in terms of the *needs* of individual organization members?
7. According to equity theory, what conditions must exist in order for a person to feel that he or she is being treated in a fair and equitable manner?
8. What are the potential outcomes of perceived inequity? How might these be dysfunctional to the organization?
9. What are the two types of expectancies hypothesized by expectancy theory? How do they differ from one another?
10. What does the term *valence of outcomes* mean?
11. How does expectancy theory hypothesize that expectancies and valences combine to determine overall motivation? Why is the theory formulated this way?
12. Discuss some of the implications of expectancy theory for managerial practice.

REFERENCES

Adams, J. S. Injustice in social exchange. In L. Berkowitz (Ed.), *Advances in experimental social psychology* (Vol. 2). New York: Academic Press, 1965, 267–299.

Adams, J. S., & Freedman, S. Equity theory revisited: Comments and annotated bibliography. In L. Berkowitz & E. Walster (Eds.), *Advances in experimental social psychology* (Vol. 9). New York: Academic Press, 1976, 43–90.

Alderfer, C. P. *Existence, relatedness, and growth.* New York: Free Press, 1972.

Arnold, H. J. A test of the multiplicative hypothesis of expectancy-valence theories of work motivation. *Academy of Management Journal*, 1981, *24*, 128–141.

Arnold, H. J., & Evans, M. G. Testing multiplicative models does *not* require ratio scales. *Organizational Behavior and Human Performance*, 1979, *24*, 41–59.

Atkinson, J. W. *An introduction to motivation.* Princeton, N.J.: Van Nostrand, 1964.

Atkinson, J. W., & Raynor, J. O. *Motivation and achievement.* Washington, D.C.: R. H. Winston & Sons, 1974.

Birch, D., & Veroff, J. *Motivation: A study of action.* Monterey, Calif.: Brooks/Cole, 1966.

Campbell, J. P., & Pritchard, R. D. Motivation theory in industrial and organizational psychology. In M. D. Dunnette (Ed.), *Handbook of industrial and organizational psychology*. Chicago: Rand-McNally, 1976.

Duchon, D., & Jago, A. G. Equity and the performance of major league baseball players: An extension of Lord and Hohenfeld. *Journal of Applied Psychology*, 1981, *66*, 728–732.

Goodman, P. S., & Friedman, A. An examination of Adams' theory of inequity. *Administrative Science Quarterly*, 1971, *16*, 271–288.

Harrell, A. M., & Stahl, M. J. A behavioral decision theory approach for measuring McClelland's trichotomy of needs. *Journal of Applied Psychology*, 1981, *66*, 242–247.

Ilgen, D. R., Nebeker, D. M., & Pritchard, R. D. Expectancy theory measures: An empirical comparison in an experimental situation. *Organizational Behavior and Human Performance*, 1981, *28*, 189–223.

Lawler, E. E., III. *Motivation in work organizations*. Monterey, Calif.: Brooks/Cole, 1973.

Lawler, E. E., III, & Suttle, J. L. Expectancy theory and job behavior. *Organizational Behavior and Human Performance*, 1973, *9*, 482–503.

León, F. R. The role of positive and negative outcomes in the causation of motivational forces. *Journal of Applied Psychology*, 1981, *66*, 45–53.

Litwin, G. H., & Stringer, R. A., Jr. *Motivation and organizational climate*. Boston: Division of Research, Graduate School of Business Administration, Harvard University, 1968.

Locke, E. A. The nature and causes of job satisfaction. In M. D. Dunnette (Ed.), *Handbook of industrial and organizational psychology*. Chicago: Rand-McNally, 1976.

Lord, R. G., & Hohenfeld, J. A. Longitudinal field assessment of equity effects on the performance of major league baseball players, *Journal of Applied Psychology*, 1979, *64*, 19–26.

Maslow, A. H. *Motivation and personality*. New York: Harper, 1954.

Matsui, T., Okada, A., & Mizuguchi, R. Expectancy theory prediction of the goal theory postulate, "The harder the goals, the higher the performance." *Journal of Applied Psychology*, 1981, *66*, 54–58.

McClelland, D. C. *The achieving society*. Princeton, N.J.: Van Nostrand, 1961.

McClelland, D. C., Atkinson, J. W., Clark, R. A., & Lowell, E. L. *The achievement motive*. New York: Appleton-Century-Crofts, 1953.

Mitchell, T. R. Expectancy models of job satisfaction, occupational preference, and effort: A theoretical, methodological, and empirical appraisal. *Psychological Bulletin*, 1974, *81*, 1096–1112.

Mowday, R. Equity theory predictions of behavior in organizations. In R. M. Steers & L. W. Porter (Eds.), *Motivation and work behavior*, (2d ed.) New York: McGraw-Hill, 1979.

Murray, H. A. *Explorations in personality*. New York: Oxford University Press, 1938.

Pecotich, A., & Churchill, G. A., Jr. An examination of the anticipated satisfaction importance valence controversy. *Organizational Behavior and Human Performance*, 1981, *27*, 213–226.

Schmidt, F. L. Implications of a measurement problem for expectancy theory research. *Organizational Behavior and Human Performance*, 1973, *10*, 243–251.

Schmitt, N., & Son, L. An evaluation of valence models of motivation to pursue various post high school alternatives. *Organizational Behavior and Human Performance*, 1981, *27*, 135–150.

Stahl, M., & Harrell, A. M. Modeling effort decisions with behavioral decision theory: Toward an individual differences model of expectancy theory. *Organizational Behavior and Human Performance*, 1981, *27*, 303–325.

Steers, R. M., & Braunstein, D. N. A behaviorally based measure of manifest needs in work settings. *Journal of Vocational Behavior*, 1976, *9*, 251–266.

Vecchio, R. P. An individual-difference interpretation of the conflicting predictions generated by equity theory and expectancy theory. *Journal of Applied Psychology*, 1981, *66*, 470–481.

Vroom, V. H. *Work and motivation.* New York: Wiley, 1964.

Wahba, M. A., & Bridwell, L. G. Maslow reconsidered: A review of research on the need hierarchy theory. *Organizational Behavior and Human Performance*, 1976, *15*, 212–240.

Wicklund, R. A., & Brehm, J. W. *Perspectives on cognitive dissonance.* Hillsdale, N.J.: Lawrence Erlbaum, 1976.

CHAPTER 6
MOTIVATING INDIVIDUAL
PERFORMANCE

In the previous chapter we discussed several of the basic theoretical approaches to understanding motivation in organizations. In this chapter we extend our discussion of motivation by introducing three additional approaches which have clear implications and applications to motivating individual performance in organizations. *Goal-setting theory* focuses upon the impact of goals on the motivation and performance of organization members and provides the theoretical basis for applied management by objectives (MBO) programs. *Organization behavior modification* (O.B. Mod.) applies the principles of reinforcement theory to the management of the contingencies of rewards and punishment in organizations. Finally, *social learning theory* provides an integrative theoretical perspective for combining many of the elements of the various motivation theories into a unified framework.

GOAL-SETTING THEORY

Goal-setting theory was put forward as a comprehensive theory of motivation in organizations by Edwin Locke (1968). Locke's basic argument is that people's *conscious* goals and intentions are the primary determinants of their actions. This in turn implies that the goal-setting process is the primary means by which organizations can influence the motivation and performance of their members.

We will first provide a general overview of the theory, and follow this with a discussion of some of the critical characteristics of goals which have been found to determine the extent to which goals have an impact on behavior. Finally, management by objectives (MBO), a system of management whose basis lies in setting goals and objectives, is described and discussed.

Nature of the Theory

The basic hypothesis of goal-setting theory is that people formulate *conscious* goals and intentions and that these goals and intentions are the *primary* determinants of people's actions. The unique features of goal-setting theory are its emphasis upon conscious goals and its position that goals are *the* preeminent determinant of what people do.

The theory is presented diagramatically in Figure 6-1. According to goal-setting theory there are three cognitive processes which intervene between events which occur in the environment around a person and the person's subsequent performance on the job. The environmental events could, for example, be things such as change in the organization's pay system, or the provision of verbal feedback from one's boss about past job performance. According to goal-setting theory the first step in the motivation process is the *perception* of environmental events by the person. The individual's perceptions may or may not agree 100 percent with what actually occurred. The next step involves the *evaluation* by the person of what has been perceived in light of his or her own personal values and priorities. This evaluation process then leads to the final cognitive step of *setting goals* and formulating *intentions* for action. Here the person consciously decides what it is that he or she is going to attempt to do and

FIGURE 6-1
The sequence of mental (cognitive) processes hypothesized by goal-setting theory as intervening between environmental events and work performance.

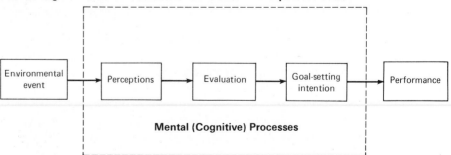

how he or she will attempt to do it. The goals and intentions thus formulated are then translated into actual behavior and job performance.

According to goal-setting theory the various types of incentives (e.g., pay, promotions, interesting assignments) employed by organizations to influence their members all have an impact on behavior via their effect upon employees' goals. Incentives are viewed simply as a way of getting people to set or accept particular work goals, and as a method of encouraging continued commitment to goals over time, as well as persistence in the face of setbacks. For example, giving instructions and setting time limits are viewed as very direct methods of encouraging employees to set goals and standards. Providing knowledge of results of work performance and setting up competitive situations are seen to be somewhat less direct but still powerful methods of suggesting performance goals to organization members. Finally, factors such as money, verbal praise and reproof, and participation in decision making are argued to be relatively indirect methods of influencing goals, and hence less powerful determinants of motivation and performance than the previously mentioned forms of incentives.

Critical Characteristics of Goals

A considerable amount of research has been carried out to investigate the effects of goals and goal-setting on behavior in organizations. Studies have been done both under controlled laboratory conditions and in ongoing work organizations. Reviews of this research are contained in articles by Locke (1968; 1978), by Latham and Yukl (1975), and by Locke et al. (1981). The basic finding of the research has been that goals can and do have an impact upon the behavior and performance of people at work. However, the research has also shown that setting just any type of goal will not necessarily produce desirable results. There are a number of critical attributes or characteristics of goals which have been found to determine whether or not goals will in fact have a positive effect on work performance.

Goal Difficulty

In general it has been found that the more difficult the goal that is set, the higher the level of performance brought about. A variety of studies in both industrial organizations and volunteer agencies have found that when difficult and challenging goals are set, higher levels of performance result than when relatively easy goals are set (Latham & Baldes, 1975; Matsui, Okada, & Mizuguchi, 1981). This pattern of results is subject to the qualification that the goal or goals must not be so difficult that they are perceived to be unrealistically high and hence impossible to attain. In such a situation, goals do not result in improved performance. However, subject to this qualification, the results quite consistently indicate that the harder the goal the better the performance (Mento, Cartledge, & Locke, 1980).

Goal Specificity

The second critical attribute of a goal is its degree of specificity. Goals can vary from the extremely general, such as "Do your best," to the highly specific, such as "Increase sales volume by $50,000 over the next three months." With this attribute, as with goal difficulty, the research results are extremely consistent. The finding is that specific goals have a consistent positive effect on performance, while vague and general goals have little if any impact. This finding has been observed for many different jobs and in a variety of types of organizations (Latham & Yukl, 1975; Locke et al., 1981). The more specifically that a goal is stated, the greater is its impact on subsequent performance.

Goal Acceptance

The previously discussed findings regarding the positive effects of difficult and specific goals upon performance are subject to one important qualification. In order for any goal to have a positive impact upon a person's performance on the job, it must first be *accepted* by that person. If people do not accept goals, do not view them as their own and as something to which they are personally committed, the likelihood of the goal influencing their behavior is almost nil. Thus, goal acceptance is an essential prerequisite to the positive influence of goals on performance. Goal acceptance requires that goals be set at realistic levels. One of the methods which has been shown to increase the likelihood that goals will be accepted is the use of a participative and supportive approach to goal setting. When people have an opportunity to participate in the process of setting their own goals it decreases the likelihood that unrealistic goals will be set and increases the degree of understanding, acceptance, and commitment to those goals on the part of those who must work to attain them (Latham & Saari, 1979a).

Management by Objectives—An Application of Goal-Setting Theory

Management by objectives, or MBO, programs involve managers throughout an organization in the process of regularly and systematically setting goals for themselves and their subordinates (Carroll & Tosi, 1973). MBO programs have been implemented in a wide variety of organizations and have a mixed record of success (Tosi, Rizzo, & Carroll, 1970; Levinson, 1970). To the extent that MBO programs facilitate the process of setting specific challenging goals which are accepted by members of the organization, goal-setting theory implies that such programs should have a positive impact upon motivation and performance.

If goal-setting theory is valid, the question arises as to why MBO should have such a mixed record of success. Why is the history of MBO not simply an uninterrupted string of success stories? The answer appears to lie not in the weaknesses of the underlying goal-setting theory upon which MBO is based, but in the faulty implementation of MBO programs in many organizations.

Our discussion of goal-setting theory indicated that goal acceptance is essential if goals are to have a positive effect on motivation and performance. Insuring goal acceptance requires skill and sensitivity on the part of managers in handling the goal-setting process with their subordinates (Latham & Saari, 1979a; Ivancevich & Smith, 1981). It now appears that while many organizations have "bought" the idea that setting specific challenging goals should improve motivation, some have failed to recognize the critical importance of goal acceptance and the accompanying need for managerial skill and sensitivity in handling the goal-setting process. Many of the "failures" of MBO appear to be traceable to a lack of attention to the need for goal acceptance and the need to train managers to handle the goal-setting process competently (Jamieson, 1973).

An excellent example of the successful application of goal setting to facilitate motivation and performance is provided by the Tenneco Corporation, a large, diversified organization with operations in eight major industries (Ivancevich, McMahon, Streidl, & Szilagyi, 1978). The goal-setting program implemented at Tenneco had the clear support and endorsement of top management, including the chairman of the board. The program was designed to encourage setting of goals both for improved performance and for the personal development of participating managers. Of equal importance, the implementation of the goal-setting system provided formal training to everyone involved in the program in the skills necessary for conducting goal-setting meetings in a constructive fashion. This type of training is probably an essential component of successful goal-setting programs in helping managers learn how to assist subordinates in setting realistic, specific, challenging goals that are acceptable to subordinates.

The results of the Tenneco goal-setting program were positive overall. In those areas of the corporation which adopted goal setting, morale improved and work-related tension was down. The organization also experienced improvements in motivation and performance as a result of the goal-setting program.

Overall, the basic notions of goal-setting theory appear to be valid and the theory has significant potential for influencing the motivation and performance of organization members. Similarly, MBO programs, when they actually result in the acceptance of challenging specific goals throughout an organization, have significant potential for positive results. However, the implementation issues are complex and the process must be managed carefully and competently if the potential is to be realized.

ORGANIZATIONAL BEHAVIOR MODIFICATION

Organizational behavior modification, or O.B. Mod., is not so much a theory as it is an overall approach to influencing the behavior of people in organizations. O.B. Mod. has its theoretical basis in the research of B. F. Skinner into the processes of learning and the ways in which rewards and punishments influence behavior. Skinner's approach differs drastically from cognitive theories such as expectancy theory and goal-setting theory in that it contains no discussion or theorizing about cognitions at all. Things like people's thoughts, feelings, beliefs, and attitudes are completely ignored. Instead, attention focuses upon how past and present patterns of rewards and punishments shape and determine what people do. Because of this, some people feel that O.B. Mod. isn't really a theory of *motivation* at all, since it doesn't try to explain the inner motives and mental states of people. Technically, such an argument is probably correct. However, from an organizational standpoint, managers are interested in motivation to the extent it helps them understand and influence the behavior of people working for them. From this point of view O.B. Mod. belongs very much in the heart of our discussion of motivation in organizations.

In what follows we'll first provide a brief introduction to the underlying theory of learning upon which O.B. Mod. is based. This introduction then provides us with a basis for a more detailed discussion of O.B. Mod. itself and the application of its principles to behavior in organizations. Finally we look at the current status of the approach and some examples of its application in organizations.

The Underlying Theory

O.B. Mod. has its intellectual roots in the work of B. F. Skinner, the noted scholar and theorist of learning. Skinner is known as a *behaviorist*, which means that his theories focus upon actual overt behavior and attempt to explain and predict overt behavior in terms of the observable environmental events which immediately precede and follow behavior. Behaviorists are not interested in cognitions. They feel that if we wish to understand, explain, and predict what people actually do (i.e., their behavior), then we should build our theories around things which we can actually physically observe. While most behaviorists don't deny that people have cognitions, they feel that little is to be gained in terms of building a sound scientific understanding of the causes and determinants of behavior from theorizing and speculating about what goes on in people's minds. Their argument is that since we'll never be able to verify theories about what goes on in people's minds (since we'll never be able to get inside someone's head to observe their cognitive processes), we may as well not waste our time speculating about these unobservable events. The behaviorists' solution is to focus upon what we can actually physically observe, which boils down to a person's actual overt behavior and the physically observable characteristics of the environment around the person immediately preceding and following the behavior.

Although Skinner is the most well known modern advocate of the behaviorist approach, he by no means invented it. The term behaviorism was in fact coined by Watson (1914) in the early part of this century. Watson argued that in order to understand why people do the things they do, we need to focus upon what the *consequences* of behavior are for the person engaging in it. In this regard Watson was building upon the earlier work of Thorndike (1911) who had stated the following *law of effect:*

> . . . of several responses made to the same situation, those that are accompanied or closely followed by satisfaction [reinforcement] . . . will be more likely to recur; those which are accompanied or closely followed by discomfort [punishment] . . . will be less likely to occur. (p. 244)

While the law of effect may appear fairly straightforward and commonsensical today, its statement was an important contribution to our understanding of human behavior and it has served as the basic underpinning to subsequent behaviorist theories.

Skinner's particular brand of behaviorism emphasizes *operant conditioning* as the primary underlying process which influences and determines how people learn and ultimately what they do. Operant conditioning is defined in terms of relationships between *stimuli* and *responses* (hence the fact that behaviorist theories are sometimes referred to as *stimulus-response* theories or *response-stimulus* theories—often shortened to *S-R* or *R-S* theories). In simplest terms, stimuli are things or events in the world outside the person, while responses are actions which a person engages in. Stimuli can both precede and follow responses. For example, in an organization a typical stimulus might be a request from one's boss to do a particular job. This stimulus might be followed by the response of doing the job. This response might itself be followed by another stimulus, such as the boss offering congratulations on doing the job so well.

Operant Conditioning

Operant conditioning is said to occur when a stimulus-response relationship (such as the relationship between the boss's request (the stimulus) and the subordinate's performance (the response)) is strengthened by following the response with another stimulus that is reinforcing (such as the boss congratulating the subordinate on a job well done). A stimulus is said to be *reinforcing* if its occurrence or administration following a response increases the likelihood of that response occurring when a person is placed in the same or a similar situation again in the future. In other words, a reinforcer is a stimulus that strengthens the response that precedes it and hence makes the response more likely to occur again.

These definitions may sound a bit circular. In fact it turns out that the circularity is more apparent than real and that it is forced upon us if we want to stick to explanations based solely on overt behavior without appealing to inner mental states. What the definition of reinforcement implies is that we can never know whether a particular stimulus is reinforcing or not until we administer it following a response and then see whether the response is more likely to be repeated. Thus, there is no a priori method of determining whether money, for example, will be reinforcing for any given response by any given person. What we must do to determine whether money is reinforcing is give someone money when we observe a particular response (e.g., working hard) and then see whether the response occurs more frequently in the future. Behaviorist theories do not address the question of *why* reinforcers are reinforcing. Trying to answer such questions takes us into the realm of mental events and cognitions, a world which behaviorists do not wish to inhabit.

The important contribution of the behaviorist theories of operant conditioning lies in their clarification of the nature of the relationships among preceding stimuli, behavioral responses, and succeeding reinforcing stimuli. The important range of applications which such theories open up for managers in organizations lies in the guidelines which are applied regarding how to design reinforcement contingencies in order to increase the likelihood of effective performance and to decrease the likelihood of ineffective performance by organization members. However, before we can move on to spell out these organizational applications in more detail, we must first discuss some important differences among different types of reinforcers.

The stimuli which follow a person's response can be experienced as either pleasant or unpleasant by the person to whom they are administered. In addition, such stimuli can either be applied contingently upon a person engaging in a particular response or alternatively, may be withheld each time the response is engaged in. This combination of either pleasant or unpleasant stimuli being either applied or withheld contingent upon a response yields a total of four possible strategies available for influencing behavior. The four combinations are outlined in Table 6-1. We'll discuss each in turn.

Positive Reinforcement

When a pleasant or desirable stimulus is applied contingent upon a person engaging in some behavior and the likelihood of the behavior being repeated goes up, positive reinforcement has occurred. An example of positive reinforcement would be an increase in productivity following the administration of pay incentives contingent upon achieving high levels of

TABLE 6-1
The combinations of contingencies and stimuli that result in positive and negative reinforcement, punishment, and extinction

	Stimulus	
Contingently	Pleasant or desirable	Unpleasant or undesirable
Applied	Positive reinforcement (behavior increases)	Punishment (behavior decreases)
Withheld	Extinction (behavior decreases)	Negative reinforcement (behavior increases)

SOURCE: Adapted from Fred Luthans, *Organizational Behavior*, 3d ed. New York: McGraw-Hill, 1981. Used by permission.

productivity. In this situation the contingent pay is a positive reinforcer since it has brought about an increase in the frequency of the desirable behavior of high productivity. The steps in the positive reinforcement process are traced through in Figure 6-2 from the initial stimulus (the supervisor's request for high productivity), to the behavioral response of high productivity, to the reinforcing stimulus of receiving increased pay as a result of the highly productive behavior. Positive reinforcement has been shown to be a powerful method of influencing behavior in many different situations and a wide variety of applications.

Extinction

Extinction occurs when positive reinforcement is discontinued. For example, members of an organization may have been regularly receiving pay bonuses even though they were achieving only moderate levels of productivity. If the organization then changes its policy and states that bonuses will no longer be paid for average or moderate productivity, the organization is said to be "extinguishing" moderate productivity. Extinction results in a reduction in the frequency of the behavior which was previously reinforced. The steps in the process are laid out in Figure 6-2. Extinction is effective in reducing the frequency of previously reinforced behavior. The removal of positive reinforcers generally results in a fairly rapid decline in the frequency of behavior. However, the disadvantage of extinction as a tool for use in organizations is that while it effectively reduces one behavior or set of behaviors, it offers no method of systematically replacing those behaviors with something better. For example, if an organization decides to attempt to extinguish average performance, it has no assurance that the average performance will not be replaced by very low levels of performance rather than very high levels. To be effective for the organization, extinction of one set of behaviors needs to be accompa-

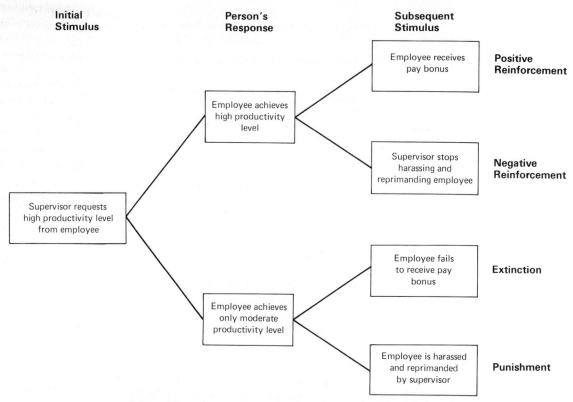

FIGURE 6-2
Example of the steps involved in the processes of positive reinforcement, negative reinforcement, extinction, and punishment.   (SOURCE: Adapted from *Introduction to Organizational Behavior* by Richard M. Steers. Copyright © 1981 Scott, Foresman and Company. Reprinted by permission.)

nied by the positive reinforcement of some new set of alternative behaviors. Use of extinction alone is risky.

Punishment

Punishment involves the application of some unpleasant or undesirable stimulus contingent upon people engaging in some behavior. In our example in Figure 6-2, employees might be reprimanded and harassed by their boss each time that their productivity was moderate. Punishment generally results in the person engaging in the punished behavior less frequently. However, punishment also has a number of shortcomings and undesirable side effects. Punishment shares with extinction the problem of not indicating to the person what behavior is in fact desirable. If for example the organization punishes people for moderate levels of performance, it has no assurance that the punished moderate level of productivity will be replaced by a higher level. All the person being punished has learned is that moderate productivity is not desired. Second, punishment tends to be effective in eliminating the punished behavior only when the source of punishment is actually present. If the punishing agent is not constantly present, the punished behavior frequently reappears quite quickly. Finally, punishment usually has the unpleasant side effect of creating feelings of anger and antipathy toward the source of the punishment. These negative feelings are sometimes manifested as aggressive behavior, sabotage, and similar undesirable conduct.

Negative Reinforcement

Negative reinforcement occurs when some unpleasant or undesirable stimulus is *withheld* or *taken away* whenever a person engages in the desired behavior. Thus, one learns that by doing what is requested one can *avoid* an unpleasant situation. Our example in Figure 6-2 indicates a situation in which employees avoid being harassed and reprimanded by their supervisor whenever they achieve a high level of productivity. At all other times, i.e., whenever they are performing at anything other than a highly productive level, they would be constantly subjected to harassment by their supervisor. The term reinforcement is employed because negative reinforcement results in an *increase* in the frequency of the reinforced behavior. The term negative is employed to indicate that reinforcement is accomplished by *removing* or taking away an unpleasant stimulus, rather than by applying or administering a desirable stimulus as in the case of positive reinforcement. Negative reinforcement shares two of the shortcomings associated with punishment. First, the source of the unpleasant stimuli must be constantly present to insure that the situation is always made unpleasant for the subjects unless they are engaging in the desired behavior. This is frequently difficult to achieve. Second, the administration of the unpleasant stimuli whenever the desired behavior is not being engaged in frequently creates feelings of frustration and anger in the people receiving such treatment. Such feelings often translate themselves into dysfunctional or destructive behavior toward the organization.

Effectiveness of the Alternative Strategies

The evidence is now quite clear from both laboratory studies and field research in organizations that of the four strategies discussed, positive reinforcement is by far the most effective and powerful for facilitating desirable, effective behavior. Positive reinforcement clearly indicates to people exactly what behavior is desired, and it is the only strategy that provides them with rewards contingent upon engaging in the desired behavior. Extinction and punishment do nothing to help people discover what it is that they should be doing; all these strategies do is point out that people are currently doing the wrong thing. Punishment has the added disadvantage of generally creating frustration, anger, and hard feelings on the part of those being punished. Negative reinforcement also creates many of these negative feelings, since it requires the administration of negative, undesirable stimuli unless the desired behavior is engaged in.

The timing of rewards has also been shown to be a critical factor in determining whether a positive reinforcement strategy will achieve its potential benefits. In order to increase the frequency of desired behavior, rewards (reinforcers) must: (1) be administered contingent upon the behavior being engaged in (they must *not* be administered if the behavior does not occur); and (2) be supplied as immediately as possible following the occurrence of the behavior. When rewards are delayed, they lose their ability to reinforce the link between the preceding stimulus and response. Timing of rewards is extremely important to the effectiveness of a positive reinforcement strategy.

Schedules of Reinforcement

In addition to timing rewards to follow behavior as immediately as possible, the effects of positive reinforcement also depend upon the way in which the rewards are *scheduled*. There are two basic approaches to the scheduling of reinforcements.

Continuous Reinforcement

Continuous reinforcement schedules require that every time the desired behavior occurs it must be rewarded. A continuous reinforcement schedule, for example, would require that every time an employee achieved a high level of productivity, the employee would receive a pay bonus. Or to take another example, if punctuality were being positively reinforced on a continuous schedule, the supervisor would have to praise (or otherwise reward) the employee each and every day the employee arrived at work on time. Continuous reinforcement schedules are very effective in the early stages of learning. They generally result in the desired behavior being acquired quite quickly. However, continuous reinforcement schedules are frequently expensive and cumbersome to maintain over long periods of time. Fortunately, there are alternatives to continuous reinforcement, alternatives which can be quite effective.

Partial Reinforcement

Partial reinforcement schedules do not require that behavior be rewarded each and every time that it occurs. Instead, under a partial reinforcement schedule the reward for the desired behavior is administered to the person only from time to time. Partial reinforcement schedules are generally less efficient than continuous schedules in the acquisition of behavior. It takes longer for the desired behavior to become established under partial reinforcement. However, partial reinforcement usually results in higher levels of performance over the long run, and behavior established under partial reinforcement tends to be quite resistant to extinction if the rewards are subsequently removed. Partial reinforcement also has the advantage of being less costly and cumbersome to implement in organizations.

There are four common approaches to establishing a partial reinforcement schedule. The approaches differ in terms of the basis upon which particular behaviors are selected for reinforcement.

Fixed-Interval Schedule. On a fixed-interval schedule the frequency of reinforcement is determined by the passage of time. Thus, a particular time interval is determined (e.g., 1 hour, 1 day, 1 week, 1 month, 1 year), and provided that the person has continued to engage in the desired behavior for the duration of the time interval, reinforcement is administered at the end of each fixed time period. Fixed-interval schedules tend to result in average and uneven levels of performance. The types of fixed intervals most frequently employed in organizations (e.g., weekly, biweekly, or monthly pay periods) tend to be too long to achieve an effective level of reinforcement for productivity.

Variable-Interval Schedule. Variable-interval schedules differ from fixed-interval schedules in that instead of reinforcement being administered at regular, fixed time intervals, the length of time separating reinforcers is varied. Thus the person never knows exactly when they are going to be reinforced. Variable-interval schedules can achieve high levels of consistent performance and tend to be quite resistant to extinction.

Fixed-Ratio Schedule. Under a fixed-ratio schedule a person is reinforced after performing an activity a fixed number of times or after producing a fixed amount of output. Piece-rate pay systems whereby workers are paid based upon the number of units they produce are a common organizational example of the use of a fixed-ratio schedule of reinforcement. Fixed-ratio schedules are capable of producing high levels of performance that are quite stable over time, provided that the timing of rewards is such that people actually receive the rewards immediately after producing the fixed amount of output.

Variable-Ratio Schedule. A variable-ratio schedule of reinforcement requires that reinforcement be based upon the quantity or amount of output produced, but the actual number of units that must be produced in order to receive a reward varies randomly around some average. For example, under a variable-ratio schedule with the production of every 10 units being rewarded on the average, workers might be rewarded after producing 6 units, then after producing 12 more units, than after producing 13 more units, then after producing 8 more units, and so on. The average level of productivity required to be rewarded is fixed, but the workers never know exactly when they will receive the next reinforcement. Fixed-ratio schedules lead to very high levels of behavior which are maintained consistently and which are highly resistant to extinction.

Implementing O.B. Mod.

Luthans and Kreitner (1974) have presented a systematic model that provides a guide to the steps required for successful implementation of O.B. Mod. in organizations. The steps in the process are outlined in Figure 6-3 and can be briefly summarized as follows.

Step 1 **Identification of critical behaviors.** The starting point of the process of O.B. Mod. must be to identify which behaviors should be reinforced. This requires a determination of exactly which behaviors are the critical determinants of success on any given job. A variety of techniques are available for use in this identification process (Luthans & Keitner, 1974; 1975). This step is greatly facilitated if an up-to-date, systematic job analysis as discussed in Chapter 2 is available.

Step 2 **Measurement of the behaviors.** Before implementing a positive reinforcement program it is necessary to measure the frequency of critical behaviors for two reasons. First, it must be determined whether it is realistic to expect improvement in the quantity or quality of the critical behaviors identified. If the critical behaviors are already being performed very rapidly and competently, there is no need for a new program of positive reinforcement. The second, and more frequent, reason for requiring measures lies in the necessity of having baseline data against which performance can be compared after positive reinforcement is introduced. Without such baseline measures it is impossible to assess systematically whether a positive reinforcement program has been successful.

Step 3 **Functional analysis of the behavior.** The goal of an O.B. Mod. program is to increase the likelihood that people will in fact engage in the behaviors which are critical to the successful performance of their jobs. Once these critical behaviors have been identified and measured, it is then necessary to determine what the causes and consequences of these behaviors are. This involves analyzing: (1) the *antecedent cues,* the factors which seem to instigate the behavior or get it started; and (2) the *consequences,* the results which accrue to the person as a result of engaging in the behavior. This process of analyzing the antecedent cues and the consequences of behavior is referred to as *functional analysis* in O.B. Mod.

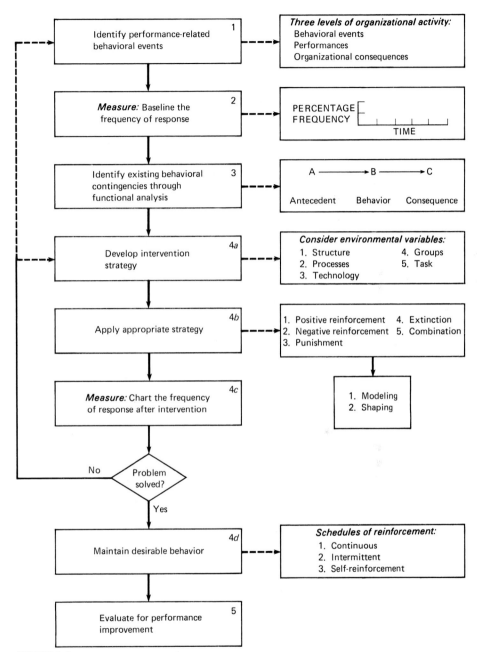

FIGURE 6-3
Steps in O.B. Mod. (SOURCE: Reprinted, by permission of the publisher, from "The Management of Behavioral Contingencies," Fred Luthans and Robert Kreitner, *Personnel*, July–August, 1974 © 1974 by AMACOM, a division of American Management Associations, p. 13. All rights reserved.)

Step 4   **Development of an intervention strategy.** The term *intervention* refers to the actions that will be taken by the manager or organization in order to increase the frequency of desirable critical behavior and to decrease the frequency of undesirable behavior. This is the critical step in the process, since it is here that the manager uses the results of the first three steps to design and implement techniques to change the behavior of his or her subordinates. The emphasis here is upon identifying rewards that can serve as positive reinforcers and establishing methods of providing these reinforcers contingent upon subordinates engaging in the desirable critical behaviors. Positive reinforcement is employed to increase the likelihood of desirable behavior. Extinction may also be used to attempt to decrease the frequency of undesirable behavior. Punishment and negative reinforcement are used as little as possible.

Step 5   **Evaluation to assure performance improvement.** In order to determine whether an O.B. Mod. program has achieved its desired results it is necessary to evaluate the effects of the program in a systematic and objective fashion. The results of such evaluation can be used both to determine whether the program should be continued or not and to "fine-tune" the interventions to increase their value and their ability to increase effective performance.

Applications of O.B. Mod.

O.B. Mod is a relatively new technique for influencing the behavior of people in organizations. Nevertheless, it has been gaining in popularity and in the frequency with which it is applied in organizations. The results of a number of these applications of O.B. Mod. techniques are summarized in Table 6-2. All of the examples cited in the figure indicate significant positive results associated with O.B. Mod. The technique appears to be extremely promising and to be capable of generating many positive outcomes for organizations.

At Michigan Bell-Operator Services for example, a program was established that involved setting productivity goals for a group of operators, providing the operators with feedback on how they were performing, and positively reinforcing performance improvements. The program resulted in service promptness (time to answer a call) improving from 94 to 99 percent of standard, average work time per call (time taken to give information) decreasing from 60 units of work time to 43 units of work time, the percentage of work time completed within ideal limits increasing from 50 to 93 percent of ideal time, and the percentage of time operators made proper use of references going from 80 to 94 percent. The

TABLE 6-2
Summary of the results of some O.B. Mod. programs in organizations

Organization	Type of employees	Specific goals	Frequency of feedback	Reinforcers used	Results
Emery Air Freight	Entire work force	(a) Increase productivity (b) Improve quality of service	Immediate to monthly, depending on task	Previously only praise and recognition; others now being introduced	Cost savings can be directly attributed to the program
Michigan Bell— Operator Services	Employees at all levels in operator services	(a) Decrease turnover & absenteeism (b) Increase productivity (c) Improve union-management relations	(a) Lower level— weekly & daily (b) Higher level— monthly & quarterly	(a) Praise & recognition (b) Opportunity to see oneself become better	(a) Attendance performance has improved by 50% (b) Productivity and efficiency has continued to be above standard in areas where positive reinforcement (PR) is used
Michigan Bell— Maintenance Services	Maintenance workers, mechanics, & first- & second-level supervisors	Improve: (a) Productivity (b) quality (c) safety (d) customer-employee relations	Daily, weekly, and quarterly	(a) Self-feedback (b) Supervisory feedback	(a) Cost efficiency increase (b) Safety improved (c) Service improved (d) No change in absenteeism (e) Satisfaction with superior & co-workers improved (f) Satisfaction with pay decreased
Connecticut General Life Insurance Co.	Clerical employees & first-line supervisors	(a) Decrease absenteeism (b) Decrease lateness	Immediate	(a) Self-feedback (b) System-feedback (c) Earned time off	(a) Chronic absenteeism & lateness has been drastically reduced (b) Some divisions refuse to use PR because it is "outdated"

Organization	Type of employees	Specific goals	Frequency of feedback	Reinforcers used	Results
General Electric	Employees at all levels	(a) Meet EEO objectives (b) Decrease absenteeism & turnover (c) Improve training (d) Increase productivity	Immediate—uses modeling & role playing as training tools to teach interpersonal ex- changes & behavior requirements	Social reinforcers (praise, rewards, & constructive feed- back)	(a) Cost savings can be directly attributed to the program (b) Productivity has increased (c) Worked extremely well in training minority groups and raising their self-esteem (d) Direct labor cost decreased
Standard Oil of Ohio	Supervisors	Increase supervisor competence	Weekly over 5 weeks (25-hour) training period	Feedback	(a) Improved supervisory ability to give feedback judiciously (b) Discontinued because of lack of overall success
Weyerhaeuser Company Gary P. Latham	Clerical, production (tree planters) & middle-level management & scientists	(a) To teach managers to minimize criticism & to maximize praise (b) To teach managers to make rewards contingent on specified per- formance levels & (c) To use optimal schedule to increase productivity	Immediate—daily & quarterly	(a) Pay (b) Praise & recognition	(a) Using money, obtained 33% increase in pro- ductivity with one group of workers, an 18% increase with a second group, & an 8% decrease in a third group (b) Currently experiment- ing with goal setting & praise and/or money at various levels in organization (c) With a lottery-type bonus, the cultural & religious values of workers must be taken into account

Organization	Employees	Performance measures	Reinforcement schedule	Reinforcers	Results
City of Detroit Garbage Collectors	Garbage collectors	(a) Reduction in paid man-hour per ton (b) Reduction on overtime (c) 90% of routes completed by standard (d) Effectiveness (quality)	Daily & quarterly based on formula negotiated by city & sanitation union	Bonus (profit sharing) & praise	(a) Citizen complaints declined significantly (b) City saved $1,654,000 first year after bonus paid (c) Worker bonus = $307,000 first year or $350 annually per man (d) Union somewhat dissatisfied with productivity measure and is pushing for more bonus to employee (e) 1975 results not yet available
B. F. Goodrich Chemical Co.	Manufacturing employees at all levels	(a) Better meeting of schedules (b) Increase productivity	Weekly	Praise & recognition; freedom to choose one's own activity	Production has increased over 300%
ACDC Electronics Division of Emerson Electronics	All levels	(a) 96% attendance (b) 90% engineering specifications met (c) Daily production objectives met 95% of time (d) Cost reduced by 10%	Daily & weekly feedback from foreman to company president	Positive feedback	(a) Profit up 25% over forecast (b) $550,000 cost reduction on $10M sales (c) Return of 1900% on investment including consultant fees (d) Turnaround time on repairs went from 30 to 10 days (e) Attendance is over 98.2% (from 93.5%)

Source: Reprinted, by permission of the publisher, from "Behavior Modification on the Bottom Line," by W. C. Hamner and E. P. Hamner, *Organizational Dynamics*, Spring, 1976, © by AMACOM, a division of American Management Associations, pp. 12–24. All rights reserved.

overall outcome was a significant improvement in the productivity of the operators.

In another example, the B. F. Goodrich Chemical plant in Avon Lake, Ohio, introduced an O.B. Mod. program at a time when the plant was in serious danger of failing. The program involved setting goals and providing feedback and positive reinforcement regarding scheduling, targets, costs, and problem areas. Supervisors received feedback once a week on sales, costs, and productivity. The plant production manager attributes the program with turning the plant around, resulting in significant cost savings and a 300 percent productivity improvement over 5 years.

These results, along with others contained in the literature of O.B. Mod., while very encouraging, must be interpreted with caution for a number of reasons. First, good news travels quickly. Organizations are usually quite happy to make their successes known but are somewhat more reticent about publicizing their failures. There is no way of knowing how many unsuccessful applications of O.B. Mod. have simply never been reported on. Second, the vast majority of the results published regarding applications of O.B. Mod. in organizations are *not* based upon careful, systematic scientific analyses of the effects of the programs. A comprehensive review of the literature from 1967 to 1976 failed to find a single example of the use of careful scientific methods in evaluating an O.B. Mod. program (McGehee & Tullar, 1978). Fortunately, this state of affairs is being rectified. For example, Luthans and his colleagues have recently begun to analyze the effects of a variety of O.B. Mod programs in a systematic scientific fashion (Luthans, 1981; Luthans & Schweizer, 1979; Luthans, Paul, & Baker, 1981; Snyder & Luthans, 1982). Komaki and her colleagues have likewise undertaken a research program which is generating a variety of encouraging research results from carefully designed and analyzed studies (Komaki, Barwick, & Scott, 1978; Komacki, Heinzmann, & Lawson, 1980). Other researchers have been systematically analyzing the impact of different reinforcement schedules on performance (Pritchard, Hollenback, & DeLeo, 1980). Overall, the results of these research programs are quite encouraging and indicate that O.B. Mod. programs can result in significant improvements in performance in organizations.

Ethical Issues in O.B. Mod.

Objections have sometimes been raised to O.B. Mod. on ethical grounds. The basic thrust of most of the criticism seems to be that O.B. Mod is a technique for controlling and manipulating the behavior of organization members. As such it is ethically undesirable since its application deprives organization members of their freedom and may result in their engaging in behavior which they would not otherwise engage in.

The basic issues of control, manipulation, and freedom are obviously extremely important, and those who raise these issues do so with considerable justification. It is extremely important to think through very carefully the ethical issues involved in the treatment of people in work organizations and to analyze the potential for misuse or misapplication of any techniques which may be developed for application to people in organizations.

Clearly, the goal of O.B. Mod. is to increase a manager's ability to control and direct the behavior of other members of the organization. But it is equally clear that the fundamental nature of a manager's job is to control and direct the behavior of the people under his or her supervision. Surely the organization is controlling the behavior of its members by insisting that in order to remain a member of the organization, people must be physically present on the job from 9 A.M. to 5 P.M. or some variant of such hours. And just as surely a manager is attempting to control and direct the behavior of members of the organization when he or she exhorts them on to higher levels of productivity or greater levels of accomplishment. O.B. Mod. simply attempts to make the process of control and direction more systematic, more effective, and more clearly based upon positive rewards rather than negative punishment.

Ethical issues regarding manipulation and freedom are by no means irrelevant in considering the application of O.B. Mod. Indeed they are very important. However, they are important issues to address in analyzing *any* technique of management, indeed any approach designed to influence the behavior of people in organizations. People who study organizations and people who work in them must all remain conscious of these ethical issues in order to insure that available techniques are not misused or placed in the service of unethical goals. Such ethical issues are pervasive and are relevant not only to O.B. Mod. but to management techniques in general.

SOCIAL LEARNING THEORY

An important question which the discussion up to this point raises is whether a manager, in looking for a way to influence the motivation and performance of others, must choose just one of the theories that we have discussed as *the* correct one to apply. If a manager decides to make use of some of the ideas from goal-setting theory by setting challenging, realistic objectives for subordinates, does that imply that the manager cannot or should not make use of any of the techniques of O.B. Mod. regarding structuring behavioral contingencies to increase the frequency with which effective performance is rewarded? It may well appear that each of the theories that we have presented so far contains certain aspects that are appealing and that appear as though they would be useful in organizational applications. What would be extremely helpful then, both from a theoretical and from a practical point of view, would be a theory of motivation and performance in organizations which pulled together the different aspects of the various theories into something of a unified whole. Social learning theory accomplishes this integrative goal by making use of both the operant conditioning notions which underlie O.B. Mod., as well as the cognitive approaches of expectancy theory and goal-setting theory.

Nature of the Theory

Social learning theory, developed by Albert Bandura (1977), acknowledges that behavior is strongly influenced and shaped by its consequences. In this sense it shares common ground with the O.B. Mod. approach by recognizing that contingencies of reward and punishment have an important effect upon the frequency with which people engage in behavior. Social learning theory has no quarrel with the important role of reinforcement in the determination of what people do.

However, social learning theory parts company with the O.B. Mod. approach regarding the role of cognitions in motivation and performance. While the theories that underlie O.B. Mod. argue that nothing is to be gained by theorizing about the unobservable mental states of people, social learning theory points out that a great deal of human behavior is initiated and maintained in the absence of any external inducements and reinforcements. For example, how do we explain in pure reinforcement terms the high levels of motivation and performance of a manager who receives a fixed amount of pay once a month and who receives systematic verbal feedback on his or her performance only once a year? Social learning theory argues that the inducements for the vast amounts of behavior that occur independent of external reinforcement must lie in the cognitions (i.e., the expectations, beliefs, and values) of the person engaging in the behavior. Thus, while not denying the importance of reinforcement in the acquisition and maintenance of behavior, social learning theory also gives primary attention to cognitions as critical determinants of motivation and behavior.

The overall social learning theory model of motivation is summarized in Figure 6-4. In what follows, each of the components of this model will be outlined and discussed.

According to social learning theory there are two major cognitive components of motivation. The first component consists of the *expectations* that a person holds in his or her mind. This aspect of the theory shares much common ground with expectancy theory. The second major cognitive component of motivation in social learning theory has to do with *goal setting* and what is referred to as the *self-regulation* of reinforcement. This aspect of the theory bears obvious similarities to goal-setting theory, but also contains some unique extensions in its treatment of how people regulate their own behavior and reinforce themselves. We'll discuss each of these cognitive components of motivation in turn.

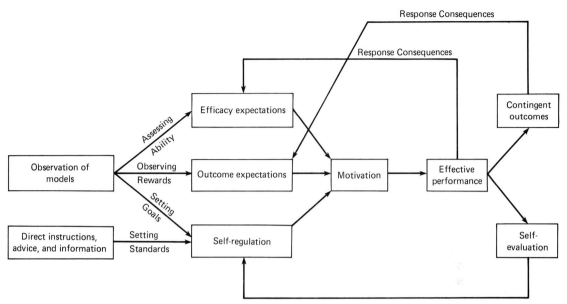

FIGURE 6-4
Summary of the social learning theory model of motivation and its determinants.

Expectations

Social learning theory hypothesizes that as a result of personal experiences and observations of the experiences of others, people develop expectations regarding: (1) their own ability to engage successfully in various types of behavior; and (2) the likelihood that engaging in various behaviors will be followed by the attainment of valued outcomes. The first set of expectations regarding one's ability to perform behaviors successfully are referred to as *efficacy expectations*. The second set, having to do with perceptions of the relationship between engaging in behavior and attaining outcomes, are known as *outcome expectations*. The role of these two types of expectations in linking the person, his or her behavior, and outcomes is diagrammed in Figure 6-5.

FIGURE 6-5
Diagrammatic representation of the difference between efficacy expectations and outcome expectations.   (SOURCE: Albert Bandura, *Social Learning Theory*, © 1977, p. 79. Reprinted by permission of Prentice-Hall, Inc., Englewood Cliffs, N.J.)

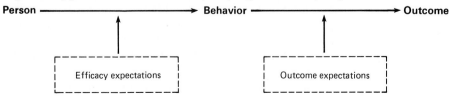

The parallels between this component of social learning theory and expectancy theory are obvious. Efficacy expectations are directly analogous to the effort $\rightarrow$ performance ($E \rightarrow P$) expectancies of expectancy theory. They both refer to the strength of the person's belief that he or she is capable of successfully performing some behavior if it is attempted. Outcome expectations are similarly analogous to expectancy theory's performance $\rightarrow$ outcome ($P \rightarrow O$) expectancies. Both refer to the person's beliefs regarding the likelihood of attaining positively or negatively valued outcomes as a result of successfully performing some behavior or set of behaviors. Just as with expectancy theory, this component of social learning theory hypothesizes that the stronger a person's efficacy expectations and the stronger the outcome expectations associated with positive outcomes, the higher the level of motivation to engage in behavior.

Goal Setting and Self-Regulation

In addition to the anticipation or expectation of attaining desirable outcomes in the future, social learning theory also argues that a critical determinant of motivation lies in the ability of people to reinforce themselves. Self-reinforcement or self-motivation requires that people set certain personal internal standards and then self-regulate their behavior with regard to these standards.

The basic idea is that people have the capacity to, and in fact do, engage in the process of evaluating their own actions (Scott & Erskine, 1980). To the extent that previous actions are viewed as desirable and effective, a person engages in self-reinforcement (feeling good about oneself), while unsuccessful or undesirable behaviors result in self-punishment (feeling badly or unhappy with oneself).

Goal setting is an essential aspect of this process since goals serve as a necessary point of comparison against which a person can compare his or her behavior in order to determine whether it exceeds some standard (the goal) and hence deserves self-reinforcement or whether it fails to reach the standard and thus requires self-punishment. For example, managers may set themselves the goal of completing an important report by a particular time. If the report is completed on time the managers will then feel good about their accomplishment, and this feeling serves as a self-reinforcer. If the managers fail to reach their goal, then self-punishment results in the form of feelings of frustration or lack of competence to get work done effectively. The important point to note is that self-evaluation, whether positive or negative, requires the existence of a standard of comparison, i.e., a goal. This aspect of social learning theory is directly analogous to goal-setting theory, and social learning theory places a similar emphasis upon the importance of goals being specific, challenging, and realistic.

Social learning theory goes beyond goal-setting theory, however, in its explanation of *how* goals influence motivation via their role in self-reinforcement and self-regulation. The emphasis upon self-reinforcement is a particular strength of social learning theory since it provides us with a basis for explaining and understanding the vast amount of behavior in organizations that occurs in the absence of any immediate sources of external control or reinforcement.

Another strength of social learning theory lies in the fact that it also addresses the issues of how the cognitive sources of motivation are acquired and influenced. This is particularly helpful, since understanding how motivation is developed is essential if we wish to be able to influence the motivation of organization members. We now turn to a discussion of the processes which underlie the acquisition and development of motivation.

The Acquisition and Development of Motivation

Recall that according to social learning theory there are two major cognitive components of motivation: (1) motivation derived from expectations of attaining valued outcomes in the future contingent upon engaging in certain types of behavior; and (2) motivation derived from goal-setting and self-regulation processes. Each of these components is acquired or developed in different ways.

Acquisition of Expectations

Social learning theory outlines two processes that form the basis for learning about the relationships between effort and behavior (efficacy expectations) and between behavior and outcomes (outcome expectations). The two processes are referred to as learning by *response consequences* and learning by *modeling*.

1. Learning by Response Consequences. Learning by response consequences is directly analogous to the learning processes that form the basis for O.B. Mod., though with one important difference. In O.B. Mod., if a consequence increases the likelihood of the behavior that preceded it, then the consequence is referred to as a positive reinforcer, and that's that. There is no attempt made to explain how or why the reinforcer caused the frequency of the behavior to increase. In social learning theory, on the other hand, it is explicitly stated that positive reinforcers increase the likelihood of previous behaviors by increasing the *outcome expectation* that the behavior is followed by a positive outcome. Thus, reinforcers operate via their effects upon expectations.

2. Learning by Modeling. Social learning theory points out that learning would be an extremely slow, cumbersome, and frequently dangerous activity if everything had to be learned by response consequences. The rate of child mortality would rise dramatically if children had to learn not to cross streets on red lights by actually crossing on red lights and

experiencing the consequences. The popularity of tennis would probably decline precipitously if tennis pros taught people to play by simply putting a racquet in the novice's hand, telling him or her to start playing, and then waiting for the novice to make correct tennis strokes and reinforcing these. The point social learning theory makes is that a tremendous amount of learning occurs by the observation of *models*. Modeling permits people to learn very quickly what behaviors they should or should not be attempting to engage in (thus facilitating the development of efficacy expectations), and what behaviors lead to pleasant or desirable outcomes (facilitating the development of outcome expectatons). Modeling speeds up the learning process and indeed makes possible the learning of many complex patterns of behavior which would be difficult or impossible to learn by trial and error alone. The observation of models, via their impact upon a person's efficacy expectations and outcome expectations, has an important impact upon an individual's motivation to engage in behavior.

Acquisition of Goal Setting and Self-Regulation

Everyone engages in self-evaluation of their own behavior. We all share a tendency to respond positively to our accomplishments and to respond negatively to our failures. What determines the extent to which self-evaluation serves as a basis for motivation is the nature of the goals or standards which we set for ourselves and which serve as the comparison point for positive or negative self-evaluation. The higher the personal standards that are set, the greater the motivation. The standards which serve as the basis for self-reinforcing responses can be influenced either by *direct instruction* or by *modeling*.

1. Direct Instruction. People may be asked or instructed to set their personal performance standards at a certain level. The likelihood that a direct instruction to set performance standards at a given level will be accepted depends upon the degree of power that the person giving the instruction has and upon the esteem in which that person is held. Direct instructions regarding standards for self-reinforcement are often influential in situations such as parent-child relationships and superior-subordinate relationships at work.

2. Modeling. Modeling is a second important determinant of how standards are set for self-reinforcement. Individuals will tend to adopt standards that they observe in use by others whom they admire or wish to emulate.

Application to Organizations

Since the development of social learning theory is quite a recent phenomenon, there are as yet relatively few examples of its application in organizations. One successful application of the theory to supervisory training was carried out by Latham & Saari (1979b). In this application, a training program aimed at improving supervisors' interpersonal skills in dealing with their employees was explicitly designed to incorporate social learning theory principles. Training films were employed that provided participants with the opportunity to observe models demonstrating effective methods of dealing with employees. According to social learning theory, observing models of effective performance can increase both efficacy expectations and outcome expectations, as well as facilitating self-regulation by encouraging goal setting. The results of the behavioral-modeling-based training were clear-cut. Trainees responded to the program very positively and evidenced significant improvements in their supervisory skills and job performance.

Several other recent studies have reported positive results from the use of behavior modeling in training programs (Decker, 1980; Dowrick & Hood, 1981). Other researchers have also begun to examine the simultaneous effects of goal setting and contingent reinforcement systems on motivation and performance (Mowen, Middlemist, & Luther, 1981). In addition, debates between advocates of goal setting on the one hand and O.B. Mod. on the other may well result in an integration of these approaches within the social learning theory approach (Locke, 1980; Komaki, 1981).

MANAGERIAL IMPLICATIONS

The approaches to motivation discussed in this chapter were explicitly chosen because of their high degree of applicability to motivating individual performance in organizations. As a result, their implications for managerial practice are quite clear-cut.

1. *Managers should encourage their subordinates to set specific, challenging, but realistic goals for performance.* Research results indicate very consistently that *specific* goals have a stronger positive impact on performance than vague, general goals. This clearly implies that managers should make every effort to insure that their subordinates are provided with clear and precise performance goals with a specific time period agreed to for their attainment. In addition, *challenging* goals that are difficult to attain result in higher levels of motivation and performance than easy goals. However, it is essential that managers not set goals at such a high level that they are totally unrealistic and impossible to attain. Setting goals that are too difficult causes problems in two ways. First, the goals may simply not be accepted and hence have no impact upon motivation. Second, even if they are accepted, evidence indicates that repeated failure to achieve goals results

in frustration and ultimately the reduction of the influence of goal setting on performance (Zander & Newcomb, 1967).

2. ***Managers must insure that goals are accepted by subordinates.*** Goal setting is conducted in vain if the goals are not accepted by those who must perform well in order to attain them. Locke (1968) pointed this out in his original statement of goal-setting theory:

> . . . it is not enough to know that an order or request was made; one has to know whether or not the individual heard it and understood it, how he appraised it, and what he decided to do about it before its effects on his behavior can be predicted and explained. (p. 174)

Thus it may do no good for a manager to *tell* his or her subordinates what their goals are or should be. Goals will only have a positive impact on performance if they are accepted by subordinates as their own. This implies a need for dialogue between manager and subordinate, and a need for sensitivity on the part of the manager to take into account the unique strengths and weaknesses of each employee in the process of setting goals and objectives. The manager who attempts to impose goals upon subordinates unilaterally runs the risk of failing to reap the potential motivational benefits which the goal-setting process is capable of yielding.

3. ***Organizations need to rely less upon punishment and negative reinforcement and instead make greater use of positive reinforcement.*** The managerial and supervisory practices in many organizations appear to be based primarily upon punishment and negative reinforcement, in spite of the fact that these techniques are relatively inefficient and have many negative side effects. For example, in many organizations first-line supervisors have very few rewards at their disposal to positively reinforce their employees. Instead, supervisors are primarily expected to punish employees for poor performance, tardiness, and so on via reprimands, warnings, suspensions, and firings. Further, when workers are paid on an hourly basis, but receive their pay only every two weeks, it is unreasonable to expect that workers come to work every day because their behavior of coming to work will be rewarded in 2 weeks' time. Rather than using positive reinforcement, such pay systems are an example of negative reinforcement: rather than coming to work Monday in order to be paid Friday the worker comes to work Monday in order to *avoid* being fired. The technique being employed is negative, not positive, reinforcement. Organizations should decrease their reliance on the negative approaches of punishment and negative reinforcement and should make greater use of positive reinforcement. This in turn implies a need for managers to become much more aware of what the contingencies of reward and punishment are in their organizations. In addition, it implies a need for managers to take an active role in managing those contingencies so that desirable and effective behavior is reinforced in a systematic fashion.

4. ***Managers must clarify and strengthen subordinates' expectations regarding their ability to perform effectively (efficacy expectations) and regarding the attainment of valued outcomes contingent on performance (outcome expectations).*** Both efficacy expectations and outcome expectations can be clarified and increased by direct inputs to the subordinate from the manager. A manager can increase a subordinate's efficacy expectations regarding his or her ability to perform effectively by insuring that a subordinate clearly understands what is to be done (i.e., what behaviors are required), and by indicating his or her faith in the ability of the subordinate to perform effectively. Outcome expectations regarding the rewards the subordinate should expect as a result of effective performance can also be clarified by a manager who takes the time to explain exactly what the contingencies are and what the subordinate can expect to obtain if he or she performs effectively.

5. ***Managers should provide their subordinates with frequent access to models who are competent, set high personal standards, and receive outcomes contingent on performance.*** Modeling has a strong influence upon the acquisition of high expectations, and upon the tendency to set high personal standards for self-reinforcement. Thus managers should insure that individuals have frequent opportunities to observe the behavior of other members of the organization who are competent at performing their jobs (thus encouraging development of efficacy expectations), who receive rewards contingent upon effective task performance (thus encouraging development of outcome expectations), and who set high personal standards for self-reinforcement (thus encouraging similar high standards and facilitating the self-regulation process).

SUMMARY

Three major approaches to motivating individual performance were outlined, and their application in organizations was described and discussed.

Goal-setting theory suggests that motivation is determined by the conscious goals that people set for themselves. Goal-setting theory also identifies three critical motivational aspects of goals: (1) goal specificity—specific goals result in higher levels of motivation than vague or general goals; (2) goal difficulty—difficult goals lead to higher motivation than easy goals, as long as the goals are not impossibly unrealistic; and (3) goal acceptance—in order to be motivational, goals must be accepted as realistic and meaningful by those who must accomplish them.

Organization behavior modification (O.B. Mod.) is based upon the theories of operant conditioning and positive reinforcement developed by B. F. Skinner. The O.B. Mod. approach does not speculate about people's cognitions or inner mental states. Instead, the focus is upon observable behavior and its observable consequences. The emphasis of the approach is upon arranging the contingencies of reinforcement in organizations in such a way that the behaviors desired by the organization are positively reinforced. The O.B. Mod. approach points out the problems created by many organizational policies and procedures which employ punishment and negative reinforcement as means of influencing behavior. Positive reinforcement has been shown to be much more effective in establishing and maintaining effective patterns of behavior and performance.

Finally, social learning theory offers a comprehensive approach which combines the cognitive elements of expectancy theory and goal-setting theory with the reinforcement principles of the O.B. Mod. approach. According to social learning theory, motivation is determined by three sets of factors: efficacy expectations, outcome expectations, and self-regulation. Efficacy expectations are analogous to the effort → performance expectancies of expectancy theory, and refer to a person's perceptions of his or her ability actually to perform effectively. Outcome expectations, analogous to expectancy theory's performance → outcome expectancies, refer to perceptions of the likelihood of attaining valued outcomes as a result of effective performance. Self-regulation refers to the processes of self-reinforcement and self-punishment which people engage in as they evaluate their own performance against their personal goals and standards. Social learning theory shows how the reinforcement processes discussed in the O.B. ·Mod. approach influence the development of expectations and self-regulation. The theory also demonstrates the critical role which models and modeling play in the development and determination of motivation.

REVIEW QUESTIONS

1. According to goal-setting theory, how do goals exert their influence upon performance?
2. What are the three critical characteristics of goals which influence the extent to which goals lead to high levels of motivation?
3. What should a manager do to put goal-setting theory to use in his or her organization?
4. What factors appear to influence the effectiveness of MBO programs in organizations?
5. Define the term *reinforcement*.
6. What is the difference between positive and negative reinforcement?
7. What are some of the problems associated with the use of punishment in organizations?
8. What is the difference between continuous and partial schedules of reinforcement? Describe several of the different types of partial reinforcement schedules.
9. Describe the steps involved in the implementation of O.B. Mod. in organizations. What issues must the manager be sensitive to at each step?
10. Describe and discuss the three major components of motivation according to social learning theory.

11. Discuss how modeling can have an impact on each of the components of motivation contained in social learning theory.
12. Discuss some of the implications of social learning theory for managerial practices in organizations.
13. Discuss the ethical issues involved in applying O.B. Mod. in organizations. How, if at all, are these ethical issues different from those raised by other methods of attempting to influence individual behavior in organizations (e.g., MBO)?
14. Do you feel that cognitive or noncognitive approaches to motivation have greater validity and applicability to motivational problems faced by managers? Defend your position.

REFERENCES

Bandura, A. *Social learning theory.* Englewood Cliffs, N.J.: Prentice-Hall, 1977.

Carroll, S. J., Jr., & Tosi, H. L., Jr. *Management by objectives.* New York: Macmillan, 1973.

Decker, P. J. Effects of symbolic coding and rehearsal in behavior-modeling training. *Journal of Applied Psychology,* 1980, *65,* 627–634.

Dowrick, P. W., & Hood, M. Comparison of self-modeling and small cash incentives in a sheltered workshop. *Journal of Applied Psychology,* 1981, *66,* 394–397.

Ivancevich, J. M., & Smith, S. V. Goal setting interviews skills training: Simulated and on-the-job analysis. *Journal of Applied Psychology,* 1981, *66,* 697–705.

Ivancevich, J. M., McMahon, J. T., Streidl, J. W., & Szilagyi, A. D. Goal setting: The Tenneco approach to personnel development and management effectiveness. *Organizational Dynamics,* Winter 1978, 58–80.

Jamieson, B. D. Behavioral problems with management by objectives. *Academy of Management Journal,* 1973, *16,* 496–505.

Komaki, J. A behavioral view of paradigm debates: Let the data speak. *Journal of Applied Psychology,* 1981, *66,* 111–112.

Komaki, J., Barwick, K. D., & Scott, L. R. A behavioral approach to occupational safety: Pinpointing and reinforcing safe performance in a food manufacturing plant. *Journal of Applied Psychology,* 1978, *63,* 434–445.

Komaki, J., Heinzmann, A. T., & Lawson, L. Effect of training and feedback: Component analysis of a behavioral safety program. *Journal of Applied Psychology,* 1980, *65,* 261–270.

Latham, G. P., & Baldes, J. J. The practical significance of Locke's theory of goal setting. *Journal of Applied Psychology,* 1975, *60,* 122–124.

Latham, G. P., & Saari, L. M. Importance of supportive relationships in goal setting. *Journal of Applied Psychology,* 1979, *64,* 151–156. (a)

Latham, G. P., & Saari, L. M. Application of social-learning theory to training supervisors through behavioral modeling. *Journal of Applied Psychology,* 1979, *64,* 239–246. (b)

Latham, G. P., & Yukl, G. A. A review of the research on the application of goal setting in organizations. *Academy of Management Journal,* 1975, *18,* 824–845.

Levinson, D. J. Management by whose objectives? *Harvard Business Review,* July–August 1970, 125–134.

Locke, E. A. Toward a theory of task performance and incentives. *Organizational Behavior and Human Performance*, 1968, *3*, 157–189.

Locke, E. A. The ubiquity of the technique of goal setting in theories of and approaches to employee motivation. *Academy of Management Review*, 1978, *3*, 594–601.

Locke, E. A. Latham versus Komaki: A tale of two paradigms. *Journal of Applied Psychology*, 1980, *65*, 16–23.

Locke, E. A., Shaw, K. N., Saari, L. M., & Latham, G. P. Goal setting and task performance: 1969–1980. *Psychological Bulletin*, 1981, *90*, 125–152.

Luthans, F. *Organizational behavior.* New York: McGraw-Hill, 1981.

Luthans, F., & Kreitner, R. The management of behavioral contingencies. *Personnel*, July–August 1974, 7–16.

Luthans, F., & Kreitner, R. *Organizational behavior modification.* Glenview, Ill.: Scott, Foresman, 1975.

Luthans, F., & Schweizer, J. How behavior modification techniques can improve total organizational performance. *Management Review*, September 1979, 43–50.

Luthans, F., Paul, R., & Baker, D. An experimental analysis of the impact of a contingent reinforcement intervention on salesperson's performance behaviors. *Journal of Applied Psychology*, 1981, *66*, 314–323.

Matsui, T., Okada, A., & Mizuguchi, R. Expectancy theory prediction of the goal theory postulate, "The harder the goals, the higher the performance." *Journal of Applied Psychology*, 1981, *66*, 54–58.

McGehee, W., & Tullar, W. L. A note on evaluating behavior modification and behavior modeling as industrial training techniques. *Personnel Psychology*, 1978, *31*, 477–484.

Mento, A. J., Cartledge, N. D., & Locke, E. A. Maryland vs. Michigan vs. Minnesota: Another look at the relationship of expectancy and goal difficulty to task performance. *Organizational Behavior and Human Performance*, 1980, *25*, 419–440.

Mowen, J. C., Middlemist, R. D., & Luther, D. Joint effects of assigned goal level and incentive structure on task performance: A laboratory study. *Journal of Applied Psychology*, 1981, *66*, 598–603.

Pritchard, R. D., Hollenback, J., & DeLeo, P. J. The effects of continuous and partial schedules of reinforcement on effort, performance, and satisfaction. *Organizational Behavior and Human Performance*, 1980, *25*, 336–353.

Scott, W. E., Jr., & Erskine, J. A. The effects of variation in task design and monetary reinforcers on task behavior. *Organizational Behavior and Human Performance*, 1980, *25*, 311–335.

Skinner, B. F. *Science and human behavior,* New York: Macmillan, 1953.

Snyder, C. A., & Luthans, F. Using O.B. Mod to increase hospital productivity. *Personnel Administrator*, August 1982, 67–73.

Thorndike, E. L. *Animal intelligence.* New York: Macmillan, 1911.

Tosi, H. L., Jr., Rizzo, J. R., & Carroll, S. J., Jr. Setting goals in management by objectives. *California Management Review*, 1970, *12* (4), 70–78.

Watson, J. B. *Behavior: An introduction to comparative psychology.* New York: Holt, Rinehart, and Winston, 1914.

Zander, A., & Newcomb, T. T., Jr. Group levels of aspiration in United Fund Campaigns. *Journal of Personality and Social Psychology*, 1967, *6*, 157–162.

Chapter 7
DESIGNING REWARD SYSTEMS

In the previous two chapters we reviewed a number of the most prominent approaches to understanding the determinants of motivation in organizations. Many of the managerial implications of these theories of motivation made reference to the importance of insuring that rewards are provided to members of the organization contingent upon their having engaged in desirable or effective types of behavior. In this chapter we deal with the concrete practical issues involved in designing reward systems in organizations in such a way that the rewards provided by organizations facilitate and encourage effective performance by their members.

The chapter begins by drawing attention to an important distinction between two basic types, or categories, of rewards, known as *intrinsic* and *extrinsic* rewards. We then go on to outline the basic requirements that an effective reward system must fulfill, the alternative functions that reward systems can serve, and the important distinguishing characteristics of some of the most frequently employed organizational rewards. Next, we discuss some innovative approaches to reward system design that have recently appeared, and several examples of organizations that have implemented innovative strategies for rewarding their members.

INTRINSIC AND EXTRINSIC REWARDS

In discussing the nature of rewards and reward systems in organizations it is helpful to draw a distinction between two basic types, or categories, of rewards. The two types are referred to as *intrinsic rewards* and *extrinsic rewards*. Some examples of intrinsic and extrinsic rewards are contained in Table 7-1 and the basis of the difference between the two types of rewards is clarified in what follows.

Intrinsic Rewards

Intrinsic rewards are rewards that are valued in and of themselves. Intrinsic rewards are inherent to an activity itself, and their administration is not dependent upon the presence or actions of any other person or thing. In this sense, intrinsic rewards are frequently referred to as *self-administered*, since in a sense one administers intrinsic rewards to oneself. The most common types of intrinsic rewards relevant to organizational behavior are different types of feelings that people experience as a result of their performance on the job. Examples of intrinsic rewards falling into this category are things such as people's feelings of personal *competence* as a result of performing a job well, feelings of personal *accomplishment* or *achievement* associated with attaining a goal or objective, feelings of *freedom* from direction and personal *responsibility* arising from being granted autonomy regarding how work activities are to be carried out, and feelings of personal *growth* and *development* resulting from success in new and challenging areas of personal endeavor.

Intrinsic rewards have the potential to exert a strong influence upon the behavior of individuals in organizations and have a number of advantages as a means of rewarding and motivating effective performance. The advantages are inherent in the fact that intrinsic rewards are self-administered and experienced directly as a result of performing effectively on the job. First, the contingent relationship between effective performance and the administration of the reward is guaranteed by the fact that the experience of intrinsic rewards arises directly from a person's

TABLE 7-1
Examples of intrinsic and extrinsic rewards

Intrinsic rewards	Extrinsic rewards
Feelings of personal competence	Pay
Feelings of personal accomplishment	Fringe benefits and perquisites
Personal responsibility and autonomy	Recognition and praise
Feeling of personal growth and development	Promotion

perception that he or she is performing well. Second, the fact that intrinsic rewards are self-administered means that their effectiveness is not dependent upon the presence of a manager to administer the rewards or on the design of an organizational reward system. Finally, since intrinsic rewards are self-generated by individuals themselves they are of low cost to the organization compared to rewards such as monetary incentives.

The primary means of increasing the likelihood that people will obtain intrinsic rewards from their work lies in the way in which the organization designs the jobs of its members. It appears that the nature of the work itself is the primary determinant of the extent to which a person will be able to experience intrinsic rewards. Thus, the primary means to improved motivation and performance via the use of intrinsic rewards lies in the design of the work itself. This is a large and important topic that we will take up in detail in Chapters 9 and 10 on the design of work. In the remainder of this chapter we will focus primarily upon ways in which organizations can design effective systems for the contingent administration of extrinsic rewards.

Extrinsic Rewards

Just as intrinsic rewards are internally generated by the person him or herself, extrinsic rewards are externally generated by someone or something else. Extrinsic rewards do not follow naturally or inherently from the performance of an activity but are administered to a person by some external or outside agent. As such, extrinsic rewards are frequently used by organizations in attempts to influence the behavior and performance of their members, and a good deal of what we will have to say in this chapter on the design of reward systems will focus on extrinsic rewards.

Money is perhaps the most frequently used extrinsic reward in organizations and is administered in a variety of forms and on a variety of bases. Salaries, bonuses, merit increases, and profit sharing plans are indicative of some of the ways in which money is used as an extrinsic reward in organizations. Although the use of money as an extrinsic reward is pervasive, it is by no means the only extrinsic reward that can be used to influence the behavior and performance of organization members. Included in the list of available extrinsic rewards are things such as recognition and praise from superiors; promotions; perquisites such as expense accounts, cars, and luxurious offices; fringe benefits such as insurance, pensions, and stock options; and social rewards such as the opportunity to make friends and meet new people.

An important point to note about these extrinsic rewards is that they are all generated by sources external to (i.e., outside) the person. In order to obtain monetary rewards, fringe benefits, and perquisites, the individual is dependent upon the pay and reward policies of the organization, while obtaining praise and promotions depends upon the perceptions and judgments of the individual by his or her boss. This dependence upon external sources for the administration of rewards, combined with the fact that the majority of extrinsic rewards carry some considerable real cost to the organization, has two important implications for the design of extrinsic reward systems. First, the organization must attempt to insure as far as is possible that the costly extrinsic rewards it is offering are in fact rewards that are highly valued (and hence experienced as rewarding) by members of the organization. Second, great care must be taken to insure that, as far as is possible, extrinsic rewards are administered to organization members *contingent* upon effective performance.

Interaction of Intrinsic and Extrinsic Rewards

Up until quite recently it was generally assumed that intrinsic and extrinsic rewards have an independent and additive effect upon the motivation of individuals in organizations. In other words, it was assumed that a person's overall level of motivation to perform effectively is determined by the sum of the person's intrinsic and extrinsic sources of motivation. While this seems to be a fairly straightforward and common-sense position, several researchers have recently begun to question whether or not it is in fact valid.

What these researchers have been suggesting is that in situations in which individuals are experiencing a high level of intrinsic rewards, the addition of extrinsic rewards for performance may cause a *decrease* in the extent to which the intrinsic rewards are capable of motivating performance (Deci, 1971, 1975; Staw, 1975). Basically, the argument is that when people are performing some activity exclusively for the intrinsic rewards derived from the activity, they perceive that the reason for their performance lies solely in the fact that they personally derive feelings of satisfaction, enjoyment, or accomplishment from the activity. However, once extrinsic rewards are added (eg., pay), people's perceptions of the reasons they are performing the activity change. Instead of feeling that they are engaging in the activity because of the feelings of satisfaction and enjoyment it generates, they feel that they are engaging in the activity *because* of the money or other extrinsic reward offered. The result is a reduction (or "undermining") in the extent to which people will experience intrinsic rewards as a result of engaging in the activity.

Because this argument that adding extrinsic rewards for performing an activity may reduce the level of intrinsic rewards experienced runs contrary to our commonsense assumptions, it has attracted a good deal of research interest recently (cf. Condry, 1977; Lepper & Greene, 1978; and Boal & Cummings, 1981 for extensive discussions). Unfortunately, the results of this research are quite ambiguous. While some researchers have found evidence for a reduction in intrinsic rewards following the administration of extrinsic rewards for an activity (eg., Deci, 1971; Staw, 1974;

Lepper & Greene, 1976), others have failed to observe such an effect (eg., Arnold, 1976; Pinder, 1976; Fisher, 1978; Phillips & Lord, 1980; Boal & Cummings, 1981). A recent review (Boal & Cummings, 1981) concluded that fourteen studies have obtained results supporting the reducing or undermining effect of extrinsic rewards on intrinsic motivation, while ten studies failed to confirm such an effect. Perhaps of more importance to the practicing manager is the fact that *all* of the evidence supporting the undermining effect of extrinsic rewards on intrinsic motivation is derived from studies of college students, high school students, and preschool children. There is not a single research study that has altered the extrinsic reward systems in an actual work organization and observed any negative effects on the levels of intrinsic rewards experienced by organization members.

From the standpoint of the practicing manager, it is important to be aware of the fact that questions have been raised regarding the potential negative impact of extrinsic rewards upon individuals' levels of intrinsic motivation. However, managers must also be aware of the fact that there is not yet a single example of extrinsic rewards having a negative impact upon the intrinsic motivation of full-time employees in work organizations.

BASIC REWARD SYSTEM REQUIREMENTS[1]

There are four basic requirements that any reward system must fulfill if it is to be effective. These requirements apply to all types of reward systems in all types of organizations.

First, an organization's reward system must *provide individual members with sufficient rewards to satisfy their basic needs for food, shelter, safety, and security*. Fortunately, it is the case in most Western nations at least that the vast majority of organizations are capable of supplying their members with sufficient rewards to satisfy these basic needs, with the possible exceptions of the need for security. Some organizations, either by choice or by force of circumstance, do not fulfill individual members' needs for security.

Second, the rewards available to members of the organization must *compare favorably with those available in other organizations*. Another way of saying this is that the organization must insure that a situation of *external equity* exists. External equity implies that when members of the organization compare themselves to people doing comparable jobs in other organizations they feel that they are being rewarded in a fair and equitable manner.

---

[1]Material contained in this and subsequent sections of the chapter is based largely on the work of Edward Lawler (1971, 1976, 1977, 1981).

Third, *the distribution of rewards within the organization must be perceived to be done fairly and equitably*. This is sometimes referred to as insuring that a state of *internal equity* exists within the organization's reward system. As our discussion of equity theory in Chapter 5 pointed out, a situation of equity exists when a person compares him or herself to someone else in the organization and perceives that the ratio of inputs or contributions compared to the level of rewards received is approximately the same for both the person him or herself and for the other individual serving as a comparison point. The importance of insuring internal equity helps to reinforce the point that the ability of organizational reward systems to accomplish the purposes for which they are designed is dependent upon the way in which they are *perceived* by the members of the organization. It is not enough that the organization's reward systems be objectively fair and equitable; in order to be effective they must be perceived to be fair and equitable by organization members.

Finally, a reward system should be *capable of dealing with members of the organization as individuals*. People differ in their needs, desires, goals, and aspirations. A reward system that insists on treating all organization members equally and providing everyone with an identical set of rewards is ignoring this individuality. Thus, an effective reward system must be flexible in the types of rewards offered and the basis upon which these rewards are administered.

FUNCTIONS OF REWARD SYSTEMS

An organization's reward systems can be designed to accomplish a variety of purposes. There are generally thought to be three broad classes of individual behavior that a reward system may be designed to influence. These three classes of behavior are organizational membership, attendance, and performance.

Membership

Organizations typically provide individuals with a wide variety of rewards simply on the basis of their being members of the organization. Provision of an adequate level of rewards for organizational membership is important for two reasons. First, it can help the organization to attract and hire new members who are competent and highly motivated. A reward system which is perceived by prospective members to be inadequate or inequitable will make it difficult for the organization to attract the types of people necessary for success. Second, reward systems can help to retain competent organization members. A large body of research indicates that people who are dissatisfied with their jobs and dissatisfied with the rewards they are receiving from their jobs are more likely to quit (Lawler, 1971; Arnold & Feldman, 1982; Porter & Steers, 1973).

While turnover is not inherently harmful to an organization (as when marginal or incompetent employees leave and create opportunities to bring in new blood), it is harmful when the individuals leaving are highly competent and valued organization members (Staw, 1980; Staw & Oldham, 1978). Thus, the organization must insure that its most valuable members perceive the reward system to be both internally equitable (so that the valuable members feel that they are being fairly treated in light of their contributions) and externally equitable (so that valuable members are not attracted to another organization offering a higher level of rewards for their services).

Attendance

Absenteeism and tardiness are clearly costly to an organization. If an individual is absent from work and no one with adequate training and experience is available to step into the person's position, then either the person's work does not get done or it gets done by someone who lacks the necessary degree of skill and expertise required to perform the job well. Both of these results are undesirable and potentially costly to the organization. If, on the other hand, a person is absent and someone with adequate training and experience is immediately available to fill in, this implies that the organization is overstaffed, a situation that is extremely inefficient and costly to the organization in the long run. However you look at it, absenteeism is undesirable and expensive. A great deal of research has shown that satisfaction and absenteeism are inversely related to one another (Breaugh, 1981; Hammer & Landau, 1981). Reward systems can serve the important organizational function of reducing absenteeism to the extent that they: (1) create feelings of satisfaction among organization members; and (2) provide rewards to members for regular attendance.

Performance

Perhaps the most obvious potential function of a reward system is to reward and encourage effective performance by organization members. Research (Vroom, 1964; Lawler, 1973) has shown that rewards can facilitate effective performance when organization members perceive that effective performance results in the receipt of valued rewards within a reasonable period of time. However, although this relationship is relatively easy to state, Lawler (1977) has pointed out that it is extremely difficult to accomplish in practice.

> . . . research shows that organizations get the kind of behavior that is seen to lead to rewards employees value. In many ways this is a deceptively simple statement of the conditions that must exist if rewards are to motivate performance. It is deceptive in the sense that it suggests all an organization

has to do is to actually relate pay and other frequently valued rewards to performance. Not only is this not the only thing an organization has to do, but it is very difficult to accomplish (Tosi, House, & Dunnette, 1972; Whyte, 1955). Tying rewards to performance requires a good measure of performance, the ability to identify which rewards are important to particular individuals, and the ability to control the amount of these rewards that an individual receives. None of these things are easy to accomplish in most organizational settings. (pp. 170–171)

Lawler goes on to point out that if employees are to perceive that rewards are linked to performance two conditions must be met. First, the relationship between performance and rewards must be clearly visible to organization members. Second, an adequate level of trust must exist between employees and the management of the organization. Trust is a necessary prerequisite to the motivational properties of reward systems, since if employees do not trust management actually to deliver the rewards which are promised for effective performance, employees will not be motivated to perform effectively. Thus, the use of reward systems to motivate effective performance requires clear and visible links between performance and rewards and a climate of trust between those doing the work and those providing the rewards. A number of the innovative approaches to reward systems discussed later in this chapter are designed to increase visibility of rewards and trust in the reward system.

TYPES OF REWARDS AND THEIR CHARACTERISTICS

The range of potential rewards that could be employed in organizations is limitless. In practice however, organizations tend for the most part to employ a relatively small number of rewards. The choice of the actual reward or rewards to be used in any particular situation must be guided by the extent to which the reward or rewards are suitable for achieving the functions of maintaining membership of valued employees, encouraging regular attendance, and motivating effective performance.

Characteristics of Rewards

Lawler (1977) has identified five characteristics that rewards should have if they are to be optimally effective in achieving these purposes.

1. *Importance.* A reward cannot influence what people do or how they feel if it is not important to them. Given the vast range of differences among people, it will obviously be impossible to find any reward which is important to everyone in the organization. Thus, the challenge in designing reward systems is to find rewards that will appeal to as broad

a range of employees as possible and to employ a variety of rewards to insure that rewards will be available that are important to all the different types of individuals in the organization.

2. **Flexibility.** If reward systems are to be tailored to the unique characteristics of individual members and if rewards are to be provided contingent upon certain levels of performance, then rewards require some degree of flexibility. Flexibility of rewards is a necessary prerequisite to the design of individualized contingent reward systems.

3. **Frequency.** The more frequently that a reward can be administered, the greater its potential usefulness as a means of influencing employee performance. Thus, the more desirable rewards are those which can be given frequently without losing their importance.

4. **Visibility.** Rewards must be highly visible if employees are to perceive a relationship between performance and rewards. Visible rewards have the additional advantage of being capable of satisfying employees' needs for recognition and esteem.

5. **Cost.** Reward systems obviously cannot be designed without consideration being given to the cost of the rewards involved. Clearly, the lower the cost the more desirable the reward from the organization's viewpoint. High-cost rewards cannot be administered as frequently as low-cost rewards, and by the very nature of the costs they incur they detract from organizational efficiency and effectiveness.

Typical Rewards

Table 7-2 evaluates some of the most commonly employed organizational rewards in light of these five characteristics of effective rewards. Although the list of rewards contained in Table 7-2 is by no means exhaustive, it does cover the rewards in most frequent and widespread use in organizations.

TABLE 7-2
Characteristics of commonly used rewards

	Average importance	Flexibility in amount	Visibility	Frequency	Dollar cost
Pay	High	High	Potentially high	High	High
Promotion	High	Low	High	Low	High
Fringe benefits	High	Moderate	Moderate	Low	High
Status symbols	Moderate	High	High	Low	Moderate
Special awards and certificates	Low	High	High	Low	Low

SOURCE: Adapted from "Reward Systems", by E. E. Lawler, III. In J. R. Hackman & J. L. Suttle (Eds.), *Improving Life at Work.* Copyright © 1977 Scott, Foresman and Company. Reprinted by permission.

Pay

The use of pay as a reward in organizations is very nearly universal. Wages or salaries can serve to reward membership and attendance, while salary increments and cash bonuses can be used as rewards for good performance. As Table 7-2 makes clear, pay has many desirable characteristics as an organizational reward. It tends to be a highly important reward to most organization members, it permits a great deal of flexibility in its administration, and it can be provided with almost any desired degree of frequency. Pay has the potential to be a highly visible reward as well, though pay secrecy policies in many organizations can inhibit this potential advantage. The sole disadvantage of pay is its high dollar cost to the organization.

Promotion

Promotions are a form of organizational reward whose average level of importance to individuals tends to be quite high. Promotions also have the advantage of being highly visible to all members of the organization. Unfortunately, promotions also suffer from a number of disadvantages as a reward. They are extremely inflexible in amount; a person is either promoted or not. It is impossible to give someone a partial promotion. By their very nature, promotions also tend to occur relatively infrequently. Given a finite number of levels in the organizational hierarchy, promotion is only feasible on a relatively infrequent basis. Finally, promotions have high dollar cost associated with the higher salaries and benefits that generally accompany more senior positions.

Fringe Benefits

Organizations commonly have one fringe benefit package for hourly employees, another for salaried personnel, and a third for top-level management. These packages usually consist of some combination of benefits such as a pension plan, life, health and dental insurance plans, stock option purchase plans, and disability income plans. The main strength of fringe benefits as rewards lies in the fact that at least some of the benefits included in such packages are usually highly important to most organization members. Fringe benefit plans have the potential to be moderately flexible and visible, though organizations have only recently begun to recognize the potential for increasing the flexibility and visibility of their benefits packages. The primary weaknesses of fringe benefits as rewards lie in the low frequency with which benefits tend to be administered and with their relatively high costs. Also, people tend to underestimate their costs and hence their value as rewards.

Status Symbols

Most organizations use various types of status symbols as rewards. Things such as a larger office, a personal secretary, a company car, a convenient parking spot, and use of the executive dining room are all visible rewards that can be administered to individuals on a flexible basis. The importance of these rewards to individuals will naturally vary, but many are of at least moderate importance to many people. Status symbols tend to be moderately costly to the organization and can generally only be provided with low frequency.

Special Awards and Certificates

Organizations frequently provide their members with small awards or certificates as a form of recognition for long service or outstanding performance. The primary advantages of such rewards lies in the fact that they are generally of low cost, can be provided with a high degree of flexibility, and are highly visible. Unfortunately, such rewards can usually be provided with only low frequency and often are not highly important to their recipients.

PAY

Because pay is such an important and widely used reward in organizations, we need to focus upon it in some detail. We'll first outline the primary methods employed for the administration of pay and then examine more carefully some alternative methods of linking pay to performance.

Methods of Pay Administration

There are obviously a tremendous variety of alternative techniques available for determining how much pay a given person performing a particular job should receive. We'll outline briefly the four most common bases used by organizations in deciding exactly how much pay their members should receive.

Job Evaluation

Pay systems based on job evaluations relate the amount of pay that a person receives to the demands and requirements of the person's job. The more complex the job and the more demands that the job puts upon the incumbent, the higher the level of pay provided to the person performing the job. Job analyses, discussed in detail in Chapter 2, provide the basic information necessary for a job-evaluation-based pay system. The results of job analyses describing all of the activities required of the job incumbent and all of the skills and characteristics which an incumbent must exhibit are used to evaluate the job. The higher the evaluation, the higher the level of pay associated with the job. Some organizations develop and apply their own methods of evaluating jobs for pay purposes. Many others employ the services of consulting firms that specialize in job evaluation. Probably the best-known firm conducting such work is the Hay Associates, whose consultants evaluate jobs in terms of "Hay points." The more complex and difficult the job, the more points are assigned to it. Pay levels are then linked to the number of points assigned to the job. Job evaluation is an extremely widely used method of determining wage and salary levels in organizations.

Skill Evaluation

A much newer and much less widely used technique of pay administration ties the amount of pay received not to what a person's job *requires* him or her to do (as in the case of job evaluation), but rather relates pay to what the individual is *capable* of doing. The level of pay that an individual receives is thus based upon the range of job-related skills that a person has developed and demonstrated, regardless of the particular skills required by the person's current job. Skill-based pay systems are extremely new and will be discussed in more detail in a later section on recent innovations in the design of reward systems.

Seniority

Some organizations link pay to length of service with the organization, although it is rare that seniority serves as the only or even the primary basis of pay administration. Linking pay to seniority serves to encourage and reward continued membership in the organization.

Performance

Almost all organizations would *claim* that the amount of pay received by their salaried personnel is related to the level of performance of the individuals involved. While it is true that most organizations *attempt* to tie pay to performance, it is much less frequently the case that organizations succeed in accomplishing this worthwhile goal. Some of the difficulties involved in linking rewards to performance have been outlined earlier in this chapter. Many of the problems are related to determining exactly what should be measured in order to obtain an accurate indication of the quality and quantity of an individual's contribution to the effectiveness of the organization. In the next section we'll examine in more detail some of the issues and alternatives involved in relating pay to performance.

Overview

The methods of pay administration that we've outlined are not necessarily mutually exclusive. An organization might use one method for nonsalaried personnel at lower levels and a different method for higher-level salaried personnel. In addition, an organization might use several of the methods in combination with one another for determining the salary of organization members. For example, it is extremely common for organizations to use job evaluation as the basis for setting wage rates for nonsalaried jobs. The precise level of pay associated with a job would be set based upon a job evaluation. At the same time, it is equally common for organizations to use job evaluations for more senior salaried positions. However, such evaluations tend not to be used to set precise salary levels, but rather to define a range within which a person performing the job should be paid. The precise level of pay within the range for a given person is then frequently determined by a combination of performance evaluation and seniority. The higher the level of performance and the longer the person has occupied the position, the more the person's salary would tend toward the high end of the range.

Pay for Performance

As pointed out in the previous section, most organizations make some attempt to relate pay to performance. The precise methods used for linking pay and performance vary widely from one organization to another. In order to get a handle on the tremendous variety of pay-for-performance schemes it will be helpful to identify three primary dimensions along which such schemes can be classified.

Organizational Unit
The first dimension has to do with the *organizational unit* where performance is measured. The three most common alternative units for performance measurement are the individual, the work group, and the total organization. It is possible to design plans to link an individual's pay to his or her own performance, to the performance of the work group of which he or she is a member, or to the performance of the total organization.

Method of Measuring Performance
The second primary dimension of performance-pay plans concerns the method or methods used for *measuring performance*. In general, performance measurement techniques can be seen as varying on a continuum from the extremely objective to the extremely subjective. Performance criteria such as profit, costs, and sales are quite objective and relatively straightforward to measure. At the other extreme are such highly subjective measures as performance ratings of an individual carried out by his or her boss or work peers.

Types of Monetary Reward
The third major dimension along which performance-pay plans can be classified has to do with the *types of monetary rewards* offered by the plan. These generally fall into the two categories of salary and cash bonuses. Salary increments have the advantage of being cumulative from year to

year, while cash bonuses provide an effective performer with a large lump sum of cash at a single time.

Evaluating the Alternatives

By classifying pay-for-performance plans on the basis of the organizational unit where performance is measured (individual, group, organization), the type of performance measure used (productivity, cost effectiveness, superior's rating), and type of reward offered (salary, cash bonus) we come up with a total of eighteen different types of pay-for-performance plans. These different alternatives are summarized in Table 7-3 (the table contains only seventeen alternatives since it is not feasible for the effectiveness of a total organization to be rated by a superior and hence this alternative is excluded).

In addition to summarizing the available alternatives, Table 7-3 also contains ratings of the effectiveness of each type of plan on a set of four critical dimensions. The ratings vary from 1 to 5; the higher the rating (the

TABLE 7-3
Ratings of various pay incentive plans

		Tie pay to performance	Produce negative side effects	Encourage cooperation	Employee acceptance
Salary reward:					
Individual plan	Productivity	4	1	1	4
	Cost effectiveness	3	1	1	4
	Superiors' rating	3	1	1	3
Group	Productivity	3	1	2	4
	Cost effectiveness	3	1	2	4
	Superiors' rating	2	1	2	3
Organization-wide	Productivity	2	1	3	4
	Cost effectiveness	2	1	2	4
Bonus:					
Individual plan	Productivity	5	3	1	2
	Cost effectiveness	4	2	1	2
	Superiors' rating	4	2	1	2
Group	Productivity	4	1	3	3
	Cost effectiveness	3	1	3	3
	Superiors' rating	3	1	3	3
Organization-wide	Productivity	3	1	3	4
	Cost effectiveness	3	1	3	4
	Profit	2	1	3	3

SOURCE: Adapted from "Reward systems" by E. E. Lawler, III. In J. R. Hackman, & J. L. Suttle (Eds.), *Improving Life at Work*. Copyright © 1977 Scott, Foresman and Company. Reprinted by permission.

closer to 5) the higher the plan is on that dimension, while the lower the rating (the closer to 1) the lower the plan is on that dimension.

1. The first dimension is the extent to which the plan succeeds in creating the perception among members of the organization that pay is in fact tied to their own level of performance. As was previously pointed out, this perception of a direct link between performance and pay is essential if the pay system is to serve to motivate effective performance.
2. The second dimension along which the alternatives are assessed is the extent to which each system produces negative side effects. Although pay-for-performance plans are designed to motivate and encourage effective performance, they sometimes create unintended negative side effects such as the social ostracism of effective performers, defensive behavior, and a tendency to supply false data about performance.
3. The third dimension is the extent to which the plan encourages cooperative behavior among organization members. The relevance of this dimension in designing a pay-for-performance plan will obviously depend upon the extent to which cooperative behavior among individuals and groups is essential for organizational success.
4. Finally, performance-pay systems can be evaluated with regard to the extent to which they tend to be accepted by organization members. No plan can hope to have an impact upon motivation and performance if it is not accepted by the people to whom it is to be applied.

The ratings reveal a number of patterns regarding the various types of plans. Looking first at the extent to which the plans create the perception that pay and performance are linked, we notice the following: *(a)* individual plans rate more highly than group plans, which in turn rate more highly than organization-wide plans; *(b)* bonus plans rate more highly than salary plans; and *(c)* plans based on objective measures rate more highly than those employing subjective measures of performance. This leads to the conclusion that an individually based bonus plan employing objective performance measures will be most successful in creating the perception that pay is tied to performance.

Turning to the issue of negative side effects we see that, in general, most of the plans fare quite well in this regard in that they have a low tendency to generate such effects. The notable exceptions are individually based bonus plans. The problem with such plans lies in their potential to create situations in which high performers may be rejected or ostracized by their coworkers, people may be encouraged to report false performance data, or employees may band together to restrict production to undermine the system.

With regard to the encouragement of cooperation, the consistent pattern is that group and organization incentive plans tend to encourage cooperation, while individually based plans tend to undermine it. When pay is based upon the performance of the work group or the total organization, people tend to perceive that they stand to gain personally from improved performance of their coworkers. This perception in turn leads to a greater willingness to be cooperative and helpful. When pay is based on individual performance, on the other hand, such cooperation is not rewarded and hence not facilitated.

Finally, regarding employee acceptance, the ratings indicate that most pay incentive plans can achieve a moderate degree of employee acceptance. The primary exception is individually based bonus plans which generally meet with only a low degree of acceptance because of their tendency to induce competitiveness among individuals and the difficulties involved in administering such plans fairly. There is also a tendency for acceptance of salary plans to be somewhat higher than bonus plans, a result that is not surprising since salary increases are cumulative from year to year, while bonuses are not.

Our discussion of the strengths and weaknesses of the various pay incentive plans makes it clear that there is no one best plan which outperforms all others on all the dimensions. Thus it is impossible to come up with a single blanket recommendation regarding which type of performance-pay plan a given organization should implement. Rather, each organization must assess its unique situation and characteristics and choose the pay incentive system which best suits its needs and goals.

THE SCANLON PLAN

Organizations have developed a wide variety of different types of pay incentive plans. Many of these employ various combinations of individual, group, and organization-wide incentives. We will briefly examine one of the best-known examples of an incentive scheme in use today.

The Scanlon plan actually refers to a variety of types of pay incentive systems based on the original ideas of Joseph Scanlon. Although differences exist in the specific details of Scanlon plans implemented in different organizations, they all share certain common characteristics.

In practice the Scanlon plan involves a combination of group and organization pay incentives, an employee suggestion system, and a participative approach to assessing and evaluating suggestions that are made. Production committees are set up for each department in the organization. These committees consist of the supervisor or senior manager in the department and representatives of the employees, who may either be elected or appointed by the union. These production committees screen suggestions for productivity improvement from both employees and managers. Experience with this system indicates that the rate of suggestions is double that of normal suggestion plans and that approximately 80 percent of the suggestions made are usable. One organization, the Atwood Vacuum Machine Company, received over 25,000 suggestions from its

2000 employees during the first 14 years the Scanlon plan was in operation.

One of the main reasons that the Scanlon plan generates such a high rate of usable suggestions is the fact that the cost savings generated by suggestions that are accepted are paid to everyone in the department from which the suggestion originated. This helps encourage suggestions from everyone involved. In addition, under the Scanlon plan gains resulting from productivity improvements are paid in the form of a monthly bonus to all employees. Everyone receives a share in proportion to his or her wage or salary level.

Overall, the record of the Scanlon plan is quite positive (Geare, 1976; Lesieur & Puckett, 1969; Schulz & McKersie, 1973). The plan has been implemented in over 100 small- to medium-sized organizations, and by at least one large organization (Midland Ross). The most frequently cited benefits associated with the plan are greater organizational efficiency, increased participation in decision making, a greater willingness on the part of employees to accept change, and an improved climate of union-management relations.

Table 7-4 provides a brief description of three companies which have

TABLE 7-4
Three companies using Scanlon plans

		Atwood Vacuum Machine Co.	Parker Pen Co.	Pfaudler Co.
Nature of the organization	Number of employees	2000	1000	750
	Number of plants	6	1	1
	Union affiliation	3 (independent)	2 (AFL-CIO)	2 (AFL-CIO)
	Product	Automotive hardware	Writing instruments	Project engineering, glassteel, stainless steel, and food-filling equipment
	Type of production	High volume; competitive	High-volume consumer item	Custom and standard fabricating
Results	Annual bonuses as percent of basic salary	High 20% Low 5%	20% 5.5%	17.5% 3%
	Percent of months in which bonus paid	87%	85%	88%
	Highest monthly bonus paid	26%	30%	22%
	Correlation of bonuses paid and division profits	High	High	High

SOURCE: Adapted from "The Scanlon Plan has proved itself" by F. G. Lesieur & E. S. Puckett. *Harvard Business Review*, 1969, *47*, 109–119. Copyright © 1969 by the President and Fellows of Harvard College; all rights reserved.

implemented the Scanlon plan and a summary of the results they have achieved. At the time they were studied, these organizations had been employing the Scanlon plan for between 14 and 17 years. As these results indicate, the Scanlon plan can have significant positive benefits both in terms of bonuses received by individual employees and in terms of the profitability of the organizations as a whole.

RECENT INNOVATIONS IN REWARD SYSTEMS

There has been increased interest recently in the design of organizational reward systems. As a result, a number of innovative approaches have been developed to the administration of pay and other rewards for effective performance. This increased interest has largely arisen from recognition of the fact that pay, far from being an almost irrelevant factor in modern organizations, as suggested by theorists such as Maslow and Herzberg, is in fact an important determinant of the satisfaction and motivation of organization members. Edward Lawler has been a leading proponent of the importance of pay in organizations and has been in the forefront of the development and study of innovative approaches to pay. Lawler (1976) recently discussed five new approaches to the administration of pay in organizations which have been shown to be effective. These innovations are discussed below and their strengths and weaknesses are summarized in Table 7-5.

Cafeteria Fringe Benefits

Almost every organization rewards its members with some combination of pay and fringe benefits such as life insurance, health insurance, and pension plans. Quite commonly an organization has one standard fringe benefit package for nonsalaried employees, another for salaried employees, and a third for senior managers. The weakness of such approaches to fringe benefits is that they fail to take into account differences among individuals in the value and importance they place upon the different benefits available. Research consistently indicates that factors such as age, marital status, and number of children influence the extent to which individuals value different types of benefits (Glueck, 1978). For example, young, single members tend to value higher salaries and more vacations, and to be less concerned regarding things like insurance and pensions. Middle-aged members with young families value salaries and bonuses but tend to be less concerned with vacation time and more concerned with various types of insurance. Older members are concerned less with current salaries and more with pensions and retirement benefits.

A fringe benefit program that ignores these differences among people and treats all organization members identically fails to obtain the maxi-

TABLE 7-5
Overview of innovative approaches to pay

	Major advantages	Major disadvantages	Favorable situational factors
Cafeteria fringe benefits	Increased pay satisfaction	Cost of administration	Well-educated, heterogeneous work force
Lump-sum salary increases	Increased pay satisfaction; greater visibility of pay increases	Cost of administration	Fair pay rates
Skill-based evaluation	More flexible and skilled work force; increased satisfaction	Cost of training; higher salaries	Employees who want to develop themselves; jobs that are interdependent
Open salary information	Increased pay satisfaction, trust, and motivation; better salary administration	Pressure to pay all the same; complaints about pay rates	Open climate; fair pay rates; pay based on performance
Participative pay decisions	Better pay decisions; increased satisfaction, motivation, and trust	Time-consuming	Democratic management climate; work force that wants to participate and that is concerned about organizational goals

mum payoff from the considerable monetary investment involved in such fringe benefit programs. If fringe benefit plans are to assist the organization by increasing the levels of satisfaction and motivation of their members, the plans must be capable of responding to the significant differences among individuals in the value they place on the benefits available.

An innovative approach to the resolution of this problem is known as a cafeteria-style fringe benefit program. The term cafeteria is employed as an analogy, since under such a plan the organization presents its employees with a whole range of alternative benefits and permits the employees to pick and choose those that they individually value most up to some set maximum value (the employee's total compensation level). At one extreme an individual could take his or her compensation entirely in the form of salary with no other benefits, while at the other extreme an individual could in any given year opt for a reduction in salary and an increase in other benefits, such as insurance or pension contributions. A variant of the cafeteria-style plan requires all employees to accept a minimal level of certain benefits such as health and life insurance and then permits free choice in allocation of compensation beyond these minimal levels.

The advantages of cafeteria-style benefit plans are twofold. First, they increase employees' perceptions of the value of their total compensation package. Second, they increase the likelihood that employees will be satisfied with their pay and benefits package. This increased satisfaction is associated with lower levels of turnover and absenteeism and greater ease in attracting new members.

Although cafeteria fringe benefits have significant advantages, they are obviously not without their drawbacks. First, they tend to create bookkeeping difficulties for the organization, which must keep track of exactly who has chosen which benefits and insure that the benefits are properly administered and dispensed. Fortunately, the use of computer systems greatly alleviates the difficulties encountered and brings the problems down to quite manageable proportions. Second, the uncertainty regarding exactly how many people will choose each benefit can make it difficult for the organization to price certain benefits such as insurance, for which the cost to the organization is partially dependent upon the number of people choosing the benefit. This difficulty is particularly salient for smaller organizations and may result in some short-term costs to the organization in the early stages of a program until the numbers of employees choosing various options have stabilized and accurate pricing can be employed. Cafeteria-style fringe benefit programs have been successfully implemented and maintained in both large organizations (e.g., the Systems Division of the TRW Corporation, with 12,000 employees) and small organizations (e.g., the Educational Testing Service with 3000 employees).

Skill-Evaluation Pay Plans

Basing a person's salary upon the job-related skills which he or she possesses was previously mentioned briefly under our discussion of alternative methods of pay administration. The most common approach to pay administration in the past has been to base an employee's pay upon what the job requires the individual to do (this is referred to as the job-requirement or job-evaluation approach to pay administration). Skill-evaluation pay plans, on the other hand, base the amount of pay not on what the current job requires of the employee, but upon what that employee is capable of doing, as indicated by the range of job-related skills that the employee has demonstrated that he or she possesses. The wider the range of skills possessed, and hence the more jobs that a person is capable of performing, the higher the salary.

Skill-evaluation pay plans have been successfully implemented in organizations in Europe as well as in a number of North American plants operated by Procter and Gamble and General Foods. The plans have frequently been employed in plants organized and designed around work groups. In such situations group members are generally highly dependent upon one another for the effective performance of their group and a high level of rotation among jobs is common. A skill-evaluation pay plan is particularly well suited to such a situation since it increases the flexibility of the work force and encourages individuals to develop a broad perspective on the operation and effectiveness of the plant.

Where skill-evaluation pay plans are in effect, new organization members typically start at a basic pay rate and move up in salary as they demonstrate the skill to perform more and more jobs. Once all of the production jobs have been mastered the individual achieves the top or "plant" rate. Further salary increases can only be obtained by acquiring a specialty rate based upon the development of expertise in a skilled trade such as electricity or plumbing.

Skill-based pay plans are successful in developing a highly skilled and flexible work force and have also been found to lead to feelings of personal growth and development among the individuals participating in them. They are also perceived to be a fair method of administering pay. On the negative side, such plans can be costly to the organization in two respects. First, they require that the organization provide individuals with formal training and other opportunities to learn, such as on the job practice. These training costs can frequently become quite high. Second, as the majority of employees develop a wide variety of skills they must be paid accordingly, resulting in a highly paid work force. A final potential problem that needs to be noted can arise when individuals who have been encouraged to grow and develop their skills reach the top level and have nowhere further to go. Such individuals may become frustrated and unhappy if new avenues for development such as interplant transfers or special assignments are not identified.

Lump-Sum Salary Increases

Almost all organizations review the salaries of their members once a year to determine the amount by which the annual salary of each of their members will be increased. The amount of increase decided upon is then averaged over the number of pay periods in a year (e.g., twelve if members are paid monthly) and then each regular paycheck is incremented accordingly. Thus, it usually takes an employee an entire year actually to collect the full amount of the annual increase, and the increase is received in small installments. The advantages of this system from the organization's viewpoint are that the organization does not have to part with large amounts of cash at any one time and, further, the organization does not put itself in a position of having paid for services prior to their being rendered by the employee. At the same time, however, the practice of integrating annual increments into regular paychecks suffers both from the fact that it is an inflexible method of administering pay as a reward and from the fact that it serves to make even quite large annual salary increases relatively unnoticeable to the employee when they are averaged over many pay periods.

An alternative that a number of organizations have begun to experiment with is the administration of annual salary increases in a single lump sum. Under such a system the individual is informed of the amount of his or her annual salary increase and is then given the choice of how and when to receive the increase. The individual may choose to take the full amount immediately, to have the increment integrated into each regular paycheck, or to receive the increment in any combination of lump-sum payments and regular increments that may be convenient. Such a system has a number of advantages. First, it is an innovative approach to pay administration and can serve to encourage innovation and experimentation throughout the organization. Second, it makes the organization's pay system much more flexible and permits it to meet the unique needs of individual members rather than treating everyone in an identical fashion. Finally, it serves to make pay increments much more visible as an organizational reward, and hence increases the likelihood that individuals will perceive a link between effective performance and the receipt of rewards. Naturally, the greater visibility afforded by lump-sum increases will only be viewed as desirable by organizations that have in place an equitable pay system that effectively links pay to performance. If an organization's pay system is inequitable or does not tie pay to performance, then the greater visibility afforded by lump-sum increases will be more likely to create than eliminate problems.

Like all innovative approaches to pay, lump-sum increases are not without their drawbacks. They clearly create bookkeeping and record-keeping difficulties of keeping track of who has chosen which specific mode of receiving salary increases. Again, computerization has made such problems eminently manageable. A more serious problem has to do with the cost to the organization of providing individuals with the full amount of their increase at a single time, prior to the individual actually having earned it. Most organizations that employ lump-sum increases deal with this problem by treating a lump-sum increase as a loan on which the employee is charged a low rate of interest until the work has been done to earn the increase. Individuals who quit prior to the end of the year for which they have received a lump-sum increment are expected to repay that portion they have not yet earned (e.g., one-third of the total if they were to quit 8 months after receiving the lump sum and hence 4 months or ⅓ of a year prior to "earning" the full increment). There will naturally be some losses associated with such a program from employees who leave without repaying the unearned amount of their lump-sum increases.

Overall, the advantages of lump-sum increases in terms of increased flexibility and visibility of the reward system appear to outweigh quite clearly the potential disadvantages.

Open Salary Information

Pay secrecy is standard practice in most organizations. The precise amount of money being earned by individual members is treated as confidential information. The most common rationale for maintaining secrecy is that members of the organization prefer a secrecy policy and would not like others to know how much they are making. However, such a justification is almost always an assumption or fabrication on the part of managers when they are asked to explain why pay is kept secret. It is extremely rare that an organization has systematically polled its members and discovered that they do indeed prefer pay secrecy. An alternative explanation for the prevalence of pay secrecy is that it permits managers to avoid having to explain and justify their pay decisions to their subordinates.

Although pay secrecy does have this advantage of making life easier and less demanding for the manager making pay decisions, it also has a number of disadvantages for the organization. Research indicates that when pay is secret individuals consistently and significantly overestimate the amount of pay being received by others at the same level in the organization. The research further shows that the degree to which people overestimate the pay of others at the same level is directly related to levels of dissatisfaction. The more a person overestimates the pay of others, the more dissatisfied that person becomes. When pay rates are kept secret, the organization is incapable of correcting such false impressions since the organization's policy is to withhold precisely that information necessary to correct the erroneous impressions.

A further disadvantage of pay secrecy is that it reduces the potential of pay to serve as a positive motivating force. As we pointed out earlier, if pay is to motivate effective performance, two factors must be present. First, individuals must perceive that pay is related to performance, and second, an adequate level of trust must exist such that individuals trust that the organization will in the future reward them with more pay if they work hard now in order to perform effectively. Pay secrecy effectively under-mines both of these essential factors. First, since pay is secret it is extremely difficult for the individual to determine whether or not the organization does or does not relate pay to performance. The individual has only his or her own personal experience to go on and is denied access to information regarding how the organization treats all the rest of its members. Second, a policy of pay secrecy is itself a manifestation of a low level of trust between the organization and its members. This low level of trust again impedes the capacity of the pay system to motivate effective performance.

The obvious alternative to pay secrecy is a policy of openness regard-ing pay. By sharing pay information openly, the organization can contrib-ute to the creation of a climate of greater trust and can help clarify for employees the relationship between pay and performance. Both these factors can lead to increased motivation if it is in fact the case that the organization's pay system does relate pay to performance. If the pay system does not successfully tie pay to performance, then sharing pay information will make the inequities more obvious and clearly would not be expected to increase motivation.

A further potential advantage of an open pay system lies in the fact that it may encourage members to make better and more equitable pay decisions. When pay is secret there may be little motivation for the manager to give a lot of attention to pay decisions since he or she knows that there is little if any chance that those decisions will be challenged or questioned. On the negative side, however, an organization implementing an open pay policy must take care that managers do not respond by paying all of their subordinates equally in order to avoid having to explain and justify their decisions. Such a practice would obviously undermine any potential benefits to be gained from open pay information.

A decision to switch from a policy of pay secrecy to one of open salary information must obviously be handled with care. If an organization is characterized by a long history of pay secrecy and low levels of trust, an abrupt switch to open pay information may be neither feasible nor desirable. A gradual opening of pay information may be more effective in such situations, beginning, for example, with publication of salary ranges and averages for various positions and moving gradually over time to full, open salary information. An organization must also attend to difficulties in measuring performance when implementing open salary information. As jobs become more complex, the criteria for evaluating performance effectiveness frequently become more ambiguous. In such situations, a policy of full salary openness may not be desirable, since individuals may disagree about the quality of performance of different individuals.

What is critical for all types of jobs at all levels is for managers to rethink their policies regarding pay information. Keeping pay information secret because "we've always done it that way" or because it makes life easier for the managers who don't have to justify their decisions is scant justification for a policy that clearly undermines the potential of pay to serve as a positive motivator of effective performance.

Participative Pay Decisions

A relatively recent innovation that has been tried by some organizations is to involve individuals in the process of setting salaries by permitting all members of the organization to participate directly in pay decisions. Several organizations that have permitted employees to participate directly in the design of salary or bonus systems found that the participatively designed systems resulted in improved attendance, reduced turnover, and higher levels of satisfaction (Lawler, 1976; Jenkins & Lawler, 1981). Other organizations that have permitted decisions regarding annual pay increments to be made by work peers have found that peer groups tend to make such decisions in a highly responsible manner and that such a system results in a high degree of satisfaction with pay and a high level of commitment to the organization.

Naturally, a participative approach to pay decisions is not without its potential difficulties, particularly in situations in which pay decisions are made by work peers and no clear-cut standards of performance (such as number of items produced and sales volume) are available. When the organization places no restriction on the total amount of money available for salary increases, peer groups frequently find it hard to say no to a raise for each member. On the other hand, when the organization does put a limit on total raises available and performance standards aren't clear-cut, there is a tendency for a peer group to decide on equal raises for everyone in order to avoid conflict and disagreement. Such an approach undermines the capacity of the pay system to motivate effective performance since all receive an equal increment regardless of their performance. Finally, as is the case with all types of participative management, the participative process itself is time-consuming and results in a reduction in the total time available for individuals to devote to their primary work responsibilities.

MANAGERIAL IMPLICATIONS

In this chapter we have presented a considerable amount of material regarding the nature of rewards, the characteristics of organizational reward systems, and the latest ideas regarding innovative approaches to reward system design. This discussion leads to a variety of implications for management practice regarding the design and operation of organizational reward systems.

1. ***If reward systems are to encourage effective performance, managers must insure that systems provide rewards contingent upon effective performance.*** Organizations invest a tremendous proportion of their resources in the rewards provided to organization members in the form of salaries, benefits, and other job perquisites. If this investment is to achieve the maximum potential payoff in terms of the effective performance of organization members, it is essential that at least some proportion of the rewards be provided *contingent* upon the performance achieved by organization members. It is further essential that the members of the organization be *aware* of the links that exist between effective performance and obtaining valued rewards.

2. ***Managers need to take into account the nature of their subordinates in the design of organizational reward systems.*** It is obvious that people differ in regard to their wants, needs, desires, and values. As a result, different individuals will find different types of rewards differentially satisfying and motivating. This implies the desirability of employing a variety of organizational rewards in a reasonably flexible fashion. In addition, people also differ in their level of education, their commitment to the goals of the organization, their desire to grow and develop new skills, and so on. Such factors will influence the likelihood of success of many of the innovative reward systems we have described. For example, a cafeteria-style fringe benefit system will be more likely to serve as a source of motivation with a relatively well-educated work force capable of making intelligent trade-offs among the alternative benefits offered. Similarly, the potential success of a skill-based salary system will depend upon the extent to which individuals care about developing their skills and abilities. Finally, the various participative approaches to reward system design can only be effective if the members of the organization share its goals and are committed to working toward the success of the total organization.

3. ***Organizations must insure that their reward systems treat employees in a fair and equitable fashion.*** Individuals who feel that they are being rewarded in an unfair or inequitable fashion are unlikely to be highly motivated to perform effectively and are much more prone to stay away from work (absenteeism) or to leave the organization altogether (turnover). As a result, it is essential that managers seek to establish equity in their reward systems and insure that the reward system is accurately *perceived* to be fair and equitable by members of the organization.

4. ***Managers need to insure that the organization's reward systems are in harmony with the overall management style of the organization.*** Problems are almost always created when an organization attempts to make a change in one part of its operations that is inconsistent or at odds with the organization's general management style and climate. Organizations can be conceived of as varying along a continuum from being very open, democratic, and participative at one extreme to being very closed, authoritarian, and directive at the other. Some of the innovative approaches to reward system design that we've discussed, particularly participative pay systems, will be much more likely to be successful in an open and participatively managed organization than in a closed and authoritarian one. Regardless of the particular reward system innovation under consideration, its likelihood of success is much higher if it is consistent with and reinforced by the organization's predominant style of management. Figure 7-1 outlines the appropriateness of the various innovative approaches based upon the type of management style in place in the organization and the fairness of the present pay system. As the figure makes clear, the range of options available for reward system innovation is greater when the management style is participative rather than authoritarian, and when pay rates are fair rather than unfair.

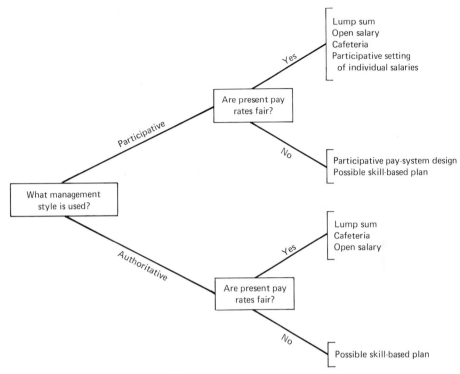

FIGURE 7-1
Guide to choosing among new approaches to pay administration. [SOURCE: Adapted from E. E. Lawler, III, "New Approaches to Pay: Innovations that Work," *Personnel*, vol. 53(5), 1976, pp. 11–23. Copyright © 1976 by AMACOM, a division of American Management Associations. All rights reserved.]

SUMMARY

Four basic requirements that a reward system must be capable of fulfilling are as follows: (1) that sufficient rewards be supplied to satisfy basic needs; (2) that the system be perceived to be equitable both internally (compared to other people in the same organization) and (3) externally (compared to others in different organizations); and (4) that the individuality of members be respected. Reward systems meeting these basic requirements can then be designed to influence the membership, attendance, and performance of individuals in an organization.

A wide variety of rewards can be employed in organizations varying from pay to promotions to fringe benefits, and so on. Rewards differ in the extent to which they are important to people, as well as in terms of the flexibility, frequency, and visibility with which they can be employed by organizations. An organization must evaluate the various rewards available to it in these terms, as well as in terms of their cost, in determining the overall design of its reward system.

Pay is the most widely employed reward in organizations. The amount of pay received by individual organization members can be determined by the complexity of their jobs, the variety of skills they possess, or the level of performance they attain. Pay-for-performance plans are quite popular since they provide a basis for using the organizational reward system to motivate effective performance. A variety of types of pay-for-performance plans have been developed and tried with varying degrees of success. One of the best-known and widely successful organization-wide approaches is the Scanlon plan.

A number of innovative approaches to the design of reward systems have appeared recently. Among these are cafeteria-style fringe benefit programs, lump-sum salary increases, skill-based evaluations, open salary information systems, and participative pay decision schemes. All of these innovations have been shown to have promise, although the applicability of any innovative technique will depend upon the management style of the organization, the fairness of the current pay system, and the characteristics of the members of the work force affected by the innovation.

REVIEW QUESTIONS

1. Discuss the distinction between intrinsic and extrinsic rewards.
2. Do intrinsic and extrinsic rewards have an additive impact upon a person's total motivation to perform effectively at work? Discuss.
3. Do you feel that organizations should attempt to influence the motivation and behavior of people primarily via intrinsic rewards or extrinsic rewards? Defend your position.
4. Outline the four basic requirements that any reward system must fulfill if it is to be effective.
5. Briefly describe three basic functions that reward systems can be designed to fulfill. Which function or functions do you feel organizations should focus their reward systems on? Why?
6. List several of the rewards most commonly employed in organizations. Discuss their relative strengths and weaknesses in terms of the critical reward characteristics presented.
7. Compare and contrast at least three different methods of determining the amount of pay that an individual should receive. Which methods would you recommend under what circumstances?
8. Discuss the relative merits of individual, group, and organization-wide merit plans.
9. What are the key characteristics of the Scanlon plan? Would you recommend its implementation in all organizations? Why?
10. Discuss the relative costs and benefits of cafeteria-style fringe benefit plans and lump-sum salary increase plans.
11. What are some of the common problems encountered with skill-based evaluation plans?

12. Under what conditions would you recommend that an organization implement an open salary information system and participative pay decisions?
13. How does the management style of the organization influence the appropriateness of various innovative approaches to reward systems?
14. Why do you think that so many organizations have a policy of pay secrecy? Do you feel that this is a healthy situation?

REFERENCES

Arnold, H. J. Effects of performance feedback and extrinsic reward upon high intrinsic motivation. *Organizational Behavior and Human Performance,* 1976, *17,* 275–288.

Arnold, H. J., & Feldman, D. C. A multivariate analysis of the determinants of job turnover. *Journal of Applied Psychology,* 1982, *67,* 350–360.

Boal, K. B., & Cummings, L. L. Cognitive evaluation theory: An experimental test of processes and outcomes. *Organizational Behavior and Human Performance,* 1981, *28,* 289–310.

Breaugh, J. A. Predicting absenteeism from prior absenteeism and work attitudes. *Journal of Applied Psychology,* 1981, *66,* 555–560.

Condry, J. Enemies of exploration: Self-initiated versus other-initiated learning. *Journal of Personality and Social Psychology,* 1977, *35,* 459–477.

Deci, E. L. The effects of externally mediated rewards on intrinsic motivation. *Journal of Personality and Social Psychology,* 1971, *18,* 105–115.

Deci, E. L. *Intrinsic Motivation.* New York: Plenum, 1975.

Fisher, C. D. The effects of personal control, competence, and extrinsic reward systems on intrinsic motivation. *Organizational Behavior and Human Performance,* 1978, *21,* 273–287.

Geare, A. J. Productivity from Scanlon-type plans. *Academy of Management Review,* 1976, *1,* 99–108.

Glueck, W. F. *Personnel: A diagnostic approach* (rev. ed.). Dallas, Texas: Business Publications, Inc., 1978.

Hammer, T. H., & Landau, J. C. Methodological issues in the use of absence data. *Journal of Applied Psychology,* 1981, *66,* 574–581.

Jenkins, G. D., Jr., & Lawler, E. E., III. Impact of employee participation in pay plan development. *Organizational Behavior and Human Performance,* 1981, *28,* 111–128.

Lawler, E. E., III. *Pay and organizational effectiveness.* New York: McGraw-Hill, 1971.

Lawler, E. E., III. New approaches to pay: Innovations that work. *Personnel,* 1976, *53*(5), 11–23.

Lawler, E. E., III. Reward systems. In J. R. Hackman & J. L. Suttle (Eds.), *Improving life at work.* Glenview, Illinois: Scott, Foresman and Company, 1977.

Lawler, E. E., III. *Pay and organization development.* Reading, Mass.: Addison-Wesley, 1981.

Lepper, M. R., & Greene, D. Turning play into work: Effects of adult surveillance and extrinsic rewards on children's intrinsic motivation. *Journal of Personality and Social Psychology,* 1976, *31,* 479–486.

Lepper, M. R., & Greene, D. Overjustification research and beyond: Towards a means-end analysis of intrinsic and extrinsic motivation. In M. R. Lepper & D. Greene (Eds.), *The hidden costs of rewards: New perspectives on the psychology of human motivation.* Hillsdale, N.J.: Erlbaum, 1978.

Lesieur, F., & Puckett, E. The Scanlon plan has proved itself. *Harvard Business Review,* Sept.–Oct. 1969, *47,* 109–118.

Phillips, J. S., & Lord, R. G. Determinants of intrinsic motivation: Locus of control and competence information as components of Deci's cognitive evaluation theory. *Journal of Applied Psychology,* 1980, *65,* 211–218.

Pinder, C. C. Additivity versus nonadditivity of intrinsic and extrinsic incentives: Implications for work motivation, performance and attitudes. *Journal of Applied Psychology,* 1976, *61,* 693–700.

Porter, L. W., & Steers, R. M. Organizational, work, and personal factors in employee turnover and absenteeism. *Psychological Bulletin,* 1973, *80,* 151–176.

Schulz, G., & McKersie, R. Participation-achievement-reward systems. *Journal of Management Studies,* 1973, *10,* 141–161.

Staw, B. M. The attitudinal and behavioral consequences of changing a major organizational reward. *Journal of Personality and Social Psychology,* 1974, *29,* 742–751.

Staw, B. M. *Intrinsic and extrinsic motivation.* Morristown, N.J.: General Learning Press, 1975.

Staw, B. M. The consequences of turnover. *Journal of Occupational Behavior,* 1980, *1,* 253–273.

Staw, B. M., & Oldham, G. R. Reconsidering our dependent variables: A critique and empirical study. *Academy of Management Journal,* 1978, *21,* 539–559.

Tosi, H. L., Jr., House, R. J., & Dunnette, M. D., (Eds.), *Managerial motivation and compensation.* East Lansing: Michigan State University Business Studies, 1972.

Vroom, V. H. *Work and motivation.* New York: Wiley, 1964.

Whyte, W. F. (Ed.). *Money and motivation: An analysis of incentives in industry.* New York: Harper & Row, 1955.

CHAPTER 8

JOB SATISFACTION: CAUSES AND CONSEQUENCES

Over the past 10 years, there has been renewed interest in job satisfaction. Comments of workers interviewed in *Work in America* (1973), a Presidential task force report on the "quality of working life," reflect some of the dimensions of this recent concern:

> I didn't go to school for four years to type. I'm bored; continuously humiliated. They sent me to Xerox school for three hours. . . . I realize that I sound cocky, but after you've been in the academic world, after you've had your own class (as a student teacher) and made your own plans, and someone tries to teach you to push a button—you get pretty mad. They even gave me a gold plated plaque to show I've learned how to use the machine." (p. 44)

> You can't wait to get out and get a job that will let you do something that's really important. . . . You think you're one of the elite. Then you go to a place like the Chicago Loop and there are all these lawyers, accountants, etc., and you realize that you're just a lawyer. No, not even a lawyer—an employee; you have to check in at nine and leave at five. I had lots of those jobs—summers—where you punch in and punch out. You think it's going to be different, but it isn't. You're in the rut like everybody else." (p. 45)

This concern for the attitudes that people hold about their jobs and the organizations in which they work, then, is important for two reasons.

First, how employees feel about their work is important in and of itself. Whether people find their work satisfying or frustrating, challenging or boring, meaningful or pointless is a strong personal concern. Second, managers are concerned about the impact of employees' attitudes on performance and productivity.

This chapter addresses the major issues in job satisfaction. First, the chapter defines job satisfaction and identifies its major sources. Second, we examine a model of job satisfaction—what determines whether, overall, an employee feels satisfied or dissatisfied. Third, we consider the consequences of job satisfaction for a variety of job behaviors—performance, absenteeism, turnover, unionization, and employee mental and physical health. Fourth, the chapter turns to some of the broader issues of job satisfaction: at the societal level, what changes have occurred in the levels of job satisfaction and dissatisfaction? Why have these changes occurred? What are the consequences of these changes? Finally, the chapter concludes with a section on the uses of job satisfaction surveys, and some guidelines are presented on how to use and interpret those surveys more effectively.

SOURCES OF JOB SATISFACTION

For our purposes, *job satisfaction* will be defined as *the amount of overall positive affect (or feelings) that individuals have toward their jobs.* When we say that an individual has high job satisfaction, we mean that the individual generally likes and values the job highly and feels positively toward it.

Identifying the sources of this overall job satisfaction is one of the most heavily researched areas in organizational behavior. Over the past 25 years alone, there have been well over 3000 studies that have tried to discover what *specific* aspects of the job situation are the most important sources of general job satisfaction. The voluminous research on the causes of job satisfaction has been driven by three major perspectives (Locke, 1976).

1. ***Industrial engineering.*** As early as the 1920s, industrial engineers were investigating the impact of working conditions and pay on job satisfaction. Variables like piece-rate incentives, rest pauses, and environmental factors such as light and noise all figured into early industrial engineering research on job satisfaction. Frederick Taylor's scientific management was predicated on the assumption that work design, working conditions, and compensation plans could all be harnessed together to insure high production and high employee morale.
2. ***Human relations movement.*** During the 1930s and 1940s, more and

more attention was paid to the role of the work group and the supervisor in determining job satisfaction. In the Hawthorne Studies of employee satisfaction at Western Electric, Mayo (1933) and Roethlisberger and Dickson (1939) found strong evidence that workers' satisfaction with their work groups and supervisors influenced their job performance. A series of studies of leadership conducted with the armed forces during World War II (e.g., Halpin & Winer, 1957) further reaffirmed the impact of supervisory practices and the informal work group on general job satisfaction.

3. ***Work itself (or growth) school.*** An important monograph published by Herzberg in 1959 signaled a new trend which was to refocus attention on the work itself as a determinant of job satisfaction. This new emphasis suggested that real satisfaction with the job could only be provided by allowing individuals enough responsibility and discretion for them to be challenged. Much of the work on job redesign in the 1960s and 1970s addressed itself to specifying which attributes of the job itself were most critical in determining job satisfaction.

In this section, we examine the six most frequently studied causes of job satisfaction: working conditions and wages (industrial engineering tradition); the work group and the supervisor (human relations tradition); the job itself and promotional opportunities (the work itself, or growth, traditions). We will discuss each of these factors in order of their importance as determinants of job satisfaction. We will see that, in general, pay and the work itself are the most important sources of job satisfaction, that promotional opportunities and supervision are moderately important sources of job satisfaction, and that the work group and working conditions are relatively minor sources of job satisfaction.

Pay

Wages do play a significant role in determining job satisfaction and are as significant to white-collar workers as to blue-collar workers. In a study of almost 2000 managers, Lawler and Porter (1963) found that the amount of wages received was very positively related to satisfaction, even with managerial level held constant. Smith and Kendall (1963) report a similarly strong relationship between the mean annual earnings of blue-collar workers in twenty-one plants and their mean job satisfaction.

While not all research ranks pay quite so important as a source of job satisfaction as the above two studies do, pay is unquestionably a key determinant of job satisfaction. First, money is very instrumental in fulfilling several important needs of the individual: it facilitates the obtaining of food, shelter, and clothing and provides the means to pursue valued leisure interests outside of work. Second, pay can serve as a symbol of achievement and a source of recognition. Employees often see pay as a reflection of management's concern for them (see Chapter 7).

Generally, benefits have not been found to have as strong an influence on job satisfaction as direct wages (Lawler, 1971). Employees tend to underestimate how much they actually receive in indirect benefits and tend to undervalue some of them (e.g., young workers tend to undervalue receiving life insurance).

The Work Itself

Since the Herzberg, Mausner, and Synderman monograph, *The Motivation to Work*, was published in 1959, increasing attention has been paid to the role the work itself plays in determining job satisfaction. The evidence accumulated since that time is that the work itself is indeed a major determinant of job satisfaction.

While a fuller treatment of job redesign appears in Chapter 9, three of the more important aspects of the work itself that are sources of job satisfaction are briefly discussed below.

Control over Work Methods and Work Pace

Scientific management advocates like the Gilbreths (1919) believed that a great deal of inefficiency in industry stemmed from the fact that workers who were given a job to do were also permitted to decide how that job should be done. Consequently, over the years, the *planning* of a job became separated from the *doing* of it. Workers lost control over how they would carry out their jobs. Early industrial engineers were equally concerned about regulating the pace of work—how quickly operations should be performed, how many rest breaks were allowable, etc. Engineers developed work systems and technologies that also took the pace of work out of the control of workers.

Evidence now suggests that control over work methods and work pace are strongly linked to job satisfaction (Hackman & Lawler, 1971). In two classic studies of the auto industry, in fact, mechanical pacing of the job was the most disliked feature of the work (Walker & Guest, 1952; Walker & Marriott, 1951).

Use of Skills and Abilities

White's (1959) pioneering work on motivation suggests that people derive pleasure from coping successfully with their environments. The organizational research on the use of skills and abilities substantiates White's work. Using valued skills and abilities provides workers with a sense of self-pride, a sense of competence, and a sense of self-confidence. For instance, Vroom (1962) found a very strong relationship between the opportunity for self-expression in the job and job satisfaction for 500 hourly blue-collar workers in Canadian oil refineries.

Variety

Another tenet of scientific management was task specialization, breaking down the job into its most basic operations and making each person responsible for (and expert in) the fewest number of basic operations possible. Indeed, it now appears that specialization and repetitiveness lead consistently to job dissatisfaction (Krech & Crutchfield, 1948; Mann & Hoffman, 1960).

Why skill variety affects job satisfaction has a lot to do with the *amount of stimulation* the worker receives. *Moderate* amounts of stimulation give workers the greatest satisfaction. Highly repetitive operations have no novelty, provide very little stimulation, and lead to psychological fatigue; too highly stimulating jobs can cause psychological "overload," physical stress, and early job "burnout" (Hebb, 1949; McClelland et al., 1953; Scott, 1966).

It seems that a moderate-sized cluster of related tasks is optimal in generating job satisfaction. Workers' feelings of accomplishment are also enhanced if they work on a "whole" piece of work or if their personal contribution to the whole is clear and visible (Hackman & Lawler, 1971).

Promotions

There is substantial evidence that promotional opportunities do affect job satisfaction. Probably the most well-known study on promotions was done in an electronics manufacturing organization by Sirota (1959). Sirota found a negative relationship between measures of promotional frustration (obtained by subtracting people's estimates of how soon they would like a promotion from their estimates of when they expected to receive it) and measures of attitudes toward the company. In a study of a Canadian oil refinery, Patchen (1960) found that people who felt that they deserved to have been promoted were absent more frequently than those who were not dissatisfied with their promotional opportunities.

Exactly how important an *independent* source of job satisfaction promotions are is more difficult to determine. As Vroom (1964) suggests, a promotion to a higher level in the same organization typically involves changes in supervision, job content, coworkers, and pay. Jobs which are high in level, either in a single organization or in society as a whole, are generally more highly paid and less repetitive, provide more freedom, and require less physical effort than other jobs lower in level. Also, what constitutes the rewards of a particular promotion differs greatly from one situation to another. One person may be promoted to a company presidency with a $50,000-a-year salary increase, whereas another person who is promoted to supervisor may receive only a $5000 salary increase.

Nevertheless, the desires to be promoted are strong, especially among business executives (Porter, 1962). Locke (1976) suggests that the roots of this desire for promotion include the desire for higher earnings, the desire for social status, the desire for psychological growth (made possible by greater responsibility), and the desire for justice (if one feels he or she has earned the promotion).

Supervision

In Chapter 11, we examine the role leadership and supervisory style have on employee motivation. Here, we briefly examine its impact on job satisfaction.

Two dimensions of leadership style seem to be most highly correlated with employee satisfaction. The first dimension is *employee-centeredness* or *consideration*. Supervisors who establish a supportive personal relationship with subordinates and take a personal interest in them contribute to their employees' satisfaction (Halpin & Winer, 1957; Fleishman, Harris, & Burtt, 1955).

The other dimension of supervisory style that seems to contribute to employee satisfaction is *influence*, or *participation*, in decision making. In two well-known field experiments in factory settings, for instance, groups that participated in decisions about changes in the work flow displayed a much higher level of job satisfaction (Coch & French, 1948; French, Israel, & As, 1960).

While employee-centeredness and influence in decision making have fairly consistently been found to be positively correlated with employee satisfaction, it is also important to note that there are personality and situational variables that determine just how much impact supervision has on general satisfaction (Graen et al., 1977). For instance, Vroom and Mann (1960) found that employees in small, highly interdependent work groups preferred more egalitarian leaders, while employees in large work groups, with little opportunity for supervisor-subordinate relationships, were found to have more positive attitudes toward authoritarian leaders. Thus, while we can say that there is a positive relationship between an employee-centered supervisory style and general satisfaction, it is not always consistent and not always strong.

Work Group

The work group does serve as a source of satisfaction to individual employees. It does so primarily by providing group members with opportunities for interaction with each other. In a study of the automobile industry, Walker and Guest (1952) found that "isolated workers disliked their jobs and gave social isolation as the principle reason" (p. 76). Zaleznik et al. (1958) found that only 43 percent of the "isolates" in work groups were highly satisfied with their jobs, compared with 75 percent of the rest of the employees. Several other studies (Kerr et al., 1951; Sawatsky, 1951; Richards & Dobryns, 1957) have found that when there was little opportunity for workers to have conversations with each other, they were more dissatisfied and were more likely to turn over.

The work group is an even stronger source of job satisfaction when members have similar attitudes and values. Having people around with similar attitudes causes less friction on a day-to-day basis. Coworkers with similar attitudes and values can also provide some confirmation of a person's self-concept: "We're OK and you're OK"; "There are lots of other people who feel the way you do." Feeling valued by the group is highly correlated with job satisfaction; in a field study among construction workers, Van Zelst (1951) found a strong relationship between feeling valued by coworkers and job satisfaction.

Ironically, while most people are very satisfied with their relationships with their coworkers, having good relationships with coworkers is not as important to employees as most other factors. In a study called "What You Really Want from Your Job," Renwick and Lawler (1978) found that while employees said they were very satisfied with the friendliness of their coworkers (more highly satisfied with that aspect of their job than any other), they rated that factor only 14th out of 18 in terms of importance—ahead of only "amount of praise you get for a job well done," "the amount of fringe benefits you get," "chances for getting a promotion," and "physical surroundings of a job." Thus, while the work group can be a particular source of job satisfaction to employees, it is not generally very important to them.

Working Conditions

There seem to be consistently positive correlations between working conditions and job satisfaction. Features such as temperature, humidity, ventilation, lighting and noise, hours of work, cleanliness of the work place, and adequate tools and equipment all affect job satisfaction (Barnowe et al., 1972). The reasons for this are fairly straightforward.

First, employees prefer pleasant working conditions because they lead to greater physical comfort. For instance, too much heat or too little light can cause physical discomfort; unclean air or poor ventilation could be physically dangerous. Second, employees prefer pleasant working conditions because they facilitate (or do not interfere with) getting the work done efficiently. Adequate tools and equipment help employees accomplish their work goals; too much noise distracts from job performance. Third, working conditions are valued by employees because they can facilitate (or do not interfere with) valued off-the-job activities, such as pursuing hobbies (Locke, 1976). Flextime, job sharing, and shorter work weeks are all management responses to employees' desires to have more time off to pursue their own interests and to have more *control* over *when* they can pursue those interests.

However, while working conditions *are* a source of job satisfaction, they are a relatively minor source. Both Herzberg (1966) and Whyte (1955) have found that complaints about physical working conditions are sometimes symbols or manifestations of deeper frustrations (e.g., personal problems or distrust of management) and soon disappear when these problems are resolved. Generally, unless working conditions are either extremely good or bad, they are taken for granted by most employees. Only when employees themselves change jobs or when working conditions change dramatically over time (e.g., a move into new facilities) do working conditions become more salient (Chadwick-Jones, 1969).

Some Conclusions about Causes of Job Satisfaction

In summary, then: pay and the work itself are the most important sources of job satisfaction, promotional opportunities and supervision are moderately important sources of job satisfaction, and the work group and working conditions are relatively minor sources of job satisfaction. In the next section, we'll consider how employee satisfactions with specific aspects of the job combine to determine overall employee satisfaction.

A MODEL OF JOB SATISFACTION

What determines whether employees feel generally satisfied or dissatisfied with their jobs? How do the specific satisfactions with pay, promotions, and the other job factors combine to produce an overall attitude of liking or disliking of the job? The model of job satisfaction presented in Figure 8-1, drawing on Lawler (1973), summarizes what we know about what determines whether employees will be generally satisfied or not.

Basically, job satisfaction is largely determined by the *discrepancy* between what individuals expect to get out of their jobs and what the job actually offers (Locke, 1976). A person will be dissatisfied if there is *less* than the desired amount of a job characteristic in the job. For instance, if a person expects to be promoted in 6 months and then is not, the person will be dissatisfied. A person will be satisfied if there is *no* discrepancy between desired and actual conditions (e.g., I expected a 10 percent raise and I received it). If there is *more* than the employee expected of some job factor and the excess is beneficial (e.g., a large bonus, extra days off), then the person will be even more satisfied than when there was no discrepancy between the desired and actual outcomes.

Current Job Satisfaction

First, let's examine more closely how workers actually evaluate how much satisfaction they are currently receiving from a job. Expectancy-valence theory (see Chapter 5) helps us here. Individuals have sets of

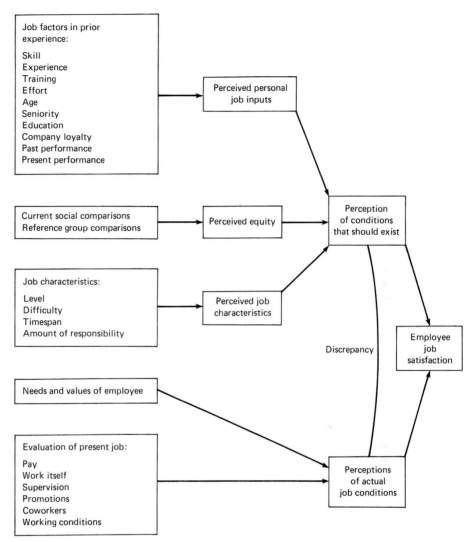

FIGURE 8-1
A model of job satisfaction. (SOURCE: Figure 4-3, p. 75, from E. E. Lawler, III, *Motivation in Work Organization*. Reprinted by permission of Brooks/Cole Publishing Company, Copyright 1973.

needs—physiological, safety, belongingness, love and esteem, and self-actualization—which they try to fulfill. Moreover, each of the job factors we discussed above—pay, work itself, supervision, promotions, coworkers, and working conditions—can fulfill one or more of these needs. An employee's satisfaction with his or her job is thus determined jointly by (1) how highly each job factor is valued (e.g., how many needs does pay fill for the person?) and (2) how instrumental the job is in attaining those valued outcomes. The more needs the job satisfies, the more satisfied the employee will be. Note, as in expectancy-valence theory, we *multiply* the value of job outcomes *by* the instrumentality of the job for their attainment to calculate job satisfaction.

Job Expectations

Next, let's consider what influences employees' job expectations, i.e., their perceptions of the conditions that *should* exist on their jobs. Three factors influence the formation of job expectations most heavily.

First, the individual makes a judgment about what assets he or she brings to the company. Generally, employees with more prior work experience, more seniority, and more successful work histories will have higher expectations about the job than younger, less experienced, less successful employees.

Second, the employee will make a judgment about what sorts of demands the job makes on the employee's ability. Do I have a lot of responsibility? Do I make important decisions? Do I work long hours? Does my job require a lot of specialized expertise? The more the job requires of the individual, the higher the individual's expectations of rewards from the job will be.

Third, the employee looks around at other employees and their circumstances to see if the benefits of his or her job are *fair and reasonable.* For instance, if I have had my M.B.A. 3 years and am making $40,000 in this firm, why am I making $5000 less than other people who graduated with me? Why is my title "assistant product manager" when other people doing the same job duties as me are product managers? If these social comparisons suggest an equitable state of affairs, the employee will be satisfied; inequity, on the other hand, leads to job dissatisfaction. All three of these factors—perceived personal job inputs, perceived job characteristics, and perceived equity—influence employees' job expectations.

The Discrepancy Model

Now, let's examine cases of both job satisfaction and job dissatisfaction, using the discrepancy model.

A newly graduating M.B.A. is hired to be an assistant brand manager at a major corporation at $30,000. Although she has no previous work experience, she expects, on the basis of job interviews, to be given significant job challenges right away. Not longer after she starts working, she realizes that (1) the job does not require M.B.A. skills for this entry-level position, (2) friends from graduate school working for other marketing corporations are doing significantly more challenging work, and (3) the salary does not cover as many expenses as expected, due to the high cost of living in a large city. In short, the actual job conditions are lacking in two significant ways (pay and challenging work). Moreover, the job expectations are seriously violated (not enough challenging work, not doing as much as friends and colleagues). The discrepancy is large, and the new graduate is dissatisfied.

Next, let's examine a case of job satisfaction. A newly graduating M.B.A. is hired to be an assistant brand manager at a major corporation at $30,000. Although the student has no previous work experience, he expects, on the basis of job interviews, to be given significant job challenges right away. Not long after he starts working, he realizes that: (1) he is doing the type of work promised in the interview; (2) he is doing the same level of work as friends from graduate school in comparable firms are doing; and (3) having lived in other major metropolitan areas, his personal estimates about how far $30,000 would go were accurate. There is no discrepancy between job expectations and what was actually found on the job, and the graduate is satisfied.

There is also a third case, where there is a discrepancy between actual job conditions and job expectations, but the job is better than expected. For instance, the new M.B.A. assistant brand manager discovers that the brand manager is being transferred to another position, and so the assistant takes on a lot of additional, challenging responsibilities and gets a corresponding pay raise. Not only are the coworkers enjoyable, but there is also an active social life with them after work. The new assistant does extremely well in the first job assignment and is promoted 6 months ahead of schedule. Since the actual job conditions exceed job expectations, job satisfaction is especially high.

CONSEQUENCES OF JOB SATISFACTION

While job satisfaction is obviously of high personal concern, managers are also concerned about the consequences of job satisfaction on employee behavior. In this section, we examine in just which ways job satisfaction affects employee behavior.

Performance

Of all the behaviors job satisfaction or dissatisfaction could affect, there is none so important to managers as performance. Are satisfied workers more productive workers? Surveys like the one by Gannon and Noon (1971) suggest that a large majority of personnel officers believe happier workers are more productive workers. It seems somehow natural that more positive feelings about work would lead to greater output and higher-quality work. Unfortunately, four decades of research into this issue do not lend support for this belief.

First, *the relationship between job satisfaction and job performance is weak.* Both Brayfield and Crockett (1955) and Vroom (1964) found that satisfaction and performance are not closely related to each other in any simple fashion. In fact, in Vroom's review, the median correlation between satisfaction and performance is only 0.14.

Second, *there is more evidence to suggest that job performance leads to job satisfaction than that job satisfaction leads to job performance.* Perhaps the model that best illustrates this point is the one put forward by Lawler and Porter (1967). According to this model (see Figure 8-2), performance leads to satisfaction rather than the other way around. Performing well brings *intrinsic* rewards to employees, who will be pleased that they have successfully accomplished their jobs. Employees who perform well should also receive more *extrinsic* rewards (e.g., pay and promotions) in recognition of their superior work. Thus, employees who perform well should receive *both* more intrinsic rewards *and* more extrinsic rewards and therefore be more satisfied with their jobs. Employees who perform poorly will probably feel worse about their competence and will probably also receive less pay and fewer promotions. Consequently, the Lawler-Porter model would predict that these poor performers will be *less* satisfied with their job experiences.

Third, *there are some conditions under which high productivity more clearly leads to high job satisfaction.* The most important condition is that employees perceive that intrinsic and extrinsic rewards are *contingent* on superior performance. Employees have to feel personally responsible for performing well, and extrinsic rewards have to be administered on the basis of good performance. The second important condition is that extrinsic rewards be *equitably* distributed. If extrinsic rewards are inequitably distributed, employees will see less connection between how hard they work and how well they are rewarded.

FIGURE 8-2
Lawler-Porter model of satisfaction and performance. (SOURCE: E. E. Lawler and L. W. Porter, "The Effect of Performance on Job Satisfaction," *Industrial Relations*, Vol. 7, 1967, p. 23. Reprinted by permission of authors and publisher. Copyright *Industrial Relations*, 1967.)

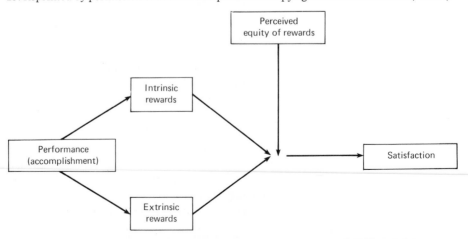

Thus, it is not true that "the happy worker is the productive worker." Rather, being satisfied and being productive are not very highly correlated. To the extent that satisfaction and performance are related, it is generally true that performance leads to satisfaction. Good performers are likely to get both more intrinsic and more extrinsic rewards from their jobs and consequently like them more. This will be especially true when rewards are distributed contingent upon performance and in an equitable fashion.

Withdrawal Behavior: Turnover and Absenteeism

We might also expect that job dissatisfaction would influence withdrawal behavior, i.e., that dissatisfied employees would be more likely than satisfied employees to stay away from work or to resign. The research evidence is consistent that, indeed, dissatisfied employees are more likely to leave their jobs permanently and to be absent temporarily from work more often.

Turnover is of considerable concern to employers because it disrupts normal operations, causes morale problems among those who remain, and increases the costs involved in selecting and training replacements. In four major reviews of the relationship of turnover to job satisfaction (Porter & Steers, 1973; Muchinsky & Tuttle, 1979; Mobley et al., 1979; Arnold & Feldman, 1982), it has been regularly demonstrated that workers who have relatively low levels of job satisfaction are the most likely to quit their jobs and that organizational units with the lowest average satisfaction levels tend to have the highest turnover rates. However, while the relationship between job satisfaction and turnover is strong, it is also important to note that the *availability of other places of employment* also influences turnover. If the labor market is tight in general or if the person does not have a variety of alternative places of employment (due to geography, family responsibilities, or very specialized skills), even if the person is highly dissatisfied with the job he or she will be unlikely to leave.

Job satisfaction is also highly related to absenteeism. Workers who are dissatisfied are more likely to take "mental health" days, i.e., days off not due to illness or personal business (Breaugh, 1981; Hammer et al., 1981). In an interesting field experiment, Smith (1977) examined what would happen if salaried employees were free to attend work or to be absent on a particular day without financial penalty. On April 2, 1975, an unexpected blizzard hit Chicago, greatly hampering the city's transportation system. Attendance on April 3 required not only the decision to attend but also considerable personal effort to get to work. Workers would not be penalized financially for absence. In work units where job satisfaction was high, attendance was high; in work units where job satisfaction was low, attendance was much lower. Those groups of workers with the highest satisfaction levels were most likely to exert the high level of effort

necessary to get to work. Because absenteeism disrupts normal operations, causes delays, increases expenses for "sick pay," and necessitates the
employment of substitute personnel, this form of withdrawal behavior,
too, seriously concerns management.

Union Activity

Many diverse groups in the business community are concerned with why
employees join unions: the National Labor Relations Board, which regulates union organizing in the private sector; employers who wish to avoid
unionization; union organizers who wish to profit by it; and labor lawyers
and management consultants who make a business of it (Brett, 1980). Why
do employees want unions? The evidence is strong that job dissatisfaction
is a major cause of unionization (Schriesheim, 1978; Allen & Keaveny,
1981).

In an important study of union organizing, Getman, Goldberg, and
Herman (1976) found that an employee's initial interest in unionization is
based on dissatisfaction with working conditions and a perceived lack of
influence to change those conditions. Employers may first violate employee expectations by not keeping wages up with inflation, by arbitrary and
capricious discipline, or by not removing safety hazards. When employers
fail to respond to employee complaints, they then violate employees'
expectations a second time—this time by denying the legitimacy of the
employees' attempt to exert influence to change the working conditions. At
this point, employees realize that their power is not strong enough to deal
with the employers and that collective action—unionization—may be the
solution. Satisfied employees are seldom interested in unions; they don't
perceive that they need them (Brett, 1980).

In their study of 31 union representation elections, Getman, Goldberg,
and Herman found that knowing an employee's initial satisfaction allowed them to predict the employee's vote with 75 percent accuracy.
Dissatisfaction with wages, job security, fringe benefits, treatment by
supervisors, and chances for promotion were all significantly correlated
with a vote for union representation (Brett, 1980). Hamner and Smith
(1978) found similar results among 62,000 salaried employees.

It is also not surprising that job dissatisfaction can have an impact on
the tendency to take action within the union, such as filing grievances or
striking (Dunham & Smith, 1979). Indeed, several studies (Fleishman et
al., 1955; Fleishman et al., 1962) have shown that departments with low
job satisfaction do have more strikes and higher grievance rates.

Physical and Mental Health

In this section, we examine the consequences of job satisfaction on the
physical and mental health of employees. While physical and mental

health are not "job behaviors" per se, we are concerned here with the impact of job dissatisfaction on employee health for two reasons: (1) for humanistic reasons, managers would like to know the impact jobs have on the well-being of their employees; and (2) there are substantial financial costs associated with poor employee health. Estimates of lost work time due to just alcoholism and drug abuse are over $20 billion per year in the United States, and this does not include the costs of insurance, workmen's compensation, and medical expenses (Reitz, 1981).

Physical Health

There is substantial evidence that job satisfaction influences temporary physical symptoms, physical illnesses, and even longevity. Job dissatisfaction has been linked to such physical symptoms as fatigue, shortness of breath, headaches, sweating, loss of appetite, indigestion, and nausea (Burke, 1969; Selye, 1956). More seriously, job dissatisfaction has been linked to such illnesses as ulcers, arthritis, high blood pressure, alcohol and drug abuse, strokes, and heart attacks. In fact, research findings suggest that medical factors like diet, exercise, heredity, and quality of medical care only account for about 25 percent of the risk factors in heart disease, the major cause of death in America. That is, if cholesterol, blood pressure, smoking, glucose level, serum uric acid, and so forth, were all perfectly controlled, 75 percent of the risk would still be "unexplained"— and a lot of that 75 percent is attributable to work-related problems (*Work in America*, 1973, p. 79). There is even strong evidence that job dissatisfaction can shorten one's life. In a convincing longitudinal study, Palmore (1969) correlated physical and attitudinal variables with subsequent longevity. The single best overall predictor of longevity was work satisfaction. Indeed, job dissatisfaction can be hazardous to one's health.

Why is it that job dissatisfaction causes such sustained effects on physical health? While more and more research is being done on psychogenic illness, one reason for the link is that increased use of tobacco, alcohol, and other types of drugs is a frequent response to job-induced tension. While taking a drink or a sedative may temporarily relieve tension, the long-run consequences for the body of repeated use of alcohol or drugs are not beneficial. In addition, tension or stress may cause some physiological reactions (like higher blood pressure) that lead to other, more serious, health problems.

Mental Health

Although mental health is a broad concept, we can conservatively say that a person who is mentally healthy has a fairly realistic view of his assets and limitations, has a good sense of self-esteem, participates in some social relationships with friends and family, and can cope with the inevitable ups-and-downs of a job. In short, the mentally healthy person feels he is leading a rewarding life and has a good self-concept (Sully &

Munden, 1962). In studies conducted at the University of Michigan's Institute for Social Research, a variety of mental health problems have been related to the absence of job satisfaction: anxiety, worry, tension, impaired interpersonal relations, and irritability. Job dissatisfaction can also lead to anger over unimportant matters, feelings of persecution, apathy, forgetfulness, and an inability to concentrate and make decisions.

What aspects of unsatisfying jobs cause such ill effects on employee mental health? The following are some of the most frequently cited factors:

1. Tedious, boring, and repetitive tasks
2. Poor relations with coworkers and supervisors
3. Uncertainty about the jobs to be performed and what level of performance is required
4. Too much work to do and too little time available to do it in
5. Conflicting expectations from different managers and from different departments
6. Rapid and continuous changes in jobs
7. Lack of job security

Probably the most well-known study of the relationship between job satisfaction and mental health is Arthur Kornhauser's *Mental Health of the Industrial Worker* (1965). In his study of 400 workers, approximately 40 percent had some symptoms of mental health problems and there was a significant relationship between job satisfaction and mental health. Feelings of helplessness, withdrawal, alienation, and pessimism were widespread and highly attributable to the job. Moreover, job dissatisfaction spread to other areas of life. Workers with the lowest mental health and job satisfaction scores were escapist or passive in their nonwork activities: they watched television a lot, did not vote, and did not participate in community organizations.

In summary, then, the evidence is very suggestive that job dissatisfaction has substantial negative consequences for both the physical and emotional health of employees. While certainly mental and physical health have other roots (personality predispositions, heredity, and prior medical care), too, job satisfaction can be prominently included on the list of contributing factors to employee well-being.

TRENDS IN JOB SATISFACTION

In the first three sections of this chapter, we looked at job satisfaction from the individual's point of view. In this section, we consider some of the more "macro" aspects of job satisfaction. Just how satisfied are workers in general today? What have been the trends in the level of job satisfaction, and why? We turn, next, to answer some of these questions.

How Satisfied Are Workers in General Today?

Despite some particularly gloomy predictions (for example, Sheppard and Herrick's *Where Have All the Robots Gone?*, 1972) major surveys of the American work force reveal that workers are generally pretty satisfied with their jobs. Probably the most highly publicized of these surveys are those carried out by the University of Michigan's Institute for Survey Research and by the National Opinion Research Center. In both these surveys, between 80 and 90 percent of employees working on a wide range of jobs across a diverse set of organizations consistently report that they are satisfied with their jobs (Weaver, 1980).

Does this mean that most workers are really happy with their jobs? The survey results are not so positive on this point. When employees were asked the question "What type of work would you try to get into if you could start all over again?" only 43 percent of the white-collar workers (including professionals) would voluntarily choose the same work that they were doing, and only 24 percent of the blue-collar workers would choose the same kind of work if given another chance (see Table 8-1). Many researchers feel this is a particularly good indicator of job satisfaction because it forces respondents to consider how the job affects their sense of self-esteem.

TABLE 8-1
Who would choose similar work again?

Professional and lower white-collar occupation	Percent	Working-class occupations	Percent
Urban university professors	93	Skilled printers	52
Mathematicians	91	Paper workers	42
Physicists	89	Skilled autoworkers	41
Biologists	89	Skilled steelworkers	41
Chemists	86	Textile workers	31
Firm lawyers	85	Unskilled steelworkers	21
Lawyers	83	Unskilled autoworkers	16
Journalists	82		
Church university professors	77		
Solo lawyers	75		
White-collar cross-section	43	Blue-collar cross-section	24

SOURCE: *Work in America.* Boston: MIT Press, 1973, p. 16.

Employees were also asked to question: "What would you do with the extra 2 hours if you had a 26-hour day?" Two out of three college professors and one out of four lawyers say that would use the extra time in a work-related activity. Strikingly, only one out of twenty nonprofessional workers would make use of the extra time in work activity (*Work in America*, 1973, pp. 14–16). A survey respondent sums up this sense of malaise in the following way: "Don't get me wrong. I didn't say it is a *good* job. It's an O.K. job—about as good a job as a guy like me might expect. The foreman leaves me alone and it pays well. But I would never call it a good job. It doesn't amount to much, but it's not bad." Thus, while there are very few employees who have classically alienating jobs, there are also very few employees who are really happy with their work. Most people have jobs which are satisfactory, not truly satisfying.

Recent Trends in Job Satisfaction

There has probably been a *very slight trend downward* in the overall level of job satisfaction over the past 10 years—probably no more than 2 to 5 percent (Quinn & Staines, 1979; Weaver, 1980). While more than 80 percent of those surveyed still report that they were either somewhat or very satisfied with their jobs, that percentage seems to have been inching down since the early 1970s. Why?

First, while the decline in overall satisfaction has been small, satisfaction with specific aspects of the job situation has declined more noticeably. In particular, satisfaction with pay and satisfaction with resources to do the job (time, help, and equipment) have both decreased substantially (see Figure 8-3). Most likely, inflation and recession have made money tight not only for the personal spending of employees but also for the capital investment of employers.

Second, demographic changes in the work force are also contributing to this downward trend. Probably the most significant of these changes is the growing number of young employees. In the United States, out of a work force of more than 85 million, 22½ million are now under age 30. The baby-boom babies of the 1950s are entering the labor market in full force—and younger employees are consistently more dissatisfied than older employees (Weaver, 1980).

Part of the reason young employees are dissatisfied is the nature of their job expectations. Young employees expect a lot of intrinsic rewards from their jobs and opportunities both to "make a contribution" and for "self-expression." Many young employees begin their jobs with unrealistic expectations about how fulfilling their jobs will be, and finding that reality falls short of expectations, they are very disillusioned in their first decade of work. After that point, expectations are modified and adjusted downward and the job is seen in a more positive light.

Another reason young employees seem to be more dissatisfied is their

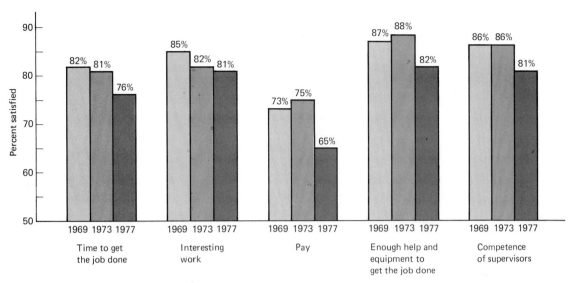

FIGURE 8-3
Trends in satisfaction with specific aspects of the job. (SOURCE: Robert R. Quinn and Graham L. Staines, *The 1977 Quality of Employment Survey,* Ann Arbor: Institute for Social Research, The University of Michigan, 1979, pp. 216–219. Reprinted by permission of the Institute for Social Research, The University of Michigan. Copyright Institute for Social Research, 1977.)

different values about authority. In 1968, over half (56 percent) of students surveyed indicated that they did not mind the future prospect of being "bossed around" on the job (*Work in America*, 1973, pp. 43–50). Today, only 33 percent of the student population see themselves willingly submitting to such authority. In the 1960s and 1970s, students received a greater voice in setting the goals of the university and in determining what was taught in the classrooms; as new entrants into the work force, they are disappointed that they have less influence as adults than they did as students. New entrants are *not* shifting away from valuing work per se; they are shifting away, however, from a willingness to take on meaningless work in authoritarian settings simply for pay.

A third factor influencing the slight downward trend in job satisfaction is the growing disenchantment of such traditionally privileged groups as the nation's 5 million middle managers. Where William H. Whyte almost parodied the subservience of these managers in his *Organization Man* (1957), today 1 out of 3 middle managers indicates some willingness to join a union. What 25 years ago was seen as dedication—late nights of work, working vacations—is seen today as compulsive behavior and evidence of "workaholism." Middle managers feel they lack influence in organization decision making, yet must implement company policy, often without sufficient authority or resources to do so effectively. Moreover, because management productivity is hard to measure and their functions often "nonessential," they are seen as the easiest place to "cut fat" during recessions. Many white-collar workers feel that their company would not act to do something about their individual problems; loyalty to the employer, once high among this group of workers, is now much lower.

In short, there is this increasing feeling in organizations that there are not enough of the good things in life to go around. More and more women and minorities are entering the workplace, only to find that discrimination is practiced in pay and promotion policies. Blue-collar workers feel "locked in" to jobs with little salary potential: they feel their children's chances of "making it" are certainly no better than their own, if not worse; they are frustrated by the fact that employers have raised credential requirements faster than they can gain them; they have the most to fear from automation. Even successful white-collar workers can hardly afford to exist on the relatively high salary they make. Today, only 14 percent of American workers come from the "traditional family"—a one-earner household in which the husband is employed and the wife and children aren't. In 1950, that figure was 70 percent (*Chicago Tribune*, Sept. 16, 1979).

USING JOB SATISFACTION SURVEYS

In this final section, we address the management and measurement of employee job satisfaction. More specifically, we are concerned with three issues: (1) When should job satisfaction surveys be utilized? (2) What are the most reliable and valid methods of measuring job satisfaction? (3) How can the results of job satisfaction surveys be interpreted and used to better manage workers? We start by examining when job satisfaction surveys can be most useful.

When Should Attitude Surveys Be Utilized?

Job satisfaction surveys can be utilized to fulfill at least six purposes of organizations.

1. ***To diagnose potential sources of problems in organizations.*** Many companies like Sears find that job satisfaction surveys serve almost as a barometer of employee satisfaction about a variety of organizational issues. If management sees a downward trend in satisfaction with pay, for instance, it will be alerted to potential future complaints about pay, and can reexamine its policies to discover why pay dissatisfaction is increasing. Conversely, if a few employees are complaining about pay scales to management but the job satisfaction survey shows a high degree of positive feelings about pay, management will be appropriately wary about broadly generalizing from the few complaints about pay they do receive.

2. ***To discover the causes of indirect productivity problems, such as absenteeism, turnover, and poor quality of work.*** We discussed earlier the tenuous link between job satisfaction and productivity: the happy worker is not necessarily the productive worker. However, we also noted that several employee behaviors that indirectly affect organizational productivity—such as absenteeism and turnover—are highly correlated with job satisfaction. If an organization is disturbed by a high rate of turnover or absenteeism, it might appropriately turn to job satisfaction surveys to discover what it is about the job situation that is leading to withdrawal behavior. Perhaps it is low pay; perhaps it is lack of promotional opportunities; perhaps it is unchallenging jobs. Without satisfaction surveys, there could be random guessing on the part of management. Moreover, management might waste money by improving the work situation in ways not valued by employees (e.g., employees may want more job responsibilities, not a raise). Job satisfaction surveys help managers both to get a better handle on why employees are leaving and to better plan solutions to problems.

3. ***To assess the impact of organizational changes on employee attitudes.*** One of the best uses of job satisfaction surveys is in the evaluation of organizational change projects. For instance, the Job Diagnostic Survey (discussed in more detail in Chapter 9) is used extensively to evaluate whether employee satisfaction with the work itself has been improved by job redesign efforts. By comparing prechange data and postchange data, researchers can determine what impact the redesigned work had on employee attitudes.

4. ***To stimulate better communication between management and workers.*** Since surveys typically guarantee anonymity to respondents, workers should feel free to communicate information that would not normally be expressed directly to management. Thus, the survey can sometimes function as a catalyst and a "safe" channel for upward communication. Surveys can stimulate downward communication, too. Feedback sessions can provide opportunities for management to discuss important issues with workers and put to rest unfounded worker concerns (Dunham & Smith, 1979).

5. ***To provide accurate information about the degree to which employees may be willing to vote for a union if given the chance.*** Since we have already noted the strong link between job satisfaction and the likelihood of voting for union representation, it makes sense for the employer who wishes to remain nonunion to systematically evaluate employee attitudes. If employees were honest in filling out the survey, management would be able to identify what working conditions were unsatisfactory and could make the changes necessary before union-organizing efforts began.

It is important to note here that it is far preferable to survey employee satisfaction *before* a union-organizing campaign begins. If a survey is conducted during a campaign, the National Labor Relations

Board might find that the employer is engaging in an unfair labor practice—implying a promise to alleviate unsatisfactory conditions (Brett, 1980, p. 57).

6. ***As an indicator of the effectiveness of organizational reward systems.*** Earlier we discussed the relationship between performance and satisfaction. Good performance is likely to lead to job satisfaction because good performers are more likely to receive both intrinsic rewards (feeling good about doing a job well) and extrinsic rewards (pay and promotions) as a result of their accomplishments. This relationship between performance and job satisfaction will be especially strong if rewards are distributed equitably and contingent upon performance.

    Looking at the relationship between job performance and job satisfaction (as measured in satisfaction surveys) can provide some clues as to the effectiveness of the organizational reward systems. If performance and job satisfaction are *not* related, then rewards are being distributed randomly; being a good worker has little to do with the amount of rewards and satisfaction derived from the job. If performance and job satisfaction are *negatively* related, then the poor performers are getting proportionately more rewards than good preformers. Here the good performer will be most likely to leave the organization. Where performance and satisfaction are *positively* related, rewards are likely based on performance. In this last case, it will be the poor performers who will most likely leave the organization. Job satisfaction surveys can help managers judge whether the best performers are receiving the most rewards and the most satisfaction from their jobs (Lawler, 1973).

How Can We Effectively Measure Job Satisfaction?

While a wide variety of instruments are available for use in surveying job-related attitudes, a few stand out as especially useful—the Job Descriptive Index (JDI), the Minnesota Satisfaction Questionnaire (MSQ), and the Porter Need Satisfaction Questionnaire (NSQ). There are several characteristics which make these instruments so well-respected (Dunham & Smith, 1979, pp. 75–86).

1. ***Validity.*** These instruments measure what they are intended to measure. Their items are highly related to other previously validated measures of job satisfaction.
2. ***Reliability.*** Reliability refers to the ability of an instrument to measure with a relative absence of error. These instruments have been demonstrated to produce stable, consistent results. They use unambiguous questions, include several items to measure each particular attitude,

and provide clear instructions and standardized survey administration conditions.

3. ***Content.*** These survey instruments identify the wide range of factors that affect work life and organizational effectiveness. They provide data on the factors most managers are interested in.

4. ***Language level.*** Writing good items is not as easy as it appears. Items have to be written so that they are understandable by the respondents and can be used across a wide variety of job incumbents. The items in these scales are appropriately worded and usable in many types of organizations and in many types of jobs.

5. ***Norm availability.*** As we will discuss in more detail later, it is very difficult to interpret job satisfaction survey data on an *absolute* basis. It is much more instructive to have baseline data (norm data) for different job categories to judge the positiveness or negativeness of survey results. These three instruments have all been developed in a diverse set of organizations and job categories and have norm data available to help interpret results.

Probably the most well-known job satisfaction survey is the Job Descriptive Index (JDI), developed by Smith, Kendall, and Hulin (1969). The JDI has separate scales for satisfaction with pay, promotion, supervision, work, and coworkers (see Figure 8-4). It has been used with a large variety of employee samples, and norms are provided for employees according to their age, sex, education, income, and type of community. It requires only 10–15 minutes to administer and is also available in a Spanish version (Katterberg, Smith, & Hoy, 1977).

The Minnesota Satisfaction Questionnaire (MSQ) was developed by Weiss, Dawis, England, and Lofquist (1967). The long form has 100 items, 5 items for each of the following 20 factors:

1. ability utilization
2. achievement
3. activity
4. advancement
5. authority
6. company policies and practices
7. compensation
8. coworkers
9. creativity
10. independence
11. moral values
12. recognition
13. responsibility
14. security
15. social service
16. social status
17. supervision—human relations
18. supervision—technical
19. variety
20. working conditions

The short form, shown in Figure 8-5, has 20 items; general satisfaction can be measured by summing the scores for all 20 items. Norms for a wide

Think of your present work. What is it like most of the time? In the blank beside each word given below, write

_Y_ for "Yes" if it describes your work
_N_ for "No" if it does NOT describe it
_?_ if you cannot decide

Work on Present Job

_____ Routine
_____ Satisfying
_____ Good
_____ On your feet

Think of the pay you get now. How well does each of the following words describe your present pay? In the blank beside each word, put

_Y_ if it describes your pay
_N_ if it does NOT describe it
_?_ if you cannot decide

Present Pay

_____ Income adequate for normal expenses
_____ Insecure
_____ Less than I deserve
_____ Highly paid

Think of the opportunities for promotion that you have now. How well does each of the following words describe these? In the blank beside each

_Y_ for "Yes" if it describes your opportunities for promotion
_N_ for "No" if it does NOT describe them
_?_ if you cannot decide

Opportunities for Promotion

_____ Promotion on ability
_____ Dead-end job
_____ Unfair promotion policy
_____ Regular promotions

Think of the kind of supervision that you get on your job. How well does each of the following words describe this supervision? In the blank beside each word below, put

_Y_ if it describes the supervision you get on your job
_N_ if it does NOT describe it
_?_ if you cannot decide.

Supervision on Present Job

_____ Impolite
_____ Praises good work
_____ Influential
_____ Doesn't supervise enough

Think of the majority of the people that you work with now or the people you meet in connection with your work. How well does each of the following words describe these people? In the blank beside each word below, put

_Y_ if it describes the people you work with
_N_ if it does NOT describe them
_?_ if you cannot decide.

People on Your Present Job

_____ Boring
_____ Responsible
_____ Intelligent
_____ Talk too much

FIGURE 8-4
Sample items from the Job Descriptive Index.   (SOURCE: Reprinted by permission of Dr. Patricia C. Smith. Copyright 1975, Bowling Green University, Department of Psychology, Bowling Green, Ohio 43403.)

variety of occupational groups are available for the MSQ, too. The long form takes about a half hour to administer; the short form, only 10 minutes.

Porter's (1961) Need Satisfaction Questionnaire (NSQ) is based on the

Ask yourself: How satisfied am I with this aspect of my job?
  Very Sat. means I am very satisfied with this aspect of my job.
  Sat. means I am satisfied with this aspect of my job.
  N means I can't decide whether I am satisfied or not with this aspect of my job.
  Dissat. means I am dissatisfied with this aspect of my job.
  Very Dissat. means I am very dissatisfied with this aspect of my job.

On my present job, this is how I feel about. . .	Very Dissat.	Dissat.	N	Sat.	Very Sat.
1. Being able to keep busy all the time	☐	☐	☐	☐	☐
2. The chance to work alone on the job	☐	☐	☐	☐	☐
3. The chance to do different things from time to time	☐	☐	☐	☐	☐
4. The chance to be "somebody" in the community	☐	☐	☐	☐	☐
5. The way my boss handles his men	☐	☐	☐	☐	☐
6. The competence of my supervisor in making decisions	☐	☐	☐	☐	☐
7. Being able to do things that don't go against my conscience	☐	☐	☐	☐	☐
8. The way my job provides for steady employment	☐	☐	☐	☐	☐
9. The chance to do things for other people	☐	☐	☐	☐	☐
10. The chance to tell people what to do	☐	☐	☐	☐	☐
11. The chance to do something that makes use of my abilities	☐	☐	☐	☐	☐
12. The way company policies are put into practice	☐	☐	☐	☐	☐
13. My pay and the amount of work I do	☐	☐	☐	☐	☐
14. The chances for advancement on this job	☐	☐	☐	☐	☐
15. The freedom to use my own judgment	☐	☐	☐	☐	☐
16. The chance to try my own methods of doing the job	☐	☐	☐	☐	☐
17. The working conditions	☐	☐	☐	☐	☐
18. The way my co-workers get along with each other	☐	☐	☐	☐	☐
19. The praise I get for doing a good job	☐	☐	☐	☐	☐
20. The feeling of accomplishment I get from the job	☐	☐	☐	☐	☐
	Very Dissat.	Dissat.	N	Sat.	Very Sat.

FIGURE 8-5
Short form of the Minnesota Satisfaction Questionnaire. (SOURCE: D. J. Weiss, R. V. Dawis, C. W. England, and L. H. Lofquist, "Minnesota Studies in Vocational Rehabilitation", Vol. 22, *Manual for the Minnesota Satisfaction Questionnaire*, Vocational Psychology Research, University of Minnesota. Copyright 1967. Reprinted by permission.)

discrepancy theory of job satisfaction discussed earlier. Each item has two questions, one for "should be" and one for "is now" (e.g., How much feeling of security should there be in this job? and, How much is there now?). An item in this scale is scored by subtracting the numerical value of the choice on the "is now" part from the numerical value of the choice on the "should be" part. The greater this difference, the more dissatisfied the respondent is with this aspect of the job. Overall job dissatisfaction can be measured by summing the scores on all of the items. Sample items appear in Figure 8-6.

Some Caveats on Survey Design and Administration

Since most of the better-validated and more-reliable instruments are copyrighted, there is a modest charge to companies who want to purchase these surveys and have them scored and interpreted. To avoid paying these fees for services, many managers are tempted to write their own questionnaires. However, as we mentioned earlier, it is very difficult to develop a reliable and valid instrument. Some of the most frequent beginner's errors in writing questionnaire items are the following:

1. Double negatives, e.g., "I don't think that I could disagree with my supervisor without being punished." (item confusing to respondent)
2. Double-barreled questions, e.g., "I am satisfied with my pay and fringe benefits." (item taps two different specific satisfactions)
3. Alien vocabulary, e.g., "I can't self-actualize in my job." (language inconsistent with that of respondents)

Thus, while ultimately a manager will want to establish the validity of a survey instrument for his or her own organization, developing a reliable and valid survey from scratch is a tall order, and demands quite a good deal of knowledge about measurement theory and statistics. Beginners,

FIGURE 8-6
Porter Need Satisfaction Questionnaire. (SOURCE: L. W. Porter, "A Study of Perceived Need Satisfaction in Bottom and Middle Management Jobs," *Journal of Applied Psychology*, Vol. 45 1961, p. 3. Copyright 1961 by The American Psychological Association. Reprinted by permission of the publisher and author.)

Examples of items from the Need Satisfaction Questionnaire

Instructions: Circle the number on the scale that represents the amount of the characteristic being rated. Low numbers represent low or minimum amounts, and high numbers represent high or maximum amounts.

1. The opportunity for personal growth and development in my management position.

   a. HOW MUCH IS THERE NOW?
   (Minimum)   1   2   3   4   5   6   7   (Maximum)

   b. HOW MUCH SHOULD THERE BE?
   (Minimum)   1   2   3   4   5   6   7   (Maximum)

2. The feeling of security in my management position.

   a. HOW MUCH IS THERE NOW?
   (Minimum)   1   2   3   4   5   6   7   (Maximum)

   b. HOW MUCH SHOULD THERE BE?
   (Minimum)   1   2   3   4   5   6   7   (Maximum)

especially, would be well-advised to use previously validated instruments. Moreover, it will be very difficult—if not impossible—to interpret the survey results of these homegrown instruments without any baseline or normative data.

How the satisfaction survey is administered can also influence how honestly people will respond to it and how useful the results will be. Some important factors that managers might want to consider in conducting job satisfaction surveys include the following:

1. *Timing.* Satisfaction surveys are most effective if they are set up as part of a regularly scheduled, long-term program. First, this resolves the problems of scheduling—managers can anticipate and plan for release time for their units to participate. Moreover, scheduling eliminates the need for "crisis" surveying, unscheduled surveying carried out in response to an acute problem (Dunham & Smith, 1979).

2. *Sampling.* Obviously it is much less expensive to sample (i.e., survey a representative subgroup of the population) than to canvass (survey the entire population). Before managers become overly influenced by this cost factor, however, they should consider the potential reactions of respondents to sampling. Imagine being bombarded with a chorus of "Why am I being singled out to participate?" and "Why am I being left out?" The hesitancy of those "singled out" can damage the validity of the survey, while the anger of those "left out" can damage management's credibility. In this situation, the added expense of a canvass might well be justified (Dunham & Smith, 1979).

3. ***Explaining the purposes of the survey.*** One of the most damaging things a manager can do in surveying employees is to create false expectations. Particularly when an organization is just starting to use attitude surveys, employees may interpret the survey as a precursor to change. Management has to be honest with employees about the purposes of the survey and what will be done with the results. If there is going to be feedback, explain when the feedback will come and in what form (i.e., aggregated by department, by division, by job categories). If changes are going to be based on survey results, explain what role employees will have in planning or discussing those changes.

4. ***Standardizing the conditions of survey administration.*** It takes a lot of lead time to administer a survey in a professional manner. Release time has to be arranged for the employees involved; meetings have to be set up; rooms for taking the survey have to be provided. It is important, too, that survey administrators be trained in how to answer frequent or typical questions, such as "Why are we doing a survey now?" Research suggests that deviations from standard practice in administering the questionnaire—including jokes and asides—can seriously lower the reliability of the results.

Interpreting and Using Survey Results

The first fact to remember about interpreting survey data results is that they are best interpreted in a *relative manner*. Knowing that a department is a 5.0 on a scale of 7 in general satisfaction tells the managers little; they also have to have some baseline data to judge just how positive this data point is (Dunham & Smith, 1979). Is the mean 4.0 or 5.5?

Depending upon the type and size of the organization, norms could be developed for job categories, level in the organization, sex differences, racial-group differences, age-group differences, line vs. staff, and geographical location. If nationally used instruments are employed, even industry-wide norms might be available. Suppose a manager found that the engineers in his or her unit were the most highly satisfied group in the organization. One might conclude from this that there were no immediate problems to be dealt with concerning the engineers. However, although the engineers might be relatively satisfied in terms of this particular organization, compared to engineers in similar organizations their satisfaction score might be relatively low. Knowing the norms can prevent managers from drawing the wrong conclusions from raw data.

One of the most useful sources of norm data can come from the organization itself *if* it has an ongoing survey program. Trends over a period of time can be especially useful in monitoring reactions to changes in organizational policies and programs.

How the survey results should be used to change management policies rests, in large part, on why management collected the data in the first place. Locating specific sources of dissatisfaction should stimulate further investigation and inquiry. Evaluations of new programs or procedures can provide organizational learning, both about what worked and what did not. Potentially, some of the causes of employee turnover, absenteeism, and prounion sentiment might be uncovered.

However, in using the results of job satisfaction surveys, it is important for managers to look not only at *overall* job satisfaction but also at *who* is job satisfied. It is not necessarily an unmitigated blessing to have low turnover, for instance, if that means even the poor and marginal performers are staying. Managers need to examine more closely who's satisfied and why. If the poor performers or the less-skilled job categories are less satisfied with pay, then that is in fact a sign of organizational effectiveness; the employees who are valued the most are receiving the greatest rewards.

It is also important for managers to remember once again that the links between job satisfaction and job behaviors are influenced by factors outside the control of the organization. Extremely dissatisfied employees may remain on their jobs for lack of other job offers; extremely satisfied employees may leave for even greener pastures. Job satisfaction is related to job behavior when all other things are equal—but they rarely are.

Finally, *feedback meetings* between managers and employees can help in both the interpretation of survey results and the planning of action steps based on them. Feedback meetings run in an open and constructive climate can elicit comments from employees that might explain results that are surprising from management's point of view. Moreover, problem-solving committees can be set up to work on specific problems identified by the attitude survey. Employee suggestions could certainly add to the quality of the proposed solutions. Good managers use job satisfaction surveys to measure the level of well-being among their employees; even better managers use surveys to encourage their employees' participation in improving upon that well-being (Dunham & Smith, 1979).

MANAGERIAL IMPLICATIONS

A better understanding of the causes and consequences of job satisfaction can help managers better diagnose and solve employee problems.

1. ***Employee disatisfaction is most frequently caused by what is perceived to be low pay and boring work.*** Too often managers delude themselves into thinking that employee dissatisfaction can be lessened by painting the work area, piping in music, giving out a few more words of praise, or giving people longer work breaks. While these issues sometimes are very important to workers, it is much more likely that the tougher issues of low pay and tedious work need to be addressed.

2. ***Employee dissatisfaction is largely influenced by feelings of inequity.*** Managers are frequently surprised by dissatisfaction of employees who, by all appearances, seem to be well-paid and well-rewarded. However, employee satisfaction is very much influenced by perceptions of a *discrepancy* between what is expected out of the job and what is received. Employees are very sensitive to, and react very negatively against, perceived inequities.

3. ***Increasing job satisfaction is not a likely solution to increasing productivity.*** Satisfaction and performance are not closely related to each other. Moreover, there is more evidence to suggest that job performance leads to job satisfaction than that job satisfaction leads to job performance. Job satisfaction is more likely to tell managers how employees feel they have performed in the past rather than how well employees are likely to perform in the future.

4. ***Managers should be more concerned about the impact of job satisfaction on employee turnover, absenteeism, and unionization.*** The research evidence is consistent that dissatisfied employees are more likely to leave their jobs permanently and to be absent temporarily from work more often. The costs of employee withdrawal behavior to organizations are high because turnover and absenteeism disrupt normal operations and cause morale problems.

Employers who wish to avoid unionization or to avoid strikes and grievances from current unions would also do well to attend to employee dissatisfaction.

5. ***In assessing the levels of job satisfaction, it is important for managers to look not only at overall job satisfaction, but also at who is job satisfied.*** If the poor performers or the less-skilled job categories are less satisfied with pay, then that is in fact a sign of organizational effectiveness; the employees who are valued the most are receiving the greatest rewards. However, if the most talented employees are leaving because of factors which are within the organization's control, then that is a legitimate—if not pressing—area of concern.

6. ***If designed and administered effectively, job satisfaction surveys can provide managers with a wealth of data about their work units.*** In addition to diagnosing sources of problems in the organization, job satisfaction surveys can be used to assess the impact of organizational changes on employee attitudes and to stimulate better communication between management and workers.

SUMMARY

This chapter focuses on job satisfaction—the amount of positive affect (or feelings) employees have toward their jobs.

The amount of compensation and the amount of challenge and interest in the work itself are the most important sources of job satisfaction. Promotional opportunities and the employee-centeredness of supervisors also contribute to job satisfaction. Most workers are generally satisfied with their relationships with coworkers and with the working conditions; however, only when the coworkers are particularly unpleasant or the working conditions particularly poor do these factors become more salient. Overall job satisfaction is largely determined by the *discrepancy* between what the individual expects to get out of the job and what the job actually offers.

The impact of job satisfaction is strongest on employee withdrawal behavior and union activity. Dissatisfied workers are more likely to be voluntarily absent from their jobs and to leave the organization altogether. Job dissatisfaction has also been closely linked to employee union activity. Employees who are more dissatisfied are much more likely to vote for union representation; once in unions, employees who are more dissatisfied are more likely to file grievances and to go on strike. There is also evidence to suggest that there is a link between job satisfaction and employee health.

The relationship between job satisfaction and productivity is more tenuous. To the extent that they are related, it is generally true that productivity leads to satisfaction rather than vice versa. Good performers are more likely to get both more intrinsic and more extrinsic rewards from their jobs and consequently like them more.

Recent surveys suggest that between 80 and 90 percent of the work force are currently satisfied with their jobs. However, it seems as if many jobs are satisfactory in terms of pay and security but are not in any real sense intrinsically rewarding. There may be a slight downward trend in job satisfaction due to a tightening economy and a growing number of under-30 employees in the work force.

Job satisfaction surveys can be utilized to fulfill at least six purposes of organizations: (1) to diagnose potential sources of problems in the organization; (2) to discover the causes of indirect productivity problems such as absenteeism and turnover; (3) to assess the impact of organizational changes on employee attitudes; (4) to stimulate better communication between management and workers; (5) to provide accurate information about prounion sentiment; and (6) as an indicator of the effectiveness of organizational reward systems.

REVIEW QUESTIONS

1. What is job satisfaction?
2. What are the major sources of job satisfaction? Which two factors are particularly important? Why?
3. Briefly describe the discrepancy model of job satisfaction.
4. What role does equity play in models of job satisfaction?
5. Comment on the following statement: "The happy worker is the productive worker."
6. What impact does job satisfaction have on turnover and absenteeism? Union activity?
7. In what ways does job dissatisfaction influence employees' mental and physical health?
8. How satisfied are workers in general today?
9. What have been the trends in the level of general job satisfaction? How do you account for those trends?
10. What are the six purposes of job satisfaction surveys?
11. What are the key attributes of a good job satisfaction survey? Which three job satisfaction surveys are most well known?
12. Identify some of the most important guidelines in administering an attitude survey.
13. Why is norm data so important in interpreting survey results?
14. What role can feedback meetings play in the interpretation of survey results and the planning of action steps based on them?

REFERENCES

Allen, R. E., & Keaveny, T. J. Correlates of university faculty interest in unionization: A replication and extension. *Journal of Applied Psychology*, 1981, *66*, 582–588.

Arnold, H. J., & Feldman, D. C. A multivariate model of job turnover. *Journal of Applied Psychology*, 1982, *67*, 350–360.

Barnowe, J. T., Mangione, T. W., & Quinn, R. P. The relative importance of job facets as indicated by an empirically derived model of job satisfaction. Unpublished report, Survey Research Center, University of Michigan, Ann Arbor, 1972.

Brayfield, A. H., & Crockett, W. H. Employee attitudes and employee performance. *Psychological Bulletin*, 1955, *52*, 396–424.

Breaugh, J. A. Predicting absenteeism from prior absenteeism and work attitudes. *Journal of Applied Psychology*, 1981, *66*, 555–560.

Brett, J. M. Why employees want unions. *Organizational Dynamics*, Spring 1980, 47–59.

Burke, R. J. Occupational and life strains, satisfaction, and mental health. *Journal of Business Administration*, Winter 1969, *1*, 35–41.

Chadwick-Jones, J. K. *Automation and behaviour*. New York: Wiley, 1969.

Coch, L., & French, J. R. P., Jr. Overcoming resistance to change. *Human Relations*, 1948, *1*, 512–532.

Dunham, R. B., and Smith, F. J. *Organizational surveys*. Glenview, Ill.: Scott, Foresman, 1979.

Fleishman, E. A., & Harris, E. F. Patterns of leadership behavior related to employee grievances and turnover. *Personnel Psychology*, 1962, *15*, 43–56.

Fleishman, E. A., Harris, E. F., and Burtt, H. E. *Leadership and supervision in industry*. Columbus: Ohio State University, Bureau of Educational Research, 1955.

French, J. R. P., Jr., Israel, J., & As, D. An experiment on participation in a Norwegian factory. *Human Relations*, 1960, *13*, 3–19.

Gannon, M. J., & Noon, J. P. Management's critical deficiency. *Business Horizons*, 1971, *14*, 49–56.

Getman, J. G., Goldberg, S. B., & Herman, J. B. *Union representation elections: Law and reality*. Russell Sage Foundation, 1976.

Gilbreth, F. B., & Gilbreth, L. M. *Fatigue study*. New York: Macmillan, 1919.

Graen, G., Cashman, J. F., Ginsburg, S., & Schiemann, W. Effects of linking-pin quality upon the quality of working life of lower participants. *Administrative Science Quarterly*, 1977, *22*, 491–504.

Hackman, J. R., & Lawler, E. E., III. Employee reactions to job characteristics. *Journal of Applied Psychology*, 1971, *55*, 259–286.

Halpin, A. W., & Winer, B. J. A factorial study of the leader behavior descriptions. In R. M. Stogdill & A. E. Coons (Eds.), *Leader behavior: Its description and measurement*. Columbus: Ohio State University, Bureau of Business Research, Research Monograph No. 88, 1957, pp. 39–51.

Hammer, T. H., Landau, J. C., & Stern, R. N. Absenteeism when workers have a voice: The case of employee ownership. *Journal of Applied Psychology*, 1981, *66*, 561–573.

Hamner, W. C., & Smith, F. J. Work attitudes as predictors of unionization activity. *Journal of Applied Psychology*, 1978, *63*, 415–421.

Hebb, D. O. *The organization of behavior*. New York: Wiley, 1949.

Herzberg, F. *Work and the nature of man*. Cleveland: World Publishing, 1966.

Herzberg, F., Mausner, B., & Snyderman, B. *The motivation to work*. New York: Wiley, 1959.

Katterberg, R., Smith, F. J., & Hoy, S. Language, time, and person effects on attitude scale translations. *Journal of Applied Psychology*, 1977, *62*, 385–391.

Kerr, W. A., Koppelmeir, G., & Sullivan, J. J. Absenteeism, turnover, and morale in a metals fabrication factory. *Occupational Psychology,* 1951, *25,* 50–55.

Kornhauser, A. W. *Mental health of the industrial worker: A Detroit study.* New York: Wiley, 1965.

Krech, D., & Crutchfield, R. S. *Theory and problems of social psychology.* New York: McGraw-Hill, 1948.

Lawler, E. E., III. *Pay and organizational effectiveness: A psychological view.* New York: McGraw-Hill, 1971.

Lawler, E. E., III. *Motivation in work organizations.* Monterey, Calif.: Brooks/Cole, 1973.

Lawler, E. E., III, & Porter, L. W. Perceptions regarding management compensation. *Industrial Relations,* 1963, *3,* 41–49.

Lawler, E. E., III, & Porter, L. W. The effects of performance on job satisfaction. *Industrial Relations,* 1967, *7,* 20–28.

Locke, E. A. The nature and causes of job satisfaction. In Marvin D. Dunnette (Ed.), *Handbook of industrial and organizational psychology.* Chicago: Rand McNally, 1976, pp. 1297–1349.

McClelland, D. C., Atkinson, J. W., Clark, R. A., & Lowell, E. L. *The achievement motive.* New York: Appleton-Century-Crofts, 1953.

Mann, F. C., & Hoffman, L. R. *Automation and the worker.* New York: Holt, 1960.

Mayo, Elton. *The human problems of an industrial civilization.* New York: Viking Press, 1960 (originally published in 1933).

Mobley, W. H., Griffeth, R. W., Hand, H. H., & Meglino, B. M. Review and conceptual analysis of the employee turnover process. *Psychological Bulletin,* 1979, *86,* 493–522.

Muchinsky, P. M., & Tuttle, M. L. Employee turnover: An empirical and methodological assessment. *Journal of Vocational Behavior,* 1979, *14,* 43–77.

Palmore, E. Predicting longevity: A follow-up controlling for age. *The Gerontologist,* 1969, *9,* 247–250.

Patchen, M. Absence and employee feelings about fair treatment. *Personnel Psychology,* 1960, *13,* 349–360.

Porter, L. W. A study of perceived need satisfaction in bottom and middle management jobs. *Journal of Applied Psychology,* 1961, *45,* 1–10.

Porter, L. W. Job attitudes in management: I. Perceived deficiencies in need fulfillment as a function of job level. *Journal of Applied Psychology,* 1962, *46,* 375–384.

Porter, L. W., & Steers, R. M. Organizational, work, and personal factors in employee turnover and absenteeism. *Psychological Bulletin,* 1973, *80,* 151–176.

Quinn, R. P., & Staines, G. L. *The 1977 Quality of Employment Survey,* Ann Arbor: Institute for Social Research, The University of Michigan, 1979.

Reitz, H. J. *Behavior in organizations.* Homewood, Ill.: Richard D. Irwin, 1981.

Renwick, P. A., Lawler, E. E., & the *Psychology Today* staff. What you really want from your job. *Psychology Today,* 1978, *11,* 53–64, 118.

Richards, C. B., & Dobryns, H. F. Topography and culture: The case of the changing cage. *Human Organization,* 1957, *16,* 16–20.

Roethlisberger, F. J., & Dickson, W. J. *Management and the worker.* Cambridge: Harvard University Press, 1939.

Sawatsky, J. C. Psychological factors in industrial organization affecting employee stability. *Canadian Journal of Psychology,* 1951, *5,* 29–38.

Schreisheim, C. A. Job satisfaction, attitudes toward unions, and voting in a union representation election. *Journal of Applied Psychology,* 1978, *63,* 548–552.

Scott, W. E., Jr. Activation theory and task design. *Organizational Behavior and Human Performance,* 1966, *1,* 3–30.

Selye, H. *The stress of life.* New York: McGraw-Hill, 1956.

Sheppard, H. L., & Herrick, N. *Where have all the robots gone?* New York: Free Press, 1972.

Sirota, D. Some effects of promotional frustration on employees' understanding of, and attitudes toward, management. *Sociometry,* 1959, *22,* 273–278.

Smith, F. J. Work attitudes as predictors of attendance on a specific day. *Journal of Applied Psychology,* 1977, *62,* 16–19.

Smith, P. C., & Kendall, L. M. Cornell studies of job satisfaction: VI: Implications for the future. Ithaca, New York: Unpublished manuscript, 1963.

Smith, P. C., Kendall, L. M., & Hulin, C. L. *The measurement of satisfaction in work and retirement.* Chicago: Rand McNally, 1969.

Sulley, C. M., & Munden, K. J. Behavior of the mentally healthy. *Bulletin of the Menninger Clinic,* Vol. 26, 1962.

Taylor, F. W. What is scientific management? In H. F. Merrill (Ed.), *Classics in management* (2d ed.). New York: American Management Association, 1970, pp. 67–71.

Van Zelst, R. H. Worker popularity and job satisfaction. *Personnel Psychology,* 1951, *4,* 405–412.

Vroom, V. H. Ego-involvement, job satisfaction, and job performance. *Personnel Psychology,* 1962, *15,* 159–177.

Vroom, V. H. *Work and motivation.* New York: Wiley, 1964.

Vroom, V. H., & Mann, F. C. Leader authoritarianism and employee attitudes. *Personnel Psychology,* 1960, *13,* 125–140.

Walker, C. R., & Guest, R. H. *The man on the assembly line.* Cambridge: Harvard University Press, 1952.

Walker, J., & Marriott, R. A study of some attitudes to factory work. *Occupational Psychology,* 1951, *25,* 181–191.

Weaver, C. N. Job satisfaction in the United States in the 1970's. *Journal of Applied Psychology,* 1980, *65,* 364–367.

Weiss, D. J., Dawis, R. V., England, G. W., & Lofquist, L. H. *Minnesota studies in vocational rehabilitation: 22, Manual for the Minnesota Satisfaction Questionnaire.* Minneapolis: University of Minnesota Industrial Relations Center, 1967.

White, R. W. Motivation reconsidered: The concept of competence. *Psychological Review,* 1959, *66,* 297–333.

Whyte, W. F. *Money and motivation.* New York: Harper & Row, 1955.

Whyte, W. H., Jr. *The organization man.* Garden City, New York: Anchor, 1957.

Work in America (Report of a special task force to the Secretary of Health, Education and Welfare). Boston: MIT Press, 1973.

Zaleznik, A., Christensen, C. R., & Roethlisberger, F. J. *The motivation, productivity, and satisfaction of workers: A prediction study.* Boston: Harvard University, Graduate School of Business Administration, 1958.

PART FOUR

THE DESIGN OF WORK

CHAPTER 9
JOB DESIGN

The topic of job design has to do with the way that organizations assign tasks and responsibilities to individual organization members. The topic is an important one, since the way in which jobs are designed can have a critical impact on the motivation, productivity, and satisfaction of organization members. In this chapter we will analyze the reasons some jobs make people unhappy, uncomfortable, and unproductive, while other types of jobs seem to unlock people's creativity, energy, and drive. We will also examine new ideas and approaches to job design that can increase the productivity and effectiveness of the organization as a whole, while at the same time permitting individual organization members to occupy jobs which they find personally meaningful and satisfying.

The chapter begins with a brief historical review of alternative approaches to the design of work, starting with scientific management and carrying on through job rotation and job enlargement to what is known as *orthodox job enrichment* (Herzberg, 1974). We then turn to a detailed examination of the *job characteristics* approach to the design of individual jobs. This approach attempts to identify specific characteristics of jobs that facilitate the motivation, satisfaction, and performance of job incumbents. The chapter concludes with a discussion of an example of the successful application of job characteristics theory to work design.

It should be pointed out that our focus in this chapter will be exclusively upon the design of work for *individuals.* Thus, our attention will center upon individual *jobs* and how jobs can be designed to increase the motivation and satisfaction of their individual incumbents. In the next chapter we will shift our focus from the individual to the group and examine ways in which groups can be assigned tasks and responsibilities in such a way that the group as a whole will be productive and group members will be satisfied and effective.

HISTORICAL BACKGROUND

Attempts to outline systematically how work should be designed for maximum efficiency and productivity date back to the early part of the 19th century. As large industrial organizations were coming into existence, the topic of the *division of labor* among various workers became a subject of considerable interest. In fact, the notion of task specialization and its advantages can be clearly seen in the following quotation from a book entitled *On the Economy of Machinery and Manufactures* written by Charles Babbage in 1835.

> That the master manufacturer, by dividing the work to be executed into different processes, each requiring different degrees of skill or of force, can purchase exactly the precise quantity of both which is necessary for each process; whereas, if the whole work were executed by one workman, that person must possess sufficient skill to perform the most difficult, and sufficient strength to execute the most laborious, of the operations into which the act is divided. (p. 190)

Scientific Management

The notions of division of labor and task specialization lie at the heart of the scientific management approach to the design of work. Scientific management is an approach to work design developed by Frederick W. Taylor in a book entitled *The Principles of Scientific Management*, published in 1911. The ideas expressed in the book have had a tremendous impact upon the design of work, especially in manufacturing organizations, right up to the present day. Basically, Taylor argued for an approach to work design that emphasized standardization, specialization, and simplification of work activities in order to maximize productive efficiency.

> Perhaps the most prominent single element of modern scientific management is the task idea. The work of every workman is fully planned out by the management at least one day in advance, and each man receives in most cases complete written instructions describing in detail the task which he is to

accomplish, as well as the means to be used in doing the work. . . . This task specifies not only what is to be done but how it is to be done and the exact time allowed for doing it. And whenever the workman succeeds in doing his task right, and within the time limit specified, he receives an addition of from 30 percent to 100 percent to his ordinary wages. . . . The task is always so regulated that the man who is well-suited to his job will thrive while working at this rate during a long term of years and grow happier and more prosperous, instead of being overworked. (p. 39)

Scientific management has had a pervasive influence on the design of work in organizations for two reasons: first, because its basic tenet that specialization and routinization of work can increase efficiency and productivity is valid (at least up to a point, as we shall see later); and second, because scientific management drew explicit attention to a number of critical managerial functions that must be handled competently if organizations are to be effective (Porter, Lawler, & Hackman, 1975).

1. ***Task Analysis.***   This is of course the heart of the scientific management approach. Management is provided with specific guidelines and criteria regarding: (*a*) how to divide the tasks to be performed among individual workers; and (*b*) how to develop rules and guidelines for the accomplishment of each particular segment of the work in the most efficient manner.
2. ***Selection.***   Scientific management places great emphasis upon insuring a good match between the skills of the worker and the demands of the job. To his credit, Taylor pointed out the dangers inherent in hiring both underqualified workers who could not perform up to standard and overqualified workers whose skills would not be well-utilized in a given position.
3. ***Training.***   Training plays a crucial role in the scientific management approach. According to Taylor, training is essential both prior to undertaking work and during work on a job. This emphasis on the role of training is clear from the fact that Taylor referred to supervisors in a scientifically managed organization as "teachers."
4. ***Rewards.***   Scientific management recognizes the fact that if high levels of productivity are to be reached and maintained, individuals must be provided with rewards contingent on their performance. Hence the emphasis on monetary bonuses when production standards are met.
5. ***Goal-setting.***   Inherent in the scientific management approach is the setting of specific and challenging goals for each individual to accomplish each workday. In Taylor's own words:

The average workman will work with the greatest satisfaction, both to himself and to his employer, when he is given each day a definite task which he is to perform in a given time, and which constitutes a proper day's work for a good workman. This furnishes the workman with a clear-cut standard, by which he can throughout the day measure his own progress, and the accomplishment of which affords him the greatest satisfaction. (pp. 120–121)

Thus we can see that the success and popularity of scientific management were no accident. First, by encouraging management to analyze how the work to be accomplished could be broken down into simple specialized tasks and then how these tasks could be performed with minimal effort and maximum speed, the overall efficiency of the organization was increased. Second, this emphasis upon standardization and simplification occurred at the same time as other significant technological developments in automation and mass production. These new production technologies were well-suited to the scientific management approach to work design. Third, scientific management had built into it a number of what are usually thought of as much more "modern" approaches to motivation and management. Specifically, it drew attention to: (1) the importance of matching individuals and jobs (via selection and training); (2) the role of contingent rewards in maintaining effective performance; and (3) the influence of specific, challenging, but realistic performance goals on motivation and performance. A final factor relevant to the popularity of scientific management among managers is its emphasis upon placing control and influence in the hands of the managers rather than the workers:

> . . . the managers assume new burdens, new duties, and responsibilities never dreamed of in the past. The managers assume, for instance, the burden of gathering together all of the traditional knowledge which in the past has been possessed by the workman and then of classifying, tabulating, and reducing this knowledge to rules, laws, and formulae which are immensely helpful to the workmen in doing their daily work. (Taylor, 1911, p. 36)

Scientific management became very popular among managers and was able to contribute significantly to increased organizational efficiency and effectiveness. At the same time, however, scientific management is not without its weaknesses and shortcomings. Primary among these short-comings is the tendency for jobs under scientific management to be highly simplified and routine, and hence monotonous and boring for those performing them. Scientific management was correct in drawing attention to the importance of matching the skills of the employee to the demands of the job. However, jobs in scientifically managed organizations tend to be so simplified and routine that all but the dullest and least skilled individuals are overqualified for them. Further, although scientific management correctly notes the importance of contingent rewards, it also assumed that the only contingent reward valued by organization members was money. There is no provision within scientific management for the use of alternative rewards such as personal recognition or opportunities for growth and development.

The outcome of all this is that although scientific management presents many potential advantages to an organization, it also tends to create high levels of monotony, boredom, and dissatisfaction among organization members. The best example of both the advantages and disadvantages of scientific management is probably the modern automobile assembly line. Although the productive efficiency of the assembly line is legend, its negative impact upon those working on the line is becoming more and more widely recognized. Figure 9-1 summarizes the feelings and reactions of individuals working on the General Motors assembly line at Lordstown in the early 1970s.

The boredom and dissatisfaction created by oversimplified and routine jobs is undesirable and costly from two points of view. First, it is costly in a societal sense in terms of the dehumanization of the individuals forced to perform such work. Individuals who are expected to behave like machines soon lose their abilities to think, take initiative, and use their skills effectively. Second, boredom and dissatisfaction are costly to the employing organizations themselves. Horror stories abound regarding acts of sabotage carried out by assembly line workers for no other reasons than either to give themselves a rest by stopping the line or to give them something interesting and challenging to do apart from their boring and repetitive jobs (eg., figuring out how you can contrive to leave a wrench in the gas tank of a car). Further, dissatisfaction is consistently related to high levels of absenteeism and turnover. Again, organizations employing highly repetitive and monotonous work systems tend to be characterized by high levels of absenteeism and turnover. Unpublished data from one large automobile manufacturing plant reported turnover among assembly line workers over 100 percent in a single year. Both absenteeism and turnover are extremely costly to organizations.

As a result of some of these shortcomings, scientific management has, not surprisingly, come in for criticism from a variety of sources. In addition, a number of alternative approaches to work design have been developed.

Job Enlargement

Job enlargement emerged in the late 1940s and 1950s in response to the perceived negative consequences of the high levels of specialization, simplification, and routinization generated by the application of the principles of scientific management to the design of work. While scientific management implies the desirability of breaking jobs down into ever smaller and simpler segments, advocates of job enlargement argued that this process could go, and in fact in many cases had gone, too far. The application of scientific management principles involves tearing a job down into its simplest and most basic components, and then assigning an individual only one of these components to perform over and over again. The advantage was a high level of productive efficiency, but the disadvantages were monotony, boredom, dissatisfaction, absenteeism, and turn-

LIFE ON THE ASSEMBLY LINE IN THE EARLY 1970s

The Vega workers (at the new Lordstown, Ohio assembly plant) are echoing a rank-and-file demand that has been suppressed by both union and management for the past twenty years: HUMANIZE WORKING CONDITIONS.

Hanging around the parking lot between shifts, I learned immediately that to these young workers, "It's not the money."

"It pays good," said one, "but it's driving me crazy."

"I don't want more money," said another. "none of us do."

"I do," said his friend, "so I can quit quicker."

"It's the job," everyone said, but they found it hard to describe the job itself.

"My father worked in auto for thirty-five years," said a clean-cut lad," and he never talked about the job. What's there to say? A car comes, I weld it. A car comes, I weld it. A car comes, I weld it. One-hundred-and-one times an hour."

I asked a young wife, "What does your husband tell you about his work?"

"He doesn't say what he does. Only if something happened like, 'My hair caught on fire,' or 'Something fell in my face.' "

"There's a lot of variety in the paint shop," said a dapper twenty-two-year-old up from West Virginia. "You clip on the color hose, bleed out the old color, and squirt. Clip, bleed, squirt, think; clip, bleed, squirt, yawn; clip, bleed, squirt, scratch your nose. Only now the Gee-Mads have taken away the time to scratch your nose."

A long-hair reminisced: "Before the Go-Mads, when I had a good job like door handles, I could get a couple of cars ahead and have a whole minute to relax."

I asked about diversions. "What do you do to keep from going crazy?"

"Well, certain jobs like the pit you can light up a cigarette without them seeing."

"I go to the wastepaper basket. I wait a certain number of cars, then find a piece of paper to throw away."

"I have fantasies. You know what I keep imagining? I see a car coming down. It's red. So I know it's gonna have a black seat, black dash, black interiors. But I keep thinking what if somebody up there sends down the wrong color interiors — like orange, and me putting in yellow cushions, bright yellow!"

"There's always water fights, paint fights, or laugh, talk, tell jokes. Anything so you don't feel like a machine."

But everyone had the same hope: "You're always waiting for the line to break down."

FIGURE 9-1

(SOURCE: Reprinted by permission of Barbara Garson c/o International Creative Management. Copyright © 1972, 1973, 1974, 1975 by Barbara Garson.)

over. In an attempt to reduce these negative consequences for the individuals performing the work, advocates of job enlargement argued in favor of "putting back together" the highly fractionalized and specialized jobs resulting from scientific management.

The rationale behind job enlargement was that "blue-collar blues" could be overcome if individuals were given jobs that involved a greater variety of operations, had longer cycle times, and required a wider range of skills than scientific management. For example, manufacturing organizations employing the principles of scientific management would generally have one person whose job was to set up jobs to run on a machine, another person to run the machine, and yet another person whose job was to inspect the work produced on the machine. The operator who finished running a job could only sit and wait until an inspector arrived to inspect the work and then wait again for the set-up person to come to set up the next job. There are numerous examples of the application of job enlargement to such situations. Rather than maintaining separate jobs for set-up, operation, and inspection, the three functions can be combined into a single, "enlarged" job. In some instances this enlargement of tasks and responsibilities was also accompanied by greater latitude for workers in determining some of the methods and procedures employed, and also some freedom (within limits) for workers to set their own work pace. Walker (1950) reports results of several such job enlargement experiments that resulted in cost savings for the organization (resulting from a reduced need for inspectors and set-up people) as well as considerable increases in both productivity and satisfaction.

A specific example of a job enlargement experiment is described by Porter, Lawler, and Hackman (1975), based upon a case description by Kilbridge (1960). The particular example involved workers who assembled a small centrifugal water pump used in washing machines.

> Prior to job enlargement, the pumps were assembled by six operators on a conveyor line, with each operator performing a particular part of the assembly. Each worker spent about ½ minute on each pump, and total pump assembly time was about 1¾ minutes. The job was changed so that each worker assembled an entire pump, inspected it, and placed his own identifying mark on the pump. In addition the assembly operations were converted to a "batch" system in which each worker had more freedom to control his work pace than had been the case under the conveyor system. The investigator reported that after the job had been enlarged, total assembly time decreased to about 1½ minutes, quality improved, and important cost savings were realized. (p. 279)

While such reported examples of the advantages and positive outcomes of job enlargement are not rare, the approach was not without its critics. For example, some members of the labor movement argued that job enlargement was essentially a management strategy designed to increase productivity and reduce the number of employees required by organizations. Others criticized job enlargement on the basis that it left the essential nature of work unchanged and simply required individuals to perform a wider variety of boring and monotonous jobs.

In addition to these specific criticisms, job enlargement also suffered from the fact that it was not based upon any well-articulated underlying theory that could explain how and why positive results should be expected when jobs were enlarged. Job enlargement was largely an intuitive approach to work design implemented by managers and consultants who could perceive some of the negative effects of overspecialization and who felt that "something had to be done." This lack of a guiding framework made it difficult to develop general principles for the redesign of work in accordance with the job enlargement approach.

Job Enrichment

The job enrichment approach to the design of work has its basis in the "two-factor" theory of motivation and satisfaction developed by Herzberg and his associates (Herzberg, 1966, 1968, 1974, 1976; Herzberg et al., 1957; Herzberg et al., 1959). According to Herzberg, characteristics of jobs fall into two separate and distinct categories labeled *motivators* and *hygiene factors*. Motivators include factors that are intrinsic to the job, such as achievement, recognition, responsibility, advancement, and personal growth and development. Hygiene factors, on the other hand, are extrinsic to the work itself and refer to things such as company policies, supervision, working conditions, salary, interpersonal relationships, status, and security. Herzberg believes that satisfaction and dissatisfaction with work are not opposite ends of a single continuum, but are separate and independent continua. Further, it is argued that the extent to which a person is satisfied and motivated by a job is solely determined by the extent to which the job contains the intrinsic motivators. Dissatisfaction, on the other hand, is caused by a lack of the extrinsic hygiene factors. Thus, hygiene factors must be present in a job in order to *prevent* dissatisfaction, but the hygiene factors *cannot* generate positive motivation and satisfaction. That can only be done by introducing the intrinsic motivators into the job.

Herzberg's theory obviously has some clear and unambiguous implications for the design of work. The theory implies that if individuals are to be satisfied by their jobs and motivated to perform effectively, then jobs must be high on the growth or motivator factors. Redesigning jobs so that they are high on the motivator factors is what Herzberg and others refer to as *job enrichment*.

A very sensible question to ask at this point would be "What's the difference between 'job enrichment' and 'job enlargement'?" Herzberg believes there's a big difference, and the difference has to do with the extent to which a job requires workers simply to *do* what others have instructed them to do versus the amount of personal *control* that an individual is given over *how* the work is to be performed. Herzberg argues that most jobs in organizations consist of a very large "doing" component and a very small "controlling" component. Herzberg refers to job enlargement as *horizontal enlargement*, since he views it as involving little if any change (in most cases) in the proportions of doing and controlling involved in jobs. When jobs are horizontally enlarged, people are given a greater variety of things to *do* but are not necessarily given any increased *control* over how these things are to be done. As a result, Herzberg believes that horizontal enlargement has relatively little capacity to increase the motivator factors in a job and a similarly small potential to affect motivation and satisfaction positively.

Herzberg refers to job enrichment as *vertical enrichment*. Vertical enrichment involves a fundamental shift in the degree of control workers have over their work. The term *vertical* is employed to indicate that job enrichment involves a downward vertical shifting in the organization of authority and responsibility for effective performance. The authority and control of management are shifted downward in the organization to those who also actually *do* the work. This downward vertical shift of control diagrammed in Figure 9-2 is inherent in jobs that are redesigned to contain more of the motivator factors. By giving individuals a greater

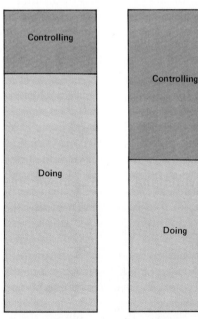

Before Vertical Enrichment

After Vertical Enrichment

FIGURE 9-2
Changes in the proportions of "controlling" and "doing" involved in typical jobs before and after vertical enrichment.

degree of freedom and control, we increase the extent to which those individuals can experience feelings of personal achievement, responsibility, growth, and competence, all factors that are believed to increase motivation and satisfaction.

Herzberg's two-factor theory of motivation and his ideas on job enrichment have achieved a wide degree of currency and popularity among practicing managers. Such awareness and popularity are not surprising. Herzberg's theory is elegant in its simplicity. If the entire world is not black and white, at least the world of work is conveniently organized into just two sets of independent factors: motivators and hygiene factors. This idea is obviously appealing to practicing managers, since it is easy to understand, easy to remember, and clear in its implications for management practice (i.e., vertically enrich all the jobs in your organization to increase the motivators they contain). In addition, Herzberg's theory is intuitively appealing to managers who can often think back to a job which they may have held which could be described as low on motivators and which they found to be uninteresting and boring, while their current jobs may be high on motivators and felt to be challenging, motivating, and satisfying.

The popularity of Herzberg's theory has had a number of positive effects. First, it has helped draw the attention of both managers and researchers to the nature of the work itself as a critical factor influencing what people do at work and how they feel about what they do. Second, it has increased awareness of the potential importance of intrinsic factors such as achievement, responsibility, and growth as factors influencing motivation, satisfaction, and performance. Finally, it has resulted in a large number of work redesign projects and experiments undertaken to enrich jobs and improve motivation and satisfaction. Many of these projects have resulted in positive improvements which are described in a variety of sources (e.g., Ford, 1969, 1973; Paul, Robertson, & Herzberg, 1969; Walters & Associates, 1975).

At the same time, however, Herzberg's theory and approach have been subjected to a good deal of criticism and appear to suffer from a number of serious shortcomings. These criticisms and shortcomings have to do with: (1) the *accuracy* of some of the reported successes of job enrichment; (2) the *validity* of the two-factor theory upon which job enrichment is based; and (3) the *completeness* of the two-factor theory approach to motivation and work design.

Accuracy of Success Reports

While a considerable number of successful examples of job enrichment have been reported, no one pretends that there have not also been failures when job enrichment has been attempted (see, for example, Hackman, 1975). At the same time, there are some individuals, particularly among trade unionists and industrial engineers, who also question the accuracy and validity of the claims made regarding what have been reported as successful cases of job enrichment. For example Mitchell Fein (1974), a consultant industrial engineer, reports that a close examination of job enrichment case histories and studies reported between 1964 and 1974 leads him to the following conclusions:

1. What actually occurred in the cases was often quite different from what was reported to have occurred.
2. Most of the cases were conducted with handpicked employees, who were usually working in areas or plants isolated from the main operations and thus did not represent a cross-section of the working population. Practically all experiments have been in nonunion plants.
3. Only a handful of job enrichment cases have been reported in the past ten years, despite the claims of gains obtained for employees and management through job changes.
4. In *all* instances the experiments were initiated by management, never by workers or unions. (p. 70)

Fein's claims draw attention to two important issues regarding job enrichment in particular and work design in general. First, there are a variety of segments of the population that are either highly skeptical or in some cases actively opposed to attempts to change the fundamental nature of work in organizations. Second, there is a tremendous need for careful, accurate, rigorous research into the effects of changes in work design on motivation, performance, and satisfaction. Vague and unsystematic anecdotes and case reports do not provide the kinds of evidence necessary to arrive at accurate and unbiased evaluations.

Validity of Two-Factor Theory

Job enrichment is based upon Herzberg's two-factor theory, which argues that only motivators can increase motivation and satisfaction, while hygiene factors can only reduce dissatisfaction. Evidence in favor of two-factor theory is reported in a number of studies carried out by Herzberg and his associates (eg., Herzberg, 1966; Herzberg et al., 1957; Herzberg et al., 1959) and in one other study (Whitsett & Winslow, 1967). However, the vast majority of other independent researchers who have attempted to replicate Herzberg's findings have consistently failed to obtain results similar to Herzberg's (eg., Dunnette, Campbell, & Hakel, 1967; Hinton, 1968; House & Wigdor, 1967; King, 1970). Researchers other than Herzberg consistently find that *both* motivators *and* hygiene factors can lead to *both* satisfaction *and* dissatisfaction. Characteristics of jobs do not appear to fall into such a neat two-way classification as Herzberg's theory suggests, and satisfaction and dissatisfaction do not appear to be two separate and independent continua. The most frequently cited explanation of why Herzberg and his associates consistently obtain results which are at variance with those obtained by almost all other researchers has to do with some peculiarities of the particular methods employed by Herzberg in his research.

Herzberg's own studies employed a research methodology known as *critical incidents*. The critical incidents technique involves asking organization members to think of experiences at work that caused them to feel either very satisfied or very dissatisfied and to describe what factors caused them to feel either positively or negatively. People tended to describe their positive feelings as being caused by intrinsic factors such as their personal accomplishments and achievements. Negative feelings, on the other hand, were described most often as being caused by extrinsic factors such as low pay and poor supervision. These findings led Herzberg to the distinction between motivators and hygiene factors. What other researchers have since pointed out, however, is that there is a widespread natural tendency among people to attribute the causes of positive events to themselves personally (intrinsic factors) and to attribute the causes of negative events to things outside themselves (extrinsic factors). This bias tends to operate regardless of what the actual source of the positive or negative feelings happens to be. As a result, critics of Herzberg's theory have argued that the nature of his findings may not be due to the fact that work characteristics consist of two distinct categories of motivators and hygiene factors. Rather, his results may simply be a reflection of the natural biases which all people share in their perceptions of the causes of positive and negative events in their lives. The critics' case is strengthened by the fact that tests of Herzberg's theory using methods other than the critical incidents technique consistently fail to find support for the existence of two independent factors.

Incompleteness of the Job Enrichment Approach

In addition to criticisms of the two-factor theory that underlies job enrichment, concern has also been raised about some important issues which the job enrichment approach does *not* address. First, advocates of job enrichment make no allowance for differences among people in their reactions to enriched work. Herzberg does not suggest that enriched jobs will be appropriate for some people and inappropriate for others, but suggests that job enrichment is *the* route to increased motivation and satisfaction for everyone. Common sense, practical experience, and research results suggest such a universal approach to be oversimplified and inaccurate (Hulin & Blood, 1968). Job enrichment is probably appropriate for some individuals and inappropriate for others. This issue is addressed by more recent theories of work design that are discussed in the next section.

A second area of incompleteness of the job enrichment approach has to do with the measurement of the presence or absence of motivating conditions in a job. Herzberg (1974) has outlined the following eight ingredients of a good job: *direct feedback, a client relationship, a learning function, the opportunity for each person to schedule his own work, unique expertise, control over resources, direct communication,* and *personal accountability.* However, Herzberg does not present any method or techniques for systematically measuring the extent to which each of these ingredients is present or absent in any given job. As a result, it is impossible to carry out rigorous and careful empirical tests of the extent to which each of these ingredients is in fact related to increased motivation and satisfaction.

JOB CHARACTERISTICS MODEL

Recently, researchers interested in the design of work and in the impact of work design on motivation, satisfaction, and performance have been focusing increasing attention upon the specific aspects or characteristics of jobs that appear to have a significant impact upon how people respond to their work. The first systematic large-scale study of job characteristics was carried out by Turner and Lawrence (1965). These researchers identified and measured six "requisite task attributes" that they theorized should be related to employee satisfaction and attendance. The six attributes were *variety, autonomy, required social interaction, opportunities for social interaction, knowledge and skill required,* and *responsibility.* Turner and Lawrence combined measures of each of the six attributes into a requisite task attribute index (RTA index) for each job and studied the relationship between the RTA Index and employees' satisfaction and attendance. Contrary to predictions, they did not find that higher scores on the RTA index were consistently related to higher levels of satisfaction and lower levels of absenteeism. What they did find, however, was that the predicted relationships were obtained for workers in small towns and rural settings, while the predictions did not hold up for workers in urban settings. They concluded that the relationship between task characteristics and employee responses was influenced by the cultural background of the employees.

Subsequent work by Blood and Hulin (1967) suggested that the underlying factor influencing individuals' responses to the design of their work may be the extent to which people are alienated from traditional middle-class work norms. Individuals adhering to such traditional work norms regarding the value of achievement, hard work, and responsibility were predicted to respond positively to interesting, challenging work. Those alienated from such values would not be expected to respond positively to more interesting, yet more demanding jobs.

An alternative approach to the impact of job characteristics on employee responses was developed by Hackman and Lawler (1971). These authors argued that four "core dimensions" of jobs determine the potential of a job to be motivating. The four core dimensions are *autonomy, task identity, variety,* and *feedback.* Hackman and Lawler also hypothesized that individuals with strong needs for personal growth and development would respond more positively to jobs high on the core dimensions than would individuals with weaker growth needs. The results obtained were largely supportive of their predictions.

The ideas put forward by Hackman and Lawler (1971) have served as a basis for further developments and refinements of the job characteristics approach to work design by Hackman and Oldham (1976, 1980). The job characteristics model put forward by Hackman and Oldham is the most well-articulated theory available regarding the impact of the design of work upon the thoughts, feelings, and actions of job incumbents. For this reason we will examine the Hackman-Oldham job characteristics model in some detail.

Internal Work Motivation

The Hackman-Oldham job characteristics model is primarily concerned with the conditions under which jobs generate high levels of *internal work motivation* in job incumbents. Internal work motivation is motivation that is self-generated by the job incumbent and is completely independent of external factors such as pay, supervision, and coworkers. When internal work motivation is high, good performance on the job generates positive feelings and serves as an occasion for self-reward. In contrast, poor performance leads to negative feelings and a denial of personal internal rewards.

Three key conditions must all be met if internal motivation is to be high. These three conditions are outlined in Figure 9-3. First, an individual must experience the work as *personally meaningful.* The person must view the work and its outcomes as something which he or she personally cares about and feels to be important. In other words, the work must be something that "makes a difference" to the person. Second, if internal motivation is to exist, the person must *experience personal responsibility* for the work and its outcomes. An individual will only experience positive feelings following good performance and negative feelings following poor performance if he or she feels personally responsible for the good or poor performance. The third key condition for the existence of internal work motivation is *knowledge of the results* of the work. Regardless of how meaningful a job is to a person or how personally responsible a person feels for the performance of a job, if the person is unable to determine whether performance has been effective or ineffective, it is impossible for the person to experience the positive or negative self-evaluative feelings that are the essential components of internal work motivation.

These three key conditions for the existence of internal work motivation are referred to as *critical psychological states.* They are given this label since the three key conditions for internal motivation are all internal to the person doing the work (hence "psychological"), and because the

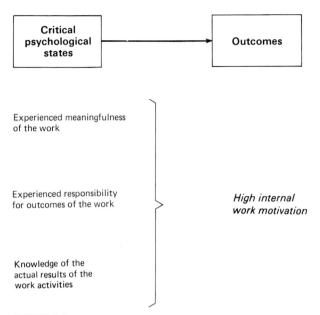

FIGURE 9-3
The three psychological states that affect internal work motivation. (SOURCE: J. R. Hackman and G. R. Oldham, *Work Redesign*. Reading, Mass.: Addison-Wesley, 1980, p. 73. Used by permission.)

presence of *all* three conditions is argued to be necessary for the existence of internal motivation (hence "critical"). Having clarified the nature of internal work motivation and the three key conditions that underlie it, we now require a specification of the relationship between particular characteristics of jobs and the key components of internal work motivation.

Core Job Characteristics

Hackman and Oldham spell out specifically the links that exist between job characteristics and the critical psychological states. These links are outlined in Figure 9-4. According to the job characteristics model there are a total of five *core* characteristics of work that influence the critical psychological states (this list is an expansion of the four core dimensions put forward by Hackman and Lawler [1971]). Three job characteristics are thought to influence the experienced meaningfulness of the work, while one characteristic each is hypothesized to have a direct impact upon experienced responsibility and knowledge of results.

Experienced Meaningfulness

Three core job characteristics are hypothesized to influence the extent to which an individual experiences work as personally meaningful. These three core characteristics are defined as follows:

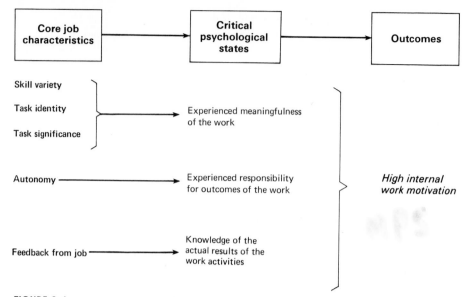

FIGURE 9-4
Job characteristics that foster the three psychological states. (SOURCE: J. R. Hackman and G. R. Oldham, *Work Redesign*. Reading, Mass.: Addison-Wesley, 1980, p. 77. Used by permission.)

> *Skill variety:* The degree to which a job requires a variety of different activities in carrying out the work, involving the use of a number of different skills and talents of the person.
> *Task identity:* The degree to which a job requires completion of a "whole" and identifiable piece of work, that is, doing a job from beginning to end with a visible outcome.
> *Task significance:* The degree to which the job has a substantial impact on the lives of other people, whether those people are in the immediate organization or in the world at large. (Hackman & Oldham, 1980, pp. 78–79)

Each of these three job characteristics contributes to the overall experienced meaningfulness of the work. A job that is high on all three job characteristics would naturally have the greatest potential to create a feeling of experienced meaningfulness for a person performing the job. However, it is important to note that a job need not be high on all three characteristics simultaneously in order to be experienced as personally meaningful. Since all three characteristics influence meaningfulness, a job that is low on one dimension and high on the other two may still be experienced as highly meaningful to the incumbent.

Experienced Responsibility

The job characteristic hypothesized to have a direct impact upon the extent to which a person experiences personal responsibility for outcomes of the work is autonomy.

> *Autonomy:* The degree to which the job provides substantial freedom, independence, and discretion to the individual in scheduling the work and in determining the procedures to be used in carrying it out. (Hackman & Oldham, 1980, p. 79)

The rationale here is fairly straightforward. If an individual is to feel that he or she is personally responsible for performing effectively or ineffectively, it is essential that the job provide the individual with some degree of freedom, independence, and discretion in determining precisely how and when the work is to be performed. Such a situation creates the conditions under which people can attribute success or failure on the job to themselves rather than to someone or something else.

Knowledge of Results

The extent to which an individual possesses knowledge of the actual results of the work activities is determined by the extent to which the job provides the incumbent with direct feedback. The relevant job characteristic is defined as follows:

> *Job feedback:* The degree to which carrying out the work activities required by the job provides the individual with direct and clear information about the effectiveness of his or her performance. (Hackman & Oldham, 1980, p. 80)

It should be pointed out that the emphasis here is upon feedback that the individual receives directly as a result of performing the job. Obviously there are other sources of feedback regarding performance such as superiors and coworkers. However, in studying the impact of work design on motivation, our interest is focused exclusively upon the extent to which the individual is able to obtain feedback directly as a result of performing the work. Feedback that a person gets directly from the job also has the advantage of letting the person know how well he or she is doing immediately, and does so in a private, nonpersonal way.

Overall Motivating Potential

As we have seen, the job characteristics model identifies five core characteristics of jobs and specifies the relationships that exist between these job characteristics and the three critical psychological states that form the basis for high levels of internal work motivation. The job characteristics model also contains a method for assessing the overall *motivating potential* of a job.

The method for determining the motivating potential score (MPS) for a job derives directly from job characteristics theory, which specifies the following:

1. *All* three critical psychological states must be present if internal motivation is to be high.
2. The psychological state of experienced meaningfulness is influenced by

the job characteristics of skill variety, task identity, and task significance.

3. The psychological state of experienced responsibility for outcomes is determined by the job characteristic of autonomy.

4. The psychological state of knowledge of results is determined by the job characteristic of job feedback.

These theoretical statements regarding the nature of high internal work motivation and the relationship between the job characteristics and the psychological states leads to the following formula for assessing a job's overall motivating potential:

$$\text{Motivating potential score (MPS)} = \frac{\text{skill variety} + \text{task identity} + \text{task significance}}{3} \times \text{autonomy} \times \text{job feedback}$$

Since the theory specifies that all three psychological states must be present if internal motivation is to be high, the job characteristics that influence each of the three psychological states are multiplied together. Multiplication is the appropriate operation, since this ensures that if any of the psychological states is at or near zero, then regardless of how high the other psychological states are, overall internal motivation will be zero or very close to it. Further, since experienced meaningfulness is determined by a total of three job characteristics, while experienced responsibility and knowledge of results are influenced by only one each, the three job characteristics influencing experienced meaningfulness are averaged prior to being multiplied by autonomy and job feedback. The MPS formula provides a very convenient basis for summarizing the nature of a job in terms of its capacity to generate high internal work motivation.

Differences among People

Unlike the job enrichment approach to work design, the job characteristics model does *not* suggest that jobs high on the core job characteristics will lead to high levels of internal work motivation for *all* people. In fact, job characteristics theory identifies three separate qualities or characteristics of people that influence or "moderate" the effect of work design on internal work motivation. As the full model contained in Figure 9-5 indicates, the theory suggests that these *individual difference moderator variables* (as they are referred to) operate in two ways. First, they influence the extent to which the five job characteristics can lead to the three psychological states. Second, they influence the extent to which the three psychological states can lead to high internal motivation.

The three characteristics of individuals that operate in this fashion as moderator variables are as follows:

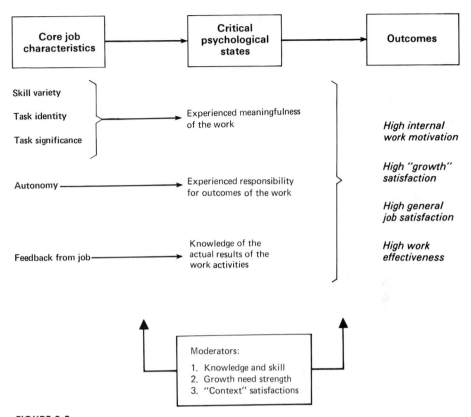

FIGURE 9-5
The complete job characteristics model.   (SOURCE: J. R. Hackman and G. R. Oldham, *Work Redesign*. Reading, Mass.: Addison-Wesley, 1980, p. 90. Used by permission.)

1. Knowledge and skill
2. Growth need strength
3. "Context" satisfactions

Knowledge and Skill

A job that is high on the five core job characteristics has the potential to generate high levels of internal work motivation. However, performance on a job is determined not only by the workers' motivation to perform, but also by their job-relevant knowledge and skill. Workers with a high degree of job-relevant knowledge and skill, when placed on a job with high motivating potential are likely to perform well and, as a result, will experience positive feelings, self-rewards, and continued high levels of internal motivation. On the other hand, workers lacking knowledge and skill required for the job will be unable to perform well regardless of the high levels of internal motivation generated by the work itself. The result will be poor performance, negative feelings, no self-rewards, and, before long, a drastic reduction in the capacity of the job to generate the key psychological states and hence high internal motivation.

Growth Need Strength

Growth needs refers to individuals' needs for such things as personal accomplishment, learning, and personal growth and development (the nature of these needs is discussed in more detail in Chapter 5). According to job characteristics theory, individuals with strong needs for growth are likely to respond much more positively to jobs high in motivating potential than are individuals with weak growth needs. In fact, the theory argues that this differential reaction occurs in two ways. First, people with strong growth needs will be more likely to experience the three critical psychological states when placed on a job high on the five core job characteristics. Second, people with strong growth needs will experience higher levels of internal work motivation when the critical psychological states are present than will individuals low on growth need strength. Both factors operating together should result in positive and enthusiastic responses to enriched jobs for individuals with strong needs for growth.

Context Satisfactions

Obviously, the nature of the work itself is not the only factor that influences a person's motivation to work and satisfaction with that work. There are a variety of other important work "context" factors such as pay, supervision, coworkers, and working conditions that also influence motivation and satisfaction. If an individual is extremely dissatisfied or unhappy with these context factors, then it is argued that the potential of an enriched job to result in high levels of internal motivation is greatly diminished. People who feel they are being unfairly paid, poorly supervised, and required to work with unfriendly coworkers in an unpleasant environment are quite unlikely to explode with enthusiasm and drive if suddenly offered more challenging and demanding jobs. Thus, it appears that a reasonable degree of satisfaction with work context factors is a necessary prerequisite for the work itself to be able to generate high levels of internal motivation.

Outcomes of Enriched Work

Up to this point the only outcome of enriched work that we have discussed is internal work motivation. In fact, job characteristics theory specifies a variety of outcomes that are influenced by work design. This full set of outcomes is summarized in Figure 9-5. These outcomes fall into two categories: personal outcomes and work effectiveness.

Personal Outcomes

Personal outcomes refers to those outcomes experienced personally by the individual performing an enriched job. There are three such outcomes influenced by the nature of the work itself. Besides generating high levels of *internal work motivation*, enriched jobs also provide individuals with greater opportunities for personal growth and development. As a result, *growth satisfaction* should be higher for individuals performing enriched work. Finally, *general satisfaction* with work should be higher on enriched jobs as a result of a spillover effect from satisfaction with the work itself.

Work Effectiveness

Work effectiveness is a summary term employed to capture both the *quality* and *quantity* aspects of work performance. Work effectiveness is predicted to be higher for enriched jobs than for more simplified and routine jobs. The argument for increased work effectiveness with regard to quality is quite straightforward. Jobs high in motivating potential generate high levels of motivation among individuals to perform *well*. As a result, high-quality performance should be observed on enriched jobs. The argument with regard to quantity of performance is less straightforward, and, in fact, the model does *not* predict improved quantity of performance as a general outcome of work redesign. However, it is argued that increases in quantity of performance will result if any of the following factors characterized the design of work in the organization *prior* to redesign: (1) individuals were "turned off" by very routine and repetitive work, (2) hidden inefficiencies existed in the use of time or support staff, or (3) redundancies or time-wasting procedures were built into the work system. By removing or correcting such problems and deficiencies, work redesign has the potential to result in improved quantity of performance.

Diagnosis and Implementation

Another positive element of the job characteristics approach to work design is its strong emphasis upon the need for careful and systematic diagnosis of the nature of work in organizations *prior* to undertaking any work-redesign projects. We'll review the techniques that have been developed for conducting such a diagnosis, the major issues and questions that a diagnosis must address, and the essential ingredients for effective implementation of work redesign.

The Job Diagnostic Survey

Hackman and Oldham (1975) have developed a questionnaire entitled the *Job Diagnostic Survey* (JDS) that is designed to measure all of the components included in the job characteristics model. The questionnaire, which has been carefully designed and validated, can be administered to all of the incumbents of a job that is being considered for redesign. The results of the incumbents' responses are then averaged in order to provide a picture of the job as it is perceived and reacted to by those who perform it and hence are most familiar with it. The JDS yields scores on a scale

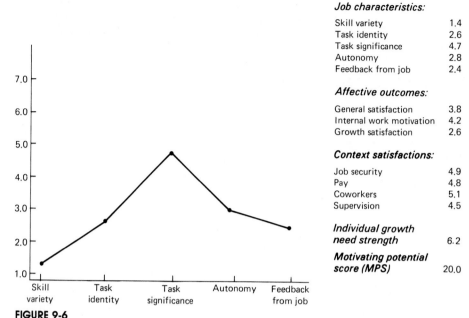

Job characteristics:

Skill variety	1.4
Task identity	2.6
Task significance	4.7
Autonomy	2.8
Feedback from job	2.4

Affective outcomes:

General satisfaction	3.8
Internal work motivation	4.2
Growth satisfaction	2.6

Context satisfactions:

Job security	4.9
Pay	4.8
Coworkers	5.1
Supervision	4.5

Individual growth need strength 6.2

Motivating potential score (MPS) 20.0

FIGURE 9-6
Diagnostic profile for keypunchers. (SOURCE: J. R. Hackman and G. R. Oldham, *Work Redesign.* Reading, Mass.: Addison-Wesley, 1980, p. 134. Used by permission.)

from 1 to 7 (1 being low and 7 high) for: (1) the five core job characteristics; (2) the three critical psychological states; (3) the three personal outcomes; (4) four context satisfactions; and (5) individual growth need strength. The motivating potential score (MPS) for the job can also be computed from the scores on the core job characteristics according to the formula presented previously (and can vary from a minimum of 1 to a maximum of 343). Figure 9-6 contains a sample profile generated from the JDS for the job of keypuncher.

In order to make a meaningful assessment of what constitutes a low or high score on any of the dimensions measured, we obviously require some standard to compare against. The best available standards are the national norms for the JDS based upon the responses to the JDS of 6930 employees who work on 876 different jobs in 56 organizations. These norms are summarized in Table 9-1. By comparing the profile for the keypuncher's job to the national norms it is possible to draw some meaningful inferences about the motivating potential of the job, the specific job characteristics on which the job is high and low, the capacity of the job to generate the key psychological states and personal outcomes, as well as the "readiness" of job incumbents for change as indicated by context satisfactions and growth need strength (at present, the JDS does not yield a measure of job-relevant knowledge and skill).

TABLE 9-1
Job Diagnostic Survey National Norms

Job characteristics	Norms
Skill variety	4.7
Task identity	4.7
Task significance	5.5
Autonomy	4.9
Feedback from job	4.9
Critical psychological states	
Experienced meaningfulness of the work	5.2
Experienced responsibility for work outcomes	5.5
Knowledge of results	5.0
Affective outcomes	
General satisfaction	4.7
Growth satisfaction	4.8
Internal work motivation	5.6
Context satisfactions	
Job security	4.9
Pay	4.3
Coworkers	5.4
Supervision	4.9
Individual growth need strength	5.0
Motivating potential score (MPS)	128.0

SOURCE: Adapted from J. R. Hackman & G. R. Oldham, *Work Redesign.* Reading, Mass.: Addison-Wesley, 1980, p. 105. Used by permission.

Diagnostic Questions

A set of six diagnostic questions needs to be addressed, in conjunction with results of the JDS, prior to undertaking work redesign. The six questions are summarized in Table 9-2. Four of the questions have to do with assessing the *need* for work redesign, and two are concerned with determining the *feasibility* of work redesign. We'll deal with each question in turn.

Question One. Is there a problem or an exploitable opportunity? Just as major surgery is nothing more than an unnecessary risk for a healthy patient, implementing job redesign in situations that evidence neither significant problems nor opportunities is more likely to cause harm than benefit. Job redesign is only appropriate if a problem exists or if a unique opportunity to achieve improvements has presented itself.

TABLE 9-2
Summary of six questions to ask in diagnosing work systems prior to work redesign

Assessing the need for work redesign

1. Is there a problem or an exploitable opportunity?
2. Does the problem or opportunity centrally involve employee motivation, satisfaction, or work effectiveness?
3. Might the design of work be responsible for the observed problems?
4. What aspects of the job most need improvement?

Determining the feasibility of work redesign

5 How ready are the employees for change?
6. How hospitable are organizational systems to needed changes?

SOURCE: Adapted from J. R. Hackman & G. R. Oldham, *Work Redesign*. Reading, Mass.: Addison-Wesley, 1980, p. 128. Used by permission.

Question Two. Does the problem or opportunity centrally involve employee motivation, satisfaction, or work effectiveness? Work design has been shown to have an impact upon employee motivation, satisfaction, and work effectiveness. If any of these three is a central component of current organizational problems, then work redesign *may* be an appropriate strategy to pursue. But if organizational problems do not involve any of these three factors (eg., if productivity is falling because of outmoded technology), then work design is clearly not called for.

Question Three. Might the design of work be responsible for the observed problems? If questions one and two have been answered in the affirmative, then it becomes appropriate to use the JDS to help answer additional questions. Even if problems exist with regard to motivation, satisfaction, or work effectiveness, the source of these problems may lie with an inadequate reward system, poor supervision, or elsewhere, rather than with the design of work. By administering the JDS and examining the motivating potential score of the job it is possible to answer question three. A low MPS would indicate that the job is at least one source of observed problems.

Question Four. What aspects of the job most need improvement? If a low MPS indicates that the job may be the source of observed problems, then additional guidance is required in order to determine exactly which aspects of the job are most in need of improvement. Answers to question four are again available from the results of the JDS, specifically in the scores for each of the five core job characteristics. Those core characteristics that are lowest will be the prime targets for redesign.

Question Five. How ready are the employees for change? Enriched jobs are not for everyone. More specifically, individuals are predicted to respond positively to enriched jobs to the extent that they: (1) possess job-relevant knowledge and skills; (2) have strong needs for personal growth; and (3) are reasonably satisfied with work context factors. It is generally feasible to assess job-relevant knowledge and skills by observing and interviewing job incumbents and their supervisors, while the JDS results yield measures of growth need strength and context satisfactions. Even if all of the previous steps indicate that problems exist with the design of work, significant changes in work design are *not* called for if incumbents do not possess the characteristics which indicate they would react positively and enthusiastically to enriched work.

Question Six. How hospitable are organizational systems to needed changes? This question is admittedly vague and cannot be straightforwardly answered from the JDS or any other single source of information. However, it is nonetheless essential to attempt to assess how receptive and supportive the organization as a whole would be to attempts to enrich a particular job or jobs. Oldham and Hackman (1980) argue that attention must be paid to the organization's technological system, personnel system, and control system in assessing whether the organization possesses sufficient flexibility and resilience to absorb and support redesigned and enriched work.

Implementation Issues

Even if careful attention to the six diagnostic questions leads to the conclusion that job redesign *is* the appropriate strategy to pursue, we still require some guidelines regarding how to go about the process of implementing changes in work design. There are really two sets of issues here: the first issue has to do with *what* specific changes should be made to jobs; the second issue is concerned with *how* the change process should be handled.

What Changes. Hackman et al. (1975) and Hackman and Oldham (1980) have developed a set of five *implementing principles* that can assist in determining what changes are most appropriate for a given job. The JDS helps clarify the specific job characteristics that are problematic. Figure 9-7 summarizes the relationships between the implementing principles and the core job characteristics.

> ***Combining tasks.*** Putting together existing, fractionalized tasks to form new and larger modules of work.

> ***Forming natural work units.*** Arranging the items of work handled by employees into logical or inherently meaningful groups. Possible

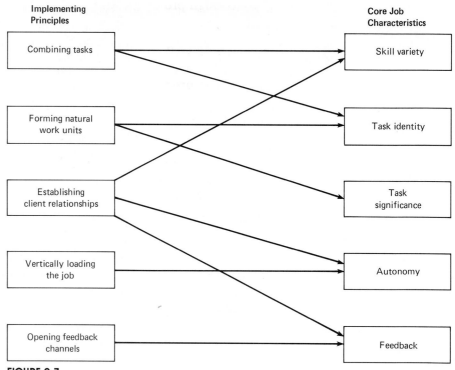

FIGURE 9-7
Links between the implementing principles and the core job characteristics. (SOURCE: J. R. Hackman and G. R. Oldham, *Work Redesign*. Reading, Mass.: Addison-Wesley, 1980, p. 135. Used by permission.)

bases for forming natural work units include geography, type of business, organization unit, and customer group.

Establishing client relationships. Putting the employee in direct contact with the recipients or "clients" of the work and giving him or her continuing responsibility for managing relationships with them.

Vertically loading the job. Giving workers increased control over the work by "pushing down" responsibility and authority that formerly were reserved for higher levels of management.

Opening feedback channels. Creating conditions for employees to learn directly from doing the job itself how they are performing and whether their performance is improving or deteriorating over time.

How Changes Are Implemented. If job redesign is to be successful, it is essential that the *process* of work redesign be managed competently. The following key ingredients have been suggested as factors that differentiate successful work redesign projects from those that turn out to be failures (Hackman, 1975, pp. 134–137).

1. Key individuals responsible for the work redesign project attack the especially difficult problems right from the start.
2. Management makes sure that a diagnosis of the changes needed in the target jobs, based on some articulated theory of work redesign, is conducted before implementation.
3. Management ensures that specific changes are publicly discussed and based explicitly on the diagnosis.
4. The people responsible for the work redesign project prepare contingency plans ahead of time to deal with both the problems and the opportunities that emerge from work design activities.
5. Those responsible for the work redesign project are prepared to evaluate the project continuously throughout its life.

Although reiterating the fact that work redesign is not a panacea for all organizational problems, Hackman (1975) reemphasizes that when work redesign projects are competently managed in accordance with these key ingredients, job redesign can improve the basic relationship between a person and his or her work and has the long-run potential to help organizations rehumanize rather than dehumanize the people who work in them.

Research on the Job Characteristics Model

Although the job characteristics model was developed only recently, it has generated a good deal of research interest in that short period of time. A large proportion of this research has been reviewed recently (Roberts & Glick, 1981). Although this review raises a variety of concerns and criticisms, it seems clear that the job characteristics identified by the model do have an important impact upon the motivation and satisfaction of people at work (Hackman & Oldham, 1980). Supportive results for various components of the model have been generated by a variety of researchers in many different types of situations (eg., Arnold & House, 1980; Brief & Aldag, 1975; Cherrington & England, 1980; Dunham, 1977; Peters & Champoux, 1979; Umstot, Bell, & Mitchell, 1976). What is less clear is whether the impact of the job characteristics upon motivation and satisfaction occurs precisely in the manner specified by the model and whether the moderator variables operate exactly as hypothesized (Roberts & Glick, 1981). Clarification of these issues should be forthcoming in future research in light of some recent methodological advances that should facilitate the appropriate testing of specific predictions of the model (Arnold, 1982; Arnold & House, 1980; Kiggundu & Vallerand, 1982). Although it cannot be stated that evidence exists in support of every aspect of the job characteristics model, it is fair to conclude overall that the model has general validity and can serve as a helpful guide both for future research and for managerial practice in redesigning work for increased motivation and satisfaction.

AN EXAMPLE OF WORK REDESIGN

There are a variety of examples of the successful implementation of work redesign employing the job characteristics approach. We'll look at a case discussed by Hackman et al. (1975) that involved the redesign of the jobs of keypunch operators working in a large insurance company. The job of keypunch operator involves transferring information from written documents onto computer cards. The keypunch department consisted of 98 operators, 7 assignment clerks, and 1 supervisor.

Work came in to the keypunch department from other client groups in the organization. Jobs were of variable size and differed in terms of whether a specific delivery date was specified or not. Jobs were received by the assignment clerks who reviewed them for obvious errors, omissions, and legibility problems. After this initial inspection the assignment clerks then broke the job up into batches that could each be performed in about 1 hour. These 1-hour batches were then each assigned to an operator who was under these constant instructions: "Punch only what you see. Don't correct errors, no matter how obvious they look."

Once a job had been punched it was then verified, a process that essentially involves doing the job a second time, to ensure that no errors were made the first time. Completed cards were then returned to the supervisor, who checked for errors and assigned corrections to any available operator.

The keypunch department was a clear problem area for the organization. A variety of factors indicated the existence of serious motivation problems. The supervisor was constantly dealing with crises and employee grievances. Operators appeared apathetic and at times openly hostile to their jobs. The output of the department (as compared to work standards) was inadequate and error rates were high. Due dates and schedules were frequently missed. Employee absenteeism was high.

Diagnosis

A diagnosis of the keypunch operators' job in light of the five core job characteristics indicated clearly that the motivating potential of the job was extremely low. Skill variety was nonexistent; operators sat at their machines and keypunched and did nothing else. Task identity was equally low. Operators were given work in 1-hour batches, not in units that had any identifiable beginning or end. Task significance was low. Since operators were insulated from the client groups by the assignment clerks and supervisor, they had no idea what impact, if any, their work had upon anyone or anything. Autonomy was near zero. Operators were to punch what they saw on the page in front of them. They had no freedom to influence what they did, how they did it, or when it was to be done. Finally, feedback from the job was nonexistent. Errors were detected by the supervisor and corrections were done by someone other than the original operator. No means existed for an operator to assess how well she was performing (all of the operators were female).

Job Redesign

Since the keypunch operator's job was so low on all of the core job dimensions, all of the implementing principles were employed in redesigning the job.

Combining tasks.   Planning and controlling activities were added to the central task of keypunching. The details of these additional activities are clarified under the remaining implementing concepts.

Forming natural work units.   Instead of performing work in unrelated 1-hour batches, each operator was given responsibility for handling all of the work for certain accounts.

Establishing client relationships.   Several direct channels were provided between operators and clients. Operators personally inspected documents received from clients for corrections and legibility. In addition, any problems arising with a job were taken up directly by the operator with the client group.

Vertical loading.   Operators were provided some freedom and discretion. First, they were given authority to correct obvious errors. Second, they were allowed to set their own schedules and plan their daily work, as long as deadlines were being met.

Opening feedback channels.   In addition to the added feedback provided by client contact, operators were also allowed to correct their own errors when these were discovered. Each operator also kept a file of her own errors in order to permit regular reviews of problems and progress.

Results

The results of the redesign and enrichment of the keypunch operators' jobs were quite dramatic. The number of operators required to perform the same volume of work dropped from 98 to 60 (this reduction was accomplished by attrition, transfers, and promotions). The quality of work produced increased by 39.8 percent, while the error rate decreased from 1.53 to 0.99 percent and the proportion of poor performers declined from

11.1 to 5.5 percent. Absenteeism, which had previously been a serious problem, declined by 24.1 percent and overall satisfaction of employees increased by 16.5 percent. Cost savings to the organization were significant. First-year savings (in early 1970s dollars) in salaries and machine rentals were $64,305, and potential future savings were estimated by the organization at over $90,000 per year.

MANAGERIAL IMPLICATIONS

The material we have discussed regarding the design of work for individuals has a variety of implications for managerial practice.

1. ***Managers need to recognize that the nature of the work itself is an important determinant of the motivation and satisfaction of employees.*** Managers sometimes tend to assume that the major determinants of employee motivation and satisfaction are extrinsic factors such as pay, security, and promotions. Managers must recognize that the nature of the work that employees are required to perform has a critical influence upon the motivation and satisfaction of organization members.
2. ***Managers must recognize that the way in which work is designed for employees is not fixed, but can be altered and manipulated.*** It is often assumed that the way in which jobs are designed or tasks are assigned to people is the way that things have to be in an organization. Frequently, managers simply haven't thought about alternative ways in which responsibilities and activities could be assigned to individuals. Managers need to recognize that within certain bounds set by technology and physical facilities, there always exist a variety of ways in which jobs can be designed for organization members.
3. ***Managers must take into account differences among people in their desire for more enriched work.*** Not everyone wants a more challenging and enriched job. As a result, redesigned work is not for everyone and will not have universal positive benefits if implemented with employees who do not desire it. Prior to undertaking a work redesign project, managers must assess their employees carefully to determine the extent to which they are likely to respond positively to more enriched work.
4. ***Managers require a theoretical model or framework to assist in the diagnosis, planning, and implementation of job redesign.*** The likelihood of achieving successful results from job redesign is directly dependent on the extent to which the redesign activities are carefully planned on the basis of a systematic diagnosis of the target jobs and employees involved. A theoretical model provides the manager with a framework that can guide the diagnosis, planning, and implementation of changes in a systematic fashion.

SUMMARY

A variety of different systems and approaches to work design have been developed, each of which seeks to maximize the productive efficiency of the organization, as well as the satisfaction of organization members.

The first and most influential approach to work design was Taylor's *Scientific Management.* According to scientific management, work is to be broken down into its simplest and most basic components. Each individual is then assigned to a highly simplified and repetitive job that suits his or her capabilities. Motivation and satisfaction are predicted to be high, since cash bonuses are offered for meeting or exceeding clearly established performance goals.

Though the simplified work procedures arising from scientific management have had many positive effects on productive efficiency, they have also tended to result in high levels of boredom, monotony, and dissatisfaction. These in turn can be costly to organizations in the areas of absenteeism, turnover, and even sabotage. One response to these negative side-effects of scientific management was *job enlargement.* Job enlargement involves giving individuals a larger variety of different tasks to perform, although it does not require that individuals be given any additional autonomy or freedom regarding how the work is to be performed. *Job enrichment* (identified primarily with Herzberg) goes beyond job enlargement by providing individual workers with increased responsibility and authority, in addition to greater variety in their work. Though job enlargement and job enrichment have both resulted in positive changes when implemented, both suffer from a lack of sound underlying theory that can adequately explain how and why they should achieve positive results.

Job characteristics theory (Hackman & Oldham) provides a well-developed systematic framework for understanding and predicting the effects of work design on the motivation, performance, and satisfaction of individuals. According to the job characteristics model a total of five distinct "core" job characteristics influence three critical psychological states, which in turn have an impact upon a variety of personal and work outcomes. In addition, the theory identifies the conditions under which positive effects would be expected when jobs are enriched and also provides tools for the diagnosis of jobs and the implementation of feasible changes in the design of work.

REVIEW QUESTIONS

1. Why is the design of work an important issue for a manager to be concerned about?
2. What is *scientific management*?

3. What assumptions does scientific management make regarding what motivates people to perform effectively?
4. Why has the scientific management approach been so influential?
5. What is job enlargement?
6. Discuss job enrichment and show how it differs from job enlargement.
7. What are the primary shortcomings of the job enrichment approach?
8. According to the Hackman and Oldham job characteristics model, what are the essential ingredients of internal work motivation?
9. Describe the relationship between the core job characteristics and the three psychological states in the job characteristics model.
10. What factors (moderator variables) are hypothesized to influence the extent to which changes in the core job dimensions will result in changes in the psychological states and the personal and work outcomes? Discuss.
11. What diagnostic steps must be taken prior to implementing job redesign?
12. Describe some of the specific implementing principles that can be employed to increase the motivating potential of a job.
13. Discuss the advantages and disadvantages of trying to influence employee motivation, satisfaction, and performance via extrinsic methods (eg., pay and other rewards) as opposed to intrinsic methods (eg., the design of jobs).
14. Is the nature of job design in an organization strictly a management prerogative, or do you feel that the employees themselves should have some say in how their jobs are designed? Defend your position.

REFERENCES

Arnold, H. J. Moderator variables: A clarification of conceptual, analytic, and psychometric issues. *Organizational Behavior and Human Performance*, 1982, *29, 143–174.*

Arnold, H. J., & House, R. J. Methodological and substantive extensions to the job characteristics model of motivation. *Organizational Behavior and Human Performance*, 1980, *25,* 161–183.

Babbage, C. *On the economy of machinery and manufactures.* Charles Knight, fourth edition enlarged, 1835. Reprints of Economic Classics, Augustus M. Kelly, New York, 1965.

Blood, M. R., & Hulin, C. L. Alienation, environmental characteristics, and worker responses. *Journal of Applied Psychology,* 1967, *51,* 284–290.

Brief, A. P., & Aldag, R. J. Employee reactions to job characteristics: A constructive replication. *Journal of Applied Psychology,* 1975, *60,* 182–186.

Cherrington, D. J., & England, J. L. The desire for nonenriched jobs as a moderator of the enrichment-satisfaction relationship. *Organizational Behavior and Human Performance,* 1980, *25,* 139–159.

Dunham, R. B. Reactions to job characteristics: Moderating effects of the organization. *Academy of Management Journal*, 1977, *20*, 42–65.

Dunnette, M. D., Campbell, J. P., & Hakel, M. D. Factors contributing to job satisfaction and dissatisfaction in six occupational groups. *Organizational Behavior and Human Performance*, 1967, *2*, 143–174.

Fein, M. Job enrichment: A reevaluation. *Sloan Management Review*, 1974, *15*, 69–88.

Ford, R. N. *Motivation through the work itself*. New York: American Management Association, 1969.

Ford, R. N. Job enrichment lessons from AT&T. *Harvard Business Review*, January–February 1973, 96–106.

Hackman, J. R. Is job enrichment just a fad? *Harvard Business Review*, September–October 1975, 129–139.

Hackman, J. R., & Lawler, E. E., III. Employee reactions to job characteristics. *Journal of Applied Psychology Monograph*, 1971, *55*, 259–286.

Hackman, J. R., & Oldham, G. R. Development of the Job Diagnostic Survey. *Journal of Applied Psychology*, 1975, *60*, 159–170.

Hackman, J. R., & Oldham, G. R. Motivation through the design of work: Test of a theory. *Organizational Behavior and Human Performance*, 1976, *16*, 250–279.

Hackman, J. R., & Oldham, G. R. *Work redesign*. Reading, Mass.: Addison-Wesley, 1980.

Hackman, J. R., Oldham, G. R., Janson, R., & Purdy, K. A new strategy for job enrichment. *California Management Review*, Summer 1975, 57–71.

Herzberg, F. *Work and the nature of man*. Cleveland: World, 1966.

Herzberg, F. One more time: How do you motivate employees? *Harvard Business Review*, January–February 1968, 53–62.

Herzberg, F. The wise old Turk. *Harvard Business Review*, September–October 1974, 70–80.

Herzberg, F. *The managerial choice*. Homewood, Illinois: Dow Jones-Irwin, 1976.

Herzberg, F., Mausner, B., Peterson, R. D., & Capwell, D. F. *Job attitudes: Review of research and opinion*. Pittsburgh: Psychological Service of Pittsburgh, 1957.

Herzberg, F., Mausner, B., & Snyderman, B. *The motivation to work*. New York: Wiley, 1959.

Hinton, B. L. An empirical investigation of the Herzberg methodology and two-factor theory. *Organizational Behavior and Human Performance*, 1968, *3*, 286–309.

House, R. J., & Wigdor, L. Herzberg's dual factor theory of job satisfaction and motivation: A review of the evidence and a criticism. *Personnel Psychology*, 1967, *20*, 369–389.

Hulin, C. L., & Blood, M. R. Job enlargement, individual differences, worker responses. *Psychological Bulletin*, 1968, *69*, 41–55.

Kiggundu, M. N., & Vallerand, R. J. Individual difference moderators in job design research: A reexamination of the empirical evidence and suggestions for future research. McGill University Working Paper, 1982.

Kilbridge, M. D. Reduced costs through job enlargement: A case. *The Journal of Business*, 1960, *33*, 357–362.

King, N. A. A clarification and evaluation of the two-factor theory of job satisfaction. *Psychological Bulletin*, 1970, *74*, 18–31.

Oldham, G. R., & Hackman, J. R. Work design in the organizational context. In B.

M. Staw & L. L. Cummings (eds.), *Research in organizational behavior* (vol. 2). Greenwich, Conn.: JAI Press, 1980.

Paul, W. J., Jr., Robertson, K. B., & Herzberg, F. Job enrichment pays off. *Harvard Business Review*, March–April 1969, 61–78.

Peters, W. S., & Champoux, J. E. The use of moderated regression in job design decisions. *Decision Sciences*, 1979, *10*, 85–95.

Porter, L. W., Lawler, E. E., III, & Hackman, J. R. *Behavior in organizations*. New York: McGraw-Hill, 1975.

Roberts, K. H., & Glick, W. The job characteristics approach to task design: A critical review. *Journal of Applied Psychology*, 1981, *66*, 193–217.

Taylor, F. W. *The Principles of scientific management*. New York: Harper, 1911.

Turner, A. N., & Lawrence, P. R. *Industrial jobs and the worker*. Boston: Harvard Graduate School of Business Administration, 1965.

Umstot, D., Bell, C. H., & Mitchell, T. R. Effects of job enrichment and task goals on satisfaction and productivity: Implications for job design. *Journal of Applied Psychology*, 1976, *61*, 379–394.

Walker, C. R. The problem of the repetitive job. *Harvard Business Review*, 1950, *28*, 54–58.

Walters, R. W. and Associates. *Job enrichment for results*. Reading, Mass.: Addison-Wesley, 1975.

Whitsett, D. A., & Winslow, E. K. An analysis of studies critical of the motivator-hygiene theory. *Personnel Psychology*, 1967, *20*, 391–415.

CHAPTER 10

QUALITY OF WORK LIFE: THE DESIGN OF WORK FOR GROUPS

In the previous chapter we examined alternative approaches to the design of work for individuals. The focus of our discussion in that chapter was upon the individual job and on how jobs could be designed to maximize the motivation, satisfaction, and productivity of individual organization members.

This chapter is also about the design of work, but here we'll be coming at the problem from a slightly different perspective. Rather than focusing upon individual organization members and the design of jobs for individuals, we'll be examining the issue of work design for groups. Many of the examples of group-based work redesign in organizations have been conducted within the context of *quality of work life* (QWL) programs. As a result, we begin the chapter with a discussion of QWL and the different forms that QWL programs can take in organizations. We then go on to discuss two alternative approaches to the design of work for groups in organizations. The first of these, known as the *sociotechnical systems approach*, involves taking a very broad perspective on the overall organization and the work which the organization must accomplish. The sociotechnical approach emphasizes the fact that organizations consist of *both* social (i.e., human) and technological components and advocates an approach to work design based upon *autonomous work groups*. The second approach, labeled *social psychological*, focuses purely and explicitly upon work groups and upon how work groups can be optimally designed to achieve both productive efficiency and satisfaction for their members.

QUALITY OF WORK LIFE

The term *quality of work life*, often abbreviated QWL, refers to a broad range of approaches and techniques that have been implemented in organizations with the common goal of improving the quality of life for people at work. Many of these types of programs had their birth in the industrial democracy movement in Western Europe, although today the QWL movement is active in North America, Japan, India, and Australia, in addition to its European roots.

In practice, QWL programs can come in many forms. Some examples of the different types of innovations that have been implemented as part of QWL programs are as follows (Chicago Tribune, Sept. 16, 1979):

1. Work teams, where the isolation of the worker doing one task repeatedly is replaced by groups of workers responsible for a variety of tasks.
2. Quality circles, a Japanese technique, in which workers meet to solve job problems, especially those related to improving the quality of their products.
3. Worker participation in the design of jobs and in decisions about their day-to-day work lives.
4. More flexible work scheduling and job assignments so that, for example, two married individuals can both work and still "manage" a household and children.
5. More flexible compensation plans, so that workers can get more of the benefits they desire and can participate in cost savings and company profits.
6. Less supervision, in which production teams, operating without direct supervision, help select and train new team members, forecast material and manpower requirements, and evaluate their own performance.
7. More attention to the design and maintenance of the physical plant and workplace, as well as to health and safety hazards.
8. In-house training programs, free tuition for higher education, or a firm policy of promoting from within.
9. Increased provision for job security.
10. New forms of union-management cooperation and increased involvement of unions in bargaining for quality of working life programs.

QWL programs have been adopted with some success by many corporations, such as General Motors, General Foods, AT&T, Xerox,

Weyerhauser, Nabisco, Procter & Gamble, and IBM. At the same time, however, the growth of QWL programs has been inhibited by a number of factors. First, QWL demands a different style of management than has frequently been practiced in the past; it requires cooperation and can't be imposed unilaterally. Second, it costs substantial amounts of money to introduce some of these organizational changes, and top management is not yet convinced that QWL programs will increase productivity. Third, and probably most important, QWL hasn't spread more quickly because workers as well as managers are suspicious of it. Unions are instinctively hesitant to cooperate with their old enemy, management, and are anxious about moving away from the bread and butter issues of wages and job security.

In spite of some of these inhibiting factors, the QWL movement has had a significant impact that managers need to be aware of and take into account. The common theme underlying all of the different types of QWL programs is an increased degree of attention to the quality of life for people at work. This involves simultaneous commitment to the provision of opportunities for workers to take personal responsibility for their work and to achieve a degree of personal dignity and pride from their work activities.

The greatest acceptance and widest application of QWL ideas in North America has occurred with regard to the design of work for groups in organizations. A common theme of many QWL projects is the use of *autonomous work groups* as the major basis for assigning responsibility for accomplishment of the work of the organization. There are two major approaches to the design of work for autonomous or self-managing groups. The first is known as the *sociotechnical systems approach,* while the second is labeled the *social psychological approach* to work design for groups. We will discuss each of these major approaches in turn.

SOCIOTECHNICAL SYSTEMS APPROACH

The sociotechnical systems approach to work design has two key distinguishing characteristics. The first major emphasis of the approach is that organizations consist of both *social* (i.e., people) and *technological* components, and that any successful strategy of work design must concurrently take into account both components. The second distinguishing characteristic of the approach is its emphasis upon organizations as *open systems,* i.e., systems that interact and are interdependent with the broader external environments in which they exist (Emery & Trist, 1969; Trist et al., 1963; Davis & Trist, 1974).

A sound question to ask at this point is, "What does conceptualizing an organization as a sociotechnical system have to do with designing work for groups?" We'll attempt to spell out the links as clearly as possible.

Relationship to Work Design for Groups

According to the sociotechnical systems approach, the process of work redesign must begin with an overall analysis of the total organization as a system. Such an overall systemic analysis must explicitly attend to: (1) the nature of the technical system employed by the organization; (2) the nature of the organization's social system; and (3) the interrelationship between the organization and its external environment. The primary goal or outcome of this systemic analysis is the identification of what are referred to as the "primary tasks" which the organization must perform if it is to be successful and continue to exist (Rice, 1958). A primary task consists of a whole, identifiable, and relatively complex set of activities that constitute a major component in the productive activity of the organization.

Once primary tasks have been identified, the next step in the sociotechnical approach involves the assignment of responsibility for the performance of each primary task to a *group* of organization members. Groups are formed in such a way that they will: (1) possess among their members all of the requisite skills necessary for the effective performance of their primary task; and (2) consist of individuals who are personally compatible with one another and likely to build into a cohesive and productive work group. A key facet of the sociotechnical approach to work design is that the groups that are given *responsibility* for performance of a primary task are also given *autonomy* regarding how the task is to be accomplished. In fact, such groups are referred to as *autonomous work groups*, since the groups are granted *responsible autonomy* for the performance of their primary task (Emery, 1972). This autonomy extends to issues such as work scheduling (what tasks will be done when), work assignments (who will perform which tasks or "jobs" at any given time), and the management of the relationships between the group and other individuals and groups in the organization.

The sociotechnical systems approach to work design pays no explicit attention whatsoever to the concept of a job, nor to the design of jobs for individual organization members. Rather, the approach focuses upon the design of autonomous work groups that are responsible for the performance of the organization's primary tasks. Further, members of autonomous work groups do not have a job as such. Rather, the group members themselves determine which *roles* each one will play in accomplishing their primary task (Davis, 1977). These roles are generally subjected to frequent change and revision (at the discretion of the group) based upon the particular skills and preferences of group members.

Sociotechnical Principles of Organization Design

A set of basic principles for organization design using the sociotechnical systems approach has been developed by Albert Cherns (1977). These principles provide some general guidance for work redesign using the sociotechnical systems approach.

1. ***Compatibility. The means to design must be consistent with the end to be achieved.*** If the goal is to design more autonomous and participative work groups, then it is essential that the organization employ an open and participative approach to the design and implementation of the new systems. Organization members will get mixed messages if an organization attempts to implement greater autonomy and responsibility in a very directive and autocratic fashion.

2. ***Minimal critical specification. What is critical should be identified and only that should be specified.*** This principle represents the operationalization of the notion of responsible autonomy. If work groups really are to be autonomous, then the organization cannot attempt to specify completely who does what and how they are to do it.

3. ***Variance control. Variances that cannot be eliminated should be dealt with as near to their point of origin as possible.*** Autonomy and decision-making authority to deal with problems should be moved to the level in the organization with first-hand knowledge of the problem and the expertise necessary to deal with it.

4. ***The multifunctional principle. Design the organization so that it can achieve its objectives in more than one way.*** Work design needs to recognize specifically that there are almost always several alternative ways to accomplish the same goal. This implies the desirability of designing for flexibility.

5. ***Boundary location. Roles that require shared access to knowledge or experience should be within the same departmental boundaries.*** When work groups or departments are set up, the determination of which persons and roles must be included should be based upon facilitating the sharing of knowledge and expertise necessary for optimal performance.

6. ***Information flow. Information systems should be designed to provide information to the organizational unit that will take action on the basis of the information.*** It is impossible to make a blanket statement that information *should* flow upward, or *should* flow downward, or *should* flow horizontally. Rather, information should flow to those who require the information in order to take intelligent and informed action.

7. ***Support congruence. The system of social support should be designed to reinforce the behaviors that the organization's structure is designed to elicit.*** If the primary unit of organization design is the work group, the other organizational systems (eg., rewards, performance appraisal, and selection) must reflect and reinforce this.

8. ***Design and human values. A prime objective of organizational design***

should be to provide a high quality of working life to its members.
The primary component of this principle involves ensuring that each
individual's role or job provides challenge, meaning, and opportunity
for learning and development.

9. *Transitional organization. There is a changeover period from old to
new that requires a transitional organization.* Organizations must
recognize that shifts from old to new forms of work design do not
occur instantly or painlessly. Organizations thus must plan for and
manage the transition process and its inherent problems.

10. *Completion. Design is an iterative process; the closure of options
opens new ones, and at the end, we are back at the beginning.* There is
no clear end to the process of work design. It is an ongoing process
requiring constant work and attention.

While neither exhaustive nor overly explicit, these principles do offer
a set of general guidelines for redesigning work in organizations using the
sociotechnical systems approach. In the next section we look at some
examples of the application of these principles to the design of work for
groups in organizations.

EXAMPLES OF WORK DESIGN FOR GROUPS

There are a considerable number of well-known examples of innovative
approaches to work design employing autonomous work groups. In this
section we will describe two of the most important and influential
examples of group-based work redesign: the Topeka plant of General
Foods and the Kalmar plant of Volvo.

General Foods' Topeka Plant[1]

In 1968 General Foods made a decision to open a new dry dog food plant in
Topeka, Kansas. The plant started production in January 1971. From its
initial conception a decision was made that this plant would attempt to
incorporate in its design and functioning the latest behavioral science
knowledge regarding work design in order to maximize both the plant's
productive efficiency and the quality of life and personal satisfaction of the
plant's employees. This commitment was made and followed through on
by the General Foods managers in charge of the design and operation of
the new plant, working in conjunction with a behavioral science consultant (Richard Walton of the Harvard Graduate School of Business Administration).

[1]This discussion of work design at Topeka is based upon descriptions by Richard Walton
(1972, 1975, 1977).

Work Design

Work in the new plant was organized around self-managing work groups, each of which were given responsibility for a major segment of the work to be accomplished. The total work force of seventy operators was divided into three *processing* teams and three *packaging* teams (one processing team and one packaging team worked each of the plant's three shifts). Each team consisted of between seven and seventeen operators and a team leader. The goal was to make the teams large enough that they could be given responsibility for a whole task requiring many different skills, but at the same time to keep the size small enough to permit face-to-face meetings for decision making and coordination.

Both job specialties and separate staff departments were avoided. Individuals were not assigned to a particular job; rather, each team reached a consensus via discussion regarding who should be assigned to perform particular tasks for a given period of time. In addition, there were no separate departments responsible for maintenance, quality control, custodial services, industrial engineering, or personnel. All of these functions were carried out by the operating teams themselves. Each team member was responsible for maintaining the equipment he operated and housekeeping his own work area. Each team was responsible for conducting its own quality testing and ensuring that quality standards were met. Team members themselves screened new job applicants and made selection decisions by consensus.

Status Differentials

The goal of the work design at Topeka was to make all of the operators' jobs equally challenging and meaningful. In order to accomplish this, the dullest and most routine jobs were eliminated from the plant either by automation (wherever possible) or by contracting work out (e.g., grounds maintenance). In addition, the set of tasks assigned to each work group always included a variety of challenging responsibilities such as planning, problem solving, and managing relationships with other work groups. In order to reinforce the perceptions of equality among all of the operators' jobs, steps were taken to minimize or eliminate status differentials within the plant. All operators were placed in a single job classification, whereas in another General Foods plant manufacturing similar products there were over twelve separate job classifications for operators. Status differences were further minimized by a lack of status symbols. For example, there was only a single parking lot used by everyone at the plant, one common entrance was used by everyone, and common decor was used throughout offices and the production area.

The minimization of status differentials was designed to facilitate the group work design in two ways. First, by creating and reinforcing only a single job classification it was possible to increase flexibility and the capacity to shift individuals from job to job within groups and also from group to group when necessary. Second, the lack of status differences helped facilitate communication and trust among operators and between operators and management. High levels of communication and trust greatly facilitate the creation of highly cohesive and highly committed work groups.

Authority and Decision Making

In line with the concept of responsible autonomy for self-managing groups, decision-making authority in the Topeka plant was shifted to the lowest feasible level in the organization. Teams were given broad scope for making decisions regarding matters affecting them. Steps were taken to facilitate decision making at the team level by ensuring that operators were provided with the economic information and decision rules necessary to permit them to make sound production decisions.

Reward System

A skills-based reward system was implemented in the plant from the outset (see Chapter 7 on reward systems for further discussion of such plans). An operator's pay was based upon the number of jobs or skills that had been mastered. Operators began at the starting rate, moved up to the single-job rate after one job had been mastered, went to the team rate when all of the jobs in the team had been learned, and finally achieved plant rate when a person was capable of performing any job in the plant. Further pay advances beyond plant rate could be obtained for learning various specialty skills, e.g., electrical maintenance. Decisions on levels of skill that had been attained were made by team leaders, with inputs from other team members as an important factor influencing the decision.

The skills-based reward system is well-suited to the system of autonomous work teams, since it permits pay progression without the existence of a complex job hierarchy. The system also provides an incentive for individuals to learn new skills and helps reinforce the importance of personal development, both of which contribute to increased work force flexibility.

Results

Overall, the innovative approach to work design for groups implemented at Topeka qualifies as highly successful, both in terms of job satisfaction and quality of work life on the one hand, and productive efficiency on the other.

Several studies have been conducted assessing the attitudes and motivation of the work force at the Topeka plant. Schrank (1974) reported high levels of work participation, freedom to communicate, expressions of warmth, minimization of status distinction, human dignity, commitment, and individual self-esteem. Another study carried out by researchers from the University of Michigan (Lawler et al., 1974) concluded that positive work attitudes were prevalent among operators at the plant. Indeed, these researchers reported that the levels of satisfaction and involvement in all parts of the plant were the highest they had ever observed in any plant they had studied.

On the economic side there is clear evidence for the productive efficiency of the plant. General Foods' corporate analysts attribute savings in the neighborhood of $1 million annually to the innovative use of self-managing groups at Topeka. This million-dollar annual saving can be appreciated in light of the fact that the plant has a total work force of approximately 100 and involved a capital investment in the $10–15 million range.

Further evidence of the effectiveness of the group work design is contained in the fact that the plant started up and ran for 3 years and 8 months (1.3 million employee hours) without a single lost-time accident. During the first 3 years of operation absenteeism ranged from 0.8 to 1.4 percent, while turnover was approximately 10 percent per year. These results were sufficiently impressive to General Foods' management that a corporate policy was developed favoring similar approaches to work design in other plants where conditions were suitable.

It should be pointed out, however, that although the available evidence does indicate the success of the Topeka work design on almost any index, the new design has not been without its problems. Any new approach to designing work is bound to generate some difficulties and have some shortcomings. A good description of the peaks and valleys in the implementation of work design for self-managing groups at Topeka is provided by Walton (1977). On balance, the picture that emerges of the Topeka plant is of an innovative and highly effective organization.

Volvo's Kalmar Plant[2]

During the late 1960s and early 1970s Volvo management was becoming increasingly concerned with labor difficulties being experienced in their manufacturing plants. Turnover was approaching 50 percent annually, absenteeism was near 20 percent, wildcat strikes were frequent, and the company was becoming increasingly dependent on foreign "guest workers," since Swedes were not interested in working in automotive manufacturing jobs. The existence of these problems, combined with the Swedish political and labor relations environment that requires in each organization a hierarchy of works councils with representation from both management and employees, resulted in Volvo undertaking a variety of work restructuring projects. Work restructuring began with a number of successful experiments and changes in the company's large existing assembly

[2]This discussion of the Volvo Kalmar plant is based upon reports by Dowling (1973), Gyllenhammar (1977), and Walton (1975).

plants near Gothenburg. However, the most dramatic and most interesting project was the new auto assembly plant that began operation at Kalmar in 1974.

The Kalmar plant was designed from the ground up with the goal of providing an optimal fit between the technical demands of productive efficiency and the human and social needs of the employees for satisfying and meaningful work. It was *not* assumed that assembly line technology was an irreversible given for automobile manufacturing and that work design for employees simply had to accommodate to that technology. Instead, both the technological and social sides of the organization were viewed as equally important and equally viable candidates for change and restructuring. The result of this approach was a new plant at Kalmar that differs radically from anything which had preceded it.

Work Design

There is no assembly line in the Kalmar plant. Instead, cars are mounted on individual battery powered carriers that move the cars from one work area to another. The movement of carriers is controlled by a computer that can be manually overridden by the employees.

The primary unit for accomplishing the task of assembling automobiles at Kalmar is the work group. The plant is designed such that semiautonomous work groups are each responsible for the assembly of a particular identifiable portion of the car, e.g., electrical system, instrumentation, interior, doors, engine compartment, and wheels and brakes. There are a total of seventeen groups in the plant, each composed of from fifteen to twenty-nine members. In line with the concept of responsible autonomy, each group is free to decide on the assignment of tasks to individual members and to set their own schedules (within established and agreed upon performance goals). The freedom to assign tasks to members has resulted in most team members learning a variety of skills, increasing the work variety for each individual as well as the flexibility of the overall work team. In addition, teams are responsible for carrying out their own inspections and for repairing any defects discovered. A computerized record of defects is maintained that is used both to draw attention to persistent problem areas and to give team members positive feedback when their work has been especially free of problems.

Physical Design

In order to increase feelings of team identity and cohesiveness, each work group is provided with its own clearly identified and relatively isolated work area. In addition, each team uses its own separate entrance to the plant that leads directly to its own work area. Each team also has next to its work area its own changing rooms (complete with showers and saunas), kitchen, and a carpeted "coffee corner" for use during breaks.

A variety of other steps were taken in order to make the work area itself more pleasant than that commonly found in automobile assembly plants. The work stations were designed to be light and airy, with the majority located along the outer wall of the plant next to large picture windows. The carriers that move the cars from place to place are equipped with a tilting mechanism that can raise cars up on their sides, greatly facilitating work on hard-to-reach areas and removing much of the physical discomfort associated with many assembly operations. Finally, great attention was paid to minimizing noise levels in the plant. The goal was to keep noise at or below the level at which normal conversation could be carried on. In order to accomplish this, assembly tools were chosen partly on the basis of their noise characteristics, and walls, screens, and roofs were specially designed to absorb and reduce noise levels.

Results

Less systematic research has been conducted to assess the effectiveness of the Kalmar plant than was the case with the innovative work design at Topeka. However, what evidence there is tends to be quite positive and indicates that the new work design at Kalmar is effective both economically and socially. Pehr Gyllenhammer, president of Volvo, states that productivity at Kalmar is good, and also reports that a union survey conducted in 1976 found that "almost all" of the employees were in favor of the new system (Gyllenhammar, 1977).

The Kalmar plant has not been without its critics, however. As Volvo management admits, the start-up costs for a plant such as Kalmar are in the range of 10 to 30 percent higher than comparable costs for a traditionally designed plant. In addition, the plant is relatively small, having a work force of only 600 employees. The applicability of the Kalmar type of design to large-scale plants has been questioned. While these points are valid and must be taken into account, it should also be noted that Volvo is sufficiently certain of the benefits from the new design that by 1977 it had not one, but five new plants organized in a nontraditional way.

SOCIAL PSYCHOLOGICAL APPROACH[3]

The social psychological approach to work design focuses its attention and emphasis squarely and explicitly upon the work group itself, rather than upon the organization as a system, or the interrelationship of technological and social systems within organizations, as was the case with the sociotechnical systems approach. Our discussion in this section is based upon a model of work design for groups that was developed by Hackman and Oldham (1980). The model focuses upon the design of *self-managing work groups*, which are defined as groups that "have the authority to

---

[3]The discussion in this section is based upon the model of work design for groups presented by Hackman and Oldham (1980).

manage their own task and interpersonal processes as they carry out their work" (p. 165). In what follows we will first outline a set of key design features for self-managing work groups and then discuss a variety of factors that influence the effectiveness of such work groups in organizations.

Key Design Features

Three key design features for self-managing groups have been identified. These three key design features are as follows.

1. The *design* of the group task (which will influence the level of effort brought to bear on the group task).
2. The *composition* of the group (which will influence the amount of knowledge and skill applied to work on the task).
3. The *group norms* about performance processes (which will influence the appropriateness of the task performance strategies used by the group).

The relationship between the key design features and the various facets or components of work group effectiveness is summarized in Figure 10-1. We will examine each of these key design features in more detail.

Design of the Group Task

The way in which the group task is designed is hypothesized to influence the effectiveness of the group by means of its impact upon the level of effort exerted by group members on the group task. According to what we know about the motivating characteristics of individual jobs, the model predicts that group members will be highly motivated and will hence exert a high level of effort when the group task is characterized by the following.

1. The group task requires the use of many different skills for successful completion (skill variety).
2. The group task is a whole and meaningful piece of work (task identity).
3. The outcomes of the group's work on the task "make a difference" to other people either inside or outside the organization (task significance).
4. The group task provides substantial latitude for members to decide together how they will carry out the work.
5. The group as a whole receives trustworthy information, preferably from doing the work itself, about the adequacy of group performance (feedback). (Hackman & Oldham, 1980, pp. 171–172)

A manager interested in increasing the extent to which a group task possesses these five characteristics can make use of the same set of "implementing principles" discussed in Chapter 9 for the design of individual tasks. These implementing principles are as follows: combining subtasks into a larger whole, forming natural work units, establishing client relationships, vertically loading the job, and opening feedback

Design Features

Facets of Work
Group Effectiveness*

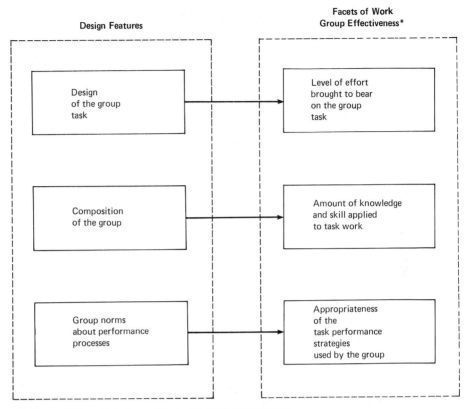

*Hackman and Oldham refer to these as "intermediate criteria of effectiveness."

FIGURE 10-1
The impact of key design features on various facets of work group effectiveness.
(SOURCE: Adapted from J. R. Hackman and G. R. Oldham, *Work Redesign*, Reading, Mass.: Addison-Wesley, 1980. Used by permission.)

channels. It is essential, however, that when these implementing principles are employed in the design of a group task that the focus of attention remains the *group* and the *group task*, not the individual tasks of group members.

Composition of the Group

The way in which a group is composed (i.e., who its members are) has a significant impact upon the amount of task-relevant knowledge and skill within the group that can be applied to work on the group task. This level of knowledge and skill is an important contributor to the group's overall effectiveness. Four aspects of group composition are particularly relevant.

1. The group should include members who have high levels of task-relevant expertise.
2. The group should be large enough to do the work—but not much larger.

3. Group members should have at least a moderate level of interpersonal skill in addition to their task-relevant skills.
4. The group should be composed to balance between homogeneity and heterogeneity. (Hackman & Oldham, 1980, pp. 174–177)

Groups that are composed in line with these criteria are more likely to possess the knowledge, information, and judgment required by the task, as well as possessing the skills necessary to work together effectively and efficiently.

Group Norms about Performance Processes

The norms shared by group members regarding performance processes will have a significant impact upon the strategies used by the group to accomplish its task. Task performance strategies are an important component of group effectiveness, since the strategy a group adopts will critically influence the extent to which the effort, knowledge, and skill contributed by group members actually result in the effective and efficient accomplishment of the group's performance goals.

Factors Influencing Work Group Effectiveness

Most organizations still assign work to individuals rather than groups and are organized around the concept of individual jobs for each organization member. As a result, the organization's policies, procedures, and management practices will tend to be oriented around a system of organization based upon individual jobs.

In light of this, a decision by an organization to assign work to self-managing groups, rather than to closely supervised individual job incumbents, usually involves a major departure from previous organizational policies and practices. As a result, the successful implementation of self-managing work groups depends to a great extent on the effective management of a number of critical *organizational* and *interpersonal* factors.

Organizational Factors

Three components of the overall organizational context are particularly important in determining the success and effectiveness of self-managing work groups. The three components are outlined in Figure 10-2, which summarizes the three components and also indicates the various facets of work-group effectiveness most directly influenced by each component.

1. Rewards and Objectives. If self-managing work groups are to be successful in generating high levels of effort among their members, it is essential that the organizational reward and control systems act to reinforce and support *group* effort rather than to undermine or interfere with it. This implies that when self-managing work groups are being set

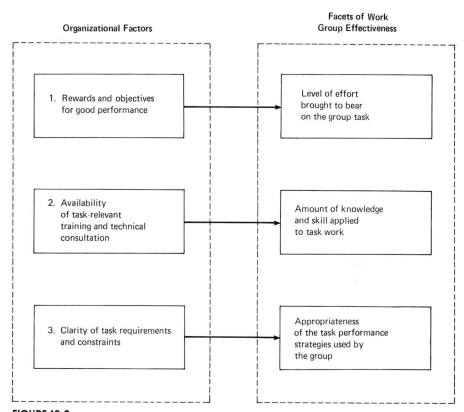

FIGURE 10-2
How organizational factors influence various facets of work group effectiveness.
(SOURCE: Adapted from J. R. Hackman, and G. R. Oldham, *Work Redesign*. Reading, Mass.: Addison-Wesley, 1980. Used by permission.)

up, managers and consultants must attend not only to the design of the new groups themselves, but also to the design of the organization's reward and control systems. No matter how much care is put into the design of self-managing groups themselves, if rewards in the form of pay, benefits, promotions, and so on are still based upon individual performance and accomplishments it is unlikely that the group will become a cohesive and productive unit. If group members are to be motivated to work *together*, then rewards must be based upon group performance and controls must be based upon a monitoring of group rather than individual performance. In addition, if the motivational properties of goals and objectives are to be taken advantage of, it is essential that specific, difficult objectives be set for the group as a whole (Zander, 1971; Umstot, 1977; Locke et al., 1981) rather than for individual members. The key point is that objectives and rewards be set and administered at the group level in a fashion that reinforces the sense of shared responsibility and shared commitment to performance among all members of the group.

2. Training and Consultation. Since the tasks being performed by self-managing groups are frequently complex and often rapidly changing, it is necessary to ensure that task-relevant training and technical consultation are provided to self-managing groups when required. The adequate provision of such training and consultation is dependent upon two factors. First, the necessary sources of expertise must be made *available* to the work group. These sources of expertise may lie outside the organization (e.g., consultants) or within the organization itself (e.g., training departments or other line or staff groups that possess task-relevant knowledge and expertise). Second, the organization must *legitimize* requests for help from the self-managing group. When self-managing work groups are set up and given responsibility and autonomy for task performance, group members may feel that this implies that they are to solve all problems and overcome all obstacles *themselves* without the benefit of outside help or assistance. To ensure that such a set of assumptions does not take hold, management must ensure that everyone, both within and without the self-managing groups, understands that requests for assistance are entirely legitimate and are to be encouraged.

3. Task Requirements and Constraints. It is essential that the members of a self-managing group clearly understand the true requirements of their task and any constraints that exist regarding what is to be done and how it is to be done. If management does not provide group members with clear information regarding task requirements and constraints, either of two undesirable outcomes may occur. First, the group may develop a performance strategy based upon a mistaken understanding of what it is to do and how it is to do it. Such a strategy will then be inappropriate and undesirable in light of actual task requirements and constraints. Second, the group may feel it has no basis for questioning or attempting to improve upon its current performance strategy, since it lacks a clear understanding of the requirements and constraints placed upon it. The outcome is an assumption that "things must be done this way because this is the way we've always done it," rather than an active search for new and better strategies for group performance effectiveness. Thus, the development of effective group performance strategies is dependent upon management providing self-managing work groups with clear and complete information about exactly what it is they are required to do.

Interpersonal Factors

The effectiveness of a self-managing work group is influenced not only by how the group is designed and by the supportiveness of the organizational context, but also by the nature of the interpersonal relationships between and among the group members themselves. Even the best-designed and most carefully supported group will be ineffective if its members cannot get along with one another and are constantly involved in disagreements and conflict. Three interpersonal factors are particularly important in determining the effectiveness of self-managing work groups. These three factors and their relationships to the facets of group effectiveness are summarized in Figure 10-3.

1. Coordinating Efforts and Fostering Commitment. The level of effort put into group work by members is influenced by both the quality of coordination of group activities and the degree of commitment of members to the group and its task. Coordination is obviously essential if optimal use is to be made of the resources that exist in the group. Inadequate coordination results in lost or wasted effort as individuals work at cross purposes, duplicate one another's efforts, or simply have nothing to do. In addition to coordination, commitment on the part of group members to the effectiveness of the group can also increase the amount of effort brought to bear on the group task. Such commitment tends to be generated when individuals value their membership in the group highly and when they enjoy working with other group members.

FIGURE 10-3
How interpersonal processes influence various facets of work group effectiveness.
(SOURCE: Adapted from J. R. Hackman and G. R. Oldham, *Work Redesign*. Reading, Mass.: Addison-Wesley, 1980. Used by permission.)

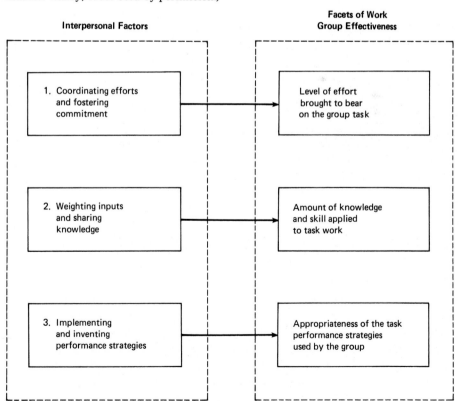

2. Weighting Inputs and Sharing Knowledge. If a self-managing group is to perform effectively, the group must make optimal use of all of the task-relevant knowledge and skill that exists in the group. This requires two sets of skills of group members, skills which management can attempt to develop and facilitate. First, group members must be willing to share their knowledge with one another and be willing to seek out information and assistance from each other. Second, members must become skilled at "weighting" information appropriately; in other words they must learn whose opinion and inputs on various issues tend to be of highest quality and put greatest emphasis (or weight) upon those inputs in making decisions.

3. Implementing and Inventing Performance Strategies. It is frequently the case that members of self-managing work groups will have had little experience developing and implementing task-performance strategies. Thus, management or consultants can frequently assist groups in their early stages in developing appropriate and effective performance strategies. Such assistance can take either of two forms. On the one hand, a manager or consultant may suggest or identify for the group some specific performance strategies that have been employed by other effective groups or that have been shown to have general applicability and utility. On the other hand, the manager or consultant may simply act as a catalyst, helping the group to think through exactly what it must accomplish, what constraints it faces, and how it might organize itself for optimal effectiveness.

INDIVIDUAL VERSUS GROUP WORK DESIGN

The final issue that needs to be addressed in this chapter has to do with the choice between individual- and group-centered approaches to work design. In the previous chapter we discussed work design focused upon the individual job, while in this chapter our attention has been turned to designing work for groups. The question we need to address now is, "Which approach is better?" or perhaps more accurately, "When is individual job redesign appropriate and under what alternative conditions are group designs for work called for?"

Hackman and Oldham (1980) provide some guidance in sorting out these issues. Table 10-1 summarizes the three-step process that they suggest for assessing which approach (if any) to work redesign is most appropriate.

The first step in the process involves assessing whether a *need* exists for work redesign (either individual or group). A set of four diagnostic questions are presented to assist the organization in assessing whether a need for work redesign exists.

TABLE 10-1
Three-step process for choosing a work redesign strategy

STEP ONE: IS THERE A NEED FOR WORK REDESIGN?

1. Is there a problem or opportunity for which work redesign would be an appropriate change strategy?
2. Does the problem or opportunity centrally involve the motivation, satisfaction, or work effectiveness of the employees?
3. Might the design of the work be responsible for the observed problems or the unexploited opportunities?
4. What specific aspects of the job, as presently structured, most need improving?

STEP TWO: IS WORK REDESIGN FEASIBLE?

A. *The feasibility of enriching individual jobs*

1. How ready for change are the employees whose jobs would be redesigned? Do they have appropriate knowledge and skill, growth need strength, and satisfaction with the work context?
2. How hospitable are existing organizational systems to the needed changes? Are the technological, personnel, and control systems likely to constrain the changes that must be made to improve the jobs? If so, can these systems be made more hospitable to work redesign?

B. *The feasibility of creating self-managing work groups*

1. Would self-managing work groups fit with the people and with the organizational context? How do employees stand on knowledge and skill, on social as well as growth need strength, and on satisfaction with the work context? Is the overall climate and managerial style of the organization likely to be supportive of self-managing groups?
2. How hospitable are existing organizational systems to the needed changes? Can intact, identifiable groups be formed that have definable products and the authority to manage their own internal processes? Given the nature of the work to be done, what design features are most important in constructing the self-managing groups? Are the technological, personnel, and control systems likely to constrain the creation of groups with these features? If so, can these systems be made more hospitable to self-managing work groups?

STEP THREE: CHOOSING BETWEEN INDIVIDUAL AND GROUP DESIGNS

1. If neither an individual nor a group design is feasible, do not proceed with work redesign.
2. If one alternative is feasible and the other is not, the choice is obvious.
3. If *both* individual and group designs are feasible, opt for the group design only if it is substantially more attractive than the best possible individual design.

SOURCE: Adapted from J. R. Hackman & G. R. Oldham, *Work Redesign*. Reading, Mass.: Addison-Wesley, 1980. Used by permission.

Once a need for work redesign has been established, the next step involves assessing the *feasibility* of work redesign for a particular organization. Separate questions are presented to assist the organization in determining the feasibility of *both* enriching individual jobs and creating self-managing work groups.

Finally, once need and feasibility of work redesign have been determined, the final step involves choosing between individual and group strategies. The first two cases are straightforward. If neither approach is feasible, work redesign is inappropriate for the organization. If one approach is feasible but not the other, no decision is required on how to proceed. A difficult decision arises only when *both* individual and group designs are feasible. The advice presented by Hackman and Oldham is to choose the group design *only* when it is *substantially* more attractive than the best possible individual design. The reason behind this preference for individual over group designs when neither approach appears clearly superior to the other lies in the greater complexity involved in implementing and managing work groups. First, work groups are inherently more complex than individuals working on jobs. Once a group is created, so are many interpersonal relationships and many issues regarding how the group should manage itself to be most effective and efficient. These issues do not arise when individuals work on their own enriched jobs. Second, creating self-managing groups frequently involves a fairly dramatic change from traditional patterns of organization. The more dramatic the changes are, the more difficult they are to manage. Finally, implementing work groups frequently requires changes well beyond the design of the work groups themselves, e.g., when reward systems must be redesigned to be based upon group, rather than individual, performance.

In general, then, it appears that work redesign based upon self-managing groups is a more difficult and more complex process than enriching individual jobs. That is not to say that work redesign for groups is never desirable or appropriate. There clearly are instances in which group-based work redesign is *the* appropriate route to pursue in improving the nature of work design. However, unless the conditions calling for a group-based approach are clear and compelling, the probability of success and ease of implementation suggest the choice of individually based job enrichment.

MANAGERIAL IMPLICATIONS

Our discussion of quality of work life programs and alternative approaches to work design for groups leads to a number of implications for managerial practice.

1. *Managers must take into account both the technological and social components of organizations when work is being designed for groups.* The nature of an organization's technology obviously places constraints upon the ways in which work can be designed. However, managers must recognize that organizations are social systems as well. The design of work must take into account the needs and capacities of the members of the organization, as well as accommodating to the nature of the organization's technology.

2. *Managers must undertake careful diagnosis of their situation prior to implementing group-based work redesign.* The implementation of autonomous self-managing work groups represents a major change for most organizations. Such changes inevitably generate complex managerial problems in supporting and managing such groups effectively. In order to ensure that coping with these complex problems is indeed worthwhile, managers need to diagnose their situations carefully *prior* to implementing group-based work redesign. Such diagnosis involves an assessment of both the *need* for work redesign and the *feasibility* of group-based work design in any particular situation.

3. *Managers must devote significant attention to the formation and design of groups when work redesign is undertaken.* When an autonomous self-managing group is established, management must ensure that the work assigned to the group is sufficiently complex and challenging to be motivational for group members. In addition, care must be taken in how the groups are composed in order to ensure that group members possess the knowledge and skill necessary to perform their work effectively. Group composition is doubly important since it is also essential that group members be capable of working effectively and harmoniously with one another.

4. *Managers must ensure that work groups receive adequate levels of organizational support.* In order to reinforce and support self-managing work groups, managers must ensure that the setting of objectives and provision of rewards by the organization is based upon the performance of the *group* as a whole. Managers must also ensure that assistance and advice are made available to the work groups when needed.

SUMMARY

Quality of work life (QWL) programs have recently been implemented in a considerable number of organizations. These programs have as their goal the provision of a high quality of life for all organization members while at work. Probably the most common technique employed in QWL programs is the redesign of work for groups. Two major approaches to group-based work design have been developed: the sociotechnical systems approach and the social psychological approach.

The sociotechnical systems approach to work design for groups has its basis in a body of theory that argues that organizations consist of *both* a social system and a technical system, and that the design of work in organizations must seek to jointly optimize both systems. Thus, work-redesign efforts should not take the organization's technology as given and then try to fit people into the technology. Rather, both technology and work design for people should be viewed as variables that can be altered and changed to suit one another most effectively. The primary vehicle for work redesign according to sociotechnical principles is the *autonomous work group.* Work groups are established and given responsibility for the performance of a significant segment of the organization's work. The group is also given the autonomy to determine how the work is to be accomplished.

The social psychological approach to work design for groups is based upon a relatively complex and detailed theory regarding the links between work-group design and organizational and personal outcomes. The approach draws attention to a number of work-group design features which influence various facets of work-group effectiveness. These design features include the design of the group task, the composition of the group, and the group norms about performance. The approach also deals with the impact of organizational and interpersonal factors upon work-group effectiveness.

Many examples exist of significant innovations in work design for groups which have been implemented in organizations. Two of the most important examples, the Topeka plant of General Foods and Volvo's Kalmar plant, are described in the chapter.

REVIEW QUESTIONS

1. What is meant by the term *quality of work life*?
2. Describe several of the types of programs which have been implemented in organizations to improve the quality of work life. Which types of programs do you feel are most likely to be successful?
3. Do you feel that quality of work life programs should be implemented in all organizations? Explain and defend your position.
4. What is a sociotechnical system?
5. What are the primary implications for managerial practice of viewing organizations as sociotechnical systems?
6. Describe the important characteristics of an autonomous work group.
7. What are the primary strengths and weaknesses of the sociotechnical systems approach to work design for groups? In your opinion, do the strengths outweigh the weaknesses, or vice versa?
8. What is a self-managing work group? Describe its major attributes.
9. Discuss the concept of work-group effectiveness and suggest some criteria which could be employed for assessing group effectiveness.
10. Describe three key design features for self-managing work groups and outline their relationship to the various facets of work-group effectiveness.

11. Discuss several organizational factors that will have a significant bearing upon the success or failure of self-managing work groups.
12. Describe the impact of interpersonal factors within a self-managing work group on the overall effectiveness of the group.
13. How should managers go about deciding whether individual or group work redesign is most appropriate for their organizations?
14. Discuss some of the factors that you believe contributed to the success of the innovative work designs at Topeka and Kalmar. Would you expect similar successes to occur any time that work is designed for autonomous work groups?

REFERENCES

Cherns, A. Can behavioral science help design organizations? *Organizational Dynamics,* Spring 1977, 44–64.

Davis, L. E. Job design: Overview and future directions. *Journal of Contemporary Business, 6,* 1977, 85–102.

Davis, L. E., & Trist, E. Improving the quality of work life: Sociotechnical case studies. In J. O'Toole (Ed.), *Work and the quality of life,* Cambridge, Mass.: MIT Press, 1974.

Dowling, W. F. Job redesign on the assembly line: Farewell to blue-collar blues? *Organizational Dynamics,* Autumn 1973, 51–67.

Emery, F. E. Characteristics of socio-technical systems. In L. E. Davis & J. C. Taylor (Eds.), *Design of jobs.* Harmondsworth, England: Penguin, 1972, 177–198.

Emery, F. E., & Trist, E. Socio-technical systems. In F. E. Emery (Ed.), *Systems thinking.* Harmondsworth, England: Penguin, 1969.

Gyllenhammar, P. How Volvo adapts work to people. *Harvard Business Review,* July–August 1977, 102–113.

Hackman, J. R. Work design. In J. R. Hackman & J. L. Suttle (Eds.), *Improving life at work.* Santa Monica, Calif.: Goodyear, 1977.

Hackman, J. R., & Oldham, G. R. *Work redesign.* Reading, Mass.: Addison-Wesley, 1980.

Lawler, E. E., III, Jenkins, G. D., Jr., & Herline, G. E. Initial data feedback to General Foods-Topeka Pet Food Plants—Selected survey items. Ann Arbor, Mich.: Institute for Social Research, July 12, 1974.

Locke, E. A., Shaw, K. N., Saari, L. M., & Latham, G. P. Goal setting and task performance: 1969–1980. *Psychological Bulletin,* 1981, *90,* 125–152.

Rice, A. K. *Productivity and social organization: The Ahmedabad experiment.* London: Tavistock, 1958.

Schrank, R. On ending worker alienation: The Gaines pet food plant. In R. Fairfield (Ed.), *Humanizing the workplace.* Buffalo, N.Y.: Prometheus Books, 1974, 119–140.

Trist, E. L., Higgin, G. W., Murray, H., & Pollock, A. B. *Organizational choice.* London: Tavistock, 1963.

Umstot, D. MBO plus job enrichment: How to have your cake and eat it too. *Management Review,* February 1977, 21–26.

Walton, R. E. How to counter alienation in the plant. *Harvard Business Review,* November–December 1972, *50,* 70–81.

Walton, R. E. From Hawthorne to Topeka and Kalmar. In E. L. Cass & F. G. Zimmer (Eds.), *Man and work in society.* New York: Van Nostrand Reinhold, 1975.

Walton, R. E. Work innovations at Topeka: After six years. *Journal of Applied Behavioral Science,* 1977, *13,* 422–433.

Zander, A. *Motives and goals in groups.* New York: Academic Press, 1971.

PART FIVE

LEADERSHIP IN ORGANIZATIONS

CHAPTER 11

LEADERSHIP: PERSONALITY AND BEHAVIOR

What is the nature of leadership? What characteristics differentiate leaders from followers, or effective leaders from ineffective ones? What sorts of things do leaders actually *do* that make them effective or ineffective? Under what conditions or in what situations will one leader be successful, while another will be unsuccessful (and will effective leadership in one set of circumstances be ineffective in a different situation)? In this chapter and the next we'll review and discuss research that has sought to throw light on these questions regarding the nature of leadership in organizations.

We begin our discussion in this chapter by looking briefly at the nature of leadership in organizations. What exactly do we mean by the term *leadership* and what does it imply? We then turn to what are known as *trait theories* of leadership, theories that have sought to identify traits or personality characteristics that distinguish leaders from followers and good leaders from poor leaders. Next we discuss several attempts to describe the *behavioral styles* of effective leaders. These approaches have sought to identify the activities that effective leaders engage in and ineffective leaders do not. In the following chapter we deal with the most recent approaches to understanding leadership in organizations, the *contingency theories* of leadership. These theories seek to understand what kinds of leaders and what kinds of leadership behavior are suitable to different kinds of situations or contexts. The basic assumption of contingency theories of leadership is not that there is a single style of effective leadership, but rather that what constitutes effective leadership depends upon (or, in other words, is *contingent* upon) the nature of the situation.

THE NATURE OF LEADERSHIP

There is no clear consensus regarding exactly what *leadership* is and how the term should be defined. This lack of consensus is not, however, a result of lack of effort. There are almost as many definitions of leadership as there are researchers who have studied the topic (and over 3000 empirical studies of leadership have been carried out [Stogdill, 1974; House & Baetz, 1979]). A sampling of some representative definitions of leadership is contained in Table 11-1. A recent comprehensive review of research on leadership came to the following conclusion regarding attempts to define the term.

> Definitions of leadership usually have as a common denominator the assumption that it is a group phenomenon involving the interaction between two or

TABLE 11-1
Some representative definitions of leadership

1. Leadership is "the behavior of an individual when he is directing the activities of a group toward a shared goal." (Hemphill & Coons, 1957; p. 7)

2. Leadership is "interpersonal influence, exercised in a situation, and directed, through the communication process, toward the attainment of a specified goal or goals." (Tannenbaum, Weschler, & Massarik, 1961; p. 24)

3. Leadership is "the initiation and maintenance of structure in expectation and interaction." (Stogdill, 1974; p. 411)

4. Leadership is "an interaction between persons in which one presents information of a sort and in such a manner that the other becomes convinced that his outcomes (benefits/costs ratio) will be improved if he behaves in the manner suggested or desired." (Jacobs, 1970; p. 232)

5. Leadership is "a particular type of power relationship characterized by a group member's perception that another group member has the right to prescribe behavior patterns for the former regarding his activity as a group member." (Janda, 1960; p. 358)

6. Leadership is "an influence process whereby O's actions change P's behavior and P views the influence attempt as being legitimate and the change as being consistent with P's goals." (Kochan, Schmidt, & DeCotiis, 1975; p. 285)

7. Leadership is "the influential increment over and above mechanical compliance with the routine directives of the organization." (Katz & Kahn, 1978; p. 528)

SOURCE: G. A. Yukl, *Leadership in Organizations.* Englewood Cliffs, N.J.: Prentice-Hall, 1981. Used by permission.

more people (Janda, 1960). In addition most definitions of leadership reflect the assumption that it involves an influence process whereby intentional influence is exerted by the leader over followers. The numerous definitions of leadership that have been proposed appear to have little else in common. (Yukl, 1981, p. 3)

Another way of saying the same thing is that leadership essentially involves one person (the leader) consciously trying to get other people (the followers) to do something that the leader wants them to do. The study of leadership then comes down to trying to understand how a leader comes to have influence over the thoughts, feelings, and actions of followers. What is it about the nature of the leader, the nature of followers, the organizational situation, or the leader's behavior that results in the leader's capacity to influence followers? And what is it that ultimately results in some leaders being labeled as *effective* and others as *ineffective*?

Leadership as a Mutual Influence Process

The very term *leadership* naturally serves to draw our attention to the leaders themselves and tends to focus our interest upon the ways in which leaders influence their followers. As a result, the vast majority of studies of leadership have tried to understand how different types of leaders and different types of behaviors by leaders *cause* followers to react in different ways (in scientific jargon, researchers have treated leadership as the *independent* or causal factor and the responses of followers as the *dependent* factor determined by leadership).

An important contribution of recent research on leadership has been to point out the shortsightedness and inadequacy of this view of leader-follower relations. While it is no doubt true that leaders can and do influence their followers, it is also true that leaders and followers engage in *interaction* with one another, which necessarily implies the existence of *mutual influence*. In other words, not only is it true that leaders influence followers, but it is equally true that followers influence leaders.

The validity of this claim has been demonstrated in a variety of empirical investigations. Farris and Lim (1969) studied the relationship between the performance of a group of research scientists and engineers and the leadership styles of their superiors. They found that the performance of the scientists had a greater impact upon the way the leaders behaved toward the scientists than the behavior of the leaders had upon the performance of the scientists. In another investigation, Lowin and Craig (1969) set up a simulated organization in which persons were hired to supervise the work of a number of secretaries. The secretaries were in fact confederates of the researchers who had been instructed to perform either effectively or ineffectively regardless of the behavior of the supervisors. The researchers found that the performance of the secretaries (i.e., followers) had a strong causal impact upon the behavior of the supervisors (i.e., leaders). Leaders whose subordinates performed incompetently tended to supervise their subordinates much more closely, to remind subordinates of their mistakes, to criticize unauthorized breaks, and to spend more time checking on the subordinates' whereabouts and activities. In addition, incompetent performance by followers resulted in leaders becoming more directive and insistent about how work should be carried out and more likely to refuse a subordinate's request to switch from one task to another. Finally, leaders of incompetent subordinates tended to be less considerate and less friendly toward their subordinates.

Further corroboration of the influence of subordinates' performance on leader behavior is contained in a recent field study (Greene, 1979). The mutual influence of leaders and subordinates was studied over a 12-month period for a group of 60 new managers in five manufacturing organizations. The results clearly indicate that the performance of subordinates had a stronger impact upon behavior of the leaders than the leaders' behavior had upon subordinate performance. Subordinates who performed effectively tended to be associated with leaders who were less directive, more personally supportive, and more likely to delegate authority to their followers.

Thus, it is clear that when we are studying leadership we are studying a mutual influence process wherein leaders influence followers and followers also influence leaders (Ilgen et al., 1981; Zahn & Wolf, 1981). Any approach that views leadership as a one-way influence process whereby what the leader does causes subordinates to react in certain ways is of necessity incomplete and oversimplified. It is essential to keep this point firmly in mind.

Sources of Leader Influence on Followers

What is it that provides a leader with the capacity to influence followers? Why will subordinates respond to the influence attempts of a leader by doing what the leader intends or wishes them to do? In other words, what is the source of the leader's *power* over subordinates?

Five distinct sources of leader power or influence have been identified (French & Raven, 1959).

1. **Reward power** refers to the leader's capacity to reward followers. To the extent that a leader possesses and controls rewards that are valued by subordinates, the leader's power increases. Rewards at a leader's disposal can be seen to fall into two categories. Rewards such as praise, recognition, and attention are sources of *personal power* possessed by the leader as an individual. In addition, a leader also usually controls certain organizational rewards such as pay raises, promotions, and

other perquisites that are sources of power that depend upon the leader's *position* in the organization.

2. **Coercive power** is the flip side of reward power and refers to the leader's capacity to coerce or punish followers. Sources of coercive power also break down into personal and positional components. Leaders *personally* possess coercive power to the extent that followers experience criticism or lack of recognition from their leader as unpleasant or punishing. In addition, leaders possess coercive power to the extent that their *position* permits them to administer organizational sources of punishment (such as demotion, withholding pay increases, or firing) to followers.

3. **Legitimate power** refers to the power a leader possesses as a result of occupying a particular position or role in the organization. In almost every organization, certain types of requests and directions by leaders of subordinates are viewed to be legitimate and valid. Subordinates are obligated to comply with such requests because of the norms, policies, and procedures accepted as legitimate by all members of the organization. Legitimate power is clearly a function of the leader's *position* in the organization and is completely independent of any of the leader's personal characteristics.

4. **Expert power** refers to power that a leader possesses as a result of his or her knowledge and expertise regarding the tasks to be performed by subordinates. Subordinates are more likely to respond positively to a leader's attempts to influence their behavior if they view the leader as competent and in possession of knowledge and information regarding effective task performance that they themselves lack. The possession of expert power by a leader obviously depends upon the *personal* characteristics of the leader (i.e., his or her personal expertise) and is not determined by the formal position that the leader occupies in the organization.

5. **Referent power** is dependent upon the extent to which subordinates identify with, look up to, and wish to emulate the leader. The more that subordinates admire and identify with the leader, the greater the leader's referent power over subordinates. Referent power, like expert power, is totally dependent upon the *personal* characteristics of the leader and does not depend directly upon the leader's formal organizational position.

Thus, there are a total of five distinct and identifiable sources of a leader's power to influence subordinates. Two of the sources (reward power and coercive power) have both personal and positional components, while legitimate power depends solely on the leader's position, and expert and referent power are determined solely by the leader's personal characteristics. Since legitimate power and the components of reward and coercive power involving organizational outcomes such as raises and firing are dependent upon the leader's *position* in the organization, these are sometimes referred to as sources of a leader's *position power*. On the other hand, expert power, referent power, and the components of reward and coercive power involving personal outcomes such as praise and criticism are dependent upon the leader's *personal* characteristics and hence are often referred to as sources of a leader's *personal power*.

Naturally, the more sources of power leaders have at their disposal, the more likely that they will be successful in influencing subordinates to do those things they would like them to do. However, possessing a high degree of power in no way assures that a leader will be *effective*. Leadership effectiveness will depend not only upon the leader's power, but also upon *what* the leader uses his or her influence to encourage subordinates to do. It is also important to note that a significant proportion of the leader's potential power derives from his or her own personal characteristics and personal style. Thus, leaders and organizations should not assume that anyone can become an influential leader purely on the basis of the position power inherent in a given job or role in the organization. Such a viewpoint ignores a large segment of the potential sources of power and influence available to a leader.

Sources of Influence on a Leader's Behavior

In a previous section we pointed out that leadership is a mutual influence process; what the leader does influences subordinates, but, likewise, what surbordinates do influences the leader. An important facet of this recognition that leadership is not simply a one-way influence process has been the increased attention that is being given to those factors that influence a leader's behavior. Previously it had been thought or assumed that leaders quite independently decided what they were going to do, and the interesting question was what influence this had on subordinates. Recent work has drawn attention to the fact that leaders are not independent actors determining what they are going to do in splendid isolation from other factors. We have already pointed out that one of the factors that has an important impact on leaders' behavior is the performance and reactions of subordinates. There are, however, a large number of additional factors that will influence what leaders do (Reitz, 1981).

Responses of Subordinates
This factor was outlined previously in our discussion of leadership as a mutual influence process. As was pointed out, the evidence is quite clear that the performance of subordinates has a critical causal impact upon what a leader does and how he or she behaves toward followers.

Characteristics of Subordinates

In addition to what subordinates do and how they perform, other identifiable traits or characteristics of subordinates may influence a leader's behavior. For example, a leader may behave differently toward males and females, older and younger people, those with a similar and those with a different personal background from his or hers, and so on.

Leader's Abilities and Traits

The leader's abilities and personal characteristics obviously influence and constrain what the leader does and how he or she behaves toward subordinates. On the ability side, task-relevant knowledge and skill, as well as supervisory skills and sensitivities, will have an important impact. In regard to traits, personality characteristics such as assertiveness, dominance, and self-confidence all have an influence on leadership behavior. These factors are discussed at greater length in the next section.

Organizational Policy and Climate

Some organizations are characterized by a very open, democratic, and participative management style. Such an organizational climate and policy will obviously influence a leader to behave as a participative manager. Very different leadership behaviors would be expected in an organization characterized by a very closed and authoritarian policy of management.

Superiors

How leaders treat their subordinates is strongly influenced by how the leaders themselves are treated by their own immediate superiors. Superiors serve both as role models and as sources of rewards and punishments for the leadership behavior of individuals toward their own subordinates. Leaders with immediate superiors who preach, practice, and reward a participative management style, for example, are unlikely to treat their subordinates in a directive and authoritarian fashion.

Peers

As in almost all things, peers have an important influence upon how leaders behave. Peer pressure has a potent homogenizing impact upon leadership behavior in an organization. Other managers in an organization are likely to exert both direct and indirect pressure on individual leaders to behave toward their subordinates in a fashion that is consistent with that practiced by other managers at that level in the organization.

The Task

The nature of the task that subordinates are performing also influences the behavior of leaders toward subordinates. A very vague and ambiguous task such as developing the design for a new product from scratch is bound to elicit different types of leadership behavior than is a highly structured and routine task such as producing a set number of units on an assembly line.

Thus, there are a multitude of factors that operate to influence what leaders do and how they behave toward subordinates (Ford, 1981). It is obviously inadequate to view leaders as being unconstrained and free to behave exactly as they wish from one moment to the next.

TRAIT THEORIES OF LEADERSHIP

The prevailing assumption among early researchers interested in leadership was that leaders are born, not made. This approach has also been characterized as the "great person" theory of leadership. It was assumed that some people are set apart from others by virtue of their possession of some quality or qualities of "greatness" and that it is such great persons who become leaders.

The implication of this approach to leadership was that understanding leaders and leadership involved identifying and measuring those personal characteristics or "traits" that differentiated the leaders (the "great") from the followers (the "not so great"). In the first half of this century a considerable amount of research was conducted that was designed to accomplish just this. This research focused on a wide variety of leader traits, including personality characteristics (e.g., adaptability, dominance, self-confidence), physical characteristics (e.g., height, weight, appearance), and ability (e.g., intelligence, task expertise, sensitivity in dealing with others).

The results of this early research on leadership traits was summarized in a review by Stogdill (1948). Stogdill carefully examined the results of 124 studies of leadership traits conducted between 1904 and 1948. The overall trend of the results was not surprising. They indicated that leaders tended to be differentiated from nonleaders by traits such as intelligence, alertness to the needs of others, understanding of the task, initiative and persistence in dealing with problems, self-confidence, and desire to accept responsibility and occupy a position of dominance and control. Although these results are consistent with the notion that leaders differ from nonleaders in regard to personal traits, the results were neither noticeably strong nor consistent. In particular, Stogdill found that results tended to vary from situation to situation, leading him to conclude that "a person does not become a leader by virtue of the possession of some combination of traits, . . . the pattern of personal characteristics of the leader must bear some relevant relationship to the characteristics, activities, and goals of the followers" (Stogdill, 1948, p. 64).

This review caused great disappointment and disillusionment among leadership researchers, resulting in many of them giving up the search for leadership traits. However, leadership trait research was carried on and, in fact, was intensified among industrial psychologists searching for traits that might predict leadership effectiveness and hence be useful for selection and screening purposes in organizations. Two important shifts in emphasis are noteworthy in this trait research following Stogdill's review in 1948. First, the focus of research shifted from identifying traits that distinguished leaders from nonleaders to a search for those that would distinguish *effective* from *ineffective* leaders. Second, the research was conducted by a group of researchers (industrial psychologists) interested specifically in predicting leadership effectiveness in managerial roles in organizations. This represented a narrowing of focus from earlier research, which had addressed the concept of leadership in a wide variety of forms and situations.

In 1974 Stogdill reported the results of a review of 163 trait studies that had been conducted between 1949 and 1974. The results of the more recent research are stronger and more encouraging than those of the earlier review. Table 11-2 summarizes the personality traits, abilities, and social skills found most frequently to be characteristic of effective and successful leaders. The findings led Stogdill (1974) to suggest the following trait profile as characteristic of successful leaders:

The leader is characterized by a strong drive for responsibility and task completion, vigor and persistence in pursuit of goals, venturesomeness and orginality in problem-solving, drive to exercise initiative in social situations, self-confidence and sense of personal identity, willingness to accept consequences of decision and action, readiness to absorb interpersonal stress, willingness to tolerate frustration and delay, ability to influence other persons'

TABLE 11-2
Personality traits, abilities, and social skills most frequently associated with effective leadership

Personality traits	Abilities	Social skills
Adaptability	Intelligence	Ability to enlist cooperation
Adjustment (normality)	Judgment and decisiveness	Administrative ability
Aggressiveness and assertiveness	Knowledge	Cooperativeness
Dominance	Fluency of speech	Popularity and prestige
Emotional balance and control		Sociability (interpersonal skills)
Independence (nonconformity)		Social participation
Originality and creativity		Tact and diplomacy
Personal integrity (ethical conduct)		
Self-confidence		

SOURCE: Reprinted with permission of Macmillan Publishing Co., Inc. From R. M. Stogdill, *Handbook of Leadership: A Survey of Theory and Research*. Copyright © 1974 by The Free Press, a division of Macmillan Publishing Co., Inc.

behavior, and capacity to structure social interaction systems to the purpose at hand. (p. 81)

The early approach to leadership, which assumed that leadership and leadership effectiveness are purely a function of the leader's traits, was obviously oversimplified. At the same time, however, there was probably an overreaction to Stogdill's 1948 review, which caused many to conclude mistakenly that personal traits and characteristics bear little or no relationship to leadership effectiveness. Both extreme positions are obviously oversimplified. While it is clear that leader traits alone do not explain leadership effectiveness, it is equally clear that such traits are not irrelevant to effective leadership. A recent review of leadership research in fact has concluded that since all leadership situations share certain common characteristics, research should continue to attempt to identify those specific traits required for effectiveness in all leadership situations (House & Baetz, 1979).

Thus, while a focus on leadership traits alone cannot explain all we need to know regarding effective leadership in organizations, leadership traits are also far from irrelevant to such an understanding. A balanced and complete understanding of leadership effectiveness in organizations must take into account the personal traits and skills of the leader (e.g., Drory & Gluskinos, 1980).

BEHAVIORAL THEORIES OF LEADERSHIP

Trait theories of leadership focus upon personal characteristics of the leader and seek to predict leadership effectiveness on the basis of what type of person the leader is. Another group of researchers argued that if we wish to understand leadership and leadership effectiveness, what we really need to focus on is not the leader's personality traits and skills but on what the leader actually *does* when he or she is dealing with subordinates. In other words, theories of leadership effectiveness should focus upon leader behavior and should seek to uncover and understand the relationship between what the leader does and how the subordinates react emotionally (satisfaction) and behaviorally (performance).

The task facing researchers who adopted this perspective was twofold. First, they had to develop some method or basis for characterizing or describing *patterns* of leader behavior. It is obviously impossible even to attempt to study links between *every* particular thing that a leader does and how subordinates respond to each particular aspect of a leader's behavior. Consequently, general patterns of leadership behavior had to be sought that could be used to characterize and describe leadership behavior, and methods had to be developed for actually classifying a particular leader on the basis of the patterns identified. Second, the researchers had to study the relationships between the various patterns of leader behavior and the performance and satisfaction of subordinates.

There are three well-known behavioral theories of leadership, each of which happens to be identified most closely with the university at which the research underlying the theory was carried out. The three universities are the University of Iowa, the Ohio State University, and the University of Michigan. For each theory we'll outline the system of describing and classifying leader behavior developed by the theorists, and then we'll examine the relationships that have been observed between the leadership styles and subordinates' reactions.

The Iowa Studies: Authoritarian, Democratic, and Laissez-Faire Leadership

The initial attempts to classify and study the effects of different styles of leader behavior were carried out at the University of Iowa (Lewin, Lippitt, & White, 1939). The Iowa theorists focused on the decision-making component of the leader's behavior and classified leaders into three different types according to their style of handling decision-making situations.

> *Authoritarian.* The leader makes decisions alone and tells subordinates what they are to do in light of the decisions made by the leader.

> *Democratic.* The leader actively involves subordinates in the decision-making process, sharing problems with them, soliciting their inputs, and sharing the authority for arriving at decisions.

> *Laissez-Faire.* The leader avoids making a decision whenever possible and leaves it up to subordinates to make individual decisions on their own with little guidance or direction either from the leader or from the rest of the group.

A more complete description of the three leadership styles is contained in Table 11-3. The table summarizes typical behaviors that would be engaged in by leaders employing the different styles on a variety of dimensions of leadership behavior.

Research on the effectiveness of these alternative styles indicated that the democratic leadership style appears most desirable (Lewin et al., 1939). Individuals under democratic leadership were more satisfied, had higher morale, were more creative, and had better relationships with their superiors. In addition, individuals working under a democratic leader were most likely to continue working in the absence of the leader. However, the quantity of output produced by workers was highest under the autocratic leadership style, slightly lower under democratic leadership, and lowest under laissez-faire leadership.

TABLE 11-3
Differences in behavior of various styles of leaders identified by the Iowa researchers

Behavior	Authoritarian	Democratic	Laissez-faire
Policy determination	Solely by leader	By group's decision	No policy—complete freedom for group or individual decision
Establishment of job techniques and activities	Solely by leader	Leader suggests—group chooses	Up to individual
Planning	Solely by leader	Group receives sufficient information to obtain perspective needed to plan	No systematic planning
Establishment of division of labor and job assignments	Dictated by leader	Left to group decision	Leader uninvolved
Evaluation	Leader personal in praise and criticism	Evaluation against objective standards	No appraisal—spontaneous evaluation by other group members

SOURCE: Adapted from "Patterns of Aggressive Behavior in Experimentally Created Social Climates" by K. Lewin, R. Lippitt, and R. K. White, *Journal of Social Psychology*, 1939, *10*, 271–299.

Overall, the Iowa studies were important in that they helped draw attention to leadership *behavior* as a critical focus of study. In addition, they provided a helpful basis for describing and classifying alternative leadership styles.

The Ohio State Studies: Consideration and Initiating Structure

Researchers at Ohio State University identified two distinct, relatively broad categories of leader behavior. The two categories were labeled *consideration* and *initiating structure*.

Consideration. As its name suggests, *consideration* refers to the extent to which a leader is considerate of subordinates and concerned about the quality of his or her relationship with subordinates. Among the specific examples of leader behavior included in the consideration dimension are friendliness, consultation with subordinates, recognition of subordinates, open communication with subordinates, supportiveness, and representation of subordinate interests.

Initiating structure. *Initiating structure* refers to the extent to which a leader is task-oriented and concerned with utilizing resources and personnel effectively in order to accomplish group goals. Specific types of leader behavior included in the initiating structure dimension include planning, coordinating, directing, problem solving, clarifying subordinate roles, criticizing poor work, and pressuring subordinates to perform more effectively. The nature of these two dimensions of leader behavior is summarized in Table 11-4.

Probably the most well known study using this classification of leader behavior was conducted with a group of production supervisors in a manufacturing environment (Fleishman & Harris, 1962). The results of this study indicated that high levels of leader consideration were associated with lower levels of employee grievances and turnover. A large body of subsequent research has been carried out studying the relationship between consideration and initiating structure and leadership effectiveness (Kerr & Schriesheim, 1974; Stogdill, 1974; Yukl, 1971; J. F. Schriesheim, 1980). This research has consistently found that subordinates report higher levels of satisfaction with a leader who is considerate than with a leader who is inconsiderate. Neither consideration nor initiating structure has been found to be consistently related to any other measures of subordinate performance.

The Michigan Studies: Employee-Oriented and Production-Oriented Leadership

At approximately the same time as the researchers at Ohio State University were developing the concepts of consideration and initiating structure, another group of scientists at the University of Michigan was also involved in research on leadership effectiveness. The approach adopted by the Michigan researchers (e.g., Katz, Maccoby, & Morse, 1950) was first to identify leaders who were acknowledged to be either effective or ineffective, and then to study the behavior of these leaders in a search for

TABLE 11-4
Examples of behaviors engaged in by leaders high on consideration and initiating structure

Leader consideration	Leader initiating structure
Friendliness	Planning
Consultation with subordinates	Coordinating
Recognition of subordinates	Directing
Open communication with subordinates	Problem-solving
Supportiveness	Clarifying subordinates' roles
Representation of subordinates' interests	Criticizing poor work
	Pressuring subordinates

patterns of behavior that might differentiate the effective and ineffective leaders.

The Michigan research also led to the identification of two distinct dimensions of leader behavior, two dimensions which bear a significant degree of similarity to the dimensions of consideration and initiating structure that came out of the Ohio State research program. The two dimensions identified were *employee-oriented leadership* and *production-oriented leadership*. The leader behaviors associated with the dimensions are summarized in Table 11-5.

Employee-oriented. As its name implies, *employee-oriented leader behavior* is highly similar to leader behavior which is high on consideration. The employee-oriented leader is concerned with the welfare and development of subordinates, engages in two-way communication with subordinates, is supportive and nonpunitive, and delegates responsibility and authority to subordinates. An employee-oriented leader is sometimes described as employing a "general" style of supervision.

Production-oriented. The notion of a leader who is highly production-oriented is very similar to the idea of a leader who is high on initiating structure. Production-oriented leaders emphasize planning, goal-setting, and meeting schedules. They are more likely to give subordinates explicit instructions, make use of power, evaluate subordinates, and generally stress the importance of production. Leaders who are highly production-oriented are frequently described as employing a "close" style of supervision.

Initially it was thought that employee-oriented and production-oriented leadership styles were opposite ends of a single continuum. In other words, it was thought that leaders were either one or the other, and the more they tended to be employee-oriented the less they tended to be production-oriented and vice versa. Fortunately, research has disproved

TABLE 11-5
Examples of behaviors engaged in by leaders with employee-oriented and production-oriented leadership styles

Employee-oriented leadership	Production-oriented leadership
Concern with subordinate welfare and development	Concern with planning, goal-setting, and meeting schedules
Two-way communication with subordinates	Gives explicit instructions
Supportive and nonpunitive	Makes use of power
Responsibility and authority delegated to subordinates	Evaluates subordinates
	Stresses production

this assumption (Weissenberg & Kavanaugh, 1972). It appears that the two dimensions are independent of one another; the extent to which a person is high or low on one dimension does not determine where that person stands on the other dimension. As a result, a leader may simultaneously be high or low on either or both of the dimensions.

A considerable amount of research was carried out examining the relationship between employee-oriented and production-oriented leadership styles and leadership effectiveness (e.g., Katz et al., 1950; Katz & Kahn, 1952; Mann & Dent, 1954; Morse & Reimer, 1956). The eventual conclusions drawn from this research regarding employee-oriented and production-oriented leadership are very similar to those drawn for consideration and initiating structure. There does appear to be some evidence that employee-oriented leadership generates higher levels of employee satisfaction. However, there is no consistent evidence that either leadership style results in higher levels of productivity.

Leader Behavioral Style: Conclusion

The behavioral theories of leadership that we have discussed made two important contributions to the understanding of leadership in organizations. First, they helped focus the attention of researchers on what leaders actually *do* rather than on what kind of person the leader is. This was a key shift in perspective, since the effectiveness of a leader obviously ultimately depends upon what the leader actually does. Second, the behavioral theories of leadership provided us with a convenient method of describing and categorizing leadership behavior according to some underlying themes or dimensions. In fact, one of the remarkable aspects of the behavioral style research was the similarity in the dimensions of leader behavior uncovered by the three major behavioral theories. There is obviously a high degree of similarity among what the Iowa researchers labeled *democratic leadership*, what the Ohio State studies called *leader consideration*, and what the Michigan research described as *employee-oriented leadership*. Similar commonalities are evident among *autocratic leadership*, *initiating structure*, and *production-oriented* leadership styles. These commonalities increase our confidence in the existence of some underlying themes or patterns in leader behavior and provide us with a useful method for describing and analyzing what leaders actually do.

At the same time, however, the failure of the behavioral theories of leadership to uncover consistent links between different leadership styles and subordinate productivity and performance is a serious shortcoming. This shortcoming has resulted in a variety of criticisms being leveled at the behavioral theories of leadership. These criticisms have tended to focus upon two issues. First, it has been argued that trying to characterize a leader as having a single leadership style may itself be misguided. Evidence is accumulating that a leader may adjust his or her leadership style to the demands of the particular situation being faced (e.g., Hill,

1973; Vroom & Yetton, 1973). Second, it has been argued that it is highly unlikely that there exists any leadership style that will be universally effective. Hence, our attention must turn from trying to identify *the* effective leadership style to trying to understand which *different* leadership styles are appropriate to different types of organizations, different types of tasks, different types of subordinates, and so on. In other words, we need to understand the complexities involved in achieving a "fit" between the leader's behavior and the leadership demands of the situation. This approach leads us to what are labeled *contingency theories of leadership*, which are the topic of the next chapter.

MANAGERIAL IMPLICATIONS

A variety of implications for management practice follow from our discussion of the nature of leadership and the trait and behavioral style approaches to understanding leadership in organizations.

1. ***Managers need to recognize that leadership is a mutual influence process.***
   While it was once assumed that leadership was a one-way influence process, with leaders influencing their subordinates' feelings and behaviors, it is now recognized that subordinates' behavior and performance also have a strong influence on what leaders do. Thus, leadership is a *mutual* influence process between leader and subordinates. This implies that managers need to recognize and become conscious of the ways in which their subordinates' behavior is influencing and affecting their own leadership style. In addition, it implies that in judging and evaluating the performance of other managers, senior managers must recognize that each manager's leadership style is in part determined by the nature of the subordinates the manager is currently supervising.

2. ***In making appointments to leadership positions, managers must recognize that while the personal traits and characteristics of the leader are not the sole determinant of leadership effectiveness, these traits do matter and do make a difference.*** The position that a leader's effectiveness is solely determined by his or her personal traits and characteristics is oversimplified and incorrect. However, it is equally oversimplified and incorrect to argue that the personal traits and characteristics of the leader are irrelevant to leadership effectiveness. Thus, in making appointments to leadership positions, managers must take into account individuals' personal traits and characteristics in assessing their suitability. Individuals differ in their appropriateness and capacity for handling different types of leadership situations effectively.

3. ***To the extent that managers are concerned about employee satisfaction, they should adopt a considerate, employee-oriented leadership style.*** The evidence is quite consistent that employees are more satisfied with leaders who are

considerate and oriented toward employee needs. Levels of satisfaction are in turn related inversely to employee absenteeism and turnover. To the extent that absenteeism and turnover are problematic or especially disruptive to the organization, the desirability of a considerate employee-oriented leadership style is implied.

4. ***No single leader or leadership style will attain high levels of subordinate performance in all types of situations.*** The primary shortcoming of the behavioral theories of leadership was their inability to demonstrate consistent relationships between any particular leadership style and the productivity and effectiveness of subordinates. The implication is that there is no single optimal or best leadership style to facilitate the work effectiveness of subordinates. This implies the necessity of understanding how and why *different* leadership styles will be effective under *different* sets of circumstances. This issue is the topic of the next chapter.

SUMMARY

Leadership is best thought of as a mutual influence process. While the majority of research on leadership has naturally focused on the ways in which leaders influence their subordinates, it also needs to be recognized that what subordinates do (in terms of their satisfaction, productivity, etc.) also has a significant influence upon their leaders. In addition, a leader is influenced by factors such as his or her peers and superiors, the nature of the task, the climate and policies of the organization, and so on. Thus, even though our primary interest may be in how the leader's behavior influences subordinates, we must also be aware of influences and constraints that operate on the leader.

Early attempts to understand leadership focused upon the traits and personality characteristics of leaders. Considerable research led to the conclusion that no single trait or set of traits reliably differentiates leaders from followers. On the other hand, more recent research on the characteristics of effective versus ineffective leaders in managerial positions indicates that certain traits do reliably differentiate these two groups (e.g., initiative, self-confidence, willingness to accept responsibility, and persistence).

An alternative to the trait approach to understanding leadership involved searching for patterns of behavior that might differentiate leaders from followers and effective leaders from ineffective ones. Researchers at the University of Iowa identified authoritarian, democratic, and laissez-faire leadership styles. Studies at Ohio State University classified leadership behavior on the dimensions of consideration and initiating structure, while scientists at the University of Michigan identified employee-oriented and production-oriented leadership styles. Unfortunately, no single leadership style appears to be universally associated with leadership effectiveness, although democratic, considerate, and employee-oriented leadership styles tend to result in higher levels of subordinate satisfaction.

REVIEW QUESTIONS

1. What are some common threads in most attempts to define leadership?
2. What do we mean when we say that leadership is a mutual influence process?
3. Discuss some of the sources of power that may be at a leader's disposal in his or her attempts to influence subordinates.
4. Is it more important for a leader to have a high degree of personal power or a high degree of position power? Discuss.
5. Outline some of the factors that have an important influence upon a leader's behavior. Which factors do you feel are most potent in determining what a leader does?
6. What are the main strengths and weaknesses of trait theories of leadership?
7. What is the difference between trait theories and behavioral theories of leadership?
8. What are the relative advantages and disadvantages associated with authoritarian, democratic, and laissez-faire leadership styles?
9. Consideration and initiating structure are two dimensions of leader behavior identified by the Ohio State leadership studies. Discuss what is meant by these two terms.
10. What do we know about the relationship between leader consideration and initiating structure on the one hand and subordinates' satisfaction and performance on the other?
11. Would you recommend that a leader adopt an employee-oriented leadership style or a production-oriented style? Discuss the reasons for your recommendation.
12. What do you feel is the primary contribution of the behavioral theories of leadership to our understanding of leadership effectiveness in organizations?
13. What personal characteristics or traits would you look for in an individual to be appointed to a leadership position in an organization? How would the nature of the leadership position influence the traits you would be looking for?
14. What sorts of things should a leader do to attempt to increase his or her level of personal power to influence subordinates?

REFERENCES

Drory, A., & Gluskinos, U. M. Machiavellianism and leadership. *Journal of Applied Psychology*, 1980, *65*, 81–86.

Farris, G. F., & Lim, F. G., Jr. Effects of performance on leadership, cohesiveness, satisfaction, and subsequent performance. *Journal of Applied Psychology*, 1969, *53*, 490–497.

Fleishman, E. A., & Harris, E. F. Patterns of leadership behavior related to employee grievances and turnover. *Personnel Psychology*, 1962, *15*, 43–56.

Ford, J. D. Departmental context and formal structure as constraints on leader behavior. *Academy of Management Journal*, 1981, *24*, 274–288.

French, J. R. P., & Raven, B. The bases of social power. In D. Cartwright (Ed.), *Studies in social power*. Ann Arbor, Mich.: Institute for Social Research, 1959.

Greene, C. N. *A longitudinal investigation of modification to a situational model of leadership effectiveness*. Paper presented at the Academy of Management Convention, Atlanta, 1979.

Hemphill, J. K., & Coons, A. E. Development of the leader behavior description questionnaire. In R. M. Stogdill & A. E. Coons (Eds.), *Leader Behavior: Its description and measurement*. Columbus: Bureau of Business Research, Ohio State University, 1957.

Hill, W. Leadership style: Rigid or flexible? *Organizational Behavior and Human Performance*, 1973, *9*, 35–47.

House, R. J., & Baetz, M. L. Leadership: Some generalizations and new research directions. In B. M. Staw (Ed.), *Research in organizational behavior*. Greenwich, Conn.: JAI Press, 1979.

Ilgen, D. R., Mitchell, T. R., & Frederickson, J. W. Poor performers: Supervisors' and subordinates' responses. *Organizational Behavior and Human Performance*, 1981, *27*, 386–410.

Jacobs, T. O. *Leadership and exchange in formal organizations*. Alexandria, Virginia: Human Resources Research Organization, 1970.

Janda, K. F. Towards the explication of the concept of leadership in terms of the concept of power. *Human Relations*, 1960, *13*, 345–363.

Katz, D., & Kahn, R. L. Some recent findings in human relations research. In E. Swanson, T. Newcomb, & E. Hartley (Eds.), *Readings in social psychology*. New York: Holt, Rinehart & Winston, 1952.

Katz, D., & Kahn, R. L. *The social psychology of organizations* (Second Edition). New York: Wiley, 1978.

Katz, D., Maccoby, N., & Morse, N. *Productivity, supervision, and morale in an office situation*. Ann Arbor, Mich.: Institute for Social Research, 1950.

Kerr, S., & Schriesheim, C. A. Consideration, initiating structure, and organizational criteria–An update of Korman's 1966 review. *Personnel Psychology*, 1974, *27*, 555–568.

Kochan, T. A., Schmidt, S. S., & DeCotiis, T. A. Superior-Subordinate relations: Leadership and headship. *Human Relations*, 1975, *28*, 279–294.

Lewin, K., Lippitt, R., & White, R. K. Patterns of aggressive behavior in experimentally created "social climates." *Journal of Social Psychology*, 1939, *10*, 271–299.

Lowin, A., & Craig, J. R. The influence of level of performance on managerial style: An experimental object lesson in the ambiguity of correlational data. *Organizational Behavior and Human Performance*, 1968, *3*, 440–458.

Mann, F. C., & Dent, J. The supervisor: Member of two organizational families. *Harvard Business Review*, 1954, *32*(6), 103–112.

Morse, N. C., & Reimer, E. The experimental change of a major organizational variable. *Journal of Abnormal and Social Psychology*, 1956, *52*, 120–129.

Reitz, H. J. *Behavior in organizations* (Rev. ed.). Homewood, Ill.: Irwin, 1981.

Schriesheim, J. F. The social context of leader-subordinate relations: An investigation of the effects of group cohesiveness. *Journal of Applied Psychology*, 1980, *65*, 183–194.

Stogdill, R. M. Personal factors associated with leadership: A survey of the literature. *Journal of Psychology*, 1948, *25*, 35–71.

Stogdill, R. M. *Handbook of leadership: A survey of theory and research*. New York: Free Press, 1974.

Tannenbaum, R., Weschler, I. R., & Massarik, F. *Leadership and organization*. New York: McGraw-Hill, 1961.

Vroom, V. H., & Yetton, P. W. *Leadership and decision-making*. Pittsburgh, Pa.: University of Pittsburgh Press, 1973.

Weissenberg, D., & Kavanaugh, M. H. The independence of initiating structure and consideration: A review of the evidence. *Personnel Psychology*, 1972, *25*, 119–130.

Yukl, G. A. Toward a behavioral theory of leadership. *Organizational Behavior and Human Performance*, 1971, *6*, 414–440.

Yukl, G. A. *Leadership in organizations*. Englewood Cliffs, N.J.: Prentice-Hall, 1981.

Zahn, G. L., & Wolf, G. Leadership and the art of cycle maintenance: A simulation model of superior-subordinate interaction. *Organizational Behavior and Human Performance*, 1981, *28*, 26–49.

CHAPTER 12

CONTINGENCY MODELS
OF LEADERSHIP

Contingency theories of leadership have appeared over the past few years largely as a result of recognition of the fact that there is no single universal "best" leadership style. As their label implies, *contingency* theories of leadership are derived from the basic proposition that the most effective behavior for leaders to engage in is *contingent* upon characteristics of the situation in which the leaders find themselves. Thus, the types of questions we must ask ourselves regarding leadership shift from those such as, "Is employee-oriented leadership more effective than production-oriented leadership?", to new questions such as, "Under what conditions (in what types of situations) will employee-oriented leadership be effective, and under what different types of conditions will production-oriented leadership be effective?"

The basic idea behind contingency theories of leadership is that leadership effectiveness depends upon the existence of a "fit" between the leader's behavior and the demands of the situation. This basic notion is diagrammed in Figure 12-1. The contingency theories that we will be discussing draw attention to some specific dimensions of leader behavior and some specific characteristics of leadership situations in order to make predictions regarding the conditions under which a good fit will occur.

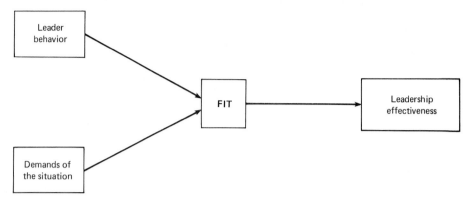

FIGURE 12-1
Leadership effectiveness depends on a fit between the leader's behavior and the demands of the situation.

FIEDLER'S CONTINGENCY THEORY

The first contingency theory we'll discuss (often referred to as *the* contingency theory of leadership) was developed by Fiedler (1964, 1967). Fiedler's theory consists of: (1) a method of classifying leaders; (2) a framework for classifying leadership situations; and (3) a model specifying which types of leaders are best suited to which types of situations. We'll discuss each of these components in turn, as well as the empirical evidence regarding the validity of the theory.

The Leader

A cornerstone of Fiedler's contingency theory is a particular method of measuring and classifying a leader's orientation. In Fiedler's theory, leaders are classified on the basis of their scores on the *least preferred coworker* (LPC) scale. An example of an LPC scale is contained in Figure 12-2. The scale consists of a series of pairs of adjectives, each of which could be used to describe a person. The leader completing the LPC scale is asked to think of the person with whom he or she works now, or with whom he or she has worked in the past, whom the leader found it most difficult to work with. The leader then describes his or her perceptions of that person (his or her "least preferred coworker") by placing X's at the appropriate points between each of the pairs of adjectives. There are eight response categories separating each adjective pair, with the most positive response for each pair given a score of 8 and the least positive response a score of 1. The leader's LPC score is determined by adding up his or her responses to the set of adjective pairs contained in the questionnaire. As a result of the way the scale is scored, higher scores indicate that the leader

Instructions:

People differ in the ways they think about those with whom they work. On the scale below are pairs of words which are opposite in meaning. You are asked to describe someone with whom you have worked by placing an "X" in one of the eight spaces on the line between the two words. Each space represents how well the adjective fits the person you are describing, as in the following example:

Very neat   :_____:_____:_____:_____:_____:_____:_____:_____: Not neat

8	7	6	5	4	3	2	1
Very	Quite	Somewhat	Slightly	Slightly	Somewhat	Quite	Very
neat	neat	neat	neat	Untidy	Untidy	Untidy	Untidy

Now, think of the person with whom you can work least well. He may be someone you work with now, or he may be someone you knew in the past. He does not have to be the person you like least well, but should be the person with whom you had the most difficulty in getting a job done. Describe this person as he appears to you.

Pleasant	:_____:_____:_____:_____:_____:_____:_____:_____:	Unpleasant
Friendly	:_____:_____:_____:_____:_____:_____:_____:_____:	Unfriendly
Rejecting	:_____:_____:_____:_____:_____:_____:_____:_____:	Accepting
Helpful	:_____:_____:_____:_____:_____:_____:_____:_____:	Frustrating
Unenthusiastic	:_____:_____:_____:_____:_____:_____:_____:_____:	Enthusiastic
Tense	:_____:_____:_____:_____:_____:_____:_____:_____:	Relaxed
Distant	:_____:_____:_____:_____:_____:_____:_____:_____:	Close
Cold	:_____:_____:_____:_____:_____:_____:_____:_____:	Warm
Cooperative	:_____:_____:_____:_____:_____:_____:_____:_____:	Uncooperative
Supportive	:_____:_____:_____:_____:_____:_____:_____:_____:	Hostile
Boring	:_____:_____:_____:_____:_____:_____:_____:_____:	Interesting
Quarrelsome	:_____:_____:_____:_____:_____:_____:_____:_____:	Harmonious
Self-assured	:_____:_____:_____:_____:_____:_____:_____:_____:	Hesitant
Efficient	:_____:_____:_____:_____:_____:_____:_____:_____:	Inefficient
Gloomy	:_____:_____:_____:_____:_____:_____:_____:_____:	Cheerful
Open	:_____:_____:_____:_____:_____:_____:_____:_____:	Guarded

FIGURE 12-2
Example of an LPC scale. (SOURCE: Adapted from F. E. Fiedler, *A Theory of Leadership Effectiveness*. New York: McGraw-Hill, 1967. Used by permission of McGraw-Hill Book Company.)

perceives his or her least preferred coworker fairly positively, while lower scores indicate a more negative impression of the least preferred coworker.

What does the LPC scale measure and how can the leader's LPC score be interpreted? According to Fiedler (1971, 1972) high LPC leaders (those who describe their least preferred coworker positively) are primarily motivated to have close interpersonal relationships with others (including subordinates), emphasize socializing with subordinates, and behave in a considerate and supportive manner toward subordinates. Achievement of task objectives is only a secondary motive to high LPC leaders and will only become important when the primary affiliation motive is satisfied. Low LPC scores, on the other hand, are interpreted by Fiedler to indicate that the leader is primarily motivated by task accomplishment. Such a leader's main concern is with doing a good job; establishing good interpersonal relationships will only receive attention if the work is going well and no serious problems exist. While many questions have been raised regarding the meaning and interpretation of LPC scores, a recent review of 25 years of research on the issue concludes that there is considerable support for the interpretation that high LPC leaders value interpersonal success, while low LPC leaders value task success (Rice, 1978).

The Situation

According to Fiedler, any managerial situation in an organization can be classified on the basis of the extent to which the situation is "favorable" to the leader. A situation is defined as favorable for the leader to the extent that the situation gives the leader influence and control over subordinate performance. Three factors are hypothesized to determine situational favorability.

1. *Leader-member relations.*   When the relationship between the leader and followers is good and the leader can count on the loyalty and support of followers, the leader's influence and control are high. Poor leader-member relations, on the other hand, impair the leader's control and contribute to a more unfavorable situation for the leader.
2. *Task structure.*   A high degree of task structure contributes to a favorable situation for the leader, since the leader can more easily monitor and influence subordinates' behavior on a highly structured task. When a task is unstructured, the leader is less likely to be sure of the best way of performing the task, and disagreements with subordinates regarding how to accomplish the task are likely. As a result, the leader's ability to control and direct subordinates is reduced.
3. *Position power.*   The greater the formal legitimate authority associated with the leader's position, and the greater the range of rewards and punishments at the leader's disposal as a result of his or her position, the greater the leader's control over subordinates and the more favorable the situation is to the leader.

According to Fiedler, these three factors arrange themselves in a hierarchy of importance according to the extent to which they influence situational favorability: leader-member relations is the most important factor, followed in turn by task structure and position power. In addition, it is argued that the three factors can be used to construct a continuum of situational favorability. This continuum is constructed by dichotomizing the three situational variables on the basis of whether leader-member relations are good or poor, task structure is high or low, and position power is strong or weak. The result is the classification of eight distinct types of leadership situations, varying from very favorable to very unfavorable, diagrammed in Figure 12-3.

The Model

When Fiedler examined the relationships among situational favorability, leader LPC, and task performance, the pattern diagrammed in Figure 12-4 emerged. Individuals with low LPC scores turned out to be most effective in highly favorable and highly unfavorable situations. When the favorability of the situation is only moderate (the central segment of Figure 12-4), low LPC leaders are not as effective. High LPC leaders, on the other hand, exhibit the opposite pattern of results. High LPC leaders are effective in situations of moderate favorability, but less effective in both highly favorable and highly unfavorable situations.

The explanation for this pattern is as follows. First, the effectiveness of low LPC leaders in highly unfavorable situations is easily explained, since such situations would clearly require the directive, task-oriented approach of the low LPC leader. Low LPC leaders can also be seen to be suitable to highly favorable situations, since they would respond very positively to a situation that facilitated the accomplishment of performance goals by the work group. The effectiveness of high LPC leaders in moderately favorable situations is less easy to explain (House & Baetz, 1979). The most plausible explanation is probably that the relationship orientation of the high LPC leader may help overcome poor leader-

FIGURE 12-3
Fiedler's classification of situation favorableness. (SOURCE: F. E. Fiedler, *A Theory of Leadership Effectiveness*. New York: McGraw-Hill, 1967. Used by permission of McGraw-Hill Book Company.)

Leader member relations	Good				Poor			
Task structure	High		Low		High		Low	
Position power	Strong	Weak	Strong	Weak	Strong	Weak	Strong	Weak
Situations	I	II	III	IV	V	VI	VII	VIII

Very favorable ← → Very unfavorable

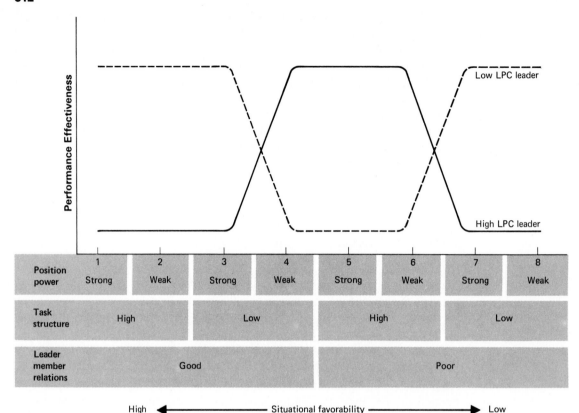

FIGURE 12-4
General pattern of results of research on Fiedler's Contingency Theory.

member relations and may facilitate a participative approach to the clarification of ambiguous task demands.

Research on Fiedler's Contingency Theory

A great deal of research has been carried out on the validity of Fiedler's contingency theory. The majority of findings have been supportive of the theory (e.g., Fiedler, 1978; Chemers & Skrzypek, 1972; Rice, 1981), although some researchers have failed to find support for the model (e.g., Graen et al., 1970; Vecchio, 1977).[1] The results of a recent comprehensive

[1]The theory has also been subjected to a wide variety of specific criticisms regarding factors such as the interpretation of the LPC score (Schriesheim & Kerr, 1977), the relative importance of the three situational factors in determining situational favorability (Shiflett, 1973), and the lack of adequate explanatory mechanisms to explain the reasons leader LPC and situational favorability interact as they do in determining group performance (Ashour, 1973). Fiedler has developed replies to most of the criticisms that have been leveled at the theory (Fiedler, 1971, 1973, 1977).

review and analysis of research on Fiedler's model (Strube & Garcia, 1981) indicate a generally high degree of overall support for the theory.

While the status of all of the detailed predictions contained in Fiedler's theory must be viewed as still tentative, it is important to keep in mind the extremely important contribution to our understanding of leadership effectiveness that Fiedler's contingency theory represents. For the first time we have a theory that: (1) explicitly recognizes that leadership effectiveness is jointly determined by the fit between the leader and the nature of the situation; and (2) is willing to make some initial attempts to become specific regarding precisely what characteristics of leaders and what characteristics of the situation are the critical factors that determine this fit and hence the effectiveness of the leader.

THE VROOM AND YETTON NORMATIVE MODEL

There is wide consensus that the process of decision making constitutes a central component of any manager's job. As a result, a critical determinant of leadership effectiveness will therefore be the extent to which the leader is an effective decision maker. Vroom and Yetton (1973) have developed a theory that focuses explicitly upon the decision-making component of the leader's role. The theory, which has subsequently been tested and extended by Vroom and Jago (Jago & Vroom, 1978; Vroom & Jago, 1978), is derived from and based upon previous research on decision-making effectiveness. The theory is referred to as a *normative model* (i.e., a *prescriptive* model, or one that tells leaders how they *should* behave), since it is designed to indicate to a leader the best or most effective method of handling a decision-making situation. It is not what is referred to as a *descriptive* theory of leadership and decision making, since it is not designed to provide a theoretical explanation (or description) of how leaders actually *do* behave (whether that behavior is effective or ineffective).

Decision Effectiveness

According to Vroom and Yetton there are three critical components that influence the overall effectiveness of a decision: quality, acceptance, and time.

Decision Quality
Decision quality refers to the extent to which a decision is "good" or "effective" in meeting the objective demands and requirements of the problem situation that initially required a decision to be made. Problem situations differ in the extent to which they possess a *quality requirement*. A situation is said to possess a quality requirement if it is clear that the problem is important *and* that alternative decisions or solutions to the

problem will clearly differ from one another in the extent to which they achieve the goals of the decision maker. Typical of situations that possess a quality requirement are decisions regarding strategic planning, setting goals and priorities, determining work procedures, solving technical problems, and assigning tasks to subordinates of differing ability. Decision situations that do not possess a quality requirement are those in which the decision concerns a trivial matter (e.g., which brand of paper clips to purchase) and those in which all of the alternatives are approximately equally desirable (e.g., which subordinate to assign to a project when all subordinates are equally competent).

Decision Acceptance

Decision acceptance refers to the extent to which subordinates will understand, accept, and commit themselves to implementing a particular decision. Decision acceptance is especially critical for those decisions in which the leader is dependent upon subordinates to implement the decision. Even if a decision made by a leader is the best available alternative in regard to its objective decision quality, the decision will not be effective if it is not implemented. Hence, attention to decision acceptance is at least as important as attending to decision quality in arriving at decisions which will ultimately be effective. Research consistently indicates that the likelihood of decision acceptance increases when subordinates are allowed to participate in the decision-making process (Maier, 1963).

Timeliness

Timeliness refers to the extent to which decisions need to be made quickly or according to a fixed schedule. It is neither efficient nor ultimately effective for the organization for leaders and subordinates to invest more time than is necessary in order to arrive at acceptable decisions of high quality. This implies the desirability of choosing a decision-making style that minimizes the time required to arrive at a decision.

Alternative Decision Styles

Vroom and Yetton identify and describe five alternative decision styles that may be adopted by a leader. These five decision styles are summarized in Table 12-1. Two of the alternatives (AI and AII) involve an *autocratic* decision style, since the leader does not tell subordinates what the problem is that he or she is dealing with. In the two *consultative* styles (CI and CII) the leader consults with subordinates by sharing the problem with them and asking for their inputs. However, in both the autocratic and the consultative styles, the leader makes the final decision alone. In the fifth style (GII), the leader employs a *group consensus* approach to decision making and shares both responsibility and authority for arriving at a decision with the entire group (i.e., leader and subordinates).

TABLE 12-1
The five alternative decision styles of the Vroom-Yetton model

AI   You solve the problem or make the decision yourself using the information available to you at the present time.

AII   You obtain any necessary information from subordinates, then decide on a solution to the problem yourself. You may or may not tell subordinates the purpose of your questions or give information about the problem or decision you are working on. The input provided by them is clearly in response to your request for specific information. They do not play a role in the definition of the problem or in generating or evaluating alternative solutions.

CI   You share the problem with the relevant subordinates individually, getting their ideas and suggestions without bringing them together as a group. Then *you* make the decision. This decision may or may not reflect your subordinates' influence.

CII   You share the problem with your subordinates in a group meeting. In this meeting you obtain their ideas and suggestions. Then, *you* make the decision, which may or may not reflect your subordinates' influence.

GII   You share the problem with your subordinates as a group. Together you generate and evaluate alternatives and attempt to reach agreement (consensus) on a solution. Your role is much like that of chairman, coordinating the discussion, keeping it focused on the problem, and making sure that the critical issues are discussed. You can provide the group with information or ideas that you have but you do not try to "press" them to adopt "your" solution and are willing to accept and implement any solution that has the support of the entire group.

SOURCE: "On the validity of the Vroom-Yetton model" by V. H. Vroom, & A. G. Jago, *Journal of Applied Psychology*, 1978, *63*, 151–162. Copyright © 1978 by the American Psychological Association. Reprinted by permission of the publisher and authors.

Choosing a Decision Style

According to Vroom and Yetton, the likelihood that an effective decision will be made is heavily determined by the decision style adopted by the leader. However, unlike Fiedler, Vroom and Yetton do not see the leader as having a single characteristic mode of making decisions or dealing with subordinates. Instead, Vroom and Yetton view the leader as highly flexible and capable of adjusting his or her decision style to the demands of the *situation*. Thus, different types of problem situations require different types of decision styles, and the effective leader must be capable of diagnosing a problem situation in order to choose the appropriate decision style that is most likely to result in an effective decision.

The Vroom and Yetton normative model contains a set of seven diagnostic questions that a manager can employ in determining which decision style to adopt in any given situation. These diagnostic questions are themselves based upon a set of seven "rules," three of which are designed to protect the quality of the decision and four of which protect the acceptance of the decision. These rules are summarized in Table 12-2.

The seven diagnostic questions that a manager can apply to any given problem situation are contained in Figure 12-5, along with the decision

TABLE 12-2
Rules underlying the Vroom and Yetton model

RULES TO PROTECT THE QUALITY OF THE DECISION

1. *The leader information rule*
   If the quality of the decision is important and the leader does not possess enough information or expertise to solve the problem by himself, then AI is eliminated from the feasible set.

2. *The goal congruence rule*
   If the quality of the decision is important and subordinates are not likely to pursue the organization goals in their efforts to solve this problem, then GII is eliminated from the feasible set.

3. *The unstructured problem rule*
   In decisions in which the quality of the decision is important, if the leader lacks the necessary information or expertise to solve the problem by himself, and if the problem is unstructured, the method of solving the problem should provide for interaction among subordinates likely to possess relevant information. Accordingly, AI, AII, and CI are eliminated from the feasible set.

RULES TO PROTECT THE ACCEPTANCE OF THE DECISION

4. *The acceptance rule*
   If the acceptance of the decision by subordinates is critical to effective implementation and if it is not certain that an autocratic decision will be accepted, AI and AII are eliminated from the feasible set.

5. *The conflict rule*
   If the acceptance of the decision is critical, an autocratic decision is not certain to be accepted and disagreement among subordinates in methods of attaining the organizational goal is likely, the methods used in solving the problem should enable those in disagreement to resolve their differences with full knowledge of the problem. Accordingly, under these conditions, AI, AII, and CI, which permit no interaction among subordinates and therefore provide no opportunity for those in conflict to resolve their differences, are eliminated from the feasible set. Their use runs the risk of leaving some of the subordinates with less than the needed commitment to the final decision.

6. *The fairness rule*
   If the quality of the decision is unimportant but acceptance of the decision is critical and not certain to result from an autocratic decision, it is important that the decision process used generate the needed acceptance. The decision process used should permit the subordinates to interact with one another and negotiate over the fair method of resolving any differences with full responsibility on them for determining what is fair and equitable. Accordingly, under these circumstances, AI, AII, CI, and CII are eliminated from the feasible set.

7. *The acceptance priority rule*
   If acceptance is critical, not certain to result from an autocratic decision, and if subordinates are motivated to pursue the organizational goals represented in the problem, then methods that provide equal partnership in the decision-making process can provide greater acceptance without risking decision quality. Accordingly, AI, AII, CI, and CII are eliminated from the feasible set.

Source: "On the validity of the Vroom-Yetton Model" by V. H. Vroom & A. G. Jago, *Journal of Applied Psychology*, 1978, *63*, 151–162. Copyright © 1978 by the American Psychological Association. Reprinted by permission of the publisher and authors.

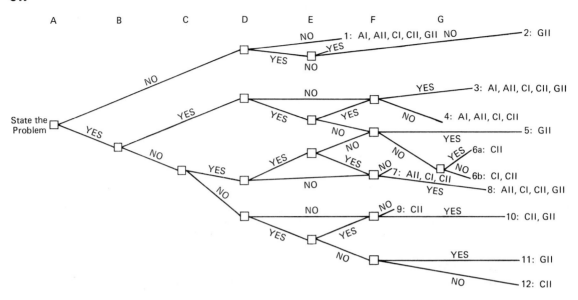

A. Does the problem possess a quality requirement?
B. Do I have sufficient information to make a high-quality decision?
C. Is the problem structured?
D. Is acceptance of the decision by subordinates important for effective implementation?
E. If I were to make the decision by myself, am I reasonably certain that it would be accepted by my subordinates?
F. Do subordinates share the organizational goals to be attained in solving this problem?
G. Is conflict among subordinates likely in preferred solutions?

FIGURE 12-5
Vroom and Yetton Decision Process Flowchart. (SOURCE: Reprinted by permission of the publisher from "Can Leaders Learn to Lead?", V. H. Vroom, *Organizational Dynamics*, Winter 1976, © 1976, by AMACOM, a division of American Management Associations, p. 19. All rights reserved.

tree developed by Vroom and Yetton that guides the manager to a "feasible set" of decision-making styles. The feasible set of decision styles for a problem situation consists of all those decision styles that do not violate any of the rules designed to protect decision quality and decision acceptance. When the feasible set contains more than one alternative, the leader must choose one style on the basis of some additional criterion. For example, the leader may choose the least time-consuming decision style. The time required to implement each decision style increases from AI (the least time-consuming) through to GII (the most time-consuming). On the other hand, a leader interested in developing his or her subordinates' decision-making skills might choose always to employ the most participative feasible decision style.

In using the Vroom and Yetton decision-tree flowchart managers begin by asking themselves the first of the seven diagnostic questions (labeled question A). They then follow the lines on the flowchart according to their answers ("yes" or "no") to each of the diagnostic questions. Each time a square is encountered on the chart the managers refer to the question corresponding to the letter above the square and continue on based upon their answers until an endpoint is reached that specifies the feasible set of alternative decision styles for the problem situation. Figure 12-6 contains an example of how the decision flowchart would be applied to a managerial problem.

Status of the Model

The Vroom and Yetton model constitutes an important contribution to leadership research and practice, since it provides a basis for a leader to choose a decision style *contingent* upon the demands of the situation.

FIGURE 12-6
An example of the application of the Vroom-Yetton model to a managerial problem requiring a decision. (SOURCE:Victor H. Vroom, "A New Look at Managerial Decision Making," *Organizational Dynamics*, Spring 1973. New York: AMACOM, a division of American Management Associations, 1973, p. 72.

> . . .You are manufacturing manager in a large electronics plant. The company's management has always been searching for ways of increasing efficiency. They have recently installed new machines and put in a new simplified work system, but to the surprise of everyone, including yourself, the expected increase in productivity was not realized. In fact, production has begun to drop, quality has fallen off, and the number of employee separations has risen.
>
> You do not believe that there is anything wrong with the machines. You have had reports from other companies who are using them and they confirm this opinion. You have also had representatives from the firm that built the machines go over them and they report that they are operating at peak efficiency.
>
> You suspect that some parts of the new work system may be responsible for the change, but this view is not widely shared among your immediate subordinates, who are four first-line supervisors, each in charge of a section, and your supply manager. The drop in production has been variously attributed to poor training of the operators, lack of an adequate system of financial incentives, and poor morale. Clearly, this is an issue about which there is considerable depth of feeling within individuals and potential disagreement between your subordinates.
>
> This morning you received a phone call from your division manager. He had just received your production figures for the last six months and was calling to express his concern. He indicated that the problem was yours to solve in any way that you think best, but that he would like to know within a week what steps you plan to take.
>
> You share your division manager's concern with the falling productivity and know that your men are also concerned. The problem is to decide what steps to take to rectify the situation.
>
> On the basis of the Vroom and Yetton model, the decision tree contained in Figure 12-5 can be used to analyze this problem situation and choose a decision style as follows:
>
> | | | |
> |---|---|---|
> | Question A | (Quality requirement?) | : Yes |
> | Question B | (Do I have sufficient information?) | : No |
> | Question C | (Problem structured?) | : No |
> | Question D | (Acceptance important for implementation?) | : Yes |
> | Question E | (Would subordinates accept my decision?) | : No |
> | Question F | (Do subordinates share organization goals?) | : Yes |
>
> Feasible set of decision styles: GII

Research that has been conducted on the validity of the model has generally been supportive (Jago & Vroom, 1980). For example, Vroom and Jago (1978) had managers describe a past decision that they had made that was successful and another previous decision that was unsuccessful. From these descriptions it was possible to determine the nature of the problem situation that had preceded the decision, as well as the decision style that the manager had employed. For those cases in which the decision style actually employed by the manager was in agreement with the feasible set prescribed by the model, 68 percent of the decisions were judged to be successful. On the other hand, only 22 percent of the cases in which the manager's decision style disagreed with the model had a successful outcome.

Overall, the Vroom and Yetton model is a promising development. It provides a model of leadership and decision making that is based upon sound theory and research and that also has the advantage of being presented in a form that permits relatively easy and direct application by the practicing manager.

PATH-GOAL THEORY

The path-goal theory of leadership is based upon research by Evans (1970, 1974) and by House and his colleagues (House, 1971; House & Dessler, 1974; House & Mitchell, 1974). The basic idea behind the theory is that a leader can influence the satisfaction, motivation, and performance of subordinates primarily by: (1) providing subordinates with *rewards*; (2) making the attainment of these rewards contingent upon the accomplishment of performance *goals*; and (3) helping subordinates obtain rewards by clarifying the *paths* to the goals (i.e., helping subordinates understand exactly what they must do to obtain rewards) and making these paths easier to travel (i.e., providing subordinates with coaching, direction, and assistance when needed). The theory argues that in order to accomplish the foregoing, a leader will have to engage in different types of leadership behavior depending upon the nature and demands of the particular situation.

Styles of Leader Behavior

Path-goal theory identifies four distinct styles of leader behavior.

1. ***Directive leadership*** is characterized by a leader who lets subordinates know what is expected of them, gives specific guidance regarding what is to be done and how it should be done, and ensures that his or her role as leader of the group is clearly understood. Such a leader also schedules work to be done, maintains definite standards of perform-

ance, and encourages group members to follow standard rules and regulations.

2. **Supportive leadership** refers to a leadership style characterized by a friendly and approachable leader who shows concern for the needs, status, and general well-being of subordinates. A supportive leader treats subordinates as equals and frequently does little things to make the work more pleasant and enjoyable.

3. **Participative leadership** is characterized by a leader who, when faced with a decision, consults with subordinates, solicits their suggestions, and takes ideas seriously in arriving at a decision.

4. **Achievement-oriented leadership** refers to a style of leadership that constantly emphasizes excellence in performance and simultaneously displays confidence that subordinates can and will achieve the high standards that are set. Such a leader sets challenging performance goals and encourages subordinates to take personal responsibility for the accomplishment of these goals.

Path-goal theory assumes that any given leader can, at different times and under different circumstances, engage in any one of these alternative styles of leadership. Like the Vroom-Yetton normative model, but unlike Fiedler's contingency theory, path-goal theory views leadership behavior as relatively flexible and adaptable.

Contingency Factors

Path-goal theory argues that no single style of leader behavior will universally result in high levels of subordinate motivation and satisfaction. Instead, the theory suggests that different types of *situations* require different styles of leader behavior. In order to provide some guidance regarding which style is likely to be appropriate in any particular situation, path-goal theory identifies two classes of situational variables. The two contingency variables are: (1) the *personal characteristics of subordinates*; and (2) the *environmental pressures and demands* facing subordinates in the accomplishment of their tasks.

Personal Characteristics

A number of personal characteristics of subordinates have been identified that are hypothesized to influence the extent to which subordinates will experience a leader's behavior as *acceptable* and *satisfying*.

1. **Ability.** When subordinates perceive their ability to be low or inadequate, they are likely to find directive leadership acceptable and to see it as helping them to perform more effectively in the future. However, when subordinates perceive their ability to be high, directive leader-

ship is likely to be perceived as unacceptable and is unlikely to have any positive effects upon satisfaction or motivation.

2. ***Locus of control.*** Locus of control refers to the extent to which people view what happens to them either as under their own direct control and influence (referred to as an *internal* locus of control), or as determined by circumstances and events outside themselves and beyond their own control (referred to as an *external* locus of control). Research indicates that internals find a participative leadership style to be both acceptable and satisfying, while externals tend to respond more positively to directive leadership (Runyon, 1973; Mitchell, Smyser, & Weed, 1975).

3. ***Needs and Motives.*** The particular needs, motives, and personality characteristics of subordinates may influence their acceptance of and satisfaction with different leadership styles. For example, subordinates with a strong need for achievement may react positively to achievement-oriented leadership, while those with a strong need for affiliation might respond more positively to a supportive or participative leadership style.

Characteristics of the Work Environment

Certain characteristics of the work environment influence the extent to which the various leadership styles will have a positive impact upon subordinate *motivation* and *performance*. The theory identifies three broad classifications of contingency factors in the environment:

1. Subordinates' tasks
2. The formal authority system of the organization
3. The primary work group

The theory suggests that an effective leadership style (in terms of motivating subordinates) is one that complements the subordinates' environment by providing direction, assistance, and support that would otherwise be missing. Thus, if subordinates are working on a highly ambiguous task in an organization with few set policies and procedures, the theory predicts that a directive leadership style will increase motivation and performance by helping subordinates understand *what* they need to do in order to perform effectively. On the other hand, the theory predicts that if subordinates are working on a highly routine and structured task in an organization with elaborate rules and regulations, directive leadership will not facilitate performance but will simply create frustration and resentment among subordinates. Thus, according to path-goal theory, the leader must analyze the nature of the situation being faced by subordinates and then choose a leadership style that, in light of this situational analysis, provides the direction and support to subordinates that would otherwise be missing.

The basic ideas of path-goal theory that leader behavior and contingency factors combine to cause subordinate attitudes and behavior are summarized in Table 12-3.

Research on Path-Goal Theory

Path-goal theory has sparked a considerable amount of interest among researchers (Filley, House, & Kerr, 1976; House & Mitchell, 1974; Schriesheim & Von Glinow, 1977; Yukl, 1981). The strongest pattern of support for the theory tends to occur for predictions regarding the effectiveness of directive and supportive leadership styles. Numerous studies have found that directive leadership will increase motivation and satisfaction for subordinates working on an ambiguous task, but leads to lower motivation and satisfaction when the task is clear-cut (House, 1971; House & Dessler, 1974; Schriesheim & DeNisi, 1981; Szilagyi & Sims, 1974). Considerable evidence also indicates that supportive leader behavior has its most positive effect on satisfaction for subordinates working on stressful, frustrating, or dissatisfying tasks (House, 1971; House & Dessler, 1974; Downey, Sheridan, & Slocum, 1975).

Path-goal theory provides a powerful framework for thinking about leadership in organizations. This framework is useful both to the manager and to the researcher. For the manager, the theory helps draw attention not only to the existence of alternative leadership styles, but also to a variety of characteristics of subordinates and leadership situations that will influence the effectiveness of any given style of leadership. For the researcher, the theory provides a rich framework to help guide future research and theorizing. The complexity of the theory undoubtedly reflects the complexity of the underlying phenomena that it seeks to model. The theory also has the advantage of being stated in such a way as to

TABLE 12-3
Summary of path-goal relationships

Leader behavior	and	Contingency factors	cause	Subordinate attitudes and behavior
Directive		Subordinate characteristics:		Job satisfaction:
Supportive		Ability		Job rewards
Achievement-oriented		Locus of control		Acceptance of leader:
Participative		Needs and motives		Leader rewards
		Environmental factors:		Motivational behavior:
		The task		Effort–performance
		Formal authority system		Performance–rewards
		Primary work group		

SOURCE: Adapted from "Path-goal theory of leadership" by R. J. House & T. R. Mitchell, *Journal of Contemporary Business*, 1974, 3. Used by permission.

facilitate its future development and expansion (House & Baetz, 1979). Overall then, path-goal theory holds significant promise both for helping develop our understanding of leadership and for helping managers select and apply effective leadership styles.

MANAGERIAL IMPLICATIONS

In this chapter and the preceding one we have reviewed and discussed a wide variety of approaches and theories regarding leadership in organizations. While our discussion has made it clear that there is no single theory of leadership that we can endorse as the "correct" or "valid" theory, an overall look at what we know about leadership does permit us to develop some relatively clear implications for managers regarding leadership in organizations.

1. ***Managers should adopt a contingency approach to leadership.*** In our discussion of the various contingency theories of leadership, we presented the strengths and weaknesses of each contingency model and concluded that no single theory could be clearly endorsed as "true" or "valid." At the same time, however, the combination of theoretical arguments, empirical results, and plain common sense leads to the clear conclusion that the nature of effective leadership is not universal but is in fact *contingent* upon the nature of the leadership situation. It is clear that factors such as the nature of subordinates (e.g., their skills, background, training, orientation, and values), the nature of the task (e.g., whether it is routine and unambiguous, or ill-defined and challenging), the nature of the work group (e.g., whether it is highly cohesive or fragmented), the nature of the organization (e.g., the extent to which it is rigid, formalized, and inflexible versus adaptive, informal, and flexible), the nature of the leader (e.g., the extent to which the leader is highly skilled and experienced), and so on, will all have an impact upon what is required of a leader in order to operate successfully.

   While no single theory adequately captures and explains the interdependent influence of all of these situational and personal factors, there is a clear implication for managers that these factors must be carefully attended to in either selecting a leader for a particular position or in personally choosing a leadership style. Effective leadership requires a match or fit between the demands of the situation and the capabilities of the leader. Managers must attend as carefully and systematically as possible to the nature of those situational demands.

2. ***Managers need to recognize that the effects of leadership are limited.*** It has not been uncommon in recent years for leadership researchers to express disappointment at the weakness of their findings. Instead of being disappointing, such findings should serve as a reminder that the behavior of the leader is but one of many factors influencing the feelings, motivation, and

performance of organization members. In addition to leadership, many other factors influence individuals in organizations, factors such as the characteristics of the individuals themselves (e.g., their needs, motives, and skills), the nature of their jobs, the nature of their peers and their work group, and the nature of the organization's policies, rules, and procedures.

The importance of such additional factors has been emphasized by Kerr and Jermier (1978), who refer to such factors as "substitutes for leadership." Kerr and Jermier have outlined a variety of subordinate, task, and organization characteristics that can either "substitute" for the effects of a leader or "neutralize" the impact of a leader. Table 12-4 summarizes a variety of substitutes and neutralizers for supportive and directive leadership styles. The important implication for the manager is that the manager or leader is only one of many factors influencing subordinates, and a change in leadership style or behavior cannot be expected to yield clear, unequivocal, and immediate changes in subordinate feelings and performance.

3. ***Managers need to take advantage of the fact that the effects of leadership can be expanded***. Our previous point drew attention to the fact that the impact of leadership is limited, since the behavior of the leader is but one of many factors influencing subordinates. At the same time, however, this awareness of the existence of additional factors and substitutes for leadership

TABLE 12-4
Substitutes and neutralizers of supportive and instrumental leadership

	Relationship-oriented supportive leadership	Task-oriented instrumental leadership
1. Subordinate characteristics		
a. Ability		Substitute
b. "Professional" orientation	Substitute	Substitute
c. Indifference toward organizational rewards	Neutralizer	Neutralizer
2. Task characteristics		
a. Unambiguous and routine		Substitute
b. Provides direct feedback concerning accomplishment		Substitute
c. Intrinsically satisfying	Substitute	
3. Organization characteristics		
a. Closely knit, cohesive work groups	Substitute	Substitute
b. Leader lacks control over organizational rewards	Neutralizer	Neutralizer

SOURCE: "Substitutes for Leadership: Their Meaning and Measurement" by S. Kerr & J. M. Jermier, *Organizational Behavior and Human Performance*, 1978, 22, 375–403.

can help leaders recognize alternative avenues and approaches to influence their subordinates. Leaders who assume that their ability to influence subordinates is limited only to face-to-face interactions with them are doomed to have relatively little influence and impact.

In addition to interacting directly with subordinates, the leader is generally in a position to influence many of the additional factors (labeled substitutes or neutralizers by Kerr and Jermier) that have a significant impact upon subordinates. For example, a leader may influence subordinates in a variety of ways: by offering coaching and direction to increase levels of ability; by influencing task characteristics through job redesign to increase the jobs' motivating potential; by attempting to change the degree of organizational formalization and flexibility by lobbying with more senior managers for changes in policies and procedures affecting subordinates; and so forth. The clear implication is that managers do not influence their subordinates' satisfaction, motivation, and performance solely on the basis of direct face-to-face interactions. To be effective, leaders must recognize and influence the many areas of leverage that are at their disposal that have an impact upon the total work experience of subordinates.

SUMMARY

Contingency theories of leadership seek to understand the different types of leadership behavior that are demanded by different situations that arise in organizations. Fiedler has developed a method of classifying leaders (on the basis of their LPC score) and management situations (on the basis of three situational dimensions), and has put forward a complex model regarding the determinants of a good fit between leader characteristics and situational demands. Vroom and Yetton have developed a systematic technique for helping managers to analyze problem situations and choose the method or style of decision making that should maximize the overall effectiveness of the decision-making process. House, with his path-goal theory, has developed an approach that can help managers understand how characteristics of subordinates and characteristics of the environment (such as the subordinates' task and their work group) influence the appropriateness and effectiveness of alternative styles of leadership.

While none of these contingency theories has obtained a sufficient degree of support to justify its being adopted as *the* valid explanation of leadership effectiveness, all three have obtained some support and provide some insight into the complexities of leadership effectiveness. They therefore offer helpful insights to the practicing manager. At the same time, the manager needs to recognize that leadership behavior is but one factor influencing subordinates. A variety of substitutes for leadership and neutralizers of leadership have been identified. To be most effective as a leader, a manager must not only choose a leadership style that fits the demands of the situation, but also take advantage of opportunities to influence and alter the multitude of additional organizational factors that have an impact upon the satisfaction and performance of subordinates.

REVIEW QUESTIONS

1. What makes a theory of leadership a *contingency* theory?
2. Describe Fiedler's contingency theory and discuss what you feel are its primary strengths and weaknesses.
3. What are the components of an effective decision that are taken into account by the Vroom and Yetton normative model?
4. Describe some of the alternative decision styles outlined in the Vroom and Yetton model. How should a manager go about choosing which style to employ?
5. What are the strategic functions of a leader according to path-goal theory?
6. Discuss the predictions of path-goal theory regarding the impact of subordinate characteristics and the nature of the work environment on the effectiveness of alternative styles of leadership.
7. Do you believe leadership makes much of a difference in the satisfaction, motivation, and performance of organization members? What other factors need to be taken into account?
8. Do you feel that a manager's leadership style is relatively fixed and unchangeable or flexible and adaptible? What are the implications of your position for organizations seeking to improve leadership effectiveness?
9. What personal traits or characteristics of leaders do you feel have the greatest impact upon their capacity to adopt alternative leadership styles?
10. Discuss some of the ways in which leaders can broaden their influence upon subordinates beyond their face-to-face interactions. Which techniques or approaches do you feel have the greatest potential to influence subordinates' work effectiveness?
11. Discuss the advantages and disadvantages of adopting a contingency approach to understanding leadership effectiveness.
12. Does leadership make any difference to the effectiveness of organizations? Defend your position.

REFERENCES

Ashour, A. S. The contingency model of leadership effectiveness: An evaluation. *Organizational Behavior and Human Performance*, 1973, 9, 339–355.
Chemers, M. M., & Skrzypek, G. J. An experimental test of the contingency model

of leadership effectiveness. *Journal of Personality and Social Psychology*, 1972, *24*, 172–177.

Downey, H. K., Sheridan, J. E., & Slocum, J. W., Jr. Analysis of relationships among leader behavior, subordinate job performance, and satisfaction: A path-goal approach. *Academy of Management Journal*, 1975, *18*, 253–262.

Evans, M. G. The effects of supervisory behavior on the path-goal relationship. *Organizational Behavior and Human Performance*, 1970, *5*, 277–298.

Evans, M. G. Extensions of a path-goal theory of motivation. *Journal of Applied Psychology*, 1974, *59*, 172–178.

Fiedler, F. E. A contingency model of leadership effectiveness. In L. Berkowitz (Ed.), *Advances in experimental social psychology*. New York: Academic Press, 1964.

Fiedler, F. E. *A theory of leadership effectiveness*. New York: McGraw-Hill, 1967.

Fiedler, F. E. Validation and extension of the contingency model of leadership effectiveness: A review of empirical findings. *Psychological Bulletin*, 1971, *76*, 128–148.

Fiedler, F. E. Personality, motivational systems, and the behavior of high and low LPC persons. *Human Relations*, 1972, *25*, 391–412.

Fiedler, F. E. The contingency model: A reply to Ashour. *Organizational Behavior and Human Performance*, 1973, *9*, 356–368.

Fiedler, F. E. A rejoinder to Schriesheim and Kerr's premature obituary of the contingency model. In J. G. Hunt & L. L. Larson (Eds.), *Leadership: The cutting edge*. Carbondale, Ill.: Southern Illinois University Press, 1977.

Fiedler, F. E. The contingency model and the dynamics of leadership. In L. Berkowitz (Ed.), *Advances in experimental social psychology*. New York: Academic Press, 1978.

Filley, A. C., House, R. J., & Kerr, S. *Managerial process and organizational behavior*. Glenview, Ill.: Scott, Foresman, 1976.

Graen, G., Alvares, K. M., Orris, J. B., & Martella, J. A. Contingency model of leadership effectiveness: Antecedent and evidential results. *Psychological Bulletin*, 1970, *74*, 285–296.

House, R. J. A path goal theory of leader effectiveness. *Administrative Science Quarterly*, 1971, *16*, 321–339.

House, R. J., & Baetz, M. L. Leadership: Some generalizations and new research directions. In B. M. Staw (Ed.), *Research in organizational behavior*. Greenwich, Conn.: JAI Press, 1979.

House, R. J., & Dessler, G. The path goal theory of leadership: Some *post hoc* and *a priori* tests. In J. G. Hunt & L. L. Larson (Eds.), *Contingency approaches to leadership*. Carbondale, Ill.: Southern Illinois University Press, 1974.

House, R. J., & Mitchell, T. R. Path-goal theory of leadership. *Journal of Contemporary Business*. Autumn 1974, *3*, 81–98.

Jago, A. G., & Vroom, V. H. Predicting leader behavior from a measure of behavioral intent. *Academy of Management Journal*, 1978, *21*, 715–721.

Jago, A. G., & Vroom, V. H. An evaluation of two alternatives to the Vroom-Yetton normative model. *Academy of Management Review*, 1980, *23*, 347–355.

Kerr, S., & Jermier, J. M. Substitutes for leadership: Their meaning and measurement. *Organizational Behavior and Human Performance*, 1978, *22*, 375–403.

Maier, N. R. F. *Problem solving discussions and conferences: Leadership methods and skills*. New York: McGraw-Hill, 1963.

Mitchell, T. R., Smyser, C. M., & Weed, S. E. Locus of control: Supervision and work satisfaction. *Academy of Management Journal*, 1975, *18*, 623–631.

Rice, R. W. Construct validity of the least preferred coworker score. *Psychological Bulletin*, 1978, *85*, 1199–1237.

Rice, R. W. Leader LPC and follower satisfaction: A review. *Organizational Behavior and Human Performance*, 1981, *28*, 1–25.

Runyon, K. E. Some interactions between personality variables and management styles. *Journal of Applied Psychology*, 1973, *57*, 288–294.

Schriesheim, C. A., & DeNisi, A. S. Task dimensions as moderators of the effects of instrumental leadership: A two-sample replicated test of path-goal leadership theory. *Journal of Applied Psychology*, 1981, *66*, 589–597.

Schriesheim, C. A., & Kerr, S. Theories and measures of leadership: A critical appraisal. In J. G. Hunt & L. L. Larson (Eds.), *Leadership: The cutting edge*. Carbondale, Ill.: Southern Illinois University Press, 1977.

Schriesheim, C. A., & Von Glinow, M. A. The path-goal theory of leadership: A theoretical and empirical analysis. *Academy of Management Journal*, 1977, *20*, 398–405.

Shiflett, S. C. The contingency model of leadership effectiveness: Some implications of its statistical and methodological properties. *Behavioral Science*, 1973, *18*(6), 429–440.

Strube, M. J., & Garcia, J. E. A meta-analytic investigation of Fiedler's contingency model of leadership effectiveness. *Psychological Bulletin*, 1981, *90*, 307–321.

Szilagyi, A. D., & Sims, H. P. An exploration of the path-goal theory of leadership in a health care environment. *Academy of Management Journal*, 1974, *17*, 622–634.

Vecchio, R. P. An empirical examination of the validity of Fiedler's model of leadership effectiveness. *Organizational Behavior and Human Performance*, 1977, *19*, 180–206.

Vroom, V. H., & Jago, A. G. On the validity of the Vroom-Yetton model. *Journal of Applied Psychology*, 1978, *63*, 151–162.

Vroom, V. H., & Yetton, P. W. *Leadership and decision-making*. Pittsburgh, Pa.: University of Pittsburgh Press, 1973.

Yukl, G. A. *Leadership in organizations*. Englewood Cliffs, N. J.: Prentice-Hall, 1981.

PART SIX

MANAGERIAL PROCESSES

CHAPTER 13

MANAGERIAL DECISION

MAKING

Regardless of their level in the organizational hierarchy, managers are constantly called upon to make decisions regarding a tremendous variety of matters, from the first-line supervisor making a decision regarding how to discipline a problem employee, to the chief executive officer making strategic organizational decisions regarding new policies, products, or procedures (Mintzberg, 1973, 1975; Stewart, 1967). In all of these situations the manager must somehow sort out what alternatives are available, try to assess the likely consequences of the various alternatives, and then make a decision regarding which alternative course of action will be pursued. In this chapter we will take a close look at this process of decision making in organizations. Our goal will be to understand exactly what's involved in organizational decision making and what can be done to improve the quality of decisions that a manager makes.

We'll begin by drawing some distinctions between different types of decisions faced by managers; more specifically, we'll differentiate programmed from nonprogrammed decisions, and personal from organizational decisions. With these distinctions in mind we'll turn to a discussion of *classical* decision theory, followed by a look at what is referred to as *behavioral* decision theory. We'll then examine more closely a couple of detailed approaches to the decision-making process, one which views decision making as a process of *muddling through* (Lindblom, 1959) and another which is known as a *conflict* theory of decision making (Janis & Mann, 1977). The chapter concludes with a discussion of the implications for managers of the various theories and approaches to decision making.

TYPES OF DECISIONS

It is possible to classify decisions on a variety of different dimensions. For our purposes it will be helpful to draw two distinctions, one between personal and organizational decisions and the other between programmed and nonprogrammed decisions.

Personal versus Organizational Decisions

Personal Decisions
Personal decisions refer to those decisions that we make as individuals that affect ourselves and our personal lives. Many of these are relatively minor decisions and of little relevance to our work lives in organizations (e.g., which movie we decide to see on Saturday night). However, some personal decisions are extremely important and highly relevant to our roles and activities in organizations. This is particularly the case for personal decisions regarding careers and regarding our membership and participation in organizations. Individuals make decisions regarding which career or occupation they will pursue, which organizations they will join, which job they will accept, and even whether they will come to work on a given day rather than stay at home. Each of these personal decisions has an impact upon both the personal life of the individual involved and the organization of which the individual is a member.

Organizational Decisions
Organizational decisions, on the other hand, refer to decisions regarding issues, problems, policies, or practices of the organization itself. Organizational decisions can vary from the trivial (e.g., which brand of paper clips to order), to the highly consequential (e.g., whether to open a new plant or launch a new product line). It should be pointed out that the distinction between organizational and personal decisions is *not* drawn in terms of *who* makes the decision, since only people are capable of making decisions. Rather, the distinction is drawn in terms of *what* the object of the decision is. Personal decisions are made by people regarding their future personal plans and activities; organizational decisions are made by people regarding the future policies and operation of the organization of which they are members.

Programmed versus Nonprogrammed Decisions

Simon (1960) has proposed a distinction between decisions that are relatively routine and frequent and those that are complicated and occur only rarely. This distinction has been widely adopted in discussions of decision making. The two types of decisions are referred to as *programmed* and *nonprogrammed* and are illustrated in Table 13-1.

Programmed Decisions

Programmed decisions take place in response to routine and repetitive situations that tend to recur frequently. By their very nature, these types of routine and repetitive situations permit the development of standardized methods or procedures for making decisions.

Personal programmed decisions are handled by the development of habits. For example, every working day each individual must make a personal decision regarding how to get to work. Instead of devoting considerable time and attention every morning to choosing among the various alternatives (e.g., subway, bus, car, motorcycle, bicycle, walking, hitchhiking), most people have arrived at a single standard solution to the problem (e.g., take the bus) or have developed a relatively simple programmed basis for making a decision (e.g., walk if the weather is pleasant, take the bus if it is unpleasant).

Organizational programmed decisions are usually handled by the development of rules, standard operating procedures, and organizational structure. For example, most organizations have standardized rules and procedures for making decisions regarding things such as when to reorder supplies, what departures from specific production standards are permissible, when and under what circumstances employees will be paid an overtime bonus, and so on.

Developing standardized procedures for dealing with programmed decision situations has a number of advantages. First, it can be economical

TABLE 13-1
Types of decisions

	Personal	Organizational
Programmed	Regular routines	Regular reorders of supplies
	When and where to shop for groceries	Standard operating procedures
	Getting to work	Conditions and rates for overtime
Nonprogrammed	Marital choice	New products
	Career choice	Major capital investment
	Job choice	Major reorganization

by simplifying and speeding up the decision-making process. Second, handling programmed decisions in a standardized fashion reduces uncertainty and frees time and attention for more critical activities. Finally, by introducing consistency and predictability into programmed decision situations, organizational coordination and control are enhanced.

Nonprogrammed Decisions

Nonprogrammed decisions occur in response to novel, complex, and important problem situations. Such problems require special attention and treatment from decision makers because they are usually vague, ambiguous, and unstructured. There are generally no established policies or procedures for dealing with nonprogrammed decisions, and such decisions hence require a high degree of insight, judgment, and creativity on the part of those making the decisions. The capacity to cope with nonprogrammed decision situations effectively is an important component of managerial success.

Personal nonprogrammed decisions arise with regard to significant nonrecurring issues that each of us faces in our personal lives at various times. Choosing a spouse, choosing a career, and choosing a job are all examples of important personal nonprogrammed decisions. The outcomes of these decisions may have either an indirect effect upon an individual's role and activities in the organization (as in the case of the spillover effects of marital harmony or conflict), or a very direct effect (as when an individual decides to quit his or her job to accept a position with a competing organization).

Organizational nonprogrammed decisions arise most frequently with regard to long-range strategic planning issues. Decisions regarding the launching of a new product, major capital investments, and significant redesign of organizational structure are all examples of organizational nonprogrammed decisions. Such decisions are obviously critically important to the long-term effectiveness, success, and continued existence of the organization. In light of their critical nature, a good deal of research has been aimed at furthering our understanding of nonprogrammed decision making and at developing improved techniques for managing these complex, ambiguous, and difficult decision situations. In the remainder of the chapter we will be reviewing major theories and approaches that have been developed to further our understanding of how individuals and organizations can cope most effectively with these organizational nonprogrammed decision situations.

CLASSICAL DECISION THEORY

Classical decision theory assumes that decision making is (or should be) a rational process whereby decision makers seek out and choose the best available alternative course of action which is most likely to maximize the achievement of their goals and objectives. According to classical theory, the decision-making process can be broken down into a series of sequential steps. These steps are summarized in Figure 13-1.

Steps in the Decision-Making Process

Perceive a Problem or Opportunity

Something has to happen in order to get the decision-making process started. The initiating event can take either of two forms. One possibility is that a decision maker perceives the existence of a problem, something that is impairing the effectiveness of the organization that is felt to require action. A second possible trigger to the decision-making process is the

FIGURE 13-1
Model of the decision-making process.

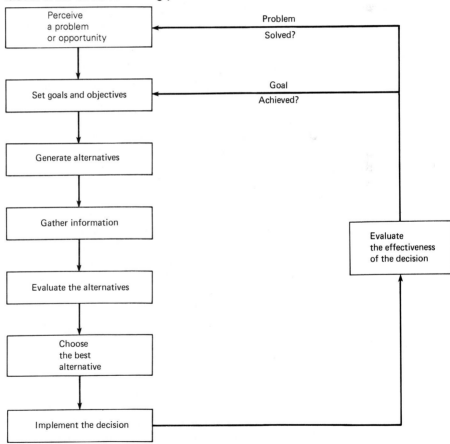

perception of a unique opportunity that may have presented itself and that should be taken advantage of. It needs to be noted that it is the *perception* of problems and opportunities, not their actual *existence*, that gets the decision-making process started. Problems and opportunities may exist all around us, but if they are not perceived and noticed, they do not instigate the decision-making process.

Set Goals and Objectives

Once a problem or opportunity has been identified, the decision maker must clearly identify the goals and objectives that a good decision should achieve. To take a personal decision-making example, if the problem experienced by the individual is a lack of satisfaction and fulfillment with his or her current job, the individual's goals for the decision-making process might be to identify, obtain, and accept a new job that is most likely to maximize his or her future satisfaction, development, and feelings of accomplishment. An organizational example might involve a problem of reduced productivity and increased turnover in a particular department. In this situation the decision maker's goals might be to identify and implement changes in the work system that are maximally likely to result in increased productivity and reduced employee turnover.

Generate Alternatives

Once goals and objectives have been set, the decision maker then generates alternative courses of action that might result in goal attainment. This is the stage in the decision-making process that requires the greatest component of creativity and imagination. Ideally, the decision maker should seek to generate as many alternatives as possible and should try to ensure that the set of alternatives is relatively diverse (i.e., all of the alternatives should not be highly similar to one another).

Gather Information

The alternatives that have been generated must be systematically evaluated. However, before evaluation can proceed, information must be collected regarding each of the alternatives and their likely consequences. More specifically, the decision maker must seek to learn as much as possible regarding: (1) the likelihood that each alternative course of action will result in the attainment of various outcomes; and (2) the extent to which those outcomes will contribute to the achievement of the goals and objectives being sought.

Evaluate the Alternatives

Once all available information has been collected regarding all of the alternatives under consideration, the decision maker must use that information to evaluate the alternatives in a systematic fashion. This requires the decision maker to develop and employ some technique that permits all of the information collected regarding each of the alternatives under consideration to be used to analyze and compare the relative advantages of each alternative. The outcome of this evaluation process should then be a rank ordering of the alternatives from best to worst according to their likelihood of leading to the attainment of the goals and objectives of the decision maker.

Choose the Best Alternative

This step should be quite straightforward if the evaluation of alternatives has been conducted comprehensively and systematically. The decision maker simply chooses the alternative that the evaluation process has indicated to be most desirable. Problems may arise at this stage, however, if the evaluation process leads to the conclusion that two or more alternatives appear equally likely to be "best."

Implement the Decision

Although, strictly speaking, the decision-making process has ended once a decision has been reached regarding the best alternative to choose, it is also true that the decision-making process is no more than a mental exercise if the chosen alternative course of action is not implemented. Further, issues of implementation (e.g., the ease and feasibility of putting a solution into practice) are frequently important factors that influence the choice of an alternative in the previous stages.

Evaluate Decision Effectiveness

The decision-making cycle should not end until the decision maker evaluates the extent to which the chosen alternative has succeeded in solving the initial problem and achieving the goals identified at the outset of the process. If such evaluation indicates success, then the decision-making cycle is concluded. However, if the chosen alternative has not solved the problem or achieved stated objectives, then the decision maker must recycle through the decision-making process to generate a new alternative course of action to be attempted.

Figure 13-2 provides an example of these steps in the decision-making process. The figure helps draw attention to the fact that there are two major phases in this process. The first several steps in the process require the active *generation* of ideas, alternatives, and information. The latter steps in the process, on the other hand, require the systematic *analysis* of the information and alternatives generated in the earlier steps. In this latter phase, the complex set of information generated in the first phase must be distilled down to a single choice regarding which course of action will be pursued.

Assumptions of Classical Theory

What distinguish the classical theory of decision making are certain assumptions that are made regarding what happens at various stages in

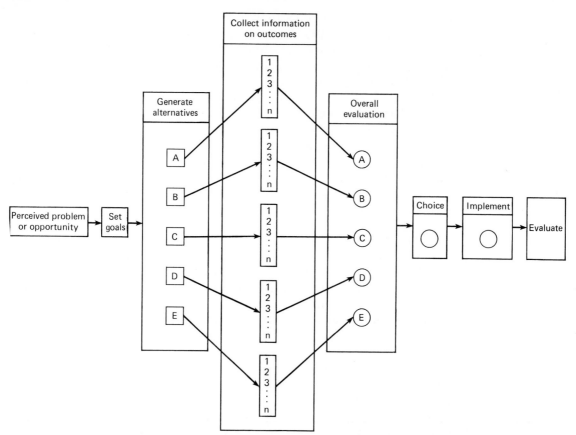

FIGURE 13-2
An example of steps in the decision-making process in which five alternatives are considered and evaluated in terms of their outcomes.

the decision-making process. We'll outline several of the most critical assumptions.

1. **Goals are given.** Classical theory assumes that the goals to be achieved in any decision situation are either predetermined or else so clearly obvious as to be straightforward. Classical theory does not address itself to situations in which goals are unclear, disagreement exists regarding goals, or several goals are in conflict with one another.

2. **All alternatives are considered.** According to classical theory, decision makers must generate and evaluate *all* possible alternative courses of action. Decision making is thus an exhaustive (and probably exhausting) process in which no potential solution to a problem is excluded from consideration.

3. **All outcomes are taken into account.** Classical theory assumes that

decision makers are aware of and take into account *every* possible outcome associated with each alternative under consideration.

4. **Perfect information is freely available.** It is assumed that decision makers either possess or can obtain (at no cost) perfect information regarding: (1) the value of every outcome that may be obtained; and (2) the likelihood that each alternative course of action will result in obtaining each of the outcomes.

5. **Decision makers are rational maximizers.** Classical theory views decision makers as totally rational. This total rationality results in the decision maker always choosing the optimal course of action, where optimal is defined as that alternative that maximizes the attainment of desirable outcomes that meet the goals of the decision maker.

Assessment of Classical Theory

Classical theory has enjoyed a good deal of popularity for a variety of reasons. First, it is intuitively appealing. It looks as though it provides a pretty good description of how people at least *should* go about making decisions (even if they aren't always quite so systematic as the theory implies they should be). Second, it does provide specific guidance to decision makers regarding how to improve the quality of decision making. Finally, when formulated mathematically, its principles of maximization turn out to be very useful in making specific predictions (in fact, most of modern microeconomic theory still assumes the validity of the classical theory of decision making).

Unfortunately, all of the assumptions of classical theory are incorrect or invalid. The theory appears to have almost no validity as a *description* of how people actually go about making decisions. In addition, the theory has some serious shortcomings as a prescriptive model of decision making (i.e., as a model of how people *should* go about making decisions). We'll look at the shortcomings of each of classical theory's assumptions in turn.

1. **Goals are given.** In almost all real decision-making situations (personal or organizational) goals are *not* given. Indeed, a central problem in most decision-making situations is determining precisely which goal or goals are most important to try to obtain. For example, does an individual making a personal decision regarding which of several jobs to accept choose the job with the highest salary (monetary goal), the best career advancement prospects (development goal), or the most interesting current work assignments (challenge and interest goal)? Similarly, when an organization is making major decisions regarding its organizational structure does the organization choose a structure that it hopes will maximize profit, total sales, market share, long-term growth, or long-term stability, or does it choose a structure that will

minimize costs, reduce overhead, or decrease turnover? In facing any nonprogrammed decision a decision maker must determine which of a multitude of goals (many of which may be conflicting) are most important to pursue. Goals are rarely, if ever, given.

2. *All alternatives are considered.* For all but the most trivial programmed decisions it is foolish to suggest that all alternatives can even be identified, much less considered. How realistic is it to suggest that an individual should consider and evaluate all possible potential spouses before choosing a marital partner? Or how should an individual go about evaluating all possible jobs before choosing one? The ambiguity and complexity of organizational nonprogrammed decisions makes this assumption even more untenable for organizational decisions. Since the number of potential organizational structures for a large multinational corporation is nearly infinite, adherence to this assumption of classical decision theory would make it impossible for such an organization ever to arrive at a new structure, since it would never finish generating and evaluating all of the alternatives available.

3. *All outcomes are taken into account.* Just as it is impossible to generate all possible alternatives, it is equally impossible to anticipate and predict all possible outcomes of each alternative.

4. *Perfect information is freely available.* Information is not free, and only rarely is perfect information even feasible to obtain regarding the ramifications of a course of action. Generating and evaluating alternatives takes time, energy, and resources (whether personal or organizational). Thus, the process of obtaining information for use in decision making frequently has high costs associated with it. As a result, almost all decisions are based upon information that is to some extent inadequate and incomplete.

5. *Decision makers are rational maximizers.* The classical model assumes that decision makers have a tremendous mental capacity both for remembering and storing huge quantities of information and for processing that information in order to assess which available alternative is *the* optimal one. A great deal of psychological research indicates that people are simply totally incapable of the kinds of mental arithmetic implied by classical theory (Miller, 1956; Simon, 1957, 1976a; MacCrimmon & Taylor, 1976). The conclusion is not simply that people *don't* make decisions in the manner suggested by classical theory; more to the point, they *can't*.

In light of these real constraints that exist to limit a manager's capacity to generate and analyze alternatives, how should a manager approach a decision situation in order to try to analyze the problem as systematically as possible and make the best possible decision within the constraints imposed by time, the complexity of the problem, the costs of information, and the limits on his or her capacity to analyze and process information? The theories of decision making discussed in the remainder of the chapter attempt to deal with this question.

BEHAVIORAL THEORY OF DECISION MAKING

Given the difficulties and shortcomings of classical decision theory we clearly need an approach to decision making that is: (1) more likely to provide an accurate *description* of how individuals actually make decisions; and (2) more likely to provide realistic guidance to decision makers regarding how they *should* approach decision situations. Behavioral decision theory provides such an alternative approach. The central ideas of behavioral decision theory have been developed by Herbert Simon, James March, and their colleagues (Simon, 1957, 1976a, b, 1978; March & Simon, 1958; Cyert & March, 1963).

Bounded Rationality

According to classical theory, decision makers are perfectly rational. They generate all possible solutions to a problem, analyze all possible outcomes of each alternative, and then choose that alternative that will maximize the likelihood of attaining their goals (in other words, they choose the best alternative of all those that exist). As previously pointed out, a major problem with this classical view of rational decision making is that it assumes that decision makers have mental capacities for analysis and evaluation which vastly exceed those possessed by real people. In addition, recent research into the underlying nature of problem complexity and techniques of searching for solutions to complex problems indicates that neither larger computers nor smarter people are likely to be able to implement the classical theory approach to decision making in the face of the enormous complexity of most real-world problem situations (Simon, 1978).

In response to this recognition of the inherent complexity of most real-world problems and the impossibility of actually implementing the classical theory approach to rational decision making, Simon (1957) has developed the notion of *bounded rationality*. According to the principle of bounded rationality, "The capacity of the human mind for formulating and solving complex problems is very small compared with the size of the problems whose solution is required for objectively rational behavior in the real world—or even for a reasonable approximation to such objective rationality" (Simon, 1957, p. 198). Thus, bounded rationality implies the following:

- Decisions will always be based upon an incomplete and to some degree inadequate comprehension of the true nature of the problem situation being faced.

- Decision makers will never succeed in generating all possible alternative solutions for consideration.
- Alternatives are always evaluated incompletely since it is impossible to foresee and predict accurately all of the outcomes associated with each alternative.
- The ultimate decision regarding which alternative to choose must be based upon some criterion other than maximization or optimization, since it is impossible ever to determine which alternative is *the* optimal one.

The validity of the principle of bounded rationality is further reinforced by recognition of the fact that if classical theory were valid and there were no limits to human rationality, there would be no need for theories of organization or organizational behavior. If everyone in every organization were perfectly rational, every individual and every organization would always be making the best possible decisions and as a result problems of organizing and managing organizations effectively would be nonexistent. It is precisely because individuals have limited abilities to agree on goals, to communicate, to cooperate, to analyze situations, and to make decisions that organizing becomes a problem.

Satisficing

If people are not perfectly rational and if they are therefore incapable of making decisions on the basis of optimization or maximization, how then can they go about determining which alternative to choose when faced with a decision? Simon has suggested that the key to understanding how people actually go about simplifying complicated decision situations lies in the notion of *satisficing*. While the principle of *maximizing* suggests that a decision maker must continue to generate and evaluate alternatives until the *best* alternative has been identified, the principle of satisficing suggests that a decision maker continues to generate and evaluate alternatives until one alternative that is *good enough* to be acceptable is identified.

The advantages of satisficing as a basis for decision making are obvious. First, it is a manageable criterion to employ since it does not require a decision maker to generate a potentially infinite list of alternatives. Second, it is a realistic criterion in light of the reality of bounded rationality and the limited mental capacities of human beings. Finally, satisficing appears to provide a valid description of how people actually go about making decisions. Given the time, effort, and expense that must go into the process of generating and evaluating alternatives, the satisficing criterion provides a realistic basis for keeping the decision-making process within manageable bounds and cutting off the process when an acceptable solution has been identified.

Procedural Rationality

Given the reality of bounded rationality and satisficing, and the impossibility of making "optimal" decisions in the sense implied by classical decision theory, what should decision makers do to ensure that they are making the best possible decisions within the constraints inherent in all real decision situations? In order to deal with this question, Simon (1976b, 1978) has introduced the concept of *procedural rationality*. Since it is impossible for decision makers ever to ensure that they have made *the* best optimal rational decision, they should turn their attention instead to the design of methods or *procedures* for decision making that will be most likely to generate the *best possible* decisions within the constraints of human judgment and insight. Such rational procedures need to be designed in such a way that they capitalize on the strengths of human beings as problem solvers and decision makers. These strengths appear to lie not in any capacity to generate, process, and analyze huge amounts of *information*, but in the ability to employ *insight* and *experience* in identifying a small number of promising alternatives for further exploration and analysis. This in turn implies that the critical scarce resource for effective decision making is not information, but rather the *attention* of decision makers. Indeed, Simon (1978) argues that for many decisions information may be an expensive luxury, since it may distract the attention of decision makers away from the truly important aspects of the problem situation.

The concept of procedural rationality implies that organizations need to design *rational procedures* for coping with problems and deciding upon solutions. These procedures must be designed to focus managers' *attention* upon key aspects of the problem and permit managers to bring to bear their insight, creativity, and experience in generating a manageable number of solutions. Information can then be brought to bear in the analysis of this small set of potential solutions. Information should not be permitted to smother the entire decision process or to distract managers' attention from the key aspects of the problem.

THE SCIENCE OF MUDDLING THROUGH

Lindblom (1959) has developed an approach that characterizes decision making as a process of *muddling through*. The interesting thing about the approach is that Lindblom doesn't think that muddling through is necessarily bad. Indeed, he characterizes muddling through as a science and argues that it may be the only feasible realistic approach to systematic decision making in the face of highly complex problems and issues.

Lindblom draws a distinction between two basic approaches to decision making. The first approach, labeled *rational-comprehensive*, is based upon the classical theory of decision making. The rational-comprehensive approach to decision making involves the determination of objectives, the development of all possible alternative courses of action, the evaluation of each alternative in terms of its anticipated outcomes, and finally the choice of the optimal alternative which is maximally likely to result in the attainment of the agreed upon objectives. The second approach, known as the method of *successive limited comparisons*, (or *muddling through*), does not require agreement on objectives, exhaustive analysis of alternatives and outcomes, or determination of the "optimal" alternative. Instead, the approach views decision making as a process of successively comparing alternative courses of action to one another until decision makers arrive at an alternative they can agree upon. The two approaches and the key characteristics that distinguish them from one another are summarized in Table 13-2.

Although the rational-comprehensive approach *sounds* like the most systematic and sensible approach to decision making, in fact it is both unrepresentative of how decisions are actually made and impossible to implement in all but the simplest types of decision situations. The method of successive limited comparisons is not only a more accurate description

TABLE 13-2
Comparison of the rational-comprehensive method of decision making with the method of successive limited comparisons ("muddling through")

Rational-comprehensive method	Method of successive limited comparisons ("muddling through")
Setting objectives is a distinct activity which must precede generating alternatives.	Setting objectives and generating alternatives are often inseparable activities.
Decision making is thus a two-stage process: first objectives are set; then alternatives are generated to achieve the objectives.	Since objectives and alternatives are frequently inseparable, a two-stage approach to decision making is often inappropriate or impossible.
A "good" decision is the alternative which rational analysis indicates is the optimal choice for achieving agreed upon objectives.	A "good" decision is one which decision makers agree upon as a good alternative (regardless of whether they agree upon objectives).
Decision making is a comprehensive analytical process; every alternative is considered and every outcome is taken into account.	Decision making is based upon drastically limited analysis; many important alternatives are not considered and many important outcomes are ignored.
Decision making relies heavily upon the use of systematic theory.	Our theories are inadequate for most complex problems; the comparison of a succession of realistic alternatives greatly reduces or eliminates reliance on theory.

of how decisions actually are made, but muddling through also may well be the best possible approach to decision making when decision makers are faced with complex and difficult problems. We'll examine the key differences between the approaches and the reason Lindblom argues in favor of the science of muddling through.

Distinguishing Objectives and Alternative Courses of Action

According to the rational-comprehensive model, the processes of setting objectives, on the one hand, and generating alternative courses of action, on the other, are viewed as separate and distinct activities. When faced with a problem, decision makers first decide which objectives are most important and then generate alternative courses of action that they think may lead to the attainment of those agreed-upon objectives. In reality it is generally difficult to obtain agreement on objectives and impossible to draw a clear distinction between objectives and alternative courses of action. Consider a simplified example of government officials developing economic policy. Two common objectives of economic policy are low inflation and low unemployment. Think of the paralysis that would be generated in the policy-making process if alternative policies could not even be generated until all decision makers had agreed upon which objective was more important, low inflation or low unemployment. In addition, even if decision makers could agree on the relative values they place upon inflation and unemployment, it is highly likely that these values could change in the course of considering alternative policies. For example, imagine that by some miracle, decision makers had all agreed that low inflation was the most important objective and low unemployment was only moderately important. Then imagine that the process of generating alternative courses of action led ultimately to the consideration of two feasible alternatives. The first alternative would be expected to result in moderate levels of inflation and moderate levels of unemployment. The second alternative would be expected to lead to slightly higher levels of inflation than the first alternative, but it would also result in extremely low levels of unemployment. What do the decision makers do? They could say, "We agreed that inflation is more important than unemployment and therefore we must choose the first alternative." Or alternatively, they might say, "In light of the alternatives available, alternative two appears to be the best course of action."

Lindblom is arguing that decision makers are much more likely to draw the latter conclusion. He is also arguing that the latter conclusion is the better choice in the situation. The reason is that it is impossible in practice to separate alternative courses of action and their outcomes. This implies that instead of viewing complex decision making as a two-stage process of setting objectives and then generating alternatives, in fact the evaluation of objectives and outcomes can only meaningfully occur within the context of concrete alternative courses of action.

Exhaustive versus Limited Analysis of Alternatives

The rational-comprehensive model requires decision makers to generate *all* possible alternative courses of action and to evaluate each alternative in terms of *all* of its anticipated consequences. As our earlier discussions of classical and behavioral theories of decision making made clear, in all but the simplest decision situations such an approach is not only impractical but in fact is clearly impossible to implement.

Rather than exhorting decision makers to try their best to accomplish the impossible, the method of successive limited comparisons involves a drastically limited analytical process that *ignores* many alternatives and many important outcomes. Instead of attempting an exhaustive analysis of all possible courses of action, the method of successive limited comparisons (as its name suggests) requires decision makers to consider only alternatives that are very *similar* to the current state of affairs, to focus analysis only upon *differences* between the current state and the alternative under consideration, and to *ignore* all outcomes of any alternative that are outside their own sphere of interest and concern. In this way the complexity of the decision-making process is brought within the feasible physical and mental bounds of decision makers.

By considering only alternatives very similar to the current course of action, decision makers limit themselves to a manageable set of alternatives and are faced only with alternatives whose outcomes may be reasonably predicted with some accuracy. By focusing attention only upon differences between alternatives, decision makers don't waste time and energy analyzing outcomes that will not help them distinguish between the alternatives. Finally, by focusing only upon outcomes within their own sphere of interest and concern, they avoid the paralysis generated by attempts to analyze and predict every possible outcome of a given course of action.

Use of Theory in Decision Making

The rational-comprehensive model implies that decision makers should, and in fact do, make heavy use of theory in analyzing alternatives and making decisions. In practice, most decision makers do not rely heavily on theory, and they are entirely correct in so doing. The method of successive limited comparisons implies that in most situations decision makers will make more progress and will make better decisions as a result of successively comparing a variety of *concrete practical alternatives* than they will by attempting a theoretical analysis of the alternatives. Successive limited comparisons requires less information and permits decision makers to focus their attention upon those facts relevant to the actual alternatives facing them.

CONFLICT THEORY OF DECISION MAKING

Janis and Mann (1977) have developed what they refer to as a *conflict theory* of decision making. The reason that Janis and Mann use the label *conflict theory* is that decision making by its very nature always generates some degree of stress in decision makers and hence the process of making decisions is one that involves *conflict* for the decision maker. Since decision making is stressful and does generate conflict within decision makers, people are always to some degree reluctant to make decisions. As a result, a variety of defensive mechanisms have developed to help people avoid having to cope with the discomfort generated by decision situations. This desire to avoid the conflict and stress inherent in decision making can frequently impede the effectiveness of the decision-making process.

Vigilant Information Processing

Janis and Mann point out that for major nonprogrammed decisions it is frequently difficult, if not impossible, to determine subsequently whether or not a particular decision was the "best" that could have been made under the circumstances. The reason that it is so difficult to assess the quality of major nonprogrammed decisions is the absence of a meaningful basis of comparison that could be used to evaluate the decision. For example, if a large organization makes a decision to launch a new product, expand into new locations, or to close an existing division, it can never know precisely what would have happened if it had *not* done any of these things and thus can never determine precisely what was gained or lost as a result of a particular decision. Similar examples are obvious in the case of individual nonprogrammed decisions. For example, an undergraduate student who makes a career choice to attend business school rather than law school can never be in a position to assess the extent to which this was the "right" decision since it is impossible simultaneously to attend both business school and law school to assess their relative merits. Similarly, a person who decides to accept a job offer from company X rather than company Y will never know exactly what would have happened if the company Y job had been accepted instead.

Since it is frequently impossible to compare systematically the desirability of alternative courses of action according to their actual outcomes and ramifications, how then are we to distinguish between "good" decisions and "bad" decisions? Janis and Mann suggest that the distinction should be drawn according to the *procedures* employed by the decision maker or decision makers in evaluating alternatives and arriving at a choice. Their conflict theory of decision making is thus an example of a theory of *procedural rationality*.

Janis and Mann argue that the likelihood of making a good decision is a direct function of the extent to which decision makers engage in *vigilant information processing* prior to making a decision. Vigilant information processing is a summary term that describes a set of activities to be undertaken in the process of decision making. The seven major criteria of vigilant information processing put forward by Janis and Mann are summarized in Table 13-3.

An examination of the criteria of vigilant information processing might lead to the erroneous conclusion that Janis and Mann are endorsing and advocating the classical theory of decision making. This is not the case. They are *not* suggesting that decision makers must generate *all* alternatives, nor that *all* outcomes of each alternative must be evaluated, nor that complex computational methods must be employed to identify *the optimal* alternative. Rather, they are suggesting that the quality of decisions will be improved to the extent that decision makers use their insight, knowledge, and intelligence in a systematic fashion to search for alternatives, to evaluate alternatives as objectively as possible, and to plan realistically for the implementation of whatever alternative is selected.

TABLE 13-3
The seven major criteria for vigilant information processing

The decision maker, to the best of his ability and within his information-processing abilities:

1. thoroughly canvasses a wide range of alternative courses of action;

2. surveys the full range of objectives to be fulfilled and the values implicated by the choice;

3. carefully weighs whatever he knows about the costs and risks of negative consequences, as well as the positive consequences, that could flow from each alternative;

4. intensively searches for new information relevant to further evaluation of the alternatives;

5. correctly assimilates and takes account of any new information or expert judgment to which he is exposed, even when the information or judgment does not support the course of action he initially prefers;

6. reexamines the positive and negative consequences of all known alternatives, including those originally regarded as unacceptable, before making a final choice;

7. makes detailed provisions for implementing or executing the chosen course of action, with special attention to contingency plans that might be required if various known risks were to materialize.

SOURCE: Reprinted with permission of Macmillan Publishing Co., Inc. from *Decision Making* by I. L. Janis and L. Mann. Copyright © 1977 by The Free Press, a division of Macmillan Publishing Co., Inc.

The Role of Stress in Decision Making

The process of choosing among alternatives whose outcomes can never be perfectly anticipated generates a degree of psychological stress and conflict. The level of stress experienced can vary from the relatively minor (as in choosing which of several pairs of shoes to buy) to the totally debilitating (as in deciding which career to pursue or which job to accept).

The conflict theory of decision making argues that a moderate level of stress must be experienced before an individual will engage in vigilant information processing. If only a low level of stress is generated by the decision problem (as in choosing a pair of shoes), then it is unlikely that the decision maker will invest the time, energy, and effort required for vigilant information processing. If, on the other hand, a decision situation generates an extremely high level of stress (as in choosing between alternative career paths), the high stress level itself may impede the decision maker's ability to engage systematically and objectively in vigilant information processing. Hence, vigilant information processing will only occur when stress levels are sufficiently high to motivate the decision maker to engage in the process but not so high as to be debilitating for the decision maker.

The Conflict Model

What then determines whether or not a decision maker will engage in vigilant information processing? Or, put slightly differently, what factors determine the likelihood that an individual will engage in a decision-making *procedure* that is likely to result in a high-quality decision? Janis and Mann have developed a model of the decision-making process that seeks to explain why and under what circumstances decision makers engage in vigilant information processing. The model is summarized in Figure 13-3.

The central idea behind the model is that when faced with a decision-making situation, people either consciously or unconsciously ask themselves a series of four questions. The way in which these questions are answered by the decision maker determines whether the person engages in vigilant information processing or whether a less effective method of coping with the decision situation is adopted.

Starting the Process

Something has to happen in order for an individual to recognize that he or she is facing a situation that requires that a decision be made. Either of two types of events can generate such recognition and hence get the decision process started. One type of event is described as *challenging negative feedback*; in other words, the individual perceives that things are going sufficiently badly or a problem has reached sufficient magnitude

START

Challenging negative feedback or opportunity

Additional information about losses from continuing unchanged

Q1

Are the risks serious if I don't change?

Low Risk Low Stress

No → Unconflicted adherence

Maybe or yes

Information about losses from changing

Low Commitment to Current Position

Q2

Are the risks serious if I do change?

No → Unconflicted change

Maybe or yes ← Intermediate Stress

Signs of more information available and of other unused resources

Q3

Is it realistic to hope to find a better solution?

No → Defensive avoidance

Maybe or yes ← Moderate Stress

Information about deadline and time pressures

Extreme Stress

Q4

Is there sufficient time to search and deliberate?

No → Hypervigilance

Maybe or yes ← Moderate Stress

Vigilance

END

Incomplete search appraisal and contingency planning

END

Thorough search appraisal and contingency planning

that something has to be done. The second type of event that can get the decision-making process started is simply the perception of the existence of a *significant opportunity* that has presented itself to the decision maker.

We can illustrate the two types of initiating events in the context of an individual deciding whether to stay with a current job or to switch to a new one. The process of making such a decision could be instigated either by the perception of challenging negative feedback or by the existence of an opportunity. Challenging negative feedback might take the form of an overwhelming feeling on the part of the individual that he or she is dissatisfied and unhappy with his or her current position and future prospects. Such feelings could start the individual into the process of deciding whether to stay on or seek new opportunities. Alternatively, the decision-making process could be started as a result of the person being approached by another company with an offer of an interesting and challenging new position.

Question One

Once the decision-making process has gotten started as a result of a perceived problem or opportunity, the individual poses the first question to him- or herself: "Are the risks serious if I don't change?" In answering this question the individual thinks about and may seek out additional information regarding any future losses or negative consequences associated with continuing unchanged. If the decision maker decides that the risks associated with continuing unchanged are not serious, the result is a state of *unconflicted adherence*. In other words, he or she adheres to the current situation and gets out of the decision-making situation without experiencing anything beyond the lowest levels of stress and conflict. Notice also, however, that the individual has not engaged in anything even approximating vigilant information processing.

Using our example of an individual who has received an offer of a new and interesting job, unconflicted adherence would occur if the individual asked him- or herself if there were any serious risks involved in simply staying with the current job, decided there weren't, and therefore decided not to give the new job offer (or any other alternatives for that matter) any further consideration.

Question Two

If the answer to the first question is positive, however, the level of stress experienced by the individual goes up slightly. The individual has now acknowledged that there are certain risks associated with the current state

FIGURE 13-3 *(opposite)*
The conflict model of decision making. (SOURCE: Reprinted with permission of Macmillan Publishing Co., Inc. from *Decision Making* by I. L. Janis and L. Mann. Copyright © 1977 by The Free Press, a division of Macmillan Publishing Co., Inc.

of affairs, and this itself creates some stress. The individual then moves to the second question: "Are the risks serious if I do change?" In answering this question the individual focuses upon what losses might be associated with changing. If the anticipated losses of changing are zero or negligible and the second question is thus answered no, the individual is predicted to accept immediately the first alternative that presents itself. This state is referred to as *unconflicted change*, since the individual decides to make a change without experiencing a great deal of stress or conflict. Notice again that there has been no systematic search for and appraisal of alternatives. Vigilant information processing has not even been approximated. Returning to our example, unconflicted change would occur if the individual had decided that serious risks were involved in remaining on the current job (yes to the first question), but no serious risks were anticipated in the first alternative job that became available (no to the second question). The individual would thus accept the first new job offered, without any systematic attempt to identify and evaluate the available alternatives.

Question Three

If the second question is answered affirmatively, stress goes up to intermediate levels. The individual has now acknowledged to him- or herself that serious risks are involved *both* in continuing unchanged and in changing. This admission naturally creates some feelings of discomfort and leads the person to the third question: "Is it realistic to hope to find a better solution?" At this stage the decision maker seeks new information regarding the likelihood of identifying new alternative feasible courses of action. If the individual determines that it is not realistic to hope to find a better solution (no to the third question), the result is a state of *defensive avoidance*. The individual has ascertained that the current alternatives all involve serious risks and that it is unrealistic to hope to find alternatives that are any better. In order to escape the feelings of stress and conflict generated by such a situation, the individual engages in defensive avoidance, a psychological defense mechanism for avoiding the need to make a decision. The person continues on in the current situation but defends him- or herself against feelings of stress and anxiety by changing and reevaluating previous perceptions of the situation to reduce discomfort. For example, a person engaging in defensive avoidance might say, "I used to think that this was a lousy job, but you know once you think about it, it's really not too bad at all."

Question Four

A positive answer to the third question results in moderate stress levels for the decision maker and leads to the fourth question: "Is there sufficient time to search and deliberate?" If an examination of the situation leads to a negative response to the fourth question, the result is extremely high levels of stress and a state labeled *hypervigilance*. A more common everyday term for this state is panic. The extremely high stress levels make it impossible to engage in vigilant information processing. Only if the response to the fourth question is yes is the outcome a state of vigilance in which the decision maker, experiencing a moderate level of stress and conflict, is motivated and capable of conducting a thorough search for alternatives, systematically evaluating the alternatives generated, and carefully developing contingency plans for the implementation of the course of action decided upon.

MANAGERIAL IMPLICATIONS

In light of our discussion of the nature of decision making and the various theories that attempt to explain and describe the process, what conclusions can we draw regarding managerial decision making in organizations? A number of implications emerge fairly clearly and forcefully from our analysis.

1. *Managers must recognize and accept that the model of decision making put forward by classical theory is impossible to implement in practice.* Classical theory, with its assumptions of rationality and comprehensive analysis, appears at first glance to offer a pretty good model of how managers should go about making decisions. However, research on decision making leads to two clear-cut conclusions regarding classical theory. First, it is not at all representative of how managers actually go about making important nonprogrammed decisions. Second, and probably more important, classical theory does *not* provide an "ideal" model of how managers *should* attempt to make decisions. The complexity of most important managerial problems and the limited intellectual capacities of all decision makers make the classical model not only inefficient but also *impossible* to implement in real decision situations.

2. *Managers need to develop methods of decision making that are suited to the limited decision-making capacities of even the brightest and most competent individuals.* Managers must face up to the reality of bounded rationality and the necessity of employing the satisficing criterion when making complex decisions. Our capacities to generate and evaluate alternative courses of action are not without limit: we are not totally rational and we cannot realistically hope to identify *the* optimal alternative course of action when faced with a decision situation. The implication is that rather than attempting the impossible, managers must use their insight, knowledge, and judgment effectively in focusing their attention on a realistic number of alternatives and knowing when further search and analysis is unlikely to pay noticeable dividends of increased decision quality.

3. *Managers must accept the fact that decision making generates stress and conflict and must design their decision-making procedures in light of this*

fact. Decision situations always involve some degree of uncertainty and unpredictability, and this in turn inevitably generates feelings of stress, discomfort, and conflict on the part of decision makers. The managerial implications are twofold. First, managers need to recognize that there is not something wrong with them because they experience stress and discomfort when faced with important and difficult decisions. Such reactions are natural and almost universal. Second, managers need to recognize that such feelings create forces on them that may cause them to try to get out of the decision situation prematurely (either by postponing or avoiding the decision or by accepting the first alternative generated). Such short-circuiting of the decision-making process is likely to result in poor decisions. Managers must learn to channel the stress of decision making into constructive generation and evaluation of realistic alternative courses of action.

4. **Managers must focus their attention on the development of effective decision-making procedures**. A common thread in most recent research on decision making is the emphasis on the impact of the decision-making *procedures* employed on the ultimate quality and effectiveness of decisions that are made. Managers must design decision-making procedures that will assist them in: a) systematically developing a manageable set of realistic alternative courses of action; b) analyzing the alternatives generated in as comprehensive a fashion as is feasible within the constraints of time, information, and attention; and c) planning for the implementation of the alternative course of action which is ultimately decided upon.

SUMMARY

Decisions can be broken down into a number of different types. *Personal* decisions are relevant to and have an impact upon the individual decision makers themselves (e.g., choosing which of several job offers to accept). *Organizational* decisions, on the other hand, refer to decisions made by managers regarding organizational issues and policies (e.g., deciding what standards to set for newly hired management trainees). *Programmed* decisions are repetitive decisions that can be handled in a standardized or routine manner (e.g., deciding when new supplies of paper must be ordered for the office photocopying machine). *Nonprogrammed* decisions arise in response to unpredictable or unique problems or opportunities that present themselves (e.g., deciding what remedial action to take in light of a recent decline in productivity).

Classical decision theory views decision making as a comprehensive rational process. According to classical theory, decision makers first agree on what their objectives are, then identify *all* possible alternative courses of action, evaluate each alternative in terms of *all* of the outcomes likely to be associated with it, and finally choose the best alternative. Unfortunately, classical theory turns out to have very little to do with how decisions actually get made in real organizational situations. First, decision makers can rarely agree on which objectives are most important and should be sought. Second, in all but the simplest types of decision situations, it is literally impossible to identify *all* of the alternative courses of action available. Finally, it is generally impossible to select the alternative that maximizes the attainment of objectives, since it is impossible to collect and analyze all of the information which would be necessary to evaluate systematically all of the alternatives under consideration.

The *behavioral theory of decision making* was developed in recognition of the shortcomings of the assumptions of classical theory. It attempts to provide a more realistic representation of how decisions are actually made. According to behavioral theory, decision makers have *bounded rationality* and employ a *satisficing* criterion for decision making (as opposed to the optimizing criterion of classical theory). The key to effective decision making in behavioral theory is the development of procedures that help decision makers make best use of their knowledge, experience, and judgment.

Two specific examples of decision-making theories that reflect the realities of human decision-making capacities were also discussed. According to the theory of *successive limited comparisons* (or "muddling through") decision making proceeds via a series of comparisons of the relative desirability of concrete courses of action. Relatively little abstract theoretical analysis of alternatives is involved. The *conflict theory* of decision making outlines the role of stress and conflict in decision making and shows how these factors may short-circuit the decision-making process. Effective decision making requires the implementation of *procedures* that facilitate the development and evaluation of realistic alternatives and that foster careful planning for the implementation of the chosen course of action.

REVIEW QUESTIONS

1. Discuss the role and importance of decision making in organizations.
2. Compare and contrast personal and organizational decisions.
3. What factors differentiate programmed and nonprogrammed decisions in organizations? What are the implications of these differences for how the different types of decisions should be handled?
4. Outline the basic assumptions of classical decision theory and describe the steps which classical theory assumes occur in the decision-making process.
5. How accurate a description of actual managerial decision making does classical theory provide? Be specific.
6. Should managers attempt to make decisions according to the procedures outlined by classical theory? If so, why? If not, why not?
7. Discuss the implications of bounded rationality and satisficing for managerial decision making.
8. What do we mean by the term "procedural rationality?" What's the relevance of procedural rationality to managerial decision making?

9. What are the strengths and weaknesses of the method of successive limited comparisons ("muddling through") as an approach to decision making?
10. Describe and discuss the criteria for "vigilant information processing."
11. According to the conflict model of decision making, what are some of the factors which cause decision makers to engage in only a limited search for and analysis of alternative courses of action?
12. What does the conflict model imply managers should do in order to improve the quality of decision making in organizations?
13. What advice would you give a manager who wanted to improve his or her ability to make good decisions?

REFERENCES

Cyert, R., & March, J. G. *A behavioral theory of the firm*. Englewood Cliffs, N.J.: Prentice-Hall, 1963.

Janis, I. L., & Mann, F. *Decision making: A psychological analysis of conflict, choice, and commitment*. New York: The Free Press, 1977.

Lindblom, C. E. The science of muddling through. *Public Administration Review*, 1959, *19*, 79–99.

MacCrimmon, K. R., & Taylor, R. N. Decision making and problem solving. In M. D. Dunnette (Ed.), *Handbook of industrial and organizational psychology*. Chicago: Rand McNally, 1976.

March, J. G., & Simon, H. A. *Organizations*. New York: Wiley, 1958.

Miller, G. A. The magical number seven, plus or minus two. *Psychological Review*, 1956, *63*, 81–97.

Mintzberg, H. *The nature of managerial work*. New York: Harper & Row, 1973.

Mintzberg, H. The manager's job: Folklore and fact. *Harvard Business Review*, July–August, 1975, 49–61.

Simon, H. A. *Models of man*. New York: John Wiley & Sons, 1957.

Simon, H. A. *The new science of management decision*. New York: Harper & Row, 1960.

Simon, H. A. *Administrative behavior* (3d ed.). New York: The Free Press, 1976a.

Simon, H. A. From substantive to procedural rationality. In S. J. Latsis, (Ed.), *Method and appraisal in economics*. Cambridge: Cambridge University Press, 1976b.

Simon, H. A. Rationality as process and as product of thought. *American Economic Review*, 1978, *68*, 1–16.

Stewart, R. *Managers and their jobs*. London: Macmillan, 1967.

CHAPTER 14
COMMUNICATION

How often do we hear managers explain an organizational problem by saying "It's a communication problem"? Implicitly, if not explicitly, we suspect that if only others were exposed to the same information we had, they would behave in a predictable way—like ourselves. Indeed, the ability to be able to communicate well is critical to effective management. It comes as no surprise that Mintzberg (1973) finds that top executives spend over 75 percent of their time in communication activities. In this chapter, our focus will be on communication—the exchange of information between people.

It is useful to think about communication as a multistage process. First, we need to *attract* people's attention to our communication. Then, we need to make sure that people *comprehend and understand* our message in the same way we mean it. Next, we would like to influence others to *accept as true* the information we have given them. Finally, we would like to ensure that people *remember* the information we have given them after our communication is over and, we hope, *modify their behavior* on the basis of that communication. We'll examine each of these four stages in the communication process in some detail and will provide some overall guidelines for improving organizational communication as well.

We begin by considering what aspects of communication attract people's attention.

ATTENTION

Every day, we are inundated with a variety of communication attempts—memos, letters, phone calls, newspapers, television and radio programs, conversations. Much of that communication literally "goes in one ear and out the other." Even within the work setting, there is a lot more information being sent to us than we are hearing; think only of the times we discarded memos without reading them carefully, phone calls where we continued to conduct business even with the phone cradled on our shoulders, meetings where we caught up on our backlog of correspondence. What communications attract our careful attention? Two key factors influence what catches our attention: (1) the situation or context in which we receive the information; and (2) the nature of the information itself. Let's examine each of these factors more closely (see Table 14-1).

Situation or Context

Amount of Communication

Probably the most important context factor that determines whether we will pay attention to a particular communication is the amount of information that we are receiving. First, managers may have *information overload*—there is so much information coming in that it cannot all be attended to equally carefully. When a manager returns from a vacation to

TABLE 14-1
Factors influencing attention to communication

1. Situation or context of communication
   a. Amount of communication
      (1) Information overload
      (2) Background "noise"
   b. Direction of communication
      (1) Upward filters out negative data
      (2) Downward filters out task-irrelevant data
   c. Communication networks
      (1) Formal vs. informal
      (2) Centralization
      (3) Status
      (4) Physical location
      (5) Gatekeepers

2. Characteristics of the message
   a. Novelty
   b. Personal importance
   c. Intensity

find reams of mail and messages piled up, proportionately more of that mail and those messages get discarded. When twelve people in a meeting are all talking with (or at) each other simultaneously, it is impossible to take notice of all the comments being made.

The most frequent response to overloading is *filtering*. Certain messages are simply not read or followed up. Junk mail is thrown away, "for your information" reports are automatically filed, phone calls from pesky salespersons are ignored. Filtering may also include ignoring certain parts of a long report (such as parts that are difficult to comprehend and parts that seem redundant with information already received). The problem with filtering, however, is that if the receiver makes an inaccurate a priori judgment about the relevance of some piece of information, some important material may be inadvertently ignored.

Second, there is often quite a bit of background *noise* behind a communication attempt. The sender's communication must compete with a number of (frequently) irrelevant stimuli: the manager is on a phone call, the receptionist buzzes that another call is waiting, the secretary brings the manager in some letters to sign; a subordinate is waiting in the office to continue the conversation the phone call interrupted. The person on the other end of the line is competing with at least three other stimuli to get a message across. Not only the *total* amount of information coming in but also the amount of *simultaneous* information coming in influences whether a manager will notice and pay attention to a specific communication.

Directionality

The direction of communication—whether subordinates are communicating upward with their supervisors or whether managers are communicating downward with their subordinates—influences how much information is transmitted and how much attention is paid to it.

Communication traveling *downward*, as one might expect, is more closely attended to than communication traveling upward. Even as a child one learns the importance of listening to those in positions of authority. People are flattered, in a sense, when their bosses initiate conversations with them; managers judge communication with their bosses to be more satisfying and valuable than communication with subordinates (Lawler, Porter, & Tennenbaum, 1968).

Managers tend to overestimate the effectiveness of their downward communication, however. In a study conducted in a public utility, 92 percent of the supervisors said that they always or nearly always told workers in advance about changes that would affect them or their work, while only 47 percent of the workers themselves said they were nearly always informed about changes in advance (Likert, 1961).

Managers may withhold information from subordinates because they feel insecure and want to maintain more control. An interesting example of their downward filtering is provided in a study conducted by Davis (1968) in a large manufacturing plant. Top management held a meeting with the middle managers and told them about a proposed change regarding tentative plans for layoffs of personnel. The middle managers were instructed to relay the information along to the supervisors below them, who were then to relay the information on to the assistant supervisors. The layoff information was passed on to 94 percent of the supervisors, but only to 70 percent of the assistant supervisors. Of course, sometimes managers are unaware that certain information they were withholding would help subordinates in the performance of their job duties.

As mentioned earlier, subordinates seem to be more hesitant about communicating *upward* than their bosses are about communicating downward. In a study of supervisors, engineers, white-collar workers, and blue-collar workers in eight companies, Vogel (1967) found that a large majority of employees believed that their boss was not interested in their problems and that they would get into "a lot of trouble" if they were completely open with their boss. Subordinates are likely to "cover up" mistakes and difficulties, so that only information that reflects positively about themselves and their units is likely to be passed upward. This distortion of upward communication is particularly strong when subordinates are ambitious for advancement and are very competitive with each other for the boss's approval (Read, 1962; Athanassiades, 1973). As a result, managers often don't receive either sufficient information to help subordinates deal with their problems or accurate enough information to make high-quality decisions.

It appears, then, that the filtering process operates in both directions but screens out different types of information. Employees transmitting information upward send information that reflects favorably upon themselves (including personal information that may help ingratiate them to their bosses) and screen out information that reflects unfavorably on their own performance. Managers passing information downward screen out information not perceived to be relevant for their subordinates' jobs (O'Reilly & Pondy, 1979).

Communication Networks

There are two patterns of communication within organizations. The first pattern is the *formal communication network,* which closely resembles the organization structure. There are formal channels through which communications are to flow. For example, an employee can only communicate with the general manager through his or her immediate supervisor. Such communication procedures protect higher-level administrators from unwanted information and reinforce the authority structure.

There is also an *informal communication network,* sometimes called "the grapevine." This informal communication occurs outside prescribed channels and most frequently is carried out either in face-to-face interaction or over the phone. This informal communication may be task-related (e.g., short-cutting long chains of command) or social-related (e.g., exchanging personal information, gossip, and rumors). The grapevine may be used by top management to make unofficial announcements (e.g., intentional leaks, "off-the-record" statements). Each person in the organization has a role in the formal communication network and a role in the informal communication network, and these two roles strongly influence how much and what type of information he or she will receive (Wexley & Yukl, 1977; Reitz, 1981).

The dimension of formal communication networks that influences the attention aspect of communication the most is their *centralization*. Some networks are highly centralized; communication must flow through the leader position. Other networks are very decentralized; people in a group can communicate directly with each other. Units with decentralized networks have more mutual communication; people in decentralized networks both send and receive a lot more information (Shaw, 1964).

There is a great deal of variance in how much information people receive in informal networks (i.e., through the grapevine). In the most well known study of grapevines, Sutton and Porter (1968) found that only 10 percent of the rank-and-file workers both received and passed on grapevine communication. More than half of the employees were "dead-enders" —they received information but did not pass it on. One-third of the employees were "isolates"—they neither received nor passed on information.

What determines whether somebody receives and sends on grapevine information? People at *higher levels* in the formal communication network receive more information through the grapevine than do people at lower levels. They also initiate more grapevine information. The predominant flow of informal communication is downward and horizontal; even if the "news" occurs at a low level in the organization, it generally first flows upward to a person at a higher level, then it spreads downward again and horizontally. *Gatekeepers*—employees who have a lot of contact with colleagues outside the organization—also tend to initiate a lot of informal communication. These gatekeepers are most likely to pass on information about a job function in which they are interested or information about someone that they know personally. People who are *geographically isolated* and people with *low status* are less likely to receive grapevine information, and if they get it at all it will be late (Davis, 1953).

Thus, the more decentralized the communication network, the more information an employee will receive. Being at a higher level in the organization, having a lot of contact with colleagues outside the organization, and being physically near a lot of other employees also increases the chances of receiving information.

Characteristics of the Message

So far we have discussed how the situation in which the communication takes place influences whether a message will attract our attention. Of course, the *characteristics of the message itself* play an equally strong role in whether we hear the information being given us. What is it about the message itself that makes us take notice?

First of all, the *novelty*, or *newness*, of the information draws our attention. If information about potential labor problems, new business ventures, or recent job postings comes across our desk, and all the information is new and unfamiliar to us, we will pay more attention to it. Advertisers have long known the importance of the novelty of the message; hence, the variety of eye-catching animals and toe-tapping jingles that extol the virtues of their products.

Second, we pay the most attention to messages that are *important* to us, that affect us *directly*. We pay a lot more attention to information about pay raises than we do to the details of a charity drive; we pay more attention to how our bonus is calculated than to how replacement-cost accounting procedures are implemented. We may tune into tomorrow's weather forecast and tune out high school sports scores.

Third, the *intensity* of the message affects how closely we attend to it. If the boss comes to our door demanding immediate action, we take heed. If the same request is more mildly stated in a list of ten other requests, it draws less attention.

If we look at the characteristics of messages that attract our attention —novelty, importance, and intensity—we can discover why so much "communication" in organizations is ignored. Much of the information that managers receive is irrelevant to their jobs (e.g., receiving retirement notices of people they have never met), routine and uninteresting (e.g., menus for the company cafeteria), and of no immediate importance (e.g., the day of the company picnic, which is 3 months off). Managers frequently find they are missing the information they currently need but are inundated with information that they won't ever use.

COMPREHENSION AND UNDERSTANDING

Attracting people's attention is only the first step in communication. The next step is communicating the information in such a way that the people receiving the information (the receivers) comprehend and understand the information in the same way that the senders mean it. Two factors determine how completely people comprehend the messages they are sent: (1) the semantics of the message; and (2) the perceptual set of the receiver (see Table 14-2). Each of these is looked at in some detail below.

TABLE 14-2
Factors influencing comprehension and understanding of communication

1. Semantics of the message
   a. Jargon
   b. Unclear meanings of symbols
   c. Unintended associations of symbols
   d. Nonverbal cues
      (1) Ambiguity
      (2) Inconsistency between overt and latent messages

2. Perceptions of receivers
   a. Drawing unwarranted conclusions from limited facts
   b. Fitting new data into preconceived beliefs
   c. Stereotyping
   d. Projection
   e. Simplification
      (1) Leveling
      (2) Sharpening

Semantics of the Message

People communicate with each other through *symbols*—words, facial expressions, body language. We try to transmit information through symbols that we think others will clearly understand—vocabulary we think others will know, facial expressions and body gestures we think are easily interpreted. However, sometimes people do not comprehend and understand the information the way we mean it because of *semantic* problems—people do not know the symbols we are using or do not interpret them in the same way we do. Semantic problems can arise in several ways.

Jargon

Every occupational and professional group has its own specialized language. While the jargon certainly helps professionals communicate with each other more quickly and more precisely, it is easy to forget that newcomers, members of other groups in the organization, and clients may not understand some of the words that are used.

Wexley and Yukl (1977) provide an anecdote about a plumber who discovered that hydrochloric acid opened clogged drains and wrote to a government bureau to ask if it was a good thing to use. The reply was as follows: "The efficacy of hydrochloric acid is indisputable, but the corrosive residue is incompatible with metallic permanence." The plumber was not very well educated and interpreted the message to mean that it was all right to use the acid. After he thanked the bureau for their assistance, the bureau sent him another message with easier language: "Don't use hydrochloric acid, it eats the hell out of pipes!" (p. 55).

Unclear Meanings of Symbols

Some words have very clear meanings: tardy, absent, superstar. Other words have much broader meanings, like "aggressive." When a prospective employee is called "aggressive," is the term conveying praise (energy, initiative, perseverance) or criticism (pushy, belligerent, domineering)? Some symbols leave a lot more room for nuance and interpretation than others.

Unintended Associations of Symbols

Sometimes a message contains words that unintentionally evoke emotions in the recipient that the sender did not mean to elicit. These associations can bias the recipient's interpretation of the message. Haney (1973) illustrates this point with an example from the aviation industry. In the early years of commercial aviation, a flight attendant would tell the passengers: "We're flying through a *storm.* You had better fasten your *safety* belts; it will be less *dangerous.*" These instructions caused some passengers to fear that the plane was likely to crash. So the language of the instructions was eventually changed to elicit more pleasant and secure associations. Today the flight attendant says: "We're flying through some *turbulence* now. Please fasten your *seat* belts; you will be more *comfortable*" (p. 443).

Nonverbal Cues

A lot of communication is carried on nonverbally. People convey their feelings and emotions through their facial expressions, their tone of voice, their posture, their eye contact, and where they position themselves in a room. For instance, people are frequently suspicious of those who don't look them squarely in the eye. We often interpret fidgeting with hands as nervousness. When people "keep their distance" from us, we take that as a sign of negativism or hostility. Semantic problems arise in two ways in regards to nonverbal cues.

First, nonverbal cues are generally even *more ambiguous* than verbal cues. Was Sue's smile a friendly smile? a nervous smile? a smirk? Did Bob not sit near me because he feels hostile? came in late? needed to pass on some messages to Alan, whom he sat next to? A lot of nonverbal cues are very difficult to interpret.

Second, while we typically try to use nonverbal cues to help us interpret verbal communication, we sometimes find the nonverbal message is *inconsistent* with the verbal message; the tone of voice, facial expressions, and body gestures contradict what is being said orally. For example, someone may say "That's great with me," while the surly tone of voice, down-turned mouth, and slouch indicate substantial disapproval (Wexley & Yukl, 1977, p. 57). The *overt* meaning (positive feelings) is very different from the *latent* meaning (negative feelings).

This inconsistency arises when it is embarrassing for the sender to communicate explicitly his or her emotions but the emotions come out nonverbally anyway. Managers may hesitate to openly disagree with subordinates, but frowns come unavoidably to the managers' faces. Students may hesitate to tell a professor they liked a lecture because it might be perceived as "brown-nosing," but an open smile conveys the same message. The newly hired M.B.A. may be trying to sound very confident, but the stiff posture, nervous mannerisms, and unsteady voice reveal real anxiety. When the overt and latent meanings differ, the person who is receiving the communication doesn't know which message to listen to or what the sender really meant.

Perceptions of the Receiver

Semantics is the first half of the comprehension problem. The second half is perception. Listeners often hear what they *expect* to hear rather than what is actually being said. For instance, pronounce the following four words slowly:

M – A – C – T – A – V – I – S – H

M – A – C – D – O – N – A – L – D

M – A – C – B – E – T – H

M – A – C – H – I – N – E – R – Y

If you pronounced the last work *Mac-Hinery* instead of *machinery* you —like most other people—were caught in a response set (Luthans, 1981, p. 90). Having read three other *Mac* words, you expected to hear yet a fourth. That "expecting-to-hear" phenomenon remains true in organizations as well. People expect to hear certain things in a communication and sometimes do not hear what is actually being communicated. When we use the term *perception*, we are talking about the ways in which people organize and interpret the information they receive. How people perceive information influences how well they comprehend it. There are several ways we perceive information that inhibit complete comprehension of a communication.

Drawing Unwarranted Conclusions

A basic principle of perception is called the *grouping principle*: people tend to group several facts or pieces of information into a pattern. This tendency is so strong that sometimes people will perceive a whole pattern where none exists, "filling in the gaps" in the pattern.

As a result of this perceptual bias, sometimes people will group together several facts and draw a conclusion from them that is unwarranted. For example, a manager polls some subordinates about their feelings about hiring a particular job candidate. The manager receives mildly positive, noncommittal information about the prospective job candidate from subordinates. When the manager announces that the job candidate has been offered a position, several subordinates are surprised and disappointed. First, several complained they had not been asked their opinions at all. Second, their responses, while positive, were not enthusiastic. Under pressure to fill the slot, the manager perceived a pattern where none existed (assumed people not contacted were like the people spoken to) and falsely read the partial pattern (aggregated mildly positive responses into a more positive overall evaluation).

Forcing Data into Preconceived Beliefs

Another perceptual bias that people frequently exhibit is "forcing" data or information into previously held ideas. An assistant brand manager comes up with an idea for a new brand of presweetened cereal. The assistant brand manager sends a proposal to the group brand manager, who sends back a long, detailed memo about the decline of the market in presweetened cereal owing to actions of dental groups, consumer advocates, and so on. The group brand manager meant the memo to put the brakes on the development of the new product. However, the assistant brand manager was so convinced that the idea was solid that the boss's memo was perceived as supportive: "the presweetened market is poor, so your product is surely needed and desired." The assistant brand manager forced the new data into the idea he or she already strongly held.

We force data all the time when we have conversations with others. For example, suppose we think of our boss as diffident, neutral, unemotional. We notify the boss that we won't be able to be at work the next day due to a personal problem, and the boss's response is "No problem with me, take the day off." We may later relate this incident to our friends and say, "Well, my boss behaved just as I expected—didn't show any emotion and didn't ask what was wrong." The boss, on the other hand, may not have wanted to pursue the matter because he or she didn't want to upset us further and didn't want to pry into our personal affairs. We fit the data to our ideas and may not take the communication the way it was meant.

Stereotyping

The grouping principle mentioned earlier works in yet another way. The greater the similarity between people or objects, the greater is the tendency to perceive them as a common group. *Stereotyping* refers to the tendency to categorize people into a single class on the basis of some trait.

For instance, people often stereotype others on the basis of sex ("that's just like a man" or "that's just like a woman") or their functional department ("a hard-nosed engineer" or "an aggressive salesperson").

Stereotyping interferes with accurate perception because people who stereotype are unable to see the individual differences and variability among members of groups. Before we hear a 65-year-old manager talk, we may assume his or her arguments will be based on experience only and not on theory or new developments; before we hear a 25-year-old M.B.A. talk, we may assume his or her arguments will be based on solely theoretical grounds and will be impractical. We are "set" to hear certain arguments from each person. If we stereotype, we are less likely to see any theoretical aspects of the older person's position and any practical considerations in the young M.B.A.'s position. Moreover, if we stereotype others, we are more likely to discount what they say ("isn't it just like a new M.B.A. to come up with an idea like this?") without seriously considering the merits of the specific case at hand.

Projection

Projection is the perceptual process by which we attribute *our own* thoughts and feelings onto others. A manager calls in her subordinate to ask him to redo some financial analyses. There are some careless calculation errors that need to be fixed. The manager displays no real emotion, but the subordinate later describes her as angry and hostile. In truth, the surbordinate was angry *at himself* and if he had been the manager he would have been even angrier. As a consequence, he *projects* an anger onto his manager where there may be none at all. Projection interferes with accurate comprehension of communication because people only perceive mirror images of their own thoughts, *not* the actual images trying to be conveyed by others.

Simplification

As information proceeds from person to person in an organization, it tends to get simplified in two ways (Lewis, 1980). First, the information gets leveled: the details of the message get dropped; the context of the message and the qualifications to the message get simplified. Second, the information gets sharpened; the message is retold more vividly and dramatically as time goes on. A systematic perceptual bias that people often have is the need to simplify information. The nuances get dropped and the major points become highlighted and made even more dramatic. As a result, messages get conveyed with a force and an unequivocality that the sender never meant.

For instance, a division manager may ask her assistant to arrange a meeting for her with her subordinates to facilitate cooperation in problem solving. The assistant relays the following message: "Ms. Jones will meet with you on April 10 to discuss problems you are having." First of all, the context of the message is completely deleted—the meeting is to help subordinates, not to punish them. Second, the message is relayed more vividly than it was intended: *problem solving* became *problems*; problems *in general* became the subordinates' *own* problems. This simplification clouds comprehension of the message, as important qualifications are dropped and the amount of emotion or force behind the communication gets exaggerated.

In summary, then, both semantics and perceptions influence whether people comprehend and understand the information in the same way that the sender meant it. Semantic problems arise because the words and gestures we use to convey information are often ambiguous; they can mean different things to different people. Perceptual problems arise because people have expectations about what they are about to hear, and have difficulty hearing messages that "break" some response set.

ACCEPTANCE OF THE INFORMATION AS TRUE

When managers use the expression *communicate effectively*, what they frequently mean is *persuade*. We don't want to settle for others merely understanding what we mean; we also want them to *agree* with us. In fact, much of our communication in organizations is aimed at *converting* others to our point of view. Two sets of variables most strongly influence whether the information we communicate to others is accepted as true. The first set of variables has to do with the *characteristics of the communicator that increase his or her credibility*. The second set of variables has to do with *defensive communication*—whether the communication poses some *threat* to the individual who is receiving it. Each set of variables is considered in turn below (see Table 14-3).

Characteristics of the Communicator

What makes a communicator credible? The answers are expertise, trustworthiness, and attractiveness.

Expertise
We are more likely to be persuaded by people with special competence in the subject we are concerned about. We more readily accept the engineer's advice on what type of concrete to use, the personnel department's advice on EEOC guidelines, the legal department's advice on tax law questions. However, it is important to note that people also put *bounds* on the expertise of those they listen to. When the engineer proffers suggestions on personnel matters, when the personnel manager dispenses financial advice, and when the corporate lawyer favors a particular advertising

TABLE 14-3
Factors influencing the acceptance of information as true

1. Characteristics of the communicator

    a. Expertise

    b. Trustworthiness
       (1) Past behavior
       (2) Argues against self-interest
       (3) Status or formal power

    c. Attractiveness

2. Defensive communication

    a. Personally threatening messages
       (1) Denial
       (2) Modification and distortion
       (3) Recognition, but refusal to change
       (4) Change in perception

    b. Dissonant information
       (1) Avoids exposure
       (2) Rejects validity
       (3) Easily forgets
       (4) Memory distorts

strategy, their comments about subject *outside* their realm of expertise are taken with much skepticism (Aronson, 1976).

Trustworthiness

"Would you buy a used car from this man?" is the everyday equivalent of the concept of trustworthiness. Is the communicator giving us a straight story? Three factors, in particular, influence a communicator's trustworthiness.

The first factor is the *past behavior of the communicator.* We tend to believe people who have carried through on their promises and tend to discount those who do not deliver. If a subordinate is told, "Don't worry about your pay raise, it's all taken care of," and he or she gets the promised pay raise, the trustworthiness of the supervisor increases. If no raise is given, substantial doubt is cast on the manager's credibility. Similarly, if the information we have received from somebody in the past has been accurate, we are more likely to believe him or her again. If an account executive strongly argues for a particular ad campaign and the ad campaign fails miserably, then the account executive's future credibility is very much decreased. We tend to listen most closely to people with a string of successes.

The second factor is that people seem more trustworthy to us if they *argue against their own self-interest*. If the medical school faculty argues for a greater allocation of funds to the medical school, we suspect its motivation: of course it will present data and arguments to support a position that will personally benefit its unit. On the other hand, if the medical school faculty argues against cutbacks in classical languages, its argument seems more credible and trustworthy. It has nothing to personally gain from such an argument (and, indeed, may possibly stand to lose some funds), so it must *really* support programs in the classics to take this position (Aronson, 1976).

The third factor is that *status* or *formal power* can enhance a communicator's credibility. The higher one's status, the more likely one will be seen as having better access to data and as having good intentions. The example of Richard Nixon during the Watergate scandal illustrates this point. President Nixon's extremely high status convinced many people that he had good reason for what he did. Many people simply refused to believe that the President of the United States would lie or knowingly do anything that was illegal or criminal. Only after months of intensive news reporting, with a steady stream of incriminating evidence, did a majority of the public finally come to believe in his guilt. Even then, though, many individuals with a special reverence for the office of the president still refused to believe that President Nixon's actions were intentionally and deliberately dishonest (Secord et al., 1977, p. 145). While very few managers are held with the same awe as a president or prime minister, most employees expect especially their top executives to be very knowledgeable. People in positions of authority are *presumed* to be credible until proven otherwise.

Attractiveness

If we look at people on television who are promoting products, we certainly couldn't conclude that they were particularly expert about the products they were selling or that they were motivated to communicate with us without bias. Is a football player like Joe Namath really knowledgeable about men's support socks? What does O. J. Simpson really know about the rental car market? And when we read about the six-figure salaries paid performers to make commercials, can we assume these people are trying to get us to shave with a certain razor only out of the goodness of their hearts and their concern for our facial texture?

It seems inconsistent at first that movie stars could influence our beliefs about the products they are selling when they are not particularly expert or trustworthy. However, Mills and Aronson (1965) found that physically attractive people—simply because of their attractiveness—could have a major impact on the opinions of an audience on a topic wholly irrelevant to their physical appearance. We might infer from the advertising industry that physical attractiveness would be enough to persuade us to change our minds.

Fortunately, the answer to this paradox lies in the nature of the issue being discussed. On important issues, expertise and trustworthiness still matter; we wouldn't take somebody's advice on key issues just because they were attractive to us. However, we *are* influenced by people we are attracted to on *trivial issues*. We might not be influenced by their opinions about whether to build a new headquarters facility, but we might be influenced by their opinions about how to decorate our office. Expertise and trustworthiness are still the key dimensions of communicator effectiveness in organizational life (Aronson, 1976).

Defensive Communication

When people perceive or anticipate some sort of threat in a communication, they behave defensively. They are unable to concentrate upon what is being said to them. They are less able to perceive the motives and the emotions of the people who are talking. They are so concerned with escaping some punishment or trying to dominate the conversation that they can't hear other people accurately. Moreover, defensive behavior on the part of one partner engenders defensive behavior on the part of others in the conversation; if unchecked, the cycle becomes increasingly destructive. Defensive communication, in short, interferes with the accurate comprehension of communication, too (Gibb, 1961).

The most frequent example of defensive communication in organizations, of course, is performance evaluation interviews (see Chapter 15). Subordinates are so concerned with being criticized and preparing their rebuttals that they cannot pay careful attention to what is being said to them. They overreact to even minor criticisms. They try to take the offensive with the manager, trying to get the manager to take some of the responsibility for performance shortcomings. The manager then also gets defensive; the manager's criticisms get sharper, the subordinate gets more angry, and the hostility escalates. Neither the subordinate nor the manager can listen to the other objectively.

Two aspects of a communication in particular can produce defensive listening: (1) a message that is personally threatening to the receiver; and (2) a dissonant message, i.e., a message that is inconsistent with the beliefs of the receiver. Each of these is considered in some more detail below.

Personally Threatening Messages

People may build defenses against hearing information or messages that are personally threatening. For instance, a second-year M.B.A. student may be interviewing for a lot of advertising jobs and getting turned down repeatedly. It is very upsetting, difficult, and threatening to hear the message of rejection over and over again.

What do people do when they receive a message that is personally threatening? Haire and Grunes (1950) have identified the four most frequent responses.

1. Denial. A few people will block out or refuse to recognize the message altogether. To continue with our example, a few students will simply not let themselves hear the negative feedback from the marketplace, and will not change either their job goals, their job-hunting strategy, or their self-perceptions.

We do not perceive emotionally disturbing information as readily as we perceive neutral information. As a result, we often don't see warning signs of problems that will affect us personally (Luthans, 1981).

2. Modification and distortion. Some people will change, color, or distort the information so they won't have to deal with its full impact. For instance, the student in our example might say, "I still haven't heard from a lot of places," or "The letter said that they didn't need me *at this time* . . . maybe I'll hear from them later." Part of the communication has been received, but the disturbing information has been distorted and is not perceived accurately.

3. Recognition, but refusal to change. A third response to threatening messages is to recognize the information but refuse to change perceptions or behaviors. For example, the M.B.A. student acknowledges having no luck getting an advertising job and, furthermore, that the consistent reason given is poor social skills. The student recognizes this data, but does not change his or her own self-perceptions: "They don't know me well enough" or "The interviewers have no social skills, so they couldn't recognize them in me." These students concur with Jonathan Swift's observation that "when a true genius appears in the world you may know him by this sign—that the dunces are all in confederacy against him."

4. Change in perception. Finally, some people will actually change their perceptions. The student recognizes that he or she is not a good fit for advertising agencies for whatever reasons. However, these changes in perceptions are generally very subtle. The student is most likely to shift into brand management or market research, not into a radically different area. As we discussed in Chapter 13 on decision making, even when perceptions do change they change incrementally. As Luthans (1981) suggests, such findings explain why some supervisors and subordinates in organizations have "blind spots." They do not 'see' or they consistently misinterpret negative events and information.

Dissonant Information

Above, we discussed what happens when people receive information which is personally threatening. In recent years, a great deal of psychological research has also been conducted on how people cope with information that *runs counter* to other information the receiver possesses—information that is dissonant with other beliefs. This research on *cognitive dissonance* suggests that there are very strong differences between reactions to information that is consistent with what the receiver already believes and reactions to new information that is inconsistent with those beliefs (Aronson, 1976; Strauss & Sayles, 1980).

1. When communication is consistent with existing beliefs, the receiver seeks additional information. When the communication is dissonant with existing beliefs, the receiver *avoids exposure* to the message.
2. When communication is consistent with existing beliefs, the receiver accepts the information as valid. When the communication is dissonant, the receiver *rejects its validity*.
3. When the communication is consistent with existing beliefs, the receiver remembers what is heard. When the communication is dissonant, the receiver *easily forgets it*.
4. When the communication is consistent with existing beliefs, the receiver remembers it accurately. When the communication is dissonant, the receiver's *memory distorts the information*.

Reactions to a recent *Time* magazine cover story on M.B.A.'s (April 28, 1981) provide perfect illustrations of cognitive dissonance at work. The article was rather critical of new M.B.A.'s, on both personal and professional grounds: they were not well-trained, not interpersonally sensitive or competent, and often caused more problems than they solved. Faculty reactions and student reactions were completely different. For many faculty members, *Time*'s critique of M.B.A.'s was well-deserved. They read the article thoroughly, thought most of the points made were valid, could remember certain quotes and sections as particularly cogent, and even a month later could reproduce the arguments of the article quite faithfully. In contrast, student reactions were very negative to the article. They felt they had been caricatured and not done justice to. Most of the M.B.A. students either didn't read the article or only glanced through it. They dismissed its validity out of hand (idiosyncratic, journalistic, not rigorous), they couldn't remember many details from the article, and what they did remember was quite distorted.

Cognitive dissonance helps explain why it is so difficult to get people to change their opinions or accept new information as accurate. People avoid exposure to dissonant information, reject its validity, distort it, and easily forget it. Consequently, most dissonant information is *presumed* to be inaccurate.

Thus, communication can be rejected by the receiver as inaccurate on two grounds. First, the credibility of the communicator may be impugned; he or she may be seen as untrustworthy or inexpert on the topics under discussion. Second, any information that is threatening in content or the way in which it is presented is unlikely to be heard accurately. Much of the information will be blocked out, and what is heard is often substantially distorted.

RETENTION AND ACTION

The final step in the communication process is getting the receiver to *remember* the information presented and, where appropriate, to take some *action* consistent with the new information. Indeed, we often judge the effectiveness of our communication by looking at whether the people we communicate with remember what we said and follow through with behaviors on the basis of it. If we are trying to persuade workers not to join a union, for instance, we may gauge how effective our message is by looking at whether the workers remember management's position and vote against union representation. If we want to assess whether our subordinates heard what we were trying to convey in performance appraisal meetings, we may ask them directly if they remember our comments and look to see if there are any improvements or changes in their performance. *How the message is presented* and *the nature of the organization's reward systems* both influence the long-run effectiveness of our communication.

Presentation of the Message

There are several dimensions of the way the message is presented that determine its effectiveness (see Table 14-4).

TABLE 14-4
Factors influencing retention and action

1. Presentation of messages

    Logic versus emotion
    Explicit versus implicit conclusions
    One-sided versus two-sided arguments
    Primacy versus recency
    Extreme versus moderate positions
    Oral versus written communication
    Single presentation versus repetition

2. Reward systems

    Intrinsic rewards for new behaviors
    Extrinsic rewards for new behaviors
    Informal and formal reward systems are similar
    Reward systems from management are internally consistent

Logic versus Emotional Appeals

There is a lot of folklore about whether it is better to appeal to people's minds or to their hearts. If you want to convince workers to follow plant safety regulations, is it better to point out the logical negative consequences of personal injury (loss of health, loss of pay, loss of job) or is it better to post graphic pictures of injured employees around the plant? Will the fear motivate workers to be safe, or will it cause them so much anxiety that they won't be able to think about the safety issue at all (i.e., "it can't happen to me")?

The research suggests that, all things being equal, *the more frightened a person is by a communication, the more likely he or she is to take preventive action* (Aronson, 1976, pp. 64–65). In a particularly well done experiment, Leventhal (1970) tried to induce people to stop smoking in three ways: (1) by recommending to subjects that they stop smoking and get their chests x-rayed (low-fear treatment), (2) by showing a film depicting a young man whose chest x-rays revealed that he had lung cancer (moderate-fear treatment), (3) by showing a gory color film of a lung-cancer operation (high-fear treatment). The people who were most frightened were most eager to stop smoking and were most likely to take chest x-rays.

Emotional appeals have even greater impact if *explicit directions for action* are given. Some managers will arouse fear by saying something like, "Things better shape up around here, or else." While the employees become more anxious and fearful, they are not sure what it is they are supposed to "shape up." There is more fear, but still no focus for behavior change. The message, "I'll file formal complaints against every worker who comes into this work area without a hard hat on, even for 1 minute" arouses as much fear, but also gets more behavioral change (Zimbardo et al., 1977, p. 99).

Explicit versus Implicit Conclusions

Should managers explicitly draw conclusions from the facts that they present, or should they let the audience draw its own conclusions?

In general, it is more effective to draw conclusions *explicitly*. No matter how cogently the facts are marshaled, the audience may still not interpret the message the way the sender meant it—there could be either semantic misunderstandings or perceptual distortion of the information. For instance, a manager may be trying to convince a subordinate to accept a transfer to New York City and is extolling the excitement and opportunities a city like New York offers. However, the mind set of the subordinate may be opposed to big city living, and he or she may be hearing the manager's arguments as good reasons for *not* moving. Drawing explicit conclusions allows the manager a second chance to reduce ambiguity in the message (Aronson, 1976).

Advertisers are well aware of this principle. Commercials can be extremely clever and humorous. Some of the best-known recent commercials are the "Mother, *please*, I'd rather do it myself," the "No matter what shape your stomach is in," and the "I can't believe I ate the *whole* thing" ads. However, sometimes advertisements are too clever for their own good; people remember the commercial *better than the product*! The message—buy Product X—is so subtle we forget it more easily than the vivid jingle. (Test yourself: do you remember what products these three commercials were selling?)

One-sided versus Two-sided Arguments

Consider the case where management is trying to convince workers to vote against the union. Is it more effective to present only the arguments against the union (a one-sided argument) or is it more effective to address both sides of the unionization argument and attempt to refute the union's position? Will presenting two sides of the argument confuse the workers even further, or will it make management seem more fair-minded?

By and large, it is more effective to present *both sides of the argument* in organizational settings. Most of the people a manager will be communicating with are fairly well informed. When the communicator avoids mentioning the counterarguments, the listeners are likely to conclude that the speaker is either unfair or is unable to refute the opponent's arguments (Aronson, 1976, pp. 67–68).

If the receivers of the information are *predisposed to disagree* with the speaker, then it is even more important to present both sides of the argument. In the union campaign example, if management knows workers are favorably inclined toward unions, it is in management's best interest to acknowledge the pro-union position before attempting to discredit it. Otherwise, the audience will be even more hostile, since the union position is being dismissed out of hand as completely worthless (Zimbardo et al., 1977, p. 98).

Finally, by presenting both sides of the argument, a speaker can *forewarn* the audience of how the other side will try to manipulate them: "The union will try to persuade you we are insensitive to your needs and care only about the almighty dollar. Let me address those issues head-on." Forewarning substantially decreases the effectiveness of the other side's position. In fact, this phenomenon is so strong it is called the *inoculation effect*. By presenting a small dose of negative information about their position, speakers inhibit those negative pieces of information from being seriously believed (Zimbardo et al., 1977).

Primacy versus Recency Effects

Let's consider the union election example again. Both management and the union will have the opportunity to address the workers. Is it better to speak first or last? The advantage of speaking first, of course, is the impact of first impressions. The second speaker will not only have to sell his or her own position but will also have to unsell the effectiveness of the position of the first speaker. The relative effectiveness of the first argument is called the *primacy effect*. On the other hand, the person who speaks last might have the advantage because the audience may remember the last thing they heard. The relative impact of the last argument is called the *recency effect* (Aronson, 1976, p. 69).

The answer to the question hinges on *how soon the audience will have to take some action or express their preference after they get the communication*. If management and the union will be presenting their arguments back to back and the election is being held that afternoon, then the *recency* effect is stronger and management should try to go last. The second speaker has the advantage of greater *retention*; the second position will be fresher in the audience's mind.

If the election is still days or weeks away, then the *primacy* effect is stronger. The first speaker's arguments will interfere with or inhibit the listener's abilities to learn the second speaker's position (analogous to forewarning). With the election still some time away, any differences in retention between the two positions are negligible (Aronson, 1976, p. 70).

Extreme versus Moderate Positions

Consider a scenario where managers are in strong disagreement over whether to acquire a new subsidiary. Imagine you are a manager taking a strong pro position. Is it better to present your argument in its most extreme form, or is it better to tone down your argument when you are communicating with people who strongly disagree with you?

If you as the communicator have high credibility, then taking the *extreme* position is the more effective strategy. Because of your credibility, people listening to you will have a hard time discounting your arguments or dismissing your position lightly. On the other hand, if you are not seen as terribly credible, then taking a more *moderate* position is appropriate. Taking an extreme position only makes you as the communicator seem *less* credible (Aronson, 1976, p. 77).

For instance, consider a meeting among members of a brand management group to discuss marketing strategies for the next year. An experienced, successful group brand manager can assert a very strong position even when others in the group may disagree heartily; if the group brand manager is highly credible, he or she will be able to at least force others to defend their arguments and to consider the differing viewpoints. A brand new assistant product manager, on the other hand, will not be effective even if he or she uses *the exact same extreme position*. The assistant's credibility is low, and others will attribute the extreme viewpoint to naiveté or ignorance.

Oral versus Written Communication

The bulk of the research evidence suggests oral communication is more effective than written communication and is preferred by most employees (O'Reilly & Pondy, 1979).

First, face-to-face communication allows the sender to obtain some *feedback* from the receiver. The speaker can explicitly ask the listeners if they understand the communication, or at the least, can get a feel from nonverbal behavior how the listeners are reacting. People remember *two-way conversation* longer than one-way communication.

Second, we usually ascribe more *credibility* to what we hear spoken than to words attributed to someone in print. Employees are conditioned to discount the slick releases of corporate public relations offices (Strauss & Sayles, 1980, p. 143).

Third, when a manager is trying to communicate negative information, written criticism tends to provoke stronger emotional reactions than do oral warnings. Face-to-face exchange can soften the blow of bad news. Moreover, the impact of praise is stronger when given in person than when relayed in memo (Rue & Byars, 1980).

Of course, written communication is much less expensive, especially in regard to time, than oral communication. When communicating information of a general nature, lengthy and detailed procedures, or information for future reference, written communication is more effective. When a message is particularly important, *both* oral and written communication should be used. New policies or procedures could first be outlined orally, and the manager could make clarifications and answer questions. Then, the information could be put in writing to reinforce the message and for future reference (Rue & Byars, 1980).

Single Presentation versus Repetition

Finally, we need to consider whether it is more effective to say something forcefully *once* or whether it is more effective to repeat the same information *several times*. On one hand, we feel just a little demeaned and our status feels just a little threatened if we have to repeat ourselves—what's wrong with us that people aren't paying attention? Moreover, we don't want to feel like a broken record, going over and over the same material. On the other hand, as we pointed out earlier, there is so much information coming in at one time and so much background noise that our message—if only delivered once—may not be heard at all.

If we need to err, it is better to err on the side of *repeating* the message. First of all, repetition of a message is attention-getting; it increases our sensitivity and alertness to the information (Morgan & King, 1966). If every day we are reminded about a report that is due, we take more notice of it. Moreover, repeating a communication *prolongs* its influence (Zimbardo et al., 1977, p. 100). We tend to remember things we hear over and over again. Most commercials, for instance, repeat the name of the product or a jingle over and over again, both to attract our attention and to implant the product name in our memories. Sometimes we do find the repetition annoying (Call GR5-5600 right now, that is GR5-5600, call GR5-5600 before midnight tonight . . .), but in fact we remember those messages longer.

Thus, by designing the presentation of a message carefully, managers can increase the likelihood that others will remember their communications. An effective presentation strategy can make the message more vivid, can reinforce the information in several ways, can reduce any ambiguity in the content of the message, and can cast serious doubts upon opposing viewpoints.

Reward Systems

Besides presentation style, the other factor that influences the persistence of a communication and the likelihood of follow-through behavior is *organizational reward systems*. During the early 1930s a sociologist named Richard LaPiere traveled throughout the United States in the company of a young Chinese couple. Unknown to the young couple, LaPiere maintained a record of their travels, noting especially how the two Chinese were received by clerks in hotels and restaurants. Only *once* was the couple not treated hospitably. However, LaPiere didn't just observe how the Chinese couple was treated. He also sent a letter to each hotel and restaurant asking whether Chinese clients would be accommodated. Over 93 percent of the responses said *no*, they would *not* accommodate the Chinese couple. People had *negative affect and beliefs* about the Chinese, but still *acted positively* toward the couple when they met them (LaPiere, 1934).

Since that classic study, many other studies have demonstrated that *behaviors do not consistently follow from attitudes and beliefs*. Why is this the case?

1. **The rewards for expressing a belief or attitude and acting on that belief can be widely different.** We may hate our jobs and constantly complain about them, but there are strong negative sanctions against quitting our jobs altogether. We may believe safety hats are good *in theory*, but we sweat in them *in practice*. The hotel and restaurant proprietors may not have liked the Chinese, but it is also illegal to discriminate on the basis of national origin.

2. **Immediate environmental factors have as much influence on our behavior as our attitudes and beliefs.** If we are all sitting around a bar after work complaining about our bosses, we may get caught up in the spirit of the moment and bring up anecdotes about our own supervisor, stories we really don't care very much about. Everyone else is complaining, so what's the harm? Similarly, we may have every intention of wearing hard hats and bringing them to work, but when we walk onto the floor and see no one else is wearing one, we leave ours in the locker. Quite frequently, our attitudes toward the situation influence our behavior a lot more than our attitudes toward people or objects. The "set" of being sociable with friends after work influences what we

say about the boss more than our own internal feelings. The set of not sticking out like a sore thumb on the shop floor influences our not wearing the hard hat more than our beliefs about its reducing safety hazards (Rokeach, 1966).

3. ***Finally, some beliefs and attitudes are intellectualized but have no real action implications.*** Mann (1969), for instance, suggests that just because proprietors express negative beliefs about Chinese people in general doesn't mean they have committed themselves to behaving angrily to every Chinese person they might encounter. We may believe tobacco contributes to cancer but have no intention of stopping smoking. We may believe safety hats prevent personal injury but still have no intention of wearing them.

Abelson (1968) suggests that an individual's beliefs and attitudes are often composed of isolated *opinion molecules*. Each molecule is made up of: (*a*) a belief; (*b*) an attitude; and (*c*) a perception of social support for them. Each molecule thus contains *a fact, a feeling, and a following.* "Nobody wants to let Chinese people into their hotels (following), and neither do I (feeling). Other guests might not register here (fact)." These opinion molecules are really only conversational units that give us something to say when the topic comes up. These attitudes are not deeply held and bear little relationship to behavior (Bem, 1970).

In short, there is *not* a one-to-one relationship between beliefs and behaviors. There is a link, but it is a weak one (Zimbardo et al., 1977). When do organizational reward systems encourage people to follow through with behaviors based on new information?

1. ***When the new behaviors are intrinsically rewarding.*** If subordinates try out new suggestions or ideas and find their work is easier to do (e.g., a short cut, a simpler method of completing work, the idea saves time or helps save money), then they are more likely to keep on engaging in the new behavior. On the other hand, if the new suggestion makes subordinates' lives more difficult (e.g., the suggestions the boss made for dealing with angry customers only made things worse), then the new behaviors are unlikely to persist.

2. ***When people get extrinsically rewarded for the new behaviors.*** Employees are very sensitive to the reward systems in their environments. When subordinates find they will receive praise or pay for new behaviors (e.g., coming to work on time or changing the way they write reports), they are more likely to change their behaviors. If subordinates feel their bosses are "all talk and no action" ("nothing ever happens when I'm late"), there is no incentive to change.

3. ***When the informal reward system and the formal reward system are similar.*** William Whyte (1955) found that employees often restrict

output, *not* because they couldn't produce more and *not* because they didn't realize they would make more money if they increased production, but because the *informal* reward system has strong norms about keeping output low. Any "ratebusters" might make other workers look poor in comparison, or give management new ideas about changing the piece rate (see Chapter 17). Sometimes employees understand communications from supervisors, but the costs of complying with them are too high.

4. **When the reward systems from management are internally consistent.** Sometimes employees are confused by the inconsistency between what their managers say and what their managers do. For instance, a manager may joke around with male subordinates about all the problems of having females around and the next day blast them for not making rapid enough progress in meeting EEOC quotas.

At other times, managers can suffer from what Kerr (1975) calls "the folly of rewarding A while hoping for B." Sometimes reward systems are so fouled up that the behaviors that get rewarded are those that the manager is trying to discourage, while the behaviors that are desired are not being rewarded at all. For instance, managers may consistently encourage subordinates to be autonomous, yet only praise those who come to have the manager check their work before sending it out. The desired behavior—autonomy—is not rewarded at all, while the undesired behavior—dependence—is indeed reinforced. Only when the manager's rhetoric and rewards are consistent will subordinates change their behaviors.

Thus, while presentation style can reinforce the communication in people's minds, the ongoing rewards for compliance (and punishments for noncompliance) serve as daily, constant reminders of what is *really* wanted and valued in the organization. Moreover, when communications suggest people behave in ways that make their lives more difficult, either personally or in dealing with other people, we can expect little behavior change at all—no matter how well they understand the message.

MANAGERIAL IMPLICATIONS

As we have seen throughout the chapter, communication is simpler in theory than it is in practice. What should be a relatively easy job—giving people information they can understand and use—is a lot more difficult than we would like. Because there is so much information coming in at the same time, people do not always pay attention to our communication. Because of the language we use, people do not always comprehend what we mean. Because of our listeners' own perceptions, they do not always understand our messages in the way we mean them. Particularly if the information we are communicating is personally threatening or is inconsistent with our audience's other beliefs, our message may be ignored or distorted. Even if our listeners do understand our communication, they may not remember it and may not change their behaviors on the basis of it.

However, there are some common themes that run throughout the communication literature that give us some clues on how to improve communication in organizations. Before concluding, let's examine some strategies for making communication more effective (see Table 14-5).

TABLE 14-5
Improving communication in organizations

1. Controlling the flow of information

    "Exception principle"
    "Need to know principle"
    Queuing
    Critical timing
    Prevent isolation from subordinates
    Off-site meetings

2. Increase redundancy and repetition

    Multiple channels for the whole message
    Redundancy within a message

3. Reduce ambiguity in the message

    Use simple and direct language
    Avoid unnecessary associations

4. Use as much face-to-face oral communication as possible

    Obtain feedback
    Effective listening
       Limit your own talking
       Put the talker at ease
       Remove distractions
       Be empathic

5. Avoid putting listeners on the defensive

    Go easy on argument and criticism
    Use descriptive, nonevaluative language
    Don't club subordinates with your status

6. Address objections and arguments to the communication head-on

    Two-sided arguments
    Forewarning
    Repeat main points
    Draw explicit conclusions
    Take extreme position if highly credible
    Make explicit recommendations for action

7. Reinforce words with actions

1. ***Managers need to more effectively control the flow of information.*** A primary reason some communication is ignored is that there is so much information coming in simultaneously that it cannot all be processed carefully. Moreover, managers are frequently inundated with information that they cannot use and don't receive some of the information that they really could use, especially information from subordinates. Regulating the flow of information can substantially increase the efficiency of communication, and could be accomplished in several ways.

    a. ***Exception principle.*** This guideline suggests that only communications regarding *deviations* from orders, plans, and policies be communicated upward on a routine basis. Thus, only information that really demands attention will be transmitted, and a great deal of unimportant information would be filtered out.

    b. ***Need-to-know principle.*** Just as superiors need to be protected from information overload, so do subordinates. This principle, analogous to the exception principle, suggests that managers be selective about transmitting information downward and only send subordinates information that is important for carrying out their immediate tasks or for their strategic planning.

    c. ***Queuing.*** A third response to overloading can be to postpone the processing of low-priority messages until a slack period. For example, unimportant mail, phone calls, and reports could be put on hold, and low-priority meetings and appointments could be postponed or rescheduled. Queuing is particularly effective when managers can block out some periods of time for serious thinking, planning, and analyzing, and set aside other blocks of time for more routine, "bureaucratic" activity.

    d. ***Critical timing.*** Sometimes communication comes too early; the receivers are being given information about problems they have not yet experienced. Some training of new recruits suffers from such poor timing; people are given instructions about how to handle problems whose nature they do not yet understand (e.g., how to administer effective discipline, when they have not yet supervised anyone). At other times, only *after* a problem has arisen and has been botched up do instructions for dealing with the problem get issued. Managers need to become more sensitive to sending employees information at the time that they need it—not 3 months early so that it is discarded as irrelevant and not 3 months late when it is no longer of any use.

    e. ***Off-site meetings.*** Frequently, taking employees away from their regular work environment—either to a company retreat or to a different location—helps "unfreeze" people from their old routines and sensitizes them to hearing new information. For this reason a lot of training and corporate planning activity takes place outside the organization. For these two activities, fresh perspectives are particularly important.

f. **Lessen isolation from subordinates.** We have already noted the paradox faced by managers receiving communication from subordinates. On one hand, managers need to control the amount of information coming to them from their subordinates. On the other hand, subordinates may be afraid to initiate communication with their supervisors about problems they are experiencing—and thus managers are deprived of information they need to make decisions, and subordinates are deprived of help the managers could provide.

To lessen this isolation from subordinates, managers can meet periodically with various groups to discuss operations and problems. They can also get out of their offices occasionally and check on how things are going; or, they can have some "unprotected" office hours, during which subordinates could come in without going through a phalanx of secretaries and assistants. Managers also need to encourage subordinates to bring them problems they need help on and refrain from criticizing subordinates at that time for causing the problems. In addition, managers would do well to pay more attention to some of the rumblings coming through the grapevine. The facts might not be completely accurate, but at least managers will discover what issues their subordinates are most concerned about (Strauss & Sayles, 1980, p. 141).

2. **Managers can increase the effectiveness of their communication by increasing redundancy and repetition.** A major principle of communication technology is to provide *multiple* channels of communication that reinforce each other. For example, a verbal request may be followed up with a memo, or a written report might be followed up by a phone call. Because there is so much information coming in simultaneously, any one piece of communication may get lost. Repeating the message increases the chances that it will be heard at least once.

Even *within* a message, it is probably good to have some redundancy. In addressing a group, managers might want to make their main arguments early in the speech, give several examples that illustrate their main points, and then reiterate the key points in conclusion. That way, if any particular word or phrase is misunderstood, there are other elements in the communication that will carry the message.

3. **Managers should try to reduce as much ambiguity in their communication as possible.** Independent of all the other sources of confusion in communication, a major cause of misunderstanding can reside in the message itself. People do not understand what is being communicated when the information given them is in vague or amorphous terms. We have only to think of some excruciating college lectures or convoluted government forms to recognize the truth of that point. What can managers do to reduce ambiguity?

First, managers can use simpler, more direct languages. Simple, direct language is usually easier to understand than abstract, difficult language. "Teach your employees how to write an executive summary" is easier to understand than "Remediate your staff's expressive skills." The level of language and the vocabulary should be that of the receiver, not the sender. A series of short messages with a few ideas in each is easier to understand than a long message with many different ideas. A nonverbal response *alone* is ambiguous; the appropriate response to a question is not a smile, but a verbal "yes."

Second, managers can avoid unnecessary associations with their messages. As we suggested earlier, sometimes a communication will trigger some unintended associations. For instance, a manager may be trying to teach a subordinate how to access data on a computer and may intersperse the instructions with anecdotes about how hard it was teaching his or her 10-year-old child math. The subordinate begins to view the manager as condescending, associations come up like "I'm being treated like a child" or "my supervisor thinks I'm as dumb as a 10-year-old." The manager might have had no intention of putting the employee down, but the remarks about teaching the child math brought up a lot of negative feelings. Using emotionally charged words and examples of other employees (especially the unsuccessful ones) in communication are particularly harmful in this regard.

4. ***Managers should utilize face-to-face communication where feasible.*** On almost every dimension of communication effectiveness, face-to-face oral communication rates higher than written. People enjoy it more. It enhances the impact of praise and softens the impact of criticism. In addition, people believe information more when they get it "straight from the horse's mouth."

From the manager's point of view, too, face-to-face oral communication is more effective. First, the manager can use the opportunity to get feedback—did my subordinates understand what I meant? Do they have any questions? What are their reactions? Second, people tend to remember two-way conversations longer than one-way communication. Third, and perhaps most important, the manager can use the opportunity of oral communication to build a climate of trust so that there can be more, and better, communication in the future. By being a good listener, a manager can reinforce a subordinate to be a good communicator. There are several guidelines for more effective listening (Davis, 1978, p. 387).[1]

a. ***Limit your own talking.*** You cannot do an effective job listening when you are spending all your "down time" preparing your next remark. Don't constantly interrupt.

b. ***Put the talker at ease.*** Help the person relax. Sometimes it takes a lot of psychic energy to get out one's thoughts to a supervisor, so be patient. Ask questions—this encourages a talker. Show that you're interested in what he or she has to say.

c. ***Remove distractions.*** Don't doodle, tap, or shuffle papers. Shut the door if

[1]Reprinted with permission from K. Davis, *Human relations at work* (5th ed.), p. 387. Copyright 1978 McGraw-Hill Book Company.

necessary. Don't read your mail while someone else talks. Don't schedule appointments so closely that you are constantly looking at your watch or edging toward the door.

    d. **Be empathic.** Try to figure out what is going on in the mind of the subordinate. When you speak to the subordinate, think how he or she will interpret what you're saying.

5. **As much as possible, managers should avoid putting listeners on the defensive.** A consistent finding throughout the communication literature is that people do not clearly hear information that they find personally threatening or is inconsistent with what they already believe. They block it out, they distort it, they forget it. As a result of this, managers need to pay extra careful attention not to put their subordinates on the defensive. Several strategies can help in this regard.

    a. **Go easy on argument and criticism.** Confrontation puts people on the defensive, and they may "clam up" or get angry themselves.

    b. **Use descriptive, nonevaluative language.** It encourages others to reciprocate with neutral, accurate information rather than with emotions and half-truths.

    c. **Don't club your subordinates with your status.** Managers often underestimate how well aware subordinates are of status differences in organizations. Mistakenly, managers sometimes feel they need to reinforce their authority with a superior tone or air when they communicate with subordinates. Such a tone elicits defensive behavior; subordinates react by not hearing the message, by forgetting it, by competing with the manager, by becoming jealous, or by causing problems to prove the manager wrong (Gibb, 1961).

6. **Managers should address objections and arguments to their communications head-on.** We frequently have to communicate information with which we think our audience is likely to disagree. In such situations, we need to acknowledge that counterarguments to our position do indeed exist. Without such an acknowledgement, the listeners are likely to conclude that we are either unfair or unable to refute the objections to our position.

      Consequently, an effective presentation strategy in these situations might include: (1) presentation of both sides of the argument; (2) forewarning the audience of the objections to our position and systematically refuting them; (3) drawing explicit conclusions; and (4) making explicit our own recommendations for action. Obviously, someone who is dead set against a communication can find every way to avoid hearing it or believing it, but the strategies above can be effective in dealing with the true undecideds and even the undecideds leaning in the opposite direction.

7. **Reinforce words with action.** Finally, it is critical to remember that words by themselves are suspect. Employees are skeptical when they see a large disparity between the rhetoric of their managers and their managers' behavior. The consistent reinforcement of management communication by management action serves three purposes: it reminds workers of the

communication; it makes explicit the behaviors that are desired; and it raises management's credibility (Strauss & Sayles, 1980, p. 145). Moreover, once management has acquired a reputation for accuracy and credibility, it can do an even more effective job of communicating with employees on future problems.

SUMMARY

This chapter examines organizational communication—the exchange of information between people in organizations. Communication is a multistage process, consisting of four parts: (1) attracting people's attention to the communication; (2) ensuring that the message is comprehended and understood as it is meant; (3) influencing the receiver to accept the information as true; and (4) reinforcing the information so that it will be remembered and acted upon. Each of these four stages is explored in some detail.

Probably the most important factor that determines whether people pay attention to a particular communication is the amount of information they are receiving. Three characteristics of the message itself also attract attention: novelty, personal importance, and intensity.

Sometimes people do not comprehend and understand information the way it was meant because of semantic problems: the jargon might be difficult to comprehend, some words might have unclear meanings, other words might evoke unintended associations. Moreover, nonverbal cues are particularly difficult to interpret, especially when they seem to conflict with the verbal message. Perceptual problems are the other reason messages might not be understood accurately; people have expectations about what they expect to hear and have difficulty hearing messages that "break set." Some perceptual biases that distort information are stereotyping, projection, drawing unwarranted conclusions from limited facts, simplification, and fitting new data into preconceived beliefs.

Communicator expertise and trustworthiness both increase the credibility of the information being presented. When people perceive or anticipate some sort of threat in a communication, that decreases the likelihood the communication will be heard accurately. People avoid, distort, and forget information that threatens them. Two aspects of a communication can produce defensive listening: (1) a message that is personally threatening to the receiver; and (2) a message that is inconsistent with the beliefs of the receiver.

How the message is presented influences whether the receiver remembers the communication and takes some action consistent with the new information. The dimensions of presentation style that are discussed in terms of communication effectiveness are: (1) logic versus emotional appeals; (2) explicit versus implicit conclusions; (3) one-sided versus two-sided arguments; (4) primacy versus recency effects; (5) extreme versus moderate positions; (6) oral versus written communication; and (7) repetition versus single presentation. Also, the consistent reinforcement of management communication by management action both reminds workers of the communication and makes explicit the behaviors that are desired.

REVIEW QUESTIONS

1. Define communication.
2. What three aspects of the context of the communication influence which communications attract attention?
3. What is information overload?
4. Which characteristics of the informal communication network influence how much grapevine information employees send and receive?
5. Identify the three aspects of the message itself that attract people's attention.
6. What semantic problems frequently arise in communication, and how do they influence the way the communication is understood?
7. Briefly describe five common perceptual biases that distort accurate comprehension of information.
8. Why are people influenced by commercials in which the communicator is seen as neither expert nor trustworthy, but don't believe coworkers who also have low credibility?
9. What four predictions does cognitive dissonance research make about people's reactions to new information that is inconsistent with their previous beliefs?
10. Which is more effective in communication:
    a. Logic or emotional appeals?
    b. Explicit or implicit conclusions?
    c. One-sided or two-sided arguments?
    d. Primacy or recency effects?
    e. Extreme or moderate positions?
    f. Oral or written communication?
    g. Single presentation or repetition?
11. What is the inoculation effect?
12. Is there a one-to-one relationship between beliefs and behaviors? Why or why not?
13. What is the folly of rewarding A while hoping for B? What are some examples you have seen of this phenomenon?

REFERENCES

Abelson, R. P. Computers, polls, and public opinion—Some puzzles and paradoxes. *Transaction*, 1968, *5*, 20–27.

Aronson, E. *The social animal* (2nd ed.). San Francisco: W. H. Freeman, 1976.

Athanassiades, J. The distortion of upward communication in hierarchical organizations. *Academy of Management Journal*, 1973, *16*, 207–226.

Bem, D. J. *Beliefs, attitudes, and human affairs*. Belmont, Calif.: Brooks/Cole, 1970.

Davis, K. Management communication and the grapevine. *Harvard Business Review*, 1953, *31*, 43–49.

Davis, K. Success of chain-of-command oral communication in a manufacturing group. *Academy of Management Journal*, 1968, *11*, 379–387.

Davis, K. *Human relations at work* (5th ed.). New York: McGraw-Hill, 1978.

Gibb, J. Defensive communication. *Journal of Communication*, 1961, *3*, 141–148.

Haire, M., & Grunes, W. F. Perceptual defenses: Processes protecting an organized perception of another personality. *Human Relations*, 1950, *3*, 403–412.

Haney, W. V. *Communication and organizational behavior*. Homewood, Ill.: Irwin, 1973.

Kerr, S. On the folly of rewarding A while hoping for B. *Academy of Management Journal*, 1975, *18*, 769–783.

LaPiere, R. T. Attitudes vs. actions. *Social Forces*, 1934, *14*, 230–237.

Lawler, E. E., III, Porter, L. W., & Tennenbaum, A. Managers' attitudes toward interaction episodes. *Journal of Applied Psychology*, 1968, *52*, 432–439.

Leventhal, H. Findings and theory in the study of fear communications. In L. Berkowitz (Ed.), *Advances in experimental social psychology* (Vol. 5). New York: Academic Press, 1970, 119–186.

Lewis, P. V. *Organizational communication: The essence of effective management* (2nd ed.). Grid Publishing: Columbus, Ohio, 1980.

Likert, R. *New patterns of management*. New York: McGraw-Hill, 1961.

Luthans, R. *Organizational behavior* (3rd ed.). New York: McGraw-Hill, 1981.

Mann, L. *Social psychology*. New York: Wiley, 1969.

Mills, J., & Aronson, E. Opinion change as a function of communicator's attractiveness and desire to influence. *Journal of Personality and Social Psychology*, 1965, *1*, 173–177.

Mintzberg, H. *The nature of managerial work*. New York: Harper & Row, 1973.

Morgan, C. T., & King, R. A. *Introduction to psychology* (3rd ed.). New York: McGraw-Hill, 1966.

O'Reilly, C. A., & Pondy, L. R. Organizational communication. In S. Kerr (Ed.), *Organizational behavior*. Grid Publishing: Columbus, Ohio, 1979, pp. 119–150.

Read, W. H. Upward communication in industrial hierarchies. *Human Relations*, 1962, *15*, 3–16.

Reitz, H. J. *Behavior in organizations*. Homewood, Ill.: Irwin, 1981.

Rokeach, M. Attitude change and opinion change. *Public Opinion Quarterly*, 1966, *30*, 529–548.

Rue, L. W., & Byars, L. Communication in organizations. In L. L. Cummings & R. B. Dunham (Eds.), *Introduction to organizational behavior: Text and readings*. Homewood, Ill.: Irwin, 1980, pp. 556–572.

Secord, P. F., Backman, C. W., and Slavitt, D. R. Impression formation and interaction. In B. M. Staw (Ed.), *Psychological foundations of organizational behavior*. Santa Monica, Calif.: Goodyear, 1977.

Shaw, M. Communication networks. In L. Berkowitz (Ed.), *Advances in experimental social psychology* (Vol. I). New York: Academic Press, 1964.

Strauss, G., & Sayles, L. R. *Behavioral strategies for managers*. Englewood Cliffs, N.J.: Prentice-Hall, 1980.

Sutton, H., & Porter, L. W. A study of the grapevine in a governmental organization. *Personnel Psychology*, 1968, *21*, 223–230.

Vogel, A. Why don't employees speak up? *Personnel Administration*, 1967, *30* (May–June), pp. 20–22.

Wexley, K. N., & Yukl, G. A. *Organizational behavior and personnel psychology.* Homewood, Ill.: Irwin, 1977.

Whyte, W. F. *Money and motivation: An analysis of incentives in industry.* New York: Harper & Row, 1955.

Zimbardo, P. G., Ebbesen, E. B., & Maslach, C. *Influencing attitudes and changing behavior* (2nd ed.). Reading, Mass.: Addison-Wesley, 1977.

CHAPTER 15
PERFORMANCE APPRAISAL

Performance appraisal refers to the process of measuring and assessing the level of performance of organization members. Most organizations are rightfully quite interested in determining the quality and quantity of performance of their members, in assessing the potential their members demonstrate for future development, and in identifying areas of weakness that may require assistance and training. The process of appraising the performance of organization members is made difficult by the fact that the criteria of effective and ineffective performance are frequently difficult to define, the areas of performance for which a single individual is responsible are often unclear, and evaluations tend often to be based not on measurements of actual performance but on the perceptions and judgments of an individual's immediate supervisor or boss. Some of these vague, ambiguous, and judgmental characteristics of performance appraisal in organizations are unavoidable because of the complexity of managerial jobs and the difficulties inherent in clearly defining concrete criteria of effective performance. At the same time, however, a considerable proportion of the vagueness and ambiguity associated with the appraisal process can be attributed to inadequate attention being paid by the organization to the design and functioning of its performance appraisal systems. This chapter is devoted to a careful analysis of the performance appraisal process in organizations, with special emphasis upon ways in which organizations can improve their performance appraisal systems.

The chapter begins with a discussion of the various uses to which performance appraisal systems can be put by organizations. A wide variety of potential purposes exists, and the optimal route to take in the design and implementation of an appraisal system will obviously depend in part upon the uses to be made of the evaluations generated by the system. From this consideration of the purposes of performance appraisal, we then turn our attention to the specific methods and techniques that have been developed for conducting performance appraisals. The strengths and weaknesses of a variety of both traditional and more modern techniques are discussed and evaluated. Finally, we look in some detail at the issues and problems involved in implementing a performance appraisal system, with particular emphasis upon the actual appraisal interview between the manager who is doing the appraisal and the subordinate who is being evaluated. Such interviews frequently generate problems of miscommunication and misunderstanding, problems that can be avoided if the appraisal system is well-designed and the person conducting the appraisal is well-trained.

USES OF PERFORMANCE APPRAISAL

The primary goal of a performance appraisal system is to generate accurate and valid information regarding the behavior and performance of members of the organization. The more accurate and valid the information generated by the system, the greater its potential value to the organization.

While all organizations share this basic primary goal for their performance appraisal systems, a tremendous amount of variety exists in the specific uses that organizations make of the information on performance generated by their appraisal systems. These uses can be categorized under three broad headings: individual evaluation and motivation, individual development, and organizational planning.

Individual Evaluation and Motivation

The results of performance appraisals frequently serve as the basis for the regular evaluation of the performance of members of the organization. Whether an individual is judged to be competent or incompetent, effective or ineffective, promotable or unpromotable, and so on is based upon the information generated by the performance appraisal system. In addition, organizations frequently attempt to influence the motivation and future performance of their members by tying the administration of various rewards, such as salary increases and promotions, to the ratings generated by the appraisal system. As discussed in Chapter 7, pay for performance plans can have a positive impact on motivation and performance, and it is the performance appraisal system that provides the information and ratings upon which such plans are based.

Individual Development

In addition to serving as a basis for the administration of organizational rewards and punishments, the information generated by an appraisal system can also be employed to facilitate the personal development of organization members. A sound appraisal system can generate valid information regarding the areas of personal strength and weakness of individual employees. If such information is fed back to individuals in a clear, unambiguous, and nonthreatening manner, the information can serve two valuable purposes. First, if the information indicates that the person is performing effectively, the feedback process itself can be reinforcing and rewarding to the recipient by increasing feelings of self-esteem and personal competence. Second, if the information identifies an area of weakness, this can serve to stimulate a process of training and development in order to overcome the weaknesses identified. The appraisal process itself also provides a means of monitoring and assessing the results and improvements arising from a program of personal training and development.

Organizational Planning

Besides providing the basis for the evaluation, motivation, and development of individual organization members, an effective performance appraisal system also generates information that can be of significant value to the organization in planning its future human resource needs and policies. The members of an organization can be thought of as the human capital of the organization. A performance appraisal system generates information that permits the organization as a whole to assess the state of its human capital and plan its recruiting, staffing, and development policies in an informed, systematic, and rational manner.

Some information on the frequency and extent to which organizations use their performance appraisal systems for each of these purposes is summarized in Table 15-1. The findings contained in the table are the results of a survey of 216 organizations conducted in 1977 (Locher & Teel, 1977). The results indicate that by far the most frequent use of appraisals is in making compensation decisions, one of the ways in which appraisals can be used to attempt to influence motivation and performance. The only other use of appraisals cited by a majority of the organizations surveyed was performance improvement. The other uses that appear to be quite widespread are feedback (a second means of attempting to influence personal development) and promotion (a use aimed at influencing motivation). Of the remaining seven uses of appraisals covered in the survey, none appear to be employed by more than about 10 percent of the

TABLE 15-1
Uses made by organizations of information generated by performance appraisals

Individual Evaluation and Motivation

Uses	Small organizations (percent)	Large organizations (percent)	All (percent)
Compensation	80.6	62.2	71.3
Promotion	29.1	21.1	25.1
Transfer	7.4	8.3	7.9
Discharge	2.3	2.2	2.3
Layoff	0.6	0.0	0.3

Individual Development

Uses	Small organizations (percent)	Large organizations (percent)	All (percent)
Performance improvement	49.7	60.6	55.2
Feedback	20.6	37.8	29.3
Training	8.0	9.4	8.7

Organizational Planning

Uses	Small organizations (percent)	Large organizations (percent)	All (percent)
Documentation	11.4	10.0	10.7
Manpower planning	6.3	6.1	6.2
Research	2.9	0.0	1.4

SOURCE: Adapted from "Performance appraisal—A survey of current practices" by A. H. Locher & K. S. Teel, *Personnel Journal*, May, 1977. Costa Mesa, Calif., Copyright © 1977. Used by permission.

organizations, and some uses such as research and layoffs are extremely rare. It is also worthy to note that the various uses falling into the *organizational planning* category are not at all widespread. Organizations appear to recognize the potential utility of appraisal information for rewarding and punishing their members, as well as for facilitating their personal development. However, organizations are much less likely to make systematic use of the information generated by the appraisal system in planning their future human resource needs and policies.

THE FOCUS OF PERFORMANCE APPRAISAL

A performance appraisal system is essentially a measurement device. It consists of a series of steps or procedures that are designed to generate measures of the performance of individual organization members.

An important issue that must be addressed in designing a perform-ance appraisal system involves defining the nature of effective perform-ance and determining what constitute meaningful criteria of effective performance. The term *criterion* refers to any factor or variable that provides an indication of the effectiveness of the performance of an individual performing a particular job. Appropriate criteria of effective performance must be identified for each job for which a performance appraisal system is to be applied. Job analysis, discussed in detail in Chapter 2, can be extremely helpful in identifying appropriate criteria of effective performance for a job. Job analysis yields both a job description outlining all of the behaviors and activities that the job incumbent must perform, and a job specification that describes the traits and characteris-tics that the job incumbent must possess. As a result, the process of developing criteria of effective performance is greatly facilitated if the organization possesses up-to-date job analyses for the positions to be appraised.

The vast majority of jobs are sufficiently complex and multifaceted that it is impossible to identify a single criterion of effective performance that would adequately capture the overall performance effectiveness of a job incumbent (Dunnette, 1963). All but the simplest jobs have many dimensions and aspects; as a result, a performance appraisal system that hopes to reflect adequately the performance of a job incumbent must of necessity employ multiple criteria of effectiveness.

Characteristics of "Good" Criteria

Although it is impossible to identify any universal criteria of performance that are applicable to all jobs, it is possible to specify a number of characteristics that a criterion should possess if it is to be useful for performance appraisal.

1. A good criterion must be capable of being measured *reliably*. The concept of reliability of measurement has two components: stability and consistency. Stability implies that measures of the criterion taken at different times should yield approximately equal results. Consistency implies that measures of the criterion taken by different methods or by different people should be approximately equal to one another.
2. A good criterion should be capable of *discriminating* among individuals according to their performance. One of the purposes of performance appraisal is to evaluate the performance of organization members. If a criterion is such that scores or ratings on the criterion are identical for everyone, the criterion is of no use for distributing pay for performance, recommending candidates for promotion, assessing training and devel-opment needs, and so on.
3. A good criterion should be *sensitive* to the inputs and actions of the job incumbent. Since the purpose of performance appraisal systems is to

assess the effectiveness of individual organization members, the criteria of effectiveness employed in those systems must be primarily under the discretionary control of the person being assessed.

4. A good criterion should be *acceptable* to those individuals whose performance is being assessed. It is important that the people whose performance is being measured feel that the critera being employed provide a fair and accurate indication of their performance (Landy et al., 1980).

Activities versus Results

A final important issue regarding criteria of effectiveness has to do with whether the criteria adopted for use in performance appraisal should focus on the *activities* engaged in by the job incumbent or on the *results* achieved by the incumbent (Porter, Lawler, & Hackman, 1975). To take a sales job as an example, an appraisal system employing criteria focused on *activities* might assess total number of calls made, number of "cold" calls, courtesy in dealing with clients, speed with which complaints are handled, and so on. All of these criteria involve assessment of the activities engaged in by the salesperson. Criteria focusing upon *results* on the other hand might include measures of total sales volume, number of new customers added, percentage increase in sales volume, and so on. Measures of results pay no attention to how the results were achieved or what activities on the part of the person are responsible for generating the results.

Research indicates that measures of activities and measures of results each have advantages and disadvantages associated with them as criteria of performance effectiveness (Tosi, Rizzo, & Carroll, 1970). Since most organizations are, in the final analysis, concerned primarily about the results they achieve, it comes as no surprise that appraisal systems that focus on results have the advantage of encouraging and rewarding the attainment of those results desired by the organization. If individuals know that they are to be assessed on the basis of the actual results they achieve, this can serve as a strong motivational force to produce effectively.

A potential disadvantage associated with results-oriented criteria of performance lies in the fact that they may produce dysfunctional behavior regarding results not measured by the appraisal system. For example, an appraisal system that measures sales volume may result in salespersons selling a great deal, but these sales may have been facilitated by unrealistic claims and promises made by the sales staff. If the appraisal system does not include other measures, such as customer satisfaction or repeat business, as additional criteria of performance, the organization may not become aware of the dysfunctional behavior until irreparable damage has been done to the organization's reputation. A second disadvantage of results measures as criteria is that they may lead to frustration when failure to achieve results is caused by factors outside the direct control of the person being appraised, e.g., by faulty tools and equipment, by lack of support and cooperation from others, etc. (Peters & O'Connor, 1980; Peters et al., 1980). Finally, results measures as criteria of performance suffer from the fact that they generate no descriptive information regarding a person's activities that can be used in counseling and assisting an individual whose results are inadequate.

This latter shortcoming of results measures is a primary strength of measures of activities as criteria. When an appraisal system generates measures of the activities or behavior that an individual is or is not engaging in, the organization has information that can be helpful in designing a program of training and development for poor performers. However, it must be kept in mind that the organization will be unable to identify just who those poor performers are if it does not also have measures of results available. In addition to this inherent incompleteness of measures of activities, such measures also suffer from the fact that they may serve only to motivate the activities measured rather than the actual results that the activities are designed to facilitate. This runs the risk of generating excessive bureaucratic emphasis on the means and procedures employed rather than on actual accomplishments and results. The successful nonconformist cannot be accommodated within an appraisal system focusing purely on activities.

Our discussion of the advantages and disadvantages of each approach should make it clear that an effective appraisal system needs to include measures of *both* results *and* activities. Since actual results are the primary concern of the organization, it makes sense that individual members should be appraised and evaluated in regard to their actual contribution to those results. At the same time, however, in order to avoid some of the potential dysfunctional consequences of results measures, and also to facilitate the use of performance appraisal for personal development as well as evaluation and motivation, an appraisal system must include some measures of activities in addition to measures of results. A well-balanced appraisal system that can both motivate effective performance and assist in the development of individuals' skills and abilities requires both types of criteria of effectiveness.

TRADITIONAL METHODS OF APPRAISAL

The traditional approaches to performance appraisal are all based upon the judgments made by a superior regarding the performance of his or her subordinates. The methods differ from one another with regard to the precise types of judgments that the rater (superior) is required to make regarding the ratee (subordinate). We will discuss the three most common traditional appraisal techniques: graphic rating scales, global evaluations, and ranking methods.

Graphic Rating Scales

The graphic rating approach to performance appraisal requires the superior to rate the extent to which a subordinate possesses or has demonstrated each of a variety of traits or characteristics such as quantity of work, quality of work, initiative, job knowledge, cooperation, and so on. A typical example of a graphic rating scale is contained in Figure 15-1. As

FIGURE 15-1
Example of a typical graphic rating scale. (SOURCE: W. F. Glueck, *Personnel: A Diagnostic Approach*. Dallas: BPI, 1978, p. 302. Used by permission.)

Name_____ Dept. _____ Date_____	Out-standing	Good	Satis-factory	Fair	Unsatis-factory
Quantity of work: Volume of acceptable work under normal conditions Comments:	☐	☐	☐	☐	☐
Quality of work: Thoroughness, neatness, and accuracy of work Comments:	☐	☐	☐	☐	☐
Knowledge of job: Clear understanding of the facts or factors pertinent to the job Comments:	☐	☐	☐	☐	☐
Personal qualities: Personality, appearance, socia-bility, leadership, integrity Comments:	☐	☐	☐	☐	☐
Cooperation: Ability and willingness to work with associates, supervisors, and subordinates toward common goals Comments:	☐	☐	☐	☐	☐
Dependability: Conscientious, thorough, accurate, reliable with respect to attendance, lunch periods, reliefs, etc. Comments:	☐	☐	☐	☐	☐
Initiative: Earnestness in seeking increased responsibilities. Self-starting, unafraid to proceed alone Comments:	☐	☐	☐	☐	☐

can be seen, the superior is required to indicate on the graphic rating scale the extent to which he or she believes that the subordinate being rated has effectively demonstrated each of the characteristics listed.

The validity and utility of graphic rating scale appraisals will depend in part upon how the specific characteristics upon which the individual is rated were identified. In some organizations the characteristics or dimensions of performance are identified only intuitively by the people designing the performance appraisal system as characteristics that they personally think effective employees should exhibit. Such an approach is not to be recommended. The potential value of a graphic rating scale is greatly enhanced if the specific dimensions and characteristics to be rated are uniquely defined for each job on the basis of careful job analysis.

Graphic rating scales can take a wide variety of forms, of which the sample provided in Figure 15-1 is only a single example. Figure 15-2 illustrates nine different graphic rating formats that could be employed for assessing a single dimension of performance. Although there is no one best way to design a graphic rating scale, in general it is desirable to employ scales for which the meaning and interpretation of each of the response alternatives is clearly identified and defined for the rater.

Although graphic rating scales are extremely popular and in extremely wide use in organizations, they are not without a number of fairly serious drawbacks. Their primary weakness lies in the fact that graphic rating scales are not directly tied to the *behavior* of the person being rated. Such scales rate an individual on the basis of the superior's *judgments* regarding various work outcomes such as quantity and quality of performance, as well as the superior's *judgments* regarding the extent to which the individual possesses certain personal traits such as initiative and cooperativeness. Thus, graphic rating scales *require the rater to draw inferences and make personal judgments regarding the performance and personal characteristics of the person being rated. Graphic rating scales do not contain ratings or evaluations of the frequency of actual job behaviors that are related to successful performance.* This has a number of negative consequences when graphic rating scales are used to appraise performance.

1. It is extremely difficult for the ratees to determine how they should change their job behavior in order to obtain improved ratings. For example, being told as a ratee that your personality is unacceptable, or that your conscientiousness is only adequate does not provide you with much guidance regarding exactly what you need to start doing differently in order to obtain improved ratings.
2. A closely related problem lies in the difficulty of designing a program of training and development for employees whose ratings are low. If the ratings do not identify precisely which behaviors are deficient, then it is impossible to design training activities that could remedy the deficiencies.

(a) Quality   High |____|__✓__|____|____| Low

(b) Quality   High |____|__✓__|____|____| Low
                    5   4   3   2   1

(c) Quality |____|____|__✓__|____|____|

| Exceptionally high-quality workmanship | Work usually done in a superior way | Quality is average for this job | Work contains frequent flaws | Work is seldom satisfactory |

(d) Quality |____|____|____|____|_✓__|

| Too many errors | About average | Occasional errors | Almost never makes mistakes |

(e) Quality   5   (4)   3   2   1

(f)

Performance factors	Performance grade			
	Consistently superior	Sometimes superior	Consistently average	Consistently unsatisfactory
Quality: Accuracy Economy Neatness	☐	☒	☐	☐

(g) Quality

1 2 3 4 5	6 7 8 9 10	11 12 13 14 15	16 17 18 19 20	21 22 23 24 25
Poor	Below average		Above average	Excellent

(g) Quality — marked box at 16

(h) Quality of Work

    15   13   (11)   9   7   5   3   1

| Rejects and errors consistently rare | Work usually OK; errors seldom made | Work passable; needs to be checked often | Frequent errors and scrap; careless |

(i) Quality of Work

Judge the amount of scrap; consider the general care and accuracy of his work; also consider inspection record.
Poor, 1–6; Average, 7–18; Good, 19–25.   20

3. It is extremely difficult to use the results of appraisals to set specific goals for improvement. When the appraisal is based upon fairly vague and general traits such as cooperation and initiative, it is extremely difficult to set anything other than vague and general goals for improvement, such as "try to be more cooperative."

4. Since graphic rating scales do not assess specific concrete behavior it is difficult to use appraisal systems employing such scales to tie rewards to effective behavior. If appraisals are not based on specific behaviors, then reward systems based on the results of appraisals are likewise prohibited from rewarding specific effective work behavior.

Graphic rating scales also suffer from *resistance on the part of the superiors doing the ratings*. The fact that graphic rating scales require large leaps of inference on the part of raters from actual observed job behavior to ratings on general traits has a tendency to make raters uncomfortable. The rating scale forces raters to draw such inferences even if they do not feel in possession of adequate information to do so accurately. As a result, raters frequently express displeasure with graphic rating scales and also frequently experience extreme difficulty in discriminating among their subordinates in regard to the degree to which they possess such general traits and characteristics.

Finally, graphic rating scales frequently *generate defensive reactions and arguments when the ratings are fed back to the employee being rated*. People are generally quite willing to admit that they have certain shortcomings and that they may have made mistakes or performed less than optimally on certain occasions. However, people also tend to react very negatively and defensively when they feel that they are being stereotyped or classified as an undesirable type of person. Telling workers that their personalities are unsatisfactory or that they lack initiative can often strike at the very heart of their self-concepts and self-esteem and leave them feeling that they have no alternative but to fight back in order to defend themselves. Such fighting back will frequently take the form of arguing with the raters, challenging them to cite examples of the undesirable characteristics, and countering the raters' observations and inputs with examples designed to refute the negative personality classification implied by the ratings. Such interchanges are generally unpleasant and, more important, do nothing to help the ratees learn about areas of strength and weakness in their work behavior in order to improve in the future. This tendency to generate defensive reactions and arguments in appraisal interviews is thus a serious shortcoming of graphic rating scales.

FIGURE 15-2 *(opposite)*
Examples of alternative rating scale formats.   (SOURCE: R. M. Guion, *Personnel Testing*. New York: McGraw-Hill, 1965, p. 98. Used by permission.)

Single Global Evaluations

Graphic rating scales require superiors to rate subordinates on a variety of different dimensions. An alternative approach to appraisal is the single global evaluation which requires the superior to make only a single rating of the overall work effectiveness of each subordinate. Such single global evaluations have a number of advantages to recommend them (Porter, Lawler, & Hackman, 1975). First, there is evidence that such global ratings are highly reliable; i.e., the ratings by a superior tend to be quite stable over time and there also tends to be a relatively high degree of agreement when different raters are asked to rate the same subordinate. Second, since such ratings are based upon the rater's observations of all of the ratee's behavior and activities, the ratings tend to be quite inclusive. Third, single global ratings facilitate comparisons of employees relative to one another. This characteristic also facilitates use of global evaluations for purposes such as decision making regarding who should receive raises and promotions. Finally, supervisors and managers tend to be quite willing to make such overall global evaluations of performance.

Of course, single global ratings are not without their weaknesses and disadvantages, many of which they share with graphic rating scales. Most important is the fact that a single global rating is a judgment by a ratee's superior and is not directly tied to the concrete behavior of the person being rated. As a result, the global rating does not provide ratees with helpful feedback regarding precisely what they need to do in order to improve their performance in the future. The single global rating does not provide information that can be used for setting goals, designing personal training and development programs, and so on. In addition, global ratings are highly likely to generate defensiveness and conflict when ratings are low, particularly when the level of trust between superior and subordinate is not high.

Ranking Methods

An alternative traditional approach to graphic rating scales and single global evaluations involves having superiors rank their subordinates in order of their performance effectiveness. Ranking methods are advantageous when the results of performance evaluations must be used for making concrete personnel decisions, since rankings do not permit people to be rated equally. If one person is to be promoted, then the person ranked first can be chosen to receive the promotion. When rating scales are used there may be more than one person who received the highest possible rating, and thus the results of the appraisal process may not provide unambiguous guidance for personnel decision making.

Ranking methods are not without their weaknesses however. First, as is the case with single global evaluations, rankings must be based on only a single global dimension of work effectiveness and hence cannot take into account the complex and multi-faceted nature of work effectiveness. Second, ranking becomes cumbersome and practically impossible as the number of subordinates to be ranked becomes large. Finally, although an advantage of rankings is their ability to facilitate personnel decisions, this advantage has an accompanying risk in that ranking procedures may *force* superiors to distinguish *artificially* between individuals whose performance is in fact equally effective. A superior with two equally outstanding subordinates can give them both outstanding ratings on a global evaluation rating scale, but must rate one of them first and the other second if a ranking procedure is employed. Thus, rankings may make it appear that individuals differ from one another in their competence and effectiveness when in reality (and in the judgment of their superior) no differences exist between the two.

It is also important to note that the 1978 U.S. Civil Service Reform Act prohibits the use of ranking methods for the appraisal of U.S. federal employees. The act requires that employees of the federal government be appraised on the basis of how well they are performing their jobs, not on the basis of a comparison with other individuals. It remains to be seen whether this prohibition will spread to other jurisdictions or whether it will be incorporated into government guidelines or regulations regarding employment practices outside government.

Common Rating Errors

In addition to the problems already identified regarding the various traditional performance appraisal techniques, there also exist a number of fairly common errors to which people are prone when making judgments and ratings about others.

Strictness and Leniency

Some individuals, when filling out rating scales on their employees, have a tendency to rate everyone quite strictly or harshly. A person prone to such a bias would tend to rate good employees as only average and average employees as poor. All of their ratings are lower or more strict than the actual performance of their subordinates warrants. Individuals who rate their employees in such a manner are said to exhibit a strictness or harshness bias in their ratings.

Just the opposite problem is involved in a leniency bias. Superiors with a leniency bias would tend to rate all their subordinates more positively than the subordinates' performance actually warranted. Such a bias is undesirable since it results in subordinates appearing to be more competent than in fact they are.

Examples of strictness and leniency biases are contained in Figure

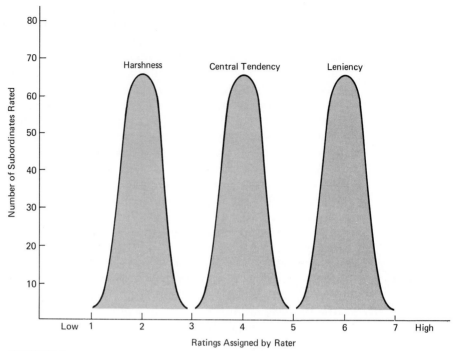

FIGURE 15-3
Examples of ratings that would be generated by raters exhibiting harshness, central tendency, and leniency errors.

15-3. The distribution of ratings on the left of the figure would indicate a strictness bias, since the ratings vary only from 1 to 3, with an average of 2. The right-hand distribution indicates a leniency bias, since everyone in this case is rated between 5 and 7, and the average rating is 6.

Central Tendency

Some raters are somewhat timid about using the extreme endpoints of rating scales. They dislike being too harsh with anyone by giving them an extremely low rating, and they also may feel that no one is really good enough to get the highest possible ratings. The outcome of this sort of attitude can be everyone being rated very close to average, ratings that tend to be at or close to the central point of the rating scale. Individuals whose ratings all converge near the midpoint of the rating scale are said to be exhibiting a central tendency bias. Figure 15-3 also shows what the distribution of ratings would look like for a rater with a central tendency bias. Everyone gets a rating between 3 and 5 and the average rating is 4. The problem created by a central tendency bias is that it makes perform- ance ratings almost useless for identifying either highly effective employees who are candidates for promotion on the one hand, or problem employees who require counseling and training on the other.

Halo

Some individuals have a tendency when filling out performance rating scales to rate a subordinate very similarly on all of the dimensions or characteristics being assessed. Thus, the person who is rated high on quantity of performance will also be rated high on quality, high on initiative, high on cooperation, and so on. This is not a problem as long as the person being rated really *is* high on all of the dimensions being assessed (or low on all of them, as the case may be). However, it is frequently the case that an employee may be very high on some dimensions, average on some, and low on still others. A superior who rates such a person the same (whether high, medium, or low) on all dimensions is said to exhibit a halo effect. The term *halo* is used, since all of the superior's ratings fall within a narrow range or halo of one another. The problem created by a halo effect is that it makes it impossible to identify the areas of strength of employees who are generally weak and, conversely, the areas of weakness which need development for employees who are generally strong (Cooper, 1981).

Recency

Ideally, ratings of employee performance should be based upon systematic observations of an employee's performance over the entire rating period (frequently 1 year). Unfortunately, it is often the case that a superior rating a subordinate is strongly influenced by the most recent events and observations of the subordinate's performance. Things that happened recently tend to be remembered more clearly and to be most salient in the mind of the rater. Thus, "annual" reviews tend to be inordinately influenced by what the rater has observed of the subordinate over the few weeks or months immediately preceding the performance appraisal.

Personal Bias

Some individuals are, unfortunately, prone to be personally biased toward others. Such bias may be based upon the past history of the relationship between the two individuals, stereotypes regarding racial or ethnic groups, role stereotypes, and so on. Regardless of its basis or cause, personal bias is a source of error in performance appraisal and impedes the capacity of an appraisal system to serve the organizational purposes for which it was designed.

Contrast Effect

Managers are frequently involved in appraising several subordinates within a fairly short time. When this is the case, the manager's appraisal of each subordinate can be influenced by the evaluation of the preceding subordinate. Thus, a subordinate whose true performance is only average, but who is evaluated immediately after someone whose performance is extremely poor, may receive a fairly positive rating. This can occur as a result of the contrast created in the mind of the person doing the appraisal between the very poor performer and the average performer. Exactly the opposite effect could occur if the average performer had the misfortune to be evaluated immediately after a truly outstanding performer.

Attribution Errors

Attributions refer to the assumptions that we make regarding the reasons for or causes of our behavior or the behavior of others (Kelley, 1973). Attributions fall into two general categories: internal and external. When we assume that the reason or cause for a person's behavior was some characteristic of that person (e.g., his or her personality), we are making an *internal attribution* (e.g., "She performed effectively in that situation because she is an intelligent and persistent person."). *External attributions*, on the other hand, occur when we conclude that the primary cause of a person's behavior resides not within the person, but somewhere in the external environment (e.g., "She performed effectively in that situation because her boss instructed her in precisely what to do every step of the way.").

The relevance of attribution processes to performance appraisal has been pointed out by J. Feldman (1981). In evaluating subordinates, managers are formalizing and recording the extent to which they *attribute* the subordinates' performance to positive or negative internal characteristics of the individuals. Subordinates evaluated most positively are those who have performed effectively *and* whose performance is attributed by their supervisors to the possession of positive personal characteristics. Subordinates evaluated negatively are those who have performed poorly *and* whose poor performance is attributed by the supervisor to shortcomings in the person (i.e., internal factors) rather than to difficulties encountered in the situation (i.e., external factors). This effect is particularly strong when poor performance is attributed to lack of *effort* on the part of the subordinate rather than to lack of ability (Knowlton & Mitchell, 1980).

What is particularly important for organizations to take into account in designing appraisal systems is the fact that untrained individuals are prone to make what is referred to as the *fundamental attribution error* (Ross, 1977). The fundamental attribution error refers to the tendency of individuals to make internal attributions regarding the behavior of others even when such attributions are unwarranted or inaccurate. In simpler language, what this means is that we all have a tendency to assume that the behavior of others is determined primarily by some fairly small number of very consistent personality traits or characteristics. In observing and attempting to understand the reasons for another person's behavior we tend to discount the importance of external situational factors and to overemphasize internal personality characteristics as causes of the behavior. The implication of the fundamental attribution error for performance appraisal is that superiors, in evaluating subordinates, will tend to attribute positive performance to positive personality characteristics and negative performance to negative personality characteristics and will tend to overlook situational factors that may be influencing behavior. The fundamental attribution error will not create errors in appraisal if it turns out to be the case that those examples of behavior upon which the superiors base their evaluations turn out by chance to all have been instances in which the subordinates' effectiveness was purely determined by their personal characteristics. If, however, as is much more likely, the superior draws inferences about subordinates' personal characteristics on the basis of observations of performance in situations where success or failure was in part determined by situational factors beyond the subordinates' control, serious errors in evaluation may result.

Reducing Rating Errors

Since rating errors can seriously undermine the value to an organization of its performance appraisal system, a good deal of effort has been focused upon the development of methods for reducing or eliminating rating errors (Bernardin & Walter, 1977; Burnaska & Hollman, 1974; Latham & Wexley, 1981). The following steps can help an organization reduce errors and problems in its appraisal system.

1. Superiors should be encouraged to observe the performance of their subordinates regularly and to keep a record of their observations.
2. Rating scales should be carefully constructed in the following manner:
   a. Each dimension on the rating scale should be designed to assess only one single important work activity.
   b. The dimensions included on the rating scale should all be important, meaningful, and clearly stated.
   c. The words used to define various points along the rating scale (e.g., "excellent," "poor," etc.) should be clearly and unambiguously defined for the rater in terms of employee behavior.
3. Raters should not be required to evaluate a large number of subordinates at any one time.
4. Raters should be made conscious of common rating errors such as strictness and leniency, central tendency, halo, and attributional errors and trained to avoid them.

Providing managers with training in the effective use of performance appraisal techniques bears special emphasis. There is now considerable evidence that errors in performance appraisal *cannot* be overcome purely by focusing upon the development and design of better rating instruments. However, carefully developed training programs such as that designed by Latham, Wexley, and Pursell (1975) have been found to minimize rating errors in the appraisal process (Borman, 1979; Bernardin & Buckley, 1979; Bernardin & Pence, 1980).

MODERN APPRAISAL TECHNIQUES

Because of the pervasiveness and importance of performance appraisal in organizations, a good deal of effort has been invested in the development of new performance appraisal techniques over the past few years. The goal of these efforts has been to design new methods of appraising and evaluating performance that are free of the errors and difficulties associated with the more traditional techniques. We will examine three of the modern appraisal techniques that have been developed: behaviorally anchored rating scales (BARS), behavioral observation scales (BOS), and management by objectives (MBO).

Behaviorally Anchored Rating Scales (BARS)

Behaviorally anchored rating scales (BARS), which are sometimes also referred to as behavioral expectation scales (BES), were first developed by Smith and Kendall (1963). BARS are similar to graphic rating scales in that both appraisal techniques present the rater with a series of dimensions or qualities along which the rater is asked to rate or appraise the person being evaluated. However, BARS differ dramatically from graphic rating scales: (1) in the way in which the dimensions along which subordinates are to be rated are identified; and (2) in the way in which the various alternative responses along the rating scale are described or "anchored."

Graphic rating scales usually consist of a list of general personal characteristics or personality traits such as initiative, cooperativeness, and judgment. The rater then judges the person being appraised on each dimension on a scale varying from *low* to *high* or from *poor* to *excellent*, or some similar terms. The characteristics being judged are usually extremely broad and general, and the rater is generally given little or no specific guidance regarding what types of work behavior qualify a person for each of the possible ratings along the scales. The rater must use his or her personal judgment in deciding how the employee's work performance can be classified into one of the available alternative responses on the rating scales.

BARS, on the other hand, require the rater to evaluate the ratee on a list of dimensions of work behavior that have been carefully derived for the specific job being performed by the person being evaluated. BARS do not evaluate individuals on the basis of their possession of general personality characteristics, but on the basis of the extent to which they exhibit effective behavior relevant to the specific demands of their jobs. Further, each response alternative along the dimensions of a **BARS** is labeled or "anchored" with examples of specific job behaviors corresponding to good performance, average performance, poor performance, and so on. These examples help the raters to tie their ratings directly to the job behavior of the person being rated.

An example of a BARS is contained in Figure 15-4. The example consists of a single dimension of a BARS developed for the job of grocery clerk. The dimension of the grocery clerk's job being evaluated by the scale contained in the figure is *judgment and knowledge*. As the example makes

FIGURE 15-4
A behaviorally anchored rating scale designed to assess the dimension of judgment and knowledge for the job of grocery clerk. (SOURCE: L. Fogli, C. L. Hulin, and M. R. Blood, "Development of First-Level Behavioral Job Criteria," *Journal of Applied Psychology,* 55, 1971, pp. 3–8. Copyright © 1971 by the American Psychological Association. Reprinted by permission of the authors.)

Extremely good performance	7	—
	—	—By knowing the price of items, this checker would be expected to look for mismarked and unmarked items.
Good performance	6	—
	—	—You can expect this checker to be aware of items that constantly fluctuate in price. —You can expect this checker to know the various sizes of cans — No. 303, No. 2½.
Slightly good performance	5	—
	—	—When in doubt, this checker would ask the other clerk if the item is taxable.
	—	—This checker can be expected to verify with another checker a discrepancy between the shelf and the marked price before ringing up that item.
Neither poor nor good performance	4	—
	—	—When operating the quick check, the lights are flashing, this checker can be expected to check out a customer with 15 items.
Slightly poor performance	3	—
	—	—You could expect this checker to ask the customer the price of an item that he does not know.
	—	—In the daily course of personal relationships, may be expected to linger in long conversations with a customer or another checker.
Poor performance	2	—
	—	—In order to take a break, this checker can be expected to block off the checkstand with people in line.
Extremely poor performance	1	—

clear, **BARS** facilitate the evaluation process by providing the person doing the evaluation with precise examples of the type of expected job behavior associated with each of the alternative ratings along the scale. This reduces the amount of personal judgment and inference required of the rater and helps to tie the appraisal process directly to work behavior.

Advantages and Disadvantages of BARS

Although **BARS** have the advantages of evaluating individuals along dimensions relevant to their own jobs and tying evaluations directly to job behavior, one of their primary disadvantages lies in the considerable time and expense involved in their design and development. The process requires the active involvement and participation of a large number of employees of the organization in determining the *dimensions* of effective performance on the job as well as *behavioral examples* of the various levels of performance along each dimension. Given the complexity involved in this development process, it is essential that an organization carefully examine the expected costs and benefits prior to undertaking the development of BARS.

A wide variety of *potential advantages* have been claimed for **BARS**. Among them are the following:

1. A reduction in rating errors as a result of the following facts:
   a. Job dimensions are clearly defined for the rater and relevant to the job being performed by the person being rated.
   b. The behavioral anchors (critical incidents) clearly define the response categories available to the rater.
2. A performance appraisal system that is more reliable, valid, meaningful, and complete since the system is developed with the active participation of employees who possess full knowledge of the demands and requirements of the job.
3. A higher degree of acceptance and commitment to the appraisal system on the part of both employees and supervisors as a result of their having been actively and directly involved in the design of the system.
4. A reduction in the degree of defensiveness and conflict generated by appraisals, since individuals are evaluated on the basis of their specific job behavior, not their personalities.
5. An improved ability to identify clearly areas of specific performance deficiency and needs for training and development activities.

While **BARS** clearly possess a broad range of potential advantages, it is equally clear that there are a number of *disadvantages* associated with them.

1. A primary drawback of BARS is the time, effort, and expense involved in their development.

2. The drawback of high development costs is compounded by the fact that separate BARS are needed for each job (or at least each family of jobs) in an organization. The investment required for development may thus be justifiable only for jobs having a large number of incumbents.

3. BARS are primarily applicable to jobs whose major components consist of physically observable behavior. Jobs having a high component of mental activity, e.g., a research scientist or creative writer, do not lend themselves as readily to evaluation using behaviorally anchored techniques.

4. Raters sometimes experience difficulty in determining the degree of similarity between the behavior of the employee that they have observed and the particular critical incidents employed as anchors of the BARS (Borman, 1979).

BARS do provide an effective approach to performance appraisal. BARS clearly outperform graphic rating scales made up on the spur of the moment by a manager in need of an appraisal device for immediate use. At the same time, however, research does not indicate that BARS are clearly superior in accuracy or validity to other appraisal techniques that have been carefully designed, researched, and tested (Bernardin, 1977; Jacobs et al., 1980; Kingstrom & Bass, 1981; Landy & Farr, 1980; Schwab et al., 1975). BARS should still be considered a serious candidate for use in an organization's appraisal system, however. Recent research has begun to clarify some of the problems in the development and use of BARS (Bernardin & Smith, 1981), and new results indicate a number of positive spin-offs to the organization from the implementation of BARS in terms of improved attitudes and reduced tension regarding appraisals (Ivancevich, 1980).

Behavioral Observation Scales (BOS)

Behavioral observation scales, or BOS, are an approach to performance appraisal developed in an attempt to capitalize on some of the strengths of the BARS approach while avoiding some of its weaknesses (Latham & Wexley, 1977; Latham, Fay, & Saari, 1979). In the BARS approach, critical incidents of work behavior are used to "anchor" the various rating points along each performance dimension. These behavioral anchors are stated in terms of the types of behavior that might be *expected* of the job incumbent being evaluated. The BOS approach also employs critical incidents of work behavior. However, for each performance dimension evaluated by a BOS, a *number* of critical incidents are listed, and the appraiser *rates* the extent to which he or she has actually *observed* the person being rated engaging in that behavior on a 5-point scale varying from *almost never* to *almost always*. An example of one performance dimension from a BOS is contained in Figure 15-5. An employee's total

I. Overcoming Resistance to Change*

(1) Describes the details of the change to subordinates.

Almost Never   1   2   3   4   5   Almost Always

(2) Explains why the change is necessary.

Almost Never   1   2   3   4   5   Almost Always

(3) Discusses how the change will affect the employee.

Almost Never   1   2   3   4   5   Almost Always

(4) Listens to the employee's concerns.

Almost Never   1   2   3   4   5   Almost Always

(5) Asks the employee for help in making the change work.

Almost Never   1   2   3   4   5   Almost Always

(6) If necessary, specifies the date for a follow-up meeting to respond to the employee's concerns.

Almost Never   1   2   3   4   5   Almost Always

Total = _____

Below Adequate 6-10	Adequate 11-15	Full 16-20	Excellent 21-25	Superior* 26-30

*Scores are set by management.

FIGURE 15-5
An Example of a BOS Performance Dimension for evaluating managers. (SOURCE: G. P. Latham and K. N. Wexley, *Improving Productivity through Performance Appraisal.* Reading, Mass: Addison-Wesley, 1981, p. 56. Used by permission.)

score on each dimension is determined by adding up his or her ratings on each of the critical incidents (or *behavior items*) included in that dimension. The development of a BOS for a job follows a series of steps that bear a high degree of similarity to the comparable process for BARS. Job incumbents, working with expert job analysts, identify the *performance dimensions* of the job, as well as *behavioral examples* of effective and ineffective behavior on each dimension.

Advantages and Disadvantages of BOS

BOS share with BARS the advantages of: (1) being relatively reliable and valid as a result of being based upon actual employee *behavior*; (2) generating high levels of employee *acceptance* and *understanding* as a result of employee involvement in their development; and (3) providing employees with *useful feedback* on their job behavior that can be employed for the design of plans for development and performance improvement. The developers of BOS also argue that since BOS focus attention on *actual observed* job behavior, rather than expected behavior, that the behavioral items included in a BOS help focus a manager's attention on what to look for during an appraisal period and also help facilitate the manager's recall of employee behavior during the appraisal process (Latham & Wexley, 1981).

Naturally, BOS share many of the disadvantages of BARS as well. BOS are relatively time-consuming and expensive to develop and are difficult to apply to jobs whose primary components may not be physically observable.

Unfortunately, no empirical comparisons of BARS and BOS have yet been conducted in industrial settings. Comparisons carried out in university settings have found BOS to be as good as or better than BARS in reducing rating errors and biases (Bernardin, 1977; Bernardin et al., 1976). BOS appear to be an interesting and promising development on the appraisal scene, although some disagreement exists regarding whether they are superior or inferior to BARS as an appraisal technique (Bernardin & Kane, 1980; Latham et al., 1980).

Management by Objectives (MBO)

Management by objectives, or MBO, programs were discussed in Chapter 6 as an example of an application of goal-setting theory to increasing the motivation and performance of organization members. In addition, an MBO system can also serve as the basis for the design of an organization's performance appraisal system, and is particularly well-suited to higher-level managerial jobs for which techniques such as BARS and BOS may be inappropriate or inapplicable.

MBO is an example of a results-based method of performance appraisal. Under MBO, individuals are evaluated on the basis of *what* they accomplish, not *how* they get the job done. There are two important steps involved in the application of MBO to performance appraisal: the first step is goal-setting and the second step is performance review.

In the goal-setting phase of MBO each individual meets with his or her immediate supervisor to discuss plans for the coming performance period (usually 1 year) and to agree on performance goals for the period. As pointed out in our discussion of goal-setting theory in Chapter 6, if goals are to maximize motivation, they must be clear and specific, sufficiently difficult to be challenging, and personally accepted by the individual seeking them. Thus, in the goal-setting phase of MBO the manager's role is to help subordinates to identify specific, realistic, and challenging performance goals for the coming year. Ensuring that goals are specific implies a need both: (1) to identify specific measurement criteria that can be employed in determining whether a goal has been met or not; and (2) to agree on time deadlines and intermediate review dates at which agreed-upon levels of progress should have been attained. Ensuring that goals are both challenging and realistic implies a need for the manager to involve the subordinate actively in the goal-setting process. The active participation of the individual performer can help to ensure that goals are set at a sufficiently difficult level to be challenging but not at such a high level as to be completely unrealistic and hence unattainable. Thus, the outcome of the goal-setting phase of MBO is a set of specific measurable goals (each with agreed-upon dates for review and accomplishment) that the individual personally identifies with and views as challenging but realistic.

In the second performance review phase of MBO, the manager and subordinate meet to discuss the subordinate's progress in attaining his or her goals. The subordinate's performance is appraised and evaluated with regard to the specific goals and objectives agreed to in the initial goal-setting meeting. Appraisal is thus based upon performance and concrete results. It is not based upon what activities the subordinate engaged in to obtain those results, nor is it based on the extent to which the subordinate's boss feels that he or she possesses vague and general personality characteristics such as cooperativeness or initiative. Table 15-2 contains an example of a hypothetical MBO evaluation report for a salesperson. The first column of the report, headed *period objective*, would have been the outcome of the initial goal-setting meeting between the salesperson and his or her manager. At the end of the performance period the *accomplishments* and *variance* columns would be filled in and serve as the basis for the salesperson's evaluation in the performance review meeting.

Advantages and Disadvantages of MBO

The major advantages claimed for MBO are as follows:

- By encouraging individuals to set specific, challenging goals, MBO has the potential of increasing employee motivation and performance, in addition to serving as the basis for performance appraisal.
- Since organizations are ultimately concerned with concrete results, it makes sense to evaluate employees on the basis of results they have personally accomplished.

TABLE 15-2
An MBO evaluation report for a salesperson

Objectives set	Period objective	Accomplishments	Variance
1. Number of sales calls	100	104	104%
2. Number of new customers contacted	20	18	90
3. Number of wholesalers stocking new product 117	30	30	100
4. Sales of product 12	10,000	9,750	92.5
5. Sales of product 17	17,000	18,700	110
6. Customer complaints/Service calls	35	11	66⅔
7. Number of sales correspondence courses successfully completed	4	2	50
8. Number of sales reports in home office within 1 day of end of month	12	10	80

SOURCE: W. F. Glueck, *Personnel: A diagnostic approach.* Dallas: BPI, 1978, p. 307. Used by permission.

- Employees know precisely what is expected of them and exactly what they must achieve if they are to be evaluated positively.
- Systematic goal setting throughout the organization facilitates planning and coordination.

However, a decision to adopt MBO as a performance appraisal technique must take into account not only the foregoing advantages of MBO, but also the following disadvantages:

- The heavy emphasis of MBO on results may lead to a lack of attention to *how* those results are being accomplished. This has two potential negative side effects. First, individuals may be accomplishing their goals in a fashion that will have negative long-run side effects for the organization, e.g., by cutting corners or by engaging in illegal or unethical behavior. Second, although individuals may know very clearly *what* they are supposed to accomplish, they may be very unclear regarding *how* they should go about achieving their goals. Thus, there is a risk that managers may not give enough attention to providing their subordinates with advice and assistance regarding how to achieve their goals effectively.
- MBO makes it difficult to compare the level of performance of different individuals. Since each person is evaluated with regard to his or her personal goals, valid comparisons of individuals require comparisons of both their levels of accomplishment and the difficulty of their goals. Such comparisons can only be based on the judgment of the manager making the comparisons. This shortcoming is particularly salient when personnel decisions regarding promotions, replacements, etc., must be made.
- MBO programs are difficult to implement effectively. We address this problem in more detail in the next section.

Implementation Problems

Although MBO programs have the potential both to increase motivation and performance and to provide a sound results-based appraisal system, their track record in organizations is decidedly mixed (Tosi, Rizzo, & Carroll, 1970). The primary factor that appears to distinguish effective and ineffective MBO programs seems to be the extent to which the implementation of MBO recognizes the need for special skills on the part of managers conducting MBO goal-setting and performance appraisal meetings (Jamieson, 1973).

In order for MBO to be effective both from the motivational and the appraisal viewpoints, managers must be especially skilled at conducting goal-setting and appraisal interviews. The goal-setting process must be *participative*; the manager must be a skilled *listener*, taking into account the skills, needs, and aspirations of the individual involved. If the manager simply *tells* the subordinate what his or her goals *should* be for the upcoming period, it is extremely unlikely that the subordinate will personally *accept* those goals and be *committed* to attaining them. Similarly, in the appraisal phase of MBO the manager requires skills in *listening* and *coaching*, so that the process serves not only to evaluate the past performance of the individual but also serves to *help* the subordinate to perform even more effectively in the future.

It is rarely the case that all of the managers in an organization possess all the necessary skills for conducting effective goal-setting and appraisal meetings. This implies that a critical component of the successful implementation of MBO must be a program of management training and development designed to assist managers in the acquisition of the necessary skills. MBO programs that fail to address this critical skill component are very likely doomed from the outset.

Comparison of Appraisal Techniques

We have now discussed three traditional methods of performance appraisal: graphic rating scales, global evaluations, and rankings. We have also discussed three more modern appraisal techniques: behaviorally anchored rating scales (BARS), behavioral observation scales (BOS), and management by objectives (MBO). Table 15-3 compares these six approaches to performance appraisal on a number of dimensions relevant to the organization in the design of its appraisal system. As the table makes obvious, there is a good deal of variation among the different techniques in regard to their strengths and weaknesses, and no single approach is without its shortcomings. The design and implementation of an appraisal system obviously demands that trade-offs be made. What is essential, given the importance and pervasiveness of the appraisal process in organizations, is that these trade-offs be made in an intelligent and informed fashion. The material that we have presented regarding each of the techniques (summarized in Table 15-3) provides a basis for such intelligent and informed decisions.

MANAGING THE APPRAISAL PROCESS

Up to this point we have looked at the different uses to which performance appraisals can be put, discussed alternative aspects of work performance that appraisals may focus upon, and reviewed a variety of the methods and techniques employed by organizations in evaluating the performance of their members. We now turn to an examination of the actual implementation of the appraisal process in organizations. We'll discuss *who* does (or should do) performance appraisals, *when* and how often appraisals are (or

TABLE 15-3
Evaluation of performance appraisal techniques on a variety of critical dimensions

	Traditional Techniques			Modern Techniques		
	Graphic rating scales	Single global evaluations	Rankings	BARS	BOS	MBO
Accuracy of evaluations	Low	Moderate	Low	High	High	High
Usefulness for personnel decisions	Moderate	High	High	Moderate	Moderate	Moderate
Usefulness for reward allocation	Low	Moderate	Moderate	High	High	High
Usefulness for identifying training and development needs	Very low	Very low	Very low	High	High	Moderate
Costs of development (time and money)	Low	Very low	Very low	High	High	Moderate/high
Costs of administration (time and money)	Low	Very low	Low	Moderate	Moderate	Moderate/high
Potential to motivate ratees	Low	Low	Low	Moderate	Moderate/high	High
Acceptability to ratees	Low/moderate	Low/moderate	Low	High	High	High
Acceptability to raters	Low/moderate	Moderate	Low	High	High	High
Skills required of raters	Low	Low	Low	Moderate	Moderate	High

should be) done, and finally we'll take a close look at the actual *appraisal interview* between the person doing the evaluation and the person being evaluated.

Who Evaluates

In the vast majority of organizations performance appraisals are conducted by the *immediate* superior of the person being evaluated (Bureau of National Affairs [BNA] Survey, 1975). This practice is so common that many individuals and organizations assume that it is the *only* feasible way to conduct performance appraisals. The fact of the matter is that there are a variety of options available that are worthy of consideration when appraisal systems are being designed.

Beyond the basic assumption that the immediate superior should and must conduct employee evaluations, there are a number of factors indicating the desirability of such a practice. First, the immediate supervisor is often in the best position to observe the employee's performance frequently over the evaluation period. Second, the superior is well-positioned to analyze and interpret the performance of the subordinate in light of the goals and plans of the organization. Finally, depending upon the design of the organization's reward systems (discussed in Chapter 7), the superior may be able to link rewards to the evaluations he or she assigns to subordinates.

A slight variation on this basic approach to appraisal involves having evaluation conducted by a *group or panel of superiors*. The superiors may be all from the same hierarchical level, or may also include managers from the next higher level in the hierarchy. Such an approach will only be desirable when all of the managers involved in the process have been in a position actually to observe the subordinate's performance during the evaluation period. If this is the case, such a group evaluation has the potential for greater reliability and validity of ratings as a result of the pooling of the perceptions and opinions of a variety of observers (Cummings & Schwab, 1973). In spite of these potential benefits, the results of the BNA (1975) survey referred to previously indicate that such group evaluations are almost never used.

A more radical departure from evaluation by the immediate superior is *peer evaluation*. As its name suggests, peer evaluation requires individuals to be evaluated by a group of their work peers from the same hierarchical level in the organization. There are a number of conditions that must be met if peer evaluations are to be successful: first, the peers doing the evaluations must be in a position that permits them frequent opportunities to observe each other's behavior and effectiveness; second, there must be a high level of trust among the peers evaluating one another; and finally, the peers must not be in a position where they are in direct competition for the same raises or promotions (Glueck, 1978). When these conditions are met, research indicates that peer evaluations can have a variety of positive outcomes for the organization (Lewin & Zwany, 1976). In spite of this, the use of peer reviews for appraisal is extremely rare (BNA Survey, 1975), primarily because of resistance to their use from organization members (Love, 1981; Cederblom & Lounsbury, 1980).

Subordinates can also be involved in the appraisal process, the argument being that subordinates are often well-placed to observe a great deal of their superior's performance. Subordinate evaluations are infrequently used and when they are used tend to be focused upon providing useful developmental feedback to the superior rather than being used as the primary basis for the superior's evaluation (Ghorpade & Lackritz, 1981).

Self-evaluations similarly tend to be used more for purposes of development than for evaluation itself. Self-evaluation appears to be in slightly wider use than some of the other, alternative approaches to evaluation (5 percent of firms in the BNA survey reported use of self-evaluations). Self-evaluations can be particularly helpful in stimulating an individual to think realistically about his or her areas of personal strength and weakness (Levine, 1980; Levine et al., 1977).

A final option, again infrequently used, involves employing *outside experts* to observe and evaluate the performance of organization members (this technique is sometimes referred to as *field review*). The potential advantage of this approach is that uninvolved outside experts evaluate individuals in a standardized and unbiased fashion. The infrequent use of the approach is probably justified in light of the fact that: (1) it is extremely costly; (2) it forces evaluations to be based upon observations of an extremely small sample of an individual's behavior; and (3) by removing the superior from the evaluation process, the likelihood of the superior becoming actively involved in the development and coaching of his or her subordinates is greatly diminished.

When to Evaluate

The BNA (1975) survey found that 75 percent of white-collar workers and 58 percent of blue-collar workers were evaluated annually, while 25 percent of white-collar and 30 percent of blue-collar workers were evaluated semiannually. Only about 10 percent of those surveyed were evaluated more often than once every 6 months. Unfortunately, there is no straightforward rule that can be applied in determining when and how often individuals should be evaluated. There are, however, certain guidelines that may be applied.

From the standpoint of employee counseling and development, frequent appraisals are desirable. Research indicates that feedback is most effective in influencing and changing behavior when it follows almost immediately after the behavior involved (Cook, 1968). This implies the desirability of frequent, if not continuous, appraisal meetings between supervisor and subordinate.

From the standpoint of employee evaluation, on the other hand, such frequent appraisals may not be desirable. Glueck (1978) has suggested the potential advantage of tying appraisals into the natural work cycles of the subordinate. In a similar vein, Porter, Lawler, & Hackman (1975) point out the desirability of timing evaluations such that they correspond to points at which the positive or negative results of an employee's performance will have had an opportunity to manifest themselves. If concrete results cannot be expected to show up for a year, insistence on a semiannual appraisal will be viewed as unfair by the employee. Similarly, if an employee's job is such that results appear quickly but may change rapidly, an annual review may be perceived to be unfair, since it would fail to take adequate account of positive results produced 6 or 8 months previously by the individual.

Glueck also points out the undesirability of superiors scheduling the evaluations of all of their subordinates at the same time. While such a practice may give the appearance of efficiency, it frequently results in fatigue for the superior and a tendency to give inadequate attention to the unique factors relevant to the case of each individual employee.

Thus, while there is no single correct approach to the scheduling of performance appraisals, it does appear desirable to: (1) schedule frequent feedback meetings to facilitate coaching and development; and (2) schedule formal evaluation reviews at times appropriate to the cycles of the employee's job.

The Appraisal Interview

If the performance appraisal process is to have any potential whatsoever for improving the level of performance of organization members, it is obviously essential that the results of the appraisal process be fed back to the individuals being evaluated. Only in this way can people learn where their strengths and weaknesses lie, and subsequently take steps to improve their future performance. In fact, of those organizations that report that they have a performance appraisal system, 97 percent indicate that they do provide feedback on appraisals to individuals, usually via an appraisal interview (BNA Survey, 1975). However, the fact that some feedback is provided via an interview does not ensure that the feedback is constructive or that the appraisal interview will have a positive motivational influence on the individuals involved. In fact, there are many factors that can serve to make the appraisal interview an uncomfortable and unproductive event. Fortunately, most of the potential negative factors can be overcome by careful planning and training of those conducting appraisal interviews.

One major factor that frequently creates difficulties in the appraisal interview is the inherent conflict experienced by the subordinate being evaluated. The subordinate can easily be torn between trying to present him- or herself in the best possible light in order to obtain the highest positive evaluation on the one hand, while on the other hand wishing to be open and candid about problems and weaknesses in order to obtain assistance and coaching that will facilitate improvement. Whether the subordinate opts for presenting him- or herself most positively or opts for being honest about strengths and weaknesses will depend primarily upon the attitudes and behavior of the superior conducting the interview. If honesty and candidness are themselves rewarded by the superior, and if the superior does in fact engage in helpful coaching and development activities that assist subordinates in correcting weaknesses and improving performance, then the likelihood of open discussion is greatly increased. Such open discussion is an essential prerequisite to the use of the appraisal process for the training and development of organization members.

A second major source of potential conflict and misunderstanding in appraisal interviews arises from the tendency for critical comments by the superior to elicit defensive reactions from the subordinate (Kay, Meyer, & French, 1965). This is obviously a natural reaction. When we are criticized or our shortcomings are pointed out, our self-concept and self-esteem are threatened and we feel a need to defend ourselves in order to permit us to maintain a positive self-image and a modicum of self-respect. But the problem is that such automatic defensive reactions interfere with our ability to face our shortcomings realistically and to discuss ways in which we might improve on them in the future. Again, the attitude and behavior of the superior in presenting negative information can greatly reduce the likelihood of defensive reactions and increase the potential for positive development.

If the attitude of the superior is simply to *present* his or her evaluation to the subordinate and then to convince the subordinate of the accuracy of the evaluation, the likelihood of defensive reactions is high and the chances of progress are poor. Such a "selling" approach frequently results in unproductive arguments between superior and subordinate regarding the accuracy and justification for the evaluation. If, on the other hand, the superior's attitude is not to present and justify evaluations but to discuss and explore past problems in order to facilitate future improvement, the likelihood of progress is much higher. Such an approach requires that the superior be willing to *listen* to the subordinate's side of the story and perhaps to change the evaluation in light of the new information. A supervisor who adopts such a "listening" approach rather than a "selling" stance is much more likely to be viewed by subordinates as a sympathetic and sensitive individual who is genuinely committed to helping subordinates improve, rather than to be viewed as arbitrary, intransigent, and unhelpful (Maier, 1976).

In addition, the likelihood of positive results and progress arising from appraisal interviews is very much dependent upon *how* negative information is communicated to subordinates. The likelihood that negative information will be listened to and acted upon by subordinates depends largely on the extent to which such information is *specific*, *descriptive* of actual behavior or performance, and oriented toward *future* performance improvement rather than simply assigning blame for past problems (Gibb, 1961). The value of appraisal techniques such as BARS, BOS, and MBO can be appreciated in this light since they are designed to focus appraisals upon specific examples of job behavior or specific performance results. The problems associated with graphic rating scales are also obvious. For example, telling a person that he or she lacks initiative is general rather than specific, evaluative rather than descriptive, and has no clear implications for how future improvement might be pursued. Negative comments that are general, evaluative, and past-oriented can be almost guaranteed to generate strong defensive reactions and very little constructive dialogue in an appraisal interview. By focusing the discussion upon descriptions of specific problems with a view toward future improvement, a superior can vastly increase the likelihood of constructive dialogue and real performance improvement.

It should not be forgotten that effective performance appraisal interviews also focus upon a subordinate's areas of strength. In discussing and praising these strengths it is equally desirable that the superior be specific and descriptive of actual events and behaviors that are the sources of positive evaluations. Only in this way does the appraisal process help the subordinate to understand exactly which areas of behavior and performance are those most valued by the organization and, therefore, which areas should continue to receive attention and emphasis (Dipboye & dePontbriand, 1981).

The failure to attend to the crucial role of the appraisal interview in the evaluation process and the failure to recognize the need for special skills on the part of superiors to manage appraisal interviews competently are major weaknesses in many organizations' appraisal systems. If the performance appraisal process is to achieve its potential for facilitating individual development, organizations must attend more carefully to the essential need for the development of the behavioral skills among their managers necessary for conducting appraisal interviews in a constructive positive fashion.

MANAGERIAL IMPLICATIONS

The quality and effectiveness of an organization's performance appraisal system are extremely important, both to the organization as a whole and to its individual members. The organization is dependent upon the performance appraisal system for the information necessary for making critical personnel decisions regarding placement, promotion, development, and termination. The quality of these decisions is directly dependent upon the quality of the information upon which they are based. Likewise, the career development of individual members is largely determined by the ratings and evaluations of their performance generated by the organization's performance appraisal system. As a result, individuals' opportunities and prospects for growth and development are influenced in no small part by the nature and validity of the organization's performance appraisal system. In light of these factors, the implications for managerial practice that follow from our discussion of performance appraisal are particularly important.

1. ***Managers must recognize and take advantage of the multiple uses to which performance appraisals can be put.*** Too often, managers tend to view the performance appraisal system as a means *solely* for judging and evaluating their subordinates. While judgment and evaluation are clearly central components of the performance appraisal process, they are not its only desired outcomes. The appraisal process can and should be a key component in an organization's program of employee development. By reinforcing strengths, identifying weaknesses, and serving as a vehicle for coaching and guidance from the supervisor, performance appraisal can contribute significantly to employee development. In addition, the information generated by the appraisal system can provide essential inputs to the organization's overall human resource planning process.

2. ***An organization's performance appraisal system should include measures of both activities and results.*** Since an organization ultimately succeeds or fails on the basis of the results it achieves, it seems sensible to include some measures of results attained in the evaluation of individual organization members. At the same time, it must be recognized that results are almost always influenced by a number of factors beyond the control of the individual. In light of this, an effective performance appraisal system should also include measures of the activities or behaviors engaged in by the individual. These activities measures not only serve to supplement results measures but also provide the manager with the information on employee behavior that is essential for feedback, coaching, and development.

3. ***Organizations must recognize the severe limitations and shortcomings of many of the widely used traditional methods of performance appraisal.*** Graphic rating scales, global evaluations, and ranking methods have serious weaknesses as appraisal methods. They tend not to generate information that can be helpful to the subordinate in improving his or her behavior. In addition, they are subject to a wide range of perceptual and judgmental biases which seriously hamper the validity of the appraisals they generate. Such appraisal methods are not to be recommended.

4. ***Organizations should seriously consider the implementation of more modern appraisal techniques such as BARS, BOS, and MBO.*** The more recently developed appraisal techniques presented in this chapter go a long way in overcoming many of the disadvantages associated with the more traditional appraisal methods. These modern appraisal techniques generate more accurate and valid evaluations, and are more likely to provide a sound basis for improved employee motivation, career planning, and personal development.

5. ***Managers need to recognize that the effectiveness of performance appraisals depends largely upon their own interpersonal skills in managing the appraisal process effectively.*** Frequently, organizations and managers tend to

assume that the success of the organization's performance appraisal system is determined solely by the quality of the system's design and the nature of the forms and paperwork that go with the system. This assumption has been the downfall of many *potentially* successful appraisal systems. The value of performance appraisal to organizations and their members is critically determined by the skills and sensitivities of the managers who actually conduct appraisal interviews. Managers must recognize this factor and work hard at developing and improving the communication skills essential for managing the appraisal process effectively.

SUMMARY

Almost all organizations have some system or procedure that is used for appraising and evaluating the performance of organization members. Performance appraisal systems can serve a variety of purposes. First and most obviously, they provide a basis for evaluating, judging, and rewarding members of the organization on the basis of their performance. Second, the information generated by an appraisal system can be used for counseling employees and planning programs of training and development. Finally, the appraisal system provides information that can greatly facilitate organizational planning for current and future human resource needs.

A primary problem that must be faced in the design of appraisal systems is the determination of exactly what should be measured in order to assess how well a person is performing. This is often referred to as the *criterion problem.* Potential criteria may include measures of the activities engaged in by organization members, measures of the results of these activities, or some combination of the two.

A wide variety of alternative techniques have been developed for performance appraisal in organizations. Among the most common traditional methods of appraisal are graphic rating scales, single global evaluations, and ranking methods. More recent work has resulted in the development of a number of modern techniques that overcome some of the difficulties inherent in the traditional methods. Among these modern techniques are behaviorally anchored rating scales (BARS), behavioral observation scales (BOS), and management by objectives (MBO).

Regardless of which specific technique is employed, a number of issues must be addressed regarding the management of the appraisal process. The organization must determine who will actually conduct appraisals and when and how often appraisals will occur; it must also ensure that those involved in appraising subordinates possess the skills necessary to manage the appraisal process in a positive and constructive fashion.

REVIEW QUESTIONS

1. Discuss some of the alternative uses to which an organization may put its performance appraisal system.

2. How would the uses to be made of performance appraisal information influence the design of an appraisal system?
3. What is meant by the term *criterion*?
4. What are the advantages and disadvantages of using measures of activities versus measures of results as criteria in an appraisal system? Would you recommend using one or the other or both in an appraisal system?
5. Why are graphic rating scales so popular in performance appraisal?
6. Under what conditions (if any) would you recommend ranking as an appraisal technique?
7. Outline several of the common errors that arise in the use of rating scales for appraisals. How might some of these errors be overcome or eliminated?
8. What is a behaviorally anchored rating scale (BARS)? How is a BARS developed and what are its strengths and weaknesses?
9. What is the difference between a BARS and a BOS? What do you see as the primary strengths of the BOS approach to performance appraisal?
10. How can a management by objectives (MBO) program be employed for performance evaluation? In what types of situations would you recommend an MBO-based appraisal system?
11. Who should carry out performance evaluations? Defend and explain your recommendation.
12. How frequently should performance appraisals be conducted? Explain the reasons behind your recommendation.
13. Describe some of the conflicts inherent in an appraisal interview and discuss how these conflicts can be overcome.
14. What types of ethical issues do you feel are raised by the performance appraisal process?

REFERENCES

Bernardin, H. J. Behavioral expectation scales vs. summated ratings: A fairer comparison. *Journal of Applied Psychology, 1977, 62,* 422–427.

Bernardin, H. J., & Buckley, M. R. A consideration of strategies in rater training. Unpublished manuscript, 1979.

Bernardin, H. J., & Kane, J. S. A second look at behavioral observation scales. *Personnel Psychology, 1980, 33,* 809–814.

Bernardin, H. J., & Pence, E. G. The effects of rater training: Creating new response sets and decreasing accuracy. *Journal of Applied Psychology, 1980, 65,* 60–66.

Bernardin, H. J., & Smith, P. C. A clarification of some issues regarding the development and use of behaviorally anchored rating scales (BARS). *Journal of Applied Psychology, 1981, 66,* 458–463.

Bernardin, H. J., & Walter, C. S. The effects of rater training and diary keeping on psychometric error in ratings. *Journal of Applied Psychology, 1977, 62,* 64–69.

Bernardin, H. J., Alvares, K. M., & Cranny, C. J. A recomparison of behavioral expectation scales to summated scales. *Journal of Applied Psychology, 1976, 61,* 564–570.

Borman, W. C. Format and training effects on rating accuracy and rater errors. *Journal of Applied Psychology,* 1979, *64,* 410–421.

Bureau of National Affairs, Employee performance: Evaluation and control. *Personnel Policies Forum no. 108,* February, 1975.

Burnaska, R. G., & Hollman, T. D. An empirical comparison of the relative effects of rater response bias on three rating scale formats. *Journal of Applied Psychology,* 1974, *59,* 307–312.

Cederblom, D., & Lounsbury, J. W. An investigation of user acceptance of peer evaluations. *Personnel Psychology,* 1980, *33,* 567–579.

Cook, D. The impact on managers of frequency of feedback. *Academy of Management Journal,* 1968, *2,* 263–277.

Cooper, W. H. Ubiquitous halo. *Psychological Bulletin,* 1981, *90,* 218–244.

Cummings, L. L., & Schwab, D. P. *Performance in organizations.* Glenview, Ill.: Scott, Foresman, 1973.

Dipboye, R. L., & dePontbriand, R. Correlates of employee reactions to performance appraisals and appraisal systems. *Journal of Applied Psychology,* 1981, *66,* 248–251.

Dunnette, M. D. A note on *the* criterion. *Journal of Applied Psychology,* 1963, *47,* 251–254.

Feldman, J. M. Beyond attribution theory: Cognitive processes in performance appraisal. *Journal of Applied Psychology,* 1981, *66,* 127–148.

Ghorpade, J., & Lackritz, J. R. Influences behind neutral responses in subordinate ratings of supervisors. *Personnel Psychology,* 1981, *34,* 511–522.

Gibb, J. Defensive communication. *Journal of Communication,* 1961, *3,* 141–148.

Glueck, W. F. *Personnel: A diagnostic approach.* Dallas, Texas: Business Publications, Inc., 1978.

Ivancevich, J. M. A longitudinal study of behavioral expectation scales: Attitudes and performance. *Journal of Applied Psychology,* 1980, *65,* 139–146.

Jacobs, R., Kafry, D., & Zedeck, S. Expectations of behaviorally anchored rating scales. *Personnel Psychology,* 1980, *33,* 595–640.

Jamieson, B. D. Behavioral problems with management by objectives. *Academy of Management Journal,* 1973, *16,* 496–505.

Kay, E., Meyer, H., & French, J. R. P. Effects of threat in a performance appraisal interview. *Journal of Applied Psychology,* 1965, *49,* 311–317.

Kelley, H. H. The processes of causal attribution. *American Psychologist,* 1973, *28,* 107–128.

Kingstrom, P. O., & Bass, A. R. A critical analysis of studies comparing behaviorally anchored rating scales (BARS) and other rating formats. *Personnel Psychology,* 1981, *34,* 263–289.

Knowlton, W. A., Jr., & Mitchell, T. R. Effects of causal attributions on a supervisor's evaluation of subordinate performance. *Journal of Applied Psychology,* 1980, *65,* 459–466.

Landy, F. J., & Farr, J. L. A process model of performance ratings. *Psychological Bulletin,* 1980, *87,* 72–108.

Landy, F. J., Barnes-Farrell, J., & Cleveland, J. N. Perceived fairness and accuracy of performance evaluation: A follow-up. *Journal of Applied Psychology,* 1980, *65,* 355–356.

Latham, G. P., & Wexley, K. N. Behavioral observation scales for performance appraisal purposes. *Personnel Psychology,* 1977, *30,* 255–268.

Latham, G. P., & Wexley, K. N. *Improving productivity through performance appraisal.* Reading, Mass.: Addison-Wesley, 1981.

Latham, G. P., Fay, C. H., & Saari, L. M. The development of behavioral observation scales for appraising the performance of foremen. *Personnel Psychology,* 1979, *32,* 299–311.

Latham, G. P., Saari, L. M., & Fay, C. H. BOS, BES, and baloney: Raising Kane with Bernardin. *Personnel Psychology,* 1980, *33,* 815–821.

Latham, G. P., Wexley, K. N., & Pursell, E. D. Training managers to minimize rating errors in the observation of behavior. *Journal of Applied Psychology,* 1975, *60,* 550–555.

Levine, E. L. Introductory remarks for the symposium "Organizational Applications of Self-Appraisal and Self-Assessment: Another Look." *Personnel Psychology,* 1980, *33,* 259–262.

Levine, E. L., Flory, A., III, & Ash, R. A. Self-assessment in personnel selection. *Journal of Applied Psychology,* 1977, *62,* 428–435.

Lewin, A., & Zwany, A. Peer nominations: A model, literature critique, and a paradigm for research. *Personnel Psychology,* 1976, *29,* 423–447.

Locher, A. J., & Teel, K. S. Performance appraisal—A survey of current practices. *Personnel Journal,* 1977, *56,* 245–254.

Love, K. G. Comparison of peer assessment methods: Reliability, validity, friendship bias, and user reaction. *Journal of Applied Psychology,* 1981, *66,* 451–457.

Maier, N. R. F. *The appraisal interview: Three basic approaches.* La Jolla, Calif.: University Associates, 1976.

Peters, L. H., & O'Connor, E. J. Situational constraints and work outcomes: The influences of a frequently overlooked construct. *Academy of Management Review,* 1980, *5,* 391–397.

Peters, L. H., O'Connor, E. J., & Rudolf, C. J. The behavioral and affective consequences of performance-relevant situational variables. *Organizational Behavior and Human Performance,* 1980, *25,* 79–86.

Porter, L. W., Lawler, E. E., III, & Hackman, J. R. *Behavior in organizations.* New York: McGraw-Hill, 1975.

Ross, L. The intuitive psychologist and his shortcomings: Distortions in the attribution process. In L. Berkowtiz (Ed.), *Advances in experimental social psychology* (Vol. 10). New York: Academic Press, 1977.

Schwab, D. P., Heneman, H. G., III, & DeCotiis, T. Behaviorally anchored rating scales: A review of the literature. *Personnel Psychology,* 1975, *28,* 549–562.

Smith, P. C., & Kendall, L. M. Retranslation of expectations: An approach to the construction of unambiguous anchors for rating scales. *Journal of Applied Psychology,* 1963, *47,* 149–155.

Tosi, H. L., Rizzo, J. R., & Carroll, S. J. Setting goals in management by objectives. *California Management Review,* 1970, *12,* 70–78.

PART SEVEN

GROUPS IN

ORGANIZATIONS

CHAPTER 16

INTRODUCTION

TO GROUP DYNAMICS

"Two heads are better than one" or "Too many cooks spoil the broth"? "The more the merrier" or "Two's company, three's a crowd"?

As Herold (1979) suggests, these conflicting beliefs about groups are not signs of our irrationality but reflect instead our own ambivalence about groups. We have all been members of groups where we greatly enjoyed the companionship of our coworkers, but we have also all been in groups where we felt personally uncomfortable. At times groups have substantially reduced the amount of effort we individually had to put into a project, but at other times we have had to carry most of the group's work by ourselves. Whatever our own personal feelings about groups, however, groups are becoming increasingly important in organizational life. As organizations continue to expand, they will need to rely more heavily on groups to make key business decisions. Moreover, only those employees skilled in working with others in groups are likely to be successful in modern organizations.

In this first chapter on groups, we address some of the most basic issues in the area. First, we'll define what we mean by a *group* and describe the different types of groups people belong to in organizations. Second, we'll explore why the bonds among different members of different work groups are not uniformly strong, i.e., what makes some groups more *cohesive* than others. Third, we discuss the consequences of group cohesiveness. Do cohesive groups have higher morale? Are they more productive? Finally, we'll examine the nature of *group norms*—the informal rules and regulations created and enforced by group members. We'll look at how and why group norms develop and what they tell us about underlying *group dynamics*.

In this chapter, then, we plan to sort out fact from fiction about the ways groups operate in organizations. In so doing, we hope to help the reader to become a better diagnostician of group dynamics, a more effective member of work teams, and a more skillful designer of productive work groups.

GROUP MEMBERSHIP

By the term *group* we mean a collection of two or more people who: (1) interact with each other; (2) perceive themselves to share some common interests or goals; and (3) come together or are brought together to accomplish some work activity. This definition of *group* is somewhat more limited than the layman's use of the term, but for good reason. In studying groups in organizations we are concerned with how group membership influences individual behavior and feelings. If people are not psychologically aware of each other and don't perceive themselves to be a group, then the question of how groups influence individual behavior becomes superficial and meaningless. A hundred people might be eating in the company cafeteria "together" at the same time and might randomly speak to each other, but we would not expect these hundred people to think of themselves as a group, or "membership" in this collection of people to seriously influence behavior.

We further restrict our definition of group to *work groups*. There are many types of *social groups* to which people might belong, such as the garden club, the softball league, college alumni associations, or the local country club. While all these collections of people are indeed groups, for our purposes we will only be examining groups that are work-related or accomplish a work-related project.

Formal Groups

We also make an important distinction between formal and informal groups. *Formal groups* are those that are deliberately created to perform a specific task. For example, brand management groups are formal groups created by marketing companies to coordinate the development and sales of commercial products. Audit teams are formal groups created by accounting firms to perform audits at client organizations.

The *command group* is the most frequent type of formal group. It is specified by the organization chart and is composed of a supervisor and his or her subordinates. A dean and respective department heads, a head nurse and respective floor nurses, and a supervisor and respective assembly-line workers are all command groups.

The other type of formal group is the *temporary task group*. A temporary task group consists of employees who work together to complete a particular task or project, but who do not necessarily report to the same supervisor. For instance, when a problem involving many departments arises, a task force made up of representatives from each of the affected departments might be formed to examine the problem and suggest solutions. These task forces eliminate a lot of circular and disjointed communication between departments. Moreover, they provide both a more efficient mechanism for gathering information about problems, and a more effective mechanism for disseminating proposed solutions to other members of the organization (Galbraith, 1974). For example, federal governments frequently use task forces to deal with problems like immigration laws and import/export tariffs, problems that cut across the Departments of Commerce, Justice, Treasury, State, and Defense.

Informal Groups

While membership in formal groups is assigned and deliberate, *informal* groups evolve naturally. Membership is voluntary and changes. Dalton (1959), in an important study of informal work groups, describes the three most common types of informal work groups: (1) horizontal cliques; (2) vertical cliques; and (3) random cliques.

Horizontal cliques consist of people who are of similar rank in the same work area. For instance, a group of recently hired M.B.A.'s working for the same advertising agency might constitute an informal work group. They might meet for lunch regularly to discuss common problems or to share information about different parts of the organization.

Vertical cliques consist of people from different hierarchical levels within the same department. For instance, some students, secretaries, professors, and administrators might develop networks for passing along information within a division of the university. The sort of "hall talk" that gets shared in these vertical cliques can be about potential problems that are arising, how well new programs or practices might be accepted, or for passing along praise or warnings that cannot be made formally (e.g., "people really liked your class," "the reason no one showed up today is that Procter & Gamble is interviewing in placement." "don't plan a test for Friday, it's homecoming").

Random cliques consist of people from various departments, locations, and hierarchical levels. Often these random cliques are composed of people who share a common interest in "getting things done," avoiding red tape, and bypassing the bureaucracy. For example, employees in various departments might be in random cliques with people from payroll, accounting, and finance so that they can get advances on paychecks, won't get questioned about travel-expense forms, can get supplies without waiting 4 weeks, and so on.

Why People Join Groups

Membership in formal groups is mandated, and most employees belong to only two or three formal groups in an organization. However, employees can simultaneously belong to a variety of informal groups. These informal groups can develop within formal groups or across or outside formal groups. The key point to remember about membership in informal groups is that people will join them *only if they satisfy some important needs*. Moreover, the more needs that any informal group can fulfill, the more the group becomes an important reference point or anchor for individual members.

Probably the reason most informal groups form is for *goal accomplishment*. Our random cliques of clerks and administrators "get things done" with less work for themselves. The vertical cliques of students, secretaries, professors and administrators are effective at "testing the waters" before implementing policy. The horizontal cliques of account executives provide a forum for testing new ideas and swapping information.

Another reason people join informal groups is to *enhance their own careers*. The employee who cuts through the red tape not only accomplishes the work quickly but also receives the praise of coworkers (who benefit from the efficiency) and a reputation as a competent "operator." The meetings of account executives give their members some informal scuttlebutt about personnel changes and the political currents in the organization. More subtly, these meetings also provide the opportunity for account executives to size each other up and to see what the competition is up to. The student who belongs to the vertical clique might get the inside story on whose courses to avoid or how to get into a closed course.

Employees also form informal groups to *sustain friendships*. People enjoy being around others who share common interests. Individuals may seek out others at work who share common hobbies (e.g., golf, video games, opera) or common backgrounds (e.g., come from the same hometown). Especially when people are new to an organization, they are eager to find friends with whom they can check out their perceptions of a new, or uncertain, environment (e.g., "is it only me, or is Tom hard to work with?"). For example, students from the same business school who barely knew each other 3 months earlier frequently seek each other out when they start working at the same organization to reduce some of their newcomers' anxiety.

Some people join informal work groups to *enhance their own personal status*. In one organization, those employees who perceived themselves to be "fast-trackers" formed a gourmet cooking group. While the ostensible purpose of this informal group was to enjoy elegant food, the real purpose was to reinforce to its members and to others in the organization that this group was comprised of the next generation of "movers and shakers" in the corporation. This became even more evident when people who really were gourmet cooks tried to join the group but were not allowed in.

Informal groups as well as formal groups influence the way people behave in organizations. However, not all of these groups influence our behavior equally, and the bonds among members of these groups are not uniformly strong. In the next section, we examine what makes some groups more cohesive than others and how that cohesiveness influences the behavior of group members.

GROUP COHESIVENESS

By the term *cohesiveness* we mean how much members of a group like each other and want to remain members of the group (Shaw, 1981).

We notice differences in cohesiveness among sports teams, groups of friends, work groups, and even families. In some groups there is genuine liking and mutual respect among group members, an almost tangible sense of group spirit. In other groups there is only a modicum of attraction between group members and being a member of a group is only a tangential part of members' lives. Recently there has been a great deal of attention paid to the Japanese style of management, where workers identify strongly with their companies and spend much of their nonwork time engaging in leisure activities with coworkers. This contrasts sharply with the 9-to-5, punch-the-timeclock culture of much of American industry. In the next sections, we examine both the sources of group cohesiveness and the consequences of cohesiveness on group functioning.

Sources of Group Cohesiveness

Interaction
Chief among the sources of group cohesiveness is the amount of contact among group members. Groups become more cohesive when individual members spend more time with each other.

Probably the most well-known illustration of interaction leading to cohesiveness is Festinger, Schachter, and Back's study of married-student housing at M.I.T. (1950). At M.I.T. the apartments varied in physical distance from each other. They also varied in functional distance from each other (i.e., whether it was necessary to pass other people's doors to get into one's own apartment, how close an apartment was to central services such as garbage collection, laundry room, and the mailboxes). Festinger and his collegues found that both physical distance and functional distance strongly predicted observed friendship patterns.

For instance, next-door neighbors were more likely to make friends with each other than with people who lived in a different entryway. Also, people who lived next to such central services as the laundry room would "bump into" the most other residents of the apartment complex and tended to be the most popular. Subsequent research suggests that members of work groups who have offices or work spaces near each other and frequently interact with each other are more likely to become cohesive.

Shared Goals

Groups that share common goals are likely to be more cohesive than those that do not. If the group agrees on the purpose and direction of its activities, this serves to bind the group together. The sports team that is united around team goals rather than individual glory or the sales team that has a well-developed, well-articulated strategy is much more likely to triumph over a bickering group of athletes or a disorganized group of salespeople. What determines whether group goals become shared and a binding force?

First, how *cooperatively* or *democratically* the goals have been set influences how cohesive the group will become. The more the group cooperates and participates in setting goals, the higher the group cohesiveness. A good example of this was seen in the professional baseball players strike of 1981. Union leadership very actively and wisely kept in close communication with the players, meeting not only with representatives of the union membership but with as many of the individual union members as they could. The union representatives had a clear agenda of what they wanted in negotiations (mainly free agent issues); they knew the players were united behind them. The players were very cohesive during the long and costly strike.

The owners, on the other hand, did not share common goals during the strike. Several of the newer owners had different priorities from the veteran owners, in regard to both what they were willing to negotiate on and how quickly they wanted to settle the strike. The newer owners also felt they were not adequately represented on the owners' negotiating team. As a result, several of the owners broke rank during the strike, and the owners as a group appeared fractious to the press and public. Most people felt the players won both more issues and more public support from the strike.

Second, *shared success in meeting goals* increases group cohesiveness. When the group meets its goals, it reaffirms its self-image as a "good group" and solidarity is sustained. Group failure, on the other hand, makes group members question the wisdom of their position collectively and the wisdom of some of their coworkers individually. In the television industry, for example, the success and cohesiveness of the cast is easily detected at the "wrap party," the party given after the last taping of the season. In shows where the ratings have been high, the party is lavish, the main stars remain at the party well into the night, and spirits run high. When the show has done poorly, the food is meager, most of the big stars do not show up or only make a brief appearance, and people leave as soon as they can politely do so. People want to revel in success with those who helped make success possible; they want to avoid being reminded of failure by avoiding those with whom they failed.

Similarity of Attitudes and Values

One of the strongest sources of group cohesiveness is shared attitudes and values among group members. As to the folksaying "birds of a feather flock together," the research is in strong agreement.

Why do we feel attracted to people like ourselves? Aronson (1976) suggests at least two reasons. First, the person who shares the same opinions we do provides us with a kind of social validation for our beliefs—he or she provides us with a feeling that we are right. If someone disagrees with us, this might evoke fear in us that we are wrong. Second, we are likely to make certain negative inferences about the character of a person who disagrees with us on important issues. If we disagree with this person on this issue, we feel much more likely that we will disagree with him or her on other issues.

For instance, in discussions about budgets, the person from personnel may argue strongly to keep funds available for training. If you are favorably disposed to training programs, you will sense some relief that the in-house specialist on these matters is in agreement with you. You might also assume you will agree with him or her on other issues—how to best manage subordinates, for example. If you are in disagreement with the personnel manager, you will feel somewhat threatened by his or her position. You might also attribute other negative characteristics to the personnel officer that you associate with the protraining stance: "soft-hearted," "no business sense," etc. You suspect you will disagree on affirmative action programs and occupational safety and health regulations, too. The result is a management group that is low on cohesiveness.

One frequently observes that companies recruit the "right type", people who will "fit in" to the corporate climate, to sustain group cohesiveness. The *Wall Street Journal* notes, for instance, that one manager wasn't hired because he spoke with enthusiasm about coaching his son's Little League baseball team. While in most cases Little League baseball might seem safe enough, in this case "it made the company president feel the executive's work wasn't really his top priority." In another case cited, a job applicant was rejected because he wore a short-sleeved shirt. Sneered the recruiter, "How far would I have to look up your sleeve before I found a shirt?" A third executive was rejected because he revealed at dinner with the chairman that he didn't know the appropriate way of eating an artichoke; "the chairman said he just didn't want a guy who didn't know how to eat properly" (*WSJ*, 1979, p. 1).[1]

There is no question that groups seek out people like themselves during selection, and that groups with similar tastes and values are more cohesive. Whether that cohesiveness is good for the organization is another question altogether and one we consider next.

Consequences of Group Cohesiveness

Morale

On almost every index of satisfaction and morale, cohesive groups rank higher than noncohesive groups. Members of cohesive groups like each other more as individuals and like the group as a whole more, too. They spend more time with each other and communicate with each other more frequently. Members of cohesive groups show greater sensitivity to each other; they are more accurate in perceiving the behaviors and feelings of other group members. There is less conflict in cohesive groups, for group members tend to view the work setting in the same way. Members of cohesive groups feel less tense and anxious and feel less pressure at work (Lott & Lott, 1965; Aronson, 1976).

The impact that group cohesiveness has on morale can be easily observed in the classroom. In classes where there is group cohesiveness, students show more understanding of each other. There is less ridicule and scapegoating of classmates, and more cooperative behavior. There is frequently more joking and kidding around. Students spend more time hanging around before and after class. The cohesiveness often extends to greater rapport between the students and the professor. In noncohesive classes, there is more tension in the air. People don't know where they stand with their classmates and are hesitant to participate in class. Comments are frequently taken in the wrong light. Students gravitate to the back of the classroom, often coming in late and leaving early. There is very little two-way communication between the professor and students. In fact, these courses are marked by very little "groupness" at all.

Productivity

The single most important study examining the impact of group cohesiveness on productivity was conducted by Seashore (1954). In a study of 228 small manufacturing work groups, Seashore found the relationship between cohesiveness and productivity was not as clear and unidimensional as the relationship between cohesiveness and morale.

---

[1]Reprinted by permission of *Wall Street Journal*. ©Dow Jones & Company, Inc., 1979. All rights reserved.

One of the strongest influences group cohesiveness has on productivity is that it *decreases productivity differences among members of a work group*. Cohesive groups exert stronger pressures toward uniformity than noncohesive groups. Members of a cohesive group value the group's good opinion and are unlikely to risk losing the group's esteem by producing much more or less than the group expects (Tajfel, 1969; Schachter et al., 1951).

A good example of this phenomenon is described by Newcomb (1954, cited by Golembiewski, 1962, pp. 223–224). A cohesive group had established a production norm of fifty units a day, but one worker wanted to produce much more than that. This worker's attempts to produce more were actively discouraged by peers, and as a result the eager worker's output dropped even below the fifty-unit norm. Some months later, the work group was split up and the individual in question no longer worked with the group that enforced the fifty-unit norm. The worker's output soon doubled.

As the above example also illustrates, group cohesiveness does *not* necessarily lead to *higher* productivity. In Seashore's study and in subsequent studies, high cohesiveness is sometimes associated with high productivity and sometimes with low productivity. Whether high cohesiveness leads to high productivity depends upon *the degree to which group members feel management is supportive of them*.

An excellent example of high cohesiveness leading to lower productivity is William Foote Whyte's study of quota restriction (1955). There is a natural antagonism between piece-rate workers and time-and-motion engineers. Piece-rate workers feel if they produce "too much" in an hour, the industrial engineers will reevaluate their jobs so that they will have to produce more units to get the same amount of pay. In these threatening situations, cohesive groups strongly ostracize any "rate busters" who refuse to abide by the informally established ceiling. Cohesiveness here works against productivity.

In a study of the British coal-mining industry, we find an example of high cohesiveness leading to *increased* productivity (Trist & Bamforth, 1948). Prior to World War II, coal was mined by the short-wall method. Coal was gathered by six-person teams who worked together and shared various coal-gathering functions in the mine. This method encouraged a high degree of teamwork and cohesiveness among group members, but there was very little task specialization. After World War II, the conventional "long-wall method" of coal mining was introduced. The conventional long-wall method was based on using a conveyor belt; it allowed the company to fractionalize the group tasks into individual jobs to increase efficiency. When work groups were no longer needed, morale decreased and labor conflict increased. Moreover, the coal companies did not realize their expected profits from the new method.

Trist and Bamforth, called in by the coal companies, discovered that a new work system, called the composite long-wall method, could combine the social benefits of the short-wall method with the technological benefits of the conventional long-wall method. Group cohesiveness in the new composite method was achieved, among other ways, by having the work groups select their own members and receive payment based on group performance instead of individual effort. As a result of both the new technology and the revived group cohesiveness, the productivity of the new composite-wall method went up 17 percent from the conventional long-wall method and absenteeism went down 50 percent.

In short, cohesiveness will decrease the amount of variability in performance among members of a work group but will not necessarily increase the productivity of the group as a whole. Whether that happens depends on the group norms and whether the group feels management is supportive rather than threatening. We turn now to examine the nature of group norms more closely.

GROUP NORMS

By the term *norm* we mean an *informal rule that a group adopts to regulate group members' behavior*. While rarely written down and mostly unspoken, these norms can regularize group behavior with a consistency and a power that even formal organizational dictates fail to engender. Porter, Lawler, and Hackman (1975) identify three salient characteristics of norms.

1. ***Norms apply only to behavior, not to private thoughts and feelings.***
   What group members *say* they believe or feel is very much under the normative control of the group. However, complying with the group's wishes about silence does not necessarily reflect changes in the true private attitudes and beliefs of group members. Norms can regulate only visible behavior of group members.

   An example from Janis's (1972) book, *Victims of Groupthink*, illustrates this point nicely. One of President John Kennedy's closest advisors, Arthur Schlesinger, Jr., had serious reservations about the Bay of Pigs invasion and presented his strong objections to the Bay of Pigs plan in a memorandum to Kennedy and Secretary of State Dean Rusk. However, Schlesinger was pressured by the President's brother, Attorney General Robert Kennedy, to keep his objections to himself. Remarked Robert Kennedy to Schlesinger: "You may be right or you may be wrong, but the President has made his mind up. Don't push it any further. Now is the time for everyone to help him all they can." Writes Schlesinger later in his memoirs: "I can only explain my failure to do more than raise a few timid questions by reporting that one's impulse to blow the whistle on this nonsense was simply undone by the circumstances of the discussion." The Kennedy Cabinet's norms influenced what Schlesinger said, but not what he thought.

2. *Norms are generally developed only for behaviors which are viewed as important by most group members.* Groups don't have the time or the energy to regulate each and every action of group members. Only those behaviors that are viewed as most important in the eyes of the group members will be brought under normative control. In Whyte's discussion of the rate-busting norm, we see clearly why production groups enforce production standards: if the jobs are reevaluated, group members will have to work harder.

3. *While groups might give the most approval to a certain amount of behavior, for most group norms there is a range of acceptable behavior.* There is at least some latitude for individual discretion, even for norm-regulated behavior. For instance, while producing 50 widgets an hour might be the most desirable level of production, producing between 40 and 60 widgets an hour is likely to be acceptable to the group as well.

Jackson's Model of Norms

Jackson (1965, 1966) has developed a model (sometimes referred to as the *Return Potential Model*) that helps us describe and analyze group norms more closely. By using Jackson's model, we can discover the pattern and intensity of approval of various group members' behaviors (e.g., how much approval or disapproval group members will receive for producing different numbers of widgets).

As can be seen in Figure 16-1, Jackson graphically represents his model along two dimensions. Along the y axis (abscissa), Jackson plots the *amount of a given behavior exhibited*. Along the x axis (ordinate), he plots the *amount of approval or disapproval felt*. One could obtain from members of a group the amount of approval or disapproval associated with a behavior and then plot the *return potential curve* based on that data. Jackson's model lets us identify five distinct indices of group norms.

1. *The point of maximum return.* The amount of behavior that generates the most approval from others (indicated by *a* in Figure 16-1).
2. *The range of tolerable behavior.* The range of behavior which receives at least some approval by others (indicated by *b* in Figure 16-1).
3. *The potential return difference.* The amount of approval versus disapproval associated with a behavior, e.g., whether the norm is a "thou shalt" or "thou shalt not" norm. (This could be roughly estimated by looking at whether most of the curve is above or below the neutral

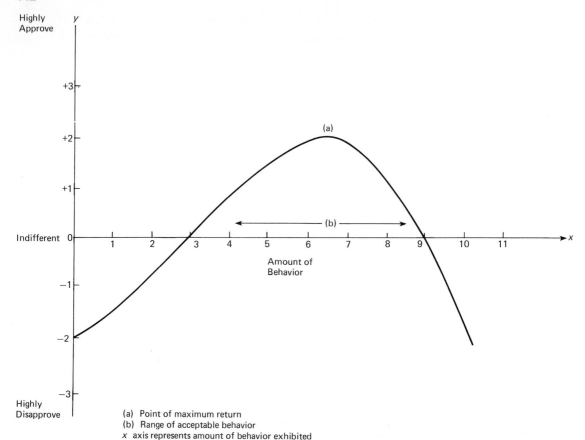

(a) Point of maximum return
(b) Range of acceptable behavior
x axis represents amount of behavior exhibited
y axis represents amount of approval or disapproval

FIGURE 16-1
Jackson's return potential model.   SOURCE: Adapted from J. Jackson, "Structural Charac-
teristics of Norms," in I. D. Steiner and M. Fishbein (eds.), *Current Studies in Social
Psychology*. New York: Holt, 1965, p. 303.

point of the approval dimension; Jackson provides a more precise
computational formula).

4. **Intensity.** The overall strength of approval or disapproval associated
   with a behavior, e.g., how strongly group members feel about a norm.
   (This can be roughly estimated by looking at the height, or depth, of a
   curve. Once again, Jackson provides a more precise computational
   formula).

5. **Crystallization.** The degree of consensus among group members about
   the amount of approval or disapproval associated with a behavior, e.g.,
   whether group members agree about the norm. (If one were to analyze
   individual responses of group members to questions about group
   norms, there would be very little variance among members about a

highly crystallized norm and a lot of variance among members about a poorly crystallized norm.)

Types of Group Norms

Using the models of Jackson (1965, 1966) and March (1954) we see that there are three basic types of norms: (1) preferred-value norms; (2) unattainable-ideal norms; and (3) attainable-ideal norms. Each of these types of norms is diagrammed in Figure 16-2 and is discussed in more detail below.

Preferred-Value Norms

We might facetiously label preferred-value norms "Goldilocks" norms: "not too hot and not too cold, but just right." In *preferred-value norms*, too little of the behavior is disapproved of, but so is too much. Only a certain range of behavior is acceptable. (Our illustration of Jackson's return potential model in Figure 16-1 is also a preferred-value norm.)

Preferred-value norms frequently regulate participation in group meetings. The person who sits back and says nothing is not appreciated, but the person who monopolizes the conversation also receives disapproval. Consider classroom situations in this light. The student who says nothing may be considered shy, lazy, or unintelligent; the student who monopolizes class discussion may be considered too forward, too eager, or too much a show-off.

Another preferred-value norm regulates the use of humor. Being completely humorless receives disapproval, for it makes other members feel uncomfortable and awkward. The person who is completely flip also receives disapproval and earns a reputation as a group fool or clown. Some appreciation and use of humor is expected, but not too much.

Production norms among the piece-rate workers are yet another example of preferred-value norms. If a person produces too little, he or she is ostracized for not carrying enough of the group's weight. If a person produces too much, he or she is ostracized for bringing about job reevaluations. There is a range of acceptable productivity, and deviation on both sides is negatively evaluated.

Preferred-value norms are by far the most frequent type of norm in organizations. They regulate most of the day-to-day behavior in groups. Moreover, they are probably the most difficult type of norm for newcomers or outsiders to learn. Individuals have to learn not only what behaviors are desired but also how to modulate their behavior so that neither too much nor too little is exhibited.

Unattainable-Ideal Norms

The unattainable-ideal norm is, in essence, the "the more, the better" norm (Porter et al., 1975). The more a group member engages in a behavior, the more approval he or she will receive from the group.

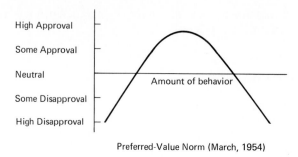

Preferred-Value Norm (March, 1954)

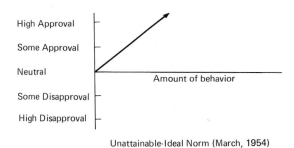

Unattainable-Ideal Norm (March, 1954)

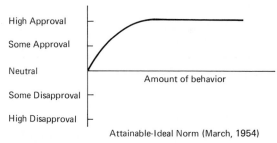

Attainable-Ideal Norm (March, 1954)

FIGURE 16-2
Types of group norms. SOURCE: James G. March, "Group Norms and the Active Minority,"
American Sociological Review, 1954, *19*, pp. 733–741. Reprinted with permission of *American
Sociological Review* and the author.

In an advertising group, the more creative an advertising campaign,
the more a person receives group approval. In a consulting firm, the more
clients a partner brings in, the more positive feedback he or she will
receive from colleagues. In an engineering company, the more precise and
thorough an engineer's plans, the more favorably the engineer will be
viewed.

In general, these unattainable-ideal norms regulate job behaviors that
are *central* to group effectiveness, such as generating creative ideas in ad

agencies, bringing in clients in a consulting firm, or doing precise and thorough plans in an engineering company.

Attainable-Ideal norms

Attainable-ideal norms encourage behaviors of group members, but only up to a point. After a sufficient amount of the behavior is engaged in, the group will not continue rewarding its members for ever-increasing amounts.

A good example of an attainable-ideal norm in organizations comes from socializing with other organization members. Groups expect their members to make some effort to socialize with each other, either at lunch, Christmas and retirement parties, or at TGIFs. Groups don't generally approve of members being totally standoffish and will give increasing approval for some attendance at these social gatherings. However, after a group member has demonstrated he or she is social *enough*, there is no increased approval. For instance, groups might give increasing approval to members who go to lunch with others four times a month, or roughly once a week. However, members will not receive *more* approval for going twice or three times a week.

In general, attainable-ideal norms regulate the more peripheral aspects of group life, such as purely social behavior and dress codes.

How Norms Develop

Norms usually develop gradually and informally as members learn what behaviors are necessary for the group to function. However, it is also possible for this process to be short-cut if group members agree consciously to set a norm (Porter et al., 1975, p. 393). Most norms develop in one of the following five ways:

1. *Individual carry-over from past situations.* Many group norms in organizations emerge because individual group members bring certain expectations with them from other work groups in other organizations. Accountants expect to behave toward those they audit in organization B as they behaved toward those in organization A. Nurses expect to behave toward doctors in hospital B as they behaved toward those in hospital A. In fact, much of what goes on in professional schools is giving new members of the profession the same standards and norms of behavior that practitioners in the field hold. Management consultants have a highly ritualized set of norms about entertaining clients. As new consulting firms form, the same norms for entertainment get replicated.

2. *Primacy.* The first behavior pattern that emerges in a group often sets group expectations. If the first group meeting is marked by very formal interaction between supervisors and subordinates, then the group often expects future meetings to be conducted in the same way. Where people

sit in meetings or rooms is frequently developed through primacy. People generally continue to sit in the same seats as they sat in at their first meeting, even though those original seats are not assigned and people could change where they sit at every meeting. Most friendship groups of students develop their own "turf" in a lecture hall and are surprised or dismayed when an interloper takes "their" seats.

Another example of primacy is seen in role differentiation among group members. The first person who takes on a group responsibility might be expected to continue accepting it. The first person who volunteers to take notes is sometimes automatically expected to continue doing so; the first person who breaks the tension with humor, likewise, is expected to continue.

It is important to note, though, that who takes what role in a group is also highly influenced by individuals' personal needs. The person with a high need for structure often wants to be in the note-taking role to control the structuring activity in the group; the person who breaks the tension might dislike conflict and uses the humor role to circumvent it.

3. ***Critical incidents.*** Sometimes there is an important incident in the group's history that establishes a precedent. In one organization, the head of a unit invited the entire staff to his house for dinner. The next day, people discovered that not one person on the staff had attended. The unpleasantness that this incident caused established the norm of no outside entertaining for several years. In another organization, some employees availed themselves of the "option" of not signing performance appraisal assessments they strongly disagreed with. The next day they were fired. The norm of "sign now, disown later" was established instantaneously. Norms about not dating coworkers often emerge after unpleasant break-ups of these romances cause too much awkwardness for other group members.

4. ***Explicit statements by supervisors or coworkers.*** Quite frequently a supervisor or a coworker might go up to new recruits and say, "That's not the way we do things around here." Sometimes this is followed by "because . . ." and other times no reason is given at all. Most frequently, norms develop this way to prevent any threats to the status quo.

For instance, new recruits who are too proactive in their respective units are often told explicitly to "cool their jets," that new recruits should be seen and not heard. Sometimes the older members don't want to be upstaged by the young upstarts. At other times, the older members might be trying to prevent the new recruits from making fools of themselves. For whatever reason, though, the norm is reestablished by explicit statements by coworkers.

5. ***Conscious decision of the group.*** Sometimes a group will explicitly address the norms that it has (or doesn't have) and discuss what works most effectively or ineffectively. These decisions are often provoked by a particularly good or bad experience the group has had.

To illustrate, a group might have had a particularly constructive meeting, and be very pleased with how much it accomplished. Several people might say, "I think the reason we got so much accomplished today is that we met really early in the morning before the rest of the staff showed up and the phone started ringing. Let's try to continue to meet at 7:30 a.m." Others might agree, and the norm is set.

Or, the group's Christmas party might have been a bust, and as members reconstruct the party the next day, someone might say, "I think the reason the party never got off the ground was having spouses there. They don't know other people at the party well, and the conversation is really stilted. Let's go back to employees-only parties next year." If others agree, another norm is set.

Why Norms Are Strongly Enforced

Groups, like individuals, try to operate in such a way that they maximize their chances of success and minimize their chances of failure. Groups want to facilitate group performance and prevent threats to reaching group goals. Moreover, groups want to ensure the satisfaction of their members and prevent any interpersonal discomfort. Norms are likely to be strongly enforced if they help groups meet their two aims of performing successfully and keeping morale high.

1. ***Norms are likely to be strongly enforced if they ensure group success or survival.*** A group will develop norms to protect itself from interference or harassment by members of other groups. For instance, a group might develop a norm not to discuss its salaries with members of other groups in the organization, so that attention will not be brought to pay inequities in its favor. Or, the group might have a norm about not discussing hiring with others in the organization, so there will be less competition for the good talent. The norms about productivity among piece-rate workers develop to ensure group success, too. The group will be less "successful" if it allows its jobs to be reevaluated. Any rate-busters have to be ostracized.

2. ***Norms are likely to be strongly enforced if they reflect the preferences of supervisors or other powerful group members.*** Most people are very sensitive to the preferences of those in power. When a supervisor's preferences about some issue are known, for instance, norms that cater to those preferences are established and strongly enforced.

   For instance, supervisors might have particular preferences for a way of analyzing problems or presenting reports. Strong norms will develop to ensure compliance with supervisor preferences. If the norms were not set, individual members would have to redo their work and/or would receive lower performance appraisals.

   Norms that cater to supervisor preferences are frequently established even when they are not objectively necessary to group functioning. For instance, while organizational norms may be very democratic in regard to everybody calling each other by their first names, some groups have strong norms about calling the supervisor Mr. or Ms. to comply with supervisor preferences. Although the form of address used in the work group does not influence group effectiveness, complying with the norm bears little cost to the group member, whereas noncompliance could cause daily friction with the supervisor.

3. *Norms are likely to be strongly enforced if they simplify, or make predictable, what behavior is expected of group members.* Group members may be uncertain about how to behave in certain types of situations. For instance, when attending meetings where proposals are presented and suggestions are requested, do the presenters really want feedback or are they simply going through the motions? Groups may develop norms that reduce this uncertainty and provide a clearer course of action, e.g., make suggestions in small, informal meetings but not in large, formal meetings.

Another example comes from norms that regulate more social behavior. For instance, when colleagues go out for lunch together, there can be some awkwardness about how to split the bill at the end of the meal. A group may develop a norm that gives some highly predictable or simple way of behaving, e.g., split evenly, take turns picking up the tab, pay for what each ordered.

4. *Norms are likely to be strongly enforced if they reinforce specific individual members' roles.* While groups obviously create pressure toward uniformity among members, there is also a tendency for groups to create and maintain *diversity* among members (Hackman, 1976). A number of different *roles* might emerge in groups. These roles are simply expectations that are shared by group members regarding who is to carry out what types of activities under what circumstances (Bales & Slater, 1955).

For instance, a group might have one person whom others expect to break the tension when tempers become too hot. Another group member might be expected to keep track of what's going on in other parts of the organization. A third member might be expected to take care of the "creature" needs of the group—making the coffee, making dinner reservations, etc. A fourth member might be expected by others to take notes, keep minutes, or maintain files. None of these roles are *formal* duties, but they are activities that the group needs accomplished and has somehow parceled out among members. If the role expectations are not met, some important jobs might not get done or other group members might have to take on additional responsibilities.

5. *Norms are likely to be strongly enforced if they help the group avoid embarrassing interpersonal problems.* Groups might develop norms discouraging certain topics of conversation that might prove awkward to some group members. For instance, a group might have a norm

about not discussing children, so that group members who have troubled or unhealthy children will not have to talk about them in public. A group might have a norm about only getting together socially in restaurants or public places and not in people's homes, so that differences in taste or income do not become salient.

Goffman's work on "facework" gives us some more insight on this point. Goffman (1955) argues that each person in a group has a "face" he or she presents to other members of the group. This face is analogous to what we would call "self-image," the person's perceptions of himself or herself and how he or she would like to be seen by others. Groups want to ensure that no one's self-image is damaged, called into question, or embarrassed. Consequently, they will establish norms that discourage topics of conversation or situations where face is too likely to be inadvertently broken.

A good illustration of Goffman's facework occurs in the classroom. There is always a palpable tension in a room when either a class is totally unprepared to discuss a case or a professor is totally unprepared to lecture or lead discussion. One part of the awkwardness stems from the fact that the other partner in the interaction cannot behave as they were prepared to or would like to. The professor can't teach if the students aren't prepared, and the students can't learn if the professors aren't teaching. Another part of the awkwardness stems from self-images being called into question. While faculty are aware that not all students are serious scholars, it is shaming to deal with the fact that the class as a group does not even show a pretense of wanting to learn. While students are aware that many faculty are mainly interested in research and consulting, it is demeaning to deal with the fact the professor does not even show a pretense of caring to teach. Norms almost always develop between professors and students about what level of preparation and interest is expected by the other. Some classes and professors are more demanding of each other than others, but all want to avoid a confrontation.

MANAGERIAL IMPLICATIONS

How does our knowledge of group membership, group cohesiveness, and group norms help us manage work groups more effectively? Let's examine some of the managerial implications of this material more closely.

1. ***In general, the evidence suggests group cohesiveness increases group effectiveness—but not in the ways most managers suspect.*** First, cohesiveness makes life much more pleasant on a day-to-day basis when colleagues enjoy each other and value the work group. The climate is more relaxed, less tense.

Second, cohesiveness facilitates group effectiveness by increasing worker cooperation. Cohesive groups are likely to have less absenteeism, turnover, and conflict. However, the link between cohesiveness and productivity is much more tenuous. Cohesiveness reduces the variance of productivity among group members, but does not necessarily increase the overall productivity of the group.

2. ***It is possible, however, for managers to induce a positive productivity bias in cohesive groups.*** Back (1951) induced three types of cohesiveness in experimental groups. In the *personal attraction* condition, the managers tried to engender group cohesiveness by getting group members to like each other personally. In the *prestige* condition, the managers tried to engender group cohesiveness by making salient to group members the high status of the group. In the *task itself* condition, the managers tried to engender group cohesiveness by creating in group members the desire to do an excellent job.

   The results of Back's research suggest that only where cohesiveness is induced on the basis of the task itself will cohesive groups be more productive. In the personal attraction condition, group members tended to engage in long, rambling conversation and had trouble settling down to work. In the prestige condition, members paid more attention to how they were being perceived by coworkers than to the work itself. In the task-based cohesiveness condition, in contrast, there was more debate before reaching consensus than in the other two conditions. There, group members tended to ignore interpersonal issues and to work rather intensely and efficiently to complete the task activity. Managers should attempt to induce group cohesiveness by making salient to group members both the extrinsic rewards and intrinsic satisfactions that would result from doing the group task well.

3. ***There seem to be two situations where group cohesiveness will systematically lead to decreased group effectiveness.*** The first situation is when the work itself is not intrinsically enough motivating to generate true group commitment, as in many production jobs. Instead of generating commitment to the job, the task may be so uninteresting that the group becomes cohesive in "avoiding hard work." In the second situation, group cohesiveness can lead to decreased group effectiveness in high-prestige, high-status groups. Being in a high-prestige, high-status group may be so reinforcing that "not rocking the boat" overwhelms "doing the task well" (Hackman, 1976). In these circumstances, managers may be better off not encouraging group cohesiveness.

4. ***The group's norms also play a large role in determining whether the group will be productive or not.*** If the work group feels management is supportive, group norms will develop that facilitate—in fact, enhance—group productivity. In contrast, if the work group feels management is antagonistic, group norms that inhibit and impair group performance are much more likely to develop.

5. ***Managers can play a major role in setting and changing group norms.*** By

explicitly setting task-facilitative norms in the group at its outset, the leader can help get the group off to a positive start. It is much easier to set norms (e.g., through example, through critical incidents) early in the group's life than to change long-standing norms. Managers can also continuously monitor whether the group's norms are functional and explicitly address counterproductive norms with subordinates. In so doing, the manager can force the group to openly examine its processes more closely and consciously develop more effective behavior patterns.

6. *Understanding how norms develop and why they are enforced helps managers better diagnose the underlying tensions and problems their groups are facing.* A set of group norms is as distinctive as an individual's fingerprints. A group of specific individuals will evolve a unique set of norms to deal with the specific challenges and problems they face. No two groups will develop the exact same set of norms or enforce them the same way. Unlike the set of individual fingerprints, however, the set of group norms can reveal a lot about the group's nature: what the group thinks is important, what its self-image is, where it thinks it is vulnerable.

   While there is no quick and easy way of diagnosing group dynamics by looking at group norms, there are some guideposts we can use to discover what the key issues in the group might be.

   a. *About what behaviors are there the most norms?* Where there is a lot of smoke, there is at least some fire. If a group develops many norms about a limited set of behaviors, it is very likely that the group sees these behaviors as critical to continued group success or survival.

      For instance, management consulting firms have a very elaborate set of norms about personal appearance and social etiquette with clients. At least in their minds, tightly prescribed norms about personal appearance and social etiquette are essential to the cultivation and maintenance of good client relationships. Brand managers frequently establish strong norms in their groups about working 10–20 hours a week overtime. Their perception is that all the work of the job cannot be done in the 8-hour day, and the extra hours are needed to ensure task completion and individual recognition.

   b. *About what nontask areas do norms cluster?* The norms about nontask-related behavior generally reveal where the interpersonal soft spots of the group lie. For instance, in some organizations there are highly ritualized norms about lunch. There might be different dining rooms for different job levels of the organization, with varying levels of stylish decor, dress required, and quality of food. There can be norms about going out to lunch or eating at one's desk. There can be norms about eating with others in the formal work group on a routine basis or each day eating with different people.

      These lunchtime norms evolve to deal with some thorny interpersonal problems the group is trying to resolve or avoid. For instance, the "company" dining rooms might fulfill the status needs that some managers might feel are not being adequately met in their day-to-day jobs. Or, managers and workers might want to avoid socializing with each other, and the lunchrooms make it socially acceptable not to. Regulating whether people go out for lunch or stay in for lunch may reflect some fears that people will take too much time for lunch and inconvenience coworkers, or some self-consciousness that people who go out for lunch "aren't serious enough." Having norms about whom one eats with can avoid feelings of being left out, or can eliminate the time and energy that goes into getting people together for lunch each day.

c. ***Where are there inconsistencies between what the group says are its norms and how people actually behave?*** There are times in groups when what people *say* is the group norm and how people actually *behave* are very inconsistent. For instance, sometimes companies will hire new managers and tell them to be entrepreneurial, to run their own units autonomously, to be independent. There will be a lot of rhetoric—almost too much—about how much freedom the organization allows its managers. Yet the harder data suggest that the more conservative, more dependent, more deferring managers consistently get rewarded and the more aggressive, dynamic managers get passed over. The official explanation, of course, is always: "He's a little too offbeat" or "She went a little too far." What can we make of this inconsistency?

First, the inconsistency can reveal a major source of *ambivalence* in the group. On one hand, the group knows it needs to encourage more entrepreneurial effort so the organization can grow and be successful. On the other hand, entrepreneurial efforts create competition, some older people might be surpassed, the status quo is threatened. The ambivalence gets channelled into this dichotomy between rhetoric and behavior.

Second, the inconsistency can reveal major *subgroup differences*. It is conceivable that group members are split about what type of behavior they approve. Some people value and encourage entrepreneurial behavior, but others do not—and they may control the group's rewards. The subgroup differences crop up in this dichotomy between rhetoric and behavior.

Third, the inconsistency can reveal a source of the group's *self-consciousness*, a dichotomy between what the group is really like and how it would like to be perceived. The group may realize that it is too conservative and complacent, yet be unable or frightened to address its problem. Instead, it pretends it is something it is not. By saying it is enterpreneurial often enough, it hopes to allay its anxiety that it is not entrepreneurial at all. The tension between reality and self-image gets translated into the dichotomy between rhetoric and behavior.

All three of these questions provide a starting point for further exploration of group dynamics. There is very little behavior in groups that is random. The good group diagnostician, like the good detective, looks for underlying patterns of behavior that reveal the really important issues.

SUMMARY

This chapter examines group membership, group cohesiveness, and group norms. By the term *group* we mean a collection of two or more people who: (1) interact with each other; (2) perceive themselves to share common interests or goals; and (3) come together or are brought together to accomplish some work activity.

Formal groups are those that are deliberately created to perform a specific task, such as command groups and temporary task forces. Membership in informal groups is voluntary and evolves naturally. Generally, people join informal groups to facilitate goal accomplishment, to enhance their own careers, or to fulfill social and esteem needs.

The bonds among memberships of all groups are not uniformly strong. By the term *cohesiveness* we mean the amount of interpersonal attraction among group members and their desire to remain members of the group. Groups will be more cohesive if: (1) they have a high level of interaction; (2) individual members share the group goals; and (3) members have similar attitudes and values. On almost every index of satisfaction and morale, cohesive groups rank higher than noncohesive groups.

The relationship between cohesiveness and productivity is not that direct. Cohesiveness does decrease the productivity differences among members of a work group. However, group cohesiveness does not necessarily lead to higher productivity. Group norms will largely influence whether group cohesiveness gets translated into higher group performance.

Norms are informal rules that a group adopts to regulate group members' behavior. March (1954) distinguishes between three types of norms. Unattainable-ideal norms give increasing approval the more the desired behavior is exhibited. Attainable-ideal norms give increasing approval the more the desired behavior is exhibited, but only up to a point. After a sufficient amount of the behavior is engaged in, the group will not continue rewarding its members for ever-increasing amounts. For preferred-value norms, both too little and too much of a desired behavior are disapproved; only a certain range of behavior is acceptable.

Norms usually develop gradually and informally. They can develop as a result of carry-over from past situations, as a result of the first behavior pattern that emerges in the group, or as a result of an important incident in the group's history that establishes a precedent. Norms can also be developed as a result of a conscious decision of the group or by explicit statements by supervisors or coworkers.

Groups will strongly enforce norms either to enhance the likelihood of group success, or to protect the group at its most vulnerable spots. Norms will be strongly enforced if: (1) they ensure group success or survival; (2) they reflect the preferences of authority figures; (3) they simplify, or make predictable, what behavior is expected of group members; (4) they reinforce specific members' roles; and (5) they help the group avoid embarrassing interpersonal problems.

REVIEW QUESTIONS

1. Define the term *group*.
2. What is the difference between a formal group and an informal group?
3. Identify the two most common types of formal groups. Give an example of each.
4. Why do people join informal work groups?
5. Define group cohesiveness.
6. What are the major sources of group cohesiveness?
7. Discuss the relationship between group cohesiveness and morale.
8. Discuss the relationship between group cohesiveness and productivity.
9. Define the term *group norm*.
10. Why can't norms regulate the private attitudes and beliefs of group members?
11. Identify the five indices of group norms developed in Jackson's Return Potential Model. How is each reflected in the return potential curve?
12. Distinguish between unattainable-ideal norms, attainable-ideal norms, and preferred-value norms. Give an example of each.
13. What are the five ways in which most norms develop?
14. Groups strongly enforce norms either to enhance the likelihood of group success or to protect the group at its most vulnerable spots. Discuss the five situations where norms are most likely to be strongly enforced.
15. How does Goffman's work on "facework" help us understand why groups try to avoid embarrassing interpersonal problems?

REFERENCES

Aronson, Elliot. *The social animal*. San Francisco: W. H. Freeman, 1976.

Back, Kurt W. Influence through social communication. *Journal of Abnormal and Social Psychology*, 1951, *46*, 190–207.

Bales, R. F., & Slater, P. E. Role differentiation in small groups. In T. Parsons, R. F. Bales, et al., *Family, socialization, and interaction process*. Glencoe, Ill.: Free Press, 1955.

Dalton, Melville. *Men who manage*. New York: Wiley, 1959.

Festinger, L., Schachter, S., & Back, K. *Social pressures in informal groups*. Stanford: Stanford University Press, 1950.

Galbraith, Jay R. Organization design: An information processing view. *Interfaces*, 1974, *4*, 28–36.

Goffman, Erving. On face-work: An analysis of ritual elements in social interaction. *Psychiatry*, 1955, *18*, 213–231.

Golembiewski, R. T. *The small group*. Chicago: University of Chicago Press, 1962.

Hackman, J. R. Group influences on individuals. In M. Dunnette (Ed.), *Handbook of industrial and organizational psychology*. Chicago: Rand McNally, 1976.

Herold, David M. The effectiveness of work groups. In S. Kerr (Ed.), *Organizational behavior*. Columbus, Ohio: Grid Publishing, 1979.

Jackson, J. Structural characteristics of norms. In I. D. Steiner & M. Fishbein (Eds.), *Current studies in social psychology*. New York: Holt, 1965.

Jackson, J. A conceptual and measurement model for norms and roles. *Pacific Sociological Review*, 1966, *9*, 35–45.

Janis, Irving L. *Victims of groupthink: A psychological study of foreign-policy decisions and fiascos*. New York: Houghton Mifflin, 1972.

Lott, A. J., & Lott, B. E. Group cohesiveness as interpersonal attraction: A review of relationships with antecedent and consequent variables. *Psychological Bulletin*, 1965, *64*, 259–309.

March, James G. Group norms and the active minority. *American Sociological Review*, 1954, *19*, 733–741.

Porter, L. W., Lawler, E. E., III, & Hackman, J. R. *Behavior in organizations*. New York: McGraw-Hill, 1975.

Schachter, S., Ellertson, N., McBride, D., & Gregory, D. An experimental study of cohesiveness and productivity. *Human Relations*, 1951, *4*, 229–238.

Seashore, Stanley. *Group cohesiveness in the industrial work group*. Ann Arbor: Institute for Social Research, University of Michigan, 1954.

Shaw, Marvin E. *Group dynamics* (3rd ed.) New York: McGraw-Hill, 1981.

Tajfel, H. Social and cultural factors in perception. In G. Lindzey & E. Aronson (Eds.), *The handbook of social psychology* (2nd ed.). Reading, Mass.: Addison-Wesley, 1969.

Trist, E. L., & Bamforth, K. W. Some social and psychological consequences of the longwall method of coal-getting. *Human Relations*, 1951, *4*, 1–38.

Wall Street Journal, Sept. 19, 1979. New York: Dow Jones, p. 1.

Whyte, W. F. *Money and motivation*. New York: Harper, 1955.

CHAPTER 17

CONFORMITY AND DEVIANCE

We are probably more ambivalent about conformity than any other aspect of group interaction. On one hand, we often resent having to bend our wishes to those of the group, yet we often get annoyed with colleagues who are intractable, stubborn, or argumentative in group meetings. When we are subordinates, we often resent having to do things just because our bosses ask us to, but when we are the bosses ourselves we become infuriated with those who won't follow our orders. We acknowledge the right of the organization that pays us to demand our obedience, but we also feel an obligation to act on the basis of our own individual conscience and reason.

In the last chapter, we examined why groups develop norms and why groups try to enforce norms strongly. In this chapter, we will be addressing more closely how *individuals* respond to those group pressures. First, we'll look at when group members are likely to *conform*, i.e., change their behaviors and beliefs as a result of group pressure. Second, we'll examine how groups respond to *deviants*, i.e., those who fail to respond to group pressure. Third, and most important, we'll examine at what point conformity becomes *dysfunctional* for the organization and deviance becomes functional; while conformity can facilitate the group getting its work done smoothly, it can just as readily stifle creativity and inhibit change.

We'll turn first to the issues of conformity.

CONFORMITY

"Get along by going along." That phrase captures much of what we have been taught over the years about how to succeed in groups and organizations. In school, we learn what happens to the "troublemakers"—they are punished by the teachers and thought of as "different" by their classmates. When we start looking for jobs, we get further reinforced for following standard practices. Résumés should look a certain way, we should dress a certain way, we should behave in our job interviews in a certain way. Of course, we don't have to conform, but we notice, too, that people who don't conform have a much more difficult time getting good jobs, or any jobs at all. As we work in organizations, we observe that people are nervous around those who "rock the boat." People who get impatient with the system and try to change it generally beat their heads against the wall. If they ignore the pressures of their colleagues, they lead a lonely existence at work; if they seriously confront their bosses, their days in the organization are numbered.

During the 1960s and 1970s, current events made especially salient the power of the group over the individual. The trial of Lieutenant Calley for allegedly murdering Vietnamese women and children, the endless string of Watergate trials for cover-ups of political dirty tricks in the Nixon administration, and the belated trials of Nazi war criminals all seemed to reverberate with one refrain—"I was only following orders; I knew it was wrong but everybody else was doing it; I assumed my superiors knew what they were doing." Two studies on obedience that were done during that period crystallized people's worst fears about conformity and demonstrated just how powerful group influences on individual behavior were.

Milgram's Obedience Study

Stanley Milgram (1965) set up an experiment at Yale University to test how much pain one person would inflict on another, simply because he or she was ordered to do so by someone in a position of authority. Two people took part in each experiment, which was described as a study of the effects of punishment on learning. One person, the "learner," was seated in a chair, wrists strapped down and wired with electrodes. The learner was told that he would read lists of simple word pairs, and that he would then be tested on his ability to remember the second word of a pair when he heard the first one again. The other person in the experiment, the "teacher," would administer increasing amounts of shock to the learner for wrong answers. The shocks would be administered via a dial labeled *slight, moderate, strong, very strong, intense, extremely intense,* or *dangerously severe shock*. The learner, however, was a confederate of the experimenter. He received no shocks at all, but was paid to respond to increasing "shocks" with loud complaints, vehement protests, emotional outcries, agonized screams, or at the very highest amounts of "shock," dead silence. The focus of the experiment was thus on the teacher and how much pain he or she would inflict on the protesting victim.

Before the experiments, Milgram asked psychiatrists for their predictions about the results of the study. The psychiatrists predicted that most subjects would not go beyond moderate shock, when the learner made his first explicit demand to be free. They expected only 4 percent of the subjects would administer very strong shocks, and only 1 in 1000 would administer the highest shock of *dangerously severe*. Their predictions were very wrong. Almost two-thirds of the subjects punished the victim with the most potent shock available. These results were true not only for college students but for professionals, white-collar workers, unemployed persons, and blue-collar workers as well. While some subjects showed considerable discomfort and great relief at the end of the experiment others displayed only minimal signs of tension from beginning to end.

The Stanford Prison Study

Haney and Zimbardo's Stanford Prison Study (1973) reveals equally startling results. As social psychologists, the authors were interested in studying the behavioral and psychological consequences of imprisonment on both the prisoners and those who maintain and administer the prison. In their experiment, they used a group of twenty Stanford students who had previously undergone extensive psychological testing and had been diagnosed as psychologically healthy. In the experiment, some students took the role of guard and others took the role of prisoner. Much to the surprise and dismay of the experimenters, in a very short time most of the subjects ceased distinguishing between their prison role and prior self-identities. The guards took sadistic pleasure in harassing and degrading the prisoners, actually going out of their way to humiliate them. Prisoners, too, became totally controlled by the reality of the prison. They became passive and submissive in demeanor; they accepted and adopted the guards' negative attitudes toward them. The experiment was cut short after only 6 days of the planned 2-week simulation.

The Milgram Obedience Study and the Stanford Prison Study reveal three important aspects of the pressure to conformity, above and beyond its sheer strength.

1. *Our bias is to give the organization and its appointed leaders the benefit of the doubt where the rationale for what we are being asked to do is either unclear to us or seems insufficient to justify our behavior.* We reason that if there is brutality in prisons, then the prisoners must have done something to deserve it or they wouldn't be in prison in the first place. If the experimenter asks the subject to shock the learner, it

must still be all right, since the experimenter is a Yale professor and he must know what he's doing (Haney & Zimbardo, 1973).

2. ***Our "role" can completely overwhelm other aspects of our self-identity***. The situation and the actions it requires of us can be so powerful that we lose sight of where our role ends and our self begins. As one subject in the Stanford Prison study put it: "It's almost like a prison that you create yourself—you get into it, and it becomes almost the definition you make of yourself, it almost becomes like walls, and you want to break out and you want just to be able to tell everyone that 'this isn't really me at all, and I'm not the person that's confined in there . . .'" (Haney & Zimbardo, 1973).

3. ***Most frightening, however, these studies suggest that evil or immoral behavior is not the sole province of pathological personalities***. Indeed, the people who shocked the victims in Milgram's study or who tormented the prisoners in Haney and Zimbardo's study were "ordinary people" who did so out of a sense of obligation and not from any peculiarly aggressive tendencies (Milgram, 1965).

Despite these rather gloomy overall findings, there was some ray of hope. Even in experiments as intense as these, not everyone conformed. For instance, fully one-third of Milgram's students did not administer the painful shocks. To illustrate, one subject who firmly refused to go further with the shocks said to the experimenter: "Well, I'm sorry, I think when shocks continue like this they are dangerous. You ask him if he wants to get out. It's his free will. . . . I don't want to be responsible for anything happening to him." As Milgram (1974) suggests, this subject's straightforward behavior made disobedience seem simple and rational, the sort of behavior he had envisioned from almost all his subjects.

When People Will Conform

The pressures to conform—to change one's behavior and beliefs as a result of group influence—come at individuals from many directions. Below, we look at seven particular circumstances in which individuals are most likely to bow to group influence.

Individuals will be more likely to conform when the work environment is uncertain and individuals need the group for information.

Individuals are unable to obtain either a very complete or very accurate view of their work environment if they rely only upon their own senses and experiences. This is particularly true if they are new to the group or if the group is undergoing a lot of change. There is simply too much going on for any one individual to observe and interpret alone. When the work environment is uncertain, individuals are more likely to turn to other group members for information and to accept that information as true.

The classic experiment illustrating how individuals conform in situations of uncertainty was done by Sherif (1936). In the Sherif study, each subject was seated alone in a dark room. A spot of light was flashed momentarily at the front of the room. On a series of trials, each subject was asked to judge how much the light "moved." In reality, the light did not move at all. There is an optical illusion called the "autokinetic effect" which occurs when a pinpoint of light is flashed into a totally dark room. The light *appears* to move to the beholder, but does not actually move at all. In this first part of the experiment, Sherif was allowing each individual to develop his or her own subjective standards for how much the light moved.

Next, Sherif put subjects together in a dark room, and had individuals publicly announce their estimates of the amount of movement. Very shortly, all the individual answers started hovering around a common standard; the individual responses converged to the same answer. Sherif's subjects were using the group for informational purposes; in the absence of "hard" sense data, they used the subjective reports of other members as information (Hackman, 1976).

In organizational settings, it is very important for individuals to have a more complete and accurate view of the work environment than they can get on their own. People need to know: (1) what rewards are available in the group and who controls them; (2) what penalties or punishments are administered to group members and who administers them; and (3) what they need to do to obtain the rewards and avoid the punishments.

For instance, when students first enroll in business schools, they are most anxious to obtain information about professors and grading policies, since these two factors most strongly influence their rewards and punishments (dean's list, financial aid, academic probation, failure). First-year students are not only susceptible to influence from second-year students, but also actively seek out information from them (e.g., What's Professor Jones really like? What are the easy-A courses? Does anybody ever flunk out?). As graduation approaches, the work environment becomes uncertain once again. Students are unsure about what jobs are available, what the jobs are like, and how to obtain them. They are constantly searching for "the inside scoop" about the job market and are generally willing to give serious credence to whatever information they do pick up (e.g., "I heard we should wear maroon ties"; "I heard they don't like to hire people over 30"). Lacking "hard" data (i.e., whether people over 30 actually get discriminated against), graduating students are more open to listening to, and accepting as true, whatever subjective information they can garner from their peers.

Individuals will be more likely to conform when they are unsure of themselves, and need the group for affirmation.

When individuals are new to a group, they often feel unsure about themselves and their abilities to perform well in the organization. At times like this, individuals look to the group for information about how they are perceived, and quite readily accept the group's opinion of them as true.

Jones and Gerard (1967) make a distinction between two ways groups can influence an individual's beliefs about his or her own abilities. In *comparative appraisal*, individuals determine their relative standing vis-à-vis others by simply observing other members of the group. In *reflected appraisal*, individuals obtain information about themselves by observing and interpreting how others actually behave toward them. Reflected appraisal is analogous to Cooley's (1922) concept of "looking glass self," whereby individuals come to gain self-understanding by inferring what they "must be like" given the way others are behaving toward them.

When individuals are new to an organization, they obtain feedback on their performance through *both* comparative and reflected appraisal (Feldman, 1980). New recruits take careful note of how they are doing relative to others—if they get their work done faster, if they make more errors than others, if others look more puzzled. They also try to figure out how they are doing by making attributions about how others behave toward them. If they are given more responsibilities and are given more autonomy, they infer they are doing well; if they are given no additional responsibilities and supervisors keep on checking their work, they infer they are doing poorly.

As surprising as it may seem, individuals even turn to groups for information about what emotions they should be experiencing (Schachter & Singer, 1962). Individuals often look to other group members to see how they should be reacting to novel situations. For instance, when a new manager first meets with his or her subordinates, group members will look to each other to see how they should be responding. Should they be relieved? apprehensive? angry? Was the manager's joke a put-down or was it funny? When individuals are unsure of themselves, they are more likely to turn to other group members for support and affirmation, and to accept the group's view of reality as true (Gerard and Rabbie, 1961).

Individuals are more likely to conform when they value group membership highly.

An individual will be more open to group influence if he or she values membership in the group and accepts the group as a relevant point of reference. The more we value membership in a group, and the more needs group membership fulfills for us, the more we accept the group's position as legitimate (Lewicki, 1981; Siegel & Siegel, 1957).

No study illustrates this point better than Newcomb's research on Bennington College students (1963). Up until recently, Bennington was an all-female, very liberal college in Vermont. Interestingly enough, however, most of the women who went to Bennington were the children of conservative, Republican parents. Newcomb found that each class of students became increasingly more liberal politically during their 4 years at Bennington. Some accepted more liberalism as a revolt against parents, others because they found it "more intellectually respectable," others because they found expressing liberal attitudes had prestige value.

However, not all the students became more liberal. Those who remained conservative did not accept Bennington as an important *reference group*. They were least absorbed in college community affairs, they spent less time on campus, and they accepted their parents' influence as more legitimate. Being a member of a group is not enough in and of itself to bring about conformity; the group membership has to be valued and the group seen as an important reference point.

We see the same phenomenon in business schools. Those students who are getting on the entry-level escalators to finance, marketing, accounting, personnel, or operations jobs accept their associates as a much more central reference group than do those pursuing less traditional business careers. Those students who are going into public administration, health services, or corporate law do not see the business school students as an equally relevant, or legitimate, reference group. These "nontraditional" students do not perceive their interests or their career plans to be similar to those of their peers. Moreover, they see business school faculty as less expert and credible about the nontraditional organizations in which they will ultimately be working.

This example points out yet another aspect of reference groups. Individuals may take as a reference group a group to which they *aspire* to belong. Individuals may begin to socialize themselves to what they perceive to be a group's norms *before* they are even group members (Merton & Rossi, 1968; Hyman & Singer, 1968). While business school students are not yet managers, they may start to conform to some of the demands they perceive will be required of them later—conservative dress, short hair, politically conservative values, concern with personal finances, etc. In fact, one of the reasons graduates adjust so readily to their new organizations is that they have conformed so much during their *anticipatory socialization* (Feldman, 1976).

Individuals are more likely to conform when there is a lot of interaction among group members.

In Chapter 16, we observed that the greater the interaction between the individuals in a group, the greater the group cohesiveness. It is also the case that the greater the interaction between an individual and other members of the group, the more likely the individual will conform to the group's beliefs and behaviors.

By repeatedly making explicit statements about how they view the job, other members of the group can influence an individual member's beliefs. If coworkers continuously maintain that a job is horrible, boring, or undesirable, the individual is unlikely to reject their judgments. The worker may want to agree with the coworkers simply to fit in (Salancik & Pfeffer, 1978, p. 229).

Lieberman's research (1956) on unions illustrates just how groups influence individual attitudes through day-to-day interaction. The study took place over a 3-year period at a unionized Rockwell manufacturing plant.

During the first year of the study, twenty-three workers were promoted to supervisor, and thirty-five workers were elected union stewards. Then, a year and half later, eight of the new supervisors were returned to the worker role (because of cutbacks associated with an economic recession) and fourteen of the union stewards returned to the worker role (because they chose not to run again in union elections or ran and were defeated).

Workers who were promoted to the job of supervisor became much more pro-management and much more critical of the union. They were exposed to much more anti-union propaganda. The accomplishments of management and the flaws of the union were both made more salient. Supervisors who remained supervisors kept their new attitudes. On the other hand, those who went back to being workers eventually became pro-union and anti-management once again.

The pattern of results for workers who became union stewards was similar. New union stewards became more pro-union; demoted union stewards became less pro-union. Thus, we see that being in frequent contact with other group members can indeed increase the degree to which an individual will conform to the group's position.

It is also important to note here that groups can condition our attitudes through daily interaction *without our conscious awareness*. Staats and Staats (1958) have demonstrated how we can be conditioned to hold certain attitudes simply by hearing evaluative adjectives paired continuously with the name of a group. For instance, if we constantly hear the adjective *flashy* associated with marketing, we may begin to think of brand managers and advertising executives as clothes-conscious and extroverted. The influence is much more subtle and much more covert, but is influence nonetheless.

Individuals are more likely to conform when they have made some sort of public commitment to the group.

In Chapter 14, we briefly discussed cognitive dissonance. There, we noted that most people feel uncomfortable when they have to deal with the fact that their behaviors are inconsistent with their attitudes. In these situations, most individuals try to achieve some consistency between their attitudes and their behaviors by shifting their attitudes to be more consistent with their behaviors.

When a group can get an individual to publicly comply with some behavior or request against his or her initial inclination, the group is creating cognitive dissonance for the individual. The individual has made a public statement or engaged in a behavior that is inconsistent with internal beliefs and attitudes. Since the behavior is public and can *not* be changed, most individuals are likely to change their *attitudes* to the group's position to achieve consistency. Let's look at a couple of examples of this.

Justification of Effort. Dissonance theory predicts that if a person works hard to attain a goal, that goal will be more attractive to him or her than to someone who achieves the same goal with little or no effort. When groups can get individuals to put in a lot of effort, they create some dissonance for the unenthusiastic group member: "I'm working like hell"; "I don't like what I'm doing." Most often, this dissonance is reduced by changing the cognition "I don't like what I'm doing" to "This job must be okay or I wouldn't be working so hard." It is much harder to acknowledge "I am working like hell, and it isn't worth it."

Festinger and Carlsmith (1959) demonstrated this point nicely in a very well-done experiment. They asked subjects to perform a very boring and repetitive series of tasks—packing spools, turning screws, etc. The experimenter then induced the subjects to lie about the task, to tell a person waiting to participate in the experiment that the tasks she would be performing would be interesting and enjoyable. Some of the students were offered $20 for telling the lie, while others were offered only $1 for telling the lie. After the experiment was over, the experimenter asked the subjects how they had enjoyed the tasks (packing spools, turning screws, etc.) they had been performing. The students who had been paid $20 said the tasks were very dull. In contrast, the students who had been paid only $1 rated the tasks as very enjoyable.

The students who were paid $20 had sufficient monetary justification for doing the boring job and didn't have to justify their effort by saying the job was enjoyable. On the other hand, the students who were paid only $1 didn't have sufficient justification for stating the task was enjoyable. Consequently, they increased the positiveness of their attitudes about the work to compensate for their lack of pay.

Severity of Initiation. Dissonance theory also predicts that the more severe the initiation to the group, the more the individual will value group membership and comply to group pressure (Aronson & Mills, 1959). By getting new members to go through a severe initiation, companies create the following set of perceptions in individuals' minds: "This initiation is really rough"; "The company must be worth it."

The job interview process works very much in this way. If students have to go through several company call-backs and undergo stress interviews, they have made substantial investments in the organization. If the students are finally offered jobs and accept them, they go into the organization with a perceptual set of *expecting* to like the organization very strongly. They figure, "Any organization that could get me to go through this process must be worth joining."

We observe the same situation on college campuses with fraternity and sorority rush. Those houses that are most popular and which demand the greatest loyalty are often those that engage in the most serious hazing. Having gone through a bad "hell week", the pledges compensate by overvaluing group membership.

Individuals are more likely to conform when the group pressure is moderate rather than severe.

If the group can get an individual to comply on a minor issue, the individual will be much more likely to conform to much larger requests later on (Kiesler & Kiesler, 1969). This "foot-in-the-door" technique lowers the individual's resistance to the group's influence and creates some commitment and involvement between the individual and the group. For instance, if the group can get an individual to come to work a half hour early initially, it is easier 6 months later to get him or her to come in to work an hour early or on an occasional Sunday.

However, if the group pressure to conform is too severe, the individual is likely to show *reactance* (Brehm, 1966). When an individual feels that the group is reducing his or her freedom beyond tolerable limits, he or she will purposely *not* conform simply to demonstrate independence. If the group is pressuring individuals too strongly to change their position, they may dig in their heels and refuse to change—not because they care that strongly but because they resent the amount of pressure being brought to bear on them. While we all recognize we are subject to group pressure, we resent being subjected to strong-arm tactics.

Individuals are more likely to conform when they are alone in opposition to the group's position.

Being a minority of one puts an individual in a very vulnerable position. There is no one to turn to for support, or for self-affirmation. Under these circumstances, the lone individual is very likely to conform to group pressure. In Chapter 16, we saw a case of that with Arthur Schlesinger, who was the only dissenter in the Kennedy cabinet decision on the Bay of Pigs invasion plan.

We see similar results in a variation of the Milgram study. Here, three teachers (two actors and a real subject) administered a test and shocks to "learners." When the two actors disobeyed the experimenter and refused to go beyond a certain shock level, thirty-six of forty subjects joined their disobedient peers and refused as well. The confederates served as a counterbalance to the strong influence of the experimenter (Milgram, 1965). Even having just *one* supporter will seriously lessen an individual's propensity to conform.

When we look at this finding, we begin to understand why single representatives to important committees (such as a student representative on a university governance committee or a worker representative on the board of directors) are so ineffective. Since the single representative is generally from a lower status group, he or she often has lower credibility and lower expertise than other committee members. Consequently, he or she will find it more difficult to change the attitudes of other committee members. Also, as a single representative the individual may have no real allies on the committee to turn to for support or affirmation. In fact, the single representative is much more likely to be persuaded by the arguments of other group members than vice versa.

Normative versus Informational Influences of Groups

In real life, it is very difficult to distinguish between the *normative* influences of groups (changing what people say they believe to avoid ridicule) and *informational* influences of groups (changing what people honestly believe because they accept the group's data as true). Most messages are "double-barreled." A group member may be given a helpful report of "the way things are" in the organization as a matter of information—but behind the informational content is the added message that the individual is expected by others to perceive things that way and act accordingly (Deutsch & Gerard, 1955).

In probably the most famous experiment ever done on conformity, Asch (1951) asked subjects to match the length of a given line with one of three unequal lines. It was obvious in each case what the correct answer was. Subjects in groups of eight (seven confederates and one real subject) were required to state their answers aloud. The experiment was set up so that the real subject answered last—after all the confederates had unanimously given the wrong response. One-third of the subjects conformed and agreed with the wrong answer of the confederates.

At first glance it might appear that the subjects in the Asch experiment were conforming strictly because they feared being ridiculed—that is, for normative reasons. However, Asch (1951, p. 178) reports that postexperiment interviews with subjects revealed that not all subjects were conforming for those reasons. He found three types of responses from the conformers.

1. ***Distortion of perception***. A few subjects were unaware that their estimates had been distorted by the majority and believed that they were giving the correct estimates throughout.
2. ***Distortion of judgment***. Most of the subjects reported that they felt that somehow their own perception was incorrect since everyone else had responded differently.
3. ***Distortion of action***. These subjects were aware that their judgments

were correct but deliberately chose to go along with the majority out of a need not to appear different from, or inferior to, others.

Thus, while some subjects consciously conformed only to avoid ridicule, the basic perceptions and judgments of others were impaired by the group.

Conversely, our first explanation for the results of Sherif's study on conformity with the autokinetic effect (discussed earlier) is that Sherif's subjects were using the group solely for informational purposes. In the absence of "hard" sense data on how much the light moved, they used the subjective reports of other members as information. However, it is also possible that subjects changed their initial private estimates after hearing the reports of others because of the fear of appearing foolish by saying aloud what they really thought they saw (Hackman, 1976).

Thus, while we have individually discussed each of the seven conditions when individuals are most likely to conform, it is important to remember that in most situations there are several sources of pressure to conformity operating on individuals. The pressures to conformity almost always have an element of normative influence and an element of informational influence, and it is hard for individual group members to untangle the two.

Compliance, Identification, and Internalization

So far, we have been using the term conformity rather generally to talk about when people will change what they say or do to meet with group approval. Yet, it makes a big difference whether people are changing what they are *saying* or what they are *believing*. We would expect that people who conform only in what they are saying are unlikely to conform over the long run, or when push comes to shove.

Kelman (1961) makes a useful distinction between three types of social influence.

1. **Compliance** is said to occur when an individual conforms because he or she hopes to achieve a favorable reaction from other group members. He or she may hope to attain specific rewards from the group (like group membership) or avoid specific punishments (like ridicule or ostracism).
2. **Identification** is said to occur when an individual conforms because he or she desires to be like other group members. He or she is attracted to other group members, finds relationships with them to be intrinsically satisfying, and wants to express attitudes that others in the group will find compatible.
3. **Internalization** is said to occur when individuals conform because what they are conforming to is consistent with their own value system. These

individuals take the group's message to heart because they find it useful information, or relevant to the solution of a problem, or because it is consistent with their own personal orientation.

Compliance is the least enduring type of social influence and has the least effect on the individual. The complier understands the force of the circumstance and can easily change his or her behavior when the circumstance no longer prevails (Aronson, 1976). Where compliance is the main way of ensuring conformity, we find that people's behavior is governed by the dictum, "out of sight, out of mind." When the threat of punishment is absent, the individual no longer conforms.

For instance, Milgram (1965) found that when the experimenter went out of the room and issued orders by telephone, the number of fully obedient subjects dropped dramatically. Moreover, several of the subjects who did continue with the experiment "cheated;" specifically, they administered shocks of lower intensity than they were supposed to and never bothered to tell the experimenter that they had deviated from the proper procedure.

Identification is somewhat more enduring than compliance. As long as the individual values group membership and wants to be attractive to other group members, the group's influence will be strong. However, if the individual finds a new group of friends or colleagues with whom to associate, then the force of identification fades quickly.

For instance, in the Bennington College study of student liberalism, those women who became more liberal solely to appear more attractive to their college classmates lost much of their liberalism after college was over. Bennington became a much less important, and much less attractive, reference group.

Internalization is the most enduring form of social influence. As long as the group-supplied information is consistent with their own experiences and beliefs and helps them function better at work, people will accept the group's influence as valid and credible.

For example, some people will comply to rate-busting norms because they fear punishment from other group members (compliance). Others will conform because they value group membership and want to express attitudes that others in the group will find compatible (identification). However, if the company changed the production system so that individuals could produce more without coworkers knowing it, or if there were new supervisors with whom the workers could better identify, the group influence on these individuals would be lost. Those individuals who *internalized* the beliefs about the functionality of the rate-busting norm— individuals who had seen the rates readjusted by industrial engineers or who believed management was trying to squeeze out 2 days' labor for 1 day's pay—those individuals would continue to restrict production *independent* of whether the production system or supervisors changed.

Needless to say, internalization is the most powerful type of conformity. With it, groups have to worry less about whether norms are broken; without it, groups have more trouble controlling and coordinating individual behavior. However, groups often can't obtain this type of conformity—what they are "selling" just doesn't jibe with individuals' past experiences or the group just isn't important enough to the individuals to obtain their loyalty and compliance. What happens to people who won't conform? And what happens to the groups of which they are members? We turn to consider these issues of deviance next.

DEVIANCE

Groupthink: A Case of Conformity Gone Awry

An important study of American foreign policy fiascos brought to managers' attention the fact that too much conformity might be dysfunctional for group effectiveness. In *Victims of Groupthink: A Psychological Study of Foreign-Policy Decisions and Fiascos*, Irving Janis (1972) presents a fascinating set of case studies of foreign policy decision-making fiascos over the last 40 years. For instance, Janis recounts how the Kennedy Cabinet backed a plan for Cuban exiles to invade Cuba against Fidel Castro, even when news of the "surprise" invasion of the Bay of Pigs was leaked in the *New York Times*. He also examines how the Johnson administration kept on misreading the strategic problems of winning a war in Vietnam and rationalized away continuous "setbacks" (as opposed to "defeats"). Janis discusses, as well, the Roosevelt administration's inability to recognize the imminent threat of the Japanese attack on Pearl Harbor, and President Truman's strategic errors in the Korean police action.

It is Janis's argument that when groups become too cohesive and demand too much conformity, they are also likely to develop patterns of behavior that interfere with, if not completely undermine, good decision making. Maintaining the pleasant atmosphere of the group (in these case studies, presidential cabinets) can become more important to members than coming up with high-quality decisions. As a result, decision making suffers tremendously.

Janis outlines the seven most salient symptoms of this "groupthink" phenomenon.

1. ***The illusion of invulnerability***. Groups with too much pressure to conformity share an illusion of invulnerability. They overestimate their ability to succeed against high odds and extraordinary risks.
2. ***Collective rationalization***. Victims of groupthink are much less likely to perceive any blind spots in their plans. When faced with feedback that suggests the plans are failing, victims of groupthink put a lot of energy

into thinking of rationalizations for the failure and ways to discount the warnings.

3. ***Belief in the inherent morality of the group***. Groups that demand too much conformity develop a sense of self-righteousness, that what they are doing is not only logically but also ethically correct. This belief dulls members' sensitivity to the ethical and moral consequences of their actions.

4. ***Stereotypes of out-groups***. Victims of groupthink hold biased, or stereotyped, views of competing groups. They assume the competition is too inept or too impotent to counter their offensives.

5. ***Direct pressure on dissenters***. Groups that demand a lot of conformity apply a great deal of pressure on people who call into question the rightness or morality of the group's position. These groups often have self-appointed "mindguards" who exert this pressure. Group members are reinforced only when they acknowledge the "goodness" of the group.

6. ***Self-censorship***. These groups also pressure members to keep silent about their misgivings about the group's decisions and to minimize the importance of their self-doubts. The analogy between this aspect of groupthink and the fable about "The Emperor's New Clothes" is clear.

7. ***Illusion of unanimity***. Largely as a result of self-censorship and the pressures to affirm the rightness of the group's decisions, the victims of groupthink share an illusion of group unanimity. They mistake silence for conversion to the group's position, and lukewarm assent for genuine agreement.

In short, groups that demand too much conformity are less likely to accurately examine the risks of their proposed courses of action. They are less likely to process negative data carefully. When faced with failure, they are less likely to reconsider other alternatives. Convinced by the rightness of their position, they fail to work out ahead of time any contingency plans for operations going wrong. All of these factors taken together contribute to the increased likelihood of decision-making fiascos.

While there has been very little research to directly test Janis's work (Longley & Pruitt, 1980), the amount of theoretical and empirical work that indirectly supports Janis's propositions is sizeable and lends credence to at least the core of his thesis. Moreover, more and more examples of groupthink in industry are emerging. How could Ford have produced a car like the Pinto knowing ahead of time its potential safety hazards and the relatively minor cost of fixing the problems? Why did Chrysler refuse to believe that the energy crisis of the 1970s was real and that the days of the big gas-guzzling car were over, despite daily reminders of long gas lines and increased small-car imports? Why were the design and maintenance problems of the DC-10 ignored for so long until the crash of American Flight 191 in May of 1979? Janis's work gives us some useful perspectives on these questions, and reminds us again of how important the day-to-day consequences of overconformity can be.

Deviance Defined

We use the term *deviance* to refer to *behaviors that other members of the group consider so threatening, embarrassing, or irritating that they bring special sanctions to bear against the persons who exhibit them* (Erikson, 1966, p. 6). Rate-busting is threatening to the survival of production groups—and is deviant; unattractive and unstylish clothing is embarrassing and irritating to executives—and is deviant.

When we discussed group norms in the last chapter, we noted that each group would develop a unique set of norms. These norms would facilitate the group's reaching its task goals and prevent uncomfortable interpersonal situations from occurring. What is deviant in a group is likewise unique. Within each group, people will *label* as deviant those behaviors they find threatening, embarrassing, or irritating (Erikson, 1966, p. 6). For instance, rate-busting is threatening in production groups, but individual competitive behavior is positively rewarded among executives. In contrast, unattractive and unstylish clothing is irritating and embarrassing to executives, but is almost the norm on production lines. What a group labels deviant reflects its own internal standards.

Functions of Deviance

What functions does labeling behavior deviant serve for the group? Punishing the deviant serves at least three functions.

1. **Labeling behavior deviant gives expression to the group's central values.** Labeling behavior deviant gives the group a chance to express what its central values are. It clarifies what is distinctive about the group and central to its identity (Hackman, 1976). When the production group labels rate-busting deviant, it says "we care more about maximizing group security than about individual profits." When an advertising agency labels unstylish clothes deviant, it says "we think of ourselves, personally and professionally, as trend-setters, and being fashionable conveys that to our clients and our public."
2. **Labeling behavior deviant makes salient the power and authority of the group.** Each time a group punishes a deviant, it reinforces in the minds of the group members the power and authority of the group. Punishment of group deviants reminds other group members what will happen if they do not conform. Ostracism and ridicule of deviants both convey the same message to coworkers: "This will happen to you, too, if you step out of line."
3. **Labeling behavior deviant makes clear the "boundaries" of the group.**

By publicly labeling and punishing deviance, the group can make clearer what its norms are. As a result of observation of deviant behavior and the consequences that ensure, other group members are reminded of the *range* of behavior that is acceptable to the group (Dentler & Erikson, 1959). For example, group members might not really understand what production level is expected without observing some examples of what happens when *unacceptable* behavior is exhibited. By observing a series of incidents (a person produces 50 widgets and is praised; a person produces 60 widgets and receives some sharp teasing; a person produces 70 widgets and is ostracized), group members learn the *limits* of the group's patience: "This far, and no further."

Amount of Deviance

Thus, we see that in some sense the group *needs* the deviant. The group needs the deviant to make clear the power and authority of the group, to define more clearly the "boundaries" of the group, to express the group's central values and to deal with its self-doubts. Even if a group were able to simply to lop off its most marginal members—say, by denying them further group membership and not dealing with them again—it is unlikely that the amount of deviance in the group would really be reduced. The group would turn its attention to other behaviors it wanted to control, and new offenders would move into the vacuum in place of their departed fellows (Erikson, 1966). Durkheim (1958), the founder of empirical sociology, puts it most succinctly:

> Imagine a society of saints, a perfect cloister of exemplary individuals. Crimes, properly so called, will there be unknown; but faults which appear venial to the layman will create there the same scandal that the ordinary offense does in ordinary consciousness. If, then, this society has the power to judge and punish, it will define these acts as criminal and will treat them as such. (pp. 68–69).[1]

Let's consider the history of one type of "deviant" behavior, marijuana use. The use of marijuana is illegal. Twenty years ago, smoking marijuana was really fringe behavior; there was no company that would hire a person who was known to smoke marijuana. Ten years ago, smoking marijuana was more frequent and a drug counterculture had developed—but the use of the term *counterculture* itself implies that the use of drugs was still deviant behavior, especially in the conservative business community. Even someone who had experimented with drugs, but did not still use them, was somewhat suspect. Today, marijuana use is still illegal, but is widespread both among business students and young managers. During

[1]Reprinted by permission from E. Durkheim, *The Rule of Sociological Method* (Translated by S. A. Solovay and J. H. Mueller). Copyright 1958 by Free Press of Glencoe, Ill.

1980, the Chicago police made national news for their huge drug bust at the Chicago Board of Trade, where traffickers were openly dealing to the investment brokers.

This example illustrates two points about the amount of deviance in a group. First, the group uses deviance to show its *strength*. However, if a behavior becomes so widespread that it becomes impossible to control, then the labeling of the widespread behavior as deviance becomes problematic. It simply reminds members of the *weakness* of the group. At this point, the group will redefine its job as that of keeping deviance *within bounds* rather than that of obliterating it altogether (Erikson, 1966). Now, the implicit norm in most organizations is: "What you do on your own time is your business. Don't carry, use, or sell drugs at work, since it is illegal; don't be under the influence of drugs at work, since it interferes with your job performance."

Secondly, the amount of deviance in a group remains relatively *constant and small*. While there is always some deviance in a group, as we discussed above, the group can only invest so much time and energy in patrolling deviant behavior. After the behavior becomes too widespread, the group tends to redefine "what is deviant" more narrowly or to monitor a different type of behavior altogether. In fact, Schur (1965) notes that even law enforcement of drug use has changed in response to its quick spread. A greater distinction is made between "hard" drugs and other controlled substances. Less penalty is given to those apprehended with small amounts than large amounts; there is greater attention focused on capturing the large-scale smugglers and traffickers than the occasional user. A group, unconsciously if not consciously, learns how much behavior it is capable of labeling deviant *and* punishing effectively.

Rejection of the Deviant

Imagine you are on a jury trying to decide on the sentencing of Johnny Rocco. Johnny is a juvenile delinquent who has been found guilty of a minor offense, a misdemeanor. However, Johnny's is surely a hard luck story if ever there was one—disadvantaged background, family problems, and so on. While most of your colleagues recommend leniency for Johnny Rocco, one of your peers in particular is obstinate in his opposition to the group's position and will not budge. How do you think the group will react to this devil's advocate?

This Johnny Rocco case was the experimental task in Schachter's research on the treatment of group deviants (Schachter, 1951). Schachter constituted groups of nine to discuss the Johnny Rocco case with six "real" subjects and three paid confederates. The "modal" confederate merely reiterated agreement with the consensus of group opinion. The "deviant" confederate chose a position of extreme disagreement with the six real subjects, and maintained it throughout the discussion. The "slider" confederate initially chose the position of extreme deviance but allowed himself to be gradually influenced so that at the end of the discussion he was at the modal position. The modal person was liked most, and the deviant was liked least, by the six real group members. Despite its negative feelings for the deviant, though, the group increased its communications to the deviant to try to change his mind. Only *late* in the group meeting did communications to the deviant drop off.

The Johnny Rocco case reminds us once again of the interesting paradox about groups and deviants. Deviants obviously make their colleagues feel uncomfortable and embarrassed, yet the group rarely does anything to directly exclude the offenders. The group is almost always hesitant to reject the deviant (Dentler & Erikson, 1959). It is generally a case of "There but for the grace of you go I." While attention is focused on one deviant, the less deviant behavior of others goes unnoticed. However, there are three circumstances in which groups do seem more willing to exclude the group deviant.

1. ***The group is more likely to reject the deviant when the deviant has not been a "good" group member previously***. Hollander (1958, 1964) suggests that group members can earn "idiosyncrasy credits" within a group. Group members generate idiosyncrasy credits mainly by being "good group citizens"—that is, generally conforming to the expectations of the group and by contributing effectively to the attainment of group goals (Hollander, 1961). Individuals expend these credits when they deviate—either by failing to comply with group norms or by performing poorly at work. When a group member no longer has a positive "balance" of credits to draw on when he or she deviates, the group is much more likely to reject that deviant.

    For instance, consider a veteran production worker whose output has climbed too sharply over the past couple of months. The group will be hesitant to ostracize the worker, since he or she has been such a good group member over the past years, producing acceptable amounts and being a congenial coworker. However, if a new worker produces too much in his or her first 2 months, that deviance will be punished. The new worker hasn't earned any laurels to rest on. Another example might be a successful ad executive who will come to work in jeans and sportshirts. If the executive has been a successful group member, coworkers might object to the deviance, but hold their tongues. If a new junior ad executive came to work dressed the same way, the group would not show similar restraint. As far as deviance goes, it is often the case that "it's not what you do, but who does it, that matters."

    Generally, new group members have not had the opportunity to build up a balance of idiosyncrasy credits to draw upon, and therefore do not have much freedom to deviate early in their careers. Hughes

(1946), for instance, found that new members of production groups were expected by coworkers to conform more closely to group production norms than were other group members. However, an individual who commands great respect among others in the profession or is being recruited strongly for a position may be able to *bargain* for some special working conditions during recruitment as a condition for employment. The high-status, highly skilled worker may be able to negotiate for some extra "credits" to start off with—being able to hire and fire with more discretion, change some policies unilaterally, etc. In these cases, the new members will be allowed to deviate more readily than would otherwise be the case (Feldman, 1976).

2. **The group is more likely to reject the deviant when the group is failing in meeting its goals successfully**. When the group is successful, it is somewhat tolerant of deviant behavior. The group may disapprove of deviant behavior, but it has some margin for error. When the group is faced with failure, then deviance is much more sharply punished. Any behavior that negatively influences the success of the group becomes much more salient and threatening to group members.

For instance, if there have been no job reevaluations for a while and the overall organization is making sufficient profits, deviance from the rate-busting norm—while undesirable—is less threatening. The group figures the one high producer will be a barely noticed "blip" in the pretty routine production figures. However, when job reevaluations are imminent or the organization is making concerted efforts to cut all costs, then deviance from the rate-busting norm is much more threatening. Even one case of deviance could draw attention to the group's restrained pace, and all deviance must be viewed as a potential "straw that could break the camel's back."

Similarly, if a brand manager starts working fewer hours than is the norm, the group may be tolerant of the deviance if the brand manager's products are doing well in the marketplace. After all, if the brand is succeeding and the brand manager can get the work done in less time, what's the problem? However, if the brand is doing poorly, then the same deviance will be strongly punished. If anything, the brand manager will be expected to work *longer* hours, not shorter. If the brand continues to do poorly and the brand manager continues to work shorter hours, he or she will likely be replaced.

It is also important to note here that even a high-status person is free to deviate only so long as his or her activities are not severely detrimental to group goal achievement. When the group is successful, high-status members receive *fewer* negative reactions for deviance than lower-status members do for the same behavior. However, when the group is unsuccessful, high-status members receive *more* hostility from peers than do lower-status members who are equally deviant (Wiggins et al., 1965; Alvarez, 1968). Because the high-status member's deviance is so clearly and seriously dysfunctional to an unsuccessful group, he or she receives much stronger reactions for norm-breaking.

For example, if a company is doing well and the chief executive officer (CEO) pursues some risky new ventures, then he or she is unlikely to be censured seriously, if at all. The CEO's new ventures, in fact, might be labeled "exciting" or "visionary." If the company is doing poorly and the CEO pursues the same new ventures, the board of directors and employees might be up in arms. "Why go out on a limb when our position is already so tenuous?" they'll ask. Ironically, when the organization is doing poorly it is unlikely to reward innovative behavior—yet that may be precisely what the organization needs to turn itself around.

3. ***The group is more likely to reject the deviant when the deviant is seen as completely incorrigible or uninfluenceable.*** Some research by Sampson and Brandon (1964) suggests that groups will try to change a deviant member when they can, and will revert to rejection of the deviant *only when change seems hopeless*. Sampson and Brandon constituted discussion groups with "real" subjects and two confederates. One confederate, the "opinion deviant," disagreed substantially with the group's position during the group discussion. The other confederate, the "role deviant," announced even before the group discussion began that he was completely different from the other group members and utterly rejected their world view. Sampson and Brandon's results show that the opinion deviants did receive a lot more communication from other group members, but were rarely rejected at all. The role deviants, on the other hand, were rejected very frequently. When the group sees it has a chance to "convert" group members, they will continue to try to influence them. When the group sees no hope for change, it rejects the deviant outright.

For instance, consider a student who disagrees with the solution to a particular case the class is doing. Both the professor and other classmates will volunteer to address the student's objections, and a lot of communication will be addressed to the "opinion deviant" to try to get him or her to understand the class's point of view. However, if a student repeatedly states that he or she doesn't see the utility of doing cases, or hates the subject matter and finds it irrelevant, then others will tune the deviant out. Psychologically the deviant will be rejected. Neither the professor nor fellow classmates will seriously address the student's objections to the case solution since they know that no answer would ever be satisfactory.

Janis (1972) recommends as a possible solution to the groupthink problem instituting the role of "devil's advocate" in the group. This devil's advocate would constantly challenge and question the group's decision-making processes. While this idea sounds good in theory, we see now why it is unlikely to be successful. The devil's advocate role is a singularly unattractive role to play, and the person who holds that solo role in the group is very likely to be ignored after a while.

MANAGERIAL IMPLICATIONS

Caught between the need to keep the deviant and the desire to reject him or her, all too often the group resolves the dilemma by *institutionalizing the role of deviant* within the group. The person is labeled an "oddball," and no one much listens to the deviant's opinions or pays attention to his or her behaviors. "Don't mind Bob, he's always like that" or "Carol's at it again" are phrases used to brush away the offending statement or behavior. People recognize the deviance but functionally ignore it (Dentler & Erikson, 1959).

Group members simply find themselves unable and unwilling to handle the sensitive interpersonal issues that would be involved in rejecting a fellow worker. By gradually defining a "role" of deviant for the offending member, the problem of the deviant's behavior can be defused in the short run without any emotional upheaval. This short-term solution for deviants may be satisfactory for "easy" task problems (e.g., How can we get John to shut up so we can get back to work?), but is not functional for more basic and important problems (Porter et al., 1975).

There are least four reasons why managers need to tolerate more deviance without dismissing the offenders out of hand.

1. *Without deviance, the group is less likely to examine the flaws in its planning and decision-making activities.* When groups become too cohesive and demand too much conformity, their planning and decision making are seriously undermined. They fail to accurately examine the risks of their proposed course of action and do not process negative data carefully. Victims of groupthink are much less likely to perceive any "blind spots" in their plans. Imbued with their own sense of self-worth, they overestimate their ability to succeed against high odds and neglect to work out ahead of time contingency plans for failure.

2. *If individuals comply solely because of group pressures, the result may be public compliance at the expense of private acceptance and personal commitment to what is being done* (Kelman, 1961; Kiesler, 1969). As we discussed earlier, it makes a big difference whether people are changing what they are *saying* or what they are *believing* in response to group influence. If people conform only as a result of group pressure, they are not going to be energetic in performing their jobs or committed to the group's goals. They will be lackluster, almost withdrawn, group members.

Moreover, when a group is heavily populated by individuals who are saying and doing one thing, but thinking and feeling another, high effectiveness in the long haul is not very likely (Hackman, 1976). If each person goes along with an uneasy consensus for fear of being rejected, the group will come up with a poor decision—one that is ineffective or that people don't agree with or that people feel uncomfortable about. Reaching a unanimous decision in this way is only a Pyrrhic victory: the unanimous decision rests solely on pillars of sand.

3. *By not tolerating deviance, the group loses the fresh perspectives of new members and diminishes their enthusiasm for improving the group.* As has emerged several times in the chapter, new members of a group are most likely to conform to the group's wishes and to be punished for deviance. The low-status member has few idiosyncrasy credits, so he or she has little freedom to deviate without incurring sanctions. Moreover, because of their low status, the new members also run greater risks of being rejected from the group altogether.

When the group stifles dissent or a questioning attitude among new recruits, it sends a distinct message to them: "Get along by going along." Their enthusiasm, even if it is overeager, is too seriously diminished. Their ideas for innovation, even if they are somewhat fanciful, are too sharply curtailed. Two of the greatest assets new recruits bring with them to organizations are a fresh perspective and a desire to improve the group, and overbearing punishment for deviance deadens both of these quite quickly.

4. *Finally, by extinguishing any signs of deviance, the group loses the opportunity to explore the usefulness and ultimate validity of the very norms it is enforcing* (Hackman, 1976). As we discussed in the previous chapter on norms, groups develop norms to facilitate task accomplishment and to circumvent thorny interpersonal problems. The set of group norms reveals a lot about the group's nature—what the group thinks is important, what its self-image is, where it thinks it is vulnerable. The deviant calls into question these basic assumptions the group makes about itself and its activities.

By ignoring the issues raised by deviance, the group will be unable to discover whether a norm is still helpful to the achievement of group goals and maintenance of group morale. Perhaps a norm about working long hours developed when the organization was short-staffed, but is no longer appropriate with fuller employment. Perhaps the norm about stylish clothing developed when the organization was of low status, but is no longer appropriate when the organization has a better reputation.

Moreover, some of these norms may be not only obsolete but also dysfunctional. The norm about long work hours might impair recruitment or encourage turnover. The norms about expensive clothing may simply be seen as pretentiousness and turn people off.

Robert Frost, in his poem, "Mending Wall," observes:

> Before I built a wall I'd ask to know
> What I was walling in or walling out,
> And to whom I was like to give offense.

Most groups would do well to heed Frost's advice. When a group makes more open and conscious decisions about what norms to enforce and what deviance to curtail, the long-term effectiveness of the group can be greatly enhanced.

SUMMARY

This chapter focuses on individual conformity to, and deviance from, group norms. By conformity we mean changing one's behaviors and beliefs as a result of group influence. By deviance we mean behaving in a way that is so threatening, embarrassing, or irritating to the group that the group brings special sanctions against the offending person.

The pressures to conform to group pressure are very strong. Individuals are most likely to conform: (1) when the work environment is uncertain, and the individual needs the group for information; (2) when the individual is unsure of himself or herself, and needs the group for affirmation; (3) when the individual values group membership highly; (4) when there is high interaction among group members; (5) when the individual has made some sort of public commitment to the group; (6) when the group pressure is moderate rather than severe; and (7) when the individual is alone in his or her opposition to the group's position.

Janis (1972) raises serious questions about whether too much conformity is functional for organizations. Groups that demand too much conformity fail to accurately examine the risks of their proposed course of action, do not process negative data carefully, and fail, to work out ahead of time any contingency plans for operations going wrong. Decision-making fiascos often occur as a result of this "groupthink" phenomenon.

Deviants are most likely to be rejected by groups when: (1) they have not been "good" group members previously; (2) when the group or organization is failing in meeting its goals successfully; or (3) when the deviants are seen as completely incorrigible or uninfluenceable.

However, rejection of the deviant is the last-ditch step in handling nonconformity. The group is very hesitant to exclude the deviant. First, deviance serves several functions for the group. Labeling behavior deviant gives the group a chance to express what its central values are. It makes salient the power and authority of the group, and makes clearer what the "boundaries" of the group norms are. Second, group members simply find themselves unable and unwilling to handle the sensitive interpersonal issues that would be involved in rejecting a fellow worker.

Caught between the need to keep the deviant and the desire to reject him, all too often the group resolves the dilemma by institutionalizing the role of the deviant within the group. However, groups need to tolerate more deviance without dismissing the offender out of hand. Without deviance, the group is less likely to examine the flaws in its planning and decision-making activities. Moreover, by not tolerating deviance, the group loses fresh perspectives of new members and diminishes their enthusiasm for improving the group.

REVIEW QUESTIONS

1. Define conformity and deviance.
2. Briefly describe Milgram's Obedience Study and the Stanford Prison Experiment. What do these two pieces of research reveal about the nature of group influence?
3. What are seven particular circumstances in which individuals are most likely to bow to group influence?
4. Distinguish between comparative and reflected appraisal. How do individuals learn about their own abilities from comparative and reflected appraisal?
5. What are reference groups? How do reference groups influence whether people will conform to group norms?
6. Briefly describe cognitive dissonance theory. How does cognitive dissonance theory explain why people who have undergone a severe initiation to the group like the group more than people who have undergone a more easy-going initiation?
7. What happens when a person experiences reactance?
8. Why is it difficult to distinguish between normative influences on attitude change and informational influences?
9. What are the differences between compliance, identification, and internalization? Which is most enduring? Which is least enduring? Why?
10. What is *groupthink*? Give some examples of the phenomenon.
11. What are the seven most salient symptoms of groupthink?
12. What functions does labeling behavior *deviant* serve for the group?
13. Why is the amount of deviance in a group small and constant?
14. What are the three circumstances when the deviant is most likely to be rejected from the group?
15. Why are groups hesitant to reject the deviant? What do they do with the deviant instead?
16. Why do groups need to tolerate more deviance without dismissing the offender?

REFERENCES

Alvarez, R. Informal reactions to deviance in simulated work organizations: A laboratory experiment. *American Sociological Review*, 1968, *33*, 895–912.

Aronson, E. *The social animal* (2nd ed.). San Francisco: W. H. Freeman, 1976.

Aronson, E., & Mills, J. The effect of severity of initiation on liking for a group. *Journal of Abnormal and Social Psychology*, 1959, *59*, 177–181.

Asch, S. Effects of group pressure upon the modification and distortion of judgment. In M. H. Guetzkow (Ed.), *Groups, leadership, and men*. Pittsburgh: Carnegie, 1951, 117–190.

Brehm, J. W. *A theory of psychological reactance*. New York: Academic Press, 1966.

CHAPTER 18

GROUP PERFORMANCE AND
GROUP DECISION MAKING

In this chapter we will be focusing attention on the key question managers have about groups: How can groups be used more effectively to increase productivity and to make better decisions? In this chapter, we will be trying to answer that question in a systematic way. The first half of the chapter will examine performance groups—groups whose main activity is producing goods and services. The second half of the chapter will examine decision-making groups—groups whose main activity is analyzing information and making decisions.

Group effectiveness has been defined in a variety of different ways. Defined by Herold (1979, p. 96), group effectiveness is how well a group carries out the tasks which it has been assigned in regard to quality and quantity of group output. Hackman (1976) proposes a more encompassing definition of group effectiveness. He considers a group effective if: (1) the group meets or exceeds acceptable levels of quantity and quality; (2) the group experience satisfies, rather than frustrates, the personal needs of members; and (3) the group experience maintains or enhances members' abilities to work together on subsequent tasks. We see, though, that no matter which definition of group effectiveness we take, group effectiveness is not a unidimensional concept. There are *several* aspects of group effectiveness, and a group can be effective in some ways and ineffective in others.

For both performance and decision-making groups, we will consider several aspects of group effectiveness. Moreover, for each aspect we will examine: (1) whether groups are more effective than individuals acting alone; and (2) what factors determine the group's effectiveness in each area. We'll start with the discussion of performance groups.

GROUP PERFORMANCE

The Hawthorne Studies

Probably the most well-known study of group performance and productivity was conducted during the 1920s by the Western Electric Company at its Hawthorne Works plant in Chicago. At the time, Western Electric was the largest producer of telephone equipment in the United States. Its management enlisted the help of some Harvard Business School professors—Elton Mayo, F. J. Roethlisberger, and William Dickson—to help increase the output of workers assembling telephone relays. The research started out as an investigation of the effects of physical working conditions on worker productivity but ended up very differently.

The researchers originally began experimenting with the amount of lighting, expecting that productivity would rise as illumination increased to an optimum level. However, this hypothesis was strongly disproved when, after several experiments in large departments of the plant, it was discovered that changes in productivity occurred quite independently of the level of illumination. In most cases, output of telephone relays tended to increase over time as the experiment proceeded, whether the level of illumination was raised or lowered. In some cases, high productivity was maintained even after it became so dark that workers could scarcely see (Blumberg, 1969).

The investigators then started experimenting with introducing rest pauses of different lengths and different frequencies during the workday, supplying coffee breaks at various points in the day, and shortening the length of the workday and the workweek. The results of the second part of the experiment were even more startling. There was an upward trend in output, regardless of the introduction or withdrawal of rest periods, lunches, coffee breaks, shorter workdays, or shorter workweeks. Furthermore, when the experiment ended after a year and the original conditions of work were restored and all previous privileges withdrawn, "the daily and weekly output rose to a point higher than at any other time." (Mayo, 1933, pp. 62–63). In addition, morale among the relay assembly room workers improved dramatically. There was a sharp increase in the amount of socializing among workers after hours. Moreover, absenteeism decreased 80 percent (Roethlisberger & Dickson, 1939).

The researchers had two potential explanations for these unexpected results. First, an informal network of interpersonal relations might have developed within the formal organization that facilitated job performance. Higher morale might have led to higher productivity, the researchers argued. Another potential factor in higher productivity might have been the workers' perception of themselves as "special." Perhaps productivity increased because the workers chosen for the experiment were accorded special treatment and privileges by the company—the so-called Hawthorne effect (Blumberg, 1969).

Of course, some of the early findings of the Hawthorne Studies have been substantially modified by subsequent research. For instance, as we saw in Chapter 8, the link between worker morale and worker productivity posited by the researchers at the Hawthorne plant is tenuous at best. However, the Hawthorne Studies did have a tremendous impact on industrial and organizational psychology and inspired substantial further research on the impact groups have on productivity.

The Steiner Model

Steiner (1966) provides us with a useful framework for understanding the impact groups have on individual productivity (see Figure 18-1). If groups could take advantage of all the efforts and abilities of group members, then the larger the group the greater its potential productivity would be. Theoretically at least, potential productivity would increase linearly with group size. However, when we look at what actually happens as groups get larger, we see that groups do not perform up to their ideal potential. There is some loss of productivity when individual contributions are combined. *Actual productivity* is lower than *potential productivity*—and the difference

FIGURE 18-1
Steiner model of group performance. (SOURCE: Adapted from I.D. Steiner, "Models for Inferring Relationships between Group Size and Potential Group Productivity." *Behavioral Science*, 1966, *11*, pp. 273–283. Reprinted by permission.

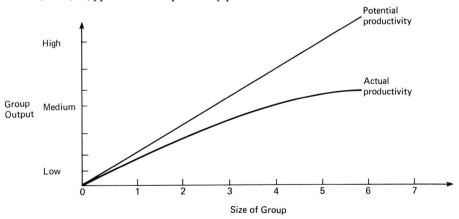

between the two gets larger as the group size increases (see Figure 18-1). Steiner argues that by looking at the *assets* of groups we can discover why both potential and actual group productivity increase as the group gets larger. Conversely, by looking at the *liabilities* of groups, we can discover why there is some loss of effectiveness as groups grow larger.

In the next few pages, we will be examining both the positive and negative influences groups have on individual productivity, as well as the circumstances when groups will most likely enhance individual performance.

Potential Assets of Groups

Groups can potentially enhance the productivity of individual members in three ways: (1) by increasing their job-relevant knowledge and skills, (2) by increasing their level of job satisfaction, and (3) by increasing the level of effort they exert. Let's look at each of these more closely.

Job-Relevant Knowledge and Skills

There is substantial evidence to suggest that groups *do* increase individual productivity by increasing individual members' job-relevant knowledge and skills. The group can assist members in developing job-relevant knowledge and skills in three ways: (1) by direct instruction, (2) by providing feedback about behavior, and (3) by serving as "models" of correct or appropriate behavior (Hackman, 1976).

First, group members can give direct instruction to coworkers on how to do their jobs more effectively. They can show them shortcuts; they can teach individuals how to work more efficiently; they can help them better organize their work. Clerical workers often help each other out in these ways.

Second, group members can give individuals some feedback about the appropriateness of their behaviors. By being told whether their behavior is right or wrong, group members can learn how to function in the group more effectively. For instance, when line managers are given feedback from colleagues about the inappropriate way in which they are treating staff members (e.g., "if you yell at the people in public relations, they'll just work more slowly to get even with you"), they learn how to treat staff support groups more effectively.

In fact, groups can change the behavior of a given group member by selectively reinforcing certain behaviors with feedback (Bavelas et al., 1965). For instance, Sarbin and Allen (1968) found that groups can increase the level of participation of initially recalcitrant group members by giving them positive feedback, and can decrease the participation of overly verbal members with negative feedback.

Third, individuals can learn correct behavior by modeling the behavior of other group members. By observing how other members of the group perform, an individual can indirectly observe what behaviors are desired in the group even without direct reinforcement. For example, most people pick up cues about how formal or informal to be in interactions with employees at different levels of the organization (secretaries, superiors) by observing how their coworkers behave.

Thus, to summarize, groups do increase the performance effectiveness of their members by increasing their job-relevant knowledge and skills. Moreover, the more complex the job, the more the individual is likely to need *all three* types of aids (i.e., direct instruction, feedback, role models) a group can provide (Hackman, 1976).

Satisfaction of Group Members

As we discussed in Chapter 8, the relationship between job satisfaction and job performance is relatively weak and the direct impact of job satisfaction on individual productivity is small. However, the social rewards of working with other individuals can increase productivity *indirectly*.

Particularly when the jobs are uninteresting and routine, having good coworkers can be the difference in making the workday more enjoyable. Indeed, most employees are more satisfied with their coworkers than they are with any other aspect of the work environment (see Chapter 8). In addition, congenial coworkers can alleviate individuals' anxieties during periods of high stress. When workers are in stressful situations, they actively seek out others and prefer to spend their time in groups rather than alone (Schachter, 1959; Gerard & Rabbie, 1961; Rabbie, 1963). These coworkers can help employees cope more effectively with stress so that good performance can be sustained until the high-stress period passes (Feldman & Brett, 1981).

Moreover, as even the Hawthorne Studies pointed out, satisfied workers have lower absenteeism, lower turnover, and less industrial conflict. All of these, too, can get translated into higher productivity.

Level of Effort

Groups have the potential to increase the level of effort and intensity individual members will put into their jobs. The term *social facilitation* refers to how an individual's performance is affected by working in the *presence* of other individuals. Zajonc (1965) found that simply working in the presence of others does have an "energizing effect" on individuals, causing them to work with greater intensity. This was found to be especially true when the others who were around the individuals might be *evaluating* their performance (Cottrell et al., 1968; Henchy & Glass, 1968). When workers are being observed by other people, especially managers, their level of effort and work intensity will increase substantially.

However, it is important to note here a major exception to the above findings. If individuals are working on more "cognitive" jobs like planning, creative work, or research and development, working in the presence of others gets in the way of performance. In these situations, people get overly nervous and lose their concentration. Their anxiety *debilitates*, or gets in the way of, better performance. This is so for several reasons.

First of all, it is hard for these employees to think with someone looking over their shoulders. Second, in any job with a lot of thinking involved, the pace of work will be uneven. Sometimes people will have bursts of energy, and at other times there is a lull in their activity. It makes people nervous when they are observed "doing nothing"—even though the "doing nothing" is essential to later "doing something." People lose energy trying to "look busy." Third, working in the presence of others presents distractions and interruptions (like hearing everyone else's phone ring) that interfere with task performance.

To summarize, then, when individuals are working on routine performance tasks, the presence of other people increases their level of effort and work intensity and their performance increases. When individuals are working on more cognitive tasks, the presence of other people has the opposite effect—the distractions and anxiety debilitate job performance.

Potential Liabilities of Groups

Just as it is possible for individuals working together to produce some benefits, the opposite is also true. Sometimes, the group is less than the sum of its parts. Somewhere along the line, the group doesn't marshal its resources effectively and a lot of individual talent is untapped or wasted. What are some of the liabilities of groups?

Groups can potentially decrease the productivity of individual members in three ways: (1) by decreasing their motivation to perform well, (2) by creating problems of coordination among group members, and (3) by decreasing individual feelings of responsibility. We'll examine each of these in more detail below.

Motivation Losses

Steiner (1966) suggests that when individuals work in groups, they often experience a loss of motivation. When we think back to what motivates individuals, we can see why this might be the case.

If individuals are being rewarded *contingent* upon their own performance, they will be motivated to perform at a high level. However, if the individuals are being rewarded contingent upon the *group's* performance, the performance-outcome link is much less clear. The individuals could work very hard but be pessimistic about the ability of the group as a whole to perform effectively. As a result, the individuals might estimate the probability of obtaining personal outcomes to be low even if they perform well. Motivation thus drops.

Group projects for classes are ideal examples of this phenomenon.

Most students put a lot more energy into studying for exams than in doing group projects. If the exam performance is poor, the individuals know they are *certain* to get low grades. Moreover, the individuals *alone* control whether the exam preparation is good or haphazard. On the other hand, even if some students work diligently at their parts of the group project, other students might not. It is difficult to pressure other group members to work harder. Consequently, there is a good chance that some students could receive lower grades than their own *individual* efforts justified. Students put more energy into exams because there is a higher certainty they will be rewarded for their individual efforts.

The class project provides another illustration of how groups can demotivate individual effort. Often in class projects the better students are at the mercy of lazy students. The lazy students might figure, "Why knock myself out? We know Joe and Sue are in this group, and they're both gunning for A's. They'll pick up the slack." These individuals' motivation is low because they can obtain outcomes *without* exerting any effort. Note, too, that Joe and Sue lose no matter what they do. If they don't cover for the slackards, they are penalized because the group product suffers. If they do cover for the slackards, they are penalized anyway because they have to do extra work.

It is also appropriate to point out here again that group norms can potentially decrease individual productivity. As we discussed in Chapters 16 and 17, group norms have a double-edged effect on how much effort individuals will exert on their jobs. If there are good relationships between workers and managers, then pro-productivity norms can be established. Group norms can encourage good performance, help the individual become highly committed to the group goal, and make the individual feel personally responsible for helping the group reach that goal. However, if there are untrusting or antagonistic relationships between workers and managers, then quota restriction norms are *more* likely to develop. These groups will decrease individual effort by discouraging good performance, by discrediting management's motives, and by demonstrating how working hard is against personal self-interest. The climate of the work group can work as easily against productivity as for it.

Thus, motivation losses are greatest when individual contributions to group projects cannot be measured and rewarded directly, and when the relationships between managers and subordinates are poor.

Coordination Losses

If ten group members are each willing to commit 10 hours to a project, the group potentially has 100 manhours to expend on work. However, some of those manhours are going to be spent merely in *getting ready* to do work. Actual performance falls short of potential performance because groups can lose a lot of productive time in trying to coordinate individual members' activities (Steiner, 1966; Reitz, 1981).

First, setup time is required—the group must be assembled, a suitable meeting place located, and an agenda established. Second, there is extra start-up time involved with group projects—the initial social pleasantries, deciding on an appropriate strategy for doing the work, etc. Third, it takes time to divide all the work and then put different parts of the project back together again after they have been completed. Thus, group projects frequently take more manhours than projects undertaken by individuals working alone. While an individual working alone might need 50 hours to do a job, it might take ten people 10 hours apiece, or 100 manhours, to complete the project together. This problem is exacerbated if the work cannot be broken down into subproblems so that group members can work on the project simultaneously instead of sequentially (Davis, 1969).

In Chapter 16, we discussed the use of temporary task forces to solve interdepartmental problems. These groups are particularly vulnerable to coordination losses. Because people are in different departments, the mere logistics of scheduling meetings takes a significant amount of time. The inevitable absence of some members requires further coordination even after group meetings are over. Some time is spent in dividing the work among group members, and additional time is spent trying to synthesize and integrate individual members' contributions. When key individuals are unavailable or haven't completed their duties, the whole group is held up. Some losses of efficiency on account of coordination problems are inevitable, but these groups lose quite a bit of their energy in this way.

The time losses due to coordination are particularly strong, then, when: (1) it is difficult to break the work down into subproblems so that group members can work on the project simultaneously instead of sequentially; and (2) group members belong to different departments.

Diffusion of Responsibility

When everyone is supposed to be responsible for some activity, it often happens that *no one* actually takes responsibility for it (Shaw, 1981). When all the waiters and waitresses in a restaurant are responsible for cleaning up, each one does what he or she perceives to be "a fair share"—and if the restaurant is still dirty, too bad. Or, if all the salespersons are responsible for taking back returns and handling exchanges, these customers are shunted from one salesperson to the other like hot potatoes. No one wants to handle these customers because no new sales commission will result. Each salesperson claims he or she "just had a return," so it's somebody else's turn. In group situations, individuals are more likely to shirk responsibilities that are not theirs *alone*. Consequently, some important organizational duties—such as maintaining a clean restaurant or providing customer service—fall through the cracks. In most group settings, diffusion of responsibility presents a real liability unless specific individual members can be given personal responsibility for completing specific parts of the project.

We see this at the societal, as well as at the organizational, level. In New York City in March, 1964, Kitty Genovese was attacked and killed on her way home from work at 3 a.m. Thirty-eight of her Kew Gardens neighbors came to their windows when she cried out in terror, yet none came to her assistance. Even more startling was the fact that although it took Ms. Genovese's assailant over a half hour to murder her, not one neighbor even so much as called the police.

The public outrage that resulted from this event sparked a good deal of research on bystander apathy. The research findings suggest that the more bystanders that are present at an emergency, the *less* likely any one bystander will intervene and provide aid. The more people that are around, the more likely people will depend on *others* to take action. In fact, a victim is more likely to get help the *fewer* people who are available to take action (Latane & Darley, 1969).

Group Size

Before moving on, it is important to note here that the larger the *size* of the group, the worse these three potential liabilities become (Thomas & Fink, 1963). O'Dell (1968), for instance, found that as group size increased, group members showed greater disagreement and greater antagonism toward each other. Shaw (1981) points out that as groups get larger, subgroups are more likely to form and there is more potential for conflict. It is harder to coordinate work. Latane and Darley (1969) have found that individual motivation also decreases as groups get larger.

Of course, there are no hard-and-fast rules about the optimum size of groups. So many aspects of group life change as the group gets larger— manager-subordinate relationships, task specialization, amount of com- munication—that is hard to sort out the direct effects group size has on group functioning. In general, though, the larger the immediate work group grows, the more potential problems arise. This is particularly true as the immediate work group gets larger than five (Slater, 1958; Berelson & Steiner, 1964).

Summary

There can be some "value added" when individuals are brought together to work on a common task. In psychology, this value added is called *assembly effects* (Collins & Guetzkow, 1964); in more popular parlance, it is known as *synergy*. However, as we have seen, groups will not necessarily enhance individual productivity. Let's briefly summarize when groups will be most effective in increasing productivity:

1. When individuals can make use of the coaching and instruction from other group members

2. When the interpersonal relationships between managers and subordinates are positive
3. When the individual jobs are relatively routine, or rote, by nature; when the jobs do not involve a lot of sustained, or creative, thinking
4. When workers' individual contributions to group projects can be measured and rewarded directly
5. When specific individual members can be given personal responsibilities for completing specific parts of a group project
6. When the group project can be broken down into several subparts so that different group members can work on different portions of the project simultaneously
7. When the size of the group can be kept relatively small

We turn next to consider group decision making.

GROUP DECISION MAKING

Brainstorming

A new management technique developed around 1940 by an advertising executive drew attention to the benefits of group decision making, in much the same way that the Hawthorne Studies had earlier turned attention to the benefits of group performance. In 1939, Alex Osborn, a partner in the Madison Avenue advertising agency of Batten, Barton, Durstine, and Osborn, developed a group decision-making technique called *brainstorming*. The purpose of the technique was to enhance creativity through group discussion. Certain procedural rules were enforced to encourage "free thinking" and to offset group processes (such as critical evaluations) that might inhibit creativity. Three rules, in particular, were central to the technique.

1. Free-wheeling discussion was encouraged. No idea was to be considered too far-out.
2. Using or building upon others' ideas was supported. No idea was any one member's property. All ideas belonged to the group.
3. Criticism was completely forbidden. Ideas were to be generated, not evaluated (Osborn, 1957).

Osborn's enthusiastic advocacy of brainstorming, coupled with his agency's success in the advertising industry, argued persuasively for the creative potential of this technique. Even today, many organizations still use brainstorming or a similar procedure in making group decisions.

Just as the early findings of the Hawthorne Studies were substantially revised, so, too, were the early findings of Alex Osborn. As we will see later, the follow-up research on brainstorming did not justify Osborn's initial enthusiasm. However, this work did focus attention on four aspects of decision-making that groups affect strongly: (1) the accuracy of decisions; (2) the creativity of decisions; (3) the riskiness of decisions; and (4) the acceptance of decisions. We will be considering each of these four aspects of group decision making in more detail below.

Accuracy of Decisions

Do groups make more accurate judgments than individuals? Generally, the answer to that question is *yes*. This is true for two reasons.

First, groups can bring a *greater sum total of knowledge and information* to bear on a problem. A single individual who makes a decision is constrained to rely on his or her own limited personal knowledge. When several people make a decision jointly, more information can be brought to bear on the issue. Other individuals might be able to fill in "missing pieces of the puzzle" (Maier, 1967). In fact, some studies have shown that groups are five to six times as likely to correctly solve judgment problems as individuals working alone (Shaw, 1981).

For example, a manager may be trying to decide how to allocate funds for pay raises among entry-level subordinates. If the manager were to sit down alone to make the pay-raise decisions, he or she would have only formal performance evaluations and some random anecdotal evidence about the performance of these employees. By meeting with their immediate supervisors to discuss worker evaluations, the manager would elicit much richer data about the employees' individual performances.

Second, groups provide a *greater number of approaches to a problem*. Sometimes individuals can get into ruts in how they approach problems. If we're from marketing, we tend to focus primarily on the advertising and selling aspects of business decisions. If we're from finance, we focus mostly on the accounting and cash-flow aspects of business decisions. If we're from operations, we focus mainly on the logistics of producing and distributing products when we make business decisions. When a decision has to be made that affects many parts of the organization, it is often useful to use a group so that "blind spots" in the decision can be identified early and better solutions devised (Maier, 1967; Shaw, 1981). Groups can point out errors or false assumptions that any one individual member might be unaware of.

For example, a consumer goods company may be trying to decide whether to introduce a new product into the market. From a marketing standpoint, it may be "all systems go"; from the financial standpoint, it may seem a little risky; from an operations standpoint, it may seem impossible. Someone from marketing may be unaware of a potential labor strike at a major plant; someone from operations may not be aware of corporate cash-flow problems that affect the expansion into new areas;

someone from finance may not realize the very positive results of market research and market pretests. By bringing these points of view together, not only is more information brought to bear on the decision but also more *different types* of information. Each person's assumptions can be tested by others.

Group Composition

However, groups are no guarantee of accurate decisions. The composition of the group most influences how much advantage groups have over individuals in accuracy of decisions.

The potential source of the group's advantage over individuals in making decisions derives from its *heterogeneity*. As we discussed earlier, having people with different perspectives interacting with each other can lead to both the generation of more innovative suggestions and the elimination of poor proposals. The research consistently suggests that groups make better judgments than individuals when the group members have varied skills and experiences (Shaw, 1981). Just adding more people to a group without increasing its diversity is unlikely to add to the accuracy of group decisions.

The group should be composed of individuals with skills and experiences *relevant* to the problem at hand. Allen and Marquis (1964) provide us with a perfect example of this point. They compared the abilities of four groups of engineers to successfully solve design problems. One group was composed of only engineers who had experienced previous success with similar problems. The second group was composed of engineers who had had both successful and unsuccessful experiences on similar design problems. The third group consisted of engineers who had only unsuccessful experiences, and the fourth group was composed of engineers with no prior relevant experience at all. The results revealed that the "successful" engineers correctly solved 80 percent of the problems, the "mixed success" engineers correctly solved 50 percent of the problems, the "no experience" group correctly solved 43 percent of the problems, and the "unsuccessful" engineers solved only 25 percent of the problems. Cleariy, experience can facilitate the group's decision making *only if* members have the right kind of experience (Reitz, 1981).

Another group composition factor that will determine how good a decision a group will make is whether the individuals with the most *competence* in an area have the most *influence* on the decision. If people with the most information have the least influence, then the decision suffers; if people with the most information have the most influence, then the decision quality is enhanced (Maier, 1970).

Needless to say, the competence of the leaders strongly influences the accuracy of a group decision. When the leaders play a dominant role in influencing a decision on which they have little expertise, the decision quality suffers (Hoffman & Maier, 1961). Low-status members are often unwilling to criticize the suggestions of high-status members, even if the lower-status members have more expertise. Moreover, people tend to overestimate the expertise of group leaders and tend to underestimate the competence of lower-status members (Harvey, 1953; Sherif, White, & Harvey, 1955). Groups make more accurate decisions when the people with the highest status have the most expertise on the topic under discussion.

It has been frequently noted in the group performance literature that the quality of group judgments *exceeds* that of the *average* individual. However, the quality of group judgments rarely exceeds that of the *most* competent group member (Shaw, 1981). The reasons for these findings are now clearer. Groups use the diversity of their members' points of view to eliminate clearly faulty reasoning so that groups will generally do better than the average individual member would have done alone. However, it is frequently the case that the most proficient group members do not have the highest status or cannot argue their views the most persuasively. Thus, there is some "process loss" which leaves the group with a better decision than the average group member would have made—but not the *best* decision that could have been made with the data available.

Creativity of Decisions

Do groups come up with more creative, imaginative ideas than individuals? Unfortunately, the general answer to this question seems to be *no*.

The initial statement of brainstorming by Alex Osborn (discussed earlier) brought in its wake a systematic evaluation of its impact on creativity. Most of that research has failed to support Osborn's enthusiasm that "the average person can think up twice as many ideas when working with a group than working alone" (Osborn, 1957, pp. 228–229).

A series of studies conducted at Yale University disclosed that four individuals, working alone, consistently generated a greater number of ideas than did four-person brainstorming groups. The four solo individuals produced, on average, nearly twice as many ideas as a four-person group. Moreover, independent judges also evaluated the creativity of the ideas generated. These judges rated the ideas of the four individuals as "more original" and "qualitatively superior" to those of the brainstorming groups (Taylor, Berry, & Block, 1958). The research has consistently found that groups do not increase creativity and that they also frequently inhibit it (Bouchard, 1971; Van de Ven & Delbecq, 1974).

Why do groups get in the way of creativity? First of all, groups can fall into a rut and pursue a single train of thought for long periods of time. Instead of trying to generate different *types* of ideas, brainstorming groups often tend to go off on tangents or on variations of *one* idea (Dunnette et al., 1963).

Second, despite rules against criticism in brainstorming, some individuals still feel that covert judgments are being made about them, even if they are not expressed (Collaras & Anderson, 1969). This further inhibits the expression of unconventional or unusual ideas.

Third, the interpersonal dynamics of the group can negatively influence whether the group comes to a creative, high-quality solution. In some groups, the desire to be a good group member and to be accepted can silence disagreement. Majority opinions get accepted regardless of whether their objective quality is logically and scientifically sound. Reaching consensus is confused with finding the best solution. In other groups, individuals try to "win" their case through sheer stubbornness and high participation. Caught up in a competitive spirit, some members become more committed to winning the argument than to finding the best solution (Maier, 1973).

At each stage in the decision-making process, different interpersonal problems emerge. Wexley and Yukl (1977) enumerate some of the most frequent ones in Table 18-1. As you can see, the pitfalls of group decision-making processes are very similar to those of individual decision makers we discussed in Chapter 13.

However, groups sometimes can come up with more creative solutions than individuals working alone. Sometimes one person's idea sparks a different and better idea from another group member. At other times, a new proposal no *one* individual had advocated might emerge as a result of group give-and-take. Using groups differently at different *phases* of the problem-solving process can enhance groups' utility in generating creative solutions.

Creativity in generating new ideas is inhibited, in part, by fear of criticism. However, it is precisely this "critical" ability of groups that makes them so effective in evaluating ideas and alternative solutions. The collective judgment of the group, with its wider range of views, seems superior to that of the individual decision maker (Harrison, 1975; Vroom, Grant, & Cotton, 1969). While individuals are better than groups in *generating* new ideas, groups are better than individuals in *evaluating* them. Groups can contribute to creative solutions by being used only for evaluative purposes.

In fact, two more recent techniques for group problem solving try to take advantage of the creativity of individual members and the critical ability of groups. These two methods are called the *Delphi technique* and the *nominal group technique*.

Delphi Technique

Developed by researchers at the Rand Corporation, the Delphi method aims at providing members with each others' ideas while avoiding the inhibitions characteristic of face-to-face interaction. Indeed, in Delphi groups, there is no face-to-face contact at all. There are five steps to the Delphi technique.

TABLE 18-1
Process problems in group decision making

PROBLEM DIAGNOSIS
Confusing facts with opinions
Confusing symptoms of problems with root causes
Scapegoating, looking for people to blame for the problem
Proposing solutions before the problem is clearly understood
Biasing the problem diagnosis to favor a preferred solution

SOLUTION GENERATION
Suggesting solutions that are irrelevant to the problem
Discussing what should have been done in the past instead of what can be done in the present
Discussing the advantages and disadvantages of a solution before everyone has had a chance to suggest solutions
Focusing on solutions that have been used in the past without any attempt to create novel solutions

SOLUTION EVALUATION
Failure to devote adequate attention to forecasting the multiple consequences of a solution
Biasing estimates of consequences and estimates of probability to support a "favorite" solution
Making verbal attacks on other members instead of limiting discussion to the solutions themselves
Making a hasty choice before the solutions are properly evaluated

SOLUTION CHOICE
Confusing silence with consensus agreement
Little influence of minority views
Individuals trying to win the argument at the expense of reaching a high-quality decision
Steamroller effect: The first solution that gets positive attention tends to be adopted too quickly

SOURCE: Adapted from K. N. Wexley and G. A. Yukl, *Organizational behavior and personnel psychology*, pp. 132–135. Homewood, Ill.: Richard D. Irwin, © 1977. Reprinted by permission.

1. Each individual member independently and anonymously writes down comments, suggestions, and solutions to the problem confronting the group.
2. All the comments are sent to a central location, where they are compiled and reproduced.
3. Each member is sent the written comments of all other members.
4. Each member provides feedback on the other comments, writes down new ideas stimulated by their comments, and forwards these to the central location.

5. Steps 3 and 4 are repeated as often as necessary until consensus is reached (Dalkey, 1969).

Nominal Group Technique

The nominal group technique has also gained some currency in industry. The term "nominal" refers to the fact that individuals are not allowed to communicate verbally; the collection of people is a group "nominally", or "in name only". The process of decision making in nominal groups has five steps.

1. The group meets face-to-face, but each member is given the problem in writing and silently and independently writes down ideas on the problem.
2. Each member in turn verbally presents one idea to the group. There is no discussion until all ideas are exhausted.
3. The group discusses ideas, both to clarify and elaborate on them, and to provide evaluation.
4. Each individual independently and anonymously ranks the ideas.
5. The group decision is determined to be the idea with the highest aggregate ranking (Delbecq, Van de Ven, & Gustafson, 1975).

The research on the effectiveness of these two techniques is encouraging (Jewell & Reitz, 1981). To be sure, the procedures are time-consuming, and there is some artificiality in not being able to communicate more openly with other group members (especially in the Delphi technique). However, both techniques allow for fuller expression of creative ideas by individuals and for fuller assessment of ideas by groups. Unfortunately, many managers today still strongly advocate brainstorming and do not even know about Delphi and nominal groups. Ironically, these latter two techniques offer much greater promise.

Risk of Decisions

Are groups bolder in taking risks than individuals, or are groups more cautious and less willing to be adventurous? The research suggests there is no systematic bias in groups toward *either* risk *or* conservatism. The group decision will not necessarily be more risky than the average individual decision would have been (Shaw, 1981).

William Whyte, in *The Organization Man* (1957), had argued convincingly that organizations intimidated managers into passivity and caution. Afraid of taking a misstep, managers would avoid taking risks to avoid the punishments for failure. Moreover, individual risk taking was inconsistent with being a "good" team player. However, in a series of studies developed to measure individual and group propensity to take risks, Stoner (1961) found just the opposite result. His research results consistently showed groups to be more willing to take risks than individuals. Two hypotheses were suggested to explain this "risky shift."

1. ***Diffusion of responsibility***. Since the individual knows the responsibility for the decision is spread among several others, he or she may experience fewer feelings of personal responsibility. This feeling of less personal responsibility might account for the greater willingness to make a risky decision in a group situation.

2. ***Risky leaders***. As we discussed early in the chapter, leaders have a greater influence on group decisions than other members. They participate more and are perceived to be more competent. If leaders are more aggressive and assertive than other group members, perhaps they persuade their followers to become more risky, too.

However, the research that followed Stoner's original findings cast serious doubts on the conclusion that groups consistently take greater risk than individuals. Neither one of these hypotheses was consistently supported in later research. Moreover, in some group problems, groups became more *conservative*. It appears now that the *content of the group decision* dictates whether the group decision is riskier or more conservative. On decisions where managers value risk (e.g., bringing out new products), group decisions become *riskier*. On decisions where managers value caution (e.g., firing personnel), group decisions become more *cautious* (Brown, 1965).

For instance, when managers make group decisions about expanding product lines, those decisions tend to be riskier than the decisions individuals would have made alone. Bringing out new products is by definition risky, so managers are used to being bolder in making those decisions. They bolster each other's confidence. However, in making decisions about firing personnel, managers tend to be more cautious in groups than when acting alone. Firing a person is personally unpleasant, has ramifications for other employees' morale, and can potentially bring about legal problems. A manager, in the heat of anger, might be ready to move quickly to fire a subordinate. In a meeting with colleagues where all the spin-off problems of firing are aired more fully, the group decision tends to be more cautious.

Group discussions do *polarize* members' individual preferences; after group discussions, there is less *variance* among group members in their preferred course of action. When individuals make decisions in groups, they try to demonstrate that they hold similar *values* to other group members. After the group discussion, individuals see what the "norm" response is and adjust their views accordingly. This explains why individuals' preferences tend to converge after group discussions.

The relationship between groups and risk taking, then, is analogous to the relationship between group cohesiveness and productivity we looked at in Chapter 16. In both cases, using groups reduces *variance* in individual preferences and behaviors. However, in both cases the *direction* of the group response is due to an external factor. In the case of group cohesiveness and productivity, whether cohesive groups are more, or less, productive depends on the amount of trust and goodwill between workers and management. In the case of groups and risk taking, it depends upon whether managers value risk or caution in the content of the decision.

Acceptance of Decisions

Does participation in group decision making increase the amount of understanding and acceptance individual members have of group decisions? Does participation in group decision making increase members' commitment to execute group decisions? The answers to these questions are generally *yes*.

When a decision is made by an individual, he or she still has to communicate that decision to others and persuade them of its merits. Oftentimes the failure to communicate the reasoning behind the decision can create problems of equal magnitude to the initial problem that was to be solved. When other group members work together in solving a problem or making a decision, the chances for communication failure are greatly reduced. People who participated will understand the solution because they saw it develop. Moreover, they will be aware of several other alternatives that were considered and why they were discarded. The common assumption that decisions advanced by superiors are arbitrarily reached will thus disappear (Maier, 1967, p. 240).

Participation has similarly positive results on individual members' acceptance of, and commitment to, group goals. While one person may be formally authorized to make a policy decision, he or she will likely be dependent upon the support of others to carry the decision out. A manager can decide to increase minority hiring, but unless subordinates who actually do the recruitment and screening share the same goal, it will be difficult to accomplish. When groups make decisions, a greater number of people accept and feel responsible for making the policy work (Maier, 1967; Shaw, 1981).

Two studies, in particular, have illustrated these points nicely. A field study by Lawler and Hackman (Lawler & Hackman, 1969; Scheflen Lawler, & Hackman, 1971) provides strong support for the proposition that participation increases comprehension and understanding of organizational policies. A utilities company was trying to combat high absenteeism among janitorial employees. In one experimental group, a new bonus pay plan was participatively developed among the janitorial staff to address the absenteeism problem. Then, the company imposed this same pay plan on a similar group elsewhere in the organization. Thus, the quality of the pay plan was held constant and only participation varied between groups.

The research findings suggest that the plan was not as effective where it was imposed as where it was participatively developed. The group that designed the new reward system responded both more quickly and more positively to the new pay plan than did the group which had the identical plan imposed upon them by company management. First, the participative group simply understood their pay plan better and had fewer uncertainties and worries about it. Second, the nonparticipative group saw the pay plan as simply another management device to get them to come to work.

The interesting field experiment conducted by Coch and French (1948) on participation at the Harwood Manufacturing Corporation illustrates that participation increases acceptance of organizational policies and increases commitment to execute them. Harwood produced pajamas in its plants. However, style changes and engineering improvements frequently necessitated changing work routines and work procedures. Employees resisted these changes strongly, experienced high absenteeism and turnover, and took a long time to reach their former production levels after job changes took place. Coch and French introduced change into the Harwood Corporation in three different ways to three different groups.

1. In the control groups, change was introduced in the "traditional" way. Supervisors told production employees that the changes were necessary because of competitive conditions and that a new piece rate had been set.
2. In the representative condition, representatives of the workers met with management to help with the redesign of the job, the setting of the piece rate, and the training of the production employees in the new methods. These representatives were then partially responsible for enlisting the aid of all the other operators in making the changes.
3. In the participative condition, all employees (in small groups) met with management and participated directly in the redesign of the job, the setting of the piece rate, and the design of operator training.

The results showed that the participative group "relearned" their jobs much more quickly and experienced much lower turnover. Participation facilitated the acceptance of the new procedures as a *group* goal. Moreover, the participative groups developed norms around this new group goal and exerted pressures on individuals to comply. In the participative groups, workers accepted the new piece rate as reasonable and exerted effort to meet their former levels of productivity as quickly as possible. In the control group, in contrast, the workers purposely restricted production to "prove" that the new piece rates were arbitrary and unreasonable and that the old rates should be reinstated.

A Caveat about Participation

As beneficial as group participation can be, it is often used indiscriminately. Vroom and Yetton's model of managerial decision making (see Chapter 11) points out that there are some circumstances when group participation is more effective than others. The research underlying Vroom and Yetton's model gives us some guidelines to follow (Vroom & Yetton, 1973).

1. Participation is more appropriate when the managers do not possess enough information to solve the problem by themselves. In these circumstances, the leaders need the expertise of subordinates to reach a high-quality decision.
2. Participation is more appropriate when the nature and the dimensions of the problem are unclear. Then, the group's help is needed to define the problem and to separate symptoms of the problem from the true problem.
3. Participation is more appropriate when subordinates share the leader's goals in solving a problem. If subordinates sense that the "best" solution might work against their own personal interest, the probability of reaching a good group decision is substantially lowered.
4. Participation is more appropriate when acceptance of the decision by subordinates is critical to effective implementation. Participation is necessary when a course of action (even a "technically correct" one) is likely to fail because it is resisted or opposed by those who have to execute it.
5. Participation is more appropriate when there are no pressing time constraints. Since group decision making takes much more time, participation is most appropriate when there is not a close deadline at hand.
6. Participation is more appropriate when the decision or problem is important and relevant to subordinates. Employees often find extended consultation on matters of little interest to them to be a waste of their time, not a favor.
7. Participation is more appropriate when subordinates have strong desires to exercise their own judgment. Individuals differ in how much they care about influencing what goes on around them and how much they care about exerting direct influence themselves. Employees with low needs for independence are just as satisfied being given orders without having to participate in decision making.

In short, participation does bring many benefits to groups and organizations. Used more discriminately, it can bring even more benefits to organizations at less cost.

Summary

Groups can enhance the quality of organizational decisions, but they do not guarantee it. Let's briefly summarize.

1. ***Groups generally increase the accuracy of group decisions.*** Groups can bring a greater sum total of knowledge and information to bear on a problem, as well as a greater number of approaches.

   The composition of the group most influences how much advantage groups yield over individuals in accuracy in making decisions. Groups will make more accurate decisions if their membership is heterogeneous, if members have skills and experiences relevant to the problems at hand, and if individuals with the most competence in an area have the most influence on the decision.

2. ***Groups generally do not increase the creativity of solutions to problems; they frequently inhibit it.*** Groups can fall into a rut and pursue a single train of thought for a long time. Despite rules against criticism in brainstorming, some individuals still feel that covert judgments are being made about them, even if they are not expressed. The interpersonal dynamics of the group can lead to a false consensus about a low-quality decision, or strong competition among individuals to "win their case."

   However, while individuals are better than groups in generating new ideas, groups are better than individuals in evaluating ideas. Groups can contribute to creative solutions by being used *only* for evaluative purposes, as the Delphi and nominal group techniques recognize.

3. ***Groups do not bias decisions toward either risk or conservatism.*** On decisions where managers value risk (e.g., in bringing out new products), group decisions become riskier. On decisions where managers value conservatism (e.g., firing personnel), group decisions become more cautious.

   Group discussions do polarize members' individual preferences. After group discussions, there is less variance among group members in their preferred course of action. After the group discussion, individuals see what the "norm" response is and adjust their views accordingly.

4. ***Participation in group decision making does increase members' acceptance of decisions.*** When people participate in group decision making, they become more aware of the rationale for the decision and the reasons other alternatives were discarded. Also, when groups make decisions, a greater number of people accept and feel responsible for implementing group decisions.

   Participation is most appropriate: when the leaders don't have enough information to define and solve the problem themselves; when group members share the leaders' goals in solving a problem; when acceptance of the decision by subordinates is critical to effective implementation; when there are no pressing time constraints; when the problem is important and relevant to subordinates; and when subordinates have strong desires to exercise their own judgment and exert influence.

MANAGERIAL IMPLICATIONS

Leaders serve a very different function from other group members. Rather than trying to simply impose their will on the group, the main function of leaders is *integrative* (Maier, 1967). Leaders facilitate communication among group members, synthesize information from various sources, and coordinate group activities so that the group can act in a unified, purposeful way. Additionally, they have to be sensitive to, and protect, minority points of view (even when they disagree with them personally) and deal with the emotional issues that arise as group members come into conflict. In short, the leader's main task is to harness the energy and contributions of individual group members in the most constructive way.

The leader's integrative functions, then, are really twofold: (1) making sure that the group accomplishes its work; and (2) providing sufficient personal satisfactions to members so that they will remain in the group. Bales (1958) calls the first of these activities *task performance duties* and the second *social maintenance duties*. It is the responsibility of the leader to balance both sets of duties, and that is a tough job indeed.

It is very difficult to meet both of these needs *simultaneously*. If several arguments are offered, the negative evaluation of one argument reflects poorly upon its sponsor. Those who are shown to be wrong suffer some loss of esteem. On the other hand, if all ideas must be received with enthusiasm, then reaching a high-quality decision is also made more difficult. Moreover, the individuals who really do have good ideas will not be motivated to continue doing high-quality work—since all work, regardless of quality, receives positive regard (Brown, 1965, p. 685).

In these concluding pages, let's consider more fully five strategies managers can use to lead work groups more effectively.

1. ***Managers need to control group membership more carefully to increase group effectiveness.*** As we stressed repeatedly in the earlier sections of the book, selection of competent organization members is vital to organizational effectiveness. Without competent employees, the organization can not possibly compete in the marketplace. Moreover, employees who have a poor fit with the organization are likely to be less motivated, less satisfied, and more likely to turn over.

   Controlling group membership is just as important at the group level. To take advantage of two key potential assets of groups—a greater sum total of knowledge and a greater number of approaches to a problem—managers have to be especially careful in how they compose decision-making groups. Group members should have competencies *relevant* to the problem at hand, and the group as a whole should represent *diverse* points of view. Moreover, the size of the group should be kept *moderately low* so that these potential assets are not wiped out by interpersonal problems and coordination problems that get worse as the group grows larger. Controlling the input at the front end takes a lot of the pressure off managing the group process at the back end.

2. ***Managers need to use work groups more selectively.*** In this chapter we saw that groups are more appropriate for some activities and less appropriate for others. For instance, groups are better at evaluating ideas than generating them—so that using groups to come up with creative ideas is ineffective but using groups to evaluate a range of alternative courses of action is very effective. Groups facilitate individual performance when group members are doing routine, or rote, tasks, but they inhibit group members who are doing tasks that are more cognitive in nature—so that having group assembly lines is more effective than open-office "think tanks." It is the manager's responsibility to use groups selectively and only for those activities for which groups bring a "value added."

3. ***Managers need to motivate and reward group-related activity.*** When we talked about the path-goal theory of motivation in Chapter 12, we noted that the leader's strategic functions include: (*a*) clarifying employees' goals for performance, (*b*) increasing personal payoffs to subordinates for work-goal attainment, and (*c*) reducing barriers to effective performance. Nowhere is the path-goal behavior of the leader more critical than in managing groups.

    First, because participation in group activities often conflicts with employees' personal duties, managers need to make clear to subordinates what their expectations are about how much energy and time are to be devoted to group projects. Moreover, managers need to get some feedback from subordinates about the reasonableness of their expectations. If not done on an ad hoc basis, this needs to be done at least at performance appraisal time.

    Second, managers need to "put their money where their mouth is." If managers want to reinforce individuals for taking group responsibilities seriously, they need to reward for it. Individuals need to be rewarded for their own contributions, and successful groups need to be rewarded as well. Managers often fall prey to what Kerr (1975) calls "the folly of rewarding A while hoping for B." If managers hope for enthusiastic contributions to group projects but only reward nongroup (individual) activities, then they are actually *discouraging* the behaviors they allegedly desire.

    Third, managers also need to reduce barriers to effective performance. The leader should assume responsibility for assuring accurate communication between members, for clarifying individual members' duties, for scheduling meetings, for summarizing and feeding back data from different sources, and for monitoring the preparation of the final group product. Sometimes groups fail because the "simple" day-to-day logistics of coordinating and scheduling group work overwhelm group members. The leader should be responsible for making sure that doesn't happen.

4. ***Managers can use groups effectively to increase acceptance of decisions.*** Frequently managers view their main task—if not their only task—as coming up with a *high-quality* decision or solution. They operate under the assumption that a good solution is "intuitively obvious" and will be treated as such by subordinates.

   However, as we have discussed in this chapter, coming up with a high-quality decision is only half the battle. The other half is getting it *accepted as reasonable* by other group members. Often, the failure to communicate the reasoning behind the decision can create problems of equal magnitude to the initial problem that was to be solved.

   Managers need to spend more energy than they typically do on gaining commitment and acceptance of group decisions *and* doing so *before* the decision is finalized. Subordinates who participated in the decision making all along will understand the solution because they saw it develop. Moreover, they will be aware of several alternatives that were considered and why they were discarded. Especially when the manager needs subordinate cooperation to effectively execute a decision, this early participation is critical.

5. ***Managers can put more energy into skillfully handling group discussions.*** As we saw in Table 18-1, there are a lot of interpersonal problems that emerge as groups try to reach decisions. At each stage in the group decision-making process, the group leader can manage group discussions in such a way that more contributions and insights of members are brought to bear on a problem without much "process loss." Wexley and Yukl (1977, pp. 132–135) suggest some of the most important strategies managers need to employ at each stage of the decision-making process.

   In *problem diagnosis*, managers need to focus the group's attention on problem diagnosis itself and discourage premature consideration of solutions. The group should be encouraged to explore any differences in members' perceptions of the problem and to propose alternative diagnoses before reaching any conclusion about what is "really" the problem. Analyses of factual data from organizational records, surveys, and other sources should be used whenever possible to supplement subjective opinions about the causes of the problem.

   In *solution generation*, managers need to encourage members who are shy or inhibited to contribute their ideas. The managers need to help the group avoid focusing on solutions that have already been tried and failed. It is important here to include personnel who will be responsible for implementing the decision, so that the decision can be implemented in a knowing, enthusiastic way. Most important, the managers need to refrain from showing a favoritism to any particular solution or proposing their own solutions until other members have finished suggesting their solutions.

Otherwise, the managers will unduly influence which solutions are considered.

In *solution evaluation*, managers need to encourage group members to systematically evaluate the costs and benefits of different solutions, using quantitative data where possible. The managers also have to prevent verbal attacks of members on each other, biasing estimates of success of an alternative to support a "favorite" solution, and rushing to make a decision just to be done with it.

In *solution choice*, managers need to ensure that everybody participates and that no "false consensus" develops. Sometimes some more vocal members can silence their opponents, and it is the managers' responsibility to make sure whether silence indicates agreement or dissent. It is also their responsibility to determine what choice procedure is appropriate. If the managers fear that coalitions will form and unproductive conflict will escalate, they may strive for a consensus decision. At other times the managers may seek only to reach a majority decision.

On the occasion of the fiftieth anniversary of the Hawthorne Studies, Western Electric commissioned a series of state-of-the-art papers on the behavioral aspects of management that the Hawthorne Studies brought so dramatically to light. Writing about the state of group research, in a paper entitled "Suppose We Took Groups Seriously," Leavitt (1975) concludes that groups will become the basic building blocks of the organizations of tomorrow. We share Leavitt's enthusiasm for the future of groups in organizations. By attending to both task and social maintenance duties, managers can capitalize upon the strengths of individual members with minimal losses due to interpersonal problems.

SUMMARY

The chapter examines how groups can be used more effectively to increase productivity and to make better decisions.

Groups can potentially enhance the productivity of individual members in three ways: (1) by increasing their job-relevant knowledge and skills; (2) by increasing their level of job satisfaction; and (3) by increasing the level of effort they put forth at work. The group frequently assists members in developing job-relevant knowledge and skills through direct instruction, through the feedback that it gives, and through the role models of appropriate behavior that it provides. Second, the social rewards of working with other individuals can increase productivity indirectly. Congenial co-workers can alleviate individuals' anxieties during periods of high stress and can help them cope more effectively with stress so that good performance can be sustained.

Groups can also increase the level of effort individual members will put forth while doing their jobs. When individuals are working on well-learned (or rote) tasks, this presence of other people further energizes and facilitates their performance. When individuals are working on more "cognitive" tasks, the presence of other people has the opposite effect. Under these circumstances, the distractions and anxiety debilitate job performance.

Groups can potentially decrease the productivity of individual members: (1) by decreasing their motivation to perform well; (2) by creating problems of coordination among group members; and (3) by decreasing individual feelings of responsibility. These problems are exacerbated the larger the size of the group. These liabilities of groups account for the difference between the potential productivity of groups and their actual productivity.

Four criteria for the effectiveness of group decision making are discussed: accuracy, creativity, riskiness, and acceptance of group decisions. Groups generally do make more accurate decisions than individuals acting alone because they can bring both a greater sum total of knowledge and a greater number of approaches to bear on a problem. This is particularly true when the group membership is heterogeneous in terms of skills and perspectives. Participation in group decision making also generally increases members' acceptance of group decisions and their commitment to executing them faithfully.

Groups do not come up with more creative problem solutions than individuals. People are hesitant to be criticized for "oddball" ideas in front of a group, and groups fall into ruts and pursue a single train of thought for long periods of time. Groups are more effectively used for evaluating problem solutions, while individuals are more effective in generating new ideas. Delphi groups and nominal groups are more effective than brainstorming groups for this reason. As for risk, the research suggests that there is no systematic bias in groups toward either risk or conservatism.

The manager plays a key role in determining whether the group experiences "synergy" or "process losses." The manager of the group can enhance group effectiveness by: (1) controlling group membership; (2) using groups more selectively; (3) motivating and rewarding appropriate behavior; (4) building acceptance and commitment to group decisions; and (5) skillfully handling group discussions.

REVIEW QUESTIONS

1. Describe the Hawthorne experiments. What did they reveal about group influences on individual productivity?
2. In what three ways can groups increase individuals' job-relevant knowledge and skills? Give an example of each.
3. Define social facilitation. When will working in the presence of others decrease individual performance?
4. Why do individuals (a) feel less motivation to perform well in group settings, (b) have more coordination problems in group settings, and (c) feel less personally responsible for doing a good job in group settings?

5. Discuss the relationship between group size and group effectiveness.
6. Do groups make more accurate judgments than individuals acting alone? Why or why not?
7. Describe brainstorming. Evaluate its effectiveness as a method of generating creative ideas.
8. Describe the Delphi technique and the nominal group technique. Evaluate their effectiveness as methods of generating creative problem solutions.
9. Is there a "risky shift" in group decision making?
10. Describe Coch and French's experiment on introducing change in the pajama factory. What does this experiment teach us about the effects of participative group decision making?
11. Under what circumstances is group participation most effective?
12. Distinguish between the task performance and social maintenance duties of managers. Why is each important?
13. What is "the folly of rewarding A while hoping for B"? How does it apply to managing work groups?
14. Discuss some strategies managers can use to more skillfully handle group discussions.

REFERENCES

Allen, T. J., & Marquis, D. G. Positive and negative biasing sets: The effects of prior experience on research performance. *IEEE Transactions on Engineering Management*, 1964, *EM-11*, 158–161.

Bales, R. F. Task roles and social roles in problem-solving groups. In E. Maccoby, T. M. Newcomb, & E. L. Hartley (Eds.), *Readings in social psychology* (3rd ed.). New York: Holt, 1958.

Bavelas, A., Hastorf, A. H., Gross, A. E., & Kite, W. R. Experiments on the alteration of group structure. *Journal of Experimental Social Psychology*, 1965, *1*, 55–70.

Berelson, B., & Steiner, G. A. *Human behavior: An inventory of scientific findings*. New York: Harcourt, Brace, & World, 1964.

Blumberg, P. *Industrial democracy: The sociology of participation*. New York: Schocken, 1969.

Bouchard, T. J. Whatever happened to brainstorming? *Journal of Creative Behavior*, 1971, *5*, 182–189.

Brown, R. *Social psychology*. New York: Free Press, 1965.

Coch, L., & French, J. R. P., Jr. Overcoming resistance to change. *Human Relations*, 1948, *1*, 512–532.

Collaras, P. A., & Anderson, L. R. Effect of perceived expertise upon creativity of members in brainstorming groups. *Journal of Applied Psychology*, 1969, *53*, 159–163.

Collins, E. B., & Guetzkow, H. *A social psychology of group processes for decision-making*. New York: Wiley, 1964.

Cottrell, N. B., Wack, D. L., Sekerak, F. J., & Rittle, R. H. Social facilitation of dominant responses by the presence of an audience and the mere presence of others. *Journal of Personality and Social Psychology*, 1968, *9*, 245–250.

Dalkey, N. *The Delphi method: An experimental study of group opinion.* Santa Monica: Rand Corporation, 1969.

Davis, J. H. *Group performance.* Reading, Mass.: Addison-Wesley, 1969.

Delbecq, A. L., Van de Ven, A. H., & Gustafson, D. H. *Group techniques for program planning.* Glenview, Ill.: Scott, Foresman, 1975.

Dunnette, M. D., Campbell, J., & Jaastad, K. The effect of group participation on brainstorming effectiveness for two industrial samples. *Journal of Applied Psychology*, 1963, *47*, 30–37.

Feldman, D. C., & Brett, J. M. The transfer and promotion process. Paper presented at the National Academy of Management Meetings, August 1981.

Gerard, H. B., & Rabbie, J. M. Fear and social comparison. *Journal of Abnormal and Social Psychology*, 1961, *62*, 586–592.

Hackman, J. R. Group influences on individuals in organizations. In M. D. Dunnette (Ed.), *Handbook of industrial and organizational psychology.* Chicago: Rand McNally, 1976.

Harrison, E. F. *The managerial decision-making process.* Boston: Houghton Mifflin, 1975.

Harvey, O. J. An experimental approach to the study of status relations in informal groups. *American Sociological Review*, 1953, *18*, 357–367.

Henchy, T., & Glass, D. C. Evaluation apprehension and the social facilitation of dominant and subordinate responses. *Journal of Personality and Social Psychology*, 1968, *10*, 446–454.

Herold, D. M. The effectiveness of work groups. In S. Kerr (Ed.), *Organizational behavior.* Columbus, Ohio: Grid Publishing, 1979.

Hoffman, L. R., & Maier, N. R. F. Quality and acceptance of problem solutions by members of homogeneous and heterogeneous groups. *Journal of Abnormal and Social Psychology*, 1961, *62*, 401–407.

Jewell, L. N., & Reitz, H. J. *Group effectiveness in organizations.* Glenview, Ill.: Scott, Foresman, 1981.

Kerr, S. On the folly of rewarding A while hoping for B. *Academy of Management Journal*, 1975, *18*, 769–783.

Latane, B., & Darley, J. M. Bystander apathy. *American Scientist*, 1969, *57*, 244–268.

Lawler, E. E., & Hackman, J. R. The impact of employee participation in the development of pay incentive plans: A field experiment. *Journal of Applied Psychology*, 1969, *53*, 467–471.

Leavitt, H. J. Suppose we took groups seriously. In E. L. Cass & F. G. Zimmer (Eds.), *Man and work in society.* New York: Van Nostrand Reinhold, 1975, 67–77.

Maier, N. R. F. Assets and liabilities in group problem solving: The need for an integrative function. *Psychological Review*, 1967, *74*, 239–249.

Maier, N. R. F. *Problem solving and creativity in individuals and groups.* Belmont, Calif.: Brooks Cole, 1970.

Maier, N. R. F. *Psychology in industrial organizations.* Boston: Houghton Mifflin, 1973.

Mayo, Elton. *Human problems of an industrial civilization*. New York: Macmillan, 1933.

O'Dell, J. W. Group size and emotional interaction. *Journal of Personality and Social Psychology*, 1968, *8*, 75–78.

Osborn, A. F. *Applied imagination*. New York: Scribner, 1957.

Rabbie, J. M. Differential preferences for companionship under threat. *Journal of Abnormal and Social Psychology*, 1963, *67*, 643–648.

Reitz, H. J. *Behavior in organizations* (2nd ed.). Homewood, Ill.: Irwin, 1981.

Roethlisberger, F. J., & Dickson, W. J. *Management and the worker*. Cambridge, Mass.: Harvard University Press, 1939.

Sarbin, T. R., & Allen, V. L. Increasing participation in a natural group setting: A preliminary report. *The Psychological Record*, 1968, *18*, 1–7.

Schachter, S. *The psychology of affiliation*. Stanford, Calif.: Stanford University Press, 1959.

Scheflen, K. C., Lawler, E. E., & Hackman, J. R. Long-term impact of employee participation in the development of pay incentive plans: A field experiment revisited. *Journal of Applied Psychology*, 1971, *55*, 182–186.

Shaw, M. E. *Group dynamics* (3rd ed.). New York: McGraw-Hill, 1981.

Sherif, M., White, B. J., & Harvey, O. J. Status in experimentally produced groups. *American Journal of Sociology*, 1955, *60*, 370–379.

Slater, P. E. Contrasting correlates of group size. *Sociometry*, 1958, *21*, 129–139.

Steiner, I. D. Models for inferring relationships between group size and potential group productivity. *Behavioral Science*, 1966, *11*, 273–283.

Stoner, J. A. F. A comparison of individual and group decisions including risk. Unpublished master's thesis, School of Industrial Management, M.I.T., 1961.

Taylor, D. W., Berry, P. C., & Block, C. H. Does group participation when using brainstorming facilitate or inhibit creative thinking? *Administrative Science Quarterly*, 1958, *3*, 23–47.

Thomas, E. J., and Fink, C. F. Models of group problem solving. *Journal of Abnormal and Social Psychology*, 1961, *68*, 53–63.

Van de Ven, A. H., & Delbecq, A. The effectiveness of nominal, Delphi, and interaction group decision-making processes. *Academy of Management Journal*, 1974, *17*, 605–632.

Vroom, V. H., Grant, L., & Cotton, T. The consequences of social interaction in group problem-solving. *Organizational Behavior and Human Performance*, 1969, *4*, 75–95.

Vroom, V. H., & Yetton, P. W. *Leadership and decision making*. Pittsburgh: University of Pittsburgh Press, 1973.

Wexley, K. N., & Yukl, G. A., *Organizational behavior and personnel psychology*. Homewood, Ill.: Irwin, 1977.

Whyte, W. H., Jr. *The organization man*. New York: Simon and Schuster, 1957.

Zajonc, R. B. Social facilitation. *Science*, 1965, *149*, 269–274.

CHAPTER 19

INTERGROUP BEHAVIOR AND

MANAGING CONFLICT

In previous chapters we have focused on the manager's responsibilities toward individual employees and the group as a whole. In this chapter we focus on yet another aspect of the manager's job—managing the relations between different groups within organizations. Conflict between groups in organizations is not unusual. In fact, it is quite frequent and highly visible. Just a few examples of such intergroup conflict include labor vs. management, line vs. staff (e.g., brand management vs. market research), two functional areas dissatisfied with each other's performance (e.g., production vs. quality assurance), and two project teams competing for scarce resources.

In this chapter we examine the key issues in managing intergroup conflict—overt expressions of hostility between groups and intentional interference with each other's activities. First, the chapter explores diagnosing the causes of intergroup conflict. Second, we describe the dynamics of intergroup conflict: what happens within conflicting groups, what happens between groups, what strategies groups use to advance their causes, and how groups change as a result of winning or losing a conflict. Finally, we explore the range of resolution strategies available to managers, and discuss the circumstances when each strategy is most effective. We begin now with diagnosing the causes of intergroup conflict.

DIAGNOSING THE CAUSES OF INTERGROUP CONFLICT

Intergroup conflict most frequently results from two key factors: (1) coordination of work between groups; and (2) organizational control systems. Let's consider each of these factors more closely.

Coordination of Work

Probably the most common source of intergroup conflict is task interdependence. Organizations need coordination among several departments' activities to produce a desired product or to provide a service, and friction arises in several ways in the process of coordinating different departments.

Task Interdependence

In *sequential* task interdependence, the product (output) of one group becomes the raw material (input) of another group. For example, the consumer surveys of a market research function become the raw data for the design of promotional activities in advertising; the specifications of an architect's construction plans provide the starting point for the engineering function's activities.

In *reciprocal* task interdependence, some outputs of each group become inputs to the other group. Probably the best example of reciprocal task interdependence is production and quality assurance: production produces goods for quality assurance to test for safety and other standards, and quality assurance sends back products to production that are substandard and need to be altered. Another example of reciprocal task interdependence is production and sales. Production provides the goods for the sales force to sell, and sales orders and sales estimates provided by the sales force help determine how many products production will turn out.

In both cases, conflict arises from differences in performance expectations. In the examples above, advertising could feel that it is not getting sufficiently accurate data from market research to do its own job effectively. Engineering may be dissatisfied with the technical competence of the architect's plans or with what seems to engineering to be the architect's grandiose ideas. Production may feel quality assurance has set standards that are too high for production to meet consistently, and quality assurance may be upset at the high reject rate on production's output. The sales force may be angry at production because of consumer complaints about their products, and production may be angry at sales for not bringing in enough new orders.

In general, intergroup conflict as a result of task interdependence will be worse: (1) the more the activities of one group affect the performance of other groups; (2) the wider the range of activities in a group that are affected by another; and (3) the more unstructured the workflow is (how unclearly the responsibilities of each group are outlined, how unclearly the standards for evaluation are specified, etc.).

Task Ambiguity

Another important source of intergroup conflict arises when it is unclear which group is responsible for performing certain activities; "things fall between the cracks," and both groups are upset with each other. An area where this task ambiguity is frequently seen is in M.B.A. recruitment. Both the personnel department and the specific functional areas (e.g., marketing, operations, finance) have responsibilities in recruiting M.B.A.s: identifying candidates, interviewing candidates, making selection decisions, and negotiating salaries. Sometimes there is conflict over who has the final authority to make and execute selection decisions, and personnel and the functional areas each assert what they perceive to be their prerogatives. Other times, task ambiguity causes intergroup conflict because both groups want to avoid doing a task. Dutton and Walton (1965) describe just such a conflict between sales and production departments, each of which wanted to avoid some responsibilities for establishing production levels.

Task ambiguity often arises when the organization is growing quickly or the organization's environment is changing rapidly. New areas of task responsibility emerge before the formal organization structure can assign formal authority for them. Task ambiguity can also result from unstructured, nondirective leadership. The work is so unstructured that groups come into conflict both about performance expectations and job assignments.

Differences in Work Orientation

How employees go about doing their work and dealing with others varies widely across functional areas of an organization (Lawrence & Lorsch, 1969). First, functions differ in their time perspectives. For example, research and development (R&D) scientists have much longer-range goals than do manufacturing groups. Manufacturing is evaluated on how quickly it can turn out high-quality proudcts, while R&D scientists can only be evaluated after a long period of product development and testing. Second, the goals of different functions vary greatly. The goals of a manufacturing unit are more specific and clear-cut than the goals of R&D units: manufacturing has precise targets for volume, cost savings, and percent of rejects, while R&D has much broader and less easily measurable goals such as developing basic science knowledge and suggesting potential market applications. Third, the interpersonal orientations of people in different departments vary. R&D labs need and encourage a level of informality, looseness of structure, and collegiality that would be dysfunctional in a manufacturing group. The greater the differences in goal, time, and interpersonal orientation, the more likely conflict will arise between groups.

These differences in work orientation lead groups to be frustrated with, and misinterpret, the behavior of other groups. Manufacturing may feel it is being too closely monitored, while the people in R&D are getting away with murder. People in manufacturing may interpret the casual atmosphere of R&D people as lack of seriousness, while people in R&D may view manufacturing's concern with volume and cost indices as narrow and as "missing the forest for the trees." When the two groups need to cooperate on a project, e.g., translating a product idea into the production phase, conflict can arise on two fronts. First, each group may get angry about the work style of the other group. Second, the conflict can escalate because of the attributions each group makes about the other's behavior: manufacturing may attribute R&D's slow pace to laziness, when in fact the slowness could be a result of the difficulty of the problem and the methodicalness of basic scientists.

Organizational Control Systems

The second set of causes of intergroup conflict arises from the ways in which organizations monitor group performance and distribute resources (e.g., money, personnel, equipment). Groups come into conflict as they compete for scarce resources and struggle to "look good" on the criteria on which they are distributed.

Resource Interdependence
Frequently, groups are relatively independent of each other in getting their work done, but compete with each other for resources. Two separate manufacturing plants making the same product may compete for additional budget allocations or additional personnel from corporate headquarters. Two departments or project groups may compete for the limited services of a support group; for example, different product groups may compete for the time of the marketing research department. Two staff departments that have little direct interaction with each other, such as personnel and public relations, may still compete with each other for budget allocations. When organizations are experiencing slow growth or no growth, the inevitable conflict over resources becomes even more intense.

Competitive Reward Systems
Sometimes the ways in which reward systems in organizations are designed create a situation in which one group can only accomplish its goal at the expense of other groups. If departments are rewarded for cost reductions, for example, they will be unwilling to share or lend personnel or equipment to other departments without substantial adjustments in

cost allocations (Jewell & Reitz, 1981). Another common example of competitive reward systems leading to intergroup conflict occurs when staff departments are rewarded for cutting costs and personnel, and line departments are rewarded for increasing the amount of products sold or services provided. To increase the amount of products sold, the line groups may have to lean even more heavily on staff groups such as advertising. However, the staff groups are being rewarded for cutting costs and personnel, and providing the types of services asked for by line groups can prevent them from meeting their own goals.

Dysfunctional Consequences of Control Systems

In trying to get subunits of an organization to comply with organization-wide policies and procedures, sometimes organizations actually generate additional conflict between groups.

Merton (1940) provides an excellent example of how organization rules and procedures can inadvertently cause more conflict. Organizations frequently impose rules and procedures to increase the reliability and predictability of subunit performance. For instance, there are rules and procedures for how staff groups are to process the demands for services from line groups so that those services will be provided in an equitable and timely fashion (e.g., the controller's office processing requisition orders). However, sometimes complying with the rules and procedures gets in the way of organizational effectiveness and causes conflict. A line group may need a job done at the last minute, and a staff group may not "bend the rules" because it is so closely monitored and punished for not complying with strict organizational procedures. This type of rigid, defensive behavior can cause conflict between groups, as the line group expresses anger over not being helped and the staff group expresses frustration at being put in a lose-lose situation. Complying with the rules gets in the way of cooperating; the rules that were made to increase organizational effectiveness get in the way of it.

Using Competition as a Motivational Strategy

Managers sometimes use competition between groups as a way of motivating better performance from the subunits. The rationale behind this strategy is that people will produce more under pressure and that competition between groups is healthy for the organization.

Unfortunately, as seductive as this theory may seem, competition between groups frequently *increases* conflict between groups *without* increasing productivity. When examined systematically, the research on this issue asserts that *non*competition results in higher productivity for groups. Groups that cooperate with each other can coordinate their activities better and have a fuller exchange of information and ideas. As a result, cooperative groups generally produce more and higher-quality products (Deutsch, 1949; Hammond & Goldman, 1961).

Moreover, if the groups who are competing are highly task interdependent, productivity decreases substantially. The reason productivity declines with task interdependence has to do with the strategies groups use when they are in competition. If groups are not task interdependent, the only way they can gain an advantage is to produce more. However, if the groups are task interdependent, they also can spend time and energy *blocking* the activities of other groups. This blocking simultaneously lowers the productivity of other groups and detracts productive time and energy away from the blocking group (Miller & Hamblin, 1963).

A good example of the effects of cooperation and competition on productivity is seen in sales groups. Frequently, sales groups are pitted against one another in a competitive fashion so that the group that sells the most receives some special bonus. However, organizational productivity might be even higher if the sales groups cooperated, shared expenses for clerical and support groups, tried to sell several product lines to the same customer, etc.

Competition between different product management groups is another example of potential productivity losses. Generally, different product groups are forced to compete with other groups for scarce advertising and promotion funds. Much of the time that could have been used to develop better marketing strategies within a product management group is used to research the other product management groups and develop arguments for why *other* groups do *not* deserve additional funding.

A Caveat on Diagnosing Intergroup Conflict

There is a real tendency on the part of many managers to misdiagnose intergroup conflict. The first manifestation of intergroup conflict in organizations is generally interpersonal conflict: two people from different groups expressing a lot of anger and frustration with each other. Frequently, this conflict is labeled a "personality problem" and the ensuing problems between other people in the two groups are seen as a result of this initial personality problem. For instance, the vice president of sales and the vice president of operations may continually be in disagreement; this conflict is labeled a "personality problem," and the problems between other people in sales and operations are seen as a result of the interpersonal conflict between the two vice presidents.

However, the causal relationship often goes the other way: there are systematic problems between the two groups, and their conflict is expressed through the leaders. The conflict between the two leaders is the *result* of intergroup problems, not the cause of them.

How can we tell whether this conflict between the vice president of sales and the vice president of operations is a "personality problem" or the result of intergroup conflict? It would be useful to look at some other indicators.

1. Did the previous vice presidents of sales and operations have frequent conflict?
2. Did the current vice presidents of sales and operations have problems dealing with each other before they became vice presidents?
3. Over time, have members from sales and operations been in frequent conflict?

If other members of sales and operations have been in conflict historically, and past vice presidents have had similar conflicts, then the conflict is much more likely a result of group membership than personality. There is probably some systematic problem with coordination of work between groups or some dysfunction in the control system. On the other hand, if the sales and operations departments have not had conflict previously but the current vice presidents did have problems with each other when they were in different roles, then the problem is more likely to be interpersonal. Systematic data needs to be collected to ensure that the causes of interpersonal and intergroup conflict are diagnosed accurately.

THE DYNAMICS OF INTERGROUP CONFLICT

When intergroup conflict is occurring in an organization, there are systematic changes in the perceptions, attitudes, and behaviors of the participants. In the now classic study of intergroup conflict between youth groups, Sherif and Sherif (1953) first outlined the impact conflict has on what happens within competing groups, what happens between competing groups, and the consequences of winning or losing on group dynamics. This next section looks at these changes in group dynamics more closely. We'll also examine what strategies groups use to gain power in intergroup conflict situations.

Changes within Each Group

The changes in intragroup dynamics that most frequently occur as a result of intergroup conflict include the following.

1. *Loyalty to the group becomes more important.* In the face of an external threat, the group demands more loyalty from individual members. Not only is social interaction with people outside the group not encouraged, it is expressly discouraged. Such interaction could lead to inadvertent betrayal of group strategy and secrets. Deviance is more closely monitored and punished.
2. *There is increased concern for task accomplishment.* There is additional pressure for the group to perform at its best. Therefore, the concern

for group members' personal needs declines and the concern for the task increases. The climate of the group becomes much less informal and casual.

3. ***Leadership in the group becomes more autocratic.*** It is even more important, with intergroup conflict present, for a group to be able to respond quickly and in a unified manner to the activities of other groups. A democratic work style can slow down the group's capacity to respond quickly. Moreover, democratic leadership also allows a lot of expression of diverse opinions. A more autocratic leadership style, in contrast, facilitates the group being able to respond quickly to external threats and strengthens the group's ability to present a united front.

4. ***The organization and structure of the work group become more rigid.*** Consistent with both the increased concern for task accomplishment and a more autocratic leadership style, the organization and structure of the work group also become more rigid. There is increased coordination of activities, additional rules and procedures are outlined and enforced, and specific responsibilities are allocated to different group members.

5. ***Group cohesiveness increases.*** As a result of an external threat, past differences and difficulties between group members are forgotten. The group closes ranks to meet the challenge. Individual group members find both the group as a whole and other group members more attractive.

A good illustration of these intragroup dynamics appears at the peak of the annual planning cycle in most organizations. Once a year, each subunit in the organization prepares to meet with top management to set group performance objectives for the upcoming year and to obtain as many resources as possible to meet those objectives. Groups are competing with each other for scarce resources, and many of the dynamics discussed above are often observed. For instance, the groups become more task-oriented: there is both an increased work load (preparing the next year's plans) and increased need for the group to perform well. Lunchtime tennis games become business lunches. People are expected to work longer hours and weekends, even at the expense of their personal lives. The leader becomes more directive, assigning additional responsibilities of the planning review to specific group members and coordinating their activities. Differences of opinion between group members become deemphasized and feelings about the group become more positive.

Changes in Relations between Groups

There are also systematic changes in perceptions, attitudes, and behaviors between groups when there is intergroup conflict.

1. ***There are distortions of perception, both about one's own group and about the other group.*** First, there is substantial selective perception about one's own group; people see only the best aspects of their own group, and deny any weaknesses or negative data about their own group's performance.

    More important, there is systematic distortion of perceptions about the other groups. Groups see only the worst parts of other groups and deny others' positive accomplishments. Blake and Mouton (1961) found, for instance, that even when members of a group were forced to listen to representatives of other groups, people systematically tuned out or denigrated the rival group's representative.

2. ***There is a shift from a problem-solving orientation toward other groups to a win-lose orientation.*** Filley (1977) outlines several facets of this shift in orientation.

    a. There is a much clearer *we-they* distinction drawn between the groups, rather than a "we versus the problem" orientation.

    b. All exchanges with the other groups are evaluated in regard to victory or defeat.

    c. The groups see the issue only from their own point of view, rather than defining the problem in terms of the needs of both groups.

    The parties emphasize the benefits of winning the conflict in the short run and tend to ignore the long-term consequences of the conflict for the relationship between the groups.

3. ***There is increased hostility toward the rival group.*** LeVine and Campbell (1972) label as *ethnocentrism* this natural progression from perceived competition among groups to perceived hostility. Members of other groups are seen as the enemy; they are viewed as contemptible and inferior, deserving of losing the conflict.

4. ***Interaction and communication between groups decrease.*** Because group members already feel hostile toward members of rival groups, there is less desire for interaction with them. Moreover, decreased interaction makes it easier for each group to maintain its negative stereotype of the other. When groups are forced to interact with each other, those interactions become fairly rigid and formal. People look for data to confirm their negative stereotypes of the other group's members. Whatever information is passed between groups is very carefully rationed and sometimes deliberately distorted.

Union-management relationships during contract negotiations illustrate some of these dynamics. It becomes difficult for each side to see anything positive about the other side; each party appeals to the good it is doing for its side and undervalues the interests of the other side. The relationship is adversarial in tone, not problem solving. Each side tries to engineer a solution that it can label as victory for itself. The relationship is viewed as a win-lose proposition. Short-run outcomes loom much more important than long-run consequences. When the two sides are forced to interact with each other, these interactions are very formalized. Each side tries to withhold as much information from each other as is allowed legally. Each side overstates its position and adds demands simply so they can be bargained away. There is marked hostility and mistrust between the two parties.

Strategies Groups Use to Gain Power

There are several strategies groups can use to gain power in an intergroup conflict situation. Some of these strategies, like contracting, allow for more cooperation and sharing between groups. Other strategies, like controlling information, increase the power of one group at the expense of others. Each of the most frequently used strategies is discussed in some detail below.

Contracting
Contracting refers to the negotiation of a quid pro quo (this for that) agreement between two groups. Each group guarantees the other some predictability and stability in its behavior; the two groups also decide how to split the profits from their relationship.

As mentioned earlier, a common example of contracting occurs between labor and management. Collective bargaining agreements are the results of such contracting. The union guarantees to management that its workers will work so many hours for so many weeks under specified work conditions. The management guarantees to the union some due process in the hiring, disciplining, and termination of employees and in changing the design of the work. Union and management both agree on how to divide the economic gains of the enterprise; the union knows precisely what the wage rates, benefits, and profit-sharing formula will be.

Co-opting
A second power acquisition strategy is *co-opting*. In co-optation, a group will give members of other groups some leadership positions in their groups or include them in their policy-making committees. By "absorbing" people from other groups into their own groups, the criticism and threat from these out-groups is blunted: how can they attack or criticize a group of which they themselves are a part?

Several university administrations used co-optation as a means of controlling student groups during the 1960s and 1970s. Students were demanding that universities divest themselves of stocks held in war-related industries, that they loosen up the rigidity of university curricula, that they respond more quickly and more affirmatively to student issues. As a way of managing this conflict, universities put students on all types of committees dealing with these issues. The students were very subtly co-opted. By being put on all these committees they could no longer protest that they were not being heard by administration. Moreover, the students on these committees were in such a minority position that there was no way they could seriously influence decisions. By "sharing power" with the students, university administrations could exert even more power than they could previously.

A frequent co-optation strategy in industry occurs through the use of boards of directors. In order to maintain stable relationships with financial lending institutions and to blunt any criticism from them, corporations may add to their boards of directors representatives of the banks on whom they are most dependent for financial support.

Forming Coalitions

A third form of power acquisition is *coalition formation*. In forming a coalition, two or more groups cooperate or combine their resources in order to increase their power over groups not in their coalition. It is an interesting mix of cooperation and competition: some groups cooperate with each other in order to compete more effectively with noncoalition members.

A well-known example of a coalition formation is the formation of the AFL-CIO. The conflict between the two large blocks of unions was hindering labor's overall position in dealing with management, in organizing a greater number of nonunion employees, and in obtaining legislation favorable to unions from Congress. In order to gain power over management, the AFL and the CIO formed a coalition, figuring that they would "surely hang separately if they did not hang together."

In recent years, the managements of major airlines have also developed cooperative arrangements with each other so that if one airline is having a strike, it will still receive 25 percent of the revenues it would have received had it been operating under normal business conditions. The reasoning behind the coalition formation is the same. Although obviously the managements of competing airlines stand to gain by the loss of one competitor during a strike, there are greater benefits to be gained by exerting general management's power against the union.

Influencing Decision Criteria

Pfeffer (1977) suggests that organizations cannot make decisions about resource allocation among groups using strictly "rational" criteria. As we discussed in Chapter 13, "purely rational" decision making is very difficult (if not impossible) to achieve because organization members disagree about what the goals of the organization should be and what criteria should be used in measuring contribution to organizational effectiveness.

Since there is no way for organizations to make "purely rational" decisions in allocating resources, groups can exert power by *influencing which criteria are selected* as the bases of distributing resources. Groups look at the *relative* position of their subunit on several criteria, and then argue that those criteria on which their subunit is relatively high be adopted as the bases of distributing resources. For instance, in budget allocation, there are several criteria on which funds might be allocated—total revenues produced, returns on investment, revenue produced per capita, etc. To gain power in a struggle for resources, a group tries to identify those criteria on which it is relatively high and then tries to get those criteria adopted in the decision-making process.

Controlling Information

Another very competitive strategy groups can use to exert power in intergroup conflict situations is to *control important information*. Gaining sensitive and revealing information and limiting other groups' access to sensitive information increases the power of the information-rich group vis à vis other subunits.

For example, getting inside information on projected annual profits can help a subunit better estimate "how much the traffic will bear" in requesting funds. Another example comes from a university, where a powerful department learned well in advance of other departments of a major bequest to the school. This department then prepared well-developed plans for spending the funds long before other departments knew anything about the money. As a result, this department was much more persuasive and successful in gaining funds for itself than the less well prepared departments.

Keeping information secret also increases a group's power (Pfeffer, 1977). By keeping information about itself secret, a group can prevent or forestall other groups making unflattering comparisons: "How come they got so much money when we have made more profit?"

Providing Critical Services

Much of the power that a group can exert in an intergroup conflict situation derives from its ability to *provide needed services* to the organization as a whole and to other subunits. If other units are dependent on a group for accomplishing its own tasks, then that group is able to exert more power against them. Groups can gain an edge over other subunits by taking on critical tasks that no other group in the organization can handle.

For example, management information systems (MIS) departments frequently exert power in this way. They are the only unit that can effectively handle data collection, analysis, and interpretation, and almost all other units in their respective organizations are highly dependent upon them. Moreover, they have a very specialized language that members of other groups are unlikely to understand. Furthermore, there are a set of organizational problems that only MIS specialists can solve. As a result, MIS groups can use withdrawal or slowdown of their services to influence other groups in the organization.

Consequences of "Winning" or "Losing" a Conflict

Sherif's work (1953) also addresses the consequences of winning or losing a conflict on group dynamics. As we would expect, the "winners" and "losers" react in substantially different ways.

1. **Effects of success.** The most systematic change in the perceptions of the winning group is a stronger belief in the negative stereotype of the losing group. Winning the conflict reaffirms the group's positive self-image and reconfirms its negative evaluation of the other group.

   In regard to group climate, the winning group becomes much more concerned again with the satisfaction and needs of individual members. The work atmosphere becomes more casual, more complacent. Success also increases how positively group members evaluate the group, and group cohesiveness and group cooperation are likely to increase as well.

   At least in the short run, the concern for work and task accomplishment decreases. The winning group has little reason to reexamine its operations and little incentive to think about ways of improving. The winning group loses some of its fighting spirit.

2. **Effects of failure.** The most noticeable change in the perceptions of the losing group is its efforts to deny or distort the reality of losing. A lot of energy is put into finding some excuses for losing (e.g., "the deck was stacked."). It is very unlikely that the losing group will simply admit that other groups were better, more deserving, and that nothing would have changed the results of the conflict.

   There is also a noticeable decline in the quality of interpersonal relationships. Unresolved conflicts come to the surface as different factions of the group blame each other for the loss. The group becomes more tense. There is lower group cohesiveness, less cooperation, and less concern for individual members' needs.

   However, if the group gets over its initial disappointment and anger and accepts its loss realistically, there can be some positive changes in the way it operates. The group can learn a lot about itself as a group because its stereotypes have been upset; the group is forced to reevaluate its own strengths and weaknesses. The group is also likely to reorganize to become more effective and to commit itself to working even harder in the future.

Thus, neither winning nor losing a conflict has unambiguous results for the participants in intergroup conflict. Winning increases self-satisfaction but at the expense of complacency; losing decreases group morale but can provide an impetus for improving group performance.

Political campaigns are good places to look for illustrations of the consequences of winning and losing on group dynamics. Consider, for instance, the Carter-Kennedy primary races in 1980, where President

Carter and Senator Kennedy were competing for the Democratic Presidential nomination. In the early phases of the campaign, Kennedy was consistently and convincingly defeated in the primaries. The Kennedy camp distorted the reality of losing—while indeed they lost, they did better than they had expected, they had won some delegates, and so on. The Kennedy people blamed the Carter people for the loss—Carter stayed in the White House, hid behind the Iranian hostage crisis, and refused to debate. There was little attention to the internal problems of the Kennedy campaign organization. The Kennedy people also became somewhat disenchanted with the Democratic Party and briefly flirted with the independent campaign of Representative John Anderson. However, after months of negative feedback, the Kennedy campaign got better organized and developed clearer and more forceful positions. While it was still too little, too late, the Kennedy faction came out of the campaign better organized and prepared the way for future runs at the presidency.

President Carter, on the other hand, received consistently positive feedback throughout the first two-thirds of the campaign. The Committee to Reelect the President had a sense of invulnerability, that things were going their way and that Mr. Carter would be hard to beat. The defeats Senator Kennedy suffered only reinforced to the Carter camp the superiority of Carter's qualifications and its negative stereotypes of Kennedy. However, as a result of all the primary victories, Carter did not examine as closely as possible why there were still substantial numbers of voters who categorically rejected him. Moreover, Carter refused to reevaluate his "Rose Garden strategy" of acting presidential and remaining in the White House. The strategy that had worked so well during the primaries was very ineffective in the fall campaign against Ronald Reagan, and Carter was stunned by the overwhelming defeat he suffered at Reagan's hands in November.

CONFLICT RESOLUTION STRATEGIES

Since dealing with conflict is such a central part of a manager's job, in this section we examine the most frequently used strategies for managing and resolving intergroup conflict and the situations where each strategy is most appropriate.

Traditional View of Conflict

Traditionally, conflict in organizations has been viewed very negatively. It has been considered dysfunctional primarily because of the adverse consequences it could have on organizational functioning. Conflict could cause losses in productivity because groups wouldn't cooperate in getting projects finished and wouldn't share important information. Conflict could be distracting and reduce concentration on the job.

Conflict has also been considered undesirable because of the adverse consequences it could have on the morale of employees. Prolonged conflict could cause stress, frustration, and anxiety. Moreover, conflict has traditionally been viewed as avoidable. Sound recruitment policies, specific job descriptions, clear rules and procedures, and orderly organizational structures were seen as preventing "personality conflicts" or intergroup conflicts from arising.

The traditional view of conflict also lays the blame for conflict squarely on the head of the manager. It is the manager's responsibility to avoid conflict, and managers should be rewarded substantially for the absence of conflict in their work groups. Should intergroup conflict arise, the traditionally preferred solution has been top management imposing its will on the warring factions.

Contemporary View of Conflict

More recently, however, a broader view of conflict has been emerging, a view that sees the functional, as well as the dysfunctional, aspects of conflict.

While the potential negative consequences of conflict are certainly costly, the costs of avoiding all conflict can be even higher. Without conflict, no attention will be called to problem areas; organizations are likely to become complacent about the status quo. More important, conflict can force organizations to reexamine organizational goals and priorities and to make corresponding changes in company policies, procedures, and resource allocation. Conflict can provide both the opportunity and incentive for adaptation and innovation.

The contemporary view of conflict also sees conflict as inevitable. Organizational systems of coordination and control are so complex that no organization design or management strategy could or should prevent all conflict. Confrontation and problem solving, as well as some other strategies of conflict resolution, now seem to be more effective than imposing a solution by top management.

Finally, since conflict can be either functional or dysfunctional, the manager's job is to diagnose the cause of conflict, to establish rules that allow some optimal level of conflict to surface, and to resolve conflicts in a way that enhances organizational effectiveness without creating hostility or destructive behavior. It is conflict diagnosis, management, and resolution that should be recognized and rewarded.

Types of Conflict Resolution Strategies

Intergroup conflict resolution strategies vary widely in how openly they address the conflict. Some of the strategies used to resolve intergroup conflict depend quite heavily on conflict *avoidance*—keeping the conflict from coming into the open at all. A second group of strategies depends instead on conflict *defusion*—keeping the conflict in abeyance and "cooling" the emotions of the parties involved. A third group of strategies depends upon conflict *containment*—allowing some conflict to surface but tightly controlling which issues are discussed and the manner in which they are discussed. A fourth set of strategies depends on conflict *confrontation*—getting all the issues of the conflict into the open and trying to find a mutually satisfactory solution.

In general, which strategy is most appropriate depends on how *critical* the conflict is to task accomplishment and how *quickly* the conflict needs to be resolved. When the conflict is over a trivial issue or needs to be resolved quickly, avoidance and defusion are more likely to be employed; when the conflict is over an important work issue and does not have to be solved in a short time frame, then containment and confrontation are more likely to be used.

We begin our closer examination of intergroup conflict resolution with the conflict avoidance strategies (see Table 19-1).

Conflict Avoidance Strategies

Ignoring the Conflict

This "strategy" is most aptly defined by the absence of behavior: the manager avoids dealing with the dysfunctional aspects of the conflict. Quite often, managers who utilize this strategy also disregard searching for the causes of the conflict, and as a result, the conflict situation frequently continues or gets worse over time.

While ignoring the conflict is generally ineffective for resolving important policy issues, there are some circumstances when it is at least a reasonable way of dealing with problems. One circumstance where ignoring the conflict satisfices is when the conflict issue is trivial. For instance, there may be differences in opinion over the wisdom of giving employees release time to go to some one-shot company training program. This is such a short-run, temporary issue that it does not warrant much attention. Another circumstance where ignoring the conflict is a reasonable strategy is when the issue seems symptomatic of other, more basic conflicts. For example, two groups may experience conflict over the amount and quality of office space. While office space is not in and of itself a trivial issue, conflicts over space reflect more important conflicts about relative power and status. Resolving the office space problem simply does not address the key issues, and attention would be more fruitfully directed to the more basic concerns (Thomas, 1977).

Imposing a Solution

This strategy consists of forcing the conflicting parties to accept a solution devised by a higher-level manager. In effect, imposing a solution does not allow much conflict to surface nor much room for the participants to air

TABLE 19-1
Conflict resolution strategies

Conflict resolution strategy	Type of strategy	Appropriate situations
Ignoring the conflict	Avoidance	When the issue is trivial When the issue is symptomatic of more basic, pressing problems
Imposing a solution	Avoidance	When quick, decisive action is needed When unpopular decisions need to be made and consensus among the groups appears very unlikely
Smoothing	Defusion	As a stop-gap measure to let people cool down and regain perspective When the conflict is over nonwork issues
Superordinate goals	Defusion	When there is a mutually important goal that neither group can achieve without the cooperation of the other When the survival or success of the overall organization is in jeopardy
Representatives	Containment	Before group positions become fixed and made public When each side is represented by groups of representatives rather than by a solo spokesperson
Structure the interaction	Containment	When previous attempts to openly discuss conflict issues led to conflict escalation rather than to problem solution When a respected third party is available to provide some structure and could serve as a mediator
Bargaining	Containment	When the two parties are of relatively equal power When there are several acceptable alternative solutions that both parties would be willing to consider
Problem-solving	Confrontation	When there is a minimum level of trust between groups and there is no time pressure for a quick solution When the organization can benefit from merging the differing perspectives and insights of the groups in making key decisions
Organization redesign	Confrontation	When the sources of conflict come from the coordination of work Self-contained work groups are most appropriate when the work can be easily divided into clear project responsibilities; lateral relations are more appropriate when activities require a lot of interdepartmental coordination but do not clearly lie within any one department's responsibilities.

their grievances. Like ignoring the conflict, imposing the solution is generally an ineffective conflict resolution strategy. The peace it achieves is frequently short-lived. The real issues do not get addressed, and conflict reappears under other guises and in other situations.

However, forcing a solution can be appropriate at times. One situation where it is useful is when quick, decisive action is needed. For instance, when there is high conflict over some investment decisions where delays can be very costly, forcing a solution may be the only strategy available to top management. Another situation where forcing a solution may be necessary is when unpopular decisions need to be made and there is very little chance that the participants involved could ever come to an agreement (Thomas, 1977). A frequent occurrence of this situation is when universities have to cut back on the funding of different academic programs. It is unreasonable to expect that any department would agree to substantially cut its staff and students for the greater good, and yet ultimately some hard, unpleasant decisions have to be made.

Conflict Defusion Strategies

Smoothing

One way a manager can deal with conflict is try to "smooth over" the conflict by playing down the importance and magnitude of the conflict. The manager might try to persuade the groups that they are not so far apart in their viewpoints as they think they are, point out to the groups their similarities rather than their differences, try to "stroke" group members whose feelings have been hurt, or downplay to the groups the importance of the issue. By smoothing the conflict, the manager hopes to decrease the intensity of the conflict and avoid an escalation of open hostility. Like forcing a solution, smoothing is generally ineffective because it does not address the key points of conflict that are likely to keep resurfacing.

However, sometimes smoothing can be effective as a stopgap measure to let people cool down and regain perspective. In the heat of battle, people may make statements that are likely to *escalate*, rather than deescalate, the conflict, and smoothing can bring the disagreement back to a manageable level. For instance, when unpopular actions or decisions are discussed in meetings, tempers often run high and hostile behavior increases dramatically. Smoothing helps get the groups back to a point where they can deal with each other with less friction (Thomas, 1977).

Smoothing may also be appropriate when the conflict is over nonwork issues. For instance, as Alderfer (1977) points out, frequently intergroup conflict occurs between older and younger employees because of their different political beliefs and moral values. Smoothing can help defuse the tension enough so that the conflict does not spill over into more central work issues.

Appealing to Superordinate Goals

Another way managers can defuse conflict is to focus more attention on the overarching goals that the groups share. Instead of emphasizing the current conflict, the manager diverts attention instead to longer-run aims that both groups have in common. The manager defuses anger over the current problem by making it seem insignificant beside the more important common goals the groups share (Sherif, 1958).

Finding such superordinate goals is not easy. The goal must be important to both groups. Obtaining the goal must require cooperation between the groups. The rewards from obtaining the common goal must be high.

Perhaps the most frequently used superordinate goal is organizational *survival*: if the subunits do not cooperate sufficiently, the continued existence of the larger organization is severely jeopardized. A recent example of appealing to superordinate goals to reduce intergroup conflict comes from the Chrysler Corporation. Ordinarily, contract negotiations between union and management would have entailed a great deal of conflict and bargaining over wages, working conditions, and benefits. However, given Chrysler's recent economic troubles, a large wage increase for the workers would have seriously hurt Chrysler's chances of economic survival. Such a wage increase would have both depleted Chrysler's already low resources and lowered Chrysler's chances of obtaining more federal loan guarantees. The superordinate goal of sustaining Chrysler as an ongoing enterprise—and as an employer—defused what would have been, under other circumstances, a very conflictful contract negotiation.

Conflict Containment Strategies

Using Representatives

One of the strategies managers use to contain conflict is the use of representatives. In order to decide an issue, many managers find it easier to meet with representatives of opposing groups rather than dealing with the groups in their entirety. The additional rationale is that a representative of a group both knows the problems of a group well and can argue the group's point of view accurately and forcefully (Blake & Mouton, 1961).

While on the face of it the use of representatives seems a logical way of proceeding, the research evidence on the use of representatives as a means of solving intergroup conflict is fairly negative. The core of the problem is that representatives are not entirely free to engage in compromise. Rather, representatives have to act out of loyalty and are motivated to win (or at least avoid defeat) even though a solution to an intergroup problem is sacrificed in the process. A representative who "gives in" is likely to face suspicion or rejection from group members. If a representative cannot win, he or she will try to deadlock a solution or at least forestall defeat. In fact, in one study, only two of sixty-two representatives capitulated to the opposition; in all the other situations, the representatives ended in deadlock (Blake & Mouton, 1961).

Negotiations between foreign diplomats, as representatives of different governments, illustrate some of the problems of this form of conflict resolution. In a self-mocking story, Copley News Service provided this guide on how to interpret the jargon used to describe negotiations between diplomats:[1]

"Useful" —No progress, but we learned where the other side stands, and that could be useful.

"Fruitful" —This round was deadlocked, but the next could be useful.

"Productive" —Still no agreement, but we are proceeding in an atmosphere that is frank and open.

"Frank and open"—Complete and total disagreement, but something may come of it.

"Meaningful" —Everybody enjoyed the tour of the museum.
(Copley News Service, *Reader's Digest*, 1975, p. 82)

While individual representatives have difficulty in negotiating an agreement because of their fear of rejection by their own groups, using *groups* of representatives from each side can overcome some of this anxiety. Members of each team can provide each other mutual support when they have to make some concessions in order to achieve an agreement. Also, groups of negotiators may receive broader-based support and trust from their respective sides, since each representative may represent a different constituency or bring a different expertise to the negotiations. In fact, most labor negotiations take place between several representatives of management and labor.

Structure the Interaction between the Groups

Sometimes managers assume that one way to decrease conflict is to increase the *amount* of contact between the groups—if only the groups interacted more, they would like each other more and fight less. However, simply increasing the amount of interaction between groups is ineffective in resolving conflict. Increased interaction will probably add fuel to the fire; the two groups will just look for additional reasons to reinforce their negative stereotypes.

However, *structuring* the interaction between the groups *can* be effective in resolving conflict. Providing constraints on how many issues get discussed and the manner in which the issues get discussed can

---

[1]Reprinted with permission from the November 1975 Reader's Digest, and with permission from Copley News Service.

facilitate conflict resolution. While there are many ways to structure the interaction between groups to deal with conflict, some of the most frequently used and effective strategies include: (1) decreasing the amount of direct interaction between the groups in the early stages of conflict resolution; (2) decreasing the amount of time between problem-solving meetings; (3) decreasing the formality of the presentation of issues; (4) limiting how far back historically and how widely precedents can be cited; and (5) using third-party mediators.

All these strategies try to allow some conflict to surface and be addressed but prevent the conflict from getting out of hand and the parties from hardening their positions. For instance, decreasing the amount of direct interaction between groups early in the conflict helps prevent the conflict from escalating: as mentioned earlier, when the groups are hostile, they just use additional interaction to confirm their negative stereotypes of each other. Decreasing the amount of time between problem-solving meetings decreases the amount of time groups will have to backslide from tentative agreements and harden their original positions. Decreasing the formality of the presentation of issues helps induce a problem-solving, rather than a win-lose, orientation to the conflict. Limiting how far back historically, and how widely, precedents can be cited helps the parties focus on finding a solution to the current conflict; if a lot of past conflicts and solutions are discussed, hostility will increase again and the likelihood of finding a solution consistent with all the precedents cited decreases. Finally, a mediator can act as a go-between who transmits offers and messages, can help the groups clarify their positions, can present each group's position more clearly to the other, and can suggest some possible solutions not obvious to the opposing parties (Wexley & Yukl, 1977).

As with the use of representatives, structuring the interaction between groups as a means of intergroup conflict resolution is seen most frequently in governmental relations and in union-management relations. In the Carter-Begin-Sadat Middle East talks, many of the principles discussed above were used. Issues were discussed informally at Camp David, not at the UN. Rather than having the Israeli and Egyptian presidents lock horns with each other day after day, Carter acted as a mediator, going from party to party with each other's proposals and counterproposals, clarifying positions and suggesting possible solutions. Rather than trying to solve all the tangled conflicts between several Middle East countries and all the issues that these several countries faced with each other, Carter focused on only two countries and on only a limited set of issues, leaving the others go for another time. Labor-management mediators use similar tactics: no announcement of interim agreements; "shuttle diplomacy" between groups; limiting the amount of time between rounds of contract talks; and putting some boundaries on how liberally each party can cite precedents.

While structuring the interaction can frequently be used to help resolve conflict, it is especially useful in two situations: (1) when previous attempts to discuss conflict issues openly led to conflict escalation rather than to problem solution; and (2) when a respected third party is available to provide (and enforce) some structure to the interactions between the groups and could serve as a mediator.

Bargaining

Bargaining can be defined as the process of exchanging concessions until a compromise solution is reached. Bargaining can certainly lead to the resolution of an intergroup conflict, but usually without much openness on the part of the groups involved and without much real problem solving.

Typically what happens in bargaining is that each side begins by demanding more than it really expects to get. Both sides realize that some concessions will be necessary in order to reach a solution, but neither side wants to make the first concession because it will be seen as a sign of weakness. A lot of what happens in bargaining is *tacit communication*: each party signals a willingness to be flexible in exchanging concessions without actually making an explicit offer or promise. There is thus little danger of appearing weak, since a tacit proposal can later be denied if it fails to elicit a positive response from the other party (Pruitt, 1971). Bargaining continues until some sort of mutually satisfactory agreement is reached. Note that this solution can be reached *without* much open discussion of the central conflict issues and *without* much concern for solving the real organizational problems.

It is also important to note that bargaining often results in a compromise agreement that fails to deal with the underlying problem in a rational manner and is not in the long-term interests of the parties. Wexley and Yukl (1977) demonstrate this point quite clearly with their example of two departments competing for control over a new production process. The conflict was resolved by an agreement to divide the new machines and personnel equally between the two departments. The cost of running duplicate operations became so excessive that departments had to continually compete for available work. Ultimately, the compromise turned out to be not only unprofitable for the company but also unsatisfactory to both departments as well (p. 182).

For bargaining to be feasible at all as a conflict resolution strategy, both parties should be of relatively equal power. Otherwise, one group could simply impose its will upon the other, the solution would not be mutually acceptable, and the weaker group would have no recourse in obtaining its concessions from the more powerful group. In addition, bargaining is more likely to work if there are several acceptable alternatives that both parties would be willing to consider. If each party has only one acceptable settlement, bargaining will likely end in deadlock.

Trading players among professional sports teams probably illustrates bargaining at its best. Each sports team generally has several players it wants and several players it would like to trade, and there are often several potential trade deals between the teams—particularly when future draft choices and money are also considered as items to be traded. Moreover, because the sports teams are members of larger professional associations (like the National Football League), there are rules and procedures that guide how bargaining is to occur and how contracts and agreements are to be enforced.

Conflict Confrontation Strategies

Problem Solving

Problem solving is a conflict resolution strategy that attempts to find a solution that reconciles or "integrates" the needs of both parties. The two groups work together both to define the problem and to identify mutually satisfactory solutions. Moreover, there is open expression of feelings as well as exchange of task-related information. Wexley and Yukl (1977, p. 183) summarize the most critical ingredients to successful problem solving.

1. Definition of the problem should be a joint effort that is based on "shared fact finding" rather than on the biased perceptions of separate groups.
2. Problems should be stated in terms of specifics rather than abstract principles.
3. Points of initial agreement in the goals and beliefs of the parties should be identified along with the differences.
4. Discussions between the groups should consist of specific, nonevaluative comments. Questions should be asked to elicit information, not to belittle the other party.
5. The groups should work together in developing alternative solutions. If this is not feasible, each group should present a range of acceptable solutions rather than promoting the solution that is best for them while ignoring or concealing other possibilities.
6. Solutions should be evaluated in terms of both "objective" considerations of quality and acceptability to the differing groups. When there is a solution that maximizes joint benefits but favors one party, some way should be found to provide special benefits to the other party to make the solution equitable.
7. All agreements on separate issues should be considered tentative until every issue is dealt with since some issues are probably interrelated and cannot be settled independently in an optimal manner (Blake & Mouton, 1962, 1964; Walton & McKersie, 1965).

Walton and McKersie (1965, p. 130) provide a good example of a successful integrative problem solution:[2]

---

[2]From R. E. Walton and R. B. McKersie, *A behavioral theory of labor negotiations: An analysis of a social interaction system,* p. 130. Copyright McGraw-Hill Book Company, 1965.

In the closing down of the McCormick Works of International Harvester, the following issue arose: As soon as the company announced the shutdown of the plant, the union wanted employees released so that they could apply for work at other International Harvester plants. For its part, the company desired to keep many of these employees since they were necessary in the phasing-out operation. The solution reached established a "pegged" seniority date at other plants. . . . The employee continued on in the plant being terminated, all the time acquiring seniority at the plant to which he would be eventually transferred.

More recently, a technology has been developed to reduce intergroup hostility and to reorient groups toward a problem-solving orientation (Blake, Shepard, & Mouton, 1964; Blake, Mouton, & Sloma, 1965). The process begins with *bringing in an outside consultant*, who tries to establish some initial trust between the conflicting groups and to set up the ground rules for future discussions (Alderfer, 1977).

The second stage of the intergroup conflict resolution is for the two groups to *exchange impressions of each other* (Burke, 1972). Each group is asked to prepare answers for the following three questions:

1. How do we see ourselves?
2. How do we see the other group?
3. How do we think they see us?

Burke (1972, p. 259) provides the following examples of characteristics from an intergroup problem-solving session between engineering and manufacturing groups.[3] During this phase, the groups first work separately to generate these images of each other and then present them publicly. Because there is a lot of emotion involved at this stage and thus some

Engineering		Manufacturing
Stable	—We see ourselves—	Competent
Cooperative		Error prone
Creative		Hard working
Unstable	—We see them—	Error prone
Not creative		No sense of urgency
Industrious		Unified as a group
In ivory towers	—They see us—	Constantly changing
Error prone		Error prone
Intrusive		Inflexible

[3]Reproduced by special permission from *Theory and Method in Organization Development: An Evolutionary Process* by John D. Adams (Ed.), p. 259, ©1972, National Training Laboratories Institute.

danger of escalating the conflict, the consultant permits only questions of clarification when these images are exchanged (Alderfer, 1977).

In the third phase, the groups work on *problem identification*. Each group works separately on identifying intergroup problems, and then these lists are exchanged with the other group. Next, several members from each group work together to generate a master list of problems (eliminating overlap and redundancy of the separate groups' lists) and to identify the problems of the highest priority.

In the final phase, the groups engage in some actual *problem solving*. Members from each group volunteer to work on the different problems which have been identified. When the problem-solving groups have completed their work, the results are shared with the larger groups, plans for implementation in the work setting are developed, and arrangements for a future meeting to assess the effects of the solutions are made (Alderfer, 1977).

There are two preconditions for integrative problem solving to work. The first is a minimal level of trust between the groups. Without this minimal trust, each group will fear it will be taken advantage of—each group will be unlikely to reveal its true preferences and will expect the other group to give it inaccurate information in return. Second, integrative problem solving takes a lot of time and can only really succeed in the absence of excessive pressure for a quick settlement. However, as the International Harvester example illustrates, the gains from integrative problem solving can be high. When the organization could benefit from merging the differing perspectives and insights of the two groups in making key organizational decisions, integrative problem solving is especially needed.

Organization Redesign

Redesigning or restructuring the organization can be an effective intergroup conflict resolution strategy, especially when the sources of conflict come from the coordination of work among different departments or divisions. Unlike the other strategies we have discussed so far, however, organization redesign can be used either to decrease conflict *or* to increase conflict. One way of redesigning organizations is to reduce task interdependence between groups and give each group clear work responsibilities; this, in effect, reduces conflict. The other way of redesigning organizations is to structure in overlapping or joint work responsibilities; this makes most use of the different perspectives and abilities of different departments but also tends to create conflict. Let's look more closely at when each of these redesign strategies is most appropriate.

Probably the most frequently used method of reducing conflict through organization redesign is to *create self-contained work groups* that have enough resources to accomplish their goals. Chapple and Sayles (1961) provide a good illustration of one such restructuring. Mechanics in a plant belonged to a separate maintenance department with their own supervisor. A lot of conflict developed between the mechanics and the production supervisors—and among the production supervisors—because of competition over whose machines should be repaired first by the mechanics. Attempts to establish standard criteria for processing requests for service failed, and higher-level managers were being inundated with requests for help. Finally, the organization was redesigned so that the mechanics also reported to the head of production. In some cases, mechanics were also assigned to individual production supervisors. No additional mechanics were needed for this reorganization, and the result was an end to the conflict and reduction in work-flow delays.

Creating self-contained work units is an appropriate strategy when the work can be easily divided into distinct, separate projects. Each group would have both clear project responsibilities and all the resources needed to reach its goals and wouldn't have to compete with other groups for resources. A potential cost of this strategy is duplication and waste of resources, particularly when no one group could fully utilize equipment or staff personnel. Also, innovation and growth may be restricted to existing project areas (Duncan, 1979); no one group would have the incentive or responsibility for coming up with new ideas.

There can also be projects which do not fall clearly into any one department's responsibilities but require the contributions and expertise of several departments. Developing new products is one such activity that requires a lot of interdepartmental coordination but does not clearly lie within any one department's responsibilities. If the organization arbitrarily assigned new product development to one department, it would decrease potential conflict but at a high cost to the quality of the product. Instead, the organization might try to sustain task-based conflict but structure in mechanisms for better managing the conflict. *Providing "integrators" or integrating teams* facilitates communication and coordination between the members of interdependent departments (Galbraith, 1974).

There are several types of integrating mechanisms organizations can use. Individuals in *liaison roles*, particularly at lower and middle management, can facilitate communication between two departments and can bypass long lines of communication involved in upward referral. When several departments or functions are involved, *task forces*, made up of representatives from each of the affected departments, become more appropriate. Some organizations create new *integrator roles*, such as product or program managers, to coordinate the activities of several departments working on the same project over time. Some organizations even adopt a *matrix* structure, in which each employee reports directly to two supervisors, one a project supervisor and the other a function (or departmental) supervisor.

Using research on companies in various industries, Lawrence and

Lorsch (1967) have outlined the necessary conditions for integrator roles or teams to work. As much as possible, integrator roles should be formalized and given formal power. This will ensure that the integrators are not ignored or rebuffed by the groups involved. Integrators should have considerable technical knowledge about the functions to be coordinated. Expertise provides integrators with additional power and influence. Moreover, an integrator who can "speak the language" of different specialist groups is better able to facilitate accurate communication among them.

The basis for evaluating and rewarding integrators should be the success of the products or projects that the integrator is responsible for coordinating. This will help to ensure that the integrator is primarily concerned about organizational effectiveness rather than short-run harmony or pleasing strong departments at the expense of weaker ones. Finally, integrators need to be able to understand and appreciate the goals and concerns of different departments and be able to serve as a "neutral" third party in resolving conflicts.

MANAGERIAL IMPLICATIONS

Above, we outlined some of the most frequently used strategies of intergroup conflict resolution and the circumstances when each strategy is most appropriate. There are some common themes that run through these strategies that suggest some overall implications for managing conflict in organizations.

1. *Work-flow arrangements, job designs, and work responsibilities should be modified not so there will be no conflict, but so that conflict will arise on policy-related issues rather than on day-to-day irritations.*
2. *Managers should monitor control systems to eliminate any win-lose conflicts among groups they might be inducing inadvertently.* Groups should be rewarded for cooperation rather than managed through competition. The contribution of different groups to overall organizational effectiveness and to the effectiveness of other groups should be both recognized and rewarded.
3. *Avoiding and smoothing conflict are generally ineffective in resolving conflict because they do not address the key sources of the conflict.* In addition, conflict which is suppressed in one area frequently reappears in other areas. They might succeed as stopgap measures or when the conflicts are over relatively unimportant issues.
4. *Using representatives and bargaining to resolve conflict are also frequently ineffective because these strategies often result in deadlock or low-quality solutions.*
5. *Managers need to establish rules and standard procedures to regulate conflict.* These rules and procedures might allow some conflict to be

expressed but carefully check the conflict from escalating or getting off on tangents. Third-party mediators or consultants can facilitate this type of intergroup conflict resolution. In-house personnel should also be trained on how to better cope with conflict.

6. ***When groups share a superordinate goal that no one group can achieve without the cooperation of other groups, appealing to this superordinate goal can help defuse conflict.*** However, this strategy only works when the goal is a very highly valued goal, like organizational survival.

7. ***Finally, when high-quality decisions and solutions are needed, managers should sustain constructive confrontation between the groups.*** This open confrontation leads to higher-quality decisions and reduces the need for groups to rely on coercive or destructive behavior.

These common approaches to managing group relations maximize the benefits of conflict while minimizing conflict's potential dysfunctions to organizations.

SUMMARY

The chapter examines intergroup conflict—the overt expressions of hostility between groups and intentional interference with each other's activities.

Intergroup conflict most frequently results from two key factors: (1) coordination of work between groups; and (2) organizational control systems. Conflict due to the coordination of work between different groups arises from disappointment in the quality of other groups' work, ambiguity over job responsibilities, and differences in work style and goal orientations between groups. Conflict due to organizational control systems arises from groups competing for scarce resources, competitive reward systems (in which one group can only accomplish its goal at the expense of other groups), and rigid rules and procedures which inhibit cooperation between groups.

When intergroup conflict is occurring in an organization, there are systematic changes in the perceptions, attitudes, and behaviors of the participants. Relations between groups also change systematically. First, there is substantial selective perception; groups only see the best aspects of their own group and only the worst aspects of the other group. Second, there is increased hostility between the rival groups and a shift to a real "win-lose" orientation. Third, rival group members spend less time with each other, and whatever information is passed between groups is very carefully rationed and sometimes deliberately distorted.

There are a variety of strategies groups can use to gain power in an intergroup conflict situation. Some of these, like contracting, coopting, and coalition formation, are relatively cooperative. Other strategies are much more competitive: influencing the criteria on which conflicts over resources will be decided; controlling vital information; and providing (or withholding) other groups with critical services. Neither winning nor losing a conflict has unambiguous results for the participants in intergroup conflict.

Intergroup conflict resolution strategies vary widely in how openly they address the conflict. Avoidance strategies try to keep the conflict from coming into the open at all, while defusion strategies try to keep the conflict in abeyance and "cool" the emotions of the parties involved. Conflict containment strategies allow some conflict to surface but tightly control which issues are discussed and the manner in which they are discussed, while conflict confrontation strategies rely on getting all the issues of the conflict into the open and trying to find a mutually satisfactory solution. Among the conflict resolution techniques discussed, appealing to superordinate goals, structuring the interaction between conflicting groups, problem solving, and organization redesign are most effective in producing high-quality conflict solutions.

REVIEW QUESTIONS

1. Why does conflict between groups arise from coordination of work activities? What three factors contribute to difficulties in coordinating activities between groups?
2. How do jurisdictional disputes over work responsibilities cause intergroup conflict? When will these jurisdictional disputes be worst?
3. What are the differences in time, goal, and interpersonal orientations between personnel and production which might cause intergroup conflict?
4. In what three ways do organizational control systems contribute to intergroup conflict?
5. How effective is competition between groups as a motivational strategy? Why?
6. What should a manager look for to determine whether a conflict between two subordinates is a "personality problem" or an intergroup conflict?
7. What are the systematic changes in the perceptions, attitudes, and behaviors of group members during intergroup conflict? What are the changes in intergroup dynamics? What are the changes in relations between groups?
8. What strategies can groups use to gain power in intergroup conflict? Which strategies are most cooperative? Most competitive?
9. What are the effects of winning a conflict on group dynamics? the effects of losing a conflict?
10. Compare and contrast the traditional and contemporary views of conflict in organizations.
11. Identify and define the four types of intergroup conflict resolution strategies.
12. When are avoidance stategies most appropriately used?
13. How effective is appealing to superordinate goals in resolving intergroup conflict?
14. Why do representatives of groups so frequently end in deadlock when they are trying to resolve conflict?

15. How can interactions between groups be structured to facilitate conflict resolution?
16. What are the key elements to integrative problem solving? What are its biggest advantages? disadvantages?
17. When should organization redesign be used to reduce conflict? When should it be used to increase conflict?

REFERENCES

Alderfer, Clayton P. Group and intergroup relations. In J. Richard Hackman & J. Lloyd Suttle, *Improving life at work*. Goodyear: Santa Monica, 1977, 227–296.

Blake, Robert R., & Mouton, Jane S. Comprehension of own and of outgroup positions under intergroup competition. *Journal of Conflict Resolution*, 1961, *5*, 304–310.

Blake, Robert R., & Mouton, Jane S. Loyalty of representatives to ingroup positions during intergroup competition. *Sociometry*, 1961, *24*, 177–183.

Blake, Robert R., & Mouton, Janes S. *The managerial grid*. Houston: Gulf Publishing, 1964.

Blake, Robert R., & Mouton, Jane S. The intergroup dynamics of win-lose conflict and problem solving collaboration in union-management relations. In Muzafer Sherif (Ed.), *Intergroup relations and leadership*. New York: Wiley, 1962.

Blake, Robert R., Mouton, J. S., & Sloma, R. L. The union-management intergroup laboratory: Strategy for resolving intergroup conflict. *Journal of Applied Behavioral Science*, 1965, *1*, 25–57.

Blake, Robert R., Shepard, H. A., & Mouton, J. S. *Managing intergroup conflict in industry*. Houston: Gulf Publishing Co., 1964.

Burke, W. W., Managing conflicts between groups. In J. D. Adams (Ed.), *Theory and method in organization development: An evolutionary process*. Arlington: NTL Institute, 1962, 255–268.

Chapple, E., & Sayles, L. R. *The measure of management*. New York: Macmillan, 1961.

Copley News Service, *Reader's Digest*, November, 1975, p. 82.

Deutsch, Morton. A theory of cooperation and competition. *Human Relations*, 1949, *2*, 129–152.

Deutsch, Morton. An experimental study of the effects of cooperation and competition upon group process. *Human Relations*, 1949, *2*, 199–232.

Duncan, Robert B. What is the right organization structure? *Organizational Dynamics*, 1979, *7*, 59–80.

Dutton, J. M., & Walton, R. E. Interdepartmental conflict and cooperation: Two contrasting studies. *Human Organization*, 1965, *25*, 207–220.

Filley, Alan C. Conflict resolution: The ethic of the good loser. In R. C. Huseman, C. M. Logue, & D. L. Freshly (Eds.), *Readings in interpersonal and organizational behavior*. Boston: Holbrook Press, 1977, pp. 234–252.

Galbraith, Jay R. Organization design: An information processing view. *Interfaces*, 1974, *4*, 28–36.

Hammond, Les K., & Goldman, Morton. Competition and noncompetition and its relationship to individual and group productivity. *Sociometry*, 1961, *24*, 46–60.

Jewell, Linda N., & Reitz, H. Joseph. *Group effectiveness in organizations*. Glenview, Ill.: Scott, Foresman, 1981.

Lawrence, Paul R., & Lorsch, Jay W. New management job: The integrator. *Harvard Business Review*, 1967, *45*, 142–151.

Lawrence, Paul R., & Lorsch, Jay W. *Organization and environment: Managing differentiation and integration*. Homewood, Ill.: Irwin, 1969.

LeVine, R. A., & Campbell, D. T. *Ethnocentrism: Theories of conflict, ethnic attitudes, and group behavior*. New York: Wiley, 1972.

Merton, Robert K. Bureaucratic structure and personality. *Social Forces*, 1940, *18*, 560–568.

Miller, L. Keith, & Hamblin, Robert L. Interdependence, differential rewarding, and productivity. *American Sociological Review*, 1963, *28*, 768–777.

Pfeffer, Jeffrey. Power and resource allocation in organizations. In Barry Staw & Gerald Salancik (Eds.), *New directions in organizational behavior*. Chicago: St. Clair, 1977.

Pruitt, D. G. Indirect communication and the search for agreement in negotiations. *Journal of Applied Social Psychology*, 1971, *1*, 205–239.

Sherif, Muzafer. Superordinate goals in the reduction of intergroup conflict. *American Journal of Sociology*, 1958, *63*, 349–358.

Sherif, Muzafer, & Sherif, Carolyn W. *Groups in harmony and tension*. New York: Harper and Bros., 1953.

Thomas, Kenneth W. Toward multidimensional values in teaching: The example of conflict behaviors. *Academy of Management Review*, 1977, *2*, 484–490.

Walton, Richard E., & McKersie, Robert B. *A behavioral theory of labor negotiations: An analysis of a social interaction system*. New York: McGraw-Hill, 1965.

Wexley, Kenneth N., & Yukl, Gary A. *Organizational behavior and personnel psychology*. Homewood, Ill.: Richard D. Irwin, Inc., 1977.

PART EIGHT

CONCLUSION

CHAPTER 20 FUTURE PROSPECTS IN ORGANIZATIONAL BEHAVIOR

CHAPTER 20
FUTURE PROSPECTS IN
ORGANIZATIONAL BEHAVIOR

Throughout the book we have presented state-of-the-art research in organizational behavior, and the most up-to-date techniques for managing individual and group behavior in organizations. In this final chapter, we are more speculative. For each section of the book we make some predictions about future trends in managing individual and group behavior. As you will see, we think the prospects are bright for both more productive *and* more humane organizations.

INTEGRATING THE INDIVIDUAL AND THE ORGANIZATION

1. *Organizations will put more energy into identifying the skills and abilities needed to do management jobs.* While job analysis has been used systematically with blue-collar and lower-level white-collar jobs, it has been seen as too difficult and too time-consuming to do for management jobs. However, increased pressures from government regulatory agencies have forced organizations to be better able to defend their selection criteria and the applicants they ultimately hire, and to do so on the basis of job analysis. Moreover, organizations are becoming aware of the relevance and usefulness of job analysis for other managerial activities, such as designing training and socialization programs, doing career

development and human resource planning, and improving performance appraisal systems.

2. ***Organizations will rely less heavily on selection interviews in choosing job applicants.*** The accumulating evidence on the low reliability and validity of selection interviews should be discouraging enough. Add to this the potentially discriminatory nature of selection interviews, and most managers will be even more hesitant about relying heavily on interviews to make selection decisions. However, interviews will continue to be used steadily to provide applicants with information about specific jobs, to project a positive image of the organization to job applicants, and to obtain from applicants missing or incomplete information that may be required for selection decisions.

3. ***Organizations will utilize assessment centers more frequently to select managers and to make promotion decisions.*** Organizations have become more aware of the impressive performance of assessment centers in predicting managerial success. In terms of measurement properties, they are relatively sound: detailed job analyses and pooled judgments of a number of raters help avoid personal biases, mistaken impressions, and unfounded inferences. Moreover, assessment centers allow organizations to make their selection and promotion decisions based upon observation of a relatively large sample of the applicants' actual behavior. Applicants are observed both as they interact with other people, and as they respond to the requirements and demands of actual job situations. In addition, assessment centers have a good record of complying with government regulations on discrimination against minority applicants. Finally, assessment centers for making promotion decisions can be useful even for applicants who don't get promoted; training and development needs can be identified, and applicants can be re-assessed at a later time.

4. ***Organizations will have to document and justify selection and promotion decisions more systematically.*** It is impossible to predict which way the pendulum of government regulation will swing in affirmative action programs. However, the days of making arbitrary and capricious selection decisions are coming to an end. Organizations now have to justify to the government not only whom they hire and promote, but also why they didn't hire or promote rejected job applicants—and why more affirmative action candidates were not in the applicant pool to begin with. Moreover, independent of government regulations, employees now expect to be treated fairly and to be told why they have been passed over for selection and promotion. Organizations no longer have the right to make unilateral decisions about employees' careers without justification to anyone.

5. ***Selection decisions will be made more frequently on the basis of systematic data rather than on intuition.*** It is still true today that many organizations don't have the knowledge and resources to develop systematic statistical models to predict job performance. It is also true that many

managers today think it "dehumanizing" to reduce a job applicant to a series of numbers and then make such an important decision based solely on those numbers. Furthermore, many personnel decision makers still believe strongly that their intuitive judgment is excellent and could never be excelled by a system lacking their personal brand of sensitivity and insight into the nature of people. However, the research evidence is becoming increasingly strong that systematic combination of numerical data yields better selection predictions than intuitive judgment. Sooner or later, most managers will realize that systematic combination makes good business sense, especially for selection decisions involving a large number of job applicants. Moreover, if there is any selection procedure that is indefensible in terms of discrimination regulations, intuition is it.

6. *Organizations will pay more attention to designing effective socialization programs and leave less of that phase of employee development to chance.* As we've pointed out, early experiences in organizations significantly influence whether employees will stay with the organization that hired them and how committed they will be if they do stay. Organizations are more aware today of how important it is to design effective socialization programs to facilitate employee adjustment. Organizational socialization programs will consist more frequently of a wide and varied series of elements: challenging work assignments; job-relevant training; timely and consistent feedback; supervisory training for managers of new recruits; relaxed orientation sessions; and increased attention to the climate of new recruits' work groups. One-shot training and orientation lectures are simply no longer sufficient.

7. *Organizations will put more energy into continually monitoring the careers and job sequences of their employees.* Organizations have become increasingly aware of the problems of middle- and later-career employees. These employees get transferred and promoted at a slower rate; the characteristics that made them attractive recruits are not so important for the jobs that lay ahead; they are being surpassed by younger employees with more current training. Organizations have been faced with an ironic situation: too many plateaued and obsolete middle-managers and a lack of promotable talent for higher management positions. Consequently, organizations will pay more attention to sequencing job assignments, doing more thorough human resource planning, providing better socialization of promoted and transferred employees, and improving corporate policies on career counseling, continuing education, and geographical relocation.

8. *Employees will exert more effort to influence and control their own careers.* Employees are much more sensitive today to the benefits which can be reaped from being active in planning and managing their own careers. We can expect job applicants to seek out more and better job-related information in choosing organizations. Employees are more likely to practice self-nomination and to make known to supervisors which

jobs they want. They are more likely to seek out different work assignments and continuing education activities. They are more likely to turn down transfers that interfere with their own career plans or their personal lives, and are more ready to leave the organization if they have to. In short, employees will put less emphasis on "seeing how things turn out" and will pressure organizations to be more responsive to their personal and professional needs.

MOTIVATION, SATISFACTION, AND PERFORMANCE

1. *Organizational reward systems will become more flexible in dealing with members of organizations as individuals.* People differ in their needs and desires and are motivated by different rewards. Reward systems that insist on treating all organization members the same and providing everyone with the same rewards is ignoring this individuality. Recent innovations in compensation plans (e.g., cafeteria-style fringe benefits, lump-sum increases, skill-based evaluations, open pay policies, and participative pay decisions) have shown substantial success. Organizations are now aware that they must be more flexible in the types of rewards they offer and how they administer them.

2. *Managers will pay more attention to employees' perceptions of equity in trying to increase employee motivation and satisfaction.* Traditionally managers have looked at "objective" indices like industrywide wages to determine whether employee complaints about pay were legitimate. However, as we have seen throughout our examination of motivation and satisfaction, employees respond to their perceptions of reality, not to any "objective" reality defined by managers. Employees are very sensitive to being treated unfairly and unjustly, and their productivity and satisfaction suffer as a result. Managers will put more energy into distributing rewards on a fair and equitable basis and on explaining the distribution system more fully to subordinates.

3. *Managers will spend more time clarifying their expectations to employees, and setting realistic work goals.* Managers consistently overestimate the extent to which subordinates pick up subtle social cues; employees need to know precisely what is expected of them. Even without increasing extrinsic rewards, managers can increase employee motivation by ensuring that subordinates clearly understand what needs to be done. Through the widespread use of management by objectives, managers are now more cognizant of the importance of setting goals in increasing motivation as well. By setting specific goals that are accepted by subordinates as realistic and challenging, managers can also increase productivity. Especially for nonstandardized, dynamic managerial jobs, the process of clarifying expectations and setting goals is likely to be particularly effective in motivating performance.

4. ***More and more rewards will be distributed contingent upon effective performance.*** There is substantial evidence now that giving rewards contingent upon effective performance does increase productivity. Organizations have discovered that giving everyone the same rewards or administering rewards on the basis of seniority has little impact on productivity. These rewards only motivate people to stay with the organization, not to produce more. As organizations face the double-edged threat of decreasing productivity and decreasing resources, they will turn more frequently to distributing rewards contingent upon effective performance. The stakes are too high now to give poor performers good raises just to avoid interpersonal conflict.

5. ***Organizations will rely more heavily on rewards other than pay to obtain some of the behaviors they desire.*** While pay is undoubtedly the most widely used reward, it is by no means the only reward that can be used to influence behavior, and by no means always the most effective. Pay is simply ineffective in motivating certain desired behaviors, such as being creative, helping out others when they get behind in their work, or building goodwill with customers and clients. Managers will become more innovative in rewarding desired performance with outcomes besides money. Included in the list of available extrinsic rewards are recognition from coworkers, praise from superiors, and social rewards such as the opportunity to make friends and meet new people. Intrinsic rewards employees might receive are feelings of competence for performing a job well, feelings of accomplishment for meeting goals, and feelings of growth and development for success in new areas of personal endeavor.

6. ***Managers will become increasingly concerned about the impact of job satisfaction on employee turnover, absenteeism, and unionization— and less about its impact on productivity.*** More and more organizations are finding that dissatisfied employees are more likely to leave their jobs permanently, to be absent temporarily from work, to vote for unionization, and to file union grievances. Because these behaviors disrupt normal operations and cause morale problems, employers are more conscientiously trying to diagnose sources of employee dissatisfaction and to remedy whatever dissatisfactions they can.

The belief that "the happy worker is the productive worker" is dying more slowly, but dying nonetheless. There is no clear link between satisfaction and performance. Indeed, one could increase employee satisfaction at the expense of performance by giving workers a lot of work breaks and not punishing poor performance. Most managers are not readily inclined to adopt such a strategy.

7. ***Managers will be more concerned with who is job satisfied and why, rather than with overall levels of job satisfaction.*** Scores on job satisfaction surveys have become false idols to many managers. Having uniformly high job satisfaction levels is an impossible ideal, particularly given the downward trend in national job satisfaction surveys. Moreover,

if poor performers are the most dissatisfied, then that is in fact a sign of organizational effectiveness; the employees who are valued the least are receiving the fewest rewards. Managers have come to realize that their most legitimate concern with job satisfaction is determining whether their most talented employees are dissatisfied, and if so, correcting the sources of their job dissatisfaction as quickly as possible.

THE DESIGN OF WORK

1. *Job redesign will be viewed more and more as a means of increasing the quality of work produced, but not the quantity of work produced.* Job redesign efforts have been successful in creating jobs that are intrinsically motivating to employees. As a result, employees working on enriched jobs take more pride in their work and produce higher-quality products. However, job redesign often entails duplication of equipment, less specialization of employees' jobs, and losses of economies of scale. As a result, productivity per person rarely increases after job redesign programs have been implemented. Managers will become more sophisticated about what job redesign can—and cannot—do for them.

2. *Much more care and attention will be paid to diagnosing job redesign problems correctly.* Prior to the 1950s, most job design problems were seen as ones of job enlargement—increasing the variety of tasks employees did. During the 1960s, managers paid more attention to job enrichment—increasing the amount of control individuals have over how their work is to be performed. Today, managers are aware of a much wider set of problems that can cause jobs to be unmotivating, including low task significance, little task identity, and little feedback from the job itself. Furthermore, managers realize that the diagnosis has to be done more systematically and prior to undertaking work redesign projects. Not all motivation problems are job redesign problems, and not all job design problems are ones of variety or autonomy.

3. *Managers who implement job redesign projects will pay increased attention to the systems which surround the focal jobs.* Many factors in the organization can inhibit, if not destroy, the success of job design projects. Some individuals simply do not value the growth opportunities enriched jobs supply. First-line supervisors may feel threatened by a perceived loss of control and try to sabotage job design efforts. Unions may be suspicious of management's motivation, particularly if pay rates are not adjusted upward for jobs utilizing additional skills. Implementing job redesign projects successfully will necessitate more effective identification of potential problems early, more explicit attention to these problems, and more preparation for the inevitable negative spin-off effects job redesign efforts produce.

4. *More and more organizations will attempt to implement group job*

redesign projects. For many organizations, especially those with heavy investments in capital equipment, job redesign at the individual level is simply not feasible. Group job design efforts, in contrast, do not demand such duplication of resources. Instead, autonomous work groups can be responsible for the performance of a major set of activities in the production process. Group members themselves can determine which "roles" each one will play in the group; these roles might change frequently, depending upon the particular skills and preferences of group members. Well-publicized group work design projects like Topeka and Kalmar have made the benefits of group job design more salient to managers.

5. *Quality of working life (QWL) programs are more likely to grow and prosper in newer organizations than older ones.* While QWL programs have been adopted with some success by several corporations, they don't spread quickly. First, QWL demands a different style of management, one that is collaborative rather than autocratic. Second, it costs substantial amounts of money to introduce some QWL programs. Third, and probably most important, QWL hasn't spread quickly because workers as well as managers are suspicious of it.

QWL programs demand whole new ways of behaving for both managers and subordinates, and QWL programs are hard to implement in systems where there are many historical traditions working against them. However, designing quality of working life programs for new plants or new organizations is much more likely to be successful. Managers and employees can be selected in part for their willingness to try new ways of operating. It is easier to create a climate of collaboration and cooperation from scratch than to change a situation marked by distrust and antagonism. While QWL has grown slowly in older organizations, it has prospered much more readily in newer ones.

LEADERSHIP IN ORGANIZATIONS

1. *Managers will vary their leadership style more from situation to situation.* The research on personality and behavioral theories of leadership has shown us that there is no one best type of leader, nor one best way of managing. Being aggressive doesn't always work; being democratic doesn't always work; and being autocratic doesn't always work. The types of subordinates a leader has, the nature of the tasks subordinates are performing, the flexibility of organizational policies, and the group's climate all influence what leadership style will be effective. Instead of looking for universal truths, managers will attempt to achieve a better fit between their behaviors and the demands of particular situations.

2. *Managers will use groups more frequently to build acceptance and commitment to important decisions.* Many managers have discovered the

hard way that a good solution that is "intuitively obvious" to them is often treated as arbitrary by subordinates. Many managers have devised "perfect" solutions on their own, only to find out that subordinates thought their solutions absurd and had little intention of executing them faithfully, if at all.

As a result, managers are now inclined to spend more energy trying to gain the commitment of subordinates to key decisions, and doing so before the decision is finalized. Subordinates who participate in such decision making will be more likely to execute those decisions in a knowing, and enthusiastic, manner.

MANAGERIAL PROCESSES

1. **Managers will become increasingly aware of their limited decision-making capacities and will develop more effective decision-making procedures.** Managers' capacities to generate and evaluate alternative courses of action are not without limit, and they cannot realistically hope to identify the optimal alternative course of action when faced with a decision situation. Perfectly logical decision making is an unreachable ideal. Managers will recognize more and more that they can only focus their attention on a realistic number of alternatives, and that endless information search and data analysis are unlikely to pay noticeable dividends. Managers will develop more effective procedures to protect the quality of decisions from the stress and anxiety that decision making evokes in them.

2. **With more and more information flowing through the organization, managers will develop better procedures for controlling information overload.** A primary reason communications are ignored in organizations is that there is so much information coming in simultaneously that it cannot all be processed carefully. Managers will regulate the flow of information more closely to increase the efficiency of communication. They can time their own communication more effectively; they can stem the flow of routine orders and procedures. Managers will also initiate more communication with subordinates to prevent becoming isolated from problems they need to know about.

3. **Performance appraisals will be used for a wider variety of purposes.** Performance appraisal forms have been used traditionally to evaluate the performance of members of the organization for pay raises and promotions. However, more and more organizations are using performance appraisal data for other personnel activities and doing so successfully. Performance appraisal information can be used to facilitate the personal development of organization members, to evaluate recruitment and staffing policies, to design training programs, and to motivate employ-

ee performance. In addition, managers will take the multiple uses of performance appraisal information into account more carefully when they are designing evaluation instruments and interviews.

4. ***Performance appraisal instruments and interviews will focus more on employee behaviors and less on employee personalities.*** Traditional methods of appraisal (such as graphic rating scales, single global evaluations, and ranking methods) have all had substantial problems because they have not been sufficiently behavior-specific. How can a manager infer if a worker is showing initiative? How can a subordinate refute the criticism that he or she is uncooperative? What does it mean if one is rated 37th out of 100 employees? Because dimensions like *initiative* and *cooperation* are so amorphous, there is a lot of unreliability in how they are measured. Moreover, because these dimensions are quasi-behavior, quasi-personality, they evoke great resentment from employees who feel they are being unfairly "psyched out" by their bosses.

Behaviorally anchored rating scales, behavioral observation scales, and management by objectives, in contrast, reduce rating errors. Job dimensions and job behaviors are clearly defined for the rater. Furthermore, there is more acceptance of and commitment to these devices on the part of both employees and supervisors because they have been actively involved in their development. As a result, these forms of appraisal will become even more popular in the future.

GROUPS IN ORGANIZATIONS

1. ***Managers will be more wary about encouraging group cohesiveness where cohesiveness is likely to lead to lower productivity.*** When cohesiveness is based on pride in the group's work, and the group feels management is supportive, then cohesiveness can indeed increase the overall productivity of the group.

However, cohesiveness will not necessarily lead to increased productivity. When cohesiveness is based on being a member of a high-prestige, high-status group, "not rocking the boat" overwhelms "doing the task well." When the work itself is not intrinsically motivating enough to generate true group commitment, the group may become cohesive in "avoiding hard work." When a cohesive group feels management is antagonistic, then it is more likely to enforce anti-productivity norms. Managers will realize more and more that cohesiveness is not a goal in and of itself, but only worthwhile when it works with, rather than against, the organization.

2. ***Managers will play a more active role in setting and changing group norms.*** Traditionally, managers have let norms develop as they would—and only if the norms interfered with group performance did they

try to change those norms. Moreover, managers were more inclined to avoid discussing norms explicitly because of the awkwardness such discussions created.

However, how norms develop is not a mysterious process that managers cannot influence. Indeed, managers can have more influence on group norms than other group members. They can explicitly set task-facilitative norms at the outset to get the group off to a positive start. They can continuously monitor whether the group's norms are functional and explicitly address counter-productive norms with subordinates. Managers will force groups to openly examine their interpersonal processes more closely so that more effective behavior patterns will develop.

3. *Managers will be more likely to use deviance constructively and less likely to reject the deviant out of hand.* There have been too many instances in both the private and public sectors in which failure to listen to divergent opinions has led to disastrous decisions. Ignoring the deviant is simply not functional for basic and important task problems. Without deviance, the group is less likely to examine the flaws in its planning and decision-making activities. By not tolerating deviance, the group loses the fresh perspectives of new members and diminishes their enthusiasm for improving the group. By extinguishing any signs of deviance, the group loses the opportunity to explore the usefulness of the very norms it is enforcing. Managers will be more open to examining why certain behaviors are punished as deviant in order to enhance the long-term effectiveness of their groups.

4. *Managers will become more selective in what activities they assign to groups.* Groups are more appropriate for some activities and less appropriate for others. Individuals are better at generating ideas than groups, but groups are better at evaluating ideas. Groups facilitate individual performance when group members do routine jobs but inhibit individuals who are doing more cognitive jobs. Since groups involve substantial costs in terms of coordination and lower individual motivation, managers will be more sensitive to using groups for only those activities for which groups bring a "value added."

5. *Managers will take greater care in how they compose the membership of work groups.* To take advantage of two key potential assets of groups—a greater sum total of knowledge and a greater number of approaches to a problem—the manager has to be very careful in how he or she composes decision-making groups. Group members should have competencies relevant to the problem at hand; diverse points of view should be represented; and the group size should be kept moderately low. Managers will learn that controlling who gets into the group at the front end takes a lot of pressure off managing the group process at the back end.

6. *Managers are becoming more aware of the need to balance task performance duties with social maintenance duties.* While the manager

has to make sure the group accomplishes its work, he or she also has to provide sufficient personal satisfactions to members so that they will remain in the group. While the task performance responsibilities are certainly primary, inattention to social maintenance duties leads to more conflict, poorer morale, and higher turnover. Social maintenance duties are especially critical in handling group discussions. Group leaders need to encourage different points of view, refrain from showing favoritism to particular solutions early in group discussions, stop one subgroup from steamrolling all the others, and prevent verbal attacks of members on each other. Only by attending to both task performance and social maintenance duties will managers be able to harness the energy and contributions of individual group members in the most constructive way.

7. *Organizations will experience more intergroup conflict as resources get tighter and organizations require greater coordination of activities between groups.* One of the major sources of intergroup conflict is competition for budgets, personnel, and equipment. As organizations have less and less slack, there will be increased competition for scarcer resources. Moreover, more organizations are using structural forms like the matrix and temporary task forces that require increased coordination of activities between groups. There will be greater task ambiguity and more differences in performance expectations between groups as a result. Intergroup conflict will become much more frequent and much more the rule than the exception.

8. *More managers will view intergroup conflict as potentially healthy for organizations.* While the potential negative consequences of conflict are certainly costly, the costs of avoiding all conflict can be even higher. Without conflict, no attention will be called to problem areas; organizations are likely to become complacent about the status quo. More important, conflict can force organizations to re-examine organizational goals and priorities and to make corresponding changes in company policies, procedures, and resource allocation. Managers will use the opportunity that conflict provides as an incentive for adaptation and innovation.

9. *Managers will rely less heavily on avoidance and smoothing as strategies for conflict resolution and more heavily on confrontation.* When conflict is over a trivial issue or the conflict needs to be resolved quickly, avoiding and smoothing conflict are reasonable strategies to pursue. However, neither strategy is generally effective in resolving conflict because neither addresses the key sources of conflict. Conflict that is suppressed in one area frequently just reappears in other areas. When high quality decisions and solutions are needed, constructive confrontation between the groups can be very valuable. Managers can use this open confrontation to obtain higher-quality decisions and to reduce the need for groups to rely on coercive or destructive behavior. Managers will try as hard to maximize the benefits of intergroup conflict as to minimize its potential dysfunctions.

A FINAL THOUGHT

In conclusion, we'd like to encourage our readers to take more risks in trying to change the way organizations are managed—and to take more chances in managing their own careers. While continuing in the old ways of behaving is the path of least resistance, it is far from the most rewarding way of life. Robert Frost best illuminates what is to be gained from such an adventuresome spirit:

> "I shall be telling this with a sigh
> Somewhere ages and ages hence:
> Two roads diverged in a wood, and I—
> I took the one less travelled by
> And that has made all the difference."

CASES

CASE 1 GIGANTIC AIRCRAFT COMPANY*

Gigantic Aircraft Company is a large firm with a plant near Santa Barbara, California. The personnel manager has called in Boyce Piersol, a management consultant specializing in personnel, for advice on selection policies. Bill Fabris invited Piersol to come in the first thing in the morning. When Piersol arrived, Fabris said:

Boyce, I'm glad you're here. I've been having a lot of trouble in selection recently. My long suit has always been collective bargaining. I'm a lawyer by training, and I think I need help. Briefly, let me outline how we handle selection here now:

Blue-collar employees—Screening interview to separate out the misfits; then a test battery—mostly abilities tests—and then interview the best of the lot. For crucial jobs, either security-wise, or if the job involves expensive equipment, get two letters of reference from prior employers.

White-collar employees—Clerical, and so forth—same as blue-collar procedures except references always are checked out.

Managerial employees—Multiple interviews, intelligence test, personality tests, and references.

I've also been making a list of what's happened in selection in the last six months since I've been in this job.

1. Our best managerial candidate was lost because she refused to take the personali-

ty test we use, The Minnesota Multiphasic Personality Inventory. She said it was an invasion of her privacy.
2. For employees who handle expensive supplies, we use a polygraph test, too. We've had a few refuse to take it. Our thefts are high. We wonder if it's any good! My boss feels the polygraph is essential.
3. One man we hired is doing a good job. We accidentally found out he has a prison record. His supervisor wants to know how we missed that and wants to let him go. We have no policy on this, but I feel he's proved himself in three months on the job.
4. We're having a lot of trouble on the reference letters. When we ask people to rate the applicants on the basis of all factors, including references, we find the supervisors read different things into these letters.
5. Our turnover has been high. My boss thinks it's because we aren't matching the best people to the right jobs. I need your help.

Requirement: You are Boyce Piersol. Make a list of additional information necessary to help Gigantic. How would you go about acquiring the information? Based on what you know now, what are the biggest problems and what would you do about them?

*FROM: W. F. Glueck, *Cases and Exercises in Personnel.* Dallas, Texas: Business Publications Inc., 1974. Used by permission.

CASE 2   HOVEY AND BEARD COMPANY*

PART 1

The Hovey and Beard Company manufactured wooden toys of various kinds: wooden animals, pull toys, and the like. One part of the manufacturing process involved spraying paint on the partially assembled toys.

The toys were cut, sanded, and partially assembled in the wood room. Then they were dipped into shellac, following which they were painted. The toys were predominantly two-colored; a few were made in more than two colors. Each color required an additional trip through the paint room.

For a number of years, production of these toys had been entirely handwork. However, to meet tremendously increased demand, the painting operation had recently been re-engineered so that the eight workers who did the painting sat in a line by an endless chain of hooks. These hooks were in continuous motion, past the line of workers and into a long horizontal oven. Each worker sat at a separate painting booth so designed as to carry away fumes and to backstop excess paint. Workers would take a toy from the tray beside them, position it in a jig inside the painting cubicle, spray on the color according to a pattern, then release the toy and hang it on the hook passing by. The rate at which the hooks moved had been calculated by the engineers so that each worker, when fully trained, would be able to hang a painted toy on each hook before it passed beyond her reach. (All of the workers were women.)

The employees working in the paint room were on a group bonus plan.

*FROM: W. F. Whyte, *Money and Motivation.* New York: Harper & Row, 1955, pp. 90–94. Used by permission.

Since the operation was new to them, they were receiving a learning bonus which decreased by regular amounts each month. The learning bonus was scheduled to vanish in six months, by which time it was expected that they would be on their own—that is, able to meet the standard and to earn a group bonus when they exceeded it.

PART 2

By the second month of the training period trouble had developed. The employees learned more slowly than had been anticipated, and it began to look as though their production would stabilize far below what was planned for. Many of the hooks were going by empty. The workers complained that they were going by too fast, and that the time study man had set the rates wrong. A few people quit and had to be replaced with new workers, which further aggravated the learning problem. The team spirit that the management had expected to develop automatically through the group bonus was not in evidence except as an expression of what the engineers called "resistance." One worker whom the group regarded as its leader (and the management regarded as the ringleader) was outspoken in making the various complaints of the group to the supervisor: the job was a messy one, the hooks moved too fast, the incentive pay was not being correctly calculated, and it was too hot working so close to the drying oven.

PART 3

A consultant who was brought into this picture worked entirely with and through the supervisor. After many conversations with the consultant, the supervisor felt that the first step should be to get the workers together for a general discussion of the working conditions. He took this step with some hesitation, but he took it on his own volition.

The first meeting, held immediately after the shift was over at four o'clock in the afternoon, was attended by all eight workers. They voiced the same complaints again: the hooks went by too fast, the job was too dirty, the room was hot and poorly ventilated. For some reason, it was this last item that they complained of most. The supervisor promised to discuss the problem of ventilation and temperature with the engineers, and he scheduled a second meeting to report back to the employees. In the next few days the supervisor had several talks with the engineers. They and the superintendent felt that this was really a trumped-up complaint, and that the expense of any effective corrective measure would be prohibitively high.

The supervisor came to the second meeting with some apprehensions. The workers, however, did not seem to be much put out, perhaps because they had a proposal of their own to make. They felt that if several large fans were set up so as to circulate the air around their feet, they would be much more comfortable. After some discussion, the supervisor agreed that the idea might be tried out. The supervisor and the consultant discussed the question of the fans with the superintendent, and three large propeller-type fans were purchased.

PART 4

The fans were brought in. The workers were jubilant. For several days the fans were moved about in various positions until they were placed to the satisfaction of the group. The employees

seemed completely satisfied with the results, and relations between them and the supervisor improved visibly.

The supervisor, after this encouraging episode, decided that further meetings might also be profitable. He asked the workers if they would like to meet and discuss other aspects of the work situation. They were eager to do this. The meeting was held, and the discussion quickly centered on the speed of the hooks. The employees maintained that the time study man had set them at an unreasonably fast speed and that they would never be able to reach the goal of filling enough of them to make a bonus.

The turning point of the discussion came when the group's leader frankly explained that the point wasn't that they couldn't work fast enough to keep up with the hooks, but they couldn't work at that pace all day long. The supervisor explored the point. The workers were unanimous in their opinion that they could keep up with the belt for short periods if they wanted to. But they didn't want to because if they showed they could do this for short periods they would be expected to do it all day long. The meeting ended with an unprecedented request: "Let us adjust the speed of the belt faster or slower depending on how we feel." The supervisor agreed to discuss this with the superintendent and the engineers.

The reaction of the engineers to the suggestion was negative. However, after several meetings it was granted that there was some latitude within which variations in the speed of the hooks would not affect the finished product. After considerable argument with the engineers, it was agreed to try out the workers' ideas.

With misgivings, the supervisor had a control with a dial marked "low, medium, fast" installed at the booth of the group leader; she could now adjust the speed of the belt anywhere between the lower and upper limits that the engineers had set.

PART 5

The workers were delighted, and spent many lunch hours deciding how the speed of the belt should be varied from hour to hour throughout the day. Within a week the pattern had settled down to one in which the first half hour of the shift was run on what the employees called a medium speed (a dial setting slightly above the point marked "medium"). The next two and one-half hours were run at high speed; the half hour before lunch and the half hour after lunch were run at low speed. The rest of the afternoon was run at high speed with the exception of the last forty-five minutes of the shift, which was run at medium.

In view of the workers' reports of satisfaction and ease in their work, it is interesting to note that the constant speed at which the engineers had originally set the belt was slightly below medium on the dial of the control that had been given the employees. The average speed at which they were running the belt was on the high side of the dial. Few, if any, empty hooks entered the oven, and inspection showed no increase of rejects from the paint room.

Production increased, and within three weeks (some two months before the scheduled ending of the learning bonus) the workers were operating at 30 to 50 percent above the level that had been expected under the original arrangement. Naturally their earnings were correspondingly higher than anticipated. They were collecting their base pay, a considerable piece rate bonus, and the learning bonus which, it will be remembered, had been set to decrease with time and not as a function of current productivity. They were earning more now than many skilled workers in other parts of the plant.

PART 6

Management was besieged by demands that this inequity be taken care of. With growing irritation between superintendent and supervisor, engineers and supervisor, superintendent and engineers, the situation came to a head when the superintendent revoked the learning bonus and returned the painting operation to its original status: the hooks moved again at their constant, time-studied designated speed, production dropped again, and within a month all but two of the eight original workers had quit. The supervisor himself stayed on for several months, but, feeling aggrieved, then left for another job.

CASE 3   PROBLEMS IN PERFORMANCE EVALUATION*

In a large electric power plant in Saskatoon, Saskatchewan, Canada, they have been having difficulty with their performance evaluation program. The organization has an evaluation program by which all operating employees and clerical employees are evaluated semiannually by their supervisors. The form which they have been using appears below. It has been in use for ten years. The form is scored as follows:

FROM: W. F. Glueck, *Cases and Exercises in Personnel* (Revised edition). Dallas: BPI, 1978, pp. 56–57. Used by permission.

Excellent = 5, above average = 4, average = 3, below average = 2, and poor = 1. The scores for each question are centered in the right-hand column and are totaled for an overall evaluation score.

The procedure used has been as follows: Each supervisor rates each employee on July 30 and January 30. The supervisor discusses the rating with the employee. The supervisor sends the rating to the personnel department. Each rating is placed in the employee's personnel file. If promotions come up, the cumulative ratings are considered at

Performance evaluation form of electric power plant

PERFORMANCE EVALUATION

Supervisors: When you are asked to do so by the personnel department, please complete this form on each of your employees. The supervisor who is responsible for 75 percent or more of an employee's work should complete this form on him or her. Please evaluate each facet of the employee separately.

Quantity of work	Excellent	Above average	Average	Below average	Poor	Score
Quality of work	Poor	Below average	Average	Above average	Excellent	
Dependability at work	Excellent	Above average	Average	Below average	Poor	
Initiative at work	Poor	Below average	Average	Above average	Excellent	
Cooperativeness	Excellent	Above average	Average	Below average	Poor	
Getting along with coworkers	Poor	Below average	Average	Above average	Excellent	

Total _____

Supervisor's signature _____

Employee name _____

Employee number _____

that time. The ratings are also supposed to be used as a check when raises are given.

The system was designed by the personnel manager who retired two years ago, Joanna Kyle. Her replacement was Eugene Meyer. Meyer is a graduate in commerce from the University of Alberta at Edmonton. He graduated 15 years ago. Since then, he's had a variety of experiences, mostly in utilities like the power company. About five of these years he did personnel work.

Meyer has been reviewing the evaluation system. Employees have a mixture of indifferent and negative feelings about it. An informal survey has shown that about 60 percent of the supervisors fill the forms out, give about three minutes to each form, and send them to personnel without discussing them with the employees. Another 30 percent do a little better. They spend more time completing the forms but communicate about them only briefly and superficially with their employees. Only about 10 percent of the supervisors seriously try to do what was intended.

Meyer found out that the forms were rarely retrieved for promotion or pay-raise analyses. Because of this, most supervisors may have felt the evaluation program was a useless ritual.

Where he had been previously employed, Meyer had seen performance evaluation as a much more useful experience, which included giving positive feedback to employees, improving future employee performance, developing employee capabilities, and providing data for promotion and compensation.

Meyer has not had much experience with design of performance evaluation systems. He feels he should seek advice on the topic.

Requirement. Write a report summarizing your evaluation of the strengths and weaknesses of the present evaluation system. Recommend some specific improvements or data-gathering exercises to develop a better system for Meyer.

CASE 4 THE CASE OF THE PLATEAUED PERFORMER*

E. Kirby Warren, Thomas P. Ference, and James A. F. Stoner

- What is a "plateaued performer"?
- Can George Briggs be managed?
- Will the company have to lose one of two valued employees?
- What does the company owe Briggs?

"Grow old along with me, the best is yet to be." When Robert Browning expressed this sentiment, he was not writing as a spokesman for business to promising young executives. Yet in the nineteenth century, while such poetry may have been out of place in business, the thought was very fitting.

In fact, until quite recently corporations have been able to reward capable employees with increased responsibilities and opportunities. Based on our recently completed research into nine companies, however, the more prevalent corporate sentiment might be, "Stay young along with me, or gone you well may be."

We found a large number of managers who, in the judgment of their organization, have "plateaued." That is, there is little or no likelihood that they will be promoted or receive substantial increases in duties and responsibilities. These long-service employees are being regarded with growing concern because plateauing is taking place more markedly, and frequently earlier, than in years past. Further, executives feel that plateauing is frequently accompanied by noticeable declines in both motivation and quality of performance.

While plateauing, like aging, is in-

evitable, in years past it was a more gradual process. For the most part, those who sought advancement in their managerial careers had ample opportunity to get it, within broad limits of ability, while those who did not desire advancement (including competent individuals content with more modest levels of achievement and success) could be bypassed by colleagues still on the way up.

Today the situation has changed. Declining rates of corporate growth and an ever-increasing number of candidates have heightened the competition for managerial positions. The top of the pyramid is expanding much more slowly than the middle, and the managers who advanced rapidly during the growth boom of the 1960s are now at or just below the top. Their rate of career progress has necessarily slowed, and yet they are still many years from normal retirement and with many productive years to go. As these managers continue in their positions, the queue of younger, aggressive aspirants just below them is likely to grow longer, with spillover effects on opportunities and mobility rates throughout the organization.

This is precisely the dilemma confronting Benjamin Petersen, president and chairman of the board of Petersen Electronics.

Petersen founded the company in 1944, and it grew rapidly during the 1950s and 1960s, reaching sales of $200 million in 1968. Growth since then, though, has been uneven and at an average of less than 5% per year. However, 1974 was a good year, with sales and profits showing leaps of 12% and 18%, respectively.

Despite the good year, Benjamin Petersen, now 61 years old, is concerned about the company as he nears retirement. His major problem involves George Briggs, 53, vice president of marketing, and Thomas Evans, national sales manager, who is 34 years old and one of Briggs's four subordinates. Nor have the implications of the situation between Briggs and Evans been lost on Victor Perkins, 39, vice president of personnel.

PETERSEN'S VIEW OF THE PREDICAMENT

"When we started, a handful of people worked very hard and very closely to build something bigger than any of us. One of these people was George Briggs. George has been with me from the start, as have almost all of my vice presidents and many of my key department heads.

"For the first five years, I did almost all the inventing and engineering work. Tom Carroll ran the plant and George Briggs knocked on doors and sold dreams as well as products for the company.

"As the company grew, we added people, and Briggs slowly worked his way up the sales organization. Eight years ago, when our vice president of marketing retired, I put George in the job. He has market research, product management, sales service, and the field sales force (reporting through a national sales manager) under him, and he has really done a first-rate job all around.

"About ten years ago we began bringing in more bright young engineers and MBAs and moved them along as fast as we could. Turnover has been high and we have had some friction between our young Turks and the old guard.

"When business slowed in the early seventies, we also had a lot of competition among our newcomers. Those who stayed have continued to move up, and a few are now in or ready for top jobs. One of the best of this group is Tom Evans. He started with us nine years ago in the sales service area. Later, he spent three years in product management.

"George Briggs got him to move from head of the sales service department to assistant product manager. After one year, George Briggs named him manager of the product management group, and two years later, when the national sales manager retired, George named Evans to this post.

"That move both surprised and pleased me. I felt that Evans would make a good sales manager despite the fact that he had had little direct sales experience. I was afraid, however, that George would not want someone in that job who hadn't had years of field experience.

"I was even more surprised, though, when six months later (a month ago) George told me he was afraid Evans wasn't working out, and asked if I might be able to find a spot for him in the corporate personnel department. While I'm sure our recent upturn in sales is not solely Evans's doing, he certainly seems to be one of the keys. Despite his inexperience, he seems to have the field sales organization behind him. He spends much of his time traveling with them, and from what I hear he has built a great team spirit.

"Despite this, George Briggs claims that he is in over his head and that it is just a matter of time before his inexperience gets him in trouble. I can't understand why George is so adamant. It's clearly not a personality clash, since they have always gotten along well in the past. In many ways, Briggs has been Evans's greatest booster until recently.

"Since George is going to need a

replacement someday, I was hoping it would be Evans. If George doesn't retire before we have to move Evans again or lose him, I'd consider moving Evans to another area.

"When we were growing faster, I didn't worry about a new challenge opening up for our aggressive young managers—there were always new divisions, new lines—something to keep them stimulated and satisfied with their progress. Now I have less flexibility—my top people are several years from retirement. And yet I have some younger ones—like Evans, whom I would hate to lose—always pushing and expecting promotion.

"Evans is a good example of this; I could move him, but there are not that many *real* opportunities. He could go to personnel or engineering or even finance. Evans has the makings of a really fine general manager. But I'd hate to move him now. He really isn't ready for another shift—although he will be in a few years—and despite what George claims, I think he is stimulating team work and commitment in the sales organization as a result of his style.

"Finally, while I don't want to appear unduly critical of Briggs, I'm not sure he could get the job done in these competitive times without a bright young person like Evans to help him."

BRIGGS'S ACCOUNT OF THE SITUATION

"Before I say anything else, let me assure you there is nothing personal in my criticism of Evans.

"I like him. I have always liked him. I've done more for him than anyone else in the company. I've tried to coach him and bring him along just like a son.

"But the simple truth is that he's in way over his head and showing a side of his personality I've never seen before. I brought him along through sales service and product management and he was always eager to learn. While I couldn't give him a lot of help in those areas (frankly, there are aspects of them I don't yet fully understand), I still tried, and he paid attention and learned from others as well.

"The job of national sales manager, however, is a different story. In the other jobs Evans had—staff jobs—there was always time to consult, to consider, to get more data. In sales, however, all this participative stuff he uses takes too long. The national sales manager has to be able to make quick, intuitive decisions. What's more, like the captain of a ship, he has to inspire confidence in those below him. If the going gets rough, the only thing that keeps the sailors and junior officers from panicking is confidence in the skipper. I've been there and I know.

"Right now, with orders coming in strong, he can get away with all of his meetings and indecisiveness. The people in the field really like him and are trying to keep him out of trouble. In addition, I have been putting in 60 to 70 hours a week trying to do my job and also make sure he doesn't make any serious mistakes.

"I know he is feeling the pressure, too. Despite the fact that he has been his usual cheery self with others, when I call him in to question a decision he has made or is about to make, he gets very defensive. He was never that way with me before.

"I may have lost a little feel for what's going on in the field over the years, but I suspect I still know more about the customers and our sales people than Tom Evans will ever know. I've tried for the past seven months to get him to relax and let the old man help him, but it's no use. I'm convinced he's just not cut out for the job, and before we ruin him I want to transfer him somewhere else. He would probably make a fine personnel director someday. He's a very popular guy who seems genuinely interested in people and in helping them.

"I have talked with Ben Petersen about the move, and he has been stalling me. I understand his position. We have a lot of young comers like Evans in the company, and Ben has to worry about all of them. He told me that if anyone can bring Evans along I can, and he asked me to give it another try. I have, and things are getting worse.

"I hate to admit I made a mistake with Evans, but I plan on seeing Ben about this again tomorrow. We just can't keep putting it off. I'm sure he'll see it my way, and as soon as he approves the transfer, I'll have a heart-to-heart talk with Tom."

EVANS'S SIDE OF THE STORY

"This has been a very hectic but rewarding period for me. I've never worked as hard in my life as I have during the last six months, but it's paying off. I'm learning more about sales each day, and more important, I'm building a first-rate sales team. My people are really enjoying the chance to share ideas and support each other.

"At first, particularly with our markets improving, it was hard to convince them to take time to meet with me and their subordinates. Gradually they have come to accept these sessions as an investment in team building. According to them, we've come up with more good ideas and ways to help each other than ever before.

"Fortunately, I also have experience in product management and sales service. Someday I hope to bring representatives from this department and

market research into the meetings with regional and branch people, but that will take time. This kind of direct coordination and interaction doesn't fit with the thinking of some of the old-timers. I ran into objections when I tried this while I was working in the other departments.

"But I'm certain that in a year or so I'll be able to show, by results, that we should have more direct contact across department levels.

"My boss, George Briggs, will be one of the ones I will have to convince. He comes from the old school and is slow to give up what he knows used to work well.

"George likes me, though, and has given me a tremendous amount of help in the past. I was amazed when he told me he was giving me this job. Frankly, I didn't think I was ready yet, but he assured me I could handle it. I've gotten a big promotion every few years and I really like that—being challenged to learn new skills and getting more responsibility. I guess I have a real future here, although George won't be retiring for some years and I've gone as high as I can go until then.

"George is a very demanding person, but extremely fair, and he is always trying to help. I only hope I can justify the confidence he has shown in me. He stuck his neck out by giving me this chance, and I'm going to do all I can to succeed.

"Recently we have had a few run-ins. George Briggs works harder than anyone else around here, and perhaps the pressure of the last few years is getting to him. I wish he'd take a vacation this year and get away for a month or more and just relax. He hasn't taken more than a week off in the nine years I've been here, and for the last two years he hasn't taken any vacation.

"I can see the strain is taking its

toll. Recently he has been on my back for all kinds of little things. He always was a worrier, but lately he has been testing me on numerous small issues. He keeps throwing out suggestions or second-guessing me on things that I've spent weeks working on with the field people.

"I try to assure him I'll be all right, and to please help me where I need it with the finance and production people who've had a tough time keeping up with our sales organization. It has been rough lately, but I'm sure it will work out. Sooner or later George will accept the fact that while I will never be able to run things the way he did, I can still get the job done for him.

PERKINS'S OPINIONS

"I feel that George Briggs is threatened by Evans's seeming success with the field sales people. I don't think he realizes it, but he is probably jealous of the speed with which Tom has taken charge. In all likelihood, he didn't expect Tom to be able to handle the field people as well as he has, as fast as he has.

"When George put Tom in the job, I have a feeling that he was looking forward to having him need much more help and advice from the old skipper. Tom does need help and advice, but he is getting most of what George would offer from his own subordinates and his peers. As a result, he has created a real team spirit below and around him, but he has upset George in the process.

"George not only has trouble seeing Tom depend so much on his subordinates but I feel that he resents Tom's unwillingness to let him show him how he used to run the sales force.

"I may be wrong about this, of course. I am sure that George honestly believes that Tom's style will get him in trouble sooner or later. George is no doddering old fool who has to relive his past success in lower-level jobs. In the past, I'm told, he has shown real insight and interest in the big-picture aspects of the company.

"The trouble is he knows he was an outstanding sales manager, but I am not sure he has the same confidence in his ability as vice president. I have seen this time and again, particularly in recent years. When a person begins to doubt his future, he sometimes drops back and begins to protect his past. With more competition from younger subordinates and the new methods that they often bring in, many of our experienced people find that doing their job the way they used to just isn't good enough anymore.

"Some reach out and seek new responsibilities to prove their worth. Others, however, return to the things they used to excel in and try to show that theirs is still the best way to do things. They don't even seem to realize that this puts them in direct competition with their subordinates.

"What do we do about this? I wish I knew! At lower levels, where you have more room to shift people around, you have more options. When the company is growing rapidly, the problem often takes care of itself.

"In this case, I am not sure what I will recommend if Ben Petersen asks my advice. Moving Tom to personnel at this time not only won't help me (I really don't have a spot for him), but it won't help Briggs or Evans either. Moving Evans now would be wasteful of the time and effort we've invested in his development. It may also reverse some important trends Tom has begun in team building within the sales force.

"If Briggs were seven or eight years older, we could wait it out. If the company were growing faster, we might be able to shift people. As things stand, however, I see only one approach as a possibility. And I'm not entirely sure it will work.

"I would recommend that we get busy refocusing Briggs's attention on the vice president's job and get him to see that there is where he has to put his time and efforts. Perhaps the best thing would be to send him to one of the longer programs for senior executives. Don't forget he is a very bright and experienced person who still has a great deal to offer the company if we can figure out how to help him."

WHAT WOULD YOU SUGGEST?

Petersen has agreed to talk with Briggs about Evans tomorrow afternoon. As he thinks about the situation, he wonders what he can do that would be best for the company and everyone concerned. Should he go along with Briggs's recommendation that Evans be transferred to personnel? Or would it be preferable to do as Perkins has suggested and send Briggs to an executive program? As you consider the various perspectives, why do you think the impasse came to be and what do you think could be done to resolve it?

CASE 5 UNIVERSAL INSURANCE COMPANY*

At the Universal Insurance Company, in November, 1970, managers in the field agency department (with 90 to 100 employees) decided to create the position of coordinator (job grade 6) in the field agency department. The coordinator's function would be to ensure that the work load among secretaries was more evenly divided than it had been. Up to that time, some secretaries had been consistently overworked while others frequently had much less work than they could do.

Obviously the qualifications for such a position would include intelligence, reliability, knowledge of the work, and insight into motivational and personality differences among agency personnel, as well as ability to establish and maintain good working relationships with secretaries and supervisors. Promotion from within was company policy and job posting was a regular procedure.

To understand the importance of effective coordination among secretaries, and the difficulties to be expected in achieving it, the reader needs a minimum of information about functions of the field agency department as well as responsibilities of agency supervisors and their secretaries.

The overall function of the field agency department (in the home office) was to provide continuous contact with district managers in the field. Each of the 10 to 12 agency supervisors served a marketing group in a specific geographical area. Major objectives of all agency supervisors were to help district managers increase the number of policyholders and to prevent policy lapses. For

*FROM: Adapted from *Personnel Administration: A Point of View and a Method, 7th Edition,* by P. Pigors and C. A. Myers. Copyright © 1973 by McGraw-Hill. Used with the permission of McGraw-Hill Book Company.

both purposes it was necessary to keep company representatives in the field fully informed as to all current developments in the insurance business and any changes in home office procedures.

Meeting these liaison responsibilities required prompt and reliable response to all correspondence and telephone inquiries. To help supervisors in this part of their job, each was assigned a personal secretary. However, the amount of activity, and therefore of correspondence, differed considerably among the various geographical areas covered by the agency supervisors. And this fact accounted for the unequal work load that had to be carried by the personal secretaries.

These secretaries had no understudies (though their work was supplemented by clerical employees in information and service centers who, supervised by unit heads, could be drawn upon as needed). As is customary, the personal secretaries enjoyed a special status. In this division, the vacation of each was timed to coincide with that of her boss (though normally the secretary's vacation was shorter). And she left for lunch at the same time as he did. (During her absence from the office, telephone calls were answered by any qualified clerical employee who happened to be in the office at the time.)

In 1971, two secretaries in the division were outstanding: Marilyn Wiener and Hope Tetzeli.

Marilyn started working for Universal in 1967, as a part-time clerk, during her last 2 years in high school. Immediately after her graduation (at eighteen, in June, 1969), she began full-time employment as a secretary (job grade 4) in Agency C of the field agency division. Her work was consistently outstanding, and she had received both of the annual merit increases that were open to employees at her level. In addition to her technical proficiency and reliability (she had never been tardy and rarely absent) she was well liked because of her pleasant way with people. And, despite her quiet manner, her supervisor and associates were aware that she was ambitious. Some of her friends, but not her supervisor, also knew that by June, 1971, Marilyn had reached the conclusion that secretaries in the field agency department had little chance for promotion.[1] She was, therefore, tentatively planning to leave Universal during the next few months and to continue her education. In this way she hoped to qualify herself for a better position, if not at Universal, then in some other company.

Hope Tetzeli was another outstanding secretary in the field agency division at that time. She was secretary to Phil James (supervisor of Agency D). She first came to Universal in June, 1970, immediately after graduating from high school (at eighteen years of age). She prided herself on having been an honor student throughout her high school career, having graduated in the top 10 percent in her class of 550 students.

Her employement interviewer described her as "neat and well dressed, petite, vivacious, deeply committed to equal rights for women, and with a keen sense of social justice." In her first performance appraisal, her supervisor (Phil James) rated the quality and quantity of her work as outstanding and commended her willingness to assume extra responsibilities when necessary. Like Marilyn, Hope had never been tardy and very rarely absent.

However, Hope's office conduct had occasionally been such as to elicit from John Lord (division manager) the comment "Hope is a self-elected moralist. She has an opinion on everything that happens, inside the department and

out, and no hesitation about expressing her opinion however unfavorable it may be." In fact, Mr. Lord had gradually become convinced that Hope's outspokenness tended to create unrest in the office. That opinion had been formed on the basis of Hope's behavior in the following incidents.

Hope's "keen sense of social justice," as well as her outspokenness, first came to John Lord's attention in January, 1971, as a result of a misunderstanding that had occurred 6 months earlier. In July, 1970, Lord was orienting a group of relatively new women—including Hope. He told them that after 6 months they would receive an automatic salary increase. However, at the end of the 6 months several of the women, including Hope, did not receive the increase. Thereupon, Hope appeared in John Lord's office (with three other women whom she had apparently egged on to join her in making a protest). Serving as spokeswoman for the group, she demanded to know why they had not been given the promised increase. The division manager expressed regret for the misunderstanding, explaining that he must have forgotten to mention that the automatic increase applied only to low-level entry jobs (grades 1 through 3). He added that after this first automatic increase, pay raises were considered annually for all employees. The other women appeared to be satisfied with this explanation. But not long afterwards news reached Mr. Lord (through the grapevine) that Hope was harping on the "unjust treatment" that some of them had received in regard to the promised salary increase. When developing this theme in conversation with her friends, she reportedly cited the incident as proof that Mr. Lord "doesn't know what he's talking about when it comes to company policies."

When John Lord heard about these

comments from Hope, he requested Phil James (her supervisor) to counsel her, explaining that her remarks were inappropriate in view of his apology and explanation—which should have ended the matter. James was reluctant to criticize the office conduct of an upstanding woman with whose technical performance he was more than satisfied. It seemed to him that her social shortcomings had nothing to do with her job performance. Therefore, his "counseling" of Hope consisted merely in saying: "You can't be a spokeswoman for all the women. Just keep on doing the excellent job you have been doing, and you're sure to get ahead."

A week later, another incident occurred which was reported differently by Hope and the other woman immediately involved. After an encounter in the ladies room, one of the women returned to the office in tears, complaining that Hope had humiliated her by talking in public about a "very personal matter." When asked about this incident, Hope replied that she had merely tried to console the woman (who was pregnant though unmarried), "and other women gathered around while I was talking."

When Mr. Lord heard about this encounter he sent for Hope and reproved her for "disturbing other employees and creating unrest in the office." According to Hope, he told her that in the future she should mind her own business and ended by saying, "If you keep on like this, I shan't be able to recommend you for promotion."

Shortly after this reprimand, Hope had her first progress review with the field agency department personnel assistant, Miss Page.[2] During this interview, Hope was full of complaints—ranging from the caliber of the company's medical clinic to the "injustice" she had suffered with regard to the "promised" salary increase. Miss Page

suggested that Hope discuss her dissatisfactions with the division manager. But Hope refused. She said there would be no point in doing so because Mr. Lord was obviously prejudiced against her. To substantiate this statement, Hope asserted that ever since the difficulty about the pay raise, Mr. Lord had "consistently picked on" her. She went on to say that Mr. Lord's prejudice extended to some of the other women also; that he had a few favorites; and that, owing to his "ignorance of company policy, he was a very ineffective manager." Miss Page then suggested that Hope should speak with the department manager, Mr. O'Hara. Hope dismissed that suggestion also, saying that "everyone" knew Mr. O'Hara took no interest in personnel matters.[3] She insisted instead on having a confidential interview with Mr. Ryan (department director). Miss Page, knowing that Mr. Ryan was a firm believer in the "open-door policy," acceded to Hope's request. The interview took place shortly thereafter.

During Hope's talk with the director, she apparently expressed the same critical views and strongly negative opinions about Mr. Lord as in the interview with Miss Page, though she stated that the supervisors were "fine."

Shortly after this interview, Mr. Lord's record as a manager was discreetly investigated. The results completely exonerated him (including charges of favoritism and inadequate information as to company policies).

During the early spring of 1971, Hope became convinced that she would never get ahead in the field agency department. She therefore kept track of posted job opportunities in other departments. In May she found one that appealed to her because it would entail a promotion. She therefore told Mr. James that she would like to apply for it. James, extremely anxious to keep his competent secretary, tried to dissuade her. Hope then went to Mr. Lord, who acceded to her request. [Such a request and permission were standard operating procedure (S.O.P.) at Universal, a prepared form being signed by the management representative receiving the request.]

During the interview in the other department, Hope was told (according to her own later statement): "Don't get your hopes up, because this job requires a mature person." When the transfer failed to materialize, Hope jumped to the conclusion that Mr. Lord had stood in her way, because of his prejudice against her. Moreover, she was deeply offended by the implication that she was regarded as an immature person. On several later occasions, when criticizing behavior by other employees, she ended in a dramatic tone, "do you call *that* mature?" To cite one example: She told her friends that in the elevator one day she overheard an elderly man say to an associate: "There sure are lots of good-looking broads in this company." She added that although she regarded such a remark as evidence of extreme immaturity, she had made no official complaint because the man had a large family and could ill afford to lose his job.

On June 16, Hope had an encounter with Marilyn which brought about immediate and serious consequences. That afternoon (a Thursday), just before the end of the working day, Marilyn had been told that she was to be promoted to the position of coordinator as of the following Monday. She expressed delight at the prospect. The word spread like wildfire. Immediately after work, Hope waylaid Marilyn in the hallway. According to another woman who witnessed the encounter, Hope accused Marilyn of being unscrupulous in accepting the promotion since, by her

own admission, she intended to leave Universal and "go back to school." Hope added that such behavior on Marilyn's part was not only exceedingly immature, under the circumstances, but also selfish, and "unfair to us three women who want to make a career at Universal." According to another report that reached Miss Page, Hope's remarks were even more bitter. "She accused Marilyn of taking the bread out of other people's mouths, told her she was greedy and ruthless and also that it is typical of you to think only of yourself."

After being the victim of this tirade, Marilyn burst into tears and rushed home.

News of the incident reached Mr. Lord the next morning, by telephone. Marilyn's mother called him to say that Marilyn would not be returning to Universal. She blamed Hope for this development. Mrs. Wiener was so angry that she almost hung up at this point. But when Mr. Lord urged her to tell him what had happened, she said that Hope had done "a complete job of character assassination" on Marilyn who was "emotionally destroyed" and might require medical attention. She ended by saying that if this proved to be necessary, she would "hold the company morally and financially responsible."

NOTES

1. Usually the only way a secretary got ahead—except by a promotional transfer—was when her immediate supervisor was promoted. However, in the field agency department, even the director was only in his early forties.
2. At Universal, a departmental personnel assistant was responsible for scheduling and conducting progress reviews and for reporting her

findings to the manager. But she was not expected to initiate any other action with personnel or to make suggestions to representatives of line management.

3. This opinion of Hope's was probably based on the fact that the department manager's responsibilities related entirely to the company representatives in the field, though this information had never been relayed to nonsupervisory employees.

CASE 6   THE EXCELLENT WORKER*

James R. Bradshaw

Marie had returned to work after approximately 15 years of staying at home raising her four children to school age. She was very excited about doing a good job and believed she would enjoy the opportunity of working a few hours each day while the children were at school. She was known as very outgoing and very capable, and was well-liked and attractive. She is Oriental; and although English is Marie's second language, she speaks and understands it very well.

Helen had been working for another company and started working here shortly after Marie. She was approximately the same age as Marie. They had known each other casually the past several years and got along well whenever they met. Helen had indicated that she needed this job very much so that she and her husband could qualify for a home loan. Helen is quiet and reserved. Helen is Polynesian, but also speaks English as her second language. She preferred to let Marie do the talking whenever the need arose for information at work.

Mr. Williams was close to retirement. The impression most people have of him is that he is very good to work for. He was born and raised in the local area. One of his responsibilities is to oversee the company lunchroom where Marie and Helen were working. They were the only workers in the lunchroom, which feeds approximately 50 to 60 people each meal. The food is pre-

pared elsewhere and brought directly to the lunchroom for heating and serving.

Mr. Phillips was in his late 50s or early 60s. He formerly worked as a construction foreman/supervisor. He is the vice president in his present company, a service organization. The president is a long-time close friend of Phillips, who had spent several years in the South Pacific area in construction work.

Marie had been asked to work for a couple of weeks as a temporary employee while one of the regular lunchroom workers was on sick leave. She found the work very interesting because of the people she saw each day—and they responded by saying that she brought a "ray of light" and enjoyment to the lunchroom. Comments came directly and indirectly to Marie about how the food seemed to taste better and how much more enjoyable it was to eat in the lunchroom when she was there.

Marie worked out a number of ways in which the lunchroom service and the food could be improved while reducing the total cost. Her suggestions were accepted and some were put into effect immediately. Her two weeks of substituting were very interesting for her. She showed great concern for her job by staying overtime nearly every day to put the area in shape by cleaning, debugging, and improving the general facilities. She brought vases of fresh flowers each day, and some of her own utensils from home to help improve the service. When her two weeks were up, the majority of the regular workers made it a point to express disappointment that she would not be working regularly.

After about one week away from

*FROM: J. E. Dittrich and R. A. Zawacki, *People and Organizations*. Plano, Texas: Business Publications, 1981, pp. 121–123. Used by permission of James R. Bradshaw (author) and BPI (publisher).

her job, Phillips called Marie to see if she would work full time or at least part time on a permanent basis. She accepted the permanent part-time position eagerly. When Marie returned to work, she found that Helen had started a few days earlier, replacing one of the full-time workers who had quit. Marie began working, this time without formal orientation but merely with the comment, "We will fill you in later about your salary, and so on." She was not concerned because her main interest was working in an enjoyable atmosphere for a few hours every day.

Helen and Marie hit it off very well. Helen encouraged Marie to ask questions of Williams or Phillips whenever necessary, especially if it were to request materials or supplies that were needed. Helen was a good friend of the person she had replaced. She consistently wanted to do things in the same way as before, such as planning the menu, ordering supplies, and so on. Marie occasionally remarked that the former worker was no longer there and that she and Helen would be held responsible for whatever happened from now on. Also, since the comments had been very favorable about the changes Marie had instituted in the food and service, she felt that this was an indication that they should follow the new way of doing things. Helen seemed to agree, but periodically would revert to the old methods when Marie was not in the immediate area or had left for the day.

After about one week, Williams, in a joking sort of way, mentioned that "for the record" someone had to be listed as being in charge to fill out the time sheets, and so on. Helen and Marie looked at each other. Marie suggested that since Helen was full time she should be designated as "in charge." Helen did not object. Williams agreed

by saying, "Okay, Helen is in charge, but Marie is chief cook." They all laughed and no one said any more.

Many times in the past, too much food had been ordered. The leftovers then had to be reheated to be served the next day, or even thrown away. Marie suggested that they work on this problem together, and Helen agreed. After one or two times, however, Helen somehow turned in the menu and the food was ordered before Marie arrived. This again resulted in the old problem of too much food and the serving of old or reheated food. Helen also served the old food first and put each day's fresh food in the refrigerator. Marie thought that she had finally convinced Helen that it didn't make sense to put fresh food in the freezer and serve old food—but Helen responded, "We always did it that way." Marie was concerned. She could sense immediately whether the workers who ate there each day felt the food was good or not. She finally decided to talk with Phillips about the ordering and serving. His initial reaction fit his reputation of being abrupt and somewhat brisk, as he stated, "I have worked for people younger than me and even though I didn't like it I had to do what they said." Marie asked if they weren't supposed to be working together on such things in a place with only two workers. Phillips said that he didn't see any reason why not. He also mentioned that he had heard many favorable comments and that it seemed the atmosphere and food had never been better.

Marie left his office feeling unsure of Phillips's feelings, but she believed that he was pleased with the work and that she and Helen should decide things together. Williams was also very complimentary about the work and the food, and said that Marie had brought a "ray of light" into the place.

Although there were minor differences of opinion, Marie and Helen always seemed to talk their problems through; and they nearly always drove to and from work together.

When Marie and Helen worked on the menu together, less food was ordered, less was wasted or thrown away, there was a greater variety of food, and a very pleasant atmosphere existed in the lunchroom. Marie was feeling more and more comfortable with her situation all the time.

About a week later, Helen once again ordered the food before Marie arrived. As before, this resulted in many leftovers; and there were the usual comments from customers that the food was not as tasty as before. Marie decided to find out from Phillips exactly what the procedure for ordering the food was to be, but found him as brisk and unhelpful as the first time. Marie asked if they were satisfied with her performance. She explained how she liked seeing the people enjoy their lunch. Phillips and Williams both told her that had she wanted to work full time she would have been in full charge. They recognized her as the real organizer in the lunchroom and felt that much of the success experienced was due to her efforts. She was asked for her ideas about several things, including preparing some food items directly in the lunchroom. Marie agreed to prepare some of the items and was told that she had permission to buy and to store immediately in the freezer $200

worth of frozen food. When Marie arrived the next day, she found that Helen had already ordered the food at the request of Phillips. Marie expressed surprise and displeasure. Helen assured her that this order was an exception and that from then on they would always do it together. Marie forgot the incident and the remainder of the day (Friday) went very well.

Saturday, as Marie was leaving, Williams called her to his office. He was visibly shaken. He had great difficulty in telling her that because she had not been able to work harmoniously with Helen, Phillips had said he did not want "that woman" here any more. Williams said that Helen had gone to Phillips's office Friday evening in tears because Marie had been angry with her that morning over the ordering of the food.

Williams said that there was nothing he could do—once Phillips had made his mind up, no one could change it. Marie was shocked; and after thinking about it the rest of the day, went with her husband to Phillips's home. He was as brisk as before, insisting there was nothing more to say since she had been warned and had not changed her behavior in working with Helen. Phillips said that he needed harmony in the lunchroom and since Marie hadn't been willing to work with Helen, that was it.

Marie was completely dumbfounded. She had been told one day that she was an "excellent worker," and then fired the next.

CASE 7   PERFECT PIZZERIA*

Perfect Pizzeria in Southville, in deep southern Illinois, is the second largest franchise of the chain in the United States. The headquarters is located in Phoenix, Arizona. Although the business is prospering, it has employee and managerial problems.

Each operation has one manager, an assistant manager, and from two to five night managers. The managers of each pizzeria work under an area supervisor. There are no systematic criteria for being a manager or becoming a manager trainee. The franchise has no formalized training period for the manager. No college education is required. The managers for whom the case observer worked during a four-year period were relatively young (ages 24 to 27) and only one had completed college. They came from the ranks of night managers or assistant managers, or both. The night managers were chosen for their ability to perform the duties of the regular employees. The assistant managers worked a two-hour shift during the luncheon period five days a week to gain knowledge about bookkeeping and management. Those becoming managers remained at that level unless they expressed interest in investing in the business.

The employees were mostly college students, with a few high school students performing the less challenging

*Adapted from a course assignment prepared by Lee Neely for Professor J. G. Hunt, Southern Illinois University—Carbondale.

FROM: J. E. Dittrich and R. A. Zawacki, *People and Organizations*. Plano, Texas: Business Publications, 1981, pp.126–128. Used by permission of J. G. Hunt (author) and BPI (publisher).

jobs. Since Perfect Pizzeria was located in an area with few job opportunities, it had a relatively easy task of filling its employee quotas. All the employees, with the exception of the manager, were employed part time. Consequently, they worked for less than the minimum wage.

The Perfect Pizzeria system is devised so that food and beverage costs and profits are set up according to a percentage. If the percentage of food unsold or damaged in any way is very low, the manager gets a bonus. If the percentage is high, the manager does not receive a bonus; rather, he or she receives only his or her normal salary.

There are many ways in which the percentage can fluctuate. Since the manager cannot be in the store 24 hours a day, some employees make up for their paychecks by helping themselves to the food. When a friend comes in to order a pizza, extra ingredients are put on the friend's pizza. Occasional nibbles by 18 to 20 employees throughout the day at the meal table also raise the percentage figure. An occasional bucket of sauce may be spilled or a pizza accidentally burned. Sometimes the wrong size of pizza may be made.

In the event of an employee mistake or a burned pizza by the oven man, the expense is supposed to come from the individual. Because of peer pressure, the night manager seldom writes up a bill for the erring employee. Instead, the establishment takes the loss and the error goes unnoticed until the end of the month when the inventory is taken. That's when the manager finds out that the percentage is high and that there will be no bonus.

In the present instance, the manager took retaliatory measures. Previously, each employee was entitled to a free pizza, salad, and all the soft drinks he or she could drink for every 6 hours of work. The manager raised this figure from 6 to 12 hours of work. However, the employees had received these 6-hour benefits for a long time. Therefore, they simply took advantage of the situation whenever the manager or the assistant was not in the building. Though the night manager theoretically had complete control of the operation in the evenings, he did not command the respect that the manager or assistant manager did. That was because he received the same pay as the regular employees; he could not reprimand other employees; and he was basically the same age or sometimes even younger than the other employees.

Thus, apathy grew within the pizzeria. There seemed to be a further separation between the manager and his workers, who started out to be a closely knit group. The manager made no attempt to alleviate the problem, because he felt it would iron itself out. Either the employees that were dissatisfied would quit or they would be content to put up with the new regulations. As it turned out, there was a rash of employee dismissals. The manager had no problem in filling the vacancies with new workers, but the loss of key personnel was costly to the business.

With the large turnover, the manager found he had to spend more time in the building, supervising and sometimes taking the place of inexperienced workers. This was in direct violation of the franchise regulation, which stated that a manager would act as a supervisor and at no time take part in the actual food preparation. Employees were not placed under strict supervision with the manager working alongside them. The operation no longer worked smoothly because of differences between the remaining experienced workers and the manager concerning the way in which a particular function should be performed.

Within a two-month period, the manager was again free to go back to his office and leave his subordinates in charge of the entire operation. During this two-month period, in spite of the differences between experienced workers and the manager, the percentage had returned to the previous low level and the manager received a bonus each month. The manager felt that his problems had been resolved and that conditions would remain the same, since the new personnel had been properly trained.

It didn't take long for the new employees to become influenced by the other employees. Immediately after the manager had returned to his supervisory role, the percentage began to rise. This time the manager took a bolder step. He cut out any benefits that the employees had—no free pizzas, salads, or drinks. With the job market at an even lower ebb than usual, most employees were forced to stay. The appointment of a new area supervisor made it impossible for the manager to "work behind the counter," since the supervisor was centrally located in Southville.

The manager tried still another approach to alleviate the rising percentage problem and maintain his bonus. He placed a notice on the bulletin board, stating that if the percentage remained at a high level, a lie detector test would be given to all employees. All those found guilty of taking or purposefully wasting food or drinks would be immediately terminated. This did not have the desired effect on the employees, because they knew if they were all subjected to the test, all would be found guilty and the manager would have to dismiss all of them. This would leave him in a worse situation than ever.

Even before the following month's percentage was calculated, the manager knew it would be high. He had evidently received information from one of the night managers about the employees' feelings toward the notice. What he did not expect was that the percentage would reach an all-time high. That is the state of affairs at the present time.

CASE 8   THE "NO MARTINI" LUNCH*

Jim Lyons had just completed his second month as manager of an important office of a nationwide sales organization. He believed that he had made the right choice in leaving his old company. This new position offered a great challenge, excellent pay and benefits, and tremendous opportunity for advancement. In addition, his family seemed to be adjusting well to the new community. However, in Jim's mind there was one very serious problem which he believed must be confronted immediately or it could threaten his satisfaction in the long run.

Since taking the job, Jim had found out that the man he replaced had made an institution of the hard-drinking business lunch. He and a group of other key executives had virtually a standing appointment at various local restaurants. Even when clients were not present, they would have several drinks before ordering their lunches. When they returned it was usually well into the afternoon and they were in no condition to make the decisions or take the actions that were often the pretext of the lunch in the first place. This practice had also spread to the subordinates of the various executives and it was not uncommon to see various groups of salespersons doing the same thing a few days each week. Jim decided that he wanted to end the practice, at least for himself and members of his group.

Jim knew this was not going to be an easy problem to solve. The drinking had become institutionalized with a great deal of psychological pressure from a central figure—in this case, the man he replaced. He decided to plan the approach he would take and then discuss the problem and his approach for solving it with his superior, Norm Landy.

The following week Jim made an appointment with Norm to discuss the situation. Norm listened intently as Jim explained the drinking problem but did not show any surprise at learning about it. Jim then explained what he planned to do.

"Norm, I'm making two assumptions on the front end. First, I don't believe it would do any good to state strong new policies about drinking at lunch, or lecturing my people about the evils of the liquid lunch. About all I'd accomplish there would be to raise a lot of latent guilt which would only result in resentment and resistance. Second, I am assuming that the boss is often a role model for his subordinates. Unfortunately, the man I replaced made a practice of the drinking lunch. The subordinates close to him then conform to his drinking habits and exert pressure on other members of the group. Before you know it everyone is a drinking buddy and the practice becomes institutionalized even when one memeber is no longer there.

"Here is what I intend to do about it. First, when I go to lunch with the other managers, I will do no drinking. More importantly, however, for the members of my group I am going to establish a new role model. For example, at least once a week we have a legitimate reason to work through lunch. In the past everyone has gone out anyway. I intend to hold a business lunch and have sandwiches and soft drinks sent in. In addition, I intend to make it a regular practice to take different groups of my people to lunch at a no-alcohol coffee shop.

"My goal, Norm, is simply to let my

*FROM: J. L. Gibson, J. M. Ivancevich, and J. H. Donnelly. *Organizations: Behavior, Structure, Processes* (3rd ed.). Used by permission. © Business Publications Inc., 1979.

subordinates know that alcohol is not a necessary part of the workday, and that drinking will not win my approval. By not drinking with the other managers, I figure that sooner or later they too will get the point. As you can see I intend to get the message across by my behavior. There will be no words of censure. What do you think Norm?"

Norm Landy pushed himself away from his desk and came around and seated himself beside Jim. He then looked at Jim and whispered, "Are you crazy? I guarantee you, Jim, that you are going to accomplish nothing but cause a lot of trouble. Trouble between your group and other groups if you succeed, trouble between you and your group, and trouble between you and the other managers. Believe me, Jim, I see the problem, and I agree with you that it is a problem. But the cure might kill the patient. Will all that conflict and trouble be worth it?"

Jim thought for a moment and said "I think it will be good for the organization in the long run."

QUESTIONS FOR DISCUSSION

1. Do you agree with Norm Landy or Jim Lyons? Why?
2. Do you think anything can be done about this situation? Why? What is your opinion of Jim's plan?
3. What would you do in Jim's situation? Be specific.

584

CASE 9   THE FACULTY DECISION*

Tom Madden slipped into his seat at the meeting of the faculty of the College of Business Administration of Longley University. He was 10 minutes late because he had come completely across campus from another meeting which had lasted 1½ hours. "Boy!" he thought, "if all of these meetings and committee assignments keep up, I won't have time to do anything else."

"The next item of importance," said the Dean, "is consideration of the feasibility report prepared by the Assistant Dean, Dr. Jackson, for the establishment of our Latin American MBA Program."

"What's that?" Tom whispered to his friend Jim Lyon sitting next to him.

"Ah, Professor Madden," winked Lyon, "evidently you've not bothered to read this impressive document," passing Tom the 86-page report, "otherwise you'd know."

"Heck, Jim, I've been out of town for two weeks on a research project and have just come from another meeting."

"Well, Tom," chuckled Jim, "the report was circulated only three days ago to, as the Dean put it, 'insure we have faculty input into where the college is going.' Actually, Tom, I was hoping you'd read it because then you could have told me what was in it."

"Dr. Jackson," said the Dean, "why don't you present a summary of your excellent report on what I believe is an outstanding opportunity for our college, the establishment of an MBA program in Latin America."

"Hey, Jim," said Tom, "they've got to be kidding, we're not doing what we should be doing with the MBA we've got

here on campus. Why on earth are we thinking about doing another one 3,000 miles away?"

Jim shrugged. "Some friend of the Dean's or Jackson's from down there must have asked them, I guess."

While the summary was being given, Tom thumbed through the report. He noted that they were planning to offer the same program they offered in the United States. "Certainly," he thought, "their students' needs are different from ours." He also noted that faculty were going to be sent from the United States on one- to three-year appointments. "You would think that whenever possible they would seek local instructors who were familiar with the needs of local industry," Tom thought. He concluded in his own mind, "Actually, why are we even getting involved in this thing in the first place? We don't have the resources."

When Jackson finished the summary, the Dean asked, "Are there any questions?"

"I wonder how many people have had the time to read this report in three days and think about it," Tom thought to himself.

"Has anybody thought through this entire concept?" Tom spoke up, "I mean. . . ."

"Absolutely, Professor Madden," the Dean answered. "Dr. Jackson and I have spent a great deal of time on this project."

"Well, I was just thinking that. . . ."

"Now, Professor Madden, surely you don't question the efforts of Dr. Jackson and myself. Had you been here when this meeting started, you would know all about our efforts. Besides, it's getting late and we've got another agenda item to consider today, the safety and security of final examinations prior to their being given."

---

*FROM: J. L. Gibson, J. M. Ivancevich, and J. H. Donnelly. *Organizations: Behavior, Structure, Processes* (3rd ed.). Used by permission. © Business Publications Inc., 1979.

"No further questions," Tom said.

"Wonderful," said the Dean. "Then I will report to the President that the faculty of the College of Business Administration unanimously approves the Latin American MBA program. I might add, by the way, the president is extremely pleased with our method of shared decision making. We have made it work in this college while other colleges are having trouble arriving at mutually agreed-upon decisions.

"This is a great day for our college. Today we have become a multinational university. We can all be proud."

After the meeting, as Tom headed for the parking lot, he thought, "What a way to make an important decision. I guess I shouldn't complain though, I didn't even read the report. I'd better check my calendar to see what committee meetings I've got the rest of the week. If I've got any more I'll. . . ."

QUESTIONS FOR CONSIDERATION

1. Analyze this exercise and outline as many factors as possible which influenced the faculty decision in this case—either positively or negatively.
2. Does this exercise indicate that shared decision making cannot be worthwhile and effective? How could it be made more effective in the College of Business Administration?
3. Do you believe decision making of this type may be more worthwhile and effective in some types of organizations than in others? Discuss.

CASE 10   PHANTOMS FILL BOY SCOUT ROLLS*

David Young

The Boy Scouts have been a tradition in America for most of this century. To the public, scouting conjures up images of camping in the woods, hikes, and troop meetings. But there is another side of scouting that is not seen, a Tribune reporter discovered during a four-month investigation. It includes massive cheating on the part of paid professional staff members to make their quotas. This is the first of a two-part report on the problem.

The Boy Scouts of America—that venerable institution devoted to keeping boys physically strong, mentally aware, and morally straight—is in trouble.

A $65 million national campaign to expand scouting by more than 2 million boys in 1976 is nearly two years behind schedule.

And professionals within the Scout organization claim the problem has been aggravated by extensive cheating which has inflated membership figures. Scouting officials claim to have 4.8 million boys enrolled nationwide.

Like most charitable organizations, scouting also has been plagued with the problem of finding enough adult volunteers to run programs and raising enough money to keep up with inflation, Scout officials concede.

Many officials blame scouting's problems on the inability to recruit and keep volunteers, especially in the inner cities.

But the root of the problem is scouting's Boypower 76 program—a national effort to increase the membership rolls to include one-third of all eligible boys in America—an estimated 6 million youngsters.

Dissidents within scouting's 4,600-member professional staff, which raises funds and recruits boys and volunteers, also claim that efforts to streamline the organization and use improved business techniques have encouraged cheating.

What has happened, past and present Scout professionals claim, is that many professionals under pressure continually to make increasing membership quotas have been meeting those quotas with nonexistent boys belonging to nonexistent units. The boys exist only on rosters filed away in Scout offices throughout the country.

Actually, the cheating is confined largely to the professional organization and has had little or no effect on existing Scout programs operated by adult volunteers. Once started, the troops, packs, and posts operate almost independently of the professional organization.

Thus, the 15 Cub Scouts who meet each week in a Detroit ghetto church aren't aware that their unit has 65 members on official Scout reports. And the PTA of a West Side Chicago school is not aware it is sponsoring a nonexistent, 44-member Boy Scout troop.

Scout professionals interviewed during the Tribune's four-month investigation revealed that sometimes they cheat with federal money. The nonexistent boys and units were paid for with poverty funds from Washington.

"This thing is national in scope," claimed one Scout executive from the national organization. He asked that his name be withheld.

"They don't know themselves how many boys they have," he said.

"As far as they are concerned, the

name on a roster is a Scout until some-one proves it different."

An independent report on scout-ing in the New York area in 1971 by the Institute of Public Affairs said that many Scout professionals believe that the pressure to meet membership goals there resulted in a "numbers game and a possible cause of paper troops." The report never was publicly released.

But nowhere is the problem more critical than in Chicago—the place where scouting started in America in 1910 and the city that gave America the Boypower 76 program.

Some Scout professionals here esti-mate that anywhere from 25 to 50 per cent of the 87,000 Cub Scouts, Boy Scouts, and Explorers registered in the Chicago Area Council are inactive or exist only on paper.

A suppressed 1968 audit of Scout operations in Chicago shows that of the council's 2,555 units, 1,694 were sub-standard and 623 were phony. Though Scout officials in Chicago claimed at the time to have 75,000 boys enrolled, the actual number of Scouts was less than 40,000, the audit showed. The Scout official who ordered the audit was qui-etly reassigned elsewhere.

Joseph Klein, the head of scouting in Chicago, claims to have 87,000 members—making Chicago the largest council in the nation.

However, confidential membership reports obtained by The Tribune show that on April 12 the actual membership was about 52,000 boys—nearly 40 per cent less than quoted.

Though cheating also exists in the suburbs, it is worse in the inner city, Scout professionals said. They claim that it is extremely difficult to deter-mine the exact extent of the cheating, but said that Scout districts with wide-ly fluctuating membership totals and few promotions indicate large numbers of phony boys and units. Nonexistent boys can't be promoted.

Though 2,321 Boy Scouts were reg-istered in the Midwest District on the West Side last December, only 117 boys received promotions to the six ranks of scouting. Only 32 boys were promoted to Tenderfoot—an almost automatic jump.

The adjacent Fort Dearborn Dis-trict listed no promotions for its 1,511 Boy Scouts, although the predominant-ly white Timber Trails District on the Southwest Side had 245 promotions for its 850 registered boys for the same period.

Membership in the Midwest Dis-trict has fluctuated, widely since 1966, confidential Scout records show. On De-cember 31, 1972, the district reported having 4,577 Scouts, but 2,797 of them —more than half—had evaporated in just two months. The district claimed to have recruited 3,270 new boys during its membership drive last fall, making it the largest district in the city, with 5,050 boys. But by the beginning of April, 2,981 boys—nearly 60 percent of the district—had somehow disap-peared.

The seven Scout districts on the West Side claim to have recruited 8,630 new Scouts during last fall's member-ship drive, but lost 9,000 in the follow-ing three months. The six South Side districts in the Chicago Council lost more than 8,000 scouts during the same period—nearly half of the total mem-bership.

The worst cheating actually occurs in the federally funded programs ad-ministered through the Chicago Model Cities program, the professionals claim. The programs, collectively known as Project 13, pay the Scout dues and fees for inner city blacks and Latins, many of whom live in housing projects.

The Chicago Council has received $341,000 in federal funds for the program during the last four years, reportedly to provide a Scouting program for more than 40,000 poor youngsters, federal records show.

"It's not hard to paper your project boys," bragged one Scout professional who asked to remain anonymous. "You register all the boys in December. You can put an extra 1,000 boys in a unit because they drop out in two months and there's no record of them," he said.

An official of the Lawndale Urban Progress Center, which sponsors one federally funded program on the West Side, said that not more than 500 of the 2,000 boys on the books are actually Scouts.

Scout professionals, past and present, admitted to a Tribune interviewer that they registered thousands of nonexistent boys to meet their quotas.

One of the most common ploys the professionals claim they used was to reregister units year after year without bothering to check to see whether the units actually exist.

"You simply change a few names so the charter looks different, then reregister it," said one former professional. "Who's going to walk through those housing projects to check you out?"

"We've got to clean the cheating up," he said. "The minute we find it (cheating) we terminate the professional."

Klein said he constantly lectures his staff on maintaining a quality scouting program, "but maybe they're not hearing me."

"I firmly believe there's a hell of a lot more good in this program than there is bad," he said.

II. SCOUTING MOTTO FORGOTTEN IN SIGNUP DRIVE

With great fanfare the Boy Scouts of America announced in 1968 it was beginning a program to make scouting more relevant.

Boypower 76, it was called.

And its goal was to raise $65 million and to bring into scouting one-third (about 6 million) of all eligible boys 8 to 20 years old in the country by 1976.

Scouting wanted the poor black youths from the ghetto, and the Puerto Ricans from Spanish Harlem. It wanted the whites from the suburbs and the sons of steelworkers from Gary.

To make the traditional scouting program more relevant to the recruits, the Boy Scouts revised handbooks to include subjects of interest to urban dwellers, translated manuals into Spanish, and asked for federal funds to pay for programs for the poor.

But somewhere in the more than five years that Boypower 76 has been with us, something went wrong.

Professional Scout staff members have detailed to The Tribune widespread cheating to meet the Boypower quotas imposed on them—including cheating in the federally funded programs.

"This thing is national in scope." claimed one Scout executive assigned to the national organization.

The officials claim they were forced to cheat to make their goals. If they didn't make the goals, they were out. Scout executive, Alden G. Barber, conceded he is aware cheating has occurred.

"Some of our people cheat—quite frankly," Barber said.

He conceded that Boypower 76 is now two years behind schedule. The problem is economic, he said. There just isn't enough money to get the job done.

Though the national organization has raised $33 million and placed nearly 500 additional professionals on local staffs, donors who gave to the national effort apparently cut back on their contributions to local Scout councils. Many local councils were forced to cut back their staffs as a result.

"The actual net gain is close to 80 professionals," Barber said.

In Chicago, the local Scout council was faced with a $340,000 deficit and was forced to chop 10 professionals from its staff although the council was expected to increase its membership from 75,000 to 100,000. The result was cheating.

Past and present Scout professionals in Chicago estimate that from 25 to 50 percent of the 87,000 scouts registered here exist only on paper.

The professionals also detailed how the cheating has gradually moved into the suburbs—the traditional bastions of the Boy Scout movement.

One South Suburban professional estimated that when he was transferred into his district he found about 20 per cent of his Scouts existed only on paper.

A North Suburban staff member discovered one day that several hundred boys had somehow mysteriously appeared on his rolls. He was later told by a supervisor that the boys were put there to make a quota.

A Southwest Suburban volunteer told of how he held an anguished meeting with his professional late one night because the district was 200 boys short of its quota. The volunteer resigned himself to missing the quota, but early the next morning he got a call from a friend congratulating him for making it.

"I don't know where the boys came from," the volunteer said. "Our meeting ended at 11 p.m. and by 8 a.m. the next day we were on target."

But cheating in the suburbs is minor compared to the inflating of membership rolls going on in the inner city, professionals claim.

"When I left the Fort Dearborn District (West Side) in 1972, I had 3,000 Scouts on the books, but only 300 of them were real," said Andre Miller, a former professional.

"We had 850 boys registered in the Altgeld Gardens project on the South Side," said Bart Kencade, another former professional. "Realistically, there were 30 Scouts active."

A Detroit supervisor told his staff members to meet their quotas even if they had to register bodies in a cemetery to do it.

Nearly 20 charters for Cub Scout packs on the West Side in 1973 list as den mother a Mrs. Ollie Carter, 130 S. Franklin St. Mrs. Carter is in fact an employee of the Boy Scouts in their equipment store at that address. She said she wasn't sure why her name appeared on so many unit rosters.

"I haven't done anything with any units for four or five years," she said.

Edward Meier, a suburban Oak Lawn businessman, is listed on those same rosters as an official of the units.

"I haven't been in the area for years," he said. "Years ago," he claimed he allowed a professional to use his name for promotional purposes in Oak Lawn.

One professional sat in his suburban apartment one night and detailed to a Tribune interviewer just how the cheating is accomplished.

His favorite tactic is known in the business as "diming them in." In November and December near the end of the scouts' annual membership drive, the practice becomes common "because in those months you only have to pay a dime (dues are 10 cents a month) to register a boy for the Dec. 31 deadline. So you can sign up 100 boys for $10."

"You can go to a business for a contribution to pay the tab, you can hold back some money you raised earlier, or you can go to your field director (supervisor) for contingency funds," he said.

Some professionals admitted they paid the phony boys' dues out of their own pocket.

They claimed they got the phony names from telephone books or by visiting elementary schools to have boys fill out applications and pay their dues in advance. Once the registration cards and dues were collected, the professionals never returned to organize units, they said.

Still others claimed they reregistered entire units without checking to see whether the units still existed. In this way, units which have dissolved are carried on the books for years.

The school ploy angered the mothers at Brown Elementary School, 54 N. Hermitage Ave.

"Last September . . . a Scout representative came through the school and recruited 30 to 40 boys," one mother said. "I called them downtown (Scout headquarters) and told them we had collected the boys' money.

"They came out and picked it up but that's the last we ever saw of them."

The Scout professionals—the men who admitted cheating—blamed the problem on the Scout organization and Boypower 76.

"If you didn't make a majority of your goals, you were fired," said one 11-year veteran who was forced out after he refused to cheat.

"Membership is at one of its lowest points in the history of the district," said John P. Costello, Chicago's assistant Scout executive, in a letter to one professional last year. "Camp is 30 per cent off target," he continued.

Failure to show dramatic progress . . . will place you in a terminal employment position with the Chicago Area Council," the letter continued.

"I couldn't send anyone to camp because paper Boy Scouts can't go to camp," said the professional. He claimed he was transferred into the district only a few months before re-ceiving Costello's letter and discovered that 33 of his 47 registered units were nonexistent.

Another Scout professional was fired last year after he attempted to organize a union among the other professionals. The firing occurred a few days after the National Labor Relations Board refused to hear a complaint he filed against the Chicago Council charging it with threatening to fire employees trying to organize the union.

"I didn't want the union," the former professional said. "I wanted to find some way we could put an end to all these abuses."

Raymond N. Carlen, a steel company executive and president of the Chicago Area Council, has adopted a hard nosed attitude toward the dissident professionals:

"If you don't enjoy what you are doing, look for something else to do," he said.

However, Barber believes that many of the problems of cheating could be curbed by better training of professionals and their supervisors.

"I assumed that the middle management people knew the techniques necessary to achieve the goals," he said.

Barber, who was the Scout executive in Chicago before being named national chief executive, is credited with streamlining the Scout organization, imposing the quota system, and making the professionals accountable for making the quotas. He engineered the "Years of Decision" Scout program in Chicago during the early 1960s. "Boypower 76 was an outgrowth of that program."

He also is credited with engineering the attempt by the Scout organization to reach the inner city.

"I felt that if scouting was to reach its potential, it had to be as meaningful to the boy in the inner city as to the boy in suburbia."

CASE 11   THE RATEBUSTER*

Of the six people in the boys' department only the head was male, and he made sales only occasionally. Two of the women were high sellers—Mrs. White and Mrs. Brown. Mrs. White was fifty-nine years old, large physically and somewhat taciturn. She had worked at Lassiters for fourteen years. Mrs. Brown was a small active person, thirty-two, and had been with the store for eight years. Masters told me that when she started in the store she was much taken with Mrs. White and copied and improved upon Mrs. White's selling techniques. Then, too, Mrs. Brown had the insights that came from close personal experience in outfitting her son. Over a period of several months they developed a rivalry. For the last six years or so, according to Masters (Mike Masters, head of the boys' department), they were coldly polite to each other when it was necessary to speak. Masters regarded existence of this hostility as one of his

*The names of the individuals in this case and the department store (Lassiters) are fictional. The incidents described took place in the boys' department of Lassiters. The saleswomen in the department were all on commission.

It is common for members of work groups who are on a commission or other system of incentive payments to avoid showing each other up. In other words, there are informal standards about what members of the group perceive to be a reasonable amount of work. Individuals who produce significantly above this level are often called "ratebusters" or "grabbers" by social scientists. Members of the work group often apply less complimentary labels and even sanctions to individuals who violate the output norms. At Lassiters, ratebusters were called "saleshogs" by their peers.

FROM: Melville Dalton, "The Ratebuster: The Case of the Saleswoman," in *Varieties of Work Experience: The Social Control of Occupational Groups and Roles,* by P. L. Stewart and M. G. Cantor, eds., pp. 206–214. Copyright 1974 by Schenkman Publishing Co., Inc. Reprinted by permission.

major problems. His professed ideal was that the women should be circulating among the customers, busy all the time and cordial to each other.

The other three saleswomen were Mrs. Bonomo, thirty-five, a quiet amenable person, in the department for four years; Mrs. Selby, forty-eight, an employee for five years, who took things as they came without being much disturbed—though judging from her behavior and remarks she made, she disliked Mrs. White much more than she did Mrs. Brown. Mrs. Dawson, at twenty-two, was the youngest member of the department. She had dubbed Mrs. Brown and Mrs. White "saleshogs." She had worked there less than two years. She liked Mrs. Brown despite the epithet she had given her. Mrs. Dawson had two years of college, the most schooling in the department.

The saleswomen received from $1.75 to $2.25 per hour, depending on how long they had been in the department. Records of sales (dollar-volume) for the department were kept for the past year and varied from month to month. These records established the quota for the current year. Once this was equaled, the women started drawing commission pay at the rate of five percent. Commission was paid separately once a month.

Before describing the selling tactics of Mrs. Brown and Mrs. White, the ratebuster types, it is instructive to note the average daily sales established over a six month period[1] by the five saleswomen. Mrs. Brown with $227 average daily sales is over twice as much as Mrs. Dawson and Mrs. Selby, nearly twice as much as Mrs. Bonomo, and $74 more than the second ratebuster, Mrs. White. Masters assured me that Mrs. White slowed up noticeably in her selling over the last two years, but in terms of dollar sales and her constant challenge to Mrs.

Brown she should still be classified as a ratebuster, or a ratebuster in decline.

Saleswomen	Average daily dollar sales
Mrs. Brown	227
Mrs. White	153
Mrs. Bonomo	119
Mrs. Selby	110
Mrs. Dawson	101

Lassiters had an employee credit union. Masters had access to the complete membership which was seventy-six. He gave me *rank only* of the five saleswomen based on the individual amounts deposited in the credit union. (He was so shocked when I requested the total savings of each of the saleswomen that I gladly accepted the partial data.) Mrs. White stood third in the store, and Mrs. Brown was fourth. Mrs. Selby ranked forty-ninth and Mrs. Bonomo was sixty-sixth. Mrs. Dawson was not a member. These data alone do not tell much, but they do indicate that Mrs. White and Mrs. Brown were among the top investors, and that commission was important in their behavior.

Mrs. Brown apparently had more personal relations with customers than anyone in the boys' department. She learned from Masters when specially-priced merchandise was coming in. She telephoned customers she knew well and made arrangements to lay away items of given size and style that were scheduled to go on sale. When she had filled these private orders there was little of the merchandise left for the general public when the official sale day arrived. These sales by telephone constituted about fifteen percent of her total sales. Relatively new customers who bought heavily a time or two she filed in her retentive memory and took steps to acquaint them with her special services.

Among her repeat buyers was a working woman with four sons who treated their clothing roughly. Every six weeks this woman came in to buy nearly complete outfits for the boys. This included shirts, underwear, socks and blue jeans, which amounted to what the sales force called a "big ticket" of about $120.

Mrs. Brown had another woman customer who did not believe in having the younger boys of her five sons wear the older boys' outgrown clothing. She did not come in much oftener than once a year to buy complete outfits, usually just before Easter, which could run to two hundred dollars or more. Mrs. Brown acted as though she had an exclusive right[2] to these customers, and several others that she knew who had only two sons. When Mrs. Brown expected these people she would skip her lunch hour for fear she might miss them, or ask Masters to make the sale and ring it up on her cash drawer in case the woman came when she was out to lunch. He was glad to do this. When business was very good, whether she expected specific customers or not, she ignored the coffee breaks (ten minutes each morning and afternoon) and the lunch hour, leaving the selling floor only long enough to eat a sandwich in the dressing room.

She also had a practical monopoly on sales for boys on welfare. These boys had to be presented by an agent in the welfare organization the first time they did business with the store. Masters turned the welfare customer over to Mrs. Brown and forever afterwards[3] she made the sales. In some cases the welfare officer brought the boy, or boys, with their only clothes on their backs, to buy a complete outfit with extra socks, handkerchiefs and underwear.

(Shoes were not sold in the boys' department.) In any case, Mrs. Brown took care of the sales then and afterwards.

Mrs. Brown's housekeeping area was just inside the entrance from the parking lot. She watched this approach closely. When she was not busy, or was talking to the other members of the department, she could break off instantly—even when she was telling a joke—and move toward the door. If she did not recognize the person she formed some judgment on him based on the affluence of his dress and bearing. If the customer had a boy along, she judged whether he would be hard to fit. In her own words, she had a theory that "the kids who are tall and skinny or short and fat are hard to fit."[4] Thus she made quick appraisals of everybody who moved toward the department. If she approached a customer and learned that he was not as promising as he looked, she often brought the person to one of the other saleswomen and presented him with a statement of what he wanted as though—according to the women—she was giving them an assured sale. She made no revealing comment on the matter, but she seemed at the same time to be putting a restraint on her rivals.

Mrs. Brown's most galling behavior to the group was her practice of getting sale claims on as many prospective buyers as possible. She thus deprived the other saleswomen of a chance at the buyers. For instance, as she was serving one person, she would see another coming through the door—which she nearly always faced even when busiest. Quickly she would lay a number of items before the first person with the promise to be back in a moment, then hurry to capture the second customer. If the situation were right, she might get her claim on three or four buyers while two

or more of the saleswomen were reduced to maintaining the show cases, and setting things in order so as not to appear idle. Mrs. Brown was able to do this because her own housekeeping and stocking area (assigned by Masters) lay between the entrance to the store and the other sections of the boys' department. Only Mrs. White would challenge her by intercepting a patron. The rivalry between them never came to a visible break. As noted earlier some of the other saleswomen resented Mrs. Brown's behavior and privately called her a "saleshog." She was not called that by Mrs. Bonomo and Mrs. Selby who thought—as they said—that Mrs. Brown in action was a "show in itself."

A standard device was used by Mrs. Brown, for ends not intended, with the understanding and collaboration of Masters. On very slack days she frequently left the store shortly after one or two o'clock to do "comparative shopping," that is, to compare the selling prices of items that Lassiters sold with the prices that other local stores charged for the same or similar items. Sometimes Mrs. Brown actually did this, but often she would attend a matinee, or go home to catch up with her housework, or just take a nap. (Her time card was punched out by Masters at the official quitting time.) In any case, to the favorable implications of "comparative shopping," the further obvious inference was made that her absence from the store allowed the other salesgirls to make more commission. (Actually, business was so slow on some days, because of weather, etc., that it was not possible for any of the saleswomen to earn bonus pay.)

Mrs. Brown's conduct may suggest total indifference to the group. But possibly because she was a female in our society, she was not as nonconformist as the grim ratebusters in industry.

Some of these could work for years without exchange of words with people, only a few feet away, that they knew hated them. To a degree Mrs. Brown was concerned about her group. Every week or so she would buy a two pound box of choice chocolates from a candy store near Lassiters and bring it in to share with the group. She could have bought a less expensive grade of candy at Lassiters. Sharing of the candy was almost certainly calculated (she ate little of it herself) but it appeared spontaneous and was received without hesitation. The saleswomen could not direct an unqualified hostility toward her.

She had another uncommon practice which made her stand apart from all of Lassiters' employees. Despite her determined assault on the commission system she did not use her right to a discount on items that she might buy for herself or members of her family. She took her fifteen-year-old son to a local independent department store to buy his clothes. She vigorously declared that "I don't want anything that [Lassiters] has." She was emphatic to the group—and implicitly condemned them—that she did not want to participate in the common practice of getting legal price reductions in addition to the regular employee discount by buying items at the end of a season. For example, an assortment of women's purses would be delivered to the selling floor. This was the "beginning of the season" for that batch of purses. The saleswomen with friends in the purse department would look at the display and select ones that appealed to them. These were laid away until the "end of the season" when they could be bought at the sale price which was further reduced by the regular discount. Mrs. Brown would have nothing to do with such items. She clearly did not want it

said that she was taking advantage of her job.

A likely interpretation is that she sensed she was rejected and widely criticized for her methods and high bonus pay. She feared that some envious salesperson would report any borderline activity on her part to top management. Her own explanation implied that her esthetic taste could not be satisfied by the merchandise at Lassiters. In effect she downgraded the status of the store. As part of this complex she also implied that she was morally somewhat above the group. Also she may have been posing to hide her possible guilt feelings about her treatment of the group.

Although the aim of this paper is not to deal with morale problems, it was glaringly clear that Masters damaged group feeling by routing welfare customers to Mrs. Brown, and by ringing up some of his sales on her cash drawer. His tacit approval of her behavior discouraged the other saleswomen from attempting to control her.

NOTES

1. Masters gave me these figures based on an average of 44 hours a week and including the back-to-school buying months of August and September 1969.
2. Probably she was encouraged by the customers to think that way; certainly some customers waited for her to be free to serve them.
3. The other saleswomen knew about this and resented it. Grateful to Masters for allowing me to observe and talk with the saleswomen, I naturally did not ask him why there was not sharing of such sales among his force. I inquired, but there was no voiced conception of a "day's work"

among the saleswomen. This general practice of informal rewarding is not uncommon in industry where it is sometimes done even with the knowledge and cooperation of individual officers of the union. (Lassiters was not unionized.)

4. Alteration of coats and trousers was done free by the store's tailor. But measuring and marking and the extra trying on were time-consuming. In the extreme cases this was futile. In any case Mrs. Brown avoided customers with "odd size" boys unless she knew them to be liberal buyers and worth her time.

INDEXES

NAME INDEX

Abelson, R. P., 380, 388n.
Adams, J. S., 114, 117, 118, 126n.
Aldag, R. J., 253, 258n.
Alderfer, C. P., 110, 126n., 529,
    535–536, 541n.
Alexander, L. D., 39, 43n.
Allen, R. E., 204, 221n.
Allen, T. J., 494, 509n.
Allen, V. L., 486, 511n.
Alvares, K. M., 312, 327n., 413,
    425n.
Alvarez, R., 475–476, 480n.
Anderson, L. R., 496, 509n.
Andrews, I. R., 25, 45n.
Arnold, H. J., 72–73, 97n., 98n., 122, 126n.,
    165, 166, 189n., 203, 221n., 253, 258n.
Aronson, E., 368–371, 373, 375–377, 388n.,
    389n., 437–438, 454n., 464, 468, 480n.
Arvey, R. D., 75–76, 98n.
As, D., 196, 222n.
Asch, S., 466–467, 480n.
Ash, R. A., 40, 44n., 419, 427n.
Asher, J. J., 36, 43n.
Ashour, A. S., 312, 326n.

Athanassiades, J., 360, 388n.
Athos, A. G., 75, 100n.
Atkinson, J. W., 112, 114, 126n., 195, 223n.
Axelrod, W., 70, 98n.
Aylward, M. S., 33, 44n.

Babbage, C., 228, 258n.
Back, K. W., 435–436, 450, 454n.
Backman, C. W., 370, 389n.
Baetz, M. L., 228, 296, 305n., 311, 323, 327n.
Bailyn, L., 93, 100n.
Baker, D., 148, 160n.
Baldes, J. J., 131, 159n.
Bales, R. F., 448, 454n., 504, 509n.
Bamforth, K. W., 439–440, 455n.
Banas, P. A., 75–76, 98n.
Bandura, A., 150, 159n.
Barnes-Farrell, J., 396, 426n.
Barnowe, J. T., 197, 222n.
Barwick, K. D., 148, 159n.
Bass, A. R., 411, 426n.
Bass, B. M., 25, 44n.
Bavelas, A., 486, 509n.

SUBJECT INDEX

Absenteeism and job satisfaction, 203–204
Affirmative action, 52
Age discrimination, 51–52
Anticipatory socialization, 462
Application blanks (*see* Biographical
    Information Blanks)
Appraisal (*see* Performance appraisal)
Appraisal interview, 420–422
Appraisal process, 416–422
Assembly effect, 491–492
Assembly lines, 231–232
Assessment centers, 36–39, 77,
    93–94
AT&T Management Progress Study, 77, 94
Attitude change, 466–469
    compliance, 467–469
    identification, 467–469
    internalization, 467–469
Attitudes (*see* Communication)
Autonomous work groups, 263, 264
Autonomy, 194

Bargaining, 521, 530–534
Behavior modification (*see* Organizational
    behavior modification)

Behavioral decision theory, 341–343
Behavioral observation scales (BOS),
    411–413
Behavioral theories of leadership, 296–302
Behaviorally anchored rating scales (BARS),
    408–411
Behaviorism, 134–135
Biographical Information Blanks (BIBs),
    34–36
Bona fide occupational qualification
    (b.f.o.q.), 51
Bounded rationality, 341–343
Brainstorming, 492–493, 495–496
Bystander apathy, 491

Cafeteria fringe benefits, 178–180
Career(s), 67–101
    choice of, 69–79
    defined, 68–69
    development programs, 94–95
    early-career issues, 79–87
    later-career issues, 92–94
    middle-career issues, 87–92
    stages, 90